BOLD&
HEALTHY
FLAVORS

BOLD&
HEALTHY
FLAVORS

450 RECIPES FROM AROUND THE WORLD

BY Steven Raichlen

PHOTOGRAPHS BY GREG SCHNEIDER AND KEN WINOKUR

BLACK DOG
& LEVENTHAL
PUBLISHERS
NEW YORK

Published by
Black Dog & Leventhal Publishers
151 West 19th Street
New York, NY 10011

Distributed by
Workman Publishing Company
708 Broadway
New York, NY 10003

This material was originally published in the following books:

Steven Raichlen's Big Flavor Cookbook
Steven Raichlen's High-Flavor, Low-Fat Cooking
Steven Raichlen's High-Flavor, Low-Fat Vegetarian Cooking
Steven Raichlen's High-Flavor, Low-Fat Italian Cooking
Steven Raichlen's High-Flavor, Low-Fat Mexican Cooking
Steven Raichlen's High-Flavor, Low-Fat Pasta
Steven Raichlen's High-Flavor, Low-Fat Appetizers
Steven Raichlen's High-Flavor, Low-Fat Desserts
Steven Raichlen's High-Flavor, Low-Fat Chicken

Manufactured in China
Composition by Compset Inc.
ISBN: 978-1-57912-855-5
h g f e d c b a

DEDICATION

My first food memories came from with my grandmothers.

So it is fitting that this book be dedicated in loving memory to

Ethel Lee Fribush Raichlen (1907–1999)
and
Sarah Marks Goldman (1907–2003)

ACKNOWLEDGMENTS

A huge thanks to J.P. Leventhal, Lindley Boegehold, Christina Gaugler and Richard Rothschild and his team at Print Matters, Inc.

The photographers, Greg Schneider and Ken Winokur.

My stepson Jake, who did much of the food styling and recipe testing and my stepdaughter Betsy, the family nutritionist.

CONTENTS

INTRODUCTION

The instructions were simple enough: "Follow a low-fat diet for two weeks and avoid red meat." I had just had some minor surgery and this was part of the post-op recovery. As I lay in bed, I had plenty of time to reflect on this new eating mandate and its significance to me as a food writer. For a guy who has spent the better part of a decade promoting the virtues of barbecue, the irony was obvious. Many people know me as the host of "Primal Grilling." It's true I've written eight books and taped two TV series on my passion for, and dare I say, obsession with live-fire cooking. It's equally true that briskets and pork shoulders, T-bones and ribs have become the way markers of my culinary path. I love barbecue, I cook it and eat it often, preaching the gospel of live-fire cooking wherever and whenever I can. What you may not know is that prior to barbecue, I spent ten years writing about healthy cooking, that my work includes nine books about low-fat cooking—the source of the recipes here. That when I dine at home with my family, we *still* more often than not follow a diet that, while explosively flavorful, is low in fat and based as much as possible on vegetables, grains, beans, and seafood, with relatively small portions of meats and poultry. My involvement with healthy cooking began in the late 1980s. I had spent ten years as a restaurant critic for *Boston Magazine*, and my nightly dining out had

left me with an alarmingly high cholesterol level and a mushrooming waistline.

For better or worse, I came of culinary age in France in the 1970s—an era when butter, eggs, and cream were considered a chef's staunchest allies. Meals routinely began with *foie gras* and *brioche* and concluded with a butter-cream *gateau*. Back in this BCC (Before Cholesterol Consciousness) era, no one suspected that cheese soufflé, *blanquette* of veal, or asparagus with hollandaise sauce actually could be detrimental to your health.

Many Americans have undergone a similar attitude change about fat. A diet high in saturated fats has been shown to lead to a host of maladies, ranging from heart disease to cancer. Almost monthly, it seems, some new medical study warns us of the dangers of fat. Unfortunately, fat is delicious. The world's most gorgeous sauces—*bearnaise* or *beurre blanc*, for example—use butter as the main ingredient. Pastry-making would be almost inconceivable without butter, cream, and egg yolks. Even in a simply grilled steak or roasted rack of lamb, the most flavorful part is the fat.

Now, I've written about food and cooking for my entire adult life. Never once have I used the word "diet." I've always been a firm believer in the virtues of home-cooked meals made with fresh natural ingredients. I have never used synthetic, dietetic, or highly processed foods and I wasn't about to start. I knew I needed to make a change in my eating habits, but I wasn't willing to sacrifice flavor. As I reviewed my cooking practices, the central question became: How could I retain bold flavors in my food while reducing or eliminating the fat? I looked for ways to replace the inherent richness of animal fats, using fresh herbs, spice mixes, condiments, marinades, and other intense flavorings instead.

Ethnic cuisines, particularly those of the Mediterranean, Middle East, India, and Asia became a major source of inspiration. These cuisines share a common enthusiasm for seafood, grains, beans, fruits, vegetables, and relatively small portions of red meat. It's no accident that in these parts of the world, the incidence of heart disease is dramatically lower than in our own.

I abandoned such classical cooking methods as sautéing and deep-frying, concentrating on low-fat techniques, like grilling and "bake-frying." The non-stick frying pan became an indispensable ally, as I came to realize that I could make the same potato pancake with 1½ tablespoons of olive oil that I used to with a half stick of butter. I began to look for alternative forms of protein, turning to beans, grains, and soy products. When I did use meat, I paired it with a high proportion of vegetables, as is done in the Far East. I replaced butter with olive oil, heavy cream with low-fat dairy products, and chicken and vegetable broth. I discovered that sauces could be thickened with puréed vegetables and that custards and soufflés could be set with egg whites, not yolks.

I came to have one guiding principle in my cooking: use flavor instead of fat.

Much to my surprise, my cooking actually improved from what it had been under the influence of Escoffier and Bocuse. I came to realize that food tasted brighter and fresher without an artery-clogging shroud of fat. And so, what began as a health necessity became a pleasurable way of life.

Every revolution begets a counter-revolution, of course, and today we are experiencing a backlash.

It's hard to pick up a newspaper or magazine today without reading about the exploding popularity of high protein diets and steak houses. We guzzle martinis with the gusto we once reserved for mineral water.

Well, I believe that healthy cooking is here to stay. However many steaks we may eat or martinis we may sip at the moment, most of us remain committed to healthy eating. For those of us in the Baby Boom generation, we become ever more mindful of the health benefits of a low-fat diet as we grow older. Gen-Xers, like my step-children, grew up on a low-fat diet and will adhere to it for the rest of their days. The truth is that high-flavor, reduced-fat cooking offers something for everyone.

The *Bold & Healthy Flavors Cookbook* is a celebration of healthy cooking, featuring more than 400 of my favorite recipes created over the last 15 years. The book tells you which ingredients and cooking methods to use and which to avoid. It offers healthy, reduced-fat alternatives to your favorite appetizers, side dishes, cholesterol-laden entrées, and buttery desserts. It is truly a global cookbook, featuring recipes and cooking styles from all over the world.

The *Bold & Healthy Flavors Cookbook* is not a diet book, at least not in the conventional sense, although it helped me—and will likely help you—lose weight. It will definitely help you prepare tasty, full-flavored, deeply satisfying food using a minimum of butter, cream, egg yolks, and other fats, artificial sweeteners, or chemical additives.

As I wrote, I tried to emphasize taste, color, flavor, and esthetic appeal over strict nutritional dogma. Remember, cooking isn't pharmacy—it's an act of pleasure, nurturing, and love.

FIFTEEN PRINCIPLES FOR TASTIER, HEALTHIER COOKING

- Use intense flavorings—fresh herbs, fragrant spices, intense condiments, chili peppers, et al.—instead of fat to make food taste delicious.

- When you do use a fat, make it a flavorful, healthy fat, like extra-virgin olive oil or sesame or nut oils.

- Put the fat where you can taste it—brush or spray it on the surface of the dish. That way, a light basting of melted butter or olive oil will be the first thing you taste and it will create the impression of extra richness throughout the dish.

- Use egg whites (or egg substitute, which consists chiefly of egg whites), in addition to or instead of yolks or whole eggs to make custards, flans, frittatas, and soufflés.

- "Bake-fry" in your oven: Bake chicken, fish, eggplant, and other foods in a crust of lightly beaten egg whites and bread crumbs (lightly sprayed with oil) to create a crackling crisp crust with virtually no fat. Use this technique to make great-tasting fritters, fried chicken, and turnovers.

- Roast or grill your way to flavor: High heat oven roasting or grilling intensifies the flavor of meats, seafood, and vegetables without adding extra fat. Pan-roasting nuts, seeds, and chilies likewise boosts their flavor without adding fat.

- Use lean cuts of meat and chicken, trimming off any visible fat or skin. Substitute ground turkey for ground beef (but be sure to buy a lean ground turkey—some brands can contain as much as 30 percent fat).

- Eat less meat, and use it as a condiment. Pair meats with a high proportion of grains, beans, and vegetables, as cooks do in Asia.

- Use chicken or vegetable broth instead of oils, butter, or cream in salad dressings, soups, stews, and casseroles. There's no loss of flavor but a considerable reduction in fat. On pages 369–372 you'll find recipes for making chicken, fish, and vegetable stock from scratch. Take the time to do so (the broth can be frozen in convenient 1- and 2-cup containers): Your food will taste infinitely better than if you use canned broth.

- Use low-fat dairy products. When I began writing about low-fat cooking, this was pretty much limited to yogurt. Today, there's a wealth of great low-fat dairy products, from low- and no-fat sour cream, evaporated milk, and condensed milk to fat-free half-and-half. The latter is great for enriching chowders and soups, but remember: It will curdle with prolonged boiling.

- Get the skinny on cheese. Considerable progress has been made in improving the quality of low- and no-fat cheeses. And some popular cheeses, like Italian parmigiano-reggiano, are made with part-skim milk to begin with. You can even use regular cheese—just pick a highly flavorful variety, like feta or sharp cheddar. A little of a strong cheese goes a long way.

- Make canapé, pie, and pastry shells with wonton and egg roll wrappers. Lightly spray them with oil and bake-fry in the oven. On page 328, for example, you'll find a great recipe for low-fat cannolis made with "bake-fried" egg roll wrapper shells.

- Use cocoa instead of chocolate to make brownies and cakes.

- Use fresh fruit and fruit purées in place of icings and creams to garnish desserts.

- Finally, don't forget that how you eat is just as important as what you eat. In many parts of the world (in Europe, Mexico, India, and the Near and Far East, for example), people dine in a simple, leisurely manner almost forgotten in North America. They eat with friends and family, at home or in restaurants, and as often as possible out-doors. They eat relatively small portions of delicious food that tastes homemade—even when served in restaurants. They enjoy a diet rich in grains, beans, fresh fruits, and vegetables; and they wash their meal down with what more and more medical researchers have come to realize is an essential part of a healthy diet: wine.

APPETIZERS

MESS O' CHIPS

Remember chips? That tasty but oh-so-unhealthy snack made by deep-frying wedges of fresh tortilla? Baking produces an equally crisp chip without the fat. When making a batch of chips, I like to use white (wheat flour), yellow-corn, and blue-corn tortillas to wind up with a colorful assortment.

2 yellow-corn tortillas

2 blue-corn tortillas

2 flour tortillas

1. Preheat the oven to 350°F. Cut each tortilla into 8 wedges (10 to 12 wedges for large flour tortillas). Arrange the wedges in a single layer on nonstick baking sheets.

2. Bake the chips until lightly browned and crisp, about 10 minutes. Be especially careful with the flour tortillas, as they burn easily. Transfer the chips to a cooling rack.

Makes 48 to 72 chips, which will serve 8 to 10

6 CALORIES PER SERVING; 0.2 G PROTEIN; 0.1 G FAT; 0 G SATURATED FAT; 1 G CARBOHYDRATE; 6 MG SODIUM; 0 MG CHOLESTEROL

A New Nacho (Prepared in the Style of a Tostada)

A NEW NACHO
(PREPARED IN THE STYLE OF A TOSTADA)

Here's a nontraditional nacho prepared like a tostada (a Mexican open-faced sandwich) that's loaded with flavor, not fat. The recipe can be doubled or tripled as desired.

12 corn tortillas

1 cup no-fat sour cream

2 tablespoons minced cilantro, plus 36 whole cilantro leaves

½ teaspoon ground cumin

½ teaspoon ground coriander

salt and freshly ground black pepper

1 ripe tomato, seeded and cut into ¼-inch dice

6 pitted black olives, thinly sliced

6 drained pickled jalapeño peppers, thinly sliced

4 scallions, trimmed and thinly sliced

½ cup (1½ to 2 ounces) coarsely grated sharp cheddar cheese (preferably an orange cheese)

1. Preheat the oven to 350°F. Arrange the tortillas on baking sheets and bake until they just begin to brown, about 10 minutes. Remove from the oven and let cool; the tortillas will crisp as they cool.

2. Meanwhile, in a mixing bowl whisk together the sour cream, minced cilantro, cumin, coriander, salt, and pepper. The mixture should be highly seasoned.

3. Just before serving, preheat the broiler. Spread each tortilla with a spoonful of the sour cream mixture. Sprinkle the diced tomato, olive and jalapeño slices, scallions, cilantro leaves, and grated cheese on top. Broil the nachos until the cheese melts and the topping is hot, about 2 minutes. Transfer to a platter and serve at once.

Makes 12 nachos, enough to serve 6

81 CALORIES PER NACHO; 4 G PROTEIN; 3 G FAT; 1 G SATURATED FAT; 4 G CARBOHYDRATE; 141 MG SODIUM; 5 MG CHOLESTEROL

PITA CHIPS

Pita chips are great for dipping—not to mention for using up leftover pita bread.

3 large or 4 small pita breads

1 tablespoon extra-virgin olive oil (optional)

1 tablespoon sesame seeds

Makes 48 wedges

7 CALORIES PER SERVING; 0.2 G PROTEIN; 0 G FAT;
1 G CARBOHYDRATE; 13 MG SODIUM; 0 MG CHOLESTEROL

1. Preheat the oven to 350°F. Separate the pita breads and brush the rough side of the pita with the olive oil, if using. Cut each piece into 8 wedges (6 wedges for small breads) and sprinkle with sesame seeds.

2. Arrange the wedges on a baking sheet and bake 8 to 10 minutes, or until golden brown. Transfer the wedges to a cooling rack.

GUACAMOLE EN MOLCAJETE
(MADE IN A LAVA STONE MORTAR WITH PESTLE)

The creamy avocado dip known as guacamole is a staple at Mexican restaurants everywhere. But no one prepares it with quite the theatrics of a New York City restaurant called Rosa Mexicana. The waiter wheels over a cart with bowls of crimson diced tomatoes, pearly white chopped onion, dark green cilantro and chopped serrano chilies, and a giant molcajete, a black lava stone mortar, and tejolote, the pestle. He pounds half the flavorings (onions, chilies, and cilantro) to a fragrant paste in the molcajete, then adds the avocado, tomatoes, and remaining seasonings in large pieces, so you get pungent pointillistic blasts of flavor. The result is one of the most explosively flavorful guacamoles ever to meet a tortilla chip. If you're inclined to such drama at home, you can buy a molcajete and tejolote at a Mexican market or specialty cookware shop. If not, follow the instructions for making guacamole in your food processor.

Note: Keep the avocado seeds in the guacamole until serving; they help prevent browning.

1 clove garlic, chopped

½ medium white onion, finely chopped

3 to 6 serrano chilies, finely chopped (for milder guacamole, seed the chilies before chopping)

½ cup coarsely chopped fresh cilantro

2 ripe avocados, pitted, peeled, and diced

2 red ripe tomatoes, seeded and diced

2 tablespoons fresh lime juice, or to taste

1 teaspoon salt, or to taste

½ teaspoon freshly ground black pepper

Makes 3½ cups, enough to serve 8

89 CALORIES PER SERVING; 1 G PROTEIN; 8 G FAT; 1 G SATURATED FAT;
6 G CARBOHYDRATE; 10 MG SODIUM; 0 MG CHOLESTEROL

MOLCAJETE METHOD

1. Place the garlic and half the onion, chilies, and cilantro in a molcajete and mash to a smooth paste with the pestle.

2. Using a pestle or a wooden spoon, stir in the avocados, tomatoes, lime juice, salt, pepper, and remaining onion, chilies, and cilantro. Stir just to mix; the idea is to create a chunky dip. Correct the seasoning, adding lime juice or salt to taste. Serve with the Mess o' Chips on page 3.

MACHINE METHOD

1. Place the garlic and half the onion, chilies, and cilantro in a mini-chopper or food processor and purée to a smooth paste.

2. Add the avocados, tomatoes, lime juice, salt, pepper, and remaining onion, chilies, and cilantro and process just to mix, running the machine in short bursts. Correct the seasoning, adding lime juice or salt to taste.

Basic Mexican Salsa (Salsa Mexicana)

BASIC MEXICAN SALSA
(SALSA MEXICANA)

Here's the basic Mexican salsa, whose colors—the bright red of tomatoes, the white of the onion, and the green of the chilies and cilantro—echo those of Mexico's flag. Salsa Mexicana is the world's easiest dish to make, but unless you use juicy, red, vine-ripened tomatoes—the kind that go splat when you drop them—you won't get the full effect. With the salsa, serve the Mess o' Chips on page 3.

  2 ripe, red tomatoes, finely chopped

  2 to 6 serrano or jalapeño chilies, finely chopped, with seeds (for a milder salsa, seed the chilies)

  ½ medium white onion, finely chopped

  1 clove garlic, minced

  ⅓ cup finely chopped fresh cilantro

  2 tablespoons fresh lime juice, or to taste

  ½ teaspoon salt, or to taste

In a mixing bowl combine the tomatoes, chilies, onion, garlic, cilantro, lime juice, and salt and toss gently. Correct the seasoning, adding lime juice or salt to taste.

Makes 2 cups, enough to serve 6 to 8

20 CALORIES PER SERVING;* 1 G PROTEIN; 0 G FAT; 0 G SATURATED FAT; 5 G CARBOHYDRATE; 5 MG SODIUM; 0 MG CHOLESTEROL

Analysis is based on 6 servings.

COUNTRY-STYLE COOKED TOMATO SAUCE
(SALSA RANCHERA)

This is one of the most basic of all Mexican salsas and a good overall pick-me-up whenever you need a sauce that's packed with flavor and low in fat.

  1½ tablespoons lard or olive oil

  1 large white onion, finely chopped

  4 cloves garlic, thinly sliced

  2 to 6 serrano chilies, thinly sliced (for a milder salsa, seed the chilies)

  4 medium ripe red tomatoes (about 1½ pounds), peeled and coarsely chopped in the food processor (with juices)

  ¼ cup chopped fresh cilantro

  2 tablespoons fresh lime juice, or to taste

  salt and freshly ground black pepper

1. Heat the lard or olive oil in a nonstick frying pan. Add the onion and cook over medium heat until it is soft but not brown, 4 minutes. Add the garlic and chilies halfway through.

2. Increase the heat to high and add the tomatoes. Cook until most of the tomato liquid has evaporated, 3 to 5 minutes. Stir in the cilantro, lime juice, and salt and pepper to taste. Cook for 1 minute. Correct the seasoning, adding salt or lime juice as needed; the salsa should be highly seasoned.

Note: Salsa Ranchera is generally served hot.

Makes 3 cups, enough to serve 6

63 CALORIES PER SERVING; 1 G PROTEIN; 4 G FAT; 1 G SATURATED FAT; 7 G CARBOHYDRATE; 9 MG SODIUM; 0 MG CHOLESTEROL

COOKED TOMATO SALSA
(SALSA DE TOMATE COCIDO)

This mild, simple salsa, brimming with rich tomato flavors and virtually without heat, is what an Italian grandmother would make—if she had grown up in Mexico City. Serve it with tacos, burritos, chiles rellenos, even over pasta—in any dish that calls for lots of salsa flavor, but not too much heat.

1¾ pounds fresh plum tomatoes (7 or 8 tomatoes) or 1 (28-ounce) can plum tomatoes, with juices

½ medium white onion, cut in half again

2 to 4 serrano chilies

2 cloves garlic

1½ tablespoons lard or canola oil

4 sprigs cilantro

1 teaspoon dried oregano (preferably Mexican)

1 (2-inch) piece cinnamon

salt and freshly ground black pepper

1. Heat a comal or cast-iron skillet over medium-high heat. Roast the tomatoes in the pan until they are nicely browned on all sides, 8 to 10 minutes. Roast the onion wedges, chilies, and garlic the same way: 8 minutes for the onion; 4 minutes for the chilies and garlic. Transfer to a plate and let cool. Seed the chilies. (For a spicier salsa, leave in the seeds.)

2. Scrape most of the burnt bits off the vegetables and purée in a blender.

3. Heat the lard or oil in a deep saucepan. Add the vegetable purée, cilantro, oregano, and cinnamon. Fry the sauce until it is thick and richly flavored, about 5 minutes, stirring with a wooden spoon. Discard the cinnamon stick. Correct the seasoning, adding salt and pepper to taste.

Makes 3 cups, enough to serve 6 to 8

68 CALORIES PER SERVING;* 1 G PROTEIN; 4 G FAT; 0.3 G SATURATED FAT; 9 G CARBOHYDRATE; 13 MG SODIUM; 0 MG CHOLESTEROL

Analysis is based on 6 servings.

SMOKED CHILI SALSA WITH TOMATOES AND TOMATILLOS
(SALSA CHIPOTLE)

Here's a handsome salsa that's brimming with smoke and fire. The heat comes from chipotle chilies (smoked jalapeños) and the smoke flavor is reinforced by charring the vegetables in a comal or under the broiler.

5 tomatillos (about 6 ounces), husked

4 plum tomatoes (about 10 ounces)

5 cloves garlic

1 (3-inch) piece white onion

3 to 5 canned chipotle chilies, with 1 to 2 tablespoons juice from the can

2 tablespoons chopped fresh cilantro

½ teaspoon salt, or to taste

¼ teaspoon sugar, or to taste

1. Heat a comal or cast-iron skillet over a medium-high flame. Add the tomatillos and plum tomatoes and cook until nicely browned on all sides, about 10 minutes, turning with tongs. Cook the garlic cloves (with skins on) and the piece of onion the same way. Alternatively, preheat the broiler and broil the vegetables.

2. Place the vegetables in a food processor. Add the chipotles, cilantro, salt, and sugar. Purée to a coarse paste. Correct the seasoning, adding salt or sugar to taste.

Makes 1¾ cups, enough to serve 6 to 8

27 CALORIES PER SERVING;* 1 G PROTEIN; 1 G FAT; 0 G SATURATED FAT; 5 G CARBOHYDRATE; 136 MG SODIUM; 0 MG CHOLESTEROL

Analysis is based on 6 servings.

COOKED SALSA VERDE
(GREEN SALSA OF TOMATILLOS)

This piquant green sauce is one of Mexico's principal salsas. Sometimes it's served by itself (with chips, that is); more often, though, it's used as a flavoring for egg dishes, seafood, poultry, and all manner of tortilla dishes (especially enchiladas). Salsa verde owes its distinctive tart, fruity flavor to its main ingredient: tomatillos. A member of the gooseberry family (it's a fruit, not a vegetable), the tomatillo looks like a small green tomato encased in a tan, papery husk. The flavor lies somewhere between that of a green tomato and that of a very tart apple. There is no substitute: Fortunately, fresh tomatillos can be found at Mexican markets, natural foods stores, and most supermarkets. Canned tomatillos are widely available as well. When you husk a tomatillo, the fruit itself will feel sticky—this is perfectly normal. Simply rinse the fruit under running water before you use it.

   1 pound fresh tomatillos, husked

   2 to 4 serrano or jalapeño chilies, stemmed (for a milder salsa verde, seed the chilies)

   1 small onion, coarsely chopped

   2 cloves garlic, minced

   ¼ cup chopped fresh cilantro

   1 tablespoon olive oil or lard

   ½ teaspoon sugar, or to taste

   salt and freshly ground black pepper

   1 cup chicken or vegetable broth, or as needed

1. Cook the tomatillos and chilies in 1 quart of simmering water in a saucepan over medium heat until just tender, 4 to 6 minutes. With a slotted spoon, transfer the tomatillos and chilies to a food processor or blender. Add the onion, garlic, and cilantro and purée until smooth.

2. Heat the oil in a deep, nonstick frying pan. Add the tomatillo mixture, sugar, salt, and pepper and fry over medium-high heat, stirring steadily with a wooden spoon, for 3 to 5 minutes, or until the mixture darkens slightly and is very aromatic. (Be careful: The salsa will spatter.)

3. Stir in the stock and simmer until the salsa is richly flavored and thick but pourable, 5 to 10 minutes. If it becomes too thick, add a little more stock. Correct the seasoning, adding salt or sugar to taste. When using canned tomatillos (you'll need 1 can), there is no need to cook them. Simply drain well. In this case, skip boiling the chilies, too.

Makes about 3 cups, enough to serve 6

62 CALORIES PER SERVING; 2 G PROTEIN; 3 G FAT; 0 G SATURATED FAT; 8 G CARBOHYDRATE; 58 MG SODIUM; 0 MG CHOLESTEROL

CHILE DE ÁRBOL SALSA

This salsa from the north of Mexico may be simple to make, but it packs a wallop you can feel a thousand miles away. The salsa owes its invigorating flavor—not to mention its lip-stinging bite—to a long, slender, dried chili called chile de árbol. Serve this brute with carnitas, taquitos, grilled meats, or any dish in need of a decisive blast of heat.

   20 dried chilies de árbol, stemmed

   1 cup warm water

   ¼ white onion

   1 clove garlic

   3 tablespoons chopped cilantro

   1 tablespoon lime juice

   ½ teaspoon salt, or to taste

1. Place the chilies in a bowl and add warm water to cover, about 1 cup. Let soak until very soft, about 1 hour.

2. Place the chilies and soaking liquid in a blender with the onion, garlic, cilantro, lime juice, and salt. Purée to a smooth paste, scraping down the sides of the blender with a rubber spatula. Correct the seasoning, adding salt to taste.

Note: For a milder salsa, tear open the soaked chilies and remove the seeds.

Makes about 1½ cups, enough to serve 8 to 10

6 CALORIES PER SERVING;* 0 G PROTEIN; 0 G FAT; 0 G SATURATED FAT; 1 G CARBOHYDRATE; 2 MG SODIUM; 0 MG CHOLESTEROL

Analysis is based on 8 servings.

DOG'S-NOSE SALSA
(XNI PEC)

Warning: If you don't like fiery food, do not attempt this recipe. Don't even READ this recipe, for xni pec (pronounced "SHNEE-pek") from the Yucatán is one of the hottest salsas in the world. The name says it all: Xni is the Mayan word for "dog," pec means "nose." I've given a range of chilies. Use all six only if you dare!

2 to 10 habanero chilies (or Scotch bonnets), stemmed and finely chopped (for a milder sauce, seed the chilies)

2 medium red tomatoes, cut into ¼-inch dice (with juices)

1 medium red onion, finely chopped (about 1 cup)

¼ cup chopped fresh cilantro

¼ cup sour orange juice, or to taste (or 3 tablespoons fresh lime juice, plus 1 tablespoon fresh grapefruit juice)

salt (about 1 teaspoon)

Combine all the ingredients in an attractive bowl and toss to mix. To correct the seasoning, add sour orange juice or lime juice to taste.

Note: Sour orange is a citrus fruit that resembles a bumpy orange but tastes like a lime. To approximate its flavor, I use regular lime juice mixed with a little grapefruit juice.

Makes about 2½ cups, enough to serve 6 to 8

24 CALORIES PER SERVING;* 1 G PROTEIN; 0 G FAT; 0 G SATURATED FAT; 5 G CARBOHYDRATE; 5 MG SODIUM; 0 MG CHOLESTEROL

Analysis is based on 6 servings.

SWEET CORN SALSA
(SALSA DE MAÍZ)

There's only one word for this sauce, which was inspired by a Oaxacan corn soup: amazing—amazing in its sweet corn flavor; amazing in its creamy richness; and triply amazing that it contains only 1 gram of fat per serving. (The secret is to use evaporated skim milk instead of cream.) For the best results, use fresh corn, but frozen corn produces a surprisingly sweet, flavorful salsa.

2 cups corn kernels (fresh, frozen, or grilled)

3 tablespoons diced onion

½ clove garlic, minced

2 tablespoons chopped fresh cilantro

1 teaspoon sugar (or to taste)

1¼ cups evaporated skim milk

salt and freshly ground white pepper

1. Combine all the ingredients in a saucepan and simmer over medium heat until the corn is very soft, 5 to 8 minutes.

2. Transfer the mixture to a blender and purée until smooth. Return to the pan and correct the seasoning, adding salt or sugar as necessary. For a particularly velvety-smooth sauce, pour the sauce through a fine-meshed china cap strainer.

Makes 1½ cups, enough to serve 4 to 6

137 CALORIES PER SERVING;* 8 G PROTEIN; 1 G FAT; 0 G SATURATED FAT; 26 G CARBOHYDRATE; 360 MG SODIUM; 3 MG CHOLESTEROL

Analysis is based on 4 servings.

SAVANNAH SALSA

I love the nutty, earthy flavor of black-eyed peas.
But until recently, this distinctive legume was enjoyed p
rimarily in the South, where it is an essential ingredient in
the classic Southern New Year's Day dish, hoppin' John.
Contemporary American chefs have given black-eyed peas a
newfound respectability. I like to use a mix of red, green,
and yellow bell peppers in this salsa, but any color will do.

2 cups cooked black-eyed peas (see Note)

1 bell pepper, cut into ¼-inch dice (about 1 cup)

½ small red onion, cut into ¼-inch dice

1 stalk celery, cut into ¼-inch dice

1 clove garlic, minced

1 to 2 jalapeño chilies, minced (for a spicier salsa, leave in the seeds)

½ cup chopped fresh parsley (preferably flat-leaf), plus sprig for garnish

3 tablespoons red-wine vinegar, or to taste

2 tablespoons extra-virgin olive oil

salt and freshly ground black pepper

1. Put the peas, bell peppers, onion, celery, garlic, jalapeño, parsley, vinegar, and oil in a nonreactive mixing bowl. Season with salt and pepper, and toss to combine. Correct the seasoning with salt, pepper, and vinegar: the salsa should be highly seasoned.

2. Transfer the salsa to a serving bowl and garnish with the parsley sprig. Serve with Mess o' Chips (see page 3).

Note: Instructions for cooking black-eyed peas from scratch can be found in my book *High-Flavor, Low-Fat Vegetarian Cooking.* You can certainly use canned beans for this recipe (try to pick a low-sodium brand, which you will find in a natural foods store). If you use canned beans, rinse them thoroughly with cold water and drain well.

Makes 3 cups, which will serve 10 to 12

68 CALORIES PER SERVING; 3 G PROTEIN; 3 G FAT; 0.5 G SATURATED FAT; 9 G CARBOHYDRATE; 48 MG SODIUM; 0 MG CHOLESTEROL

PINEAPPLE SALSA

Here's a fruit salsa that's great with grilled fish or
poultry. (It's also great by itself as a salad.)
For a jazzy presentation, serve it in a pineapple shell.

1 small pineapple

1 red bell pepper, cored, seeded, and cut into 1-inch pieces

1 yellow bell pepper, cored, seeded, and cut into 1-inch pieces

1 green bell pepper, cored, seeded, and cut into 1-inch pieces

1 fresh poblano chili or 2 or 3 jalapeño or serrano chilis, cored, seeded, and finely chopped

1 small red onion, finely diced

½ cup chopped fresh mint or cilantro

3–4 tablespoons fresh lime juice

salt and freshly ground black pepper

1 tablespoon brown sugar (optional)

1. Cut the pineapple in half lengthwise, leaving the leaves intact. Using a grapefruit knife, cut out the pineapple flesh, leaving the shell intact. Core the pineapple and cut the flesh into 1-inch pieces.

2. Combine the pineapple with the remaining ingredients in a mixing bowl and gently toss. Correct the seasoning, adding lime juice, salt, and sugar to taste. This salsa tastes best served within 1 hour of being made.

Makes 3 to 4 cups

6 CALORIES PER TABLESPOON; 0 G PROTEIN; 0 G FAT; 1 G CARBOHYDRATE; 0 MG SODIUM; 0 MG CHOLESTEROL

MANGO SALSA

Once the province of Floridian cooks, the oval, orange-fleshed mango with its peachy-pineappley flavor has taken the nation by storm. When you buy mangoes, look for heavy, unblemished fruits. Let them ripen at room temperature until squeezably soft and very fragrant. Some, but not all, varieties turn red when ripe, so you really need to judge ripeness by smell and touch. This salsa is also delicious made with other fruits, such as peaches, pineapple, or melon.

2 to 3 ripe mangoes

1 cucumber, peeled, seeded, and cut into ¼-inch dice (see Note)

4 large or 8 small scallions, trimmed and finely chopped (about ½ cup)

½ red bell pepper, cut into ¼-inch dice

1 tablespoon minced candied ginger or fresh ginger

½ to 1 Scotch bonnet, habanero, or other hot chili, minced

¼ cup chopped fresh mint or cilantro

3 tablespoons rice vinegar or fresh lime juice, or to taste

2 tablespoons packed light-brown sugar, or to taste

salt and freshly ground black pepper

1. Peel the mangoes and cut the flesh off the pits. Cut the flesh into ¼-inch dice: you should have about 1½ cups.

2. Put the mango, cucumber, scallion, bell pepper, ginger, chili pepper, mint, vinegar, and sugar in a nonreactive mixing bowl, season with salt and pepper, and toss to combine. Correct the seasoning with vinegar and sugar: the salsa should be a little tart, a little sweet, and very highly seasoned. You can prepare the ingredients ahead of time, but don't mix them more than 20 minutes before serving. Serve with Mess o' Chips (see page 3).

Note: To seed cucumbers, cut them in half lengthwise and scrape out the seeds with a melon baller or spoon.

Makes about 3 cups, which will serve 10 to 12

45 CALORIES PER SERVING; 0.6 G PROTEIN; 0.2 G FAT; 0 G SATURATED FAT; 11 G CARBOHYDRATE; 3 MG SODIUM; 0 MG CHOLESTEROL

FRENCH HERBED CHEESE DIP

I first tasted this garlic-laden dip at a smoky, low-ceilinged restaurant in the Marais district of Paris. A specialty of Lyons, it bears the curious name cervelles de canuts, *literally "weavers' brains." It can be made in the food processor, but the herbs should be chopped by hand and added separately so they don't turn the cheese green. Traditionally spread on rye bread or served over boiled potatoes, this is an excellent dip for Homemade Breadsticks (page 89).*

2 cups nonfat yogurt

8 ounces low-fat, small-curd cottage cheese

4 cloves garlic, minced (4 teaspoons)

1½ tablespoons extra-virgin olive oil

1 tablespoon white wine vinegar or rice wine vinegar

1 tablespoon fresh lemon juice (or to taste)

salt and freshly ground black pepper

½ cup finely chopped fresh herbs (tarragon, thyme, oregano, basil, chervil, chives, scallions, and/or flat-leaf parsley)

1. Drain the yogurt in a yogurt funnel or cheesecloth-lined colander for 2 hours. Drain the cottage cheese in a fine-meshed strainer for 2 hours.

2. Purée the yogurt and cottage cheese in a food processor. Work in the garlic, olive oil, vinegar, lemon juice, salt, and pepper. Correct the seasoning, adding lemon juice and salt to taste. Stir in the herbs. The dip can be served right away, but its flavor will improve if you let it ripen with the herbs for 2 to 3 hours.

Serves 8

23 CALORIES PER TABLESPOON; 2 G PROTEIN; 1 G FAT; 2 G CARBOHYDRATE; 34 MG SODIUM; 2 MG CHOLESTEROL

OSTUNI CHICKPEA DIP

Ostuni is one of the most picturesque towns in southern Italy, a hilltop citadel with whitewashed stone homes and labyrinthine alleyways that recall the villages of the Greek islands. Food writers often depend on the kindness of strangers, and this particular night, a local physician who had done his residency in Boston invited our party to a restaurant we'd surely never have found on our own, as it possessed no sign or outward markings on the street. The meal opened with a tangy dip made with a local cheese called ricotta forte *("strong ricotta") that reminded me of feta. As feta is more readily available than* ricotta forte, *I call for it in this recipe. If you can find* ricotta forte, *all the better.*

FOR THE DIP:

1½ cups cooked chickpeas (1 15-ounce can, drained and rinsed)

1 tomato, peeled and diced (with juices)

1 to 2 cloves garlic, minced

1 to 2 ounces feta cheese, crumbled, with 1 to 2 tablespoons brine

1½ tablespoons fresh lemon juice, or to taste

1 tablespoon extra-virgin olive oil, or to taste

salt and freshly ground black pepper

1 to 3 tablespoons Basic Vegetable Stock (page 382), chickpea cooking liquid, or water (optional)

crostini (page 15) for serving

Combine the chickpeas, tomato, garlic, and feta in a food processor and purée to a smooth paste. Still using the food processor, work in the lemon juice, olive oil, salt and pepper to taste. If the dip seems too thick, thin it with a little vegetable stock. Serve with crostini or bruschette.

Makes 1½ cups, enough to serve 6 to 8

96 CALORIES PER SERVING;* 4 G PROTEIN; 4 G FAT; 1 G SATURATED FAT; 12 G CARBOHYDRATE; 44 MG SODIUM; 3 MG CHOLESTEROL

Analysis is based on 8 servings.

GRILLED EGGPLANT DIP

Babo ganooj (eggplant dip) is well known in North America, but few people prepare it the correct way, which is to char the eggplant on a grill to give it a rich smoky flavor. Serve with fresh or toasted pita bread wedges and fresh vegetables for dipping.

2 large eggplants (about 2 pounds)

2 cloves garlic, minced (2 teaspoons)

2 scallions, minced

¼ cup minced flat-leaf parsley, plus a few sprigs for garnish

3–4 tablespoons fresh lemon juice (or to taste)

2 tablespoons nonfat yogurt

2 tablespoons extra-virgin olive oil

½ teaspoon ground cumin

salt and freshly ground black pepper

1. Prick the eggplants in a few spots with a fork. (This keeps them from exploding.) Grill them over a medium flame, turning often, until the skin is charred on all sides and the flesh is soft. Let cool.

2. Cut the eggplants in half lengthwise and scoop out the flesh. (There should be about 2 cups.) Purée the flesh in a food processor, or finely chop it by hand. Mix the garlic, scallions, and parsley with the eggplant. Add the lemon juice, yogurt, olive oil, and cumin. Season with salt and pepper to taste. Spoon into a shallow bowl and garnish with parsley sprigs.

Serves 6 to 8

11 CALORIES PER TABLESPOON; 0 G PROTEIN; 1 G FAT; 1 G CARBOHYDRATE; 1 MG SODIUM; 0 MG CHOLESTEROL

VEGETABLE STICKS WITH DRY DIPS

Dry dips make a nice switch from the usual sour cream- and yogurt-based concoctions found on most buffet spreads. Dry dips are nothing more than spice mixes, and they adhere nicely to moist vegetables such as cucumber, pepper, and zucchini spears. Here are some of my favorites. Feel free to use vegetables other than the ones called for below.

Note: Although I've given salt in the amounts I would use, I've added the words "or to taste," since many people like to restrict the salt in their diet.

- 4 stalks celery
- 2 zucchini
- 1 cucumber, peeled and seeded
- 1 red bell pepper
- 1 yellow bell pepper
- 1 medium (12-ounce) jícama (see Note opposite)

Serves 8 to 12

20 CALORIES PER SERVING; 0.9 G PROTEIN; 0.1 G FAT; 0 G SATURATED FAT; 4 G CARBOHYDRATE; 15 MG SODIUM; 0 MG CHOLESTEROL

1. Cut the celery crosswise into 3-inch pieces, then lengthwise into ¼-inch strips. Cut the zucchini and cucumber the same way. Core and seed the peppers (the easiest way to do this is to cut the sides right off the core) and cut them into ¼-inch strips. Peel the jícama and cut it the same way.

2. Stand the vegetable sticks in bowls or arrange them on platters and serve with shallow bowls of the dips following on pages 10 and 11.

Note: Jícama is a crisp root vegetable from Mexico that tastes like a cross between an apple and a potato.

CAJUN DIP

- 3 tablespoons sweet paprika
- 2 tablespoons garlic powder
- 1 tablespoon freshly ground black pepper
- 1 tablespoon onion powder
- 1 tablespoon dried oregano
- 1 tablespoon dried thyme
- 1 teaspoon cayenne pepper
- 2 tablespoons kosher salt, or to taste

Put all the ingredients in a small bowl and whisk to combine.

Makes about ½ cup

7 CALORIES PER SERVING; 0.3 G PROTEIN; 0.2 G FAT; 0 G SATURATED FAT; 1.6 G CARBOHYDRATE; 534 MG SODIUM; 0 MG CHOLESTEROL

GREEK DIP

- 3 tablespoons dried oregano
- 1 tablespoon dried mint
- 1 tablespoon dried dill
- 1 tablespoon garlic flakes
- 2 teaspoons freshly ground black pepper
- 1 tablespoon kosher salt, or to taste

Put all the ingredients in a small bowl and whisk to combine.

Makes about ½ cup

4 CALORIES PER SERVING; 0.2 G PROTEIN; 0 G FAT; 0 G SATURATED FAT; 0.8 G CARBOHYDRATE; 267 MG SODIUM; 0 MG CHOLESTEROL

SHANGHAI DIP

- 2 tablespoons toasted white sesame seeds
- 2 tablespoons black sesame seeds
- 1 tablespoon poppy seeds
- 1 tablespoon onion flakes
- 1 tablespoon garlic flakes
- 2 teaspoons hot-pepper flakes

Put all the ingredients in a small bowl and whisk to combine.

Makes about ½ cup

23 CALORIES PER SERVING; 0.9 G PROTEIN; 1.8 G FAT; 0.2 G SATURATED FAT; 1.3 G CARBOHYDRATE; 5 MG SODIUM; 0 MG CHOLESTEROL

PROVENÇALE DIP

- 2 tablespoons dried basil
- 2 tablespoons dried oregano
- 1 tablespoon dried thyme
- 1 tablespoon dried marjoram
- 1 tablespoon dried rosemary
- 1 tablespoon dried lavender (optional)
- 1 tablespoon salt, or to taste

Put all the ingredients in a small bowl and whisk to combine.

Makes about ½ cup

7 CALORIES PER SERVING; 0.3 G PROTEIN; 0.2 G FAT; 0 G SATURATED FAT; 1.4 G CARBOHYDRATE; 1 MG SODIUM; 0 MG CHOLESTEROL

Fig Tapenade

PUMPERNICKEL TOAST POINTS

½ package thinly sliced cocktail-type mini-loaves of pumpernickel bread (22 slices)

1 tablespoon extra-virgin olive oil or spray oil

1. Preheat the oven to 375°F. Cut each pumpernickel slice on the diagonal and lightly brush each slice with oil on both sides or spray with spray oil.

2. Arrange the slices on a baking sheet and bake until crisp, 10 to 15 minutes per side. Transfer the toast points to a cooling rack.

Makes 44 toast points

95 CALORIES PER SERVING; 3 G PROTEIN; 1.8 G FAT; 0.3 G SATURATED FAT; 18 G CARBOHYDRATE; 193 MG SODIUM; 0 MG CHOLESTEROL

FIG TAPENADE

Tapenade—the olive, caper, and anchovy spread—is one of the classic hors d'oeuvres of Provence. Unfortunately for the health-conscious, its two main ingredients, olives and olive oil, are loaded with fat. I got an idea for a reduced-fat tapenade in Sarah Leah Chase's charming book The Bicycling Through Provence Cookbook, *which features a recipe for olive-and-fig tapenade. I've increased the proportion of figs to olives and replaced most of the olive oil with vegetable stock.*

2 cups dried black mission figs (about 10 ounces)

½ cup cognac

2 cups vegetable stock, chicken stock, or water

⅔ cup pitted oil- or brine-cured olives, such as kalamata

4 anchovy fillets, rinsed in warm water and patted dry

¼ cup drained capers

2 tablespoons Dijon-style mustard

2 tablespoons fresh lemon juice, or to taste

1 tablespoon extra-virgin olive oil

salt and freshly ground black pepper

Toast points or slices of bread for serving

1. Stem and cut the figs crosswise into ¼-inch slices. Put them in a saucepan with the cognac and stock. Gently simmer 10 minutes, or until the figs are soft. Meanwhile, pit the olives.

2. Transfer the figs with a slotted spoon to a food processor, reserving the poaching liquid. Add the olives, anchovies, and capers, and process to a smooth paste. Add the mustard, lemon juice, and oil, and process to combine. With the motor running, add enough fig-poaching liquid (½ to 1 cup) to obtain a soft, spreadable purée. Correct the seasoning with salt, pepper, and lemon juice: the tapenade should be highly seasoned.

3. Transfer the tapenade to a serving bowl and serve with the toast points or bread.

Makes 2 cups, which will serve 8 to 10

162 CALORIES PER SERVING; 2 G PROTEIN; 6.6 G FAT; 0.9 G SATURATED FAT; 25 G CARBOHYDRATE; 588 MG SODIUM; 2 MG CHOLESTEROL

ROASTED-VEGETABLE "CAVIAR"

Vegetable "caviars" are a popular Russian appetizer, not to mention the specialty of my friend the late Bob Ginn. While this one won't fool anyone into thinking he's eating beluga, it does have the soft, crunch-gooey texture one associates with caviar and a robust flavor that would do any zakuski *platter (Russian hors d'oeuvres) proud. My low-fat version calls for the vegetables to be roasted in a super-hot oven—a technique that provides so much flavor, you only need a fraction of the oil found in the traditional recipe.*

1 medium eggplant (10 to 12 ounces)

1 medium onion, peeled and quartered

½ green bell pepper, cored and seeded

½ red bell pepper, cored and seeded

1 carrot, peeled and cut into chunks

1 large ripe tomato, halved and seeded (see page 385)

1 large or 2 small stalks celery, thinly sliced

2 jalapeño chilies or other hot peppers, halved and seeded (optional)

3 cloves garlic, peeled

spray oil

TO FINISH THE "CAVIAR":

¼ cup chopped fresh parsley (preferably flat-leaf)

3 tablespoons chopped fresh dill or cilantro

1 to 2 tablespoons fresh lemon juice, or to taste

1 to 2 tablespoons extra-virgin olive oil

salt and freshly ground black pepper

1. Preheat the oven to 450°F. Lightly spray a nonstick baking sheet with spray oil. Prick the eggplant in several places with a fork. Place the eggplant, onion, bell peppers, carrot, tomato, celery, jalapeños, and 2 cloves of the garlic on the prepared baking sheet. (Place the garlic, celery, and jalapeños on top of the tomatoes to keep them from burning.) Roast the vegetables until very tender, 20 to 30 minutes. Stir as needed to prevent scorching. Remove the pan from the oven and let the vegetables cool to room temperature.

2. Transfer the onion, carrot, tomato, celery, garlic, and jalapeños to a food processor and process in bursts until coarsely chopped. Cut the eggplant in half lengthwise, scrape out the pulp with a spoon, and add it to the processor along with the bell peppers. Process in bursts until coarsely chopped. Mince the remaining 1 clove garlic and add along with the parsley, dill, lemon juice, and oil. Season with salt and pepper, and process to mix. Correct the seasoning with salt and lemon juice: the "caviar" should be highly seasoned. Chill and serve with Pita Chips (see page 5) or Pumpernickel Toast Points (see page 14).

Note: Alternatively, you could spoon the "caviar" into hollowed-out mushroom caps or zucchini halves and bake in a 400°F. oven until thoroughly heated, 10 to 15 minutes.

Makes about 2½ cups, which will serve 8 to 10

43 CALORIES PER SERVING; 9 G PROTEIN; 1.9 G FAT; 3 G SATURATED FAT; 6.6 G CARBOHYDRATE; 12 MG SODIUM; 0 MG CHOLESTEROL

CROSTINI WITH TOPPINGS

Crostini are the Italian equivalent of toast points. I like to brush or spray them with a little oil before baking, but you could certainly bake them dry. Crostini should be audibly crisp once they've emerged from the oven and cooled.

1 Italian- or French-style baguette

1 tablespoon extra-virgin olive oil (or a can or spray olive oil)

1. Preheat the oven to 400°F. Cut the bread on the diagonal into ½-inch-thick slices. (If you prefer thinner crostini, cut into ¼-inch-thick slices.) Lightly brush or spray the bread slices with oil on both sides and arrange on a nonstick baking sheet.

2. Bake the crostini until crisp and golden brown, 8 to 12 minutes per side. Take care that they don't burn. Transfer the crostini to a wire rack to cool. Serve with one of the following toppings (see Yellow Tomato and Arugula Topping, Sardinian "Salsa," and Tuscan Mushroom Liver Pâté).

Makes 30 to 36 crostini, enough to serve 6 to 10

145 CALORIES PER SERVING;* 5 G PROTEIN; 3 G FAT; 23 G CARBOHYDRATE; 308 MG SODIUM; 0 MG CHOLESTEROL

Analysis is based on 6 servings.

Crostini with Toppings

YELLOW TOMATO AND ARUGULA TOPPING

The Italian word for tomato is pomodoro, *literally "golden apple." The first tomatoes imported to Italy
(or at least grown there) were probably a small yellow ancestor of the modern red tomato.
That set me thinking about a gold-and-green topping made with yellow tomatoes and arugula.*

3 ripe yellow tomatoes (enough to make about 2 cups diced) or 1½ pints yellow cherry tomatoes

1 bunch arugula, washed and stemmed (see box on page 69)

2 to 3 tablespoons minced red onion

1½ tablespoons balsamic vinegar

1 tablespoon extra-virgin olive oil

salt and freshly ground black pepper

1. If using large tomatoes, cut into ¼-inch dice, reserving the juices. If using cherry tomatoes, cut each in half lengthwise. Cut the arugula widthwise into ¼-inch slivers.

2. Not more than 20 minutes before serving, combine all the ingredients for the topping, adding enough strained tomato liquid to make a mixture that is moist but not wet. Correct the seasoning, adding vinegar or salt to taste.

Makes about 2¼ cups, enough for 1 recipe of crostini

40 CALORIES PER SERVING;* 0.7 G PROTEIN; 2.4 G FAT; 4 G CARBOHYDRATE; 7 MG SODIUM; 0 MG CHOLESTEROL

Analysis is based on 6 servings.

SARDINIAN "SALSA"

This fresh tomato topping makes me think of salsa.
For a Sardinian touch, each crostino is topped with a shaving
of Pecorino, the island's famous grating cheese, a firm,
tangy sheeps'-milk cheese. Use a vegetable peeler to shave
off broad, thin strips of cheese.

3 ripe red tomatoes, cut into ¼-inch dice

6 pitted black olives, finely chopped

1 green onion or 3 scallions, finely chopped

3 tablespoons chopped flat-leaf parsley

2 anchovy fillets, finely chopped (optional)

1 tablespoon drained capers

1½ tablespoons balsamic vinegar, or to taste

1½ tablespoons extra-virgin olive oil

salt and freshly ground black pepper

a 1-ounce chunk of Pecorino cheese

1. Not more than 20 minutes before serving, combine the tomatoes, olives, scallions, parsley, anchovies, capers, vinegar, oil, salt, and pepper in a mixing bowl and gently toss to mix. Correct the seasoning, adding vinegar or salt to taste.

2. Mound the "salsa" on the crostini. Using a vegetable peeler, shave a thin slice of Pecorino on top of each crostini.

Makes about 2¼ cups, enough for 1 recipe of crostini

70 CALORIES PER SERVING;* 2 G PROTEIN; 5 G FAT; 4 G CARBOHYDRATE; 174 MG SODIUM; 3 MG CHOLESTEROL

Analysis is based on 6 servings (without anchovy fillets).

TUSCAN MUSHROOM LIVER PÂTÉ

The traditional topping for crostini in Tuscany is liver pâté.
My low-fat remake uses roasted mushrooms as the base of the
pâté, with a little liver—just enough—for flavor. I think
you'll be amazed at how "livery" this pâté actually tastes.

12 ounces portobello or button mushrooms, trimmed and quartered

½ medium onion, peeled and quartered

2 cloves garlic, peeled

1 tablespoon extra-virgin olive oil

salt and freshly ground black pepper

2 to 4 ounces chicken livers (from two birds), trimmed, rinsed and blotted dry

2 tablespoons finely chopped flat-leaf parsley

1 tablespoon brandy or to taste

1 to 2 tablespoons dried bread crumbs, as needed

1. Preheat the oven to 450°F. Place the mushrooms, onion, and garlic in a nonstick roasting pan. Toss with olive oil, salt, and pepper. Roast the mushrooms until beginning to brown, 5 to 10 minutes, stirring to ensure even cooking.

2. Add the livers and continue roasting until the mushrooms are well browned and flavorful and the liver is cooked but still pink in the center, 5 to 10 minutes more.

3. Purée the mushroom-and-liver mixture in a food processor, adding the parsley, brandy, and salt and pepper to taste. If the mixture seems watery, add a tablespoon or two of bread crumbs.

Makes 2 cups, enough for 1 recipe of crostini

60 CALORIES PER SERVING;* 5 G PROTEIN; 3 G FAT; 0.5 G SATURATED FAT; 5 G CARBOHYDRATE; 15 MG SODIUM; 35 MG CHOLESTEROL

Analysis is based on 6 servings.

A NEW SHRIMP TOAST

Remember shrimp toast? The oily, deep-fried, but oh-so-luscious appetizer from the Cantonese restaurants of our childhood? Here's a heart-healthy version that is broiled instead of fried. The idea comes from Joyce Jue, author of the excellent book Asian Appetizers.

8-ounce can water chestnuts, drained

1 pound shrimp, peeled and deveined (1¼ pounds in shells)

3 cloves garlic, minced

4 scallions, trimmed and minced

1 tablespoon minced fresh ginger

1 tablespoon Chinese or Japanese rice wine, or dry sherry

2 to 3 teaspoons sugar

1 to 2 teaspoons hot sauce (optional)

1 large egg white

salt and freshly ground black pepper

1 long, slender French bread (baguette)

1 to 2 teaspoons Asian sesame oil

spray oil

1. Finely chop the water chestnuts by hand or in a food processor and transfer to a mixing bowl. Coarsely chop the shrimp in the food processor. Add the garlic, scallion, ginger, wine, sugar, hot sauce, and egg white, and season with salt and pepper. Process briefly to mix. Add the shrimp mixture to the water chestnuts and stir to mix. Correct the seasoning with salt: the mixture should be highly seasoned. (To taste the mixture for seasoning without eating raw seafood, cook a tiny bit on the end of a spoon in boiling water.)

2. Preheat the oven to 400°F. Cut the bread on the diagonal into ½-inch-thick slices. Arrange the slices on a baking sheet and lightly spray both sides with oil. Bake until golden brown on both sides, about 6 minutes per side. Transfer the bread slices to a wire rack.

3. Preheat the broiler. Spread a generous tablespoon of the shrimp mixture on each slice of bread and brush with sesame oil or spray with spray oil. Broil the toasts until the shrimp mixture is puffed and golden brown on top and cooked through, 2 to 4 minutes.

Makes about 30 pieces

68 CALORIES PER PIECE; 5 G PROTEIN; 0.9 G FAT; 0.2 G SATURATED FAT; 9 G CARBOHYDRATE; 112 MG SODIUM; 26 MG CHOLESTEROL

6 corn tortillas

SHRIMP CEVICHE MINI-TOSTADAS

Here's a ceviche for people who don't think they can eat uncooked seafood. If you can find them, buy true baby shrimp (the kind that are so small that a dozen will fit in a tablespoon). Otherwise, you'll need to cut large cooked shrimp into ½-inch dice. I've called for the ceviche to be served on tortilla chips, canapé-style. But you can certainly present it, shrimp cocktail–style, in a martini glass.

1 tablespoon melted lard or olive oil (optional)

FOR THE SHRIMP CEVICHE:

1 cup cooked baby shrimp or diced large shrimp

½ medium white onion, finely chopped

1 ripe red tomato, peeled, seeded, and diced

½ ripe avocado, peeled and finely diced

1 or 2 serrano chilies, finely chopped
   (for a milder ceviche, seed the chilies)

¼ cup chopped fresh cilantro, plus 36 sprigs

fresh cilantro for garnish

¼ cup fresh lime juice

salt and freshly ground black pepper

1. Preheat the oven to 350°F. Brush the tortillas on both sides with the optional lard or olive oil. Cut each tortilla into six wedges and arrange them in a single layer on a baking sheet. Bake the tortillas until they are lightly browned, 8 to 10 minutes. Transfer to a cake rack to cool: They'll crisp as they cool.

2. Meanwhile, prepare the ceviche. Place the shrimp, onion, tomato, avocado, chili, chopped cilantro, and lime juice in a bowl and toss to mix. Add salt and pepper to taste.

3. At the moment of serving, arrange the tortilla chips on a platter. Top each with a spoonful of ceviche and a sprig of cilantro and serve at once.

Makes 36 pieces, enough to serve 6 as an appetizer

176 CALORIES PER SERVING;* 10 G PROTEIN; 5 G FAT; 1 G SATURATED FAT; 24 G CARBOHYDRATE; 142 MG SODIUM; 63 MG CHOLESTEROL

Analysis is based on 4 servings.

MEXICAN CHICKEN SALAD TOSTADAS

A good tostada combines the crispness of a cracker and the refreshing crunch of salad with the mouth-filling satisfaction of a sandwich. You might think that a dish whose main components are a deep-fried tortilla, refried beans, and a pile of grated cheese would be off-limits to a heart-healthy diet. But by bake-frying the tortilla and using a little strong-flavored cheese as an accent instead of a main ingredient, you wind up with a popular Mexican snack that's as good for you as it tastes good to eat.

8 corn tortillas

1 tablespoon melted lard or olive oil

FOR THE DRESSING:

¾ cup no-fat sour cream

2 tablespoons fresh lime juice

¼ teaspoon ground cumin

2 tablespoons chicken or vegetable broth

salt and freshly ground black pepper

1½ cups refried beans
  (page 298, or use a good fat-free canned brand)

1½ cups shredded cooked chicken

2 cups shredded lettuce

⅓ medium onion, diced (about 5 tablespoons)

½ avocado, peeled and diced

8 (¼-inch-thick) slices ripe red tomato

¼ cup crumbled queso fresco, queso añejo,
  or feta cheese (or ¼ cup grated Romano cheese)

1. Preheat the oven to 350°F. Brush the tortillas on both sides with the lard or olive oil. Arrange them in a single layer on a baking sheet and bake until they're lightly browned, 10 to 15 minutes. Transfer the tortillas to a cake rack; they'll crisp as they cool.

2. Meanwhile, make the dressing. Combine the sour cream, lime juice, and cumin in a mixing bowl and whisk until smooth. Whisk in enough chicken broth to make a pourable dressing, then add salt and pepper to taste. Warm the refried beans in a saucepan.

3. Just before serving, spread 3 tablespoons of the refried beans on each tortilla. Top with the shredded chicken, shredded lettuce, onion, and avocado. Drizzle the dressing on top. Place a tomato flat on top of each tostada and sprinkle it with the crumbled cheese.

Makes 8 tostadas, enough to serve 8 as an appetizer, 4 as a light entrée

214 CALORIES PER TOSTADA; 16 G PROTEIN; 7 G FAT; 1 G SATURATED FAT; 21 G CARBOHYDRATE; 251 MG SODIUM; 36 MG CHOLESTEROL

GALLOPING HORSES
(SPICED PORK ON PINEAPPLE)

I first learned of this colorfully named hors d'oeuvre from Nancy MacDermott, former Peace Corps worker, Thai cooking authority extraordinaire, and author of one of my favorite Thai cookbooks, Real Thai. *The combination of fruit and meat, sweet and salty, is a hallmark of Thai cooking, and these pineapple wedges topped with spiced pork are as refreshing as they are unusual. When buying pineapples, look for a gold rather than a green skin: this indicates a riper, sweeter pineapple.*

½ ripe pineapple (cut lengthwise)

FOR THE TOPPING:

8 to 10 ounces lean pork, such as tenderloin or center-cut boneless chops

1 tablespoon canola oil

2 cloves garlic, minced

2 shallots, minced

1 tablespoon minced fresh ginger

1 to 4 jalapeño or other hot chilies, seeded and minced (for a spicier topping, leave in the seeds)

1 teaspoon minced cilantro root (optional) (see Note)

3 tablespoons finely chopped fresh cilantro

2 tablespoons packed dark brown sugar

2 tablespoons fish sauce or soy sauce

FOR THE GARNISH:

1 to 2 tablespoons chopped unsalted dry-roasted peanuts

about 30 cilantro sprigs

1. Peel and core the pineapple. Cut the pineapple crosswise into ½-inch-thick rings, and cut each slice into 6 wedges. Arrange the pineapple pieces on a serving platter.

2. Trim any fat or sinew from the pork and mince it with a cleaver, or cut it into ½-inch cubes and grind it in a food processor. Heat the oil in a wok or a large frying pan (preferably nonstick) set over medium heat. Add the garlic, shallots, ginger, chilies, and cilantro root, and stir-fry until lightly browned, about 2 minutes.

3. Add the pork and stir-fry until cooked, about 3 minutes. Stir in the cilantro leaves, sugar, and fish sauce, and cook 1 minute. Correct the seasoning with fish sauce or sugar: the mixture should be sweet, salty, and a little spicy. Let the pork cool to room temperature. The recipe can be made ahead to this point and refrigerated. If this is done, let the dish come to room temperature before serving.

4. Mound a spoonful of the pork mixture on top of each pineapple wedge. Sprinkle with a little chopped peanut and garnish with a sprig of cilantro. Serve at once.

Note: The root of the cilantro plant is a popular Thai seasoning, with an aromatic, cilantro-like pungency and an earthy flavor reminiscent of celeriac or parsley root. Asian and Hispanic markets sell cilantro with the roots attached, and so do many gourmet shops and greengrocers. But don't worry if you can't find it—the Galloping Horses will be perfectly tasty without it. The topping can also be made with chicken breast or shrimp (10 ounces of shrimp in shells; 8 ounces of shelled shrimp). This recipe can be doubled or tripled to serve a larger crowd.

Makes about 30 pieces

24 CALORIES PER PIECE; 1.9 G PROTEIN; 0.9 G FAT; 0.2 G SATURATED FAT; 2.2 G CARBOHYDRATE; 94 MG SODIUM; 5 MG CHOLESTEROL

SMOKED TROUT MOUSSE ON CUCUMBER

Here's a handsome and refreshing canapé featuring smoked trout mousse on cucumber slices. Smoked trout is available at fish stores, gourmet shops, and many supermarkets. One excellent mail-order source is DuckTrap River Farm in Maine (telephone 800-828-3825). You could also prepare the recipe with smoked salmon or other smoked fish.

1 large English (hothouse) cucumber

1 smoked trout (8 to 10 ounces)

6 ounces low- or no-fat cream cheese, at room temperature

2 to 3 teaspoons prepared white horseradish (optional)

salt and freshly ground black pepper

Dill sprigs, for garnish

1. Peel the cucumber, leaving narrow strips of peel to create a striped effect. Cut the cucumber into ¼-inch-thick slices. Blot the slices dry with paper towels and arrange them on a serving platter.

2. Prepare the trout mousse. Skin the trout and remove the meat from the bones with a fork. Purée the trout in a food processor. Add the cream cheese and process to a smooth paste. Add the horseradish and season with pepper and, if needed, salt. Transfer the mixture to a pastry bag fitted with a large star tip. Pipe rosettes of trout mousse onto the cucumber slices. Garnish each with a dill sprig.

Makes 48 pieces

16 CALORIES PER PIECE; 1.7 G PROTEIN; 0.8 G FAT; 0.8 G SATURATED FAT; 0.6 G CARBOHYDRATE; 22 MG SODIUM; 5 MG CHOLESTEROL

PERSIAN SHRIMP KEBABS WITH POMEGRANATE DIP

Yogurt, onions, lemon, and saffron are some of the defining flavors of Persian cooking. The pomegranate dip isn't particularly traditional, but pomegranate syrup (sometimes called pomegranate molasses) is a popular ingredient in the Near East.

24 large shrimp (1 to 1½ pounds)

1 small onion

FOR THE MARINADE:

½ teaspoon saffron threads

2 teaspoons warm water

1 cup nonfat plain yogurt

¼ cup fresh lemon juice

1 medium onion, thinly sliced

salt and freshly ground black pepper

FOR THE SAUCE:

1 cup nonfat yogurt

2 tablespoons pomegranate syrup (see Note)

1 tablespoon minced fresh dill or cilantro

½ teaspoon ground coriander

1 clove garlic, minced

12 6-inch bamboo skewers

1. Peel and devein the shrimp. Peel the onion and cut it in half crosswise. Cut each half into 6 wedges.

2. Make the marinade: Put the saffron in a nonreactive mixing bowl and pulverize it with the end of a wooden spoon. Add the water and let stand 3 minutes. Stir in the yogurt, lemon juice, and sliced onion, and season with salt and pepper. Add the shrimp and marinate 30 to 60 minutes. Meanwhile, soak the skewers in cold water.

3. Make the sauce: Put the yogurt, pomegranate syrup, dill, ground coriander, and garlic in a mixing bowl, and season with salt and pepper: the mixture should be highly seasoned. Transfer the sauce to a serving bowl or ramekin.

4. Preheat the grill or broiler to high. Thread the shrimp onto the skewers, 2 shrimp to a skewer, with an onion wedge between them. Grill the kebabs until the shrimp is cooked, about 1 minute per side. If the skewer ends begin to burn, protect them with strips of aluminum foil. Arrange the kebabs on a platter and serve with the sauce for dipping.

Note: Look for pomegranate syrup at Middle Eastern and Iranian markets. If it is not available in your area, substitute balsamic vinegar syrup, made by boiling down ½ cup balsamic vinegar to 2 tablespoons.

Makes 12 kebabs

72 CALORIES PER KEBAB; 9 G PROTEIN; 0.4 G FAT; 0.1 G SATURATED FAT; 8 G CARBOHYDRATE; 98 MG SODIUM; 59 MG CHOLESTEROL

Chicken, Prosciutto, and Sage Spedini and Shrimp Spedini with Basil and Peppers

SHRIMP SPEDINI WITH BASIL AND PEPPERS

Spedini are Italian kebabs. These shrimp spedini are packed with flavor, thanks to their skewers—sprigs of fresh rosemary. You'll need fairly stiff rosemary branches: the sort you find on a small rosemary bush at a plant shop. (Besides, this is a more economical way to buy rosemary than in the plastic bags in the supermarket produce section. It helps to strip the leaves off the bottom 2 inches of each rosemary sprig.) Scallops could be prepared the same way.

24 large shrimp, peeled and deveined

1 tablespoon fresh lemon juice

1 tablespoon extra-virgin olive oil

1 clove garlic, minced

1 red bell pepper, cut into 1-inch triangles

1 bunch fresh basil, washed and stemmed

1 yellow bell pepper, cut into 1-inch triangles

salt and freshly ground black pepper

12 stiff sprigs fresh rosemary, each about 5 inches long

1. Combine the shrimp, lemon juice, olive oil, and garlic in a glass bowl and toss to mix. Marinate for 15 minutes.

2. Skewer the shrimp on the rosemary sprigs, placing 2 shrimps head to head on each skewer, as pictured. Place a red pepper triangle on one end, a fresh basil leaf and a yellow pepper triangle on the other. If the rosemary sprigs are too flexible for skewering, make holes in the shrimp with a bamboo skewer, then insert the rosemary.

3. Just before serving, preheat the grill or broiler to high. Generously season the shrimp with salt and pepper. Grill or broil the spedini until cooked, about 2 minutes per side. Baste with any excess marinade as the spedini cook.

Makes 12 spedini, enough to serve 4 to 6

33 CALORIES PER 1 PIECE SPEDINI; 3 G PROTEIN; 1 G FAT; 0.2 G SATURATED FAT; 3 G CARBOHYDRATE; 25 MG SODIUM; 22 MG CHOLESTEROL

SATÉ MIXED GRILL WITH SPICY PEANUT SAUCE

Satés (pronounced "sah-TAYS") are bite-size kebabs enjoyed throughout Southeast Asia. I've omitted the fat-laden coconut milk used in traditional recipes and added spices, lime juice, and fish sauce for flavor. If fish sauce is unavailable, you can substitute soy sauce.

Mixed Saté with Spicy Peanut Sauce

½ **pound skinless, boneless chicken breast**

½ **pound lean pork, such as loin or tenderloin**

½ **pound lean beef, such as sirloin or tenderloin**

½ **pound medium shrimp**

FOR THE MARINADE:

⅓ **cup fish sauce or soy sauce**

⅓ **cup fresh lime juice**

¼ **cup honey**

4 **cloves garlic, minced**

2 **teaspoons ground coriander**

2 **teaspoons ground turmeric**

Spicy Peanut Sauce (recipe follows)

About 40 6-inch bamboo skewers

1. Wash and dry the chicken, pork, and beef, and trim off any fat or sinew. Cut the chicken and pork into strips about 3 inches long and ½-inch wide. Slice the beef into long, thin strips. Peel and devein the shrimp. Put each ingredient in a separate nonreactive bowl.

2. Make the marinade: Put the fish sauce, lime juice, honey, garlic, coriander, and turmeric in a nonreactive mixing bowl and stir to combine. Divide the marinade among the four bowls of ingredients and marinate 30 minutes. Meanwhile, soak the skewers in cold water.

3. Preheat a grill or broiler to high. Thread the chicken, pork, beef, and shrimp onto the skewers (10 skewers of each ingredient). Grill or broil the satés until cooked through, about 1 to 3 minutes per side. If the skewer ends begin to burn, protect them with strips of aluminum foil.

4. Transfer the satés to a platter and serve with Spicy Peanut Sauce.

Makes 40 kebabs

33 CALORIES PER PIECE; 4 G PROTEIN; 0.7 G FAT; 0.3 G SATURATED FAT; 2.2 G CARBOHYDRATE; 189 MG SODIUM; 18 MG CHOLESTEROL

SPICY PEANUT SAUCE

Peanut sauce is the traditional accompaniment to satés. I've lightened the recipe by reducing the amount of peanut butter and replacing the coconut milk with chicken stock.

⅔ **cup warm chicken or vegetable stock**

⅓ **cup chunky peanut butter**

3 **tablespoons fish sauce or soy sauce, or to taste**

3 **tablespoons fresh lime juice, or to taste**

1 **tablespoon honey**

1 **ripe tomato, peeled, seeded, and chopped (about ¾ cup) (see page 385)**

4 **scallions, trimmed and minced**

2 **cloves garlic, minced**

1 **tablespoon minced fresh ginger**

1 **to 3 jalapeño chilies, seeded and minced (for a hotter sauce, leave in the seeds)**

¼ **cup finely chopped fresh cilantro, plus sprigs for garnish**

1. Put the stock, peanut butter, fish sauce, lime juice, honey, tomato, scallion, garlic, ginger, chilies, and cilantro in a nonreactive saucepan and bring to a boil. Reduce the heat and simmer, whisking, until the sauce is thick and creamy, about 2 minutes.

2. Correct the seasoning with fish sauce, lime juice, or honey: the sauce should be salty, tart, and sweet. Transfer the sauce to bowls and garnish with sprigs of cilantro.

Makes about 1½ cups

17 CALORIES PER SERVING; 0.7 G PROTEIN; 1.1 G FAT; 0.2 G SATURATED FAT; 1.4 G CARBOHYDRATE; 108 MG SODIUM; 0 MG CHOLESTEROL

YAKITORI
(CHICKEN AND SCALLION KEBABS)

Yakitori—tiny chicken-and-scallion kebabs basted with teriyaki sauce—is a popular Japanese appetizer. Replacing the traditional sugar with maple syrup adds more flavor. Traditionally, yakitori is cooked on a hibachi; it can also be cooked on a barbecue grill or under the broiler.

1 pound boneless, skinless chicken breast

1 bunch large scallions

FOR THE MARINADE:

3 tablespoons soy sauce

3 tablespoons maple syrup

3 tablespoons mirin (see Note)

1 teaspoon Asian sesame oil

2 scallions, trimmed and finely chopped

2 cloves garlic, minced

2 teaspoons minced fresh ginger

1½ teaspoons black or toasted white sesame seeds, for garnish (see Note)

12 6-inch bamboo skewers

1. Wash and dry the chicken and trim off any fat or sinew. Cut the chicken into pieces 1 inch long and ½-inch wide. Trim the roots off the scallions. Cut the white parts into 1-inch pieces and the green parts into 2-inch pieces.

2. Make the marinade: Put the soy sauce, maple syrup, mirin, sesame oil, scallion, garlic, and ginger in a mixing bowl and stir to combine. Add the chicken and marinate 30 minutes. Meanwhile, soak the skewers in cold water.

3. Preheat the hibachi, grill, or broiler to high. Thread the chicken and scallion pieces crosswise onto the skewers, alternating them. Fold the scallion greens in half before skewering. Reserve any excess marinade.

4. Grill or broil the yakitori until cooked through, 1 to 2 minutes per side, basting with the remaining marinade. If the skewer ends begin to burn, protect them with strips of aluminum foil. Sprinkle the kebabs with sesame seeds and serve at once.

Note: Mirin is a Japanese sweet rice wine used for cooking. Look for it in Japanese and natural foods markets and many supermarkets. You can substitute sake, cream sherry, or white wine sweetened with a little sugar or honey. Black sesame seeds are available at Japanese markets and natural foods stores. To toast sesame seeds, cook in a dry frying pan over medium heat until golden brown, 3 to 5 minutes.

Makes 12 kebabs, which will serve 4 to 6

55 CALORIES PER SERVING; 6 G PROTEIN; 1 G FAT; 0.2 G SATURATED FAT; 4 G CARBOHYDRATE; 271 MG SODIUM; 15 MG CHOLESTEROL

SEVILLE "SATÉ"

This dish, marinated in paprika, sherry, and sherry vinegar, has a decidedly Spanish accent. It is, in fact, a popular Spanish tapas.

1 pound lean pork loin or tenderloin

36 pearl onions

FOR THE MARINADE:

1 small onion, diced (about ¾ cup)

4 cloves garlic, minced

3 tablespoons minced parsley (preferably flat-leaf)

1 tablespoon Spanish paprika or Hungarian sweet paprika

½ teaspoon hot-pepper flakes

½ teaspoon ground cumin

½ teaspoon dried oregano

¼ teaspoon saffron threads

2 tablespoons sherry vinegar or red-wine vinegar

2 tablespoons dry sherry

2 teaspoons extra-virgin olive oil

salt and freshly ground black pepper

16 6-inch bamboo skewers

1. Trim any fat or sinew off the pork and cut it into ¾-inch cubes. Peel the pearl onions. Cook the onions in 1 quart boiling salted water until just tender, about 2 minutes. Drain the onions, rinse under cold water, and drain again.

2. Make the marinade: Put the diced onion, garlic, parsley, paprika, hot-pepper flakes, cumin, oregano, saffron, vinegar, sherry, and oil in a nonreactive mixing bowl, season with salt and pepper, and stir to combine. Add the pork and pearl onions and marinate 1 hour. Meanwhile, soak the skewers in cold water.

3. Preheat a grill or broiler to high. Thread the pork onto the skewers, alternating with pearl onions. Grill until the pork is cooked, 1 to 2 minutes per side, basting with any remaining marinade. If the ends begin to burn, protect them with strips of aluminum foil. Serve at once.

Makes 16 kebabs

59 CALORIES PER PIECE; 7 G PROTEIN; 1.7 G FAT; 0.5 G SATURATED FAT; 4 G CARBOHYDRATE; 17 MG SODIUM; 20 MG CHOLESTEROL

SESAME CHICKEN FINGERS

Instead of being deep-fried, these chicken fingers are baked in a colorful sesame crust. Black sesame seeds can be found at Japanese markets (where they are called gomen*), as well as at natural foods stores and Armenian markets. If black sesame seeds are unavailable, use more white.*

1 pound boneless, skinless chicken breasts

FOR THE MARINADE:

3 tablespoons soy sauce

2 tablespoons rice wine or sherry

1 tablespoon honey

1 clove garlic, minced

1 egg white

⅓ cup white sesame seeds, or as needed

½ cup black sesame seeds, or as needed

spray oil

Dipping Sauces (optional) (see pages 36, 38)

1. Preheat the oven to 400°F. Wash and dry the chicken breasts and trim off any fat. Cut the breasts on the diagonal into strips the size of your baby finger. Combine the ingredients for the marinade in a mixing bowl. Add the chicken fingers and stir to mix. Marinate the chicken for 3 hours, stirring once or twice.

2. Drain the chicken fingers in a strainer and blot dry with paper towels. Place the egg white in a shallow bowl and lightly beat with a fork. (Beat enough to break up the white, but not so much that it becomes foamy.) Combine the sesame seeds in another shallow bowl and stir to mix. Lightly spray a nonstick baking sheet with oil.

3. Using two forks, dip each chicken finger in the egg white, letting the excess drip off, then in the sesame seeds, taking care to coat all sides. Arrange the chicken in a single layer on the baking sheet. Bake until cooked, 8 to 10 minutes, turning once. Serve at once with the dipping sauces.

Makes 24 pieces, which will serve 6 as an appetizer

183 CALORIES PER SERVING;* 20 G PROTEIN; 9 G FAT; 1 G SATURATED FAT; 6 G CARBOHYDRATE; 564 MG SODIUM; 37 MG CHOLESTEROL

Analysis is based on 6 servings.

STUFFED ZUCCHINI FLOWERS

Crisply fried squash or zucchini blossoms are one of the happiest harbingers of summer in Italy— enjoyed as an antipasto in May and June, when the zucchini crop flowers. I discovered that audibly crisp and delectable crunchy zucchini flowers could be made by brushing the blossoms with beaten eggs and baking them with toasted bread crumbs.

2 dozen zucchini or squash blossoms

1 ounce smoked mozzarella, Bel Paese, or Parmigiano-Reggiano cheese, cut into 24 matchstick slivers

1 thin slice prosciutto, cut into 24 matchstick slivers

6 fresh basil or sage leaves, cut lengthwise into matchstick slivers (optional)

1 egg plus 2 whites, or ½ cup egg substitute, lightly beaten with a fork

salt and freshly ground black pepper

1 cup fine toasted bread crumbs (preferably homemade), in a shallow bowl (page 385)

spray olive oil

KOREAN CHICKEN KEBABS

The presentation of these colorful kebabs isn't traditional, but the sweet-salty sesame marinade is the very soul of Korean cuisine. The traditional meat would be beef, and it would be cooked at tableside on a pan that looks like an inverted wok. But I like the smoky flavor that comes with grilling chicken.

12 ounces boneless, skinless chicken breasts

FOR THE MARINADE:

¼ cup sesame seeds

¼ cup soy sauce

3 tablespoons honey or sugar

1 teaspoon Oriental sesame oil

3 cloves garlic, minced

2 scallions, trimmed and minced

1 tablespoon minced fresh ginger

½ teaspoon hot pepper flakes

½ teaspoon freshly ground black pepper

4 carrots, peeled

24 baby onions, peeled

salt (optional)

24 snow peas, stem ends and strings removed

8 eight-inch bamboo skewers, soaked in cold water for 1 hour

1. Wash and dry the chicken breasts and trim off any fat. Cut the breasts into ¼-inch cubes.

2. Prepare the marinade. Roast the sesame seeds in a dry skillet over medium heat until lightly browned, about 2 minutes. Transfer half the sesame seeds to a small bowl and set aside. Transfer the remaining seeds to a mixing bowl and add the remaining ingredients for the marinade. Whisk or stir until the honey or sugar is dissolved. Stir in the chicken and marinate for 30 minutes, stirring occasionally.

3. Meanwhile, cut the carrots on the diagonal into ¼-inch pieces. Boil the carrots and onions in lightly salted water until just tender, about 5 minutes. Drain the carrots and onions in a colander, refresh under cold water, and drain.

4. Thread the chicken pieces, carrots, onions, and snow peas onto the skewers, alternating colors. Fold the snow peas in half to make them fit. Preheat the grill to high.

5. Grill the kebabs until the chicken is cooked, 2 to 3 minutes per side, basting with the marinade. Transfer the kebabs to a platter and sprinkle with the remaining sesame seeds.

Makes 8 kebabs

157 CALORIES PER SERVING;* 11 G PROTEIN; 4 G FAT; 1 G SATURATED FAT; 20 G CARBOHYDRATE; 552 MG SODIUM; 20 MG CHOLESTEROL

Analysis is based on 4 servings.

1. Preheat the oven to 400°F. Check the zucchini flowers to be sure they are free of bugs. Carefully insert a sliver of cheese, a sliver of prosciutto, and a sliver of basil, if using, in each flower. Using a pastry brush, brush the blossoms on both sides with the egg mixture and season with salt and pepper. Dip each in the bread crumbs, turning to coat on all sides, shaking off the excess.

2. Arrange the squash blossoms on a nonstick baking sheet sprayed with oil. Spray the tops of the blossoms with oil and reseason with salt and pepper. Bake the squash blossoms until crisp and nicely browned, 10 to 12 minutes. Serve at once.

Makes 24 blossoms, enough to serve 4 to 6 as an antipasto

28 CALORIES PER BLOSSOM; 2 G PROTEIN; 0.8 G FAT; 0.3 G SATURATED FAT; 4 G CARBOHYDRATE; 67 MG SODIUM; 10 MG CHOLESTEROL

CHICKEN, PROSCIUTTO, AND SAGE SPEDINI

Spedini are Italian kebabs. Large ones are sold ready-made at Italian butcher shops, ready for home barbecues. Small ones make a great antipasto. Here's a bite-size spedini inspired by the classic Roman dish saltimbocca. Veal or pork spedini would be made the same way—you just substitute meat for the chicken.

1 pound boneless, skinless chicken breasts

12 pearl onions, unpeeled

salt

2 very thin slices prosciutto, cut into ½-inch strips

1 bunch sage leaves, stemmed

12 stiff sprigs fresh rosemary or bamboo skewers, each about 5 inches long

freshly ground black pepper

FOR BASTING:

1 tablespoon extra-virgin olive oil

1 teaspoon grated lemon zest

1. Trim any fat or sinew off the chicken breasts and cut each half breast lengthwise into finger-thick strips. (Each strip should be about 4 inches long and ½-inch wide.)

2. Place the onions in a saucepan in cold salted water to cover. Bring to a boil. Cook the onions until just tender, about 5 minutes. Drain well, refresh under cold water, and drain again. Peel the onions.

3. Assemble the spedini: Place a strip of prosciutto and a sage leaf on top of each strip of chicken. Skewer the chicken on the rosemary sprig, curving it into an S shape. Skewer an onion on the end. If the rosemary sprigs are too flexible for skewering, make holes in the chicken with a bamboo skewer, then insert the rosemary. (It helps to strip the leaves off the bottom 2-inches of each rosemary sprig.) Season the spedini with salt and pepper. The recipe can be prepared several hours ahead to this stage.

4. Just before serving, preheat the grill or broiler to high. Combine the oil and lemon zest in a small bowl and stir to mix. Brush the spedini with the lemon oil and grill or broil until the chicken is cooked, 2 to 3 minutes per side. Baste with the lemon oil as the spedini cook.

Makes 12 spedini, enough to serve 6 as an appetizer, 4 as an entrée

63 CALORIES PER 1 PIECE SPEDINI; 9 G PROTEIN; 2 G FAT; 0.5 G SATURATED FAT; 1 G CARBOHYDRATE; 65 MG SODIUM; 23 MG CHOLESTEROL

GOLDEN BASKETS

This classic Thai appetizer features crisp pastry cups filled with spiced ground chicken or pork. To create a low-fat version, I made the baskets from baked Chinese ravioli wrappers instead of the traditional deep-fried batter. You get the same audible crispness and explosive flavors with dramatically less fat and labor. The traditional golden basket has sloping, fluted sides—an effect you can achieve using miniature brioche molds. Otherwise, use small muffin tins. You will need 16 molds measuring 1½ to 2 inches across.

Asian sesame oil or spray oil

16 3- to 4-inch round Chinese ravioli wrappers

FOR THE FILLING:

12 ounces boneless, skinless chicken breast

2 teaspoons canola oil

3 cloves garlic, minced

2 shallots, minced (3 to 4 tablespoons)

1 tablespoon minced fresh ginger

1 to 3 jalapeño or other hot chilies, seeded and minced (optional)

2 teaspoons curry powder

2 tablespoons packed light-brown sugar, or to taste

2 tablespoons fish sauce or soy sauce, or to taste

FOR THE GARNISH:

1 cucumber, peeled, seeded, and cut into the finest possible dice

1 red bell pepper, cored, seeded, and minced

cilantro sprigs (optional)

1. Preheat the oven to 375°F. Brush or spray the molds with the sesame or spray oil, and press a ravioli wrapper into each mold. Trim off any excess dough. Bake until the shells are browned and crisp, 10 to 15 minutes. Transfer the molds to a cooling rack.

2. While the shells are baking, prepare the filling. Trim any fat or sinew off the chicken breast. Mince the chicken with a cleaver, or cut it into ½-inch cubes and grind it in a food processor. Heat the canola oil in a large nonstick frying pan set over medium-high heat. Add the garlic, shallots, ginger, chilies, and curry powder, and cook, stirring continuously, until lightly browned, about 3 minutes.

3. Add the chicken and sauté until cooked through, about 5 minutes, crumbling it with a wooden spoon. Add the sugar and fish sauce, and cook 1 minute, or until the mixture is thick and flavorful. Correct the seasoning with fish sauce or sugar: the filling should be salty, sweet, and spicy. The recipe can be prepared ahead to this stage and refrigerated.

4. Just before serving, place 1 tablespoon of hot filling in each pastry shell. Garnish with a teaspoon of the cucumber and bell pepper, and a cilantro sprig, if desired. Serve at once.

Makes 16 baskets

50 CALORIES PER PIECE; 4 G PROTEIN; 1.7 G FAT; 0.2 G SATURATED FAT; 5 G CARBOHYDRATE; 172 MG SODIUM; 11 MG CHOLESTEROL

Golden Baskets

JALAPEÑOS STUFFED WITH PICADILLO

Picadillo lends these stuffed chilies both sweet and salty accents—the sweetness is provided by the raisins and almonds; the saltiness comes from the capers and olives.

24 large green jalapeño peppers

**Fruit and Nut Picadillo
(see page 281)**

1. Roast, peel, and seed the peppers, as described in the recipe above.

2. Prepare the picadillo and stuff each pepper with a spoonful. You may have some filling left over. Reward yourself with a little snack.

3. The stuffed peppers can be served at room temperature or hot. (To serve hot, heat the peppers on a nonstick baking sheet in a 400-degree oven for 10 to 15 minutes.)

Serves 6 to 8

109 CALORIES PER SERVING;*
9 G PROTEIN; 3 G FAT; 1 G SATURATED FAT;
13 G CARBOHYDRATE; 28 MG SODIUM;
15 MG CHOLESTEROL

Analysis is based on 6 servings.

STUFFIES
(RHODE ISLAND STUFFED CLAMS)

I like to think of the following as low-fat clams casino. The recipe is based on Rhode Island's official state snack, stuffies (stuffed clams). A Rhode Islander would use a quahog (the large hardshell clam favored by New Englanders for making chowder). Littleneck or cherrystone make for better finger fare, but any size clam will do.

36 littleneck clams, 24 cherrystone clams, or 12 quahogs

2 cups cool water

1½ teaspoons extra-virgin olive oil

1 small onion, finely chopped

2 shallots, finely chopped

2 stalks celery, finely chopped

2 cloves garlic, minced

1 scallion, finely chopped

1 tablespoon fresh or 1 teaspoon dried marjoram

1 teaspoon fresh or dried thyme

1 tablespoon fresh or 1 teaspoon dried oregano

2 teaspoons grated lemon zest

5 tablespoons finely chopped parsley (preferably flat-leaf)

2 cups fresh bread crumbs, lightly toasted, plus more as needed

1 to 2 tablespoons fresh lemon juice

1 teaspoon hot sauce (optional)

salt and freshly ground black pepper

cayenne pepper

1. Scrub the clams with a stiff brush under cold running water to remove any sand. Place the clams in a large pot with a tight-fitting lid. Add the water, cover, bring to a boil, and cook until the shells just begin to open, about 5 minutes for cherrystones or littlenecks, 10 to 15 minutes for quahogs. Transfer the clams with a slotted spoon to a plate to cool. Strain the cooking liquid through a cheese-cloth or paper-towel-lined sieve and reserve 1½ cups. (Any excess can be saved for chowders or stews.)

2. Remove the meat from the clamshells, reserving the bottoms of the shells. Finely chop the clam meat in a food processor or meat grinder or by hand, reserving the juices.

3. Heat the oil in a large nonstick frying pan. Add the onion, shallot, celery, and garlic, and cook over medium heat until the vegetables just begin to brown, about 5 minutes. Add the chopped clams, scallion, marjoram, thyme, oregano, and zest, and 4 tablespoons of the parsley, and cook 1 minute. Remove the pan from the heat.

4. Put the bread crumbs, lemon juice, and hot sauce and 1 cup of the reserved clam broth in a nonreactive mixing bowl. Stir in the clam mixture and season with salt, pepper, and cayenne. If the mixture is too dry, add a little more clam broth; if it's too wet, add a few more bread crumbs. Spoon the clam mixture into the reserved shells, mounding it high in the center. The stuffies can be prepared ahead to this stage and refrigerated; they can even be frozen.

5. Arrange the broiler rack 6 inches under the heating element and preheat the broiler. Broil the stuffies until thoroughly heated and golden brown on top, about 15 minutes. Sprinkle with the remaining 1 tablespoon parsley and serve at once.

Serves 6 to 8

49 CALORIES PER SERVING; 6 G PROTEIN; 0.9 G FAT; 0.1 G SATURATED FAT; 4 G CARBOHYDRATE; 48 MG SODIUM; 15 MG CHOLESTEROL

STUFFED CLAMS WITH PROSCIUTTO AND OREGANO

When I was growing up, stuffed clams—loaded with butter and bacon—were part of any self-respecting antipasto platter. Here's a low-fat version that uses prosciutto and fresh oregano for flavor, with a fraction of the fat found in the original. I like the delicacy of littleneck or cherrystone clams, but you could make the recipe with a dozen large clams.

24 littleneck or cherrystone clams (1½ to 2 inches across)

2 cups dry white wine

1 tablespoon extra-virgin olive oil, plus ½ to 1 tablespoon for drizzling

1 medium onion, finely chopped

2 stalks celery, finely chopped

2 cloves garlic, minced

1 ounce prosciutto, minced

3 tablespoons finely chopped flat-leaf parsley

2 teaspoons chopped fresh oregano, plus 24 leaves or tiny sprigs for garnish

1¾ cups fresh bread crumbs, lightly toasted

1 teaspoon fresh lemon juice, or to taste

salt and freshly ground black pepper

1. Scrub the clams with a stiff brush under cold water to remove any grit or sand. Bring the wine to a boil in a large pot. Add the clams, tightly cover the pot, and cook over high heat until the shells just begin to open, 6 to 8 minutes. Transfer the clams with a slotted spoon to a plate to cool. Strain the broth (the cooking liquid) through cheesecloth or strainer lined with a paper towel and set aside 1½ cups. (Any excess can be saved for the Umbrian Clam "Chowder" on page 51.)

2. Remove the meat from the clamshells, reserving the bottoms of the shells. Finely chop the clam meat in a food processor or by hand, reserving the juices.

3. Heat the olive oil in a large nonstick frying pan. Cook the onion, celery, garlic, and prosciutto over medium heat until just beginning to brown, about 5 minutes. Add the chopped clams, parsley, and chopped oregano and cook for 1 minute. Remove the pan from the heat.

4. Stir in the clams, the bread crumbs, and enough reserved broth to obtain a moist but not wet filling. Add lemon juice, salt, and pepper to taste: the mixture should be highly seasoned. Spoon the mixture into the clamshells, mounding it high in the center. The clams can be prepared ahead to this stage. Preheat the oven to 450°F. or preheat the broiler.

5. Drizzle a little of the ½ to 1 tablespoon olive oil over each clam. Bake or broil the clams until thoroughly heated and browned on top, about 15 minutes. Garnish each clam with an oregano sprig or leaf and serve at once.

Makes 24 pieces

37 CALORIES PER CLAM; 2 G PROTEIN; 1 G FAT; 0.2 G SATURATED FAT; 3 G CARBOHYDRATE; 48 MG SODIUM; 4 MG CHOLESTEROL

OYSTERS ON THE HALF SHELL WITH MANGO MIGNONETTE

I love oysters on the half shell, especially when served with the zestily tart French dipping sauce, mignonette. The term (literally, "little darling") refers to cracked black peppercorns. (To crack peppercorns, coarsely crush in a mortar and pestle or wrap in a dish towel and smash under the edge of a heavy frying pan.) Mango adds a tropical touch to a French classic.

FOR THE MIGNONETTE SAUCE:

2 to 3 large shallots (6 tablespoons minced)

½ ripe mango, peeled, seeded, and cut into ¼-inch dice (6 tablespoons minced)

1 tablespoon cracked black peppercorns

½ cup red or white wine vinegar

½ cup dry white wine

salt

24 oysters in the shell

Makes 24 pieces

28 CALORIES PER PIECE; 2.8 G PROTEIN; 0.7 G FAT; 0.2 G SATURATED FAT; 3 G CARBOHYDRATE; 31 MG SODIUM; 14 MG CHOLESTEROL

1. Combine the ingredients for the mignonette sauce in a mixing bowl and stir to mix, adding salt to taste.

2. Just before serving, shuck the oysters. (It's a good idea to wear heavy gloves to protect your hands while shucking.) Arrange the oysters on a platter lined with ice or seaweed or both. Spoon a little Mango Mignonette sauce over each oyster and serve the remainder on the side, in a bowl with a spoon.

CRAB-STUFFED ARTICHOKES

This dish dates from my student days at the Cordon Bleu in Paris. Shrimp, lobster, or chicken breast can be substituted for the crab. For the best results, use homemade bread crumbs.
Serve with Lemon Chili Sauce (page 32) or
Horseradish "Cream" (page 32).

4 large artichokes

½ lemon

salt

FOR THE STUFFING:

½ pound crabmeat

1 teaspoon freshly grated lemon zest

3 tablespoons lightly toasted fresh bread crumbs

3 tablespoons finely chopped flat-leaf parsley

2 tablespoons finely chopped fresh dill, or more parsley

2 scallions, finely chopped

1 tablespoon Dijon-style mustard

salt and freshly ground black pepper

pinch of cayenne pepper

2 teaspoons olive oil

1. Cut the stems and crowns (the top third) off the artichokes. With scissors, cut the barbs off the leaves. Rub the artichokes with the lemon to prevent browning. Cook in at least 3 quarts of boiling salted water for 30 to 40 minutes, or until the leaves pull away easily and you can easily pierce the heart with a skewer. Refresh under cold water, invert, and drain.

2. To make the stuffing, pick through the crabmeat, removing any bits of shell. Combine the crabmeat with the zest, bread crumbs, herbs, scallions, mustard, salt, pepper, and cayenne in a bowl and mix well. Correct the seasoning, adding salt, pepper, and cayenne to taste.

3. Remove the inside leaves of the artichokes to make a 1½-inch cavity. Use a melon baller or grapefruit spoon to scrape out the fibrous "choke" at the bottom, taking care not to pierce the heart. Spoon the filling into the artichokes and sprinkle ½ teaspoon oil over each. The artichokes can be prepared ahead to this stage.

4. Preheat the oven to 400°F. Bake the stuffed artichokes for 10 to 15 minutes, or until thoroughly heated. Serve warm or at room temperature.

Serves 4

122 CALORIES PER SERVING; 8 G PROTEIN; 4 G FAT; 18 G CARBOHYDRATE; 303 MG SODIUM; 8 MG CHOLESTEROL

LEMON CHILI SAUCE

I first tasted this sauce at the Royal Orchid Sheraton Hotel in Bangkok. It was meant to be served with grilled seafood, but I soon found myself eating it straight with a spoon. For a truly authentic version, use cilantro root, which tastes like a cross between cilantro leaves and parsnips. (Asian and Hispanic markets often sell the whole plant.) Cilantro leaves produce a tasty sauce, too.

- 1 head fresh garlic, minced (¼ cup)
- 4 or 5 fresh hot red chilies, minced (¼ cup)
- 3 tablespoons minced cilantro root or leaves
- ½ cup fresh lemon juice
- ½ cup fish sauce
- 2 tablespoons sugar (or to taste)

Combine all the ingredients in a glass bowl and stir until the sugar is completely dissolved. Add more sugar as necessary. The sauce should be tart, salty, and sweet.

Makes 1¼ cups

17 CALORIES PER TABLESPOON; 1 G PROTEIN; 0 G FAT; 2 G CARBOHYDRATE; 147 MG SODIUM; 3 MG CHOLESTEROL

HORSERADISH "CREAM"

Here's another low-fat remake of a high-calorie favorite. This attractive sauce makes a great accompaniment for smoked fish, boiled shrimp (or any sort of raw or cooked seafood), steaks, and roast beef.

- 2 cups nonfat yogurt
- 1 tablespoon white horseradish or finely grated fresh root
- 1 clove garlic, minced (1 teaspoon)
- 1 shallot, minced
- 1 tablespoon minced fresh chives
- 1 teaspoon Dijon-style mustard
- 1 teaspoon fresh lemon juice
- salt and freshly ground black pepper

Drain the yogurt in a yogurt funnel or a cheesecloth-lined colander for 2 hours. Gently stir the remaining ingredients into the yogurt. Correct the seasoning, adding salt and horseradish to taste. The sauce should be very spicy.

Makes 1¼ cups

15 CALORIES PER TABLESPOON; 2 G PROTEIN; 0 G FAT; 2 G CARBOHYDRATE; 32 MG SODIUM; 0 MG CHOLESTEROL

STUFFED MUSSELS

No antipasto spread would be complete without stuffed shell-fish. These mussels can be prepared ahead of time and are equally tasty served hot or at room temperature. There are a couple of options for cheese. For a sweeter stuffing, you could use Parmigiano-Reggiano. For a sharper stuffing, you could use Pecorino Romano. Or you could omit the cheese entirely.

- 2 pounds mussels
- 1 cup dry white wine
- 1 small onion, peeled and quartered

FOR THE STUFFING:

- 1½ tablespoons extra-virgin olive oil
- 3 to 4 shallots or 1 small onion, minced (about ¾ cup)
- 1 celery stalk, minced
- 2 cloves garlic, minced
- 1¼ cups fine dry bread crumbs
- 2 tablespoons finely chopped flat-leaf parsley
- 1 teaspoon finely grated lemon zest
- 2 tablespoons grated Parmigiano-Reggiano or Pecorino Romano cheese (optional)

1. Scrub the mussels, discarding any with cracked shells or shells that fail to close when tapped. Bring the wine and quartered onion to a boil in a large, heavy saucepan. Add the mussels and tightly cover the pot. Cook the mussels until the shells open wide, about 8 minutes, stirring once or twice to give the mussels on the bottom room to open. Transfer the cooked mussels to a colander to drain, discarding any that do not open. (Strain the broth through cheesecloth and set aside.) When the mussels are cool enough to handle, remove the top shell. Arrange the bottom shells with the mussels on a heat-proof platter.

2. Prepare the stuffing: Heat half the olive oil in a nonstick frying pan. Add the shallots, celery, and garlic and cook over medium heat until just beginning to brown, about 5 minutes. Stir in the bread crumbs, parsley, lemon zest, and cheese, if using. Add 6 to 8 tablespoons mussel liquid—enough to moisten the stuffing but not so much that it will make the stuffing soggy. (Save extra mussel liquid for one of the fish soups on pages 51–53.) Place a spoonful of stuffing in each mussel shell, smoothing the top with the back of a spoon. The recipe can be prepared ahead to this stage.

3. Preheat the oven to 400°F. or preheat the broiler. Bake the mussels until thoroughly heated and the top is lightly browned, about 15 minutes, or broil for 2 minutes. Just before serving, drizzle the remaining olive oil over the mussels or spray with spray oil.

Makes 40 to 50 pieces, enough to serve 6 to 8 as an appetizer

42 CALORIES PER EACH OF 40 PIECES; 4 G PROTEIN; 1 G FAT; 0.1 G SATURATED FAT; 4 G CARBOHYDRATE; 95 MG SODIUM; 13 MG CHOLESTEROL

....

BRAZILIAN STUFFED CRAB

Casquinha de siri (literally, "crab shells") turn up in seaside communities throughout Brazil, where tiny surf crabs are stuffed with a lively mixture of crabmeat, bell pepper, and chilies. If you live in a fishing town, you may be able to find tiny blue crab shells for stuffing; otherwise, use scallop shells, mussel shells, or small gratin dishes. You will need 16 shells. You could even use the stuffing for filling crêpes (see page 111). This recipe can also be made with cooked shrimp instead of crabmeat.

1 tablespoon extra-virgin olive oil

½ large red onion, finely chopped (about ¾ cup)

2 cloves garlic, minced

½ green bell pepper, cored, seeded, and finely chopped

1 to 2 jalapeños or other hot chilies, seeded and minced (for a hotter stuffing leave in the seeds)

1 pound lump crabmeat

1 small tomato, peeled, seeded, and diced (see page 375)

2 tablespoons flour

1 cup skim milk (see Note)

3 tablespoons finely chopped cilantro or parsley (preferably flat-leaf)

2 teaspoons fresh lime juice, or to taste

salt and freshly ground black pepper

¼ cup dry bread crumbs

2 to 3 tablespoons grated fresh Parmesan cheese (preferably Parmigiano-Reggiano)

1. Heat the oil in a large nonstick frying pan set over medium heat. Add the onion, half the garlic, the bell pepper, and the chilies and cook until soft and just beginning to brown, about 5 minutes. Meanwhile, pick through the crabmeat to remove any bits of shell.

2. Increase the heat to high and add the tomato and crab. Cook until the liquid evaporates, about 1 minute. Stir in the flour and cook 1 minute. Stir in the milk and bring to a boil. Reduce the heat and gently simmer until thick, about 2 minutes. Remove the pan from the heat and stir in the cilantro and lime juice. Season with salt and pepper. Correct the seasoning with more lime juice if needed: the stuffing should be highly seasoned.

3. Fill the shells with the stuffing. Sprinkle with bread crumbs and grated cheese. The recipe can be prepared ahead to this stage and refrigerated.

4. Preheat the oven to 400°F. Just before serving, bake the stuffed crab shells on a baking sheet until the top is crusty and brown and the filling is bubbling hot, about 10 minutes.

Note: For a more authentic flavor, and if your fat budget allows, you could use lower-fat or reduced-fat coconut milk (one good brand is A Taste of Thai) in place of some or all of the skim milk.

Makes 16 stuffed crabs

39 CALORIES PER PIECE; 3 G PROTEIN; 1.3 G FAT; 0.3 G SATURATED FAT; 4 G CARBOHYDRATE; 111 MG SODIUM; 5 MG CHOLESTEROL

EMPANADAS
(HISPANIC MEAT PIES)

Empanadas are a popular snack from one end of Latin America to the other. The juxtaposition of sweet and salty flavors (raisins, capers, and olives) is a hallmark of Hispanic cooking. Traditionally, empanadas are filled with pork, made with a lard-based dough, and deep-fried. This recipe (made with chicken) achieves a similar crispness with a lot less fat—and a lot less work—by using ravioli wrappers (available in the produce section of most supermarkets) and baking the empanadas in the oven.

FOR THE FILLING:

8 ounces boneless, skinless chicken breast

1 clove garlic, finely chopped

½ small onion, finely chopped (about ¼ cup)

½ green bell pepper, cored, seeded, and finely chopped

½ tomato, seeded and coarsely chopped (see page 375)

1 tablespoon tomato paste

2 tablespoons chicken stock or water

½ teaspoon cumin, or to taste

2 tablespoons raisins

4 pimiento-stuffed green olives, coarsely chopped

1 teaspoon minced fresh cilantro or parsley (preferably flat-leaf)

salt and freshly ground black pepper

1 to 2 tablespoons dry bread crumbs

TO FINISH THE EMPANADAS:

36 3-inch round ravioli wrappers

spray oil or olive oil

1. Prepare the filling: Wash and dry the chicken breast and trim off any fat or sinew. Cut the chicken into ½-inch dice. Put the chicken, garlic, onion, green pepper, tomato, tomato paste, stock, cumin, raisins, olives, and cilantro in a saucepan, and season with salt and pepper. Gently simmer over medium heat, stirring often, until the chicken is cooked, about 5 minutes.

2. Transfer the mixture to a food processor and process until coarsely ground. The mixture should be fairly dry; if it is too wet, add 1 to 2 tablespoons bread crumbs. Correct the seasoning with cumin or salt: the filling should be highly seasoned. Refrigerate until cold.

3. Preheat the oven to 400°F. Lightly spray or brush a baking sheet (preferably nonstick) with oil. Arrange a few ravioli wrappers on a work surface. Very lightly brush the edge of each wrapper with water (this acts as glue to make a seal). Place a heaping teaspoon of the filling in the center and fold the wrapper in half to make a half-moon-shaped dumpling. Crimp the edges with a fork. Place the empanadas on a wire rack and repeat the process with the rest of the ravioli wrappers.

4. Arrange the empanadas on the prepared baking sheet. Spray or brush the tops of the empanadas with oil. Bake the empanadas until the pastry is crisp and golden brown on both sides, 4 to 6 minutes per side.

Makes 36 empanadas

22 CALORIES PER PIECE; 1.5 G PROTEIN; 0.4 G FAT; 0 G SATURATED FAT; 3 G CARBOHYDRATE; 16 MG SODIUM; 6 MG CHOLESTEROL

Empanadas (Hispanic Meat Pies)

OVEN-BAKED EGGROLLS

My discovery that eggroll and wonton wrappers could be baked instead of deep-fried came as a revelation.
(Like many revelations, it was an accident—a last-ditch attempt to salvage some soggy steamed dumplings.) To keep my family happy,
I've made these eggrolls vegetarian, but you could always add a little chopped cooked pork or shrimp.

FOR THE FILLING:

5 dried Chinese black mushrooms

8 ounces nappa (Chinese cabbage) or savoy cabbage, julienned (about 2 cups; ¼ to ½ cabbage, depending on size)

2 carrots, julienned (about 1 cup)

8-ounce can water chestnuts, julienned

4 ounces snapped and strung snow peas, julienned (about 1 cup)

2 stalks celery, julienned (about ¼ cup)

5 ounces mung bean sprouts (about 2 cups)

FOR THE COOKING SAUCE:

1 tablespoon cornstarch

1 tablespoon soy sauce

1 tablespoon rice wine or dry sherry

1 tablespoon oyster sauce

1 tablespoon sugar or honey

freshly ground black pepper

1 tablespoon canola oil

3 cloves garlic, minced

3 scallions, trimmed and minced

1 tablespoon slivered fresh ginger

36 to 40 4-inch square wonton wrappers

2 teaspoons cornstarch dissolved in 2 teaspoons cold water to make paste

spray oil or canola oil

1. Soak the mushrooms in hot water for 30 minutes. Drain and squeeze the mushrooms, reserving the soaking liquid for soups and sauces if desired. Stem the mushrooms and julienne. Put the mushrooms, cabbage, carrots, water chestnuts, snow peas, celery, and bean sprouts in a mixing bowl and stir to combine.

2. Put the cornstarch, soy sauce, wine, oyster sauce, and sugar in a small bowl, season with pepper, and whisk to combine.

3. Heat a wok (preferably nonstick) over high heat to smoking. Swirl in the canola oil. Add the garlic, scallion, and ginger, and stir-fry 30 seconds, or until fragrant but not browned. Add the vegetable mixture and stir-fry until the vegetables are crisp-tender and most of the liquid has evaporated, 4 to 5 minutes. Stir the sauce and add it to the wok. Bring the mixture to a boil: the sauce will thicken. Transfer the mixture to a bowl and let cool to room temperature, then refrigerate until cold. (If you're in a hurry, chill the bowl over ice.) The filling can be prepared ahead to this stage.

4. Preheat the oven to 450°F. Lightly spray or brush a nonstick baking sheet with oil. Arrange a wonton wrapper on a work surface on the diagonal, with a point facing you. Place about 1 tablespoonful of filling in the center. Fold the bottom third (the side closest to you) over the filling, then fold in the sides. Roll up the eggroll, securing the end with a dab of cornstarch paste. Assemble the remaining eggrolls the same way, placing the finished ones on the prepared baking sheet.

5. Lightly spray or brush the tops of the eggrolls with oil. Bake until crisp and golden brown on both sides, 15 to 20 minutes. Serve at once with Chinese mustard and duck sauce or Honey-Soy Dipping Sauce (see page 36).

Makes 36 to 40 2-inch eggrolls

44 CALORIES PER PIECE; 1.4 G PROTEIN; 1.2 G FAT; 0.1 G SATURATED FAT; 7 G CARBOHYDRATE; 67 MG SODIUM; 2 MG CHOLESTEROL

SEAFOOD POT STICKERS WITH HONEY-SOY DIPPING SAUCE

Pot stickers are pan-fried Chinese pork dumplings. I've lightened the traditional recipe by using seafood instead of pork. This recipe calls for equal amounts of shrimp and scallops, but you can use only shrimp if you prefer.

FOR THE FILLING:

8-ounce can water chestnuts, drained

4 ounces peeled and deveined shrimp (5 ounces if buying shrimp with shells on)

4 ounces scallops

1 clove garlic, minced

2 scallions, trimmed and minced

1 tablespoon minced fresh ginger

2 teaspoons soy sauce

1 teaspoon sugar

salt and freshly ground black pepper

TO FINISH THE POT STICKERS:

36 3-inch round ravioli wrappers

Canola oil

½ cup water

Honey-Soy Dipping Sauce (following)

1. Finely chop the water chestnuts by hand or in a food processor and transfer to a mixing bowl. Coarsely chop the shrimp and scallops in the food processor. Add the garlic, scallions, ginger, soy sauce, and sugar, season with salt and pepper, and pulse to mix. Stir the seafood mixture into the water chestnuts. Correct the seasoning with salt: the filling should be highly seasoned. (To taste for seasoning without eating raw seafood, cook a tiny bit on the end of a spoon in boiling water.)

2. Arrange a few ravioli wrappers on a work surface. Very lightly brush the edges of each wrapper with water (this acts as glue to make a seal). Place a teaspoon of the filling in the center and fold the wrapper in half to make a half-moon-shaped dumpling. Press the edges with your fingertips or crimp with a fork to seal. Place the pot stickers on a wire rack and repeat the process with the rest of the ravioli wrappers.

3. Heat 1 to 2 teaspoons oil in a large nonstick frying pan or sauté pan. Set over high heat. Arrange a single layer of pot stickers in the pan and cook, shaking the pan to prevent them from sticking, until the bottoms are nicely browned, 1 to 2 minutes. Turn the dumplings, add the water to the pan, and bring to a boil. Cover and cook 2 minutes. Remove the cover and continue cooking until all the water has evaporated and the bottoms of the dumplings are browned, 2 to 3 minutes. Transfer the dumplings to a platter and keep warm in a 200°F. oven or on a warming shelf over the stove. Cook the remaining dumplings in this fashion, adding more oil as necessary.

4. Arrange the pot stickers on a serving platter and serve with Honey-Soy Dipping Sauce.

Makes 36 dumplings

22 CALORIES PER PIECE; 2 G PROTEIN; 0.6 G FAT; 0.1 G SATURATED FAT; 3 G CARBOHYDRATE; 30 MG SODIUM; 9 MG CHOLESTEROL

HONEY-SOY DIPPING SAUCE

Here's a sweet-and-sour sauce for people who don't like sweet-and-sour sauce. There's nothing sticky or cloying about it.

⅔ cup low-sodium soy sauce

⅔ cup distilled vinegar

¼ cup honey, or to taste

¼ cup water, or to taste

3 cloves garlic, minced

1 tablespoon minced fresh ginger

3 scallions, trimmed and minced

Put all the ingredients in a nonreactive mixing bowl and whisk to combine. If the sauce tastes too strong, add a little more water; if it's too salty, add a little more honey. Transfer the sauce to small bowls for dipping.

Makes 1¾ cups

11 CALORIES PER SERVING (2 TEASPOONS); 0.3 G PROTEIN; 0 G FAT; 0 G SATURATED FAT; 2.7 G CARBOHYDRATE; 179 MG SODIUM; 0 MG CHOLESTEROL

SANTA FE "SUSHI"

You won't find this dish at any sushi bar, but the colorful assortment of tuna, avocado, tomato, and scallion rolled in a tortilla recalls some of Japan's maki (seaweed, rice, and fish rolls). You could also use cooked shrimp (see Note).

12 ounces fresh tuna steak

2 teaspoons extra-virgin olive oil

2 teaspoons chili powder

salt and freshly ground black pepper

2 poblano chilies or
   1 green bell pepper

1 yellow bell pepper (optional)

8 ounces fresh spinach, stemmed

Santa Fe "Sushi"

FOR THE CHILI CREAM SAUCE:

1 cup nonfat sour cream

1 tablespoon fresh lime juice

2 teaspoons chili powder

½ teaspoon ground cumin

salt and freshly ground black pepper

TO FINISH THE "SUSHI":

4 8-inch flour tortillas

1 ripe avocado

1 tomato, peeled and seeded
   (see page 385)

1 bunch cilantro, separated into sprigs

8 pickled jalapeño chilies, thinly
   sliced lengthwise (optional)

8 scallions, green part only

1. Brush the tuna with the oil on both sides, sprinkle with the chili powder, and season with salt and pepper. Heat a nonstick frying pan over high heat. Sear the tuna on both sides (1 to 2 minutes per side for rare, 2 to 3 minutes per side for medium). Transfer the tuna to a plate and let cool. (Alternatively, the tuna can be grilled or broiled.)

2. Roast and peel the poblano and yellow pepper. Cut them into long, ¼-inch strips. Blanch the spinach in boiling salted water until tender, about 30 seconds. Drain, chill in ice water, drain again, and blot dry with paper towels.

3. Make the chili cream sauce: Put the sour cream, lime juice, chili powder, and cumin in a nonreactive mixing bowl and whisk to combine. Season with salt and pepper: the sauce should be highly seasoned. Place half the cream sauce in a small serving bowl to serve as a dipping sauce.

4. Preheat the oven to 350°F. Place the tortillas on a baking sheet and heat until soft and pliable, 2 to 3 minutes. Meanwhile, peel and pit the avocado and cut it into long, ¼-inch strips. Cut the tomato into long, ¼-inch strips. Slice the tuna into long, ¼-inch strips.

5. To assemble the "sushi," lay a tortilla on a work surface. Spread 1 tablespoon of the remaining cream sauce evenly over the surface. Arrange a thin layer of spinach on top of this. Starting at the edge closest to you, arrange strips of tuna, avocado, tomato, roasted peppers, cilantro, jalapeño, and scallions in neat horizontal rows, leaving the last inch of tortilla uncovered. Roll up the tortilla tightly and wrap in plastic wrap. Repeat with the remaining tortillas. Let the "sushi" stand 10 minutes before cutting.

6. Just before serving, using a very sharp, slender knife, cut each "sushi" roll crosswise into 1-inch sections. (Do not serve end sections that look ragged.) Stand the sections on end and arrange them on a platter around the bowl of dipping sauce.

Note: You can substitute 16 large, peeled, and deveined shrimp for the tuna. Impale them end to end on a bamboo skewer to keep them straight during cooking. Poach in simmering water until just firm, about 1 minute. Season with salt and pepper, omitting the chili powder.

Makes 4 to 5 dozen pieces

33 CALORIES PER PIECE; 2.5 G PROTEIN; 1.3 G FAT; 0.3 G SATURATED FAT; 3 G CARBOHYDRATE; 27 MG SODIUM; 3 MG CHOLESTEROL

CHICKEN AND LETTUCE BUNDLES WITH VIETNAMESE DIPPING SAUCE

This unusual appetizer combines several Asian cuisines. The bundles offer the pleasing crunch and explosive flavor of spring rolls, but without the fat associated with deep-fat frying.

½ pound boneless, skinless chicken breasts

6 dried Chinese black mushrooms

1 large or 2 small heads Boston lettuce

FOR THE WOK SAUCE:

3 tablespoons fresh lime juice

2 tablespoons fish sauce or soy sauce

4 teaspoons honey, or to taste

2 teaspoons cornstarch

1 tablespoon canola oil

2 cloves garlic, minced

2 scallions, minced

1 to 2 jalapeño chilies, minced
(for a milder dish, seed the chilies before mincing)

2 stalks celery, very finely diced

½ cup water chestnuts, very finely diced

1 cup mung bean sprouts

1 tablespoon finely chopped dry roasted peanuts (optional)

salt and freshly ground black pepper

1 bunch fresh mint or cilantro, washed and stemmed

Vietnamese Dipping Sauce (follows)

1. Wash and dry the chicken breasts and trim off any fat. Chop the chicken breasts as finely as possible with a cleaver. Soak the mushrooms in hot water to cover for 30 minutes. Drain, stem, and finely chop the mushrooms. (Save the soaking liquid for later use in soups.)

2. Peel 12 large whole leaves off the head of lettuce. (Save any remaining lettuce for salads.) Arrange the leaves around the outside of a large platter. Combine the ingredients for the wok sauce in a mixing bowl and stir until the cornstarch is dissolved.

3. Heat a nonstick work or frying pan over high heat. Swirl in the oil. Add the garlic, scallions, and chilies and stir-fry until fragrant but not brown, about 15 seconds.

Add the chicken, celery, water chestnuts, and black mushrooms and stir-fry until cooked, about 2 minutes. Stir the wok sauce to redissolve the cornstarch and add it to the chicken mixture with the bean sprouts. Stir-fry for 1 minute, or until the bean sprouts are tender but not soft. Remove the wok from the heat and stir in the peanuts, if desired. Add salt and pepper to taste, and stir in the mint leaves. Transfer the chicken mixture to a serving bowl and place it in the center of the platter with the lettuce leaves. (You can serve it hot or at room temperature.)

4. To serve, have each guest place a heaping spoonful of chicken mixture in a lettuce leaf and fold it up like a blintz. Provide each guest with a small bowl of the dipping sauce.

Makes 12 bundles, which will serve 4 to 6 as an appetizer

173 CALORIES PER SERVING; 13 G PROTEIN; 5 G FAT; 1 G SATURATED FAT; 20 G CARBOHYDRATE; 565 MG SODIUM; 27 MG CHOLESTEROL

VIETNAMESE DIPPING SAUCE

This delicate sauce goes by the name of nuoc mam *in Vietnam, where it's served as an all-purpose table sauce.*

¼ cup warm water

3 tablespoons fresh lime juice

3 tablespoons fish sauce or soy sauce

1 tablespoon honey

½ carrot, shredded as finely as possible

Combine the ingredients in a mixing bowl and stir to dissolve the honey. Divide the sauce among 4 tiny bowls for serving.

Makes about 1 cup

30 CALORIES PER SERVING;* 1 G PROTEIN; 0 G FAT; 0 G SATURATED FAT; 6 G CARBOHYDRATE; 114 MG SODIUM; 2 MG CHOLESTEROL

Analysis is based on 4 servings.

MEXICAN BAR SNACKS (BOTANAS)

"Botanas" refers to a broad range of hors d'oeuvres served at a bar or with drinks at a restaurant. (Another word for botana is bocadito, meaning "little mouthful.") Order a beer or a shot of tequila and tiny plates of these simple snacks will appear on your table—usually with no extra charge to the customer. A simple botana might be chili- and garlic-spiced peanuts. A more elaborate spread could include chilied fruit, spiced cucumbers, stewed pumpkin, pickled vegetables, ceviche—the selection is almost endless. Here are some of the botanas served at a charming open-air seafood restaurant called Le Saint Bonnet in the town of Progreso on the Gulf of Mexico in the Yucatán.

CHILIED PINEAPPLE

Here in the United States, we don't usually season fruit with chili powder, but Mexicans (and, for that matter, Indians and Southeast Asians) love the way chilies and salt bring out the succulence and sweetness of fruit. For the best results, use a golden pineapple—available at gourmet shops and most supermarkets.

- 1 pineapple, peeled, cored, and cut into 1-inch pieces (4 to 6 cups)
- 2 tablespoons fresh lime juice
- 1 tablespoon hot chili powder, or to taste
- Coarse sea salt or kosher salt

Place the pineapple in a bowl and toss with the lime juice. Sprinkle with the chili powder and salt and serve at once, with toothpicks for skewering.

Serves 8 to 12

33 CALORIES PER SERVING;* 0.4 G PROTEIN; 0.4 G FAT; 0 G SATURATED FAT; 1 G CARBOHYDRATE; 10 MG SODIUM; 0 MG CHOLESTEROL

Analysis is based on 8 servings.

SPICED CUCUMBER

There's nothing more refreshing on a hot day than cool cucumber—especially when it's seasoned with fresh lime juice and cilantro.

- 1 European-style cucumber
- 2 tablespoons fresh lime juice, or as needed
- ½ cup coarsely chopped fresh cilantro
- ¼ white onion, finely chopped
- salt and freshly ground black pepper

1. Peel the cucumber and cut it lengthwise into quarters, then widthwise into 1-inch chunks.

2. Place the cucumber in an attractive serving bowl and stir in the lime juice, cilantro, onion, salt, and pepper. Correct the seasoning, adding salt and lime juice to taste. Serve with toothpicks for skewering.

Serves 4 to 6

8 CALORIES PER SERVING;* 0.3 G PROTEIN; 0.1 G FAT; 0 G SATURATED FAT; 2 G CARBOHYDRATE; 2 MG SODIUM; 0 MG CHOLESTEROL

Analysis is based on 4 servings.

STEWED PUMPKIN BOTANA

You might not think of pumpkin as a bar snack, but this one—stewed with onions and garlic and topped with grated queso fresco—is as delectable as it is unexpected. If fresh pumpkin isn't available, use butternut squash.

- 1 pound peeled pumpkin, cut into 1-inch dice
- 1 small onion, thinly sliced
- 2 cloves garlic, thinly sliced
- 1 tomato, peeled, seeded, and diced
- 2 sprigs cilantro
- salt and freshly ground black pepper
- 2 tablespoons finely grated queso fresco or feta cheese

1. Place the pumpkin, onion, garlic, tomato, cilantro, salt, and pepper in a saucepan. Add water to cover and bring to a boil. Reduce the heat to medium and simmer the vegetables until the pumpkin is just tender and most of the water has evaporated, about 10 minutes, stirring occasionally. (If the water evaporates before the pumpkin is tender, add a little more.) Correct the seasoning, adding salt and pepper to taste.

2. Transfer the pumpkin mixture to a serving bowl and let cool to room temperature. Sprinkle the cheese over the pumpkin and serve at once. Serve with toothpicks for skewering.

Serves 4 to 6

72 CALORIES PER SERVING;* 3 G PROTEIN; 2 G FAT; 0.1 G SATURATED FAT; 11 G CARBOHYDRATE; 49 MG SODIUM; 7 MG CHOLESTEROL

Analysis is based on 4 servings.

CHIPS WITH REFRIES

Most of us think of frijoles refritos (refried beans) as a burrito filling or side dish. But sprinkled with a little queso fresco, refries make an excellent dip for tortilla chips. **Note:** *If you're in a hurry, you could use a good commercial brand of fat-free refried beans.*

- ½ batch refried beans, cooled to room temperature (page 306)
- 2 tablespoons crumbled or finely grated queso fresco or feta cheese
- Mess o' Chips (made with 6 tortillas—page 3)

Mound the beans in a bowl or platter and sprinkle with queso fresco. Arrange the chips around the beans or in a bowl on the side and serve at once. (Use chips for scooping up the beans.)

Serves 6

142 CALORIES PER SERVING; 6 G PROTEIN; 3 G FAT; 0.3 G SATURATED FAT; 23 G CARBOHYDRATE; 277 MG SODIUM; 5 MG CHOLESTEROL

GROUPER CEVICHE

No botana spread would be complete without some sort of ceviche. This one features grouper marinated in sour orange juice—a local citrus fruit that has the tartness of lime with the fruity overtones of fresh orange and grapefruit. If you live in an area with a large Hispanic community, you may be able to find fresh sour oranges. Otherwise, use lime juice flavored with a little fresh orange juice and grapefruit juice.

- **1 pound fresh grouper fillets or other impeccably fresh fish**
- **½ medium white onion, finely chopped**
- **1 cup fresh sour orange juice, or ¾ cup fresh lime juice, plus 2 tablespoons each fresh orange juice and grapefruit juice**
- **1 tomato, peeled, seeded, and diced**
- **1 or 2 serrano chilies, thinly sliced**
- **¼ cup chopped fresh cilantro**
- **salt**

1. Cut the fish fillets lengthwise into 1-inch strips. Cut each strip widthwise on the diagonal into ⅛-inch slices. (The idea is to obtain pieces that are about 1-inch square and ⅛-inch thick.) Transfer the fish and onion to a mixing bowl and stir in the sour orange juice. Marinate for 15 minutes.

2. Stir in the tomato, chili, cilantro, and salt to taste; the ceviche should be highly seasoned. Marinate for 5 minutes, then transfer to an attractive bowl for serving. Serve with little plates and forks.

Serves 4

153 CALORIES PER SERVING; 23 G PROTEIN; 1 G FAT; 0.3 G SATURATED FAT; 11 G CARBOHYDRATE; 65 MG SODIUM; 41 MG CHOLESTEROL

BLACK BEAN MINI-TOSTADAS WITH QUESO AÑEJO

These crisp mouthfuls are simplicity itself, yet the striking flavors of avocado leaf-scented refried black beans (smoky, with a touch of anise flavor) and salty queso añejo (aged cheese) are downright symphonic. Queso añejo is a salty, sourish, tangy white cheese available at Mexican markets. (Feta cheese makes the best substitute.) **Note:** *If you're in a hurry, use a good commercial brand of fat-free refried beans. If epazote is unavailable, substitute sprigs of cilantro, although the flavor won't be quite the same. Also,*

you could make four large tostadas by omitting cutting the tortillas in step 1.

- **4 corn tortillas**
- **1 tablespoon melted lard or olive oil (optional)**
- **1 cup refried black beans**
- **¼ cup crumbled queso añejo**
- **24 sprigs epazote**

1. Preheat the oven to 350°F. Brush the tortillas on both sides with lard or olive oil (if using). Cut each tortilla into six wedges and arrange them in a single layer on a baking sheet. Bake the tortillas until they're lightly browned, 8 to 10 minutes. Transfer to a cake rack to cool; they'll crisp as they cool.

2. Just before serving, warm the black beans. Place a spoonful of the beans on each tortilla chip. Top with a sprinkle of cheese and a sprig of epazote. Serve at once.

Makes 24 pieces, enough to serve 4 to 6 as an appetizer

158 CALORIES PER SERVING;* 7 G PROTEIN; 6 G FAT; 0.2 G SATURATED FAT; 20 G CARBOHYDRATE; 294 MG SODIUM; 14 MG CHOLESTEROL

*Analysis is based on 4 servings

GRILLED QUESADILLAS

Quesadillas are the Mexican version of a grilled cheese sandwich. Grilling imparts a smoky flavor that makes up for the relative blandness of low-fat

cheese. *(You could also broil the quesadillas or sauté them in a nonstick frying pan brushed with a little olive oil.)*

- **2–3 ounces low-fat Monterey Jack or cheddar cheese, coarsely grated**
- **1 large ripe tomato, peeled, seeded, and finely chopped**
- **1 yellow or red bell pepper, cored, seeded, and finely diced**
- **¼ cup finely chopped cilantro**
- **3 scallions, finely chopped**
- **2 pickled jalapeño chilies (or to taste), thinly sliced**
- **8 flour tortillas**
- **salt and freshly ground black pepper**

Place the cheese, tomato, yellow or red pepper, cilantro, scallions, and jalapeños in a bowl and toss to mix. Preheat the grill. Just before serving, spread four tortillas with the cheese mixture and season with salt and pepper. Place the remaining tortillas on top, sandwich-style. Grill the quesadillas over medium heat for 1 minute per side, or until the cheese is melted and the tortillas are lightly browned. Cut into wedges and serve at once.

Serves 4 as an appetizer, 2 as a light entrée.

244 CALORIES PER SERVING; 10 G PROTEIN; 7 G FAT; 37 G CARBOHYDRATE; 113 MG SODIUM; 10 MG CHOLESTEROL

MELON, MINT, AND PROSCIUTTO

It's hard to imagine an appetizer that improves on melon with prosciutto. You could use almost any type of melon, as long as it's ripe. I like the color contrast provided by honeydew, but you can't go wrong with other old standbys, like cantaloupe or Cranshaw. To make an easy-to-eat finger food, serve the melon balls on toothpicks.

1 very ripe melon

1 bunch mint, washed and stemmed

1½ ounces very thinly sliced prosciutto, cut into 1-inch squares

Halve and seed the melon and cut it into 1-inch balls with a melon baller. Make a slit in each melon ball going half-way through to the bottom. Insert a mint leaf and a square of prosciutto in each melon ball.

Makes about 30 pieces, enough to serve 6

78 CALORIES PER SERVING; 3 G PROTEIN; 1 G FAT; 0.5 G SATURATED FAT; 16 G CARBOHYDRATE; 150 MG SODIUM; 6 MG CHOLESTEROL

VEAL CARPACCIO WITH WHITE TRUFFLES

This carpaccio, actually more a veal tartare, is a specialty of the restaurant Il Vicoletto in the city of Alba in Piedmont. Alba, of course, is the capital of Italy's white-truffle trade, and if you're lucky enough to be there during truffle season (October to January), you can order your carpaccio topped with paper-thin slices of white truffle. Alternatively, you can sprinkle a few drops of truffle oil (also available at gourmet shops) on top of each. But even if you can't find fresh white truffles, this tangy carpaccio makes a delectably different antipasto. Buy the veal at a quality butcher shop that prizes freshness.

1 pound veal loin or tenderloin, meticulously trimmed of all fat and sinew

1 to 2 anchovy fillets, rinsed, blotted dry, and finely chopped

1 large shallot or ¼ red onion, minced (about 3 tablespoons)

½ clove garlic, minced

1 to 2 tablespoons fresh lemon juice, or to taste

1½ tablespoons extra-virgin olive oil

salt and freshly ground black pepper

1 bunch arugula, stemmed, washed, and dried (see box on page 69)

¼ to ½ ounce fresh white truffle or ½ teaspoon truffle oil

crostini (see page 13) or toast points

1. Finely chop the veal by hand using a cleaver or a sharp chopping knife. Hand chopping produces a much more pleasing texture than the food processor. Transfer the veal to a mixing bowl and stir in the anchovies, shallot, garlic, and lemon juice. Add half the olive oil and salt and pepper to taste.

2. Line 4 salad plates with arugula leaves and mound the veal mixture in the center. Drizzle the remaining olive oil over the veal and arugula. Season with more salt and pepper. If using fresh truffle, shave it as thinly as possible over the veal, using a truffle shaver (see Note). If using truffle oil, sprinkle a few drops on top. Serve the crostini or toast points on the side.

Note: White truffles taste best when sliced tissue-thin. The best way to do this is with a truffle shaver, a sort of hand-held mandolin with an adjustable blade that enables you to cut slices thin enough to read through. When you dine at a good restaurant in Alba during truffle season, you often find a truffle on a plate on your table. The waiter weighs the truffle before and after slicing. Guests are charged according to the amount of truffle used. Unlike black truffles, white are almost never cooked.

Serves 4

205 CALORIES PER SERVING; 9 G PROTEIN; 11 G FAT; 3 G SATURATED FAT; 2 G CARBOHYDRATE; 122 MG SODIUM; 90 MG CHOLESTEROL

SOUPS

MEXICAN GAZPACHO

Gazpacho is a Spanish soup, of course, not Mexican, but the ingredients—luscious, ripe red tomatoes, onions, garlic, and peppers—are shared by both countries. One day I had the idea to roast the vegetables in a comal Mexican-style before puréeing them to make gazpacho: The result was a revelation. I think you'll be amazed by the complex, charred, smoky flavors that result from roasting the vegetables.

2 corn tortillas

8 large ripe red plum tomatoes (about 2 pounds)

1 red bell pepper

1 poblano chili or green bell pepper

1 medium white onion, quartered

1 to 2 jalapeño peppers

4 cloves garlic, peeled

4 scallions, white part trimmed, green part finely chopped

1 cucumber, peeled and seeded

2 tablespoons extra-virgin olive oil

2 tablespoons red wine vinegar, or as needed

¼ cup finely chopped cilantro

salt and freshly ground black pepper

6 lime wedges

1. Preheat the oven to 350°F. Cut the tortillas in half, then crosswise into ¼-inch strips. Arrange the strips on a baking sheet in a single layer. Bake until lightly browned, 6 to 8 minutes. Remove from the oven and let cool; the tortillas will crisp as they cool.

2. In a comal or cast-iron frying pan or under the broiler, roast the tomatoes, red pepper, poblano, onion, jalapeño, garlic, and scallions whites until nicely browned on all sides: 8 to 10 minutes for the tomatoes, peppers, and onions; 4 to 6 minutes for the jalapeños, garlic, and scallion whites. (Turn with tongs.) Transfer the vegetables to a plate and let cool. Cut open the pepper and chilies and remove the veins and seeds, reserving the juices.

3. Combine the roasted vegetables, cucumber, olive oil, vinegar, and cilantro in a blender and purée until smooth. Add water to thin the gazpacho to pourable consistency (1 to 2 cups). Add salt, pepper, and more vinegar (if needed); the gazpacho should be highly seasoned.

4. Pour or ladle the gazpacho into bowls. Garnish each with the chopped scallion greens and crisped tortilla slivers. Serve with lime wedges for squeezing.

Serves 6

127 CALORIES PER SERVING; 4 G PROTEIN; 6 G FAT; 1 G SATURATED FAT; 20 G CARBOHYDRATE; 33 MG SODIUM; 0 MG CHOLESTEROL

GRAPE GAZPACHO

To most people, gazpacho means an icy purée of tomatoes and other vegetables. Not so in Málaga, in southern Spain, where grapes, garlic, and almonds are turned into an uncommonly refreshing soup, ajo blanco. It is traditionally made with green grapes, but a lovely rose color and rich flavor can be obtained with red grapes.

¼ cup blanched almonds

2 pounds seedless red grapes

1 or 2 cloves garlic, minced (1 or 2 teaspoons)

2 or 3 slices firm white bread, crusts removed, diced (about 2 cups)

1 tablespoon Spanish olive oil

1 tablespoon wine vinegar (or to taste)

½ teaspoon almond extract (optional)

salt and freshly ground black pepper

¼ cup nonfat yogurt

1. Preheat the oven to 350°F. Lightly toast the almonds on a baking sheet (or use a toaster oven) for 10 minutes, or until crisp but not brown. Let the almonds cool.

2. Purée the almonds, grapes, and garlic in a blender. Add the bread, oil, vinegar, almond extract (if using), salt, and pepper, and purée until smooth. The gazpacho can be eaten right away, but it will taste better if you "ripen" it in the refrigerator for 1 hour. If too thick, stir in a few tablespoons of cold water.

3. Just before serving, correct the seasoning, adding vinegar and salt to taste. The sweetness of the grapes should be balanced by the piquancy of the vinegar and pungency of the garlic. Whisk the yogurt in a small bowl until smooth and creamy. Ladle the gazpacho into serving bowls and garnish each with a dollop of yogurt. If you like, marble the yogurt into the soup with the tip of a knife.

Serves 4

272 CALORIES PER SERVING; 5 G PROTEIN; 9 G FAT;
49 G CARBOHYDRATE; 75 MG SODIUM; 0 MG CHOLESTEROL

CINNAMON PEACH SOUP

Here's another great cold soup for a hot summer day. For the best results, use peaches that are ripe to the point of being squishy soft. A similar soup could be made with nectarines or apricots.

2 pounds ripe peaches

3 whole cloves

3 allspice berries

3 cardamom pods

2 cups freshly squeezed orange juice

3 tablespoons fresh lime juice (or to taste)

3–4 tablespoons honey or brown sugar (or to taste)

1 teaspoon ground cinnamon

1 teaspoon ground ginger

1 cup nonfat yogurt

1 tablespoon diced candied ginger

sprigs of fresh mint, for garnish

1. Drop the peaches in a pot of boiling water and boil for 30 seconds. Rinse them under cold water and slip off the skins. Pit the peaches and coarsely chop them. Tie the cloves, allspice, and cardamom in cheesecloth (or wrap in foil and piece with a fork).

2. Combine the peaches, spice bundle, orange juice, lime juice, honey, cinnamon, and ginger in a heavy saucepan. (The amount of honey needed will depend on the sweetness of the peaches.) Simmer for 5 to 10 minutes, or until the fruit is very soft.

3. Remove the spice bundle and let the soup cool to room temperature. Purée the soup in a blender and chill. Just before serving, whisk in the yogurt and candied ginger. Correct the seasoning, adding honey and lime juice to taste. Serve in glass bowls or wine goblets, garnishing each with a sprig of mint.

Serves 4 to 6

215 CALORIES PER SERVING; 5 G PROTEIN; 1 G FAT; 51 G CARBOHYDRATE;
46 MG SODIUM; 1 MG CHOLESTEROL

COLLARD GREEN AND POTATO SOUP

This soup is modeled on Portugal's caldo verde, *or "green broth," made with a leafy cabbage similar to collard greens. In Portugal, you can buy a device that looks like a meat slicer for cutting collards into paper-thin shreds. Lacking this, roll the greens lengthwise into a tight bundle, then slice them widthwise as finely as possible, using a sharp chef's knife.*

1½ tablespoons Spanish or Portuguese olive oil

1 onion, finely chopped

3 cloves garlic, minced (1 tablespoon)

2 large potatoes, peeled and finely diced

3 cups chicken stock

3 cups water

2 bay leaves

salt and freshly ground black pepper

1½ pounds collard greens, stemmed and sliced paper-thin (8 cups)

Heat the oil in a large saucepan. Cook the onion and garlic over medium heat for 3 minutes, or until soft but not brown. Add the potatoes, stock, water, bay leaves, salt, and pepper. Bring the soup to a boil, reduce the heat, and simmer for 10 minutes, or until the potatoes are tender.

Stir in the collard greens and simmer for 1 to 2 minutes, or until just tender. Correct the seasoning, adding salt and pepper to taste. Ladle the soup into large bowls and serve with crusty bread.

Serves 6 as an appetizer, 4 as an entrée

Note: The Portuguese like their greens stringier than most North Americans do. You may wish to cut the shredded greens a few times with a chef's knife.

191 CALORIES PER SERVING; 6 G PROTEIN; 6 G FAT; 31 G CARBOHYDRATE; 82 MG SODIUM; 0 MG CHOLESTEROL

GRANDMA RAICHLEN'S CABBAGE BORSCHT

To most people, borscht means beets, but this soulful soup can be made with a multitude of vegetables. My great-grandmother brought the recipe from her native Riga to America. To make the broth, she always used flanken, a cheap, flavorful cut of meat similar to skirt steak. For a vegetarian version, you could use vegetable stock or water. I dedicate this recipe to my Aunt Vivian, who loved cabbage borscht more than anything.

1 head green or savoy cabbage

1½ tablespoons olive oil

2 leeks, finely chopped

1 large onion, finely chopped

2 carrots, peeled and finely chopped

2 stalks celery, finely chopped

1 large parsnip, peeled and finely chopped

3 cloves garlic, minced (1 tablespoon)

4 or 5 ripe tomatoes (about 2 pounds), peeled, seeded, and finely chopped, or 1 28-ounce can imported plum tomatoes

2 quarts beef stock, chicken stock, or water

5 whole cloves (or ¼ teaspoon ground cloves)

2 teaspoons caraway seeds (optional)

salt and freshly ground black pepper

¼ cup brown sugar (or to taste)

¼ cup red wine vinegar (or to taste)

½ cup finely chopped scallions (4 whole scallions), for garnish

¼ cup chopped flat-leaf parsley, for garnish

Cut the cabbage in half lengthwise. Remove the core and cut the leaves widthwise into ¼-inch strips. Heat the oil in a large saucepan. Add the leeks, onion, carrots, celery, parsnip, and garlic, and cook over medium heat for 3 minutes. Stir in the cabbage and cook, stirring often, for 6 to 8 minutes, or until soft. Stir in the tomatoes, stock, cloves, caraway seeds (if using), salt, and pepper. Bring the soup to a boil, reduce the heat, and simmer for 30 to 40 minutes, or until the vegetables are very tender.

Ten minutes before the end, stir in the brown sugar and vinegar. The soup should be a little sweet and a little sour. Correct the seasoning, adding salt, sugar, and vinegar to taste. Ladle into bowls and garnish with chopped scallions and parsley.

Serves 8 to 10

160 CALORIES PER SERVING; 6 G PROTEIN; 4 G FAT; 29 G CARBOHYDRATE; 832 MG SODIUM; 0 MG CHOLESTEROL

- -

MINESTRONE WITH PESTO

Italy meets Provence in this recipe—vegetable, bean, and pasta soup with pesto. Feel free to vary the vegetables according to what's in season and what looks good. If using canned beans, choose a low-sodium brand. This recipe may look complicated because it contains a lot of ingredients, but it's actually quick and easy to make.

1 medium onion, finely chopped

1 medium leek, trimmed, washed, and finely chopped

3 cloves garlic, thinly sliced

3 stalks celery, thinly sliced

1 large or 2 medium potatoes (about 12 ounces), peeled and cut into ¼-inch dice

3 medium zucchini (about 1 pound), cut into ¼-inch dice

3 carrots (about 8 ounces), peeled and cut into ¼-inch dice

2 ripe tomatoes (about 1 pound), peeled, seeded, and cut into ¼-inch dice

4 ounces green beans, ends snapped, cut into ¼-inch pieces

½ cup green peas (ideally freshly shucked) (optional)

1 herb bundle made by tying together 2 bay leaves, 2 sprigs fresh or dried thyme, and 2 sprigs fresh or dried rosemary

6 to 8 cups water

1½ cups cooked cannellini beans (1 15-ounce can)

2 ounces thin spaghetti, broken into ½-inch pieces

salt and freshly ground black pepper

¾ cup Enlightened Pesto (page 164)

1. In a large pot combine the onion, leek, garlic, celery, potatoes, zucchini, carrots, tomatoes, green beans, peas (if using), and herb bundle and 6 cups water and bring to a boil. Briskly simmer the soup until the vegetables are almost cooked, about 15 minutes.

2. Add the cannellini beans, spaghetti, and a little salt and pepper and simmer until the pasta and vegetables are tender, 10 to 15 minutes. Add 1 to 2 cups water (or more) if necessary to keep the soup soupy. Discard the herb bundle and correct the seasoning, adding salt and pepper to taste: the soup should be highly seasoned.

3. To serve, ladle the soup into bowls. Serve the pesto on the side. Have each eater stir a tablespoon of pesto into his soup before eating.

Note: For a quicker, easier version of this soup, omit the pesto and add 1 bunch washed, stemmed, thinly slivered basil leaves. Of course, it will be minestrone with basil, not pesto.

Makes 10 cups, enough to serve 8 to 10

190 CALORIES PER SERVING;* 7.6 G PROTEIN; 4.6 G FAT; 1 G SATURATED FAT; 31 G CARBOHYDRATE; 350 MG SODIUM; 0 MG CHOLESTEROL

Analysis is based on 8 servings.

MEXICAN NOODLE SOUP
(SOPA DE FIDEOS)

Every nation has its version of chicken noodle soup. Mexico's owes its ruddy complexion and rousing flavor to the addition of fried noodles and puréed tomatoes. Although it's not customary to roast the vegetables for this recipe, I like the depth of flavor that roasting imparts.

- 2 medium ripe red tomatoes
- 1 small white onion, quartered
- 4 cloves garlic
- 1½ tablespoons lard or olive oil
- 6 ounces vermicelli (or other slender pasta), broken into 3-inch lengths
- 3 tablespoons finely chopped flat-leaf parsley, plus 6 sprigs for garnish
- 6 cups chicken stock
- salt and freshly ground black pepper

1. Heat a comal or cast-iron skillet over medium-high heat. Roast the tomatoes, onion, and garlic until nicely browned on all sides, 8 to 10 minutes for the tomatoes and onion, 4 to 5 minutes for the garlic. Transfer the vegetables to a blender and purée to a smooth paste.

2. Heat the lard in a large saucepan. Add the vermicelli and cook over medium-high heat until it is golden brown, stirring continuously, 2 to 3 minutes. Add the vegetable purée and chopped parsley and fry until thick and fragrant, 2 to 3 minutes. Stir in the stock and bring to a boil.

3. Reduce the heat and simmer the soup until the pasta is tender, 8 to 10 minutes, stirring occasionally. Add salt and pepper to taste. Ladle the soup into bowls and serve at once, garnishing each with a sprig of parsley.

Makes 6 cups, enough to serve 6 as an appetizer, 4 as a light main course

259 CALORIES PER SERVING;* 8 G PROTEIN; 6 G FAT; 2 G SATURATED FAT; 45 G CARBOHYDRATE; 37 MG SODIUM; 5 MG CHOLESTEROL

Analysis is based on 4 servings.

TORTILLA SOUP
(SOPA DE TORTILLA)

Is there anything more comforting on a chilly night than a steaming bowl of tortilla soup, its broth smoky with roasted vegetables, warmed by pasilla chilies, fragrant with meaty chicken stock, and thick with tortilla "noodles"? Tradition calls for the tortillas to be deep-fried, but I've found that baking produces the requisite crispness with dramatically less fat—especially if you use stale tortillas.

Note: *Canadian bacon isn't traditional either, but I like the way it enhances the soup's smoke flavor.*

- 10 corn tortillas
- 3 pasilla chilies
- 8 plum tomatoes (1¼ to 1½ pounds)
- 1½ medium white onions, quartered
- 6 cloves garlic
- 3 sprigs epazote (or cilantro)
- 3 tablespoons chopped flat-leaf parsley
- 1 tablespoon lard or olive oil
- 1 ounce Canadian bacon, minced
- 6 cups chicken broth (see page 369)
- salt and freshly ground black pepper
- 4 to 6 tablespoons no-fat sour cream
- ¼ cup coarsely grated queso fresco, white cheddar, or Monterey Jack cheese (about 1 ounce)
- 4 to 6 wedges fresh lime

1. Preheat the oven to 350°F. Cut the tortillas in half, then crosswise into ½-inch strips. Arrange the strips on a baking sheet in a single layer. Bake until lightly browned, 6 to 8 minutes. Remove from the oven and let cool; the tortillas will crisp as they cool.

2. Stem the chilies, tear open, and remove the veins and seeds. Place the chilies on a baking sheet and bake until they are aromatic and crisp but not burnt, 4 to 6 minutes. Transfer to a plate to cool; the chilies will crisp as they cool. Coarsely crumble the chilies.

3. In a comal or cast-iron frying pan or under the broiler, roast the tomatoes, onions, and garlic until nicely browned: 8 to 10 minutes for the tomatoes and onions; 4 to 6 minutes for the garlic. In the blender, purée the tomatoes, onion, garlic, epazote, parsley, and one of the toasted chilies.

4. Heat the lard in a large saucepan. Fry the tomato purée and Canadian bacon over high heat, stirring well, until thick, dark, and fragrant, 5 to 10 minutes. Add the chicken broth and simmer for 10 minutes. Stir in the toasted tortilla strips and salt and pepper to taste. Cook for 2 minutes.

5. To serve, ladle the tortilla soup into bowls and garnish each with a dollop of sour cream. Sprinkle the cheese and remaining crumbled pasadilla chilies on top and serve at once, accompanied by lime wedges for squeezing.

Serves 6 as an appetizer, 4 as a hearty main course

328 CALORIES PER SERVING;* 12 G PROTEIN; 9 G FAT; 2 G SATURATED FAT; 57 G CARBOHYDRATE; 312 MG SODIUM; 14 MG CHOLESTEROL

Analysis is based on 4 servings.

Tortilla Soup (Sopa de Tortilla)

SQUID AND SWISS CHARD SOUP

Zimino is a stew of Swiss chard and cuttlefish that originated in Genoa and was traditionally served on Friday. I first tasted it at the restaurant Cesarina in Santa Margherita, where it was made with seppiolini, *cuttlefish fish so tiny a half dozen would fit in a tablespoon. I know you can't buy* seppiolini *in this country or probably even* seppie *(cuttlefish). I also know that squid has a significantly different texture and flavor. Nevertheless, the combination of Swiss chard and squid makes a delicious seafood soup with distinctly Ligurian overtones.*

Note: Sometimes I make *zimino* with spinach instead of Swiss chard. You'd need a 10-ounce package of fresh spinach or 5 ounces frozen spinach.

1 pound cleaned squid
(see box on page 191)

1½ tablespoons extra-virgin olive oil

1 onion, finely chopped

2 stalks celery, finely chopped

1 small or ½ large bulb fennel, finely chopped

2 cloves garlic, finely chopped

¼ cup finely chopped flat-leaf parsley

1 bay leaf

5 to 6 cups Fish Stock
(page 381), mussel broth, Chicken Stock (page 379), or bottled clam juice

salt and freshly ground black pepper

1 bunch Swiss chard, stemmed, washed, and thinly sliced crosswise

1 teaspoon fresh lemon juice or red wine vinegar (optional)

3 tablespoons toasted pine nuts

1. Cut the squid bodies into thin rings. Leave the tentacle section whole. Heat the olive oil in a large saucepan. Add the onion, celery, fennel, and garlic and cook until lightly browned, about 6 minutes, stirring often. Add half the parsley, the bay leaf, the fish stock, the squid, and a little salt and pepper.

2. Simmer the soup, covered, until the squid are very tender, about 40 minutes. Stir in the Swiss chard the last 10 minutes of cooking. Discard the bay leaf. If a sharper-tasting broth is desired, add a little lemon juice or vinegar. Correct the seasoning, adding salt and pepper to taste. Sprinkle the remaining parsley and the pine nuts over the stew and serve at once.

Makes 5 to 6 cups, enough to serve 4

231 CALORIES PER SERVING; 22 G PROTEIN; 11 G FAT; 2 G SATURATED FAT; 12 G CARBOHYDRATE; 99 MG SODIUM; 264 MG CHOLESTEROL

THAI HOT AND SOUR SOUP

This soup is easy to make, but it requires a few special ingredients. This recipe can also be made with chicken, pork, or squid.

- 4 or 5 stalks fresh lemongrass (or 3 tablespoons dried), or 4 strips lemon zest
- 1 tablespoon minced galangal or fresh ginger (about 1 inch fresh or frozen galangal, or 3 or 4 dried slices)
- 4 cups chicken stock
- 3 tablespoons fish sauce (or to taste)
- ½–1 teaspoon Thai chili paste or other hot sauce (or to taste)
- 1 ripe tomato, cut into 8 wedges
- 1 medium-sized onion, thinly sliced
- 1 or 2 Thai, serrano, or jalapeño chilies, thinly sliced on the diagonal
- 4 ounces fresh straw, button, or oyster mushrooms, halved or quartered (about 1 cup)
- 8 ounces small shrimp
- ¼ cup fresh lime juice
- 2 tablespoons thinly sliced scallions
- ⅓ cup fresh cilantro leaves

1. Cut the top ⅔ off each lemongrass stalk, trim off the outside leaves and roots, and cut the core into ½-inch slices on the diagonal. If using dried lemongrass, soak the pieces in warm water for 20 minutes, then mince. If using lemon zest, remove it from the fruit in thin strips with a vegetable peeler and mince. If using dried galangal, soak it in warm water for 20 minutes.

2. Combine the lemongrass, galangal, chicken stock, fish sauce, and chili paste in a saucepan and bring to a boil. Gently simmer for 5 minutes. Add the tomato, onion, chilies, mushrooms, and shrimp, and simmer for 1 minute, or until the shrimp are firm and pink. The soup can be prepared ahead to this stage.

3. Just before serving, stir in the lime juice, scallions, and cilantro. Bring the soup just to a boil. It should be spicy and quite sour. If more salt is needed, add more fish sauce. If more tartness or hotness is desired, add more lime juice or chili paste. Suggest to your guests that they eat around the lemongrass pieces.

Serves 4

104 CALORIES PER SERVING; 14 G PROTEIN; 2 G FAT; 9 G CARBOHYDRATE; 272 MG SODIUM; 90 MG CHOLESTEROL

Thai Hot and Sour Soup

RHODE ISLAND RED CHOWDER

Clams or fish? Tomatoes or cream? Nothing brings out controversy like chowder. Red chowder contains no cream and (this one at least) no salt pork. Use tiny cherrystone clams if you can find them. Otherwise, use quahogs (pronounced KO-hogs—large hard-shell clams), preshucked clam meat, or even canned clams.

3 dozen tiny cherrystone clams, 16 quahogs, or 2 cups chopped clam meat

2 cups dry white wine

2–4 cups bottled clam broth, fish stock, or water

1½ tablespoons olive oil

1 large onion, finely chopped

2 stalks celery, finely chopped

3 cloves garlic, minced (1 tablespoon)

1 teaspoon minced fresh thyme (or 1 teaspoon dried)

1 bunch flat-leaf parsley, minced

2 bay leaves

4 ripe tomatoes, peeled, seeded, and chopped (or 1 28-ounce can)

1 tablespoon tomato paste

2 large potatoes, peeled, diced, and placed in cold water to cover

salt, freshly ground black pepper, and cayenne pepper

1. Scrub the clams and place them in a large pot with the wine. Tightly cover the pot and steam until the shells open. (Cherrystones will need about 6 to 8 minutes steaming, quahogs 12 to 15 minutes.) If using cherrystones, leave the clams in the shells and set aside. If using quahogs, remove the meat from the shells and finely chop, using a meat grinder or food processor. (There should be about 2 cups meat.)

2. Strain the cooking liquid through a cheesecloth-lined strainer into a large measuring cup. Add enough clam broth to make 6 cups. (If using preshucked or canned clams, omit the steaming and use 2 cups wine and 4 cups clam broth.) Heat the oil in a large pot. Add the onion, celery, garlic, thyme, half the parsley, and bay leaves.

3. Cook over medium heat for 3 to 4 minutes, or until soft but not brown. Add the tomatoes and tomato paste, and cook for 2 minutes. Add the wine–clam broth mixture, and bring to a boil. Add the potatoes, reduce the heat, and simmer for 8 to 10 minutes, or until the potatoes are tender.

4. Just before serving, stir in the cooked cherrystones or clam meat and the salt, pepper, and cayenne. Remove and discard the bay leaves. Garnish with the remaining parsley and serve at once.

Serves 6

252 CALORIES PER SERVING; 13 G PROTEIN; 5 G FAT; 28 G CARBOHYDRATE; 402 MG SODIUM; 26 MG CHOLESTEROL

Rhode Island Red Chowder

UMBRIAN CLAM "CHOWDER"

The Villa Roncalli occupies a former seventeenth-century hunting lodge on the outskirts of the city of Foligno in Umbria. To call its young chef, Maria Luisa Leocastre, gifted would be an understatement. Maria Luisa has mastered that quintessential Italian art of extracting stunning flavors from just a few simple ingredients. Consider the following clam "chowder," which is made with cannellini beans instead of potatoes. The only thing less than wonderful about this soup is the color. The parsley helps, but try to concentrate on the flavor, not the appearance.

32 littleneck clams, 24 cherrystone clams, or 12 ounces canned clams with juices (see Note)

1½ cups dry white wine

2½ to 3 cups Fish Stock (page 381), Chicken Stock (page 379), Basic Vegetable Stock (page 382), or bottled clam juice

1 tablespoon extra-virgin olive oil

1 onion, finely chopped

2 cloves garlic, finely chopped

2 stalks celery, finely chopped

¼ cup finely chopped flat-leaf parsley

1½ cups cooked cannellini beans (14-ounce can)

salt and freshly ground black pepper

1. If using fresh clams, scrub the shells, discarding any with cracked shells or open shells that fail to close when tapped. Bring the wine to a boil. Add the clams, cover the pot tightly, and cook over high heat until the clams just open, about 8 minutes. Stir the clams once or twice to give the shellfish on the bottom room to open.

2. Transfer the clams to a bowl with a slotted spoon to cool so you can shell them. Shell all but 4 of the clams and set aside. Strain the clam cooking liquid through a strainer lined with a cheesecloth or paper towels into a large measuring cup. Add enough fish stock to obtain 4 cups liquid. If using canned clams, you'll need to add 2 cups stock.

3. Heat the olive oil in a large saucepan. Add the onion, garlic, celery, and half the parsley. Cook until the vegetables

are soft but not brown, about 4 minutes. Stir in the beans, shelled clams, and clam stock and simmer until richly flavored, about 5 minutes. Purée the soup in a blender and return it to the pot. Correct the seasoning, adding salt and pepper to taste.

4. To serve, ladle the soup into bowls. Sprinkle each with parsley and float a clam in the center. Alternatively, you can garnish each bowl of soup with a few croutons.

Note: You can make a 5-minute version of this soup by using canned clams and beans. Try to buy canned baby clams (you'll need 10 to 12 ounces).

Serves 4

264 CALORIES PER SERVING; 17 G PROTEIN; 5 G FAT; 0.6 G SATURATED FAT; 24 G CARBOHYDRATE; 70 MG SODIUM; 24 MG CHOLESTEROL

FISHERMAN'S STEW
(ZUPPA DEL PESCATORE)

Here's a stunning fish stew for people who find making bouillabaisse too complicated and time-consuming. Quite literally, you can make it from start to finish in 30 minutes. You don't even need fish broth (although using it will make a tastier zuppa). The more types of seafood you use, of course, the better the stew will be. Feel free to use all or some of the seafoods called for below or make substitutions, based on what's freshest and best in your area or at your fish market.

1½ tablespoons olive oil

1 medium onion, finely chopped

2 cloves garlic, thinly sliced

1 large red ripe tomato, finely chopped, with its juices

1 large or 2 medium baking potatoes (about 1 pound)

1 quart water, or fish broth for a richer stew

3 tablespoons finely chopped flat-leaf parsley

1 bay leaf

½ teaspoon dried oregano

salt and freshly ground black pepper

FOR THE SEAFOOD:

- 12 littleneck clams, scrubbed
- 12 mussels, scrubbed, threads at the hinge of the shell removed with needlenose pliers
- 12 shrimp or prawns, peeled and deveined
- 1 pound fish fillets (possibilities include snapper, mahi-mahi, cod, bass, and swordfish)

1. Heat the olive oil in a large sauté pan (preferably nonstick). Add the onion and cook over medium heat for 2 minutes. Add the garlic and cook until the onion and garlic are soft and translucent but not brown, about 2 minutes more. Add the tomato and cook until soft, about 2 minutes.

2. Add the potatoes, the water, half the parsley, the bay leaf, the oregano, and salt and pepper and bring to a boil.

Reduce the heat to medium and gently simmer the potatoes, uncovered, until half-cooked, about 10 minutes.

3. Add the clams and mussels, cover the pan, and cook until the shells just begin to open, about 5 minutes. Discard any clams and mussels that do not open. Add the shrimp and fish and continue simmering until all the seafood is cooked and the potatoes are soft, about 3 minutes.

4. Correct the seasoning, adding salt and pepper to taste. Remove and discard the bay leaf. Serve fisherman's stew in shallow bowls, with extra bowls for holding the empty clam and mussel shells. Garnish with the remaining parsley.

Serves 4

350 CALORIES PER SERVING; 36 G PROTEIN; 8 G FAT; 1 G SATURATED FAT; 33 G CARBOHYDRATE; 174 MG SODIUM; 95 MG CHOLESTEROL

Fisherman's Stew (Zuppa del Pescatore)

GENOESE FISH SOUP
(BURRIDA)

Burrida *belongs to an extended family of fish soups and stews that includes Spain's* zarzuela *and France's bouillabaisse. Every city on the Ligurian coast has a version: this one comes from the picturesque port town of Camoglie. The traditional way to prepare the soup is to purée the vegetables through a vegetable mill, poaching the seafood in the resulting broth. But sometimes I like to serve the fish and vegetables together as a stew.*

½ teaspoon saffron threads

1 tablespoon extra-virgin olive oil

1 medium onion, finely chopped

2 cloves garlic, minced

1 stalk celery minced

1 small or ½ large bulb fennel, cut into ½-inch dice (about 1 cup)

¼ cup finely chopped flat-leaf parsley

salt and freshly ground black pepper

1 tablespoon tomato paste

4 ripe tomatoes, peeled, seeded, and diced (about 3 cups)

1 large or 2 small potatoes, peeled and cut into ½-inch dice

6 cups Fish Stock (page 381) or 4 cups bottled clam juice plus 2 cups water, or 6 cups water

1 herb bundle made by tying together a bay leaf, a sprig of thyme, and a sprig of rosemary

FOR THE SEAFOOD:

1 (1½-pound) lobster or 1 or 2 crabs

18 mussels

18 littleneck or cherrystone clams (the smallest you can find)

1½ pounds fish fillets, cut into 2-inch diamonds

18 shrimp

6 squid, cleaned, bodies cut into rings, tentacles left whole

1. Place the saffron in a bowl and grind it to a powder with the end of a wooden spoon. Add 2 tablespoons hot water and let stand for 10 minutes.

2. Meanwhile, heat the olive oil in a large pot. Add the onion, garlic, celery, and fennel and half the parsley. Add salt and pepper to taste and cook over medium heat until soft but not brown, about 5 minutes. Add the tomato paste and cook for 1 minute.

3. Increase the heat to high, add the tomatoes, and cook until the tomato juices have evaporated, about 2 minutes. Add the potatoes, fish stock, and herb bundle and bring to a boil. Reduce the heat and simmer the mixture until the potatoes are very soft, about 20 minutes. Season the soup with a little more salt and pepper and discard the herb bundle.

4. Force the soup through a vegetable mill or ricer into a wide shallow pot. (Alternatively, strain the soup into a pot, purée the vegetables in a food processor, and add the purée to the pot.)

5. If using lobster, cook it in 2 inches boiling water in another pot until the shell turns red, about 3 minutes. Drain the lobster in a colander and let cool. When cool enough to handle, break off and crack the claws. Cut the tail section into 1-inch medallions. If using crab, cook, clean, and cut into sections.

6. Just before serving, bring the soup to a boil. Add the mussels, clams, and lobster and cook just until the clam and mussel shells open, about 8 minutes. Discard any clams and mussels that do not open. Add the fish the last 4 minutes; the shrimp and squid, the last 2 minutes. Cook until all the shellfish is done. Correct the seasoning of the soup, adding salt and pepper. Sprinkle the remaining parsley on the top and serve at once.

Note: There are many possibilities for fish. The Genoese would use an assortment of bony but flavorful Mediterranean sea creatures, such as *scorfano* (rascasse or wraisse), *gallinella* (sea hen), and conger eel. In this country, you could use monkfish, snapper, halibut, cusk, sea bass, and/or swordfish.

Serves 6 as a first course, 4 as an entrée

526 CALORIES PER SERVING;* 83 G PROTEIN; 9 G FAT; 2 G SATURATED FAT; 23 G CARBOHYDRATE; 495 MG SODIUM; 508 MG CHOLESTEROL

Analysis is based on 6 servings as a first course.

VENETIAN SHELLFISH SOUP

Variations of this soup turn up all along the Italian coast. The shellfish and seasonings change from region to region: one cook might use vongole *(tiny clams with brown-striped shells); another,* fasolari *(pink clams); a third,* cannolicchi *(tiny razor clams). Here's a Venetian version, made with both clams and mussels.*

1 pound of the smallest mussels you can find
(20 to 24 mussels)

12 to 16 of the tiniest clams you can find

1 cup dry white wine

3 cups Fish Stock (page 381) or bottled clam juice

1 small onion, finely chopped

1 clove garlic, minced

1 tomato, peeled, seeded, and finely chopped

1 stalk celery, finely diced

¼ teaspoon hot pepper flakes (optional)

¼ cup finely chopped flat-leaf parsley

salt and freshly ground black pepper

1. Scrub the mussels and clams, discarding any with cracked shells or open shells that fail to close when tapped. Using tweezers or needlenose pliers, pull out any tufts of black threads clumped at the hinge of the mussels.

2. Bring the wine to a boil. Add the fish broth, onion, garlic, tomato, celery, pepper flakes, and half the parsley and bring to a boil. Add the mussels and clams, cover the pan tightly, and cook over high heat until the mussel and clam shells just open, about 8 minutes. Stir the soup once or twice to give the shellfish on the bottom room to open. Discard any mussels or clams that do not open. Add salt and pepper to taste.

3. With a slotted spoon or wire skimmer, transfer the mussels, clams, and vegetables to a tureen or 4 soup bowls. Strain the broth through a strainer lined with a cheesecloth or paper towels over the shellfish. Or, if you're in a hurry, ladle the broth over the shellfish, leaving the last ½ inch (the part where the grit gathers) in the pot. Sprinkle the remaining 2 tablespoons parsley on top and serve at once, with crusty bread for dunking.

Serves 4

117 CALORIES PER SERVING; 10 G PROTEIN; 1 G FAT; 0 G SATURATED FAT; 6 G CARBOHYDRATE; 227 MG SODIUM; 27 MG CHOLESTEROL

BASIC CHICKEN BROTH

Stock is the cornerstone of good cooking. It is easy to make and will leave your kitchen smelling great. Few dishes are more ecological—stock enables you to recycle otherwise unusable vegetable scraps and bones. Besides, most canned chicken broth is loaded with sodium and it can't touch the flavor of homemade stock.

Many people are intimidated by the idea of making stock, but nothing could be easier. There are really only two things you need to remember. First, after the initial boiling, gently simmer the stock and never let it boil again. (If you do, the fat will homogenize and the broth will become cloudy.) Second, skim the stock often with a shallow ladle. This removes any fat and impurities and keeps the stock clean.

Whenever I have chicken bones or scraps, onion skins, carrot ends, celery leaves, or other vegetable trimmings, I toss them into a plastic bag in the freezer. When the bag is full, I make stock. For convenience, the finished stock can be frozen in 1- and 2-cup containers, so you always have the right amount of hand.

3½ to 4 pounds chicken backs, wings, necks, or the carcass from a large roast chicken

FOR THE SPICE BUNDLE:

4 large parsley sprigs or parsley stems

4 fresh thyme sprigs or 1 teaspoon dried thyme

2 bay leaves

10 peppercorns

2 allspice berries

GRAMMIE ETHEL'S CHICKEN NOODLE SOUP

Is there anything quite as comforting as a bowl of chicken soup? Untold generations of Raichlens have enjoyed this golden elixir in times of illness as well as health. I can't think of better relief for a cold, flu, or whatever else ails you. Here's a chicken soup just like my Grammie Ethel makes. You can use the extra meat for one of the salads on page 85.

FOR THE BROTH:

1 3½- to 4-pound chicken

1 onion, quartered

1 leek, trimmed, washed, and cut into 1-inch pieces

2 carrots, cut into 1-inch pieces

2 stalks celery with leaves, cut into 1-inch pieces

4 cloves garlic

1 bouquet garni of bay leaf, thyme, and parsley

TO FINISH THE SOUP:

8 ounces egg noodles, thin spaghetti, fettuccine, or bow ties

salt and freshly ground black pepper

3 tablespoons chopped flat-leaf parsley

1. Remove any lumps of fat from the chicken. (For a leaner broth, remove the skin, too.) Wash the bird and drain. Place the chicken, vegetables, garlic, and bouquet garni in a large pot and add cold water to cover by 2 inches. (You'll need about 4 quarts.)

2. Bring the soup to a rolling boil, skimming off any foam that rises to the surface. Lower the heat and gently simmer the soup for 1 hour, skimming often. Add cold water as necessary to keep the bird covered and skim after you add it.

3. Strain the chicken broth into another large pot and keep hot. Transfer the chicken to a platter, and let cool. Pull the meat off the bones.

Finely dice or shred 1½ cups meat. Save the rest for chicken salad.

4. Cook the noodles in 8 cups boiling salted water until al dente, about 8 minutes. Strain, rinse under cold water, and drain. Stir the noodles and the diced chicken into the simmering chicken broth. Add salt and pepper to taste. Sprinkle the soup with the parsley and serve at once. This recipe is the next best thing to having dinner at Grammie Ethel's.

Makes 10 to 12 cups, enough to serve 6 to 8

213 CALORIES PER SERVING;* 15 G PROTEIN; 3 G FAT; 1 G SATURATED FAT; 30 G CARBOHYDRATE; 38 MG SODIUM; 29 MG CHOLESTEROL

Analysis is based on 6 servings.

---

1 large onion, quartered with skin

1 leek, trimmed, washed, and cut into 1-inch pieces

3 carrots, cut into 1-inch pieces

3 stalks celery, cut into 1-inch pieces

1 head of garlic, cut in half

4 quarts of water, or as needed

1. Remove the skin and any lumps of fat from the chicken pieces. Rinse the chicken pieces well. Make the spice bundle: Tie the herbs, peppercorns, and allspice berries in a piece of cheesecloth or wrap them in a square of aluminum foil, and pierce all over with a fork.

2. Place all the ingredients for the stock in a large stockpot with enough water to cover the chicken. Bring the stock to a boil and skim off any foam that rises to the surface. Lower the heat and gently simmer the stock until well flavored, 2 to 3 hours. Add cold water as necessary to keep the chicken covered. Skim the stock often, especially after you've added water. (The cold water brings the fat to the top.)

3. Strain the stock into a clean container and let cool to room temperature. Transfer to 1- and 2-cup containers and refrigerate or freeze. (Stock will keep four to five days in the refrigerator and for several months in the freezer.)

Note: For an extra-clear stock, pour the stock through a strainer lined with paper towels.

Makes 10 to 12 cups

COCONUT NOODLE STEW

This colorful dish was inspired by Marnie's Noodle Shop, a postage stamp–size eatery in Greenwich Village that specializes in brimming bowls of Asian-style noodles. This recipe calls for chicken, but you can substitute seafood or make a vegetarian version by using shiitake mushrooms or other vegetables. Marnie's uses a thick, chewy, fresh udon-style noodle, but any wheat noodle will do. (I've had great success with perciatelli, bucatini, *and even* linguini.*)*

8 ounces boneless, skinless chicken breast (optional)

1 tablespoon canola oil

3 garlic cloves, minced

3 shallots, thinly sliced

1½ tablespoons minced fresh ginger

2 cups lite coconut milk (see Note)

4 cups Chicken Stock (see page 379)

1 tablespoon cornstarch

4 to 5 tablespoons Asian fish sauce or soy sauce, or to taste

1 pound fresh udon noodles or 8 ounces dried udon (or other thick Asian wheat noodles) or perciatelli or bucatini

6 cups stemmed, washed fresh spinach

freshly ground black pepper

4 scallions, finely chopped

1. Wash the chicken breast, if using, and blot dry. Trim off any fat or sinew and cut the chicken breast widthwise into the thinnest possible slices.

2. Heat the oil in a nonstick wok or large saucepan. Add the garlic, shallots, and ginger and cook over medium heat until fragrant and just beginning to brown, about 2 minutes. Add the coconut milk and stock and bring to a rolling boil. Reduce the heat, add the chicken, and gently simmer until the chicken is cooked and the mixture is richly flavored, about 5 minutes.

3. Dissolve the cornstarch in the fish sauce in a small bowl. Stir this mixture into the broth and simmer for 1 to 2 minutes. The broth should thicken slightly.

4. Cook the noodles in 4 quarts of rapidly boiling water until tender, about 3 minutes for fresh noodles and 8 minutes for dried. Drain the noodles in a colander and add them to the coconut mixture. Simmer the noodles in the broth for 1 minute. Stir in the spinach and simmer until cooked, about 30 seconds. Add pepper to taste and, if needed, a little more fish sauce: The broth should be highly seasoned. Ladle the stew into bowls, sprinkle with scallions, and serve at once.

Note: Coconut milk, with its high saturated fat content, may seem like an unlikely ingredient for a low-fat cookbook, but the new "lite" coconut milk by A Taste of Thai contains only a third the fat found in regular coconut milk. A Taste of Thai Lite Coconut Milk is available in most gourmet shops.

Serves 4

370 CALORIES PER SERVING; 13 G PROTEIN; 10 G FAT; 5 G SATURATED FAT; 58 G CARBOHYDRATE; 2,166 MG SODIUM; 0 MG CHOLESTEROL

SPAETZLE SOUP

Here's a twist on classic chicken noodle soup, made with tiny homemade egg noodles called spaetzle. (The word is a German diminutive for "sparrow," a reference to the noodle's birdlike shape.) Spaetzle are the only egg noodles I know of that can be made from start to finish from scratch in ten minutes, which makes them very popular around our house. (You'll need one special piece of equipment that is described in the Note to this recipe.) Spaetzle is traditionally served as a side dish; however, I like them in chicken soup. Think of the following as the ultimate comfort food.

FOR THE SPAETZLE:

1 egg white

1 whole egg (or 2 more whites)

⅔ cup skim milk

¼ teaspoon freshly grated nutmeg, or to taste

¼ teaspoon freshly ground black pepper, or to taste

¾ teaspoon salt (optional)

1½ cups (approximately) unbleached all-purpose white flour

½ teaspoon canola oil

TO FINISH THE SOUP:

6 cups Chicken Stock (see page 379)

1 large or 2 medium carrots, cut into the finest possible dice

2 stalks celery, cut into the finest possible dice

1½ cups shredded cooked chicken

salt and freshly ground black pepper to taste

¼ cup coarsely chopped flat-leaf parsley

1. Combine the egg white and egg in a mixing bowl and whisk until smooth but not frothy. Whisk in the milk, seasonings, and enough flour to obtain a thick, sticky dough. (It should have the consistency of soft ice cream.)

2. Bring 4 quarts of water and the oil to a boil in a large, deep saucepan. Place the spaetzle machine over the pan, add the dough to the holder, and push back and forth to cut tiny droplets of dough into the water. Cook the spaetzle until the water returns to a boil and the noodles rise to the surface, about 1 minute. Remove the spaetzle with a skimmer or slotted spoon and transfer to a colander to drain. Rinse with cold water until cool. (This keeps the spaetzle from overcooking and removes the excess starch.) Continue cooking the spaetzle in this fashion until all the batter is used up. Drain well. The spaetzle can be prepared up to 48 hours ahead to this stage and refrigerated.

3. Just before serving, bring the chicken stock to a boil in a large saucepan. Add the carrot and celery and cook until soft, about 3 minutes. Stir in the chicken (if using) and spaetzle and cook until heated. Season the soup with salt and pepper to taste (it should be highly seasoned) and sprinkle with the parsley before serving.

Note: A spaetzle machine is a hand-held device consisting of a thin metal rectangle lined with rows of small holes, surmounted by a movable, open-topped box. The batter is placed in the box, which is slid back and forth over the metal plate. As it moves, tiny droplets of dough fall through the holes, forming tiny dumplings called spaetzle. Spaetzle machines can be purchased at most cookware shops.

Serves 4 to 6

234 CALORIES PER SERVING;* 9 G PROTEIN; 3 G FAT; 1 G SATURATED FAT; 43 G CARBOHYDRATE; 93 MG SODIUM; 54 MG CHOLESTEROL

Analysis is based on 4 servings.

SOPA DE LIMA—YUCATÁN CHICKEN LIME SOUP

This vibrant soup is just the thing for relieving a stubborn cold. The chilies blast open your sinuses, the lime juice loads you with vitamin C, while the garlic is believed to possess antibiotic properties. I've suggested a range of chilies: 1 seeded chili for a mild soup, 3 to 4 with seeds for liquid fire.

12 ounces boneless, skinless chicken breasts

1 corn tortilla, cut into matchstick slivers

1 tablespoon olive oil

1 medium onion, thinly sliced

8 cloves garlic, thinly sliced

1 to 4 serrano or jalapeño chilies, thinly sliced

5 cups chicken stock (see page 380)

½ cup fresh lime juice, or to taste

1 large ripe tomato, cut into ½-inch dice

salt and freshly ground black pepper

¼ cup chopped fresh cilantro

1. Wash and dry the chicken breasts and trim off any fat. Cut the chicken breasts across the grain on the diagonal into thin ⅛-inch strips. Cut these strips in half widthwise.

2. Spread the tortilla slivers on a nonstick baking sheet or on a piece of foil and bake in a 400°F. oven or toaster oven until lightly browned, about 4 minutes. Let cool on a plate.

3. Heat the olive oil in a large saucepan. Add the onion, garlic, and chili slices and cook over medium heat until lightly browned, about 5 minutes. Stir in the chicken stock, lime juice, chicken, and tomato. Gently simmer the soup until the chicken is cooked, about 3 minutes. Add salt and pepper to taste and extra lime juice if desired: The soup should be highly seasoned. Stir in the cilantro. Ladle soup into bowls and sprinkle with toasted tortilla strips.

Serves 4 to 6

221 CALORIES PER SERVING;* 19 G PROTEIN; 6 G FAT; 1 G SATURATED FAT; 23 G CARBOHYDRATE; 105 MG SODIUM; 41 MG CHOLESTEROL

Analysis is based on 4 servings.

Sopa de Lima—Yucatán Chicken Lime Soup

VELVET CHICKEN SOUP WITH CORN AND LEEKS

Here's a Western twist on a Chinese classic, a velvety chicken soup loaded with corn, leeks, and herbs.
The chicken can be either finely diced or minced. Canned corn may seem like a rather pedestrian ingredient,
but that's really how the soup is made in Chinese restaurants.

½ pound boneless, skinless chicken breast

1 tablespoon sesame oil or canola oil

1 leek, trimmed, washed, and finely chopped (trim just up to the light-green part; should be about 1 cup)

2 cloves garlic, minced

1 tablespoon minced fresh ginger

¼ cup rice wine or dry sherry

4 cups Chicken Stock (see page 379)

1 15-ounce can creamed corn

2 teaspoons honey

salt (optional) and freshly ground black pepper (to taste)

1½ tablespoons cornstarch, dissolved in 2 tablespoons water or chicken stock

2 egg whites, lightly beaten (but not foamy)

½ cup chopped flat-leaf parsley, basil, or fresh dill

1. Rinse and dry the chicken breast. Remove any fat or tendons from the chicken. Cut the chicken into a fine dice or mince with a cleaver or in a food processor.

2. Heat the oil in a large nonstick saucepan. Add the leek, garlic, and ginger and cook over medium heat until soft but not brown, 3 to 4 minutes, stirring often. Stir in the wine and bring to a boil. Add the chicken stock, corn, honey, and chicken and simmer for 10 minutes, or until the chicken is cooked and the soup is richly flavored. Add salt and pepper to taste.

3. Bring the soup to a boil. Stir the dissolved cornstarch, and add to the soup. Return the soup to a boil: It should thicken slightly. Add the egg whites in a very thin stream from a height of about 6 inches, stirring the soup a few times with a wooden spoon. You should wind up with delicate threads of egg. Just before serving, stir in the parsley. Cook for 30 seconds and serve at once.

Serves 4

235 CALORIES PER SERVING; 14 G PROTEIN; 5 G FAT; 1 G SATURATED FAT; 32 G CARBOHYDRATE; 372 MG SODIUM; 27 MG CHOLESTEROL

THAI CHICKEN COCONUT SOUP

Tom kha ghai is one of the glories of Thai gastronomy, a haunting soup that plays the tartness of lemongrass, lime juice, and kaffir lime leaves against the pepperiness of galangal and the richness of coconut milk.

1 10- to 12-ounce boneless, skinless chicken breast

3 stalks fresh lemongrass or ¼ cup dried

4 cups Chicken Stock (see page 379)

¼ cup thickly sliced galangal or fresh ginger

8 kaffir lime leaves, or 4 thin strips lime zest

1 cup "lite" coconut milk

2 cups fresh mushrooms, thinly sliced

2 teaspoons cornstarch dissolved in 1 tablespoon water

4 to 5 tablespoons fish sauce

4 to 5 tablespoons fresh lime juice

12 fresh basil leaves, julienned

1 to 4 jalapeño chilies, thinly sliced widthwise (optional)

1. Wash and dry the chicken breast and trim off any fat. Slice the chicken breast on the diagonal as thinly as possible. Trim the green leaves and root ends off the lemongrass stalks and strip off the outside leaves. Cut the lemongrass sharply on the diagonal into ¼-inch slices.

2. Combine the chicken stock, lemongrass, galangal, and kaffir lime leaves in a large saucepan and simmer for 5 minutes. Add the coconut milk and bring to a boil, stirring steadily. Reduce the heat and simmer the soup until richly flavored, about 5 minutes. Strain the soup into another saucepan, discarding the flavorings, or remove them with a slotted spoon.

3. Stir in the chicken and mushrooms and simmer until the chicken is cooked, 2 to 3 minutes. Stir in the dissolved cornstarch and bring the soup to a boil: It should thicken slightly. Remove the pan from the heat and stir in the fish sauce, lime juice, basil, and chilies. Correct the seasoning, adding fish sauce or lime juice as necessary to achieve a balance between saltiness and tartness. Ladle the soup into bowls for serving.

Serves 4

141 CALORIES PER SERVING; 15 G PROTEIN; 5 G FAT; 1 G SATURATED FAT; 9 G CARBOHYDRATE; 192 MG SODIUM; 35 MG CHOLESTEROL

CHICKEN GUMBO

Gumbo takes its name from nkgombo, an African word for okra. My low-fat version uses smoked chicken to provide the rich smoky flavor traditionally supplied by tasso ham and andouille sausage. To further lighten the dish, I've modified the procedure for making the roux and greatly reduced the amount of oil. Gumbo is traditionally served over white rice in shallow bowls or soup dishes.

2 tablespoons olive oil

1 large onion, finely chopped (about 2 cups)

4 stalks celery, finely chopped

1 green bell pepper, cored, seeded, and finely chopped

1 red bell pepper, cored, seeded, and finely chopped

4 cloves garlic, chopped

3 tablespoons flour

1 to 2 tablespoons Cajun seasoning

1 teaspoon dried thyme

½ teaspoon ground bay leaves

1 cup beer

4 cups Chicken Stock (page 379)

2 to 3 cups diced smoked chicken (8 to 12 ounces—see recipe on page 243, or use a good commercial brand)

12 ounces fresh okra, cut widthwise into ½-inch slices (about 3 cups)

1 cup corn kernels

1 tablespoon Worcestershire sauce

1 teaspoon Tabasco or other hot sauce, or to taste

salt and freshly ground black pepper

1 tablespoon filé powder (sometimes sold as filé gumbo—optional)

1. Heat the oil in a large, heavy, non-stick pot. Add the chopped vegetables and garlic and cook over medium heat until nicely browned, 6 to 8 minutes, stirring often. Stir in the flour, Cajun seasoning, thyme, and bay leaves and cook until fragrant, about 2 minutes. Stir in the beer and stock and bring to a boil.

2. Reduce the heat to a simmer and stir in the smoked chicken, okra, corn, Worcestershire and Tabasco sauces, and salt and pepper to taste. Simmer until well flavored, 10 to 12 minutes.

3. Just before serving, stir in the filé powder, if using. Simmer the gumbo for 1 minute. Correct the seasoning, adding Cajun spice, hot sauce, salt, or other seasonings to taste. The gumbo should be highly seasoned.

Serves 6 to 8

204 CALORIES PER SERVING;* 12 G PROTEIN; 5 G FAT; 1 G SATURATED FAT; 27 G CARBOHYDRATE; 465 MG SODIUM; 32 MG CHOLESTEROL

Analysis is based on 6 servings.

CHICKEN GARBANZO BEAN SOUP WITH SMOKY CHILIES
(CALDO TLALPEÑO)

I first tasted this soup at the sprawling Arroyo restaurant in Coyoacán outside Mexico City. The preparation comes from the community of Tlalpán, where an exuberant use of chipotles (smoked jalapeño chilies) gives the soup a heady smoke flavor and fiery bite. Note: *I like to cook the chicken on the bone for extra flavor, but you can certainly opt for the convenience of boneless breast.*

FOR THE CHICKEN AND BROTH:

7 cups chicken stock

1 pound bone-in but skinless chicken breasts

1 bay leaf

¼ onion

1 clove

2 sprigs cilantro

TO FINISH THE SOUP:

4 plum tomatoes

1½ tablespoons lard or olive oil

1 medium white onion, finely diced

3 cloves garlic, finely chopped

4 scallions, trimmed and finely chopped (reserve the greens for garnish)

1 carrot, peeled and finely diced

1 large potato, peeled and finely diced

1 to 3 canned chipotle chilies, minced, with 1 to 3 teaspoons juice from the can

1 cup cooked garbanzo beans

2 sprigs epazote

salt and freshly ground black pepper

6 wedges fresh lime

1. Place the stock and chicken breasts in a large saucepan. Pin the bay leaf to the onion quarter with the clove. Add this to the pot with the cilantro. Gradually bring the mixture to a boil, reduce the heat, and gently simmer the chicken until cooked, 8 to 10 minutes. Transfer the chicken to a plate to cool, then tear it off the bones into shreds and set aside. Strain the stock; you should have about 6 cups.

2. In a comal or cast-iron frying pan or under the broiler, roast the tomatoes until they are nicely browned, 8 to 10 minutes. Transfer them to a plate to cool. Purée the tomatoes in a blender.

3. Heat the lard in a large saucepan over medium heat. Cook the onion, garlic, and scallion whites until they're lightly browned, 5 minutes, stirring often. Increase the heat to high and add the tomato purée. Cook until thick and fragrant, about 5 minutes.

4. Stir in the chicken broth, carrot, potato, and chipotles with their juices and cook 5 minutes. Add the shredded chicken, garbanzo beans, epazote, and salt and pepper. Gently simmer the soup until it is richly flavored and the vegetables are tender, 5 minutes. Correct the seasoning, adding salt and pepper to taste. Ladle the soup into bowls and sprinkle with the scallion greens. Serve with the lime wedges.

Serves 6 to 8

247 CALORIES PER SERVING;* 22 G PROTEIN; 7 G FAT; 2 G SATURATED FAT; 27 G CARBOHYDRATE; 251 MG SODIUM; 51 MG CHOLESTEROL

Analysis is based on 6 servings.

BRAZILIAN CHICKEN RICE SOUP

Every nation has a version of chicken soup. One of the most satisfying is Brazil's canja. *This recipe includes instructions for making the broth. If you're in a hurry, use premade stock (page 379) and start with adding the rice in paragraph 3.*

1 3-pound chicken
1 bay leaf
1 medium-sized onion, quartered
1 whole clove
2 ripe tomatoes, quartered
1 carrot, cut into 1-inch pieces
¼ cup chopped celery leaves
20 black peppercorns, tied in a piece of cheesecloth
½ cup uncooked white rice
salt and freshly ground black pepper
3 carrots, thinly sliced on the diagonal
3 stalks celery, thinly sliced on the diagonal
¼ cup finely chopped flat-leaf parsley

1. Wash the chicken thoroughly. Remove the skin and any pieces of fat. Pin the bay leaf to 1 onion quarter with the clove. Place the chicken in a large pot with the tomatoes, onion quarters, 1 carrot, celery leaves, and peppercorn bundle. Add 10 cups cold water and bring to a boil. Using a ladle, skim off the fat and foam that rise to the surface. Reduce the heat and simmer for 1 hour, skimming often to remove the fat.

2. Remove the chicken from the broth and let cool. Strain the broth into a large saucepan, pressing the vegetables to extract the juices. (There should be about 8 cups of broth.) Pull the chicken meat off the bones and shred or finely dice it.

3. Add the rice, salt, and pepper to the broth and simmer for 10 minutes. Add the thinly sliced carrots and celery to the soup with the shredded chicken and half the parsley. Simmer the soup for another 10 minutes, or until the rice is tender. Correct the seasoning, adding salt and pepper to taste. Sprinkle with the remaining parsley and serve at once.

Serves 8 as an appetizer, 4 to 6 as an entrée

293 CALORIES PER SERVING; 33 G PROTEIN; 8 G FAT; 22 G CARBOHYDRATE; 131 MG SODIUM; 92 MG CHOLESTEROL

TIBETAN NOODLE STEW

I first tasted this dish at the Tibetan Kitchen, a charming, tiny Manhattan restaurant. The noodle favored there is a short, open-sided tube called gutse-ritu, *which closely resembles* cavatelli, *an Italian pasta widely available at gourmet shops.*

2 cups cavatelli or other thin tube-shaped pasta
1 tablespoon canola oil
2 onions, thinly sliced (about 1½ cups)
8 garlic cloves, thinly sliced
1 tablespoon minced fresh ginger
4 ounces lean lamb, thinly sliced (optional)
2 tomatoes, cut into ¼-inch dice
4 cups Chicken Stock or Vegetable Stock (see pages 379, 382)
3 to 4 tablespoons tamari or soy sauce
2 teaspoons hot paprika, or to taste
4 cups stemmed, washed spinach leaves

1. Cook the cavatelli in 4 quarts of boiling water until al dente, about 8 minutes. Drain in a colander, rinse with cold water until cool, and drain again.

2. Heat the oil in a wok or large saucepan, preferably nonstick. Add the onions, garlic, and ginger and cook over medium heat until nicely browned, about 5 minutes. Stir in the lamb, if using, and tomatoes and cook until the lamb loses its rawness, about 2 minutes.

3. Stir in the stock, tamari or soy sauce, and paprika and bring to a boil. Reduce the heat and simmer the stew until richly flavored and the lamb is tender, 5 to 10 minutes. Stir in the cavatelli and simmer for 2 minutes. Stir in the spinach leaves and cook until wilted, about 1 minute. Correct the seasoning, adding tamari or paprika to taste.

Serves 4

294 CALORIES PER SERVING; 12 G PROTEIN; 5 G FAT; 1 G SATURATED FAT; 53 G CARBOHYDRATE; 818 MG SODIUM; 0 MG CHOLESTEROL

Tibetan Noodle Stew

VIETNAMESE BEEF NOODLE SOUP

Rice noodle soup is a popular street food throughout Southeast Asia. This version, redolent with star anise and ginger, takes only 15 minutes to make. It even includes its own salad: the platter of bean sprouts and mint sprigs traditionally served with a Vietnamese meal. Asians like long noodles, and it is their custom to slurp them noisily. North Americans may prefer to cut the rice sticks into more manageable lengths.

8 ounces rice sticks, preferably ⅛-inch wide

4 scallions, whites minced,
  greens finely chopped for garnish

6 cups beef or chicken stock

6 thin slices fresh ginger

3 star anise

¼ cup fish sauce

6 ounces beef tenderloin or sirloin, partially frozen

1 large white onion

12–15 fresh basil or mint leaves

2 cups fresh mung bean sprouts

12 sprigs fresh mint or basil

1 or 2 jalapeño or serrano chilies, thinly sliced

2 limes, cut into wedges

1. Soak the rice sticks in cold water for 30 minutes, or until soft. Combine the scallion whites, stock, ginger, star anise, and fish sauce in a large pot and gently simmer for 10 minutes, or until well flavored. Remove the ginger and star anise with a slotted spoon and discard.

2. Meanwhile, slice the beef across the grain as thinly as possible. (It's easier if you have a meat slicer.) Thinly slice the onion. Thinly sliver the basil leaves. Arrange the bean sprouts, mint sprigs, sliced chilies, and lime wedges on a platter.

3. Just before serving, bring the broth to a boil. Add the rice sticks and simmer for 15 to 30 seconds, or until soft. Stir in the beef and remove the pan from the heat. (The heat of the broth should be sufficient to cook the meat. If not, simmer it for a few seconds.) Stir in the onion slices and ladle the soup into bowls. Garnish each bowl with the slivered basil and chopped scallion greens, and serve at once, with the bean sprout platter on the side. Let each person add bean sprouts, mint sprigs, chilies, and lime juice to the soup to taste.

Serves 6 as an appetizer, 4 as an entrée

341 CALORIES PER SERVING; 24 G PROTEIN; 5 G FAT; 49 G CARBOHYDRATE; 2,671 MG SODIUM; 32 MG CHOLESTEROL

VEGETABLE SOUP WITH MEATBALLS

This is Mexican comfort food at its best, a steaming bowl of broth chock-full of vegetables and tiny meatballs fragrant with spices and enriched with rice. There are probably as many different meatball recipes in Mexico as there are cooks. These feature the aromatic accents of oregano, cumin, and, for a sweet touch, cinnamon and cloves. To decrease the amount of fat, I've replaced some of the pork and beef with boneless, skinless chicken breast and used egg whites instead of a whole egg.

FOR THE MEATBALLS:

6 ounces boneless, skinless chicken breast, cut into ½-inch cubes

6 ounces lean pork loin, cut into ½-inch cubes

6 ounces lean beef (like sirloin), cut into ½-inch cubes

1 teaspoon salt, or to taste

½ teaspoon freshly ground black pepper

½ teaspoon dried oregano

½ teaspoon ground cumin

¼ teaspoon cinnamon

Pinch of ground cloves

3 tablespoons minced onion

2 cloves garlic, minced

2 egg whites

1 cup cooked rice

TO FINISH THE SOUP:

9 cups chicken stock (page 380)

1 bay leaf

1 medium onion

2 carrots

2 stalks celery

¼ medium cabbage

1 baking potato

6 ounces green beans

½ cup cooked corn kernels

½ cup cooked green peas

½ cup cooked lima beans

salt and freshly ground black pepper

1. To prepare the meatballs, place the chicken, pork, beef, salt, pepper, oregano, cumin, cinnamon, cloves, onion, and garlic in a food processor and grind to a fine paste. Add the egg whites and process to mix. Transfer the mixture to a large bowl and stir in the rice. To test for seasoning, fry a small piece of meatball mixture in a nonstick skillet. Correct the seasoning, adding salt, pepper, or any other spice to taste. Chill the meatball mixture for 30 minutes.

2. Meanwhile, prepare the soup. Bring the chicken stock with the bay leaf to a boil in a large pot. Cut the onion, carrots, celery, cabbage, potato, and green beans into ½-inch dice (the green beans will be in ½-inch pieces). Add them to the pot with the corn, peas, and lima beans. Briskly simmer the soup until the vegetables are almost cooked, 8 to 10 minutes.

3. Form the meatball mixture into 32 (¾-inch) balls. (It helps to dampen your hands when forming the balls.) Gently lower the meatballs into the soup and simmer until they are cooked through, 10 to 15 minutes. Season the broth to taste, adding salt and pepper. Ladle it into bowls and serve at once.

Serves 8 as an appetizer,
4 to 6 as a light main course

334 CALORIES PER SERVING;*
33 G PROTEIN; 6 G FAT; 2 G SATURATED FAT;
39 G CARBOHYDRATE; 140 MG SODIUM;
69 MG CHOLESTEROL

Analysis is based on 6 servings.

SALADS

A VENETIAN SALAD OF BITTER GREENS

This salad was inspired by an open-air market in Venice, where a staggering assortment of bitter greens was on display: purple and white veined radicchio, red-leafed treviso, slender jagged-leafed chicory, fleshy escarole. Combined, they make an intriguing, pleasantly bitter salad that is unexpectedly refreshing. The fennel adds a counterpoint of sweetness.

5 cups bitter greens, including chicory, escarole, radicchio, treviso (a red-leaf chicory with cream-colored veins), arugula, young dandelions, Belgian endive, etc.

1 small or ½ large bulb fennel, thinly sliced crosswise

2 stalks celery, thinly sliced

FOR THE DRESSING:

1½ tablespoons balsamic vinegar

salt and freshly ground black pepper

1½ tablespoons extra-virgin olive oil

1 ounce Parmigiano-Reggiano cheese

1. Wash and dry the greens and combine with the fennel and celery.

2. In the bottom of a large salad bowl, combine the vinegar, salt, and pepper and whisk until the salt crystals are dissolved. Whisk in the olive oil in a thin stream to make a smooth emulsion.

3. Just before serving, add the greens and vegetables and gently toss to mix. Shave curls of Parmesan over the salad, using a vegetable peeler. Serve at once.

Serves 4 to 6

105 CALORIES PER SERVING;* 4 G PROTEIN; 7 G FAT; 2 G SATURATED FAT; 6 G CARBOHYDRATE; 173 MG SODIUM; 6 MG CHOLESTEROL

Analysis is based on 4 servings.

Watercress Salad with Endive and Orange

WATERCRESS SALAD WITH ENDIVE AND ORANGE

This offbeat salad may be the oldest recipe in the book. It was inspired by a "sallet" I tasted at Plimoth Plantation, a museum devoted to the life of the 17th-century New England Pilgrims. The contrast of sweet (oranges and currants) and salty (capers and salt) has characterized New England cooking since the 1600s.

1 bunch watercress

2 Belgian endives

2 oranges

1 tablespoon balsamic vinegar

1 tablespoon extra-virgin olive oil

salt and freshly ground black pepper

2 tablespoons currants

1 tablespoon capers

1. Wash the watercress, spin dry, and tear into bite-sized sprigs. Cut the endives widthwise into ¼-inch strips. Cut the rind (both zest and white pith) off the oranges to expose the flesh. Make V-shaped cuts to remove the individual segments from the membranes, working over a large salad bowl to catch the juice. (There should be 1 to 2 tablespoons juice.)

2. Add the vinegar, oil, salt, and pepper to the orange juice in the bowl and whisk until blended. Add the currants and capers. Just before serving, add the watercress, endives, and orange segments. Gently toss to mix and serve at once.

Serves 4

85 CALORIES PER SERVING; 2 G PROTEIN; 4 G FAT; 13 G CARBOHYDRATE; 47 MG SODIUM; 0 MG CHOLESTEROL

ARUGULA AND JERUSALEM ARTICHOKE SALAD

This is my wife's favorite salad, especially when we have fresh arugula in the garden. It combines the peppery flavor of arugula with the deliciously crisp, earthy taste of Jerusalem artichokes. The latter are small, lumpy tubers in the sunflower family that taste a little like artichokes. When buying them, choose the largest tubers with the fewest possible knobby protuberances, as these are the easiest to peel.

1 bunch arugula (about 1–1½ cups leaves)

3 or 4 Jerusalem artichokes, peeled and thinly sliced or cut into julienne strips

2 tablespoons minced fresh herbs (tarragon, oregano, parsley, and/or chives)

2 teaspoons extra-virgin olive oil

1 teaspoon sherry or wine vinegar (or to taste)

salt and freshly ground black pepper

1. Stem the arugula and wash thoroughly by gently agitating the leaves in a large bowl of cold water. Transfer the leaves to a strainer and pour off the sandy water. Refill the bowl and repeat until the leaves are clean. Dry in a salad spinner.

2. Combine the arugula, artichokes, and herbs in a mixing bowl. Sprinkle the oil, vinegar, salt, and pepper on top and toss gently. Correct the seasoning and serve at once.

Serves 2

84 CALORIES PER SERVING; 1 G PROTEIN; 5 G FAT; 10 G CARBOHYDRATE; 5 MG SODIUM; 0 MG CHOLESTEROL

PEAR SALAD WITH WATERCRESS AND GORGONZOLA

This attractive salad is bursting with autumnal flavors: the sweetness of ripe pear, the woodsy flavor of walnuts, the salty tang of Gorgonzola.

1 bunch watercress, washed, spun dry, and torn into sprigs

4 ripe pears (preferably bosc)

½ lemon

8 walnuts, toasted and coarsely chopped

FOR THE DRESSING:

1 ounce Gorgonzola cheese, crumbled

1 tablespoon extra-virgin olive oil

2 to 3 tablespoons Chicken Stock (page 379) or Basic Vegetable Stock (page 382)

2 to 3 teaspoons white wine vinegar

freshly ground black pepper and salt as needed

1. Arrange a bed of watercress on each of 4 salad plates. Peel the pears (if desired), cut in quarters lengthwise, remove the cores, and rub with cut lemon to prevent discoloring.

2. Arrange the pears on top of the watercress, narrow ends facing out, like the points of a compass. Sprinkle the walnuts on top.

3. Prepare the dressing: Combine the cheese, oil, stock, vinegar, and pepper in a bowl and whisk to mix. Correct the seasoning, adding salt or vinegar to taste.

4. Spoon the dressing over the pears and watercress and serve at once.

Serves 4

188 CALORIES PER SERVING; 4 G PROTEIN; 10 G FAT; 2 G SATURATED FAT; 23 G CARBOHYDRATE; 134 MG SODIUM; 6 MG CHOLESTEROL

CAESAR SALAD

Caesar salad was first served at a restaurant called Caesar's Palace in Tijuana in 1924, the creation of an Italian immigrant turned restaurateur named Caesar Cardini. My healthy version features buttermilk in place of some of the olive oil and egg substitute instead of the coddled egg. (The egg substitute—optional here—has the added advantage of being pasteurized, so you needn't worry about the risks associated with eating raw eggs.) Cheese-and-chili-toasted tortilla chips stand in for the fried bread. Here, then, is a heart-healthy Caesar that would do Cardini proud.

2 hearts romaine lettuce

Garlic Parmesan Chili "Croutons" (page 68)

FOR THE DRESSING:

1 large clove garlic, cut in half

4 anchovy fillets, rinsed with hot water, then drained, plus 4 to 6 fillets for garnish (optional)

1 teaspoon Dijon mustard

1 tablespoon egg substitute (optional)

1¼ teaspoons Worcestershire sauce

3 tablespoons low-fat buttermilk

1 tablespoon fresh lemon juice

1 tablespoon extra-virgin olive oil

salt and freshly ground black pepper

¼ cup freshly grated Pecorino Romano cheese

1. Wash the lettuce and spin dry. Tear leaves into 2-inch pieces; you should have 6 to 8 cups. Prepare the "croutons."

2. Make the dressing. (For extra points, do this tableside before the admiring gaze of your guests.) Rub a large salad bowl with ½ clove of garlic. Mince the remainder of the garlic and the four anchovy fillets with a knife or cleaver. Place them in the salad bowl and mash to a paste with the back of a mixing spoon. Whisk in the mustard, egg substitute (if using), Worcestershire sauce, buttermilk, lemon juice, and olive oil. Add salt and pepper to taste; the dressing should be highly seasoned. The dressing can be made up to 4 hours ahead.

3. Just before serving, add the lettuce, cheese, and croutons. Gently toss the salad to mix. Mound the Caesar on salad plates, crowning each with an optional anchovy fillet.

Serves 6

172 CALORIES PER SERVING; 7 G PROTEIN; 9 G FAT; 2 G SATURATED FAT; 17 G CARBOHYDRATE; 367 MG SODIUM; 9 MG CHOLESTEROL

GARLIC PARMESAN CHILI "CROUTONS"

I first created these garlicky, cheesy, chili-charged "croutons" to go with the Mexican-style Caesar salad on this page. People liked them so much that I started serving them with other salads, soups, and even as a finger food. You can use either corn or flour tortillas; in my house, we prefer the latter.

1 clove garlic, minced

1 tablespoon extra-virgin olive oil, melted lard, or melted butter

4 (8-inch) flour tortillas

1 tablespoon pure chili powder

salt and freshly ground black pepper

3 tablespoons freshly grated Parmesan cheese

1. Preheat the oven to 350°F.

2. Stir the garlic into the olive oil. Using a pastry brush, paint the top of each tortilla with garlic oil. Sprinkle the tortillas with chili powder, salt, pepper, and Parmesan cheese. Cut each tortilla into eight wedges or other shapes, using a large knife.

3. Arrange the "croutons" on a baking sheet in a single layer. Bake until they are lightly browned, 8 to 12 minutes. Remove from the oven and let cool on the baking sheet; the croutons will crisp as they cool.

Makes 32 croutons, enough to serve 4 to 6

172 CALORIES PER SERVING;* 5 G PROTEIN; 8 G FAT; 2 G SATURATED FAT; 21 G CARBOHYDRATE; 274 MG SODIUM; 4 MG CHOLESTEROL

Analysis is based on 4 servings.

ARUGULA, TOMATO, AND ENDIVE SALAD WITH SHAVED PARMESAN

This salad is a standby at our house. My wife and I enjoy a variation of it several times a week. Sometimes we substitute watercress or spinach for the arugula. Sometimes we omit the endive. Usually, we simply toss the ingredients together, but sometimes, when we're feeling fancy, we'll carpet salad plates or a platter with arugula leaves and pile the tossed endive and diced tomato in the center.

1 large or 2 medium juicy, red ripe tomatoes

2 Belgian endives, thinly sliced crosswise

1 bunch arugula, washed, dried, and stemmed

1½ tablespoons extra-virgin olive oil

1 to 1½ tablespoons balsamic vinegar

salt and freshly ground black pepper

1 ounce Parmigiano-Reggiano cheese

1. Cut the tomatoes into ¼-inch dice and add them with the juices to a salad bowl. Just before serving, add the endive, arugula, oil, vinegar, salt, and pepper to the bowl. Gently toss to mix. Correct the seasoning, adding salt or vinegar to taste.

2. Transfer the salad to plates or a platter. Shave a few curls of Parmigiano-Reggiano cheese over each and serve at once.

Serves 4

90 CALORIES PER SERVING; 3 G PROTEIN; 7 G FAT; 2 G SATURATED FAT; 3 G CARBOHYDRATE; 140 MG SODIUM; 6 MG CHOLESTEROL

HOW TO SHAVE PARMESAN

The easiest way to shave Parmesan is to use a swivel-bladed vegetable peeler. Hold the block of cheese in your left hand (or right hand if you're left-handed) and pull the vegetable peeler over it with your left. Long, thin shavings of Parmesan will land on the salad. It's easier to start with a larger block of cheese than you actually need for serving four people.

HOW TO WASH ARUGULA

The easiest way to wash arugula is to agitate the leaves in a bowl of cold water, holding the bunch by the stems. Change the water two or three times, or until grit no longer appears; arugula tends to be very gritty, so wash well before using.

ONION SALAD

This salad—from Brazil's cattle country—is not for the fainthearted. The onions lose some of their nose-jarring pungency, however, when soaked in ice water. Choose the mildest onions you can find, such as Vidalias or Maui onions.

2 large onions

2 teaspoons Dijon-style mustard

1 tablespoon red wine vinegar (or to taste)

1 tablespoon fresh lemon juice

salt and freshly ground black pepper

2 tablespoons olive oil

3 tablespoons chicken stock

⅓ cup chopped flat-leaf parsley, for garnish

1. Peel the onions and slice them widthwise as thinly as possible. Separate the slices into rings. Place the onions in a shallow bowl with 2 cups ice cubes and cold water to cover. Refrigerate for 2 hours.

2. Combine the mustard, vinegar, lemon juice, salt, and pepper in a bowl and whisk until the salt is dissolved. Whisk in the oil and stock in a thin stream. Correct the seasoning.

3. Drain the onions and rinse under cold water. Drain again, blot dry, and arrange in a shallow bowl. Whisk the sauce and pour it over the onions. Sprinkle the salad with parsley and serve at once.

Note: Warn your guests to cut the onions with a knife and fork. It is difficult to eat the rings whole.

Serves 6 to 8

54 CALORIES PER SERVING; 1 G PROTEIN; 5 G FAT; 3 G CARBOHYDRATE; 204 MG SODIUM; 0 MG CHOLESTEROL

LIDIA'S BLOOD ORANGE SALAD

Lidia Bastianich is one of the foremost Italian chefs in New York, the owner of Felidia, Becco, and Frico Bar (and restaurants in Minneapolis and Pittsburgh), as well as the author of an acclaimed cookbook. What I come away with whenever I dine at one of her restaurants is her uncanny ability to create amazingly complex dishes with a few simple ingredients. Consider this simple but stunning salad, which she inspired. Blood oranges are a traditional southern Italian citrus fruit with striking red color and intense strawberry-orange flavor. Blood oranges are in season primarily in winter, although they turn up sporadically throughout the year. Look for them in gourmet shops, Italian markets, and specialty greengrocers. If unavailable, use regular oranges.

8 blood oranges

3 Belgian endives

1 bunch watercress, washed, stemmed, and torn into sprigs

2 to 3 teaspoons white wine vinegar

salt and freshly ground black pepper

1½ tablespoons extra-virgin olive oil

4 sprigs flat-leaf parsley

1. Using a sharp paring knife, cut the rind and white pith off the oranges to expose the red flesh. Cut each orange, crosswise, into ¼-inch slices. Remove the seeds with a fork without breaking the slices. Work over a bowl or on a grooved cutting board to collect the juices. Cut the endives on the diagonal into ¼-inch slices.

2. Combine the vinegar, salt, and pepper in a shallow bowl and whisk until the salt is completely dissolved. Whisk in the olive oil and any reserved orange juice.

3. Arrange the orange slices around the outside edge of 4 salad plates or a platter. Spoon a little of the salad dressing over the oranges. Gently toss the endive and watercress with the remaining dressing and mound the mixture in the center. Garnish with parsley sprigs and serve at once.

Serves 4

173 CALORIES PER SERVING; 3 G PROTEIN; 5 G FAT; 0 G SATURATED FAT; 32 G CARBOHYDRATE; 9 MG SODIUM; 0 MG CHOLESTEROL

CUCUMBER SALAD WITH SPICY WASABI DRESSING

Here's a Japanese version of cucumber salad made with a spicy horseradishlike condiment called wasabi. Rice wine vinegar is milder than most Western vinegars. If unavailable, mix 2 parts distilled white vinegar with 1 part water.

1½ teaspoons dry wasabi (or to taste)

2 cucumbers

2 tablespoons rice wine vinegar

1 teaspoons sugar

1 teaspoon sesame oil

salt and freshly ground black pepper

1 green onion or 2 scallions, thinly sliced

1 tablespoon black or toasted white sesame seeds

1. Mix the wasabi with ½ teaspoon warm water in the bottom of a mixing bowl and let it stand for 5 minutes. Peel the cucumbers, cut each one in half lengthwise, and use a melon baller or spoon to scoop out the seeds. Cut the cucumbers widthwise into ¼-inch crescents.

2. Add the vinegar and sugar to the wasabi and whisk until smooth. Whisk in the sesame oil, salt, and pepper. Just before serving, add the cucumbers, green onion, and sesame seeds to the dressing and mix well.

Serves 4

51 CALORIES PER SERVING; 1 G PROTEIN; 2 G FAT; 7 G CARBOHYDRATE; 25 MG SODIUM; 0 MG CHOLESTEROL

Cucumber, Yogurt, and Spearmint Salad

CUCUMBER, YOGURT, AND SPEARMINT SALAD

This salad is a popular item on a mezza platter, a salad sampler served at the start of a Middle Eastern meal. The mint of choice is spearmint, but any fresh mint will work.

2 cups nonfat yogurt

2 cucumbers

1 or 2 cloves garlic, minced (1 or 2 teaspoons)

salt

freshly ground black pepper

⅓ cup chopped fresh mint (preferably spearmint)

⅓ cup chopped flat-leaf parsley

½ teaspoon sugar (optional)

2 teaspoons extra-virgin olive oil

pita bread

1. Drain the yogurt in a yogurt funnel or cheesecloth-lined colander for 1 hour. Peel the cucumbers, cut each one in half lengthwise, and use a melon baller or spoon to scoop out the seeds. Cut the cucumbers into ¼-inch dice. Mash the garlic and salt to a paste in a mixing bowl.

2. Stir the drained yogurt into the garlic paste. Add the cucumbers, pepper, mint, parsley, and sugar, and toss to mix. Correct the seasoning, adding salt and pepper to taste. Just before serving, drizzle the salad with olive oil. Tear off pieces of pita bread and use them to scoop up the salad.

Serves 4 to 6

147 CALORIES PER SERVING; 10 G PROTEIN; 5 G FAT; 16 G CARBOHYDRATE; 107 MG SODIUM; 12 MG CHOLESTEROL

NINO'S FENNEL, TOMATO, AND SPINACH SALAD

Nino Pernetti runs the popular Caffe Abbracci in Coral Gables. His simple, tasty food—epitomized by this salad—is always served with style and generosity. For the best results buy young leaf spinach. You could also use arugula.

- 1 bunch tender, young leaf spinach
- 2 ripe tomatoes
- 1 small bulb fennel or ½ large bulb (reserve the feathery leaves for garnish)

FOR THE DRESSING:

- 1½ tablespoons balsamic vinegar (preferably white)
- 1½ tablespoons extra-virgin olive oil
- 1½ tablespoons Chicken Stock (page 379) or Basic Vegetable Stock (page 382)
- 2 tablespoons minced red onion or shallot
- salt and freshly ground black pepper

1. Wash and stem the spinach. Thinly slice the tomatoes. Thinly slice the fennel crosswise, discarding the fibrous core.

2. Combine the ingredients for the dressing (the vinegar, oil, stock, onion, salt, and pepper) in a bowl and whisk until smooth. Correct the seasoning, adding vinegar or salt to taste.

3. Carpet four salad plates or a platter with spinach leaves. Arrange the tomato slices in a circle on top and mound the sliced fennel in the center. Spoon the dressing over the salads and serve at once, garnished with feathery fennel leaves.

Serves 4

75 CALORIES PER SERVING; 2 G PROTEIN; 5 G FAT; 0.7 G SATURATED FAT; 6 G CARBOHYDRATE; 58 MG SODIUM; 0 MG CHOLESTEROL

BEET, AVOCADO, AND WATERCRESS SALAD

This colorful salad was invented by macrobiotic baker Michael Evans. The raw beets are wonderfully crunchy, but wear rubber gloves when preparing them to avoid staining your fingers.

FOR THE DRESSING:

- 1 or 2 cloves garlic
- salt and freshly ground black pepper
- 1 tablespoon Dijon-style mustard
- 2 tablespoons olive oil
- 3 tablespoons balsamic vinegar
- 1 ripe avocado, peeled, pitted, and diced
- juice of 1 lemon
- 1 pound fresh beets, peeled and diced
- 2 bunches watercress, torn or cut into 1-inch sprigs, with stems
- 2 red bell peppers, cored, seeded, and diced
- 1 red onion, diced
- 1 cup fresh or slightly thawed frozen peas
- 2 bunches stemmed and finely chopped cilantro and/or parsley

To make the dressing, combine the garlic with the salt and pepper in the bottom of a large salad bowl and mash to a smooth paste. Work in the mustard. Whisk in the oil and vinegar. Correct the seasoning, adding salt and pepper; the dressing should be highly seasoned.

Not more than 10 minutes before serving, add the salad ingredients to the dressing and toss well.

Serves 6 to 8

156 CALORIES PER SERVING; 4 G PROTEIN; 10 G FAT; 15 G CARBOHYDRATE; 72 MG SODIUM; 0 MG CHOLESTEROL

ROASTED CHILI SALAD WITH PUMPKIN-SEED VINAIGRETTE
(ENSALADA DE RAJAS CON SALSA DE PEPITAS)

It's hard to imagine Mexican cuisine without rajas, *those smoky, spicy, electrifyingly flavorful strips of roasted poblano chilies. This salad features a colorful assortment of roasted peppers, topped with a nutty pumpkin-seed vinaigrette.*

- 8 poblano chilies
- 2 yellow bell peppers
- 2 red bell peppers

FOR THE VINAIGRETTE:

- 2 tablespoons coarsely chopped pumpkin seeds
- 2 tablespoons fresh lime juice
- ½ teaspoon salt
- ½ teaspoon freshly ground black pepper
- ¼ teaspoon minced garlic
- 1½ tablespoons olive oil

Serves 4 to 6

108 CALORIES PER SERVING;* 4 G PROTEIN; 7 G FAT; 1 G SATURATED FAT; 12 G CARBOHYDRATE; 272 MG SODIUM; 0 MG CHOLESTEROL

Analysis is based on 4 servings.

1. Roast the chilies and peppers over a high flame, on a barbecue grill, or under the broiler, until the skins are charred all over, 8 to 10 minutes. Place the chilies and peppers in a paper bag and seal the top, or put them in a bowl and cover with plastic wrap. Let cool for 15 minutes.

2. Scrape the burnt skin from the chilies and peppers, using a paring knife. Seed and devein the chilies and peppers, cutting each lengthwise into ¼-inch-wide strips. Work on a grooved cutting board to collect any pepper juices. Reserve these juices for the dressing.

3. Arrange the chili and pepper strips in a star-burst pattern on round plates, alternating colors. The strips should radiate from the center of the plates like the spokes of a wheel.

4. To prepare the vinaigrette, roast the pumpkin seeds in a skillet over medium heat until they are lightly toasted and fragrant, about 2 minutes. Set aside. Combine the lime juice, salt, pepper, and garlic in a mixing bowl and whisk until the salt is dissolved. Whisk in the olive oil and pepper juices. Spoon this mixture over the salad and sprinkle with the pumpkin seeds. Serve at once.

Beet, Avocado, and Watercress Salad

MEXICAN "SLAW"

Thinly sliced white cabbage accompanies countless Mexican dishes, from flautas to tacos and taquitos. Its refreshing crispness and audible crunch make a pleasing counterpoint to stews and soft, moist tortilla dishes. From shredded cabbage, it's a short jump to slaw.

FOR THE DRESSING:

1 small clove garlic, minced

1 tablespoon sugar, or to taste

½ teaspoon salt, or to taste

½ teaspoon freshly ground black pepper

½ teaspoon toasted cumin seeds (optional)

⅓ cup fresh lime juice

FOR THE "SLAW":

3 cups white cabbage, finely shredded (about 5 ounces)

1 carrot, shredded

4 to 5 ounces jícama, shredded

1 tomato, seeded and cut into ¼-inch dice

1 or 2 jalapeño chilies, minced (for a milder slaw, seed the chilies)

⅓ cup coarsely chopped cilantro

1. In the bottom of a serving bowl, combine the garlic, sugar, salt, pepper, and cumin (if using) and mash to a paste with a wooden spoon. Stir in the lime juice.

2. Add the cabbage, carrot, jícama, tomato, jalapeños, and cilantro and toss to mix. Correct the seasoning, adding sugar or lime juice. The slaw should be a little sweet and a little sour.

Note: The sugar makes a U.S.-style slaw. To be more Mexican, you could certainly omit it.

Serves 4 to 6

56 CALORIES PER SERVING;* 2 G PROTEIN; 0 G FAT; 0 G SATURATED FAT; 13 G CARBOHYDRATE; 46 MG SODIUM; 0 MG CHOLESTEROL

Analysis is based on 4 servings.

PASTA PRIMAVERA SALAD

This salad features a painter's palate of spring colors: the oranges of baby carrots, the greens of asparagus and fresh peas, the rose of new red potatoes. The choice is limited only to your imagination.

2 cups short fusilli (or other curly pasta)

1½ tablespoons extra-virgin olive oil

4 ounces haricots verts, stem ends snapped off

6 ounces slender asparagus stalks

10 ounces fresh peas

6 ounces baby carrots

6 ounces baby red potatoes

12 basil leaves, plus a small sprig of basil for garnish

¼ cup finely chopped flat-leaf parsley

1 tablespoon tarragon vinegar or rice vinegar

1 tablespoon fresh lemon juice

½ teaspoon freshly grated lemon zest

1 garlic clove, minced

salt and freshly ground black pepper

1. Bring 4 quarts of salted water to a boil for cooking the pasta and vegetables. Cook the fusilli until al dente, about 8 minutes. Using a wire skimmer or slotted spoon, transfer the pasta to a colander, rinse under cold water until cool, and drain well. Transfer the fusilli to a mixing bowl and toss with olive oil. Return the water to a boil.

2. Cut the haricots verts into 2-inch pieces. Snap the fibrous ends off the asparagus and cut the stalks into 2-inch pieces. Shell the peas. Cut the carrots and new potatoes in half lengthwise. Cook the haricots verts, asparagus, and peas in the boiling water until crispy-tender, about 2 minutes. Drain the vegetables and transfer to a bowl of ice water. (The sudden cold helps intensify the colors.) Cook the carrots and potatoes in the boiling water until tender, 4 to 6 minutes. Drain the vegetables and transfer to the bowl of ice water. Drain all the vegetables in a colander, blot dry on paper towels, and add them to the salad.

3. Just before serving, cut the basil leaves crosswise into ¼-inch strips. Add the basil, parsley, vinegar, lemon juice, lemon zest, garlic, and salt and pepper to the salad and toss to mix. Correct the seasoning, adding lemon juice, salt, or pepper to taste. The salad should be highly seasoned. Garnish with the basil sprig and serve at once.

Serves 4

373 CALORIES PER SERVING; 13 G PROTEIN; 7 G FAT; 1 G SATURATED FAT; 66 G CARBOHYDRATE; 35 MG SODIUM; 0 MG CHOLESTEROL

Pasta Primavera Salad

SANTA FE SALAD
(WAGON WHEELS WITH ROASTED CHILIES AND CORN)

One of the most distinctive of Italy's pastas is ruote di carro, *"cartwheels." This set me thinking about the covered wagons of America's Wild West and before long I imagined a wagon-wheel pasta salad garnished with such Southwestern flavorings as chili peppers, roasted corn, and cilantro. You can certainly add 1 to 2 cups diced cooked chicken to this salad and serve it as a light main course.* Note: *For a quicker salad, you can skip roasting the peppers and simply dice them.*

FOR THE DRESSING:

4 tablespoons no-fat sour cream

2 to 3 tablespoons fresh lime juice

2 tablespoons Chicken Stock or Vegetable Stock
  (see pages 379, 382)

2 tablespoons ketchup

1 tablespoon extra-virgin olive oil (optional),
  plus 1 teaspoon for grilling the corn

1 tablespoon chili powder

1 garlic clove, minced

salt and freshly ground black pepper

TO FINISH THE SALAD:

2 cups wagon-wheel pasta (ruote di carro)

4 poblano chilies or 2 green bell peppers (see Note)

3 ears corn, shucked

½ red bell pepper, cut into ¼-inch dice (about ½ cup)

½ red onion, cut into ¼-inch dice (about ½ cup)

½ cup finely chopped fresh cilantro,
  plus a few sprigs for garnish

1 to 2 jalapeño chilies, seeded and finely chopped
  (for a hotter salad, leave the seeds in)

1. Combine the ingredients for the dressing in a large attractive serving bowl and whisk until smooth.

2. Cook the wagon wheels in 4 quarts of boiling water until al dente, 8 to 10 minutes. Drain the wagon wheels in a colander, refresh under cold water, and drain well. Stir the pasta into the dressing. Preheat a barbecue grill or broiler to high.

3. Roast the chilies over a high flame until charred on all sides, about 8 minutes. Wrap the chilies in wet paper towels and let cool. Brush the corn with the reserved 1 teaspoon oil and season with salt and pepper. Grill the corn until nicely browned on all sides, turning often, about 8 minutes. Transfer the corn to a cutting board and cut the kernels off the cobs. (The easiest way to do this is to lay the ears flat on the cutting board and make lengthwise cuts with a chopping knife.)

4. Scrape the burnt skin off the chilies, cut the chilies in half, and remove the seeds and stems. Cut the chilies into ¼-inch strips and add them to the pasta with the corn. Stir in the red bell pepper, onion, cilantro, and jalapeños. Correct the seasoning, adding salt, chili powder, and/or lime juice to taste: The salad should be highly seasoned. Garnish the salad with cilantro sprigs before serving.

Note: The poblano is a dark green, mildly hot, elongated triangle-shaped chili traditionally used by Mexicans to make *chiles rellenos.* Look for them at Hispanic grocery stores, gourmet greengrocers, and many supermarkets.

Serves 4

314 CALORIES PER SERVING; 10 G PROTEIN; 3 G FAT; 0 G SATURATED FAT;
64 G CARBOHYDRATE; 139 MG SODIUM; 0 MG CHOLESTEROL

ASIAN NOODLE SALAD

This colorful salad is great for a picnic or a summer buffet. There are several possibilities for noodles: you could use Chinese egg noodles, Japanese wheat noodles (such as ramen *or* udon*), Japanese buckwheat noodles (*soba*), or even Western spaghetti.*

8 ounces pre-steamed Chinese egg noodles,
    dried wheat noodles, spaghetti, or bucatini

1 teaspoon sesame oil

8 ounces asparagus

salt

8 ounces snow peas,
    ends snapped off and strings removed

1 red bell pepper, cored, seeded,
    and cut into matchstick slivers

1 yellow bell pepper, cored, seeded,
    and cut into matchstick slivers

1 15-ounce can baby corn, drained

6 scallions, white part minced,
    green part thinly sliced on the diagonal

FOR THE DRESSING:

1 clove garlic, minced

3 tablespoons toasted sesame seeds

¼ cup rice vinegar

¼ cup honey

1 tablespoon sesame oil

freshly ground black pepper

1. Cook the noodles in 4 quarts boiling water until al dente, 6 to 8 minutes. Drain the noodles in a colander, rinse with cold water until cool, and drain well. Transfer the noodles to a large mixing bowl and toss with 1 teaspoon sesame oil.

2. Snap the fibrous ends off the asparagus and cut the stalks sharply on the diagonal into 2-inch pieces. Cook the asparagus in 2 quarts boiling salted water until crispy-tender, about 3 minutes. With a slotted spoon, transfer the asparagus to a colander and shock-chill with ice water (see Note). Drain well. Cook, drain, and chill the snow peas the same way. (They'll need about 1 minute of cooking.)

3. Prepare the dressing. Mash the garlic and half the sesame seeds in an attractive serving bowl. Add the vinegar, honey, remaining 1 tablespoon sesame oil, salt, and pepper, and whisk until the salt crystals are dissolved. Correct the seasoning, adding salt or vinegar to taste: the dressing should be highly seasoned.

4. Add the noodles, asparagus, snow peas, peppers, baby corn, scallion whites, and half the scallion greens to the dressing and toss to mix. Sprinkle the remaining sesame seeds and scallion greens on top and serve at once.

Note: Shock-chilling means immersing or rinsing a vegetable in ice water. The sudden cold interrupts the cooking process and intensifies the vegetable color.

Serves 4 to 6

414 CALORIES PER SERVING;* 13 G PROTEIN; 10 G FAT; 1 G SATURATED FAT; 72 G CARBOHYDRATE; 231 MG SODIUM; 41 MG CHOLESTEROL

Analysis is based on 4 servings.

TUSCAN BREAD SALAD

Here's how cooks on the other side of the Mediterranean keep stale bread from going to waste. In Tuscany, the salad would be made with saltless Tuscan bread. Any dense Italian or country-style loaf will work as well.

1 clove garlic, minced (1 teaspoon)

3–4 tablespoons chicken stock or water

1½ tablespoons olive oil

1½ tablespoons red wine vinegar

1–2 tablespoons fresh lemon juice

salt and freshly ground black pepper

2 or 3 thick slices firm, dense white bread, cut into 1-inch cubes (about 3 cups)

2 ripe tomatoes, diced or cut into wedges

1 small red onion, cut into rings

1 stalk celery, cut into ½-inch diagonal slices

1 cucumber, peeled, seeded, and cut into ½-inch pieces

½ bunch flat-leaf parsley, coarsely chopped

½ bunch fresh basil (about 20 leaves), coarsely chopped, plus a few whole leaves for garnish

3 tablespoons capers

8 black olives (optional)

2 anchovy fillets, diced, plus whole or halved fillets for garnish (optional)

1. Combine the garlic, stock, oil, vinegar, lemon juice, salt, and pepper in a small bowl and whisk until smooth. (Or combine the ingredients in a jar with a tight-fitting lid and shake well.)

2. Place the remaining ingredients in a large bowl and toss with the dressing. Let the salad stand for at least 30 minutes before serving to allow the bread to absorb the juices. Toss again just before serving and correct the seasoning, adding salt and vinegar to taste. (If the bread tastes too dry, add a little more stock or water.) Decorate the salad with whole basil leaves and whole or halved anchovy fillets, if desired.

Serves 4

147 CALORIES PER SERVING; 4 G PROTEIN; 7 G FAT; 20 G CARBOHYDRATE; 295 MG SODIUM; 2 MG CHOLESTEROL

PITA BREAD SALAD

Fattoush, a pita bread salad popular throughout the Middle East, delights thrifty cooks who love to transform yesterday's leftovers into tomorrow's dish of distinction. As in many recipes in this book, I've reduced the amount of oil by using chicken stock to moisten the pita.

2 large or 4 small stale (or fresh) pita breads, torn or cut into bite-sized wedges

1 ripe tomato, seeded and diced

3 scallions, finely chopped (⅓ cup)

1 cup finely chopped flat-leaf parsley

¼ cup finely chopped fresh spearmint or other mint

1½ tablespoons olive oil

2–3 tablespoons chicken stock or water

2 tablespoons fresh lemon juice

2 tablespoons red wine vinegar

salt and freshly ground black pepper

1 pomegranate (optional)

1. Combine the pita bread wedges, tomato, scallions, parsley, and mint in a salad bowl and toss to mix. Combine the oil, stock, lemon juice, vinegar, salt, and pepper in a small bowl and whisk until smooth. (Or combine the ingredients in a jar with a tight-fitting lid and shake well.) The dressing should be highly seasoned; add salt and lemon juice to taste.

2. If using the pomegranate, cut it in half lengthwise. Working over a bowl to catch any juice, break the halves into sections and separate the sections into individual seeds.

3. Not more than 15 minutes before serving, pour the dressing over the salad and toss to mix, adding half the pomegranate seeds and any pomegranate juice. If the pita bread seems too dry, add a little more stock or water. Sprinkle the salad with the remaining pomegranate seeds and serve at once.

Serves 4

167 CALORIES PER SERVING; 5 G PROTEIN; 6 G FAT; 25 G CARBOHYDRATE; 250 MG SODIUM; 0 MG CHOLESTEROL

WILD RICE SALAD

I can't think of a better dish for a picnic than this colorful salad, since you don't need to worry about it wilting. Presoaking the rice shortens the cooking time and improves the final texture.

1 cup wild rice

2 large oranges

¼ cup sultanas (yellow raisins)

2 scallions, finely chopped

½ bunch flat-leaf parsley, finely chopped (about ½ cup), plus a few sprigs for garnish

1½ tablespoons olive oil

1½ tablespoons balsamic vinegar (or to taste)

1½ tablespoons fresh lemon juice (or to taste)

1 or 2 dashes hot sauce

salt and freshly ground black pepper

1. Rinse the rice thoroughly in cold water in a strainer. Soak it for at least 4 hours in a large bowl with water to cover.

2. Place the rice in a large pot with 6 cups cold water. Bring to a boil, reduce the heat, and simmer for 30 minutes, or until tender. Meanwhile, cut the rind (both zest and white pith) off the oranges to expose the flesh. Make V-shaped cuts to remove the individual segments from the membranes, working over a bowl to catch the juice. Soak the sultanas in the orange juice for at least 5 minutes.

3. Combine the rice, orange segments, sultanas, and remaining ingredients in a large bowl, reserving a few of the orange segments for garnish. Toss the salad, adding salt, vinegar, and orange juice to taste. Mound the salad on a platter or in a bowl and decorate the top with the reserved orange segments and parsley sprigs.

Serves 6

164 CALORIES PER SERVING; 5 G PROTEIN; 4 G FAT; 30 G CARBOHYDRATE; 6 MG SODIUM; 0 MG CHOLESTEROL

POSOLE SALAD

This salad has probably never been served in Mexico, but it's thoroughly Mexican in color, flavor, and spirit. Posole—parched, hulled, cooked corn—is traditionally served in soups and stews, but its malty flavor and softly chewy texture make it a delectable base for a salad. Here, as elsewhere in this book, for the sake of convenience I call for canned hominy (posole).

1¾ cups cooked hominy
(one 14½-ounce-can, drained and rinsed several times)

1 ripe red tomato, seeded and cut into ¼-inch dice

1 cucumber, peeled, seeded, and cut into ¼-inch dice

3 scallions, trimmed and finely chopped

½ cup chopped fresh cilantro

1 or 2 jalapeño chilies, seeded and minced
(for a spicier salad, leave in the seeds)

½ teaspoon ground cumin

3 tablespoons fresh lime juice

salt and freshly ground black pepper

4 to 6 lettuce leaves, washed and dried

1. Combine all the ingredients except the lettuce leaves in a mixing bowl and toss to mix.

2. Place a lettuce leaf on each salad plate. Mound the posole on each leaf and serve at once.

Serves 4 to 6

99 CALORIES PER SERVING;* 3 G PROTEIN; 1 G FAT; 0 G SATURATED FAT; 20 G CARBOHYDRATE; 224 MG SODIUM; 0 MG CHOLESTEROL

Analysis is based on 4 servings.

KASHA SALAD WITH DILL

Kasha is the Jewish name for buckwheat groats. This gray-brown grain has an earthy, nutty flavor that is unique. In this recipe, the groats are roasted dry with egg white to keep the grains fluffy and separate. Kasha can be found in Jewish markets, natural food stores, and most supermarkets.

1 cup buckwheat groats

½ egg white, beaten

1 small onion

1 bay leaf

1 whole clove

salt

1 small red bell pepper, cored, seeded, and diced

1 small yellow bell pepper, cored, seeded, and diced

3 scallions, finely chopped

¼ cup finely chopped fresh dill

2 tablespoons red wine vinegar

1½ tablespoons extra-virgin olive oil

1 tablespoon fresh lemon juice

½ teaspoon ground cumin

freshly ground black pepper

1. Wash the groats under cold running water, drain well, and blot dry. Combine the groats and egg white in a bowl and stir to mix. Put the groats mixture in a heavy (preferably nonstick) pan and cook over high heat, stirring steadily, for 2 to 3 minutes, or until the individual grains are dry.

2. Cut the onion in half and pin the bay leaf to one half with the clove. Add the onion, 2 cups water, and salt to the groats. Bring to a boil, stirring well. Reduce the heat and simmer for 15 to 18 minutes, or until the groats are tender but not too soft. Transfer the groats to a colander and let cool. Discard the onion.

3. Place the groats and the remaining ingredients in a large mixing bowl and toss well. Correct the seasoning, adding salt and lemon juice to taste.

Note: If the groats stick to the pan, soak it and then scour it with oven cleaner.

Serves 4

207 CALORIES PER SERVING; 6 G PROTEIN; 6 G FAT; 35 G CARBOHYDRATE; 22 MG SODIUM; 0 MG CHOLESTEROL

....

TUSCAN BEAN SALAD

Visit a restaurant in the Italian countryside and the chances are that you'll find a grandmother or grandfather sitting at a table in the kitchen or dining room shelling fagioli (white beans). If you live in an area with a large Italian community, you may be able to find fresh fagioli. If not, use dried or canned beans. If using the latter, rinse well before using.

2 cups cooked cannellini beans

1 gorgeous ripe tomato, peeled, seeded, and diced

1½ tablespoons top-quality Tuscan extra-virgin olive oil

1 tablespoon toasted pine nuts

¼ red onion, minced (3 to 4 tablespoons)

¼ cup chopped flat-leaf parsley

salt and freshly ground black pepper

lemon wedges for garnish

1. If using canned beans, rinse well under cold water. Drain well and blow dry. Warm the beans and tomato in a nonstick frying pan over medium heat. They should be warm but not hot.

2. Remove the pan from the heat and stir in the oil, pine nuts, red onion, parsley, and salt and pepper to taste. The salad should be highly seasoned. Serve the salad with lemon wedges for squeezing.

Serves 4 to 6

193 CALORIES PER SERVING;* 10 G PROTEIN; 7 G FAT; 1 G SATURATED FAT; 25 G CARBOHYDRATE; 11 MG SODIUM; 0 MG CHOLESTEROL

Analysis is based on 4 servings.

Black Bean Salad with Feta Cheese and Mint

BLACK BEAN SALAD WITH FETA CHEESE AND MINT

This salad offers a striking contrast between the inky darkness of black beans (also known as turtle beans) and the snowy white of feta cheese. Feta isn't a low-fat cheese, but because it has such a sharp flavor, you need only a little. A similar salad could be made using tofu instead of cheese.

- **2 cups dry black beans (or 4 cups cooked beans)**
- **1 small red onion, finely chopped (about ½ cup)**
- **½ cup tightly packed, finely chopped fresh mint, plus a few sprigs for garnish (or 2 tablespoons dried)**
- **2 ounces drained feta cheese, crumbled**
- **2 tablespoons extra-virgin olive oil**
- **3–4 tablespoons fresh lemon juice**
- **salt and freshly ground black pepper**

1. Wash the beans and soak them in cold water to cover overnight. The next day, drain the beans and place them in a pot with cold water to cover. Bring to a boil, reduce the heat, and simmer for 20 to 25 minutes, or until tender. Refresh under cold water and drain. (For extra flavor, add onion, carrot, celery, and garlic to the beans.)

2. Combine the beans, onion, mint, and most of the cheese in a bowl. Add the olive oil, lemon juice, salt, and pepper, and mix well. Let the beans marinate for 10 minutes and toss again. Correct the seasoning before serving, adding salt and lemon juice to taste. Garnish the salad with mint sprigs and the remaining cheese.

Serves 4 to 6

333 CALORIES PER SERVING; 18 G PROTEIN; 11 G FAT; 44 G CARBOHYDRATE; 162 MG SODIUM; 12 MG CHOLESTEROL

LENTIL SALAD WITH SMOKED TURKEY AND CHILIES

Lentils are best known as a soup ingredient, but they're delicious in salads as well. The tiny green lentils from Le Puy, France, are the best. Alternatively, you could use the red lentils found in Indian markets, but shorten the cooking time.

½ pound lentils

2 cloves garlic

2 bay leaves

6 ounces smoked turkey or smoked chicken, diced

1 large ripe tomato, peeled, seeded, and diced

2 scallions, finely chopped

¼ cup finely chopped cilantro or flat-leaf parsley, plus a few sprigs for garnish

FOR THE DRESSING:

1 clove garlic, minced (1 teaspoon)

3 tablespoons nonfat yogurt

2 tablespoons red wine vinegar

1½ tablespoons olive oil

1 tablespoon Dijon-style mustard

1 tablespoon fresh lemon juice

1 tablespoon chopped pickled jalapeño chilies

1 tablespoon pickled jalapeño juice

1 teaspoon cumin seeds (or ½ teaspoon ground cumin)

salt and freshly ground black pepper

Pick through the lentils, removing any twigs or stones. Wash thoroughly and drain. Place the lentils in a large pot with 6 cups cold water, the garlic, and the bay leaves. Bring to a boil, reduce the heat, and simmer for 20 minutes, or until the lentils are soft but not mushy. Drain in a colander, refresh under cold water, and drain well. Remove the garlic and bay leaves.

Combine the ingredients for the dressing in a large salad bowl and whisk until smooth. Mix in the lentils, turkey, tomato, scallions, and cilantro. Correct the seasoning, adding salt and vinegar to taste. Spoon the salad into a bowl and decorate with cilantro sprigs.

Serves 6

223 CALORIES PER SERVING; 16 G PROTEIN; 7 G FAT; 26 G CARBOHYDRATE; 323 MG SODIUM; 0 MG CHOLESTEROL

Chicken Salad Niçoise with Big-Flavor Vinaigrette

CHICKEN SALAD NIÇOISE WITH BIG-FLAVOR VINAIGRETTE

This salad recalls one of the most memorable meals I ever had: Lunch with Julia Child at her hillside home in Grasse in the south of France. The moment my wife and I arrived, we were put to work: chopping onions, slicing tomatoes, washing lettuce. We soon sat down to a magnificent salade niçoise, *which we ate al fresco. In this recipe pepper-seared chicken replaces the traditional tuna. The vinaigrette uses chicken stock in place of most of the olive oil for flavor with less fat.*

1 pound boneless, skinless chicken breasts, or 2 cups cooked chicken

2 teaspoons extra-virgin olive oil

2 tablespoons cracked black peppercorns

kosher salt to taste

FOR THE SALAD:

1 pound small red potatoes, scrubbed

½ pound haricots verts or green beans

2 large ripe tomatoes, very thinly sliced

4 to 5 cups mesclun (mixed baby lettuces)

¼ cup niçoise or kalamata olives, rinsed and drained

2 hard-boiled eggs, yolks discarded, whites coarsely chopped

¼ red onion, thinly sliced

FOR THE BASIL VINAIGRETTE:

¼ cup Chicken Stock (see page 379)

1 tablespoon wine vinegar, or to taste

1 tablespoon extra-virgin olive oil

1 clove garlic

1 scallion, trimmed

1 to 2 anchovy fillets, rinsed, and blotted dry (optional)

1 tablespoon capers, drained

16 basil leaves

1. Preheat the grill or broiler to high. Wash and dry the chicken breasts and trim off any fat and sinews. Brush the chicken breasts with olive oil and thickly sprinkle with cracked peppercorns and salt. Grill the breasts until cooked, 2 to 3 minutes per side. Transfer the chicken breasts to a cutting board and thinly slice widthwise across the grain. If using cooked chicken, thinly slice or dice it.

2. Place the potatoes in a pot with cold water to cover and salt. Bring the potatoes to a boil, reduce the heat, and simmer until tender, 8 to 10 minutes. Refresh the potatoes under cold water and drain. Cut any large potatoes in quarters or halves to have bite-size pieces. Snap the stems off the beans and cook them in rapidly boiling salted water until crispy-tender, about 2 minutes. Refresh under cold water and drain.

3. Fan the tomato slices out to cover the bottom edges of 4 large plates or a platter. Mound the mesclun at the top of the plate. Arrange bundles of haricots verts, clusters of potatoes, and piles of olives between the tomatoes and mesclun. Sprinkle the hard-cooked egg whites and sliced onion on top. Or use a different arrangement: The idea is to create a pretty, colorful salad.

4. Prepare the vinaigrette. Place the stock, vinegar, olive oil, garlic, scallion, anchovy fillets (if using), capers, and basil leaves in a blender and purée until smooth. Correct the seasoning, adding black pepper and salt to taste. (You probably won't need salt if you use the anchovy.) Transfer the dressing to a bowl and serve on the side.

Serves 4

297 CALORIES PER SERVING; 27 G PROTEIN; 7 G FAT; 1 G SATURATED FAT; 36 G CARBOHYDRATE; 352 MG SODIUM; 55 MG CHOLESTEROL

CURRIED CHICKEN SALAD WITH CHICKPEAS AND DATES

Curry powder lends this salad an Indian accent, while the dates add a Middle East touch of sweetness.

2 to 3 cups diced cooked chicken (without skin)

¼ pound green beans, snapped and cut into 1-inch pieces

salt

1 red bell pepper

10 pitted dates

2 cups cooked chickpeas, drained

⅓ cup raisins or currants

1 cup washed, stemmed cilantro leaves

FOR THE DRESSING:

1 cup plain non-fat yogurt

3 tablespoons lemon juice, or to taste

1 tablespoon honey

1 tablespoon curry powder, or to taste

1 tablespoon chopped candied ginger (optional)

salt and freshly ground black pepper

1. Cut the chicken into ½-inch dice. Cook the green beans in rapidly boiling water until crispy-tender, about 3 minutes. Refresh under cold water and drain. Core and seed the pepper and cut into 1- by ¼-inch strips. Cut the dates widthwise into ¼-inch slices. Have all the other ingredients for the salad ready.

2. Combine the ingredients for the dressing in an attractive serving bowl and whisk until smooth. Stir in the chicken, green beans, pepper, dates, chickpeas, raisins, and half the cilantro. Correct the seasoning, adding salt or lemon juice to taste. Sprinkle the remaining cilantro over the salad and serve at once.

Serves 4

357 CALORIES PER SERVING; 29 G PROTEIN; 5 G FAT; 1 G SATURATED FAT; 52 G CARBOHYDRATE; 432 MG SODIUM; 55 MG CHOLESTEROL

CAPRI SHRIMP AND BEAN SALAD

Call me a sucker for street life, but my favorite part of Capri wasn't the upper village, with its picture-perfect narrow streets and expensive boutiques. I preferred the hurly-burly of the docks in the lower village, where the ferries and fishing boats come in. I wandered in and out of trattorie, *chatting with cooks (no one would be so pretentious as to call himself a chef here), sampling simple fare and supremely fresh seafood, including the following salad.*

1½ tablespoons extra-virgin olive oil

1 clove garlic, crushed with the side of a cleaver and peeled

½ teaspoon curry powder

¼ to ½ teaspoon hot pepper flakes

1 pound large shrimp, peeled and deveined

salt and freshly ground black pepper

2 cups cooked cannellini beans

10 black olives

3 tablespoons chopped flat-leaf parsley

1 tablespoon red wine vinegar, or to taste

lemon wedges for garnish

1. Heat 1 tablespoon oil in a nonstick frying pan over a medium flame. Add the garlic, curry powder, and pepper flakes and sizzle in the oil until fragrant, about 30 seconds to a minute. Add the shrimp and sauté until cooked (they'll be firm and pink), 2 to 3 minutes, seasoning with salt and pepper.

2. Remove the pan from the heat and let cool. Stir in the beans, olives, parsley, and vinegar. Correct the seasoning, adding salt or vinegar to taste; the salad should be highly seasoned. Transfer the salad to a shallow serving bowl or to plates, drizzle the remaining ½ tablespoon olive oil on top, and garnish with lemon wedges for serving.

Serves 4 to 6

275 CALORIES PER SERVING;* 28 G PROTEIN; 8 G FAT; 1 G SATURATED FAT; 24 G CARBOHYDRATE; 253 MG SODIUM; 175 MG CHOLESTEROL

*Analysis is based on 4 servings.

TROPICAL CHICKEN SALAD WITH CREAMY CITRUS DRESSING

This salad is bursting with the tropical flavors of avocado, hearts of palm, and citrus fruits. The creamy vinaigrette dressing features reduced fruit juices and no-fat sour cream. If possible, use a Florida avocado, which contains about 30 percent less fat than a California Haas avocado. Florida avocados have a smooth, light green skin and are larger and sweeter than their Californian counterparts.

FOR THE DRESSING:

1 cup fresh orange juice

2 tablespoons fresh lemon juice

2 tablespoons fresh lime juice

⅔ cup no-fat sour cream

1 tablespoon extra-virgin olive oil (optional)

1 teaspoon honey (optional)

salt and freshly ground black pepper

pinch of cayenne pepper

2 to 3 cups diced cooked chicken (without skin)

1 ripe avocado, peeled, seeded, and cut into ½-inch dice

1 can hearts of palm, drained and cut into ½-inch slices

3 scallions, finely chopped

1 tablespoon lime juice

4 ripe oranges

6 to 8 Boston lettuce leaves, washed

¼ cup chopped fresh cilantro, mint, or parsley

1. Prepare the dressing. Combine the orange, lemon, and lime juices in a saucepan and boil until reduced to ¼ cup. Let this mixture cool completely, then whisk in the sour cream, olive oil and honey (if using), and salt, pepper, and cayenne to taste. The dressing should be highly seasoned.

2. Cut the chicken into ½-inch dice. Place the chicken, avocado, hearts of palm, and scallions in a mixing bowl and gently toss with the lime juice.

3. Cut the rind and pith (the white part) off the oranges. Thinly slice each orange widthwise. Line 4 large salad plates or a platter with lettuce leaves and arrange the orange slices on top. Mound the chicken mixture in the center. Pour most of the dressing over the chicken mixture, drizzling the remainder over the oranges. Sprinkle the salads with cilantro and serve.

Serves 4

291 CALORIES PER SERVING; 25 G PROTEIN; 10 G FAT; 2 G SATURATED FAT; 27 G CARBOHYDRATE; 159 MG SODIUM; 54 MG CHOLESTEROL

VIETNAMESE CHICKEN SALAD

I first tasted this salad in San Francisco's Chinatown at a noodle emporium called Golden Flower. The explosive flavors perform an intricate ballet on the palate. To simplify the recipe, use cooked chicken. (You'll need about 1½ cups thinly sliced cooked chicken.)

FOR THE DRESSING/ MARINADE:

⅓ cup fresh lemon juice

⅓ cup fish sauce

3 tablespoons honey

1½ teaspoons finely grated lemon zest

1 to 3 teaspoons Vietnamese, Thai, or other hot sauce

1 clove garlic, minced

12 ounces boneless, skinless chicken breasts, washed, dried, and trimmed of any fat

½ head iceberg lettuce, cored

½ head nappa or green cabbage, cored

¼ sweet onion, such as Vidalia, Walla Walla, or Maui

2 celery stalks, thinly sliced

2 carrots, finely julienned

1 bunch Thai or regular basil, washed and stemmed (reserve 4 whole sprigs for garnish)

1 to 4 jalapeño or other hot chilies, cut widthwise into paper-thin slices

2 tablespoons finely chopped dry roasted peanuts

1. Combine the ingredients for the dressing/marinade in a mixing bowl and whisk until the honey is dissolved. Transfer one-third of the mixture to a shallow bowl with the chicken breasts. Marinate the chicken in this mixture for 20 minutes, turning once or twice, while you prepare the remaining ingredients for the salad. Preheat a barbecue grill or broiler.

2. Slice the iceberg lettuce widthwise as thinly as possible. Do the same with the nappa and onion. Blanket 4 salad plates with the sliced lettuce. Mound the sliced cabbage on top. Then arrange neat layers of sliced onion, celery, carrots, and basil leaves.

3. Grill the chicken breasts over high heat until cooked, about 2 minutes per side. Thinly slice the chicken breasts across the grain. Fan the chicken slices out on top of the salads. Sprinkle the salads with the sliced chilies and chopped peanuts. Spoon the remaining dressing over the salads and let stand for 3 to 5 minutes before serving.

Serves 4

230 CALORIES PER SERVING; 21 G PROTEIN; 5 G FAT; 1 G SATURATED FAT; 28 G CARBOHYDRATE; 354 MG SODIUM; 47 MG CHOLESTEROL

THAI EGGPLANT AND SHRIMP SALAD

This fragrant salad comes from the restaurant Bahn Thai in Bangkok. The eggplants were roasted over charcoal to give them a rich smoky flavor. Oriental eggplants are purple or lavender in color and are more slender than the Western kind. If they are unavailable, use the skinniest Western eggplants you can find.

4–6 Oriental eggplants (about 1½ pounds), or 2 Western eggplants

2 tablespoons fish sauce

2 tablespoons fresh lime juice

1 tablespoon sugar

½ teaspoon Thai chili paste (or to taste)

1½ tablespoons canola oil

1–3 Thai chilies or other hot peppers (or to taste), seeded and thinly sliced

3 cloves garlic, thinly sliced

3 shallots, thinly sliced

1 pound fresh shrimp, peeled and deveined

½ cup fresh mint leaves

4 whole lettuce leaves

1. Grill the eggplants on all sides over a high flame, or roast them under the broiler. The skin should be completely charred. Let cool, then scrape off the burnt skin with a knife. Cut the eggplants into ½-inch chunks. Combine the fish sauce, lime juice, sugar, and chili paste in a small bowl and whisk until mixed.

2. Heat a wok until almost smoking and swirl in the oil. Add the chilies, garlic, and shallots, and stir-fry for 15 seconds, or until fragrant. Add the shrimp and cook for 1 minute. Stir in the fish sauce mixture and cook for 1 minute, or until the shrimp are cooked.

3. Remove the wok from the heat and stir in the eggplant and half the mint leaves. Correct the seasoning, adding lime juice and sugar to taste. Line salad plates with the lettuce leaves and spoon the salad on top. Garnish with the remaining mint leaves and serve at once.

Serves 4

207 CALORIES PER SERVING; 21 G PROTEIN; 7 G FAT; 17 G CARBOHYDRATE; 291 MG SODIUM; 176 MG CHOLESTEROL

SICHUAN CHICKEN SALAD

The beguiling play of textures and flavors has endeared this salad to cooks around the world. Also known as "peng peng" or "bon bon" chicken, the dish makes an intriguing appetizer, not to mention a refreshing summer entrée. Bean threads are slender white noodles made from mung bean starch. They're usually sold in 1-ounce packages bundled in netlike bags. Look for them at Asian markets and in the Chinese foods section of most supermarkets. You can also use 2 ounces rice noodles or 6 to 8 ounces soba (buckwheat noodles) or spaghetti.

2 cups cooked chicken

2 teaspoons soy sauce

1 teaspoon sesame oil,
    plus 1 teaspoon for the bean threads

FOR THE SPICY SESAME SAUCE:

¼ sesame seeds

3 scallions, white part minced, green part finely
    chopped for garnish

2 cloves garlic, minced

2 teaspoons minced fresh ginger

3 tablespoons peanut butter

3 tablespoons tamari or soy sauce

2 tablespoons rice vinegar or cider vinegar

2 teaspoons honey or sugar

1 teaspoon Chinese chili paste (or your favorite hot
    sauce), or to taste

⅓ cup Chicken Stock (see page 379), or as needed

2 one-ounce packages of bean threads

2 large cucumbers

1. Cut or tear the chicken into matchstick slivers. Transfer to a mixing bowl and toss with the soy sauce and sesame oil.

2. Prepare the sauce. Roast the sesame seeds until a light golden brown in a dry skillet over medium heat, 2 to 3 minutes. Transfer half the sesame seeds to the bowl of a food processor. Set the remainder aside for garnish. Add the white part of the scallions, the garlic, ginger, peanut butter, tamari, vinegar, honey, and chili paste to the processor and purée until smooth. Add enough stock to thin the mixture to a thick but pourable sauce. Correct the seasoning, adding soy sauce, vinegar, sugar, or chili paste to taste. The sauce should be highly seasoned.

3. Meanwhile, soak the bean threads in warm water to cover in a mixing bowl for 10 minutes. Bring 2 quarts water to a boil in a large saucepan. Drain the bean threads and cook in the boiling water until tender but not soft, 1 to 2 minutes. Drain the bean threads in a colander, rinse well with cold water, and drain again. Transfer the bean threads to a mixing bowl and toss with the remaining 1 teaspoon sesame oil. Peel the cucumbers, cut in half lengthwise, and scrape out the seeds with a melon baller or spoon. Thinly slice the cucumber halves widthwise.

4. Assemble the salad. Mound the bean threads in a large bowl or on a platter. Arrange the cucumber slices in a circle around the bean threads, overlapping slightly. Mound the chicken in the center of the bean threads. Spoon the sauce over the chicken in the center. Sprinkle the salad with the reserved sesame seeds and scallion greens.

Serves 6 as an appetizer, 3 to 4 as a main course

229 CALORIES PER SERVING;* 20 G PROTEIN; 10 G FAT; 2 G SATURATED FAT;
16 G CARBOHYDRATE; 759 MG SODIUM; 36 MG CHOLESTEROL

Analysis is based on 4 servings.

BREADS & PIZZAS

GRISSINI (BREAD STICKS)

Grissini are associated with the Piedmont city of Turin, but variations on the theme of audibly crisp bread sticks turn up the breadth and length of Italy. What you may not know is how easy bread sticks are to make at home. Here's a basic recipe, plus several regional variations.

1 envelope (2½ teaspoons) dry yeast

1 tablespoon sugar

2 tablespoons warm water, plus 1¼ cups water at room temperature

3 cups all-purpose unbleached white flour

1 cup whole-wheat flour (or more white flour)

2 teaspoons salt

1 tablespoon extra-virgin olive oil

FOR THE TOPPING:

1 egg white, beaten with a pinch of salt for glaze

1 tablespoon fennel seeds, sesame seeds, poppy seeds, cracked black peppercorns, and/or coarse salt

1. Combine the yeast with the sugar and 2 tablespoons warm water (110° to 115°F.) in a small bowl and let stand until foamy, 5 to 10 minutes.

2. Place the flours and salt in the bowl of a food processor fitted with a dough blade. With the machine running, add the yeast mixture, remaining water, and oil. Process for 1 minute, or until the dough comes together into a

Grissini (Bread Sticks)

smooth ball. (If the dough is too dry, add a little more water.) Knead the dough until smooth and springy, 3 to 4 minutes in the processor, running the machine in spurts.

2a. To make the dough in a mixer, place the yeast mixture, water, oil, sugar, and salt in the mixing bowl. Using the dough hook, incorporate the flour, mixing at low speed to obtain a stiff dough. Knead the dough in the mixer until pliable and smooth, 8 to 10 minutes.

2b. To make the dough by hand, place the yeast mixture, water, oil, sugar, and salt in a large heavy mixing bowl. Stir in the flour with a wooden spoon to obtain a stiff dough. Turn the mixture out onto a work surface and knead until pliable and smooth, 6 to 8 minutes.

3. Place the dough in a lightly oiled bowl and cover with plastic wrap. Let rise in a warm, draft-free spot until doubled in bulk, 1 to 2 hours.

4. Punch the dough down and cut it in half. Roll each half into a rectangle 14 to 16 inches long and 10 inches wide. Cut each rectangle crosswise into ½-inch strips. Stretch these strips to the desired length (16 to 18 inches) by taking an end in each hand and gently pulling and twirling. Arrange the grissini on nonstick or lightly oiled baking sheets, 1 inch apart. Loosely cover with plastic wrap and a dish towel and let rise until doubled in height, 30 to 60 minutes. Preheat the oven to 400°F.

5. Lightly brush the tops of the grissini with the egg-white mixture, taking care not to drip any on the baking sheet. Sprinkle the bread sticks with seeds, pepper, and/or coarse salt.

6. Bake the grissini until crisp and golden-brown, about 20 minutes. Transfer to wire racks to cool.

Makes 36 to 40 grissini

55 CALORIES PER BREAD STICK; 2 G PROTEIN; 0.6 G FAT; 0 G SATURATED FAT; 11 G CARBOHYDRATE; 121 MG SODIUM; 0 MG CHOLESTEROL

ALMOND GRISSINI

These bread sticks make a stunning, unexpected centerpiece for a dinner table or buffet table, yet they're easy to make, consisting of a strip of bread stick dough knotted around an almond.

1 recipe Grissini (page 89), prepared through step 3
about 40 unskinned almonds
1 egg white, beaten with a pinch of salt, for glaze

Proceed with step 4 but stretch the bread sticks out to 20 inches long. Knot the top of each breadstick around an almond as pictured on page 88. Arrange the bread sticks on nonstick or lightly oiled baking sheets, 1 inch apart. Loosely cover with plastic wrap and a dish towel and let rise until doubled in height, 30 to 60 minutes. Preheat the oven to 400°F. Proceed to step 5.

Makes about 36 to 40 grissini

60 CALORIES PER BREAD STICK; 2 G PROTEIN; 1 G FAT; 0.1 G SATURATED FAT; 10 G CARBOHYDRATE; 115 MG SODIUM; 0 MG CHOLESTEROL

TAPERED BREAD STICKS
IN THE STYLE OF SANTA MARGHERITA

The bread sticks made in the Ligurian seaside town of Santa Margherita come with pointed ends and are brushed with olive oil instead of egg-white glaze.

1 recipe Grissini (page 89), prepared through step 3
1 tablespoon extra-virgin olive oil
coarse sea salt for sprinkling

1. Tear off 1½-inch balls of the grissini dough and roll them between the palms of your hands or on the work surface to make sticks about 6 inches long and ⅛ inch in diameter. Roll the ends so that they taper to sharp points.

2. Arrange the grissini on nonstick or lightly oiled baking sheets, 1 inch apart. Loosely cover with plastic wrap and a dish towel and let rise until doubled in bulk, 30 to 60 minutes. Preheat the oven to 400°F.

3. Lightly brush the tops of the grissini with olive oil and sprinkle with sea salt. Bake the grissini until crisp and golden-brown, 15 to 20 minutes. Transfer to wire racks to cool.

Makes 36 to 40 grissini

52 CALORIES PER BREAD STICK; 1 G PROTEIN; 0.8 G FAT; 0.1 G SATURATED FAT; 10 G CARBOHYDRATE; 114 MG SODIUM; 0 MG CHOLESTEROL

TARALLI
(SPICED RING-SHAPED BISCUITS)

I first tasted these ring-shaped biscuits in Boston's "Little Italy," the North End. They looked like tiny bagels and they were sold ten to a bunch on a string. The analogy is apt: like bagels, traditional taralli *are boiled first, then baked. This produces a hard, jaw-breakingly crisp pastry that's often dipped in wine to soften it before eating. Taralli are a specialty of southern Italy, where bakeries sell both sweet and hot versions—the former flavored with fennel seed, the latter fired with cracked black pepper. For an even easier way to make* taralli, *see Note.*

1 package (2½ teaspoons) dry yeast

1 teaspoon sugar

2 tablespoons warm water (110° to 115°F.)

6 tablespoons extra-virgin olive oil,
    plus oil for the baking sheet

¾ cup dry white wine

1½ teaspoons sea salt, plus salt for the water

2 teaspoons fennel seeds or cracked black peppercorns

about 3 cups all-purpose unbleached white flour,
    plus flour for rolling

1. Combine the yeast, sugar, and water in a small bowl and let stand until foamy, 5 to 10 minutes. Transfer the mixture to the bowl of a mixer or a large mixing bowl. Stir in the 6 tablespoons olive oil and the wine, salt, and fennel. Using a dough hook, add enough flour to obtain a firm but pliable dough. (If working by hand, stir the flour in with a wooden spoon.) Knead until smooth, about 10 minutes in a mixer, 5 minutes by hand.

2. Transfer the dough to a lightly oiled bowl, turn once or twice to oil the top, then cover with plastic wrap and a dish towel. Let the dough rest for 30 minutes. Bring 3 quarts salted water to a boil in a large pot. Preheat the oven to 375°F.

3. Pinch off a fist-sized piece of dough and roll it into a tube ¼-inch thick. Cut the tube into 5-inch lengths. Bring the ends together and pinch to form a ring. Shape the remaining *taralli* the same way.

4. Gently lower the *taralli*, a few at a time, into the boiling water. Cook until they rise to the surface again. Transfer them to a wire rack on a baking sheet to drain. Boil all the *taralli* in this fashion.

5. Transfer the *taralli* to lightly oiled nonstick baking sheets. Bake until lightly browned, about 30 to 40 minutes. Transfer the *taralli* to a rack to cool. You can serve them the same day or let them harden for a few days. For a novel gift, tie the *taralli* in bunches with string.

Note: for a delectable if nontraditional variation, omit boiling the *taralli* in step **4.** Arrange the rings on a baking sheet, cover with plastic wrap, and let rise until doubled in bulk, about 1 hour. Bake the *taralli* until lightly browned, 15 to 20 minutes. This produces a bread-stick-like taralle.

Makes 4 to 4½ dozen taralli

47 CALORIES PER PIECE; 1 G PROTEIN; 2 G FAT; 0.2 G SATURATED FAT; 6 G CARBOHYDRATE; 67 MG SODIUM; 0 MG CHOLESTEROL

Onion Dill Bread

ONION DILL BREAD

This recipe uses a sponge (starter) to give the bread an extra lift. The kneading can be done by hand, in a food processor, or in a mixer fitted with a dough hook. If fresh dill is unavailable, substitute any other fresh herb.

1 tablespoon (1 envelope) dry yeast,
   or ½ ounce compressed yeast

2 teaspoons sugar

3 cups warm water

5–7 cups unbleached white flour

3 tablespoons honey

1 tablespoon sea salt

1 bunch dill, finely chopped

1 medium-sized onion, minced

1 cup whole wheat flour

2 tablespoons cornmeal (optional)

1 egg white, beaten

1. Combine the yeast, sugar, and 2 tablespoons of the warm water in a small bowl and stir to mix. Let stand for 3 to 5 minutes, or until foamy.

2. Stir 3 tablespoons of the warm water into the yeast mixture. Stir in 1 cup white flour, or enough to obtain a moist but workable dough. Roll the dough into a ball and drop it in a deep bowl filled with warm water. It will sink to the bottom. After 15 to 30 minutes, it will rise to the surface. The sponge is now activated and ready to use.

3. Transfer the sponge to a large mixing bowl. Use a wooden spoon to stir in the remaining warm water and the honey, salt, dill, and onion. Stir in the whole wheat flour, then the remaining white flour, 1 cup at a time. Continue adding flour until the dough becomes too stiff to stir. It should be dry enough to come away from the sides of the bowl but soft enough to knead. Turn the dough out onto a lightly floured work surface. Wash and lightly oil the bowl.

4. Knead the dough for 6 to 8 minutes, or until smooth and elastic. If the dough is too sticky to knead, work in a little more flour. When you press the dough with your finger, the depression should spring back.

5. Return the dough to the oiled bowl and cover with plastic wrap and a dish towel. Place in a warm, draft-free spot and let rise for 1½ to 2 hours, or until doubled in bulk. (The dough will rise at lower temperatures, even in the refrigerator, but the rising time will be longer.)

6. Lightly oil two 9-inch loaf pans. Punch the dough down and form the loaves. To make rectangular loaves, cut the dough in half, pat each half into an 8-inch-long oval, plump the ovals in the center, and drop them into the pans, seam side down. To make free-form round loaves, roll each half into a ball. Liberally sprinkle a baker's peel (or 2 tart pan bottoms) with cornmeal, if desired, and place the balls on top.

7. Cover the loaves with dish towels and let the dough rise again until doubled in bulk. Preheat the oven to 375°F. Brush the top of each loaf with beaten egg white. Using a razor blade, make a series of diagonal slashes, ¼- to ½-inch deep, in each loaf. (Slashing allows the steam to escape and the bread to expand without cracking.) Bring 2 cups water to a boil in an ovenproof pan.

8. Place the loaf pans in the oven next to the pan of boiling water. (The water helps create a crisp crust.) If baking free-form loaves, slide them onto the baking stone. Bake the loaves for about 40 minutes, or until firm and browned on all sides. Tap the bottom of the loaf; if it sounds hollow, the bread is done. You can also test for doneness with an instant-read thermometer. The internal temperature should be about 190°F.

9. Let the loaves cool for 5 minutes in the loaf pans, then turn them out onto a wire rack to cool slightly before slicing. Bread piping hot out of the oven is very hard to slice.

Makes 2 loaves

126 CALORIES PER SERVING; 4 G PROTEIN; 0 G FAT; 27 G CARBOHYDRATE; 270 MG SODIUM; 0 MG CHOLESTEROL

APULIAN POTATO BREAD

This bread was inspired by the restaurant Angelo Ricci in the town of Caglie in Apulia. Like many great Italian restaurants, it looked utterly unpretentious on the outside and seemed to be located in the middle of nowhere. The food was extraordinary, but what I really remember are the breads, which were baked in a wood-burning stone oven out back.

- 1 pound red-skinned potatoes, peeled and quartered
- 2 teaspoons sea salt for cooking the potatoes, plus 1 tablespoon salt for the dough
- 1½ envelopes (4 teaspoons) dry yeast
- 1 teaspoon sugar
- 2 tablespoons extra-virgin olive oil, plus oil for brushing
- 6 to 7 cups flour
- ½ cup cornmeal for sprinkling

1. Place the potatoes in a large pot with 2 quarts water and 2 teaspoons salt. Bring the potatoes to a boil, reduce the heat to medium, and gently simmer the potatoes until very soft, about 15 minutes. Drain the potatoes in a colander over a bowl, reserving the potato liquid. Let both cool until tepid.

2. In the bowl of a mixer fitted with a dough hook, dissolve the yeast and sugar in ¼ cup warm potato water (about 110° to 115°F.). Let stand until foamy, 5 to 10 minutes. Mash the potatoes with a potato masher or purée through a ricer or vegetable mill. (Do not purée the potatoes in a food processor, or the mixture will be gummy.) Add the olive oil, mashed potatoes, and 1½ cups potato cooking liquid to the yeast mixture. Mix at low speed to blend.

3. Running the mixer on low speed, add the 1 tablespoon salt and enough flour to obtain a pliable dough. It should be soft but not sticky. Add flour as needed. Knead the dough in the mixer until smooth, about 10 minutes. Transfer the dough to an oiled bowl and cover with plastic wrap. Let the dough rise in a warm, draft-free spot until doubled in bulk, 1 to 2 hours.

4. Turn the dough out onto a lightly floured work surface and cut it in half. Roll each half into a round or oblong loaf.

5. Place the loaves on a baker's peel or the back of a baking sheet that you've generously sprinkled with cornmeal. Cover with a clean dish towel and let rise until doubled in bulk, about 1 hour. Preheat the oven to 450°F. If you have a baker's stone, preheat it in the oven. If not, preheat a baking sheet.

6. Spray the loaves with water. Make 2 or 3 shallow slashes in the top with a razor blade and immediately slide the loaves onto the baking stone or baking sheet. Spray the loaves 2 more times with water, once before baking, again after 10 minutes. Turn the heat down to 375° after 20 minutes. Bake the loaves until crusty and brown, about 40 minutes in all. (When done, the breads will sound hollow when tapped on the bottom.) Transfer the breads to a wire rack to cool. Serve warm or at room temperature.

Note: To prepare the dough by hand, mix the ingredients in step 2 in a large mixing bowl. Stir in the salt and flour with a wooden spoon. Turn the dough out onto a floured work surface and knead until smooth by hand. Let the dough rise as described above.

To prepare the dough in a food processor (use a plastic dough blade), mix the ingredients in step 2 in the processor bowl. Add the salt and enough flour to obtain a soft, pliable dough. (You'll need a little more flour than if working in a mixer or by hand.) Run the machine in bursts to knead the dough, about 5 minutes. Let the dough rise as described above.

Makes 2 loaves

150 CALORIES PER SLICE; 4 G PROTEIN; 2 G FAT; 0.2 G SATURATED FAT; 30 G CARBOHYDRATE; 551 MG SODIUM; 0 MG CHOLESTEROL

CIBATTA

Cibatta *(pronounced "chee-BA-ta") means "slipper" in Italian. If you use your imagination, these long, flat, crusty breads do, indeed, look like slippers. The dough is wetter than most bread doughs and contains a lot more yeast, which is what makes* cibatta *so light and moist inside. (The yeast has another advantage: The dough can be made, leavened, and baked in less than 2 hours.) Here's how my friend Pino Saverino, a chef from Chiavari, makes this traditional bread.*

1 cup warm water (110° to 115°F.)

2 tablespoons yeast (preferably cake yeast, which is available from bakeries, but dry yeast will work as well)

1 tablespoon sugar

2 tablespoons extra-virgin olive oil, plus oil for the bowl

2 teaspoons salt

3½ to 4 cups all-purpose unbleached white flour, plus flour for sprinkling

¼ cup fine cornmeal or more flour

GRILLED BREAD

You don't need a degree in restaurant-going to know that grill fever has reached epidemic proportions. The latest manifestation of this delectable malady is grilled bread. I first tasted it at a revolutionary restaurant called Panache (sadly no longer around) in Cambridge, Massachusetts.

½ tablespoon (½ package) dry yeast, or ¼ ounce compressed yeast

2 tablespoons molasses

⅔ cup warm water

½ teaspoon salt

½ cup whole wheat flour

½ cup fine stone-ground cornmeal

1¼ cups unbleached white flour (approximately)

1 tablespoon extra-virgin olive oil

coarse salt and cracked black peppercorns

1. In the bowl of a heavy-duty mixer fitted with a dough hook, combine the water, yeast, sugar, and olive oil. Mix at low speed for 5 minutes to dissolve the sugar and yeast. Let stand until foamy, 5 to 10 minutes.

2. Running the mixer on low speed, add the salt and enough flour to obtain a soft, pliable dough. It should be very soft but not too sticky. Add flour as needed. Knead the dough in the mixer until smooth, about 10 minutes. Transfer the dough to an oiled bowl and cover with plastic wrap. Let the dough rise in a warm, draft-free spot until doubled in bulk, 30 to 60 minutes.

3. Turn the dough out onto a lightly floured work surface and roll it into an oblong shape. Using a pastry cutter, cut the oblong shape crosswise on the diagonal into 8 equal-size pieces. Take one end of each piece in each hand and gently stretch the dough into a slipper shape 6 to 8 inches long, 2½ inches wide, and ¼-inch thick. Sprinkle one or two nonstick baking sheets with cornmeal. Arrange the *cibatte* on the baking sheets, leaving 2 inches between each. Lightly dust the tops with flour and cover with a

clean dish towel. Let the *cibatte* rise until doubled in bulk, about 20 minutes. Preheat the oven to 400°F.

4. Bake the *cibatte* until crusty and golden brown, about 20 minutes. Transfer to a wire rack to cool. Serve as soon as possible.

Note: To prepare the dough by hand, mix the ingredients in step 1 in a large mixing bowl. Stir in the salt and flour with a wooden spoon. Turn the dough out onto a floured work surface and knead by hand until smooth. Let the dough rise as described above.

To prepare the dough in a food processor (use a plastic dough blade), mix the ingredients in step 1 in the processor bowl. Add the salt and enough flour to obtain a soft, pliable dough. (You'll need a little more flour than if working in a mixer or by hand.) Run the machine in bursts to knead the dough, about 5 minutes. Let the dough rise as described above.

Makes 8 *cibatte*

257 CALORIES PER PIECE; 7 G PROTEIN; 4 G FAT; 0.6 G SATURATED FAT; 67 G CARBOHYDRATE; 535 MG SODIUM; 0 MG CHOLESTEROL

1. Combine the yeast, molasses, and 2 tablespoons of the warm water in a large bowl. Stir to mix. Let stand 3 to 5 minutes, or until foamy. Stir in the remaining water and the ½ teaspoon salt, whole wheat flour, cornmeal, and white flour. Add enough white flour to obtain a dough that is stiff enough to come away from the sides of the bowl but soft enough to knead. Turn the dough onto a lightly floured work surface. Wash and lightly oil the bowl.

2. Knead the dough for 6 to 8 minutes, or until smooth and elastic. The dough can be prepared in a food processor (mix the dry ingredients first, then add the water and yeast mixture), but finish the kneading by hand.

3. Return the dough to the bowl and cover with plastic wrap and a dish towel. Let the dough rise in a warm place for 1 to 2 hours, or until doubled in bulk. Punch it down and let rise for ½ to 1 hour, or until doubled in bulk again. Light the grill.

4. Punch down the dough and cut it into 6 pieces. Using a rolling pin or a pasta machine, roll the pieces into circles ¼-inch thick. Place the circles on a platter, separated by floured sheets of wax or parchment paper.

5. Just before serving, brush the tops of the circles with oil and sprinkle with coarse salt and cracked pepper. Place the circles, oiled side down, on the grill and cook over medium-high heat for 1 to 2 minutes, or until the bottom is blistered and browned. Meanwhile, brush the tops with oil and sprinkle with salt and pepper. Turn the circles and cook 1 to 2 minutes more, or until both sides are puffed and golden brown. Serve at once.

Serves 6

209 CALORIES PER SERVING; 5 G PROTEIN; 3 G FAT; 41 G CARBOHYDRATE; 181 MG SODIUM; 0 MG CHOLESTEROL

SESAME GARLIC FOCACCIA

Focaccia is a cousin of pizza, a flat yeasted bread baked in the oven. (The term comes from the Latin word focus, *meaning "hearth.") Instead of being topped with tomato sauce, focaccia is brushed with olive oil and sprinkled with sesame seeds, chopped nuts, or herbs. Here, too, the dough can be kneaded in a food processor or heavy-duty mixer.*

- 1 tablespoon (1 envelope) dry yeast, or ½ ounce compressed yeast
- 1 teaspoon sugar
- 2 tablespoons plus 1⅓ cups warm water
- 1 teaspoon sea salt
- ¼ cup chopped fresh basil, rosemary, oregano, thyme, and/or parsley (optional)
- 3 cloves garlic, minced (1 tablespoon)
- 2 tablespoons minced shallots
- 3½–4 cups unbleached white flour
- cornmeal
- 2–3 teaspoons extra-virgin olive oil
- 2 tablespoons sesame seeds
- 1 teaspoon coarse salt

1. Combine the yeast, sugar, and 2 tablespoons water in the bottom of a large mixing bowl. Let stand for 5 minutes, or until the mixture is foamy. Stir in the remaining water, sea salt, herbs (if using), half the garlic, and half the shallots. Stir in the flour, adding a cup at a time, until the dough comes away from the sides of the bowl. Turn it out onto a lightly floured work surface. Wash and lightly oil the bowl.

2. Knead the dough for 6 to 8 minutes, or until smooth and elastic. Place the dough in the oiled bowl, cover with plastic wrap and a dish towel, and let rise in a warm place for 1½ hours, or until doubled in bulk.

3. Punch the dough down, then roll it into 1 large or 2 small ovals, each ½-inch thick. Transfer the oval to a baker's peel or a tart pan bottom liberally sprinkled with cornmeal. Let rise for 30 minutes, or until doubled in bulk. Preheat the oven to 375°F.

4. Poke your fingers in the surface of the focaccia to give it a dimpled appearance. Brush the top with 1 teaspoon olive oil and sprinkle with the remaining minced garlic and shallots, the sesame seeds, and the coarse salt. Bake for 25 to 35 minutes, or until crisp and golden brown.

5. Let cool slightly. Just before serving, drizzle with the remaining olive oil. Cut into wedges and serve.

Serves 8

237 CALORIES PER SERVING; 7 G PROTEIN; 3 G FAT; 45 G CARBOHYDRATE; 535 MG SODIUM; 0 MG CHOLESTEROL

RED-ONION AND ROSEMARY FOCACCIA

Thicker than pizza but flatter than a conventional loaf, the Italian bread known as focaccia *(pronounced "foh-KAH-cha") has become a North American favorite. A dark-colored baking pan will give you a crisper, browner crust.*

- 1 envelope dry yeast
- 2 tablespoons sugar
- 1½ cups warm (90°F.) water
- 2 teaspoons salt
- 3 teaspoons extra-virgin olive oil
- 4½ to 5 cups unbleached white flour
- spray oil
- coarse cornmeal
- 1 small red onion, thinly sliced
- 2 teaspoons chopped fresh or dried rosemary
- Kosher salt and freshly cracked or coarsely ground black pepper

1. Combine the yeast, sugar, and ¼ cup of the water in a large mixing bowl. Let stand until foamy, about 10 minutes. (If yeast does not foam, discard it and start over.)

2. Stir in the remaining 1¼ cups water, the 2 teaspoons salt, and 1½ teaspoons of the olive oil. Stir in the flour ½ cup at a time to form a soft, pliable dough that comes away from the sides of the bowl. Turn the dough out onto a lightly floured work surface and knead it until it is smooth and elastic, 6 to 8 minutes, adding more flour as necessary.

3. Spray a large mixing bowl with oil. Put the dough in the bowl and cover with plastic wrap. Let rise in a warm, draft-free place until doubled in bulk, 1 to 2 hours.

4. Punch down the dough and roll it out ½-inch thick into an 11x 17-inch rectangle, stretching it as you roll. Sprinkle a nonstick baking sheet with cornmeal. Transfer the focaccia to the baking sheet and cover with a clean cloth. Let rise until doubled in height, 30 to 60 minutes.

5. Preheat the oven to 375°F. Poke your fingers all over the surface of the focaccia to decoratively dimple the surface. Arrange the onion slices on top. Brush with the remaining 1½ teaspoons olive oil and sprinkle with the rosemary, kosher slat, and cracked pepper.

6. Bake the focaccia until crisp and golden brown, 20 to 30 minutes. Let cool slightly before serving. Cut into squares or rectangles and serve.

Note: The dough can also be made in a mixer with a dough hook or a food processor. (If using the latter, let the yeast, sugar, and water foam in a small bowl. Place the flour and salt in the processor bowl. Add the yeast mixture, remaining water, and olive oil. Knead the dough by pulsing the machine in bursts.

Makes 1 11 x 17-inch focaccia, which will serve 8 to 10

291 CALORIES PER SERVING; 8 G PROTEIN; 2 G FAT; .4 G SATURATED FAT; 58 G CARBOHYDRATE; 535 MG SODIUM; 0 MG CHOLESTEROL

Burgundian Spice Bread

BURGUNDIAN SPICE BREAD

Pain d'épices (spice bread) is an ancient Burgundian delicacy. This recipe comes from a beekeeper in the village of Looze in northern Burgundy. Rye flour and honey give it a moistness usually achieved by eggs in these sorts of breads. Tightly wrapped, Burgundian spice bread will keep for several days. It also freezes well and is good toasted.

¾ cup honey	½ teaspoon ground cinnamon
½ cup sugar	1½ teaspoons freshly grated orange zest
½ cup sultanas	¼ teaspoon salt
½ cup warm water	1½ cups unbleached white flour
1½ teaspoons aniseed	½ cup rye flour
1½ teaspoons ground ginger	1 tablespoon baking powder

1. Warm the honey jar in a pan of hot water. (This will make it easier to pour and measure.) Combine the honey, sugar, and sultanas in a large mixing bowl. Stir in the water, spices, zest, and salt.

2. Sift the flours and baking powder into the honey mixture. Mix with a wooden spoon to obtain a thick batter. Cover the bowl with a dish towel and let the batter rest for 1 hour. Meanwhile, spray a 9 x 4-inch loaf pan with vegetable oil spray and line it with parchment paper. Lightly spray the parchment paper with vegetable oil spray. Preheat the oven to 300°F.

3. Check the consistency of the batter. It should fall from a raised spoon in a thick, silky ribbon. Thin it, if necessary, with a little water. Spoon the batter into the pan and bake for 1½ hours, or until a skewer inserted in the center comes out clean. Cool the bread in the pan for 15 minutes, then turn it out onto a wire rack and let cool to room temperature. Slice for serving.

Serves 8 to 10

281 CALORIES PER SERVING; 3 G PROTEIN; 0 G FAT; 68 G CARBOHYDRATE; 193 MG SODIUM; 0 MG CHOLESTEROL

BANANA SULTANA MUFFINS

Unlike most banana breads, which are made with mashed fruit, this one features whole chunks of banana and sultanas (yellow raisins).

½ cup sultanas

¼ cup apple juice or orange juice

½ cup low-fat buttermilk

2 egg whites (or 1 whole egg)

1 tablespoon canola oil

3 tablespoons honey

1½ cups unbleached white flour

⅓ cup stone-ground
   white cornmeal

2 teaspoons baking powder

1 teaspoon baking soda

¼ cup brown sugar

½ teaspoon ground ginger

¼ teaspoon ground cardamom

2 ripe bananas, diced

1. Preheat the oven to 375°F. Combine the sultanas and apple juice in a large bowl and let stand for 5 minutes. Add the buttermilk, egg whites, oil, and honey, and whisk until smooth.

2. Sift the flour, cornmeal, baking powder, and baking soda into another large bowl. Whisk in the brown sugar, ginger, and cardamom. Add the bananas and toss lightly. Add the dry ingredients to the buttermilk mixture and stir just to mix with a wooden spoon. (Stir as little as possible, or the muffins will be tough. Ten to 12 strokes should do it.)

3. Line the muffin cups with parchment paper or paper liners or lightly grease with vegetable oil spray. Spoon the batter into the cups, filling each ⅔ full. Bake for 20 to 30 minutes, or until puffed and lightly browned. A skewer inserted in the center should come out clean. Turn the muffins out onto a wire rack and let cool for 5 to 10 minutes before serving.

Makes 12 muffins

160 CALORIES PER SERVING; 3 G PROTEIN; 2 G FAT; 34 G CARBOHYDRATE; 145 MG SODIUM; 1 MG CHOLESTEROL

LEMON PEPPER POPOVERS

These delicious popovers take advantage of lemon's strong affinity with freshly grated black pepper. They rise best if baked in deep molds in a very hot oven. One of the best ways to grate lemon peel is to remove the zest in strips using a vegetable peeler, then grind it to a fine powder in a spice mill.

1 cup unbleached white flour

1 cup skim milk,
   at room temperature

1 tablespoon extra-virgin olive oil

¼ teaspoon salt (or to taste)

½ teaspoon cracked or coarsely
   ground black pepper

2 teaspoons freshly grated lemon zest

3 egg whites, lightly beaten

1. Preheat the oven to 450°F. Sift the flour into a mixing bowl and gradually whisk in the milk. Add the remaining ingredients, whisking just to mix. The mixture should be the consistency of heavy cream. If necessary, add more milk.

2. Grease popover molds or muffin cups with vegetable oil spray or a little olive oil. Fill each mold ½ full. Bake for 15 minutes without opening the oven door. Reduce the heat to 375°F. and continue baking for 20 to 25 minutes, or until the popovers are puffed and well browned. Unmold and serve at once.

Makes 6 to 8 large popovers

119 CALORIES PER SERVING; 5 G PROTEIN; 3 G FAT; 18 G CARBOHYDRATE; 166 MG SODIUM; 1 MG CHOLESTEROL

BASIC NEAPOLITAN PIZZA DOUGH

My first pizza in Naples came as something of a shock. Where were the olives, the pepperoni, the gooey carpet of cheese? For a true Neapolitan pizza is a paragon of understatement, a slab or circle of moist, puffy dough, smokily browned in a wood-fired oven. The topping—when the pizza comes topped at all—is limited to a whisper of tomato sauce and perhaps a few atoms of cheese. The crust is the focal point, and the toppings are kept sparse to keep it that way. Here's the basic dough recipe: topping ideas begin on page 102. Italian flour is softer than American flour. The cake flour in the following recipe has a softening effect on the dough.

2 packages (5 teaspoons) dried yeast

1 teaspoon sugar

1⅓ cups warm water (110° to 115°F.)

2½ cups all-purpose unbleached white flour, plus flour for rolling and stretching the dough

1 cup cake flour

2½ teaspoons salt

spray oil

¼ cup cornmeal for sprinkling (optional)

2 to 3 teaspoons extra-virgin olive oil

1. Dissolve the yeast and sugar in 3 tablespoons of the warm water in a small bowl. Let stand until foamy, 5 to 10 minutes.

2. Combine the flours and salt in a large mixing bowl and whisk well to mix. Make a well in the center and add the yeast mixture and remaining water. Working with your fingertips, gradually mix in the flour mixture. Add flour as necessary to obtain a very soft, pliable, but not quite sticky dough. Turn the dough out onto a lightly floured work surface and knead until smooth, 8 to 10 minutes.

2a. If making the dough in a mixer, dissolve the yeast and sugar in the water in the mixing bowl. When foamy, add the remaining water, flours, and salt. Using a dough hook, mix the dough at low speed until it comes away from the sides of the bowl in a smooth, soft pliable ball. (Add a little flour if necessary.) This will take about 10 minutes.

2b. If using a food processor, add the flours and salt and mix with a plastic dough blade. Work in the yeast mixture and remaining 1 cup water, running the machine in bursts until the dough comes away from the sides of the processor bowl in a smooth, soft, pliable ball. When making the dough in a machine, you should still turn it onto a floured work surface and knead it a little by hand.

3. Place the dough in a large bowl lightly sprayed with oil and cover with plastic. Let the dough rise until doubled in bulk, 1 to 2 hours. Preheat the oven to 500°F. If you have a baking stone, preheat it as well. If you don't, preheat a heavy baking sheet or cookie pan.

4. Punch the dough down and cut it in half (to make two 12-inch pizzas) or quarters (to make four 6-inch pizzas). Lightly sprinkle your work surface with flour and roll, pat, or stretch each ball to form a circle. Gently stretch each circle with the palms of your hands or over your fists (pulling your fists apart in the manner of a pizzamaker), to make a 12-inch circle (or a 6-inch circle if making a small pizza) with a slightly raised rim. Transfer the pizzas to a peel (baker's paddle) or flat cookie sheet generously sprinkled with cornmeal. Garnish the pizzas with one of the toppings on pages 102 through 103. Brush the edges of the crusts with olive oil.

5. Slide the pizzas onto the baking stone or baking sheet in the preheated oven. (The hotter the better.) Bake until the crust is puffed and nicely browned, 6 to 10 minutes, turning as needed to ensure even baking.

Note: You're probably not used to baking at 500°F., but this high heat is necessary to produce a crust that's puffy, moist, and light, yet crisp. Also, to simulate the floor of a wood-fired or commercial pizza oven, I like to bake the pizza on a preheated baking stone (available at cookware shops). If you don't have a baking stone, bake the pizza on the back of a preheated baking sheet. The only disadvantage of this method is the tendency for any stray cornmeal to burn, filling your oven with smoke. Put on the exhaust fan and don't worry; your pizza isn't burning. The inconvenience is well worth producing a proper crust.

Makes two 12-inch pizzas, enough to serve 4

449 CALORIES PER SERVING; 13 G PROTEIN; 4 G FAT; 1 G SATURATED FAT; 90 G CARBOHYDRATE; 1,337 MG SODIUM; 0 MG CHOLESTEROL

MILK-BASED PIZZA DOUGH
FROM SORRENTO

This recipe comes from one Amadeo Cinque, the amiable pizzaiolo *(pizzamaker) of the Vela Bianca (White Sail) restaurant in Sorrento. Signor Cinque makes his pizza dough with milk—an innovation that produces an exceptionally sweet, moist dough. I've streamlined his recipe from the first book, but the results are still impressive.*

1½ packages (4 teaspoons) dried yeast

1 teaspoon sugar

2½ cups all-purpose unbleached white flour, plus flour
   for rolling and stretching the dough

1 cup cake flour

1½ teaspoons salt

1 cup 2 percent, 1 percent, or skim milk

spray oil

¼ cup cornmeal for sprinkling

1. Dissolve the yeast and sugar in 3 tablespoons warm water (110° to 115°F.) in a small bowl. Let stand until foamy, 5 to 10 minutes.

2. Combine the flours and salt in a large mixing bowl and whisk well to mix. Make a well in the center and add the yeast mixture and milk. Working with your fingertips, gradually mix the flour mixture into the milk mixture. Add flour as necessary to obtain a soft, pliable, but not sticky dough. Turn the dough out onto a lightly floured work surface and knead until smooth, 8 to 10 minutes.

2a. If making the dough in a mixer, dissolve the yeast and sugar in the water in the mixing bowl. When foamy, add the milk, flours, and salt. Using a dough hook, mix the dough at low speed until it comes away from the sides of the bowl in a smooth, soft, pliable ball. (Add a little flour if necessary.) This will take about 10 minutes.

2b. If using a food processor, add the flours and salt and mix with a plastic dough blade. Work in the yeast mixture and milk, running the machine in bursts until the dough comes away from the sides of the processor bowl in a smooth, soft, pliable ball. When making the dough in a machine, you should still turn it onto a floured work surface and knead it a little by hand.

3. Place the dough in a large bowl lightly sprayed with oil and cover with plastic. Let the dough rise until doubled in bulk. 1½ to 2 hours.

4. Punch the dough down, cut it in half, and roll each half into a ball. Place the balls on a lightly floured work surface and cover with plastic wrap or a slightly damp dish towel. Let the dough rise until doubled in bulk again, 30 to 60 minutes.

5. Preheat the oven to 500°F. If you have a baking stone, preheat it as well. If you don't, preheat a heavy baking sheet or cookie sheet.

6. Lightly sprinkle your work surface with flour and roll, pat, or stretch each ball to form a circle. Gently stretch each circle with the palms of your hands or over your fists (pulling your fists apart in the manner of a pizzamaker), to make a 12-inch circle (or a 6-inch circle if making a small pizza) with a slightly raised rim. Transfer the pizzas to a peel (baker's paddle) or flat cookie sheet generously sprinkled with cornmeal. Garnish the pizzas with one of the toppings following.

7. Slide the pizzas onto the baking stone or preheated baking sheet. Bake until the crust is puffed and nicely browned, 6 to 10 minutes, turning as needed to ensure even baking.

Makes two 12-inch pizzas, enough to serve 4

456 CALORIES PER SERVING; 14 G PROTEIN; 3 G FAT; 1 G SATURATED FAT; 92 G CARBOHYDRATE; 835 MG SODIUM; 5 MG CHOLESTEROL

WHITE PIZZA

This is the simplest of all pizzas and one of the most satisfying. For the best flavor, use coarse sea salt. (I like to bite into the crunchy crystals of salt.) The pepper isn't strictly traditional, but I like its flavor.

- 1 recipe Basic Neapolitan Pizza Dough (page 99) or milk dough (page 101), prepared through step 3
- 1 to 1½ tablespoons extra-virgin olive oil
- 12 sage leaves, thinly slivered
- coarse sea salt
- freshly grated black pepper (optional)
- ¼ to ½ cup freshly grated Parmigiano-Reggiano or Pecorino Romano cheese

1. Preheat the oven with a baking stone or baking sheet to 500°F. Prepare, raise, and stretch out the pizza dough as described in step 4 on page 99 to make two 12-inch crusts.

2. Drizzle the tops of the pizzas with olive oil and sprinkle with the sage, salt, pepper, and cheese. Brush the edges of the crust with oil.

3. Slide the pizza onto the baking stone or preheated baking sheet. Bake until the crust is puffed and nicely browned, 6 to 10 minutes, turning as needed to ensure even baking.

Makes two 12-inch pizzas, enough to serve 4

506 CALORIES PER SERVING; 16 G PROTEIN; 8 G FAT; 2 G SATURATED FAT; 91 G CARBOHYDRATE; 1,953 MG SODIUM; 5 MG CHOLESTEROL

TOMATO AND ARUGULA PIZZA

Wafer-thin and crackling crisp are the pizzas prepared by Mark Militello, owner-chef of Mark's Las Olas in Ft. Lauderdale. They shatter into a thousand savory shards when you take a bite. Topped with caramelized onions, shiitake mushrooms, and a tomato-arugula salad, this pizza offers an interesting contrast of temperatures, textures, and flavors.

- 2 tablespoons extra-virgin olive oil
- 1 medium red onion, thinly sliced
- 3 ounces shiitake mushrooms, stemmed and thinly sliced
- salt and freshly ground black pepper
- 1 recipe Basic Pizza Dough, prepared through step 3 (see page 99)
- ½ cup low- or no-fat tomato sauce (optional) (see Note)
- 1 bunch arugula, stems removed
- 1 ripe tomato, seeded and cut into ½-inch dice
- 2 teaspoons balsamic vinegar, or to taste

1. Preheat the oven to 450°F. Heat 1 tablespoon of the oil in a large nonstick frying pan set over medium heat. Add the onion and cook 5 minutes, stirring often. Add the shiitakes and cook, stirring, 5 minutes more, or until the onions are nicely browned and caramelized. Season with salt and pepper.

2. Roll out the dough into an 11 x 17-inch rectangle, stretching it as you roll. Transfer it to a baking sheet and flute the edges. Bake 5 minutes. Cover with the tomato sauce and the onion mixture. Bake another 5 to 10 minutes, or until the crust is browned and crisp, about 10 minutes in all.

3. Meanwhile, toss the arugula and diced tomatoes with the remaining 1 tablespoon olive oil and the vinegar. Season with salt and pepper. When the pizza is cooked, pile the salad on top of the pizza. Cut the pizza into squares and serve immediately.

Note: Recipes for low- and no-fat tomato sauce can be found in my books *High-Flavor, Low-Fat Cooking; High-Flavor, Low-Fat Vegetarian Cooking;* and *High-Flavor, Low-Fat Pasta.*

Makes 1 11 x 17-inch pizza, which will serve 8 to 10

231 CALORIES PER SERVING; 6 G PROTEIN; 4 G FAT; 0.6 G SATURATED FAT; 43 G CARBOHYDRATE; 406 MG SODIUM; 0 MG CHOLESTEROL

PIZZA MARINARA
(MARINER'S STYLE)

*This is a favorite in pizzerias in Italy, a thin crust
topped with oregano-scented tomato sauce
and a gutsy garnish of anchovies, capers, and olives.*

1 recipe Basic Neapolitan Pizza Dough (page 99)
   or milk dough (page 101), prepared through step 3

1 cup homemade tomato sauce
   or a good commercial brand

10 fresh oregano leaves or ½ teaspoon dried oregano

2 to 6 anchovy fillets, drained, rinsed,
   blotted dry, and cut into ½-inch pieces

1 to 2 tablespoons drained capers

8 black olives, pitted

coarse sea salt

1 tablespoon extra-virgin olive oil (optional)

1. Preheat the oven with a baking stone or baking
sheet to 500°F. Prepare, raise, and roll or stretch out
the pizza dough as described in step 4 on page 99 to
make two 12-inch crusts.

2. Spread the tomato sauce on top of the crust in a
thin layer and sprinkle with the oregano. Arrange the
anchovy pieces, capers, and olives on top. Sprinkle
the pizza with coarse salt. If using the olive oil,
drizzle some oil over the pizza and brush the edges
with oil.

3. Slide the pizzas onto the baking stone or preheated
baking sheet. Bake until the crust is puffed and nicely
browned, 6 to 10 minutes, turning as needed to ensure
even baking.

Makes two 12-inch pizzas, enough to serve 4

485 CALORIES PER SERVING; 14 G PROTEIN; 6 G FAT; 0.8 G SATURATED
FAT; 94 G CARBOHYDRATE; 1,611 MG SODIUM; 2 MG CHOLESTEROL

FOUR SEASONS PIZZA

*The four seasons pizza is the Italian version of "the works,"
and it says a lot about the simplicity and purity of flavors
characteristic of Italian cooking. In North America, the
toppings would be piled together in a cacophonous jumble.
In Italy, the various ingredients are arranged singly on the
pizza in quadrants—whence the name* four seasons—
so you can taste each without distraction.

1 recipe Basic Neapolitan Pizza Dough (page 99)
   or milk dough (page 101), prepared through step 3

1 recipe tomato sauce

2 ounces very thinly sliced prosciutto

4 ounces button mushrooms,
   wiped clean with a damp cloth and trimmed

2 cooked fresh artichokes or 1 13-ounce can
   artichoke hearts, rinsed and drained

2 roasted red peppers

coarse sea salt

1 tablespoon extra-virgin olive oil (optional)

1. Preheat the oven with a baking stone or baking sheet to
500°F. Prepare, raise, roll or stretch out the pizza dough
as described in step 4 on page 99 to make two 12-inch
pizzas. Cover the pizzas with a clean dish towel and let
rise until soft and slightly puffed, 10 to 20 minutes.

2. Spread the tomato sauce on top of the crust in a thin
layer. Arrange prosciutto slices on one quarter of each
pizza. Thinly slice the mushrooms and arrange them on
a second quarter of each pizza. Thinly slice the artichokes
and arrange them on a third quarter of each pizza. Cut
the peppers into thin strips and arrange them on the fourth
quarter of each pizza. Sprinkle the mushroom, artichoke,
and pepper quadrants with salt. If using the olive oil, drizzle
some over the pizza and brush the edges of the crust with oil.

3. Slide the pizzas onto the baking stone or preheated baking
sheet. Bake until the crust is puffed and nicely browned, 6
to 10 minutes, turning as needed to ensure even baking.

Makes two 12-inch pizzas, enough to serve 4

581 CALORIES PER SERVING; 23 G PROTEIN; 6 G FAT; 2 G SATURATED FAT;
115 G CARBOHYDRATE; 1,986 MG SODIUM; 12 MG CHOLESTEROL

EGG DISHES, CRÊPES, TORTILLAS, AND TAMALES

TEX-MEX TORTILLA EGG SCRAMBLE WITH CHILE VERDE AND SALSA VERDE (MIGAS)

Migas are Tex-Mex comfort food, a rib-sticking scramble of eggs and fried tortillas slathered with salsa verde or salsa ranchera. This may not sound like the best way to get your day off to a healthy start, but by bake-frying the tortillas and replacing the eggs with egg whites or egg substitute, you can make a great-tasting Tex-Mex breakfast low-fat.

8 corn tortillas

1 tablespoon lard or canola oil

1 medium white onion, thinly sliced

4 cloves garlic, thinly sliced

1 (4½-ounce) can *chiles verdes*
   (or 2 Anaheim or 1 large poblano chili, roasted,
   peeled, and diced)

2 cups egg substitute or 4 whole eggs and 8 whites

½ cup chopped cilantro, plus 4 sprigs for garnish

salt and freshly ground black pepper

2 cups Salsa Verde (page 8)

½ cup no-fat sour cream

2 tablespoons crumbled queso fresco,
   sharp white cheddar, or feta cheese

Huevos Motuleños (Eggs with Salsa, Ham, and Tortillas)

1. Preheat the oven to 400°F. Arrange the tortillas on a baking sheet and bake until they are lightly browned, 5 to 8 minutes. Remove the tortillas from the oven; they'll crisp as they cool.

2. Heat the lard or oil in a nonstick frying pan. Lightly brown the onion over medium heat, 5 minutes, stirring often, adding the garlic and chiles verdes after 3 minutes.

3. Beat the egg substitute (or whole eggs and whites), cilantro, and salt and pepper in a mixing bowl. Break the tortillas into 1-inch pieces and stir them into the egg mixture. Let soften for 5 minutes.

4. Add the egg mixture to the frying pan and cook until scrambled, 2 to 4 minutes, stirring with a wooden spoon. Correct the seasoning, adding salt and pepper to taste.

5. Transfer the migas to plates and carpet each with the salsa verde. Place a dollop of sour cream on top, sprinkle with cheese, and serve at once.

Serves 4

305 CALORIES PER SERVING; 22 G PROTEIN; 7 G FAT; 2 G SATURATED FAT; 39 G CARBOHYDRATE; 406 MG SODIUM; 10 MG CHOLESTEROL

NOODLE FRITTATA

A frittata is a cross between an omelet and a Spanish tortilla *(the egg dish, not the Mexican cornmeal flatbread). Like the former, it's started on the stove and the main ingredient is eggs; like the latter, it's finished in the oven and cut into wedges for serving. My low-fat version uses mostly egg whites, with a few whole eggs for richness. Egg substitute produces a fine frittata (after all, the main ingredient in egg substitute is egg whites), although the idea may be unsettling for a purist. Necessity may be the traditional mother of invention, but some of my best ideas come from leftovers. This colorful frittata was inspired by a bowl of leftover angel-hair pasta! The idea isn't as strange as it sounds: consider kugel (Jewish noodle pudding).*

¼ pound angel-hair pasta

salt

1½ tablespoons extra-virgin olive oil

1 small onion, thinly sliced

1 clove garlic, minced

1 red bell pepper, cut into matchstick slivers

1 yellow bell pepper, cut into matchstick slivers

1 small zucchini, cored and cut into matchstick slivers

2 eggs plus 8 egg whites, or 12 egg whites, or 1½ cups egg substitute

3 tablespoons finely chopped flat-leaf parsley

3 to 4 tablespoons freshly grated Parmigiano-Reggiano cheese

freshly ground black pepper

1. Cook the pasta in 3 quarts rapidly boiling salted water until al dente, about 5 minutes. Drain in a colander, rinse under cold water, and drain again. Blot the pasta dry with a paper towel. Preheat broiler.

2. Heat half the olive oil in a 12-inch nonstick frying pan. Add the onion, garlic, red and yellow pepper, and zucchini and cook over medium heat until soft and translucent but not brown, about 4 minutes.

3. Lightly beat the eggs and whites in a large mixing bowl. Stir in the sautéed vegetables, parsley, cheese, and angel-hair. Add salt and pepper to taste: the mixture should be highly seasoned.

4. Heat the remaining olive oil in a 12-inch nonstick frying pan. Add the frittata mixture and cook over medium heat until the mixture is set on the bottom, 3 to 5 minutes. Place the frittata under the broiler and continue cooking until the frittata is set and the top is lightly browned, 2 to 4 minutes. Let the frittata cool for a few minutes. Using a spatula or thin flexible knife, loosen the frittata from the sides of the pan. Invert it onto a round platter and cut into wedges for serving. The frittata can be served either hot or at room temperature.

Serves 6 as an appetizer, 4 as a light entrée

180 CALORIES PER 4 APPETIZERS; 12 G PROTEIN; 7 G FAT; 2 G SATURATED FAT; 18 G CARBOHYDRATE; 162 MG SODIUM; 90 MG CHOLESTEROL

Noodle Frittata

HUEVOS MOTULEÑOS

(EGGS WITH SALSA, HAM, AND TORTILLAS)

I first tasted this rich, flavorful dish at a breakfast buffet in Mérida. Scarcely a day went by when I wasn't served some version of eggs in the style of the Yucatán town of Motul. This dish has something for everyone: smoky ham, habanero-heated salsa, fresh peas for a flash of green, and refried beans to keep up your strength. To decrease the amount of fat in the traditional recipe, I bake the tortillas instead of deep-frying them, use lean Canadian bacon instead of ham, and use scrambled egg substitute instead of fried eggs. There's still so much flavor that you won't miss the fat.

FOR THE SALSA:

3 medium ripe red tomatoes

½ medium white onion, cut in half

3 cloves garlic

1 habanero chili, cut in half and seeded (for an incandescent salsa, leave in the seeds)

½ teaspoon dried oregano

½ teaspoon ground cinnamon

salt and freshly ground black pepper

4 corn tortillas

1 cup refried beans (page 306) or use a good brand of fat-free canned refried beans

FOR THE EGGS:

1 tablespoon lard or olive oil

½ medium white onion, thinly sliced

1 clove garlic, thinly sliced

1½ cups egg substitute (or 12 egg whites)

2 ounces Canadian bacon or country-style ham, cut into ¼-inch dice

½ cup cooked green peas

1 tablespoon crumbled queso fresco or feta cheese

1. To prepare the salsa, heat a comal or frying pan over a medium-high flame. Roast the tomatoes, onion, garlic, and habanero until lightly browned: 8 to 10 minutes for the tomatoes and onion; 4 to 5 minutes for the garlic and chili. Transfer the roasted vegetables to a food processor and grind to a coarse purée.

2. Transfer the purée to a saucepan. Add the oregano, cinnamon, salt, and pepper and simmer for 5 minutes, stirring with a wooden spoon. Correct the seasoning, adding salt and pepper to taste.

3. Preheat the oven to 400°F. Bake the tortillas until they are golden brown, about 5 minutes. Transfer the tortillas to plates or a platter; they'll crisp as they cool. Warm the refried beans in a saucepan.

4. Heat the lard or oil in a nonstick frying pan. Lightly brown the sliced onion and garlic over medium heat, 3 to 5 minutes. Add the egg substitute and cook until scrambled, 2 minutes, stirring with a wooden spoon. Add salt and pepper to taste.

5. Warm the Canadian bacon and peas in a nonstick saucepan over medium heat.

6. To assemble the huevos motuleños, spread the refried beans on each of the tortillas. Mound the scrambled eggs on top. Spoon the salsa over the eggs and sprinkle with the bacon, peas, and queso freso. Serve at once.

Serves 4

267 CALORIES PER SERVING; 21 G PROTEIN; 6 G FAT; 2 G SATURATED FAT; 33 G CARBOHYDRATE; 615 MG SODIUM; 13 MG CHOLESTEROL

ROASTED SWEET POTATO AND GARLIC SFORMATO
(CUSTARD)

Sformati (custards or timbales) are a popular primo piatto (first course) in Italy, and the flavorings are limited only to your imagination. This one owes rich flavor to the high-heat roasting of its main ingredients: garlic and sweet potatoes. As you've probably gathered by now, roasting is one of my favorite low-fat cooking methods: it evaporates the water in a vegetable, concentrating the flavor and caramelizing the natural sugars.

spray oil

1½ pounds sweet potatoes (2 or 3 large)

1 medium head garlic

⅓ cup grated Parmigiano-Reggiano cheese

2 tablespoons chopped flat-leaf parsley

1 egg plus 2 egg whites, or ½ cup egg substitute

salt, freshly ground black pepper,
    and a little freshly grated nutmeg

8 ½-cup timbale molds or ramekins

1. Preheat the oven to 400°F. Spray the timbale molds or ramekins with oil and freeze. Place the sweet potatoes and garlic in a nonstick roasting pan. Roast until soft, about 20 minutes for the garlic, 40 to 60 minutes for the potatoes. Transfer the vegetables to a plate to cool. Peel the sweet potatoes with the help of a paring knife. Squeeze the roasted garlic out of the skins.

2. Combine the sweet potatoes, garlic, cheese, and parsley in a food processor and purée until smooth. While still using the food processor, work in the egg and egg whites. Add salt, pepper, and nutmeg to taste: the mixture should be highly seasoned.

3. Reduce the oven temperature to 350°F. Bring 3 cups water to a boil. Remove the timbale molds from the freezer and line the bottom of each mold with an oval of baking parchment or foil. Spray the mold again. (The freezing and double oiling helps prevent sticking.) Spoon the sweet potato mixture into the molds. Set the molds in a roasting pan with 1 inch boiling water.

4. Bake the timbales until set (an inserted skewer will come out clean), 20 to 30 minutes. (If the water in the roasting pan evaporates, add more.) Transfer the timbales to a wire rack and let cool for 3 minutes. Place a plate over each one, invert, and give the mold a little shake: the timbale should slide right out.

You don't really need a sauce, but if you'd like one, the Sugo di Pomodoro on page 162 would be a nice accompaniment.

Serves 8

103 CALORIES PER SERVING; 5 G PROTEIN; 2 G FAT; 1 G SATURATED FAT; 17 G CARBOHYDRATE; 108 MG SODIUM; 30 MG CHOLESTEROL

SPINACH SOUFFLÉ

Soufflé might seem like an unlikely dish for a low-fat cookbook. The secret to my version is to replace the egg yolks with puréed roasted onions. The egg whites, which are almost pure protein, provide the puff. Serve with Red-Hot Tomato Sauce (page 138).

1 medium-sized onion

2 cloves garlic

1 teaspoon butter, melted, or vegetable oil spray

2 tablespoons lightly toasted sesame seeds or bread crumbs

12 ounces fresh spinach (or 1 package frozen)

3 tablespoons flour

1 cup skim milk

1 tablespoon Dijon-style mustard

salt and freshly ground black pepper

cayenne pepper

freshly grated nutmeg

6 egg whites

¼ teaspoon cream of tartar

Serves 4

130 CALORIES PER SERVING; 12 G PROTEIN; 4 G FAT; 13 G CARBOHYDRATE; 223 MG SODIUM; 4 MG CHOLESTEROL

1. Preheat the oven to 350°F. Roast the onion in its skin for 1 hour, or until soft. After 30 minutes, add the garlic cloves in their skins and roast until soft. Let cool.

2. Meanwhile, brush a 5-cup soufflé dish with the melted butter or spray with vegetable oil. Sprinkle the inside of the dish with sesame seeds. Steam the spinach until tender, refresh in ice water, and drain. Squeeze the spinach in your hand, wringing out as much liquid as possible. Peel the onion and garlic, and purée them in a food processor with the spinach and flour.

3. Transfer the purée to a saucepan and bring it to a boil. Stir in the milk and boil for 2 minutes, or until the mixture thickens. Whisk in the mustard, salt, pepper, cayenne, and nutmeg. (The mixture should be very highly seasoned.) Keep warm. Preheat the oven to 400°F.

4. Beat the egg whites almost to stiff peaks, adding the cream of tartar after 20 seconds. Stir ¼ of the whites into the hot spinach mixture. Gently fold this mixture into the remaining whites. Spoon the soufflé mixture into the prepared dish and smooth the top with a wet spatula. Bake for 20 to 30 minutes, or until puffed and cooked to taste. Serve at once.

LOW-FAT CRÊPES

You certainly know that Mexicans love wrapped foods (think tacos and burritos). What you may not be aware of is their unbridled enthusiasm for crêpes. These paper-thin pancakes are used as a wrapping for everything from shrimp to cajeta (Mexican caramel). My low-fat crêpes contain one ingredient that's not traditionally Mexican, however: buttermilk. The thick, creamy consistency of this low-fat dairy product allows you to eliminate the butter and most of the egg yolks that are in the traditional recipe for crêpes.

1 egg

2 egg whites

½ cup low-fat buttermilk

¾ cup water

½ teaspoon sugar

½ teaspoon salt, or to taste

1 teaspoon canola oil

1 cup unbleached all-purpose flour

spray oil

1 or more crêpe or omelet pans (approximately 7-inches in diameter)

1. Combine the whole egg and the whites in a bowl and whisk to mix. Whisk in the buttermilk, water, sugar, salt, and oil. Sift in the flour and gently whisk just to mix. (Do not overwhisk, or the crêpes will be rubbery.) If the batter looks lumpy, strain it into another bowl. It should be the consistency of heavy cream. If it's too thick, thin it with a little more water.

2. Lightly spray the crêpe pan(s) with oil and heat over a medium flame. (When the pan is the proper temperature, a drop of water will evaporate in 2 or 3 seconds.) Off the heat, add 3 tablespoons of the crêpe batter to the pan in one fell swoop. Gently tilt and rotate the pan to coat the bottom with a thin layer of batter. (Pour back any excess—the crêpe should be as thin as possible.)

3. Cook the crêpe until it is lightly browned on both sides, 30 to 60 seconds per side, turning with a spatula. As the crêpes are done, stack them on a plate. For the best results, spray the pans with oil between pouring batter.

Note: Don't worry if your first crêpe looks weird: That's usually the case. The crêpes will look better the more you make.

Makes 12 to 14 (7-inch) crêpes

40 CALORIES PER CRÊPE; 2 G PROTEIN; 1 G FAT; 0 G SATURATED FAT; 7 G CARBOHYDRATE; 78 MG SODIUM; 14 MG CHOLESTEROL

BUTTERMILK CRÊPES

Every nation has its version of pancakes, from Russian blini to Jewish blintzes. The most famous of all is France's gossamer crêpe. My low-fat version reduces the number of egg yolks and uses buttermilk to achieve the richness once acquired with butter and cream.

1 large egg plus 2 egg whites, beaten

½ cup low-fat buttermilk

¾ cup water

½ teaspoon sugar

½ teaspoon salt, or to taste

1 teaspoon canola oil

1 cup unbleached white flour

spray oil

1. Put the egg, egg whites, buttermilk, water, sugar, salt, and oil in a mixing bowl and whisk to combine. Sift in the flour and gently whisk just to combine. (Do not overmix, or the crêpes will be rubbery.) If the batter is lumpy, strain it. The batter should be the consistency of heavy cream; if it is too thick, thin it with a little more water.

2. Lightly spray a crêpe pan or 7-inch frying pan with oil and heat over medium heat. (When the pan is the proper temperature, a drop of water falling on it will evaporate in 2 to 3 seconds.) Off the heat, add a shot glass full or 1 small ladleful of batter (about 3 tablespoons) to the pan. Gently tilt and rotate the pan to coat the bottom with a thin layer of batter. (Pour back any excess: the crêpe should be as thin as possible.)

3. Cook the crêpe until it is lightly browned on both sides, 30 to 60 seconds per side, turning it with a spatula. As the crêpes are done, stack them on a plate. For the best results, spray the pan with oil after every crêpe.

Note: For extra flavor, replace ¼ cup of the flour with buckwheat flour or stone-ground fine cornmeal, use cider or beer in place of the water, or add 2 tablespoons minced chives.

Makes 16 crêpes

42 CALORIES PER CRÊPE; 2 G PROTEIN; 1 G FAT; 0.2 G SATURATED FAT; 0.6 G CARBOHYDRATE; 78 MG SODIUM; 13 MG CHOLESTEROL

SHRIMP CRÊPES WITH ANCHO CHILI SAUCE

Tortillas aren't the only flatcakes used as a wrap in Mexican cooking. Crêpes may have entered the Mexican repertoire in the 1860s, when Mexico was virtually ruled by France. But there's nothing French about the following filling, which is built on toasted ancho and guajillo chilies, roasted tomatoes and onions, Mexican herbs, and shrimp stock. Shrimp crêpes make a surprisingly elegant entrée: Given their rich flavor, you'd never guess how low they are in fat.

1 pound medium shrimp in their shells

3 cups fish stock or bottled clam broth

FOR THE SAUCE:

4 ancho chilies

4 guajillo or dried New Mexican red chilies

1 ripe tomato

1 small onion, quartered

2 cloves garlic

4 sprigs cilantro

½ teaspoon oregano (preferably Mexican)

salt and freshly ground black pepper

12 crêpes (page 109)

spray oil

¼ cup grated jack or white cheddar cheese (optional)

¾ cup fat-free sour cream

1. Peel and devein the shrimp, reserving the shells. Combine the shrimp shells and fish stock in a saucepan and simmer gently until the shrimp shells turn orange, 8 to 10 minutes.

2. Heat a comal or cast-iron skillet over medium heat. Toast the chilies until they are fragrant but not burned, 20 seconds per side. Transfer to a plate to cool. Roast the tomato, onion quarters, and garlic in the hot comal until nicely browned on all sides: 8 to 10 minutes for the tomato and onion; 4 to 6 minutes for the garlic. Transfer to a plate to cool. Place the chilies in a bowl and strain the hot shrimp stock over them. Let soak until the chilies are soft and pliable, about 20 minutes.

3. With a slotted spoon, remove the chilies from the shrimp stock. Tear open the chilies and remove the veins and seeds. Combine the chilies, roasted tomato, onion, garlic, cilantro, oregano, and shrimp stock in a blender and purée until smooth. Add salt and pepper to taste; the sauce should be highly seasoned.

4. Transfer the sauce to a saucepan and cook over medium heat until it is thick and richly flavored, 6 to 8 minutes. (If the sauce becomes too thick, add a little more stock.) Stir in the shrimp and simmer until cooked, 2 to 3 minutes.

5. Preheat the oven to 400°F.

6. Assemble the crêpes. Place a crêpe, darker side down, on a plate. Place a large spoonful of shrimp and sauce along the bottom and roll the crêpe into a tube. Assemble all the crêpes in this fashion. Arrange the crêpes in an attractive baking dish you've lightly sprayed with oil. Spoon any excess sauce over the crêpes. Lightly sprinkle the crêpes with the grated cheese (if using) and place a spoonful of sour cream in the center of each. (Alternatively, whisk the sour cream in a bowl until smooth, transfer it to a squirt bottle, and squirt decorative squiggles of cream over the crêpes.)

7. Bake the crêpes until they are browned and bubbling, 10 to 15 minutes. Serve at once.

Serves 4

314 CALORIES PER SERVING; 33 G PROTEIN; 5 G FAT; 1 G SATURATED FAT; 35 G CARBOHYDRATE; 448 MG SODIUM; 213 MG CHOLESTEROL

HOMEMADE CORN TORTILLAS

What would Mexican cuisine be without tortillas? These soft, ground-corn flatbreads have been the stuff of life in Mexico virtually since the domestication of corn some 9,000 years ago. A meal simply isn't a meal in Mexico without fresh tortillas, and small indeed is the town that doesn't have a tortilla bakery, with its rickety chain-link conveyor belt carrying freshly pressed tortillas to be cooked over open flames. In villages women pat tortillas by hand; fancy restaurants employ special cooks who make tortillas to order. The good news is that if you have a tortilla press (available in Mexican grocery stores and cookware shops), fresh tortillas are a snap to make at home. You'll need to know about one special ingredient, masa harina (ground, hulled parched corn), which is available at most supermarkets. Don't be discouraged if your first few tortillas don't come out perfect: With a little practice, you'll be turning them out like a pro.

2 cups masa harina

1¼ cups hot water, or as needed

1. In a mixing bowl, combine the masa harina and water. Mix and knead with your fingers to obtain a smooth, pliable dough, about 3 minutes. (The consistency of the dough should be like that of soft ice cream. Add a spoonful or two of water if needed.) Cover the dough with plastic wrap and let it rest at room temperature for 20 minutes.

2. Heat a comal, griddle, or cast-iron frying pan over medium-high heat. To test the temperature, spatter a drop of water on the pan: It should evaporate in a few seconds. Pinch off a walnut-size piece of dough and roll it between the palms of your hands into a ball. Sandwich this ball between two sheets of plastic (a torn-open zip-top bag works well for this) and place it in the tortilla press. Close the press to flatten the dough into a 5-inch tortilla.

3. Peel off the top layer of plastic, then the bottom layer, and place the tortilla in the hot pan. Cook for about 1 minute per side, or until the top of the tortilla puffs and the bottom begins to brown. Transfer the tortilla to a basket lined with a cloth napkin. As you make and cook the tortillas, transfer them to the basket and keep them covered. The cloth keeps in the steam, so the tortillas remain soft and tender.

Makes 14 to 16 (5-inch) tortillas

52 CALORIES PER TORTILLA; 1 G PROTEIN; 1 G FAT; 0 G SATURATED FAT; 11 G CARBOHYDRATE; 1 MG SODIUM; 0 MG CHOLESTEROL

POTATO AND CHORIZO QUESADILLAS

The first thing I do whenever I get to a new city is walk to where the sidewalk food vendors are. You can learn a lot about a place by its street food, and nowhere is this truer than in Mexico City. I'd never seen a potato quesadilla before, and this one—flavored with fried onion and fried in chorizo fat—was love at first bite. To decrease the amount of fat, I use a little chorizo to flavor the potatoes and I dry-fry the tortillas on a comal or griddle. The result is quesadillas bursting with the earthy flavors of chorizo and potato, with merely a fraction of the fat.

1 baking potato (about 14 ounces),
  peeled and cut into 1-inch pieces

salt

1 tablespoon canola oil

½ to 1 ounce chorizo sausage, finely chopped

½ medium white onion, thinly sliced

¼ cup chicken stock or skim milk, or as needed

½ cup coarsely grated sharp white cheddar or
  Muenster cheese

Freshly ground black pepper

8 (8-inch) flour tortillas

CRAB QUESADILLAS

Quesadillas go uptown in this recipe, flavored with tomatoes, corn, and fresh crab.
There are several options for crab: backfin lump meat from the blue crab (my favorite), delicate shreds of Maine crab,
Dungeness crab, or even king crab. You can also make a quesadilla from minced cooked or smoked shrimp or from baby shrimp.

½ **pound crabmeat (about 8 ounces)**

½ **cup no-fat sour cream**

½ **cup grated Muenster or white cheddar cheese (about
2 ounces)**

3 **scallions, finely chopped**

½ **cup cooked corn kernels**

1 **small tomato, seeded and diced**

3 **tablespoons coarsely chopped fresh cilantro leaves**

½ **teaspoon ground cumin**

salt and freshly ground black pepper

8 **(8-inch) fat-free flour tortillas**

Serves 4 as an appetizer or snack

297 CALORIES PER SERVING; 21 G PROTEIN; 6 G FAT; 3 G SATURATED FAT;
46 G CARBOHYDRATE; 1,160 MG SODIUM; 72 MG CHOLESTEROL

1. Preheat the grill or broiler to medium-high. Pick through the crabmeat, removing any bits of shell. Place the sour cream in a mixing bowl and stir in the crabmeat, cheese, scallions, corn, tomato, cilantro, and cumin. Correct the seasoning, adding salt or pepper to taste.

2. Lay four tortillas on a work surface. Spread the crab mixture evenly over each of them, using a spatula or the back of a spoon. Place the remaining tortillas on top to make a sort of sandwich.

3. Grill or broil the quesadillas until the tortillas are lightly browned and the filling is heated through, 1 to 2 minutes per side. Alternatively, you can cook the quesadillas in a comal, griddle, or dry skillet over high heat until the tortillas brown and blister, 1 to 2 minutes per side. (The sour cream mixture holds the halves together.) Cut each into eight wedges and serve at once.

---

1. Place the potato in a saucepan with cold salted water to cover. Bring to a boil, reduce the heat, and simmer until the potato is soft, about 10 minutes. Drain the potato in a colander, then return it to the pan and cook over medium heat for 1 minute to evaporate the excess liquid.

2. Meanwhile, heat the oil in a small frying pan. Add the chorizo and onion and cook over medium heat until the onion is golden brown, about 5 minutes. Stir this mixture into the potatoes and mash with a potato masher or pestle. Add enough chicken broth or milk to obtain a soft but thick purée. Stir in the cheese and salt and pepper to taste.

3. Arrange four tortillas flat on a work surface. Evenly spread the mashed potatoes on top. Arrange the remaining

tortillas on top to make a sort of sandwich, pressing hard to adhere the two halves.

4. Preheat a comal, griddle, or large dry frying pan over medium-high heat. Cook the quesadillas until the tortillas are lightly browned and the filling is heated, 1 to 2 minutes per side. Cut each quesadilla into eight wedges and serve at once.

**Makes 32 pieces, enough to serve 8 as an appetizer or
snack, 4 as a light main course**

329 CALORIES PER SERVING;* 9 G PROTEIN; 11 G FAT; 2 G SATURATED
FAT; 50 G CARBOHYDRATE; 429 MG SODIUM; 6 MG CHOLESTEROL

Analysis is based on 8 servings.

SHRIMP TAQUITOS COOKED IN THE STYLE OF ESCAMOTES

One of the most delectable—and disconcerting—delicacies that await a non-Mexican visitor at a fine restaurant in Mexico City is an appetizer composed of three pre-Columbian foods that are staging a rousing comeback these days: deep-fried escamotes (ant eggs), chapolinas (baby crickets), and gusanos (agave cactus worms). All three have a delicate flavor, the escamotes and gusanos being more fatty and buttery (a little like cracklings), the chapolinas somewhat shellfishy (like soft-shell crab legs or fried shrimp).

But what Mexicans really prize in these ancient foods, I suspect, is their softly crunchy texture (think chicarrones and caviar) and their superb ability to absorb other flavors. The idea of eating bugs probably sounds revolting to most of us, but Mexicans devour them with gusto. This recipe comes from the Four Seasons Hotel in Mexico City, where the pre-Columbian treats are served on a magnificent earthenware platter at a price reminiscent of caviar.

The following version calls for shrimp, which is more readily available (and certainly more socially acceptable) than insects, and while the flavor is decidedly different, you'll get an idea of just how much fun this dish is to eat. Besides, think of what a great story you'll have to tell when you serve it.

1 pound fresh shrimp

1 tablespoon olive oil

½ white onion, finely chopped

1 clove garlic, finely chopped

1 serrano chili, finely chopped
(for a milder dish, seed the chili)

1 to 2 teaspoons pure chili powder

salt and freshly ground black pepper

TO SERVE:

½ white onion, finely diced
(about ¾ cup)

¾ cup finely chopped cilantro

8 small corn tortillas (preferably freshly made)

1 batch roasted salsa verde (page 8)

1. To prepare the shrimp, peel and devein them, then cut each into ¼-inch dice. Heat the olive oil in a nonstick skillet. Add the onion, garlic, and chili and cook over medium heat until golden brown, about 4 minutes, stirring often. Stir in the shrimp and chili powder. Sauté until the shrimp are firm and pink, 2 to 3 minutes, stirring well. Correct the seasoning, adding salt or chili powder; the shrimp should be highly seasoned. Transfer the shrimp to a serving bowl and keep warm.

2. Combine the onion and cilantro in another serving bowl and toss to mix. Heat the tortillas in a 350°F oven until they are warm, soft, and pliable (3 to 5 minutes), or warm them on a comal or griddle. (If you are serving fresh tortillas, they may still be warm.) Place the tortillas in a cloth-lined basket and wrap to keep warm. Place the salsa verde in an attractive bowl.

3. To assemble, have each diner place a spoonful of the shrimp, the onion mixture, and salsa verde in the center of a tortilla and then fold it in half. To eat? Just pop it into your mouth. The appropriate beverage? The sangrita with tequila chaser on page 373 would make a great start.

**Makes 8 pieces,
enough to serve 4 as an appetizer**

334 CALORIES PER SERVING; 29 G PROTEIN; 8 G FAT; 1 G SATURATED FAT; 39 G CARBOHYDRATE; 183 MG SODIUM; 172 MG CHOLESTEROL

Chicken Fajitas

CHICKEN FAJITAS

This Tex-Mex dish, a close cousin of the taquito, *literally sizzles when you bring it to the table. The fajita takes its name from the Spanish word* faja *(literally, "girdle"), a nickname for a skirt steak. Skirt steak may have been the original meat for fajitas, but today the dish is made with seafood, vegetables, and, of course, poultry. I like the smoky flavor imparted by grilling, but you can also cook the fajitas in a skillet.*

1½ pounds boneless, skinless chicken breasts

3 tablespoons fresh lime juice, plus a few drops for sprinkling on the avocado

2 cloves garlic, minced

1 tablespoon chili powder

2 teaspoons extra-virgin olive oil

salt and freshly ground black pepper

2 red bell peppers, cored, seeded, and thinly sliced lengthwise

2 green bell peppers, cored, seeded, and thinly sliced lengthwise

2 medium onions, peeled and cut into wedges

TO FINISH THE FAJITAS:

8 flour tortillas

1 large ripe tomato, seeded and finely chopped

½ ripe avocado, thinly sliced and sprinkled with a few drops of lime juice to prevent browning

1½ cups salsa

1. Wash and dry the chicken breasts and trim off any fat. Cut the chicken breasts across the grain into ¼-inch slices. In a nonreactive mixing bowl combine the lime juice, garlic, chili powder, olive oil, and salt and pepper to taste and stir to mix. Stir in the chicken and vegetables and marinate for 1 hour. Preheat the barbecue grill with a fine-meshed vegetable grill on top.

2. Grill the chicken and vegetables on the vegetable grill. (If you don't have a vegetable grill, leave the chicken breasts whole and the peppers and onions in quarters. Grill them this way, then thinly slice them on a cutting board. Transfer the chicken and vegetables to a warm platter or preheated skillet (see Note).

3. Just before serving, warm the tortillas until soft and pliable and place them in a napkin-lined bread basket. This will take about 5 minutes on a baking sheet in a 350°F. oven or toaster oven, or about 15 seconds per side on a barbecue grill. Place the tomato, avocado, and salsa in serving bowls.

4. To serve the fajitas, have each guest place a heaping spoonful of grilled chicken and vegetables on a tortilla. Spoon the tomato, avocado, and salsa on top and roll or fold the tortilla into a neat bundle for eating.

Note: Fajitas are often served on noisily sizzling skillets at the table. To achieve this sort of theatric, preheat a cast-iron skillet in a 400°F. oven for about 20 minutes. Just before serving, transfer the grilled chicken and vegetables to the skillet; they will sizzle at once. Warn your guests not to touch the skillet.

Makes 8 fajitas

249 CALORIES PER SERVING;*
19 G PROTEIN; 7 G FAT; 2 G SATURATED FAT;
29 G CARBOHYDRATE; 540 MG SODIUM;
41 MG CHOLESTEROL

Analysis is based on 4 servings.

OAXACAN "PIZZAS"
(CLAYUDAS)

Clayudas are the Oaxacan version of tostadas—flour tortillas brushed with pork fat, crisped on a comal, and topped with beans, lettuce, tomatoes, onion, avocado, and queso fresco. The overall effect is rather like that of a pizza. To decrease the amount of fat, I've cut back on the lard, and I bake the tortillas instead of pan-frying them. (If you hate lard, you can use olive oil.) I've also increased the proportion of vegetables. Clayudas make a great snack, not to mention an unexpected hors d'oeuvre.

4 (8-inch) fat-free flour tortillas

1 tablespoon lard or olive oil

¾ cup refried beans or drained cooked pinto beans

1½ cups shredded lettuce

1 large ripe red tomato, seeded and diced

½ avocado, diced and tossed with 1 teaspoon fresh lime juice

¼ cup diced white or red onion

¼ cup crumbled queso fresco or rinsed and drained feta cheese

1. Preheat the oven to 350°F. Brush the tops of the tortillas with lard and arrange on a baking sheet. Bake them until they are just beginning to brown, 8 to 10 minutes. Let the tortillas cool on the baking sheet for 2 minutes, then arrange them on plates.

2. Spread the refried beans on top of the tortillas. Arrange the lettuce, tomato, avocado, and onion on top. Sprinkle the clayudas with queso fresco and serve at once.

Serves 4

236 CALORIES PER SERVING; 9 G PROTEIN; 12 G FAT; 2 G SATURATED FAT; 27 G CARBOHYDRATE; 396 MG SODIUM; 18 MG CHOLESTEROL

SHRIMP PANUCHOS

I like to think of this snack as a Yucatán Dagwood sandwich. Local legend credits its invention to one Señor Ucho, who ran a bar in Merida. One day, pressed by hungry customers but short on food, he piled leftover refries, turkey, and lettuce onto a puffed, fried tortilla. Today, Ucho's bread (for this is what panucho *means) is a beloved Yucatán snack. In the following recipe I give the panuchos a maritime twist, topping them with marinated grilled shrimp or shark. In Mexico, the tortillas for panuchos are often cooked on a griddle and patted with a damp cloth to make them steam and puff before deep-frying. I opt here for bake-frying the tortillas to make them crisp, like tostadas.*

1 pound shrimp, peeled and deveined, or 1 pound shark steaks

1 habanero chili

2 tablespoons fresh lime juice

2 tablespoons chopped white onion

2 tablespoons chopped fresh cilantro

1 clove garlic, minced

½ teaspoon annatto seeds

salt and freshly ground black pepper

8 corn tortillas

½ cup warm refried black beans

1 cup shredded lettuce

1 large ripe tomato, seeded and diced

2 to 3 tablespoons sliced pickled jalapeño peppers

1 cup Cooked Tomato Salsa (page 7; optional)

3 tablespoons crumbled queso fresco or Romano cheese

1. Place the shrimp or shark in a glass bowl. Make a slit in the side of the habanero, but otherwise leave the chili whole. Add the chili, lime juice, onion, cilantro, garlic, annatto, salt, and pepper to the shrimp. Toss to mix. Marinate for 30 minutes. Preheat the grill to high.

2. Thread the shrimp onto skewers and grill until cooked, 2 to 3 minutes per side. Remove from the skewers and let cool. (If you are using shark, grill until cooked, 3 to 4 minutes per side.) When cool, cut into bite-size pieces. Preheat the oven to 400°F.

3. Arrange the tortillas in a single layer on baking sheets. Bake until they are lightly browned, 6 to 8 minutes. Transfer the tortillas to a rack to cool; they'll crisp as they cool.

4. To assemble the panuchos, spread each tortilla with a little of the refried black beans. Top with the shrimp, tomato, pickled jalapeños, the optional salsa, and the cheese. Serve at once.

Serves 4

316 CALORIES PER SERVING; 31 G PROTEIN; 7 G FAT; 1 G SATURATED FAT; 31 G CARBOHYDRATE; 321 MG SODIUM; 184 MG CHOLESTEROL

SOUTH-OF-THE-BORDER "LASAGNA" (BUDÍN AZTECA)

This recipe is Mexican comfort food at its best. I like to think of budín azteca *(Aztec "pudding") as south-of-the-border lasagna. Tortillas stand in for the noodles and salsa verde for the tomato sauce. This version, lavished with shredded chicken and sour cream, tastes so rich and filling that you'd never dream it's low in fat. The recipe is really quite easy: Once you have the chicken and salsa verde, the budín takes only 10 minutes to assemble.*

3 cups salsa verde (page 8)

12 corn tortillas

1 cup hot chicken stock in a frying pan

2 cups cooked shredded chicken

2 poblano chilies, charred, peeled, seeded, and cut into strips

1½ cups no-fat sour cream

¾ cup grated sharp white cheddar cheese (about 3 ounces)

1. Preheat the oven to 400°F.

2. Spoon a little salsa verde (3 tablespoons) in the bottom of a 10-inch springform pan. Cut two tortillas in half. Cook them in the chicken stock for a few seconds to soften them, then use them to line the springform pan. (Place the cut edge of each tortilla at the top edge of the pan, bringing the rounded edge to and over the bottom.) Soften a third tortilla and place it on the bottom. The idea is to cover the sides and bottom of the pan.

3. Arrange one third of the chicken and chili strips in the pan and top with one quarter of the remaining salsa verde and sour cream. Sprinkle with 2 tablespoons of the cheese. Soften three more tortillas in the stock and use them to make a second layer. Top with a second layer of chicken, chilies, salsa verde, sour cream, and a light sprinkling of cheese. Make a third layer of tortillas, followed by a third and final layer of chicken and chilies, using half the remaining salsa verde and sour cream and a sprinkling of cheese. Soften the remaining tortillas and use them to cover the top. Spoon the remaining salsa verde and sour cream on top and sprinkle with the remaining cheese. Breathe a sigh of relief: The hard part is over.

4. Bake the budín until it is lightly browned on top and bubbling and heated in the center, 15 to 25 minutes. Cut into wedges for serving.

Serves 6 as an appetizer, 4 as an entrée

339 CALORIES PER SERVING;* 29 G PROTEIN; 8 G FAT; 3 G SATURATED FAT; 39 G CARBOHYDRATE; 360 MG SODIUM; 63 MG CHOLESTEROL

Analysis is based on 6 servings.

FLAUTAS (TORTILLA "FLUTES") WITH FRUIT AND NUT PICADILLO

Flautas (flutes) are one of the hundreds of variations on a theme of crisply fried tortillas garnished with vegetables, meat, and salsa. Tradition calls for the tortilla tubes to be deep-fried. To make a low-fat version, I brush the tortillas with lard (or olive oil) and bake them crisp in the oven: You get the same shattering crispness with just a fraction of the fat. The fillings for flautas are really limited to your imagination. I call for a fruit and nut picadillo here, but you could also use shredded chicken, shrimp, or tinga (page 248).
Note: *If you have Italian cannoli tubes, lightly spray them with oil and tie the tortillas around them. Bake until lightly browned, then gently twist the tortillas to unmold. Cannoli molds will give you perfectly tubular flautas.*

12 corn tortillas

1½ tablespoons melted lard or olive oil

1 batch of Fruit and Nut Picadillo (page 281), warmed in a small saucepan

6 cups shredded lettuce (romaine or Boston)

3 cups Cooked Tomato Salsa (page 7) or salsa verde (page 8)

1 cup no-fat sour cream

1 tomato, seeded and diced

sliced radishes, for garnish

1. Preheat the oven to 350°F. Bake the tortillas, a few at a time, until they are soft and pliable, 2 to 4 minutes. Roll up each tortilla into a cigarlike tube and tie with a piece of string.

2. Brush the tortilla tubes with lard and arrange them on a baking sheet. Bake the "flutes" until just beginning to brown, 15 to 20 minutes. Remove from the oven; the flutes will crisp as they cool.

3. Just before serving, with a small spoon stuff the picadillo into the tortilla tubes. Spread half the lettuce on a platter and arrange the flutes on top. Place the remaining lettuce atop the flutes and ladle the salsa on top. Garnish with dollops of sour cream, diced tomatoes, and the sliced radishes.

Note: To make vegetarian flautas, substitute an additional 1 cup of refried beans for the picadillo.

Makes 12 flautas, enough to serve 6 as an appetizer, 4 as a light main course

306 CALORIES PER SERVING;* 18 G PROTEIN; 9 G FAT; 2 G SATURATED FAT; 45 G CARBOHYDRATE; 68 MG SODIUM; 22 MG CHOLESTEROL

Analysis is based on 6 servings.

AMAZING BLACK BEAN BURRITOS

At first glance, burritos may seem an unlikely candidate for a heart-healthy makeover. After all, what could be worse for you than lard-laden refried beans or ground beef wrapped in flour tortillas and deep-fried? One day I tried brushing the burritos with a little lard (or canola oil) and baking them in the oven. Eureka! The burritos came out moist and creamy inside and crusty and crisp outside, with a tiny fraction of the traditional fat. The purist may want to make refried beans from scratch, following the recipe on page 306. If you're in a hurry, use a good low- or no-fat can of refries.

8 (8-inch) fat-free flour tortillas

2 cups refried beans

¼ cup chopped red or white onion

8 sprigs fresh epazote (optional)

1 to 1½ teaspoons melted lard
  or canola oil

FOR SERVING THE BURRITOS:

½ avocado, diced

1 tablespoon fresh lime juice

1 medium red onion, diced

½ cup chopped fresh cilantro

1 cup nonfat sour cream

1 batch Salsa Mexicana (page 6)

1. Preheat the oven to 400°F. Warm the tortillas in the oven until they are soft and pliable, 2 to 4 minutes. (Alternatively, you can warm the tortillas in a comal.) Spoon ¼ cup of the refried beans in a short cigar shape along the line that would represent the bottom third of the tortilla. Place a little chopped onion and a sprig of epazote on top of the refries. Roll up the tortilla, folding in the sides, as you would an egg roll. Make the remaining burritos the same way.

2. Lightly brush the bottoms and sides of the burritos with lard; brush the tops more heavily. Arrange the burritos, seam side down, in an attractive baking dish. Bake the burritos until they are lightly browned and steaming hot, 10 to 15 minutes.

3. Meanwhile, place the avocado in a serving bowl and toss with the lime juice. Place the onion, cilantro, sour cream, and salsa in serving bowls. Let each diner spoon the garnishes and salsa over his burritos to taste.

**Serves 8 as an appetizer,
4 as a light main course**

414 CALORIES PER SERVING;* 19 G PROTEIN; 8 G FAT; 2 G SATURATED FAT; 75 G CARBOHYDRATE; 682 MG SODIUM; 7 MG CHOLESTEROL

Analysis is based on 4 servings.

Amazing Black Bean Burritos

EVERYTHING-BUT-THE-KITCHEN-SINK BURRITOS

The burrito may have been born in Mexico, but it reached its apotheosis in San Francisco. As it traveled north, it grew in size and complexity, becoming a full meal wrapped in a flour tortilla. The burritos served at San Francisco burrito parlors were the inspiration for the wrap mania now sweeping the country, and they're a great way to use up leftovers. The following recipe is a rough guideline: Feel free to customize it with whatever filling ingredients you have on hand.

8 large (14- to 16-inch) fat-free flour tortillas

3 cups cooked rice

1 to 2 cups refried beans (page 306, or use a good fat-free commercial brand)

1 cup shredded cooked chicken or cooked baby shrimp

2 cups shredded lettuce or cabbage

1 tomato, seeded and finely chopped

½ white onion, diced

½ avocado, diced

¼ cup thinly sliced radishes

¼ cup chopped fresh cilantro

½ cup no-fat sour cream

2 cups of your favorite salsa (I like the salsa verde on page 8)

Serves 4

488 CALORIES PER SERVING; 27 G PROTEIN; 7 G FAT; 1 G SATURATED FAT; 85 G CARBOHYDRATE; 665 MG SODIUM; 32 MG CHOLESTEROL

1. Warm the tortillas on a comal or in a preheated 350° oven until they are soft and pliable—1 to 2 minutes per side on the comal and 2 to 4 minutes in the oven. Heat the rice, beans, and chicken.

2. Arrange a tortilla on your work surface. Place a mound of rice in the center. Top it with the beans, chicken, lettuce, tomato, onion, avocado, radishes, cilantro, sour cream, and salsa (save half the salsa for dipping).

3. Roll the tortilla up as you would an egg roll; that is, roll the bottom around the filling, fold over the left and right sides, and continue rolling to obtain a compact cylinder. Make the remaining burritos the same way. If you like, roll up the burritos in aluminum foil or waxed paper, so you can eat them out of hand. Serve the remaining salsa on the side as a dip for the burritos.

OAXACAN CHICKEN MOLE TAMALES

I first tasted these chili-chocolate-flavored tamales at the Central Market in Oaxaca. It was love at first bite. The recipe isn't complicated, particularly if you make them when you have leftover mole poblano sauce (page 227). (Oaxacans would use a black mole sauce that's similar to mole poblano, but made with a chili that is difficult to find in the United States.) The traditional wrapper for this tamale is a banana leaf—available at Mexican and Hispanic markets and via mail order. If you can't find any, use corn husks, or even cook the tamales in sheets of foil.

12 (12-inch) banana leaf squares

FOR THE DOUGH:

4½ cups masa harina

2 teaspoons salt

2 teaspoons baking powder

1¾ cups hot chicken or vegetable broth, or as needed

1 cup puréed creamed corn (purée in a blender)

2 cups Mole Poblano Sauce (page 227)

¼ cup softened lard or canola oil

2 cups cooked shredded chicken

1. Thaw the banana leaves, if frozen. Cut into 12-inch squares.

2. To make the dough, place the masa, salt, and baking powder in a mixing bowl and combine well with a wooden spoon. Stir in the broth, puréed corn, 1¼ cups of the mole poblano sauce, and the lard or oil. The mixture should be soft and pliable, like soft ice cream. If it's too firm, add more broth. Beat the mixture until it's light and fluffy, 5 to 10 minutes. For ease in preparation, do the beating in a mixer fitted with a dough hook or paddle.

3. To assemble the tamales, lay one of the banana leaves flat on a work surface, with the dark, shiny side down. Mound ⅓ cup of the masa mixture in the center of the banana leaf and pat it into a flat rectangle. Using your fingertips, make a shallow groove running the length of the corn mixture and place some shredded chicken and 1 tablespoon of the mole poblano sauce in the center. Pinch the sides of the groove together to seal in the filling. Fold the sides of the banana leaf over the filling, then the top and bottom, creating a rectangular package. Tie with string. Prepare the remaining tamales the same way. Pat yourself on the back; the hard part is over.

4. Set up a steamer in a large pot filled with 4 inches of boiling water. Stand the tamales upright in the steamer. Cover the pot and steamer. Steam the tamales until the filling is firm and set and comes away easily from the banana leaves, 1¼ to 1½ hours. To test, unwrap one tamale. If it is not done, rewrap and continue cooking.

5. Serve the tamales in the banana leaves, cutting the strings to facilitate unwrapping. Have each diner unwrap the tamale to get to the masa and filling inside.

Makes 12, enough to serve 4 to 6

274 CALORIES PER TAMALE; 10 G PROTEIN; 7 G FAT; 2 G SATURATED FAT; 45 G CARBOHYDRATE; 379 MG SODIUM; 15 MG CHOLESTEROL

SHRIMP AND GREEN CHILI TAMALES

These colorful tamales are modeled on the green chili tamales so popular in New Mexico and Arizona. There are several possibilities for chilies. You could roast your own New Mexican green or Anaheim chilies or even chiles poblanos. Alternatively, you could use canned green chilies. The shrimp simmered in salsa verde is my own touch: I think you'll like the resulting depth of flavor.

24 dried corn husks, plus 6 for lining the steamer

FOR THE DOUGH:

2½ cups masa harina

1 teaspoon salt

1 teaspoon baking powder

1 cup hot fish, chicken, or vegetable broth, or as needed

½ cup puréed creamed corn (purée in a blender)

½ cup salsa verde (plus what's needed below)

2 tablespoons softened lard or canola oil

1 cup finely chopped roasted green chilies

FOR THE FILLING:

1 cup (8 ounces) baby shrimp or chopped regular shrimp

1 cup salsa verde (page 8)

1. Soak the corn husks in a bowl with hot water to cover until they are soft and pliable, 2 hours.

2. To make the dough, place the masa, salt, and baking powder in a mixing bowl and combine with a wooden spoon. Stir in the broth, puréed corn, ½ cup of the salsa verde, the lard or oil, and the green chilies. Beat the mixture until it is light and fluffy, 5 to 10 minutes. The mixture should be soft and pliable, like soft ice cream. If it's too firm, add more broth. For ease in preparation, do the beating in a mixer fitted with a dough hook or paddle.

3. To prepare the filling, combine the shrimp and remaining 1 cup of salsa verde in a saucepan and simmer until the shrimp are cooked, about 3 minutes. Let the mixture cool to room temperature. Drain the corn husks.

4. To assemble the tamales, lay one of the corn husks flat on a work surface, tapered end toward you. Mound ¼ cup of the masa mixture in the center of the top half of the corn husk. (The mound should be somewhat rectangular, running the length of the corn husk.) Using your fingertips, make a shallow groove the length of the corn mixture and place a spoonful of the shrimp mixture in it. Pinch the sides of the groove together to seal in the filling. Fold the tapered half of the corn husk over the top to encase the filling.

5. Lay another corn husk flat on the work surface, tapered end away from you. Place the first husk (with the filling) in the center of the bottom half of the second husk. Fold the tapered end over the bottom to encase the tamale. Tie the bundle into a neat rectangle, using strips of corn husk or string. Continue forming the tamales in this fashion until all the filling and 24 of the corn husks are used up. Congratulations: The hard part is over.

6. Set up a steamer in a large pot filled with 4-inches of boiling water. Line the steamer with the remaining six corn husks. Stand the tamales upright in the steamer. Cover the pot and steamer. Steam the tamales until the filling is firm and set and comes away easily from the corn husks, 1 to 1½ hours. To test, unwrap one tamale. If it is not done, rewrap and continue cooking.

7. Serve the tamales in the husk, cutting the strings to facilitate unwrapping. Have each diner unwrap the corn husks to eat the masa and filling inside.

Makes 12, enough to serve 6 as an appetizer or light entrée, 4 as a main course

154 CALORIES PER TAMALE; 7 G PROTEIN; 4 G FAT; 1 G SATURATED FAT; 25 G CARBOHYDRATE; 210 MG SODIUM; 31 MG CHOLESTEROL

RED CHILI CHICKEN TAMALES

These satisfying chicken tamales are popular in Texas and Arizona, where they're flavored with a rust-colored salsa made from dried New Mexican chilies. You can also use guajillo chilies or even a mix of the two. You'll love the way the earthy, piquant flavor of the chili sauce is in counterpoint to the sweetness of the corn.

24 dried corn husks, plus 6 for lining the steamer

FOR THE DOUGH:

2½ cups masa harina

1 teaspoon salt

1 teaspoon baking powder

1½ cups red chile salsa

¾ cup hot chicken or vegetable broth, or as needed

¼ cup puréed creamed corn (purée in a blender)

2 tablespoons softened lard or canola oil

1 cup diced cooked chicken

1. Soak the corn husks in a bowl with hot water to cover until they are soft and pliable, 2 hours.

2. To make the dough, place the masa, salt, and baking powder in a mixing bowl and combine with a wooden spoon. Stir in 1 cup of the red chili salsa, and the broth, corn, and lard or oil. The mixture should be soft and pliable, like soft ice cream. If it is too firm, add more broth. Beat the mixture until it's light and fluffy, 5 to 10 minutes. For ease in preparation, do the beating in a mixer fitted with a dough hook or paddle. In a small bowl, stir the remaining salsa into the diced chicken. Drain the corn husks.

3. To assemble the tamales, lay one of the corn husks flat on a work surface, tapered end toward you. Mound ¼ cup of the masa mixture in the center of the top half of the corn husk. (The mound should be somewhat rectangular, running the length of the corn husk.) Using your fingertips, make a shallow groove the length of the corn mixture and place a spoonful of the diced chicken mixture in it. Pinch the sides of the groove together to seal in the filling. Fold the tapered half of the corn husk over the top to encase the filling.

4. Lay another corn husk flat on the work surface, tapered end away from you. Place the first husk (with the filling) in the center of the bottom half of the second husk. Fold the tapered end over the bottom to encase the tamale. Tie the bundle into a neat rectangle, using strips of corn husk or some string. Continue forming the tamales in this fashion until all the filling and the 24 corn husks are used up. Well done! The hard part is over.

5. Set up a steamer in a large pot filled with 4 inches of boiling water. Line the steamer with the remaining six corn husks. Stand the tamales upright in the steamer. Cover the pot and steamer. Steam the tamales until the filling is firm and set and comes away easily from the corn husks, 1 to 1½ hours. To test, unwrap one tamale. If it is not done, rewrap and continue cooking.

6. Serve the tamales in the husk, cutting the strings to facilitate unwrapping. Have each diner unwrap the corn husks to get to the masa and filling inside.

Makes 12, enough to serve 6 as an appetizer or light entrée, 4 as a main course

131 CALORIES PER TAMALE; 5 G PROTEIN; 3 G FAT; 1 G SATURATED FAT; 21 G CARBOHYDRATE; 187 MG SODIUM; 8 MG CHOLESTEROL

PASTA AND NOODLE DISHES

. . . .

HOMEMADE EGG PASTA

Is there any dish that better epitomizes the glory and comfort of the Italian table than fresh pasta?
Soft yet chewy, velvety and smooth, it's the very soul of Italian cooking. Traditional egg pasta is made with only eggs and flour,
of course, but it's still not what I'd call bad for you. An appetizer-size portion of egg pasta rings in at about 3.3 grams of fat per
serving; a main-course portion, at about 4.4 grams per serving. Tolerable. So our master recipe follows the traditional proportions.
You can trim the fat by about 30 percent by substituting 2 egg whites for 1 of the whole eggs. Or by making one of the vegetable
pastas on page 127. I also offer three methods for making pasta: one by hand, one in the food processor, and one in the mixer.
But even when mixing by machine, I like to knead the dough for a minute or two by hand to give it a "human" touch.

HOMEMADE EGG PASTA

MAKING THE DOUGH

3 large eggs

approximately 2 cups all-purpose unbleached white flour

HAND METHOD

1. Place the flour in a mound on a clean work surface. Make a 3-inch "well" (depression) in the center, using your hands or the bottom of a cup. Place the eggs in the well and beat with a fork until smooth. Using the tips of your fingers, gradually work enough flour into the eggs to form a thick paste. Using both hands, mix in the remaining flour to form a compact mass. Scrape the crumbs off your hands and the work surface and add them to the dough. If the dough is too wet (that is, if it sticks to your hands), add a little more flour. Wash and dry your hands.

2. Lightly flour the work surface. Turn dough 90°, fold over. Using the heels of your palms, knead the dough until smooth and satiny, about 8 minutes. Use as little flour as possible—just enough to keep the dough from sticking to your hands. When ready, it will feel dense, smooth, and elastic. Wrap it in plastic wrap until you're ready to roll it out. It is best to roll out the dough within 10 minutes of making it.

FOOD PROCESSOR METHOD

1. Crack the eggs into a food processor fitted with a dough blade (or metal blade, if you don't have a dough blade). Process until smooth. Mix in the flour, running the machine in bursts. The dough should form a smooth ball. If it is too wet, add a little more flour. Knead the dough in the food processor until smooth and pliable, about 3 minutes.

2. Transfer the dough to a lightly floured work surface and knead by hand for a minute or two, as described in the hand-method instructions. Wrap it in plastic wrap until you're ready to roll it out. It is best to roll out the dough within 10 minutes of making it.

MIXER METHOD

1. Crack the eggs into a mixer fitted with a dough hook. Mix until blended. Add the flour and mix at low or medium-low speed until the ingredients come together into a soft ball. If dough is too wet, add a little more flour. Knead the dough in the mixer until smooth and pliable, about 10 minutes.

2. Transfer the dough to a lightly floured work surface and knead by hand for a minute or two. Wrap it in plastic wrap until you're ready to roll it out. It is best to roll out the dough within 10 minutes of making it.

MAKING PASTA WITH AN EXTRUDER-TYPE MACHINE

Extruder-type pasta machines are based on industrial pasta presses in Italy. They vary in their quality and their success with particular types of noodles. I'm not a big fan of extruder-type machines; I find the noodles tend to clump together. But many people swear by them. Follow the manufacturer's instructions.

ROLLING OUT THE DOUGH

HAND METHOD

Rolling the dough is the only hard part about making pasta. Pat the dough into a disk. Using a long, slender rolling pin, roll the dough into as large and thin a circle as you can, rotating the dough and lightly flouring the work surface as needed. Begin rolling from the center of the dough circle and roll toward the edge. Keep the dough moving.

The trick to obtaining really thin pasta is to stretch the dough with the heels of your palms as you roll it. Continue turning, rolling, and stretching the dough until it's a little thinner than a dime.

MACHINE METHOD

Divide the dough into 2 balls. Open the rollers of the pasta machine to their widest setting. Run each ball through the rollers 4 or 5 times. Close the setting a notch and crank the dough through again. Continue closing the rollers and rolling the dough until you obtain the desired thickness.

Note: If you plan to make cannelloni, ravioli, agnolotti, tortellini, or other stuffed pasta, cover the resulting dough sheets with plastic wrap, then a slightly damp dish towel, to keep them from drying out. If you plan to make noodles, hang the sheets on a rack or hanger until they just begin to feel dry, 10 to 15 minutes. Do not let the pasta dry so much that it cracks when you try to fold it.

CUTTING THE PASTA INTO NOODLES

HAND METHOD

To cut the pasta into noodles, fold the sheet of pasta like a business letter. Using a large chopping knife, cut the dough perpendicular to the folds into strips of uniform thickness. Cut 2-inch strips to make lasagne, 1-inch strips to make pappardelle, ½-inch strips for tagliatelle, ¼-inch strips for fettuccine, ⅛-inch strips for tarelli (flat spaghetti), and ¹⁄₁₆-inch strips for capelli d'angelo (angel hair). To give lasagna or pappardelle a rippled edge, cut the pasta with a fluted pastry wheel. Maltagliati (literally, "badly cut"

noodles) are made by cutting the dough into irregular parallelograms.

MACHINE METHOD

Feed the long dough sheets through the cutting rollers of the pasta machine, using cutters of the desired size. Hang the noodles on a pasta rack or loosely coil them on a wire rack to dry. The pasta can be dried completely and stored in plastic bags, or frozen, for later use.

Instructions for making filled pastas will be found in the respective recipes.

COOKING THE PASTA

Pasta should be cooked in rapidly boiling water—at least 4 quarts for every pound of pasta. The water should be lightly salted. Depending on the size of the noodle and the freshness of the pasta, you'll need 4 to 6 minutes of cooking. Italians have a wonderful term for describing properly cooked pasta: al dente (literally "to the tooth"). That is, the pasta should be tender, but still a little firm.

Serves 4

274 CALORIES PER SERVING; 11 G PROTEIN; 3 G FAT; 0.8 G SATURATED FAT; 68 G CARBOHYDRATE; 60 MG SODIUM; 107 MG CHOLESTEROL

SPINACH PASTA

¼ cup cooked fresh or frozen spinach (tightly squeeze it between your fingers to wring out all excess water)

1 egg, plus 2 egg whites

about 2 cups all-purpose unbleached white flour

Purée the spinach, egg, and egg whites in a blender. Use this mixture, in place of the plain eggs in the basic recipe, to make pasta dough, following one of the procedures outlined above.

Serves 4

TOMATO PASTA

2 eggs, plus 2 egg whites

1 tablespoon tomato paste

about 2 cups all-purpose unbleached white flour

Combine the eggs, whites, and tomato paste in a bowl and whisk until smooth. Use this mixture to make pasta dough, following one of the procedures outlined above.

Serves 4

LEMON PEPPER PASTA

Prepare the basic pasta recipe, adding 1 to 2 tablespoons finely grated lemon zest and ½ teaspoon freshly ground black pepper. One easy way to grate lemon zest is to peel off strips with a vegetable peeler, then grind them in a spice mill.

Serves 4

WHOLE-WHEAT ORECCHIETTE

Many fancy restaurants and hotels in Italy have the sense to hire local housewives to make their pasta. Which is how I met Antonia Chiarappa, pastamaker at the luxurious Melograno ("Pomegranate") resort in Apulia. Working with a dexterity that borders on legerdemain, Antonia transforms a simple whole-wheat dough into delicate orecchiette (tiny pasta disks— the name literally means "little ears"). Don't be discouraged if your first few orecchiette look misshapen. With a little practice, you'll be turning them out the way Antonia does. Orecchiette are traditionally served with broccoli rabe sauce (page 148), or any of the tomato sauces on pages 160–162.

1 cup whole-wheat flour

1 cup all-purpose unbleached white flour

1 egg or 2 egg whites

about ½ cup hot water

1 scant teaspoon salt

HAND METHOD

1. Mix the flours in a bowl and dump them in a mound on a smooth work surface. Make a depression in the center, using your hands or the bottom of a measuring cup. Place the egg or whites, water, and salt in the center and beat with a fork. Gradually incorporate the flour, working with your fingertips. Knead the mixture into a firm but pliable dough. (If the dough looks too dry, add a little more water.) You'll need 6 to 8 minutes kneading by hand in all. Wrap the dough in plastic wrap and let stand for 30 minutes.

FOOD PROCESSOR METHOD

1a. Place the flours in a processor bowl fitted with a dough blade. With the machine running, add the egg or whites, water, and salt. Knead the mixture into a firm but pliable dough, about 3 minutes. Wrap the dough in plastic wrap and let stand for 30 minutes.

MIXER METHOD

1b. Place the flours in the bowl of a mixer fitted with a dough hook. With the machine running, add the egg or whites, water, and salt. Knead the mixture into a firm but pliable dough, about 8 minutes. Wrap the dough in plastic wrap and let stand for 30 minutes.

2. Divide the dough into 4 even portions. Roll each under the palms of your hands to form a cylinder ½ inch in diameter. Cut the cylinder into ¼-inch pieces. Lightly flour your fingers. Roll each small piece of dough into a ball with your fingers, then flatten it against your thumb by pressing with your forefinger. Peel the dough off your thumb. It should look like a tiny concave disk (or, with a little imagination, a little ear). Transfer to a lightly floured baking sheet or screen to dry. Continue making the orecchiette until all the dough is used up. Let the orecchiette dry for 30 minutes.

3. Bring 4 quarts salted water to a rolling boil. Add the orecchiette and boil until al dente, 5 to 8 minutes. Drain well before adding to the sauce.

Serves 4 to 6

234 CALORIES PER SERVING;* 9 G PROTEIN; 2 G FAT; 0.5 G SATURATED FAT; 46 G CARBOHYDRATE; 444 MG SODIUM; 53 MG CHOLESTEROL

Analysis is based on 4 servings.

Herb Spaetzle

HERB SPAETZLE

Spaetzle are tiny dumplings. The name literally means "little sparrow" in German, and with a bit of imagination, these pea-sized dumplings do, indeed, look like tiny birds. The traditional recipe for spaetzle is loaded with eggs and butter. This low-fat version omits the yolks and generously uses fresh herbs for flavor and richness. It goes particularly well with meat and poultry dishes made with sauces.

2 egg whites

1 whole egg (or 2 more whites)

1 cup skim milk

½ cup minced fresh herbs (basil, oregano, tarragon, thyme, chervil, chives, and/or flat-leaf parsley)

salt and freshly ground black pepper

freshly grated nutmeg

2 cups flour (approximately)

2 teaspoons olive oil (optional)

1. Combine the egg whites, egg, milk, 6 tablespoons herbs, salt (I use 1 scant teaspoon), pepper, and nutmeg in a large bowl and whisk until smooth. Sift in the flour. Mix with a wooden spoon to obtain a loose, sticky batter. (It should be the consistency of apple sauce. If it's too thin, add a little flour.)

2. Bring at least 2 quarts water to a rolling boil in a large, deep saucepan. Add 1 teaspoon salt. Place a spaetzle maker over the pan, load it with dough, and cut tiny droplets into the water. Cook for 1 minute, or until the water returns to a boil and the spaetzle rise to the surface. Remove the spaetzle with a skimmer or slotted spoon and transfer to a colander to drain. Continue cooking the spaetzle in this fashion until all the batter is used up.

Transfer the spaetzle to a bowl and toss with the olive oil (if using). Sprinkle with the remaining herbs and serve at once.

Note: The easiest way to make spaetzle is to use a spaetzle maker.

Serves 6 to 8

190 CALORIES PER SERVING; 8 G PROTEIN; 2 G FAT; 34 G CARBOHYDRATE; 319 MG SODIUM; 36 MG CHOLESTEROL

POTATO GNOCCHI

Gnocchi (pronounced "NYO-key") are small, soft dumplings that have the seemingly opposite virtues of being feather-light and pleasingly chewy. This is no small feat when you stop to consider that the two principal ingredients are potatoes (or another root vegetable) and flour. Bad gnocchi are simply starchy on the palate and leaden in the belly.

Here are some points to watch:

- Use a dry, starchy potato, like an Idaho baking potato.
- Mash the potatoes by hand, or put them through a vegetable mill or ricer, or mash them in a mixer fitted with a dough hook. Never purée them in a food processor.
- It's best to add the flour to the potatoes when they are still warm.
- The gnocchi dough will be very soft, sticky, and hard to work with. It's supposed to be. Use plenty of flour for rolling it out.

2 pounds baking potatoes, scrubbed but not peeled

1 egg white (or egg yolk)

1 teaspoon salt to taste

2½ to 3 cups all-purpose unbleached white flour, plus flour for rolling

1. Place the potatoes in a large pot with cold water to cover. Gradually bring to a boil. Briskly simmer the potatoes until soft (they'll be easy to pierce with a skewer), about 20 minutes. Drain and rinse them with cold water until cool enough to handle (but still hot), and drain again. Pull the skins off the potatoes with the help of a paring knife.

Potato, Beet, and Wasabi Gnocchi

2. Purée the potatoes in a large mixing bowl with a potato masher, put them through a vegetable mill or ricer, or mash them in a mixer fitted with a dough hook. Stir in the egg white, salt, and flour. Add enough flour to obtain a soft dough—it should be the consistency of soft ice cream. The dough will be sticky, but it shouldn't be wet. Bring 4 quarts lightly salted water to a boil in a large pot.

3. Generously flour your work surface. Pinch off a 3-inch ball of dough and roll it out into a long, skinny, ½-inch-thick cylinder. Using a sharp paring knife, cut the cylinder on the diagonal into ½-inch pieces. These will be your gnocchi. Continue working until all the dough is rolled and cut. At this point the gnocchi can be frozen for future use. See Note.

4. Boil the gnocchi in the water until firm, about 5 minutes. Work in several batches, to avoid crowding the pot. Transfer the gnocchi with a slotted spoon or wire skimmer to a colander to drain. The gnocchi can be served right away with your favorite sauce (see pages 160–164). Or you can layer them in a baking dish with sauce and cheese or sauce and vegetables to make a casserole that you can bake now or later.

Note: This recipe will make a rather large batch of gnocchi, which is how we make them in our house. Any excess can be frozen before cooking—they freeze well. Freeze them on a baking sheet, then transfer them to a plastic bag. To cook, add the frozen gnocchi directly to boiling water.

The roll-and-cut method described in step 3 is quick and easy and produces pleasingly rustic-looking gnocchi. For a fancier presentation, you can roll the individual gnocchi against the tines of a fork to make the traditional ridged oval shape.

Serves 8 to 10

254 CALORIES PER SERVING;* 7 G PROTEIN; 0.5 G FAT; 0 G SATURATED FAT; 55 G CARBOHYDRATE; 280 MG SODIUM; 0 MG CHOLESTEROL

Analysis is based on 8 servings.

PINO'S BEET GNOCCHI

Puréed beets give these gnocchi a stunning rose color and earthy flavor that go beautifully with a variety of sauces. Beet gnocchi are a specialty of my friend Pino Saverino, a chef from Chiavari, Italy, who now works in Miami. For a more complete discussion of making gnocchi, see the basic recipe on page 130.

1 (16-ounce) can or jar of cooked beets, drained and blotted dry

2 eggs

2 pounds baking potatoes, unpeeled

2 teaspoons salt

2½ to 3 cups all-purpose unbleached white flour or as needed, plus flour for rolling the gnocchi

1 to 2 teaspoons vegetable oil (optional)

1. Purée the beets in a food processor or blender; add the eggs and blend until you have a smooth purée. Set the mixture aside.

2. Place the potatoes in a large pot with water to cover. Gradually bring to a boil. Boil the potatoes 20 to 30 minutes, until very tender (they'll be easy to piece with a skewer). Drain the potatoes in a colander and let cool until you can comfortably handle them.

3. Pull the skin off the potatoes with the help of a paring knife and place them in a mixer fitted with a paddle or dough hook. Beat them until mashed. Alternatively, you can mash them with a pestle or purée them through a food mill. Do not purée in a food processor or the gnocchi will be gummy. Beat in the beet purée, the salt, and enough flour to obtain a soft, sticky dough.

4. Bring 4 quarts lightly salted water to a boil in a large pot.

5. Generously flour your work surface. Pinch off a 3-inch ball of dough and roll it into a long, skinny cylinder about

½-inch thick. Cut the cylinder on the diagonal into ½-inch pieces. These are the gnocchi. Continue rolling and cutting the dough until all is used up. Use plenty of flour on your hands and the cutting board to keep the gnocchi from sticking.

6. Boil the gnocchi in the water until firm, working in several batches to avoid crowding the pot. The cooking time will be 2 to 3 minutes once the water returns to a boil. The gnocchi should be light but firm. Transfer the cooked gnocchi with a wire skimmer or slotted spoon to a colander to drain. Rinse with cold water and drain again. Transfer the gnocchi to a roasting pan and toss with a little oil to prevent sticking. Continue cooking the gnocchi in this fashion until all the dough is used up.

The gnocchi can be served right away. There are a variety of great sauces for beet gnocchi, including the Enlightened Pesto on page 164 (the green and pink make a lovely com-bination), or the pumpkin sauce on page 135. Tomato sauce would be too strong and too red. Ladle the hot sauce over the gnocchi and serve.

Another way to serve the gnocchi (this is especially good for a crowd) is to arrange them in a lightly oiled baking dish, top with sauce, and sprinkle with a little freshly grated Parmigiano Reggiano. Bake the gnocchi in a 400°F. oven until bubbling and beginning to brown, about 15 minutes.

Note: To freeze the gnocchi for future use, arrange the cooked gnocchi on a baking sheet in the freezer. When frozen hard, place them in resealable freezer bags. My wife and I like to freeze two-person portions, so we always have some on hand for dinner.

Serves 8 to 10

345 CALORIES PER SERVING;* 10 G PROTEIN; 2 G FAT; 0.5 G SATURATED FAT; 73 G CARBOHYDRATE; 717 MG SODIUM; 53 MG CHOLESTEROL

Analysis is based on 8 servings.

WASABI GNOCCHI

I doubt anyone has ever made or served wasabi gnocchi in Italy. But I would be remiss in my familial if not writerly duties if I didn't include this recipe, for it comes from my stepson, chef Jake Klein. In keeping with his passion for Asian flavors (Jake and I opened a restaurant together in Hong Kong), Jake flavors the gnocchi with wasabi (Japanese horseradish). The green powder imparts a tangy flavor much in the spirit of high-flavor, low-fat cooking. I'm sure a progressive-minded Italian would approve.

1½ pounds Idaho potatoes, peeled and cut into ½-inch dice

2 ounces fresh or frozen spinach (about 3 tablespoons cooked)

1 egg

1 to 2 tablespoons wasabi powder

1 teaspoon salt

2 to 2½ cups all-purpose unbleached white flour, plus flour for rolling

1. Place the potatoes in a large pot with cold water to cover. Bring to a boil. Briskly simmer the potatoes until tender but not soft, 6 to 8 minutes. With a wire skimmer, transfer the potatoes to a colander, drain well, and let cool slightly.

2. Boil the spinach in the potato water until cooked, about 2 minutes. Transfer the spinach to a blender with 2 or 3 tablespoons cooking liquid. Purée to a smooth paste.

3. Mash the potatoes in a large mixing bowl with a potato masher, put them through a vegetable mill or ricer, or mash them in a mixer fitted with a dough hook. Do not purée in a food processor or the gnocchi will be gummy. Stir in the puréed spinach and the egg, wasabi powder, salt, and flour. Add enough flour to obtain a soft dough—it should be the consistency of soft ice cream. The dough can be a little sticky, but it shouldn't be wet (add a little flour if necessary). Bring 4 quarts lightly salted water to a boil in a large pot.

ROMAN-STYLE SEMOLINA GNOCCHI

These dumplings are a cross between traditional flour-based gnocchi and polenta. If you live near an Italian market, you may be able to buy semolina (coarse-grained particles of durum wheat). Quick-cooking Cream of Wheat works well, too, and is available at any supermarket. The chicken broth isn't traditional, but it replaces some of the flavor traditionally provided by egg yolks and oceans of butter.

2 cups skim, 1 percent, or 2 percent milk

2 cups chicken broth

1 cup semolina or quick-cooking Cream of Wheat

2 egg whites or ¼ cup egg substitute

½ cup freshly grated Parmigiano-Reggiano cheese

salt and freshly ground black pepper

spray oil

1½ tablespoons extra-virgin olive oil or butter

1. Bring the milk and broth to a simmer in a heavy saucepan. Add the semolina in a thin stream, whisking steadily. Simmer the mixture over medium heat until cooked and thick, 5 to 10 minutes, whisking to obtain a smooth consistency. Let the mixture cool to warm. Whisk in the egg whites, ¼ cup of the cheese, and salt and pepper to taste. Spread the semolina mixture on a nonstick baking sheet with a spatula (the layer should be about ¼-inch thick) and let cool until firm, about 1 hour.

2. Using a 2-inch cookie cutter, cut the semolina mixture into circles. Transfer the scraps to an attractive 10- to 12-inch by 6- to 8-inch baking dish you've lightly sprayed with oil. Press the scraps into a mostly smooth layer. Drizzle 2 teaspoons olive oil or butter over this layer and sprinkle with 1 tablespoon of the remaining cheese.

3. Arrange the gnocchi circles on top of the scraps, slightly overlapping each circle on the one before it. (The idea is to create an effect that looks like a tiled roof.) Drizzle the remaining oil or butter over this layer and sprinkle with the remaining cheese. The recipe can be made up to 48 hours ahead to this stage. Store in the refrigerator.

4. Generously flour your work surface. Pinch off a 3-inch ball of gnocchi dough and roll it out into a long, skinny, ½-inch-thick cylinder. Using a sharp paring knife, cut the cylinder on the diagonal into ½-inch pieces. These will be your gnocchi. Continue working until all the dough is rolled and cut. At this point the gnocchi can be frozen for future use. (For instructions on how to freeze, see Note on page 131—basic gnocchi.)

5. Boil the gnocchi in the water until firm, about 5 minutes. Work in several batches, so you don't crowd the pan. Transfer the gnocchi with a slotted spoon or wire skimmer to a colander to drain. The gnocchi can be served right away with your favorite sauce. (Jake favors a nondairy tomato "cream" sauce made with silken tofu.) To prepare for later use, shock-chill the gnocchi by rinsing in ice water. Reheat them in water or the sauce.

4. Preheat the oven to 425°F. Bake the gnocchi until thoroughly heated and lightly browned on top, 15 to 20 minutes. Serve at once.

Note: For a richer, more substantial dish, alternate the gnocchi layers with one of the tomato sauces on pages 160–162 and bake as described above.

Serves 6 to 8

279 CALORIES PER SERVING;* 8 G PROTEIN; 1 G FAT; 0.4 G SATURATED FAT; 58 G CARBOHYDRATE; 380 MG SODIUM; 36 MG CHOLESTEROL

Analysis is based on 6 servings.

Serves 6

213 CALORIES PER SERVING; 12 G PROTEIN; 7 G FAT; 2 G SATURATED FAT; 25 G CARBOHYDRATE; 546 MG SODIUM; 14 MG CHOLESTEROL

GNOCCHI WITH TURKEY SAUSAGE AND MUSTARD GREENS

This dish is fairly brimming with flavor. Turkey sausage can be found at gourmet shops and most supermarkets. (Choose the leanest you can find.) Grilling gives the sausage a smoky flavor and allows you to cook out the excess fat. The arugula adds color and heat. Gnocchi is a tiny Italian potato dumpling, of course, but there's also a gnocchi pasta that looks like an elongated ridged shell.

12 ounces turkey sausage (2 links)

8 ounces gnocchi pasta (or small shells)

1 tablespoon extra-virgin olive oil

1 large onion, finely chopped

2 stalks celery, finely chopped

1 red bell pepper, cored, seeded, and diced

2 garlic cloves, minced

1 teaspoon ground coriander

½ teaspoon ground cumin

½ cup dry white vermouth or white wine

2 ripe tomatoes, cut into ½-inch dice

2 cups Chicken Stock (see page 379)

salt and freshly ground black pepper

1 large bunch arugula (3 to 4 cups), stemmed, washed, and cut crosswise into ½-inch strips

3 to 4 tablespoons grated romano cheese

1. Bring 4 quarts water to a boil in a large pot for cooking the pasta. Preheat the grill or broiler. Prick the sausage all over with a pin or toothpick. (This allows the steam to escape.) Grill or broil the sausage until cooked, about 4 minutes per side. Thinly slice the sausage on the diagonal. Transfer the slices to a plate lined with paper towels and blot dry.

2. Cook the gnocchi pasta in the rapidly boiling water until al dente, about 8 minutes. Drain the pasta in a colander.

3. Meanwhile, heat the olive oil in a large non-stick frying pan. Cook the onion, celery, pepper, garlic, coriander, and cumin over medium heat until lightly browned, about 4 minutes. Stir in the vermouth and bring to a boil. Stir in the tomatoes, sausage, stock, salt, and pepper and simmer the sauce until richly flavored and slightly reduced, about 4 minutes.

4. Stir in the pasta and cook until thoroughly heated and the stock is partially absorbed, about 2 minutes. Stir in the arugula and serve at once, with the cheese on the side for sprinkling.

Serves 4

477 CALORIES PER SERVING; 27 G PROTEIN; 13 G FAT; 4 G SATURATED FAT; 57 G CARBOHYDRATE; 839 MG SODIUM; 61 MG CHOLESTEROL

....

TYROLEAN DUMPLINGS
(CANEDERLI TIROLESI)

Most of us think of Italy as the epicenter of Mediterranean cooking. But majestically mountainous northern Italy shares the Alpine soul—and cuisine—of its northern neighbors, Austria and Switzerland. Consider the following dumplings, which are reminiscent of Austria's Semelknoedeln *(bread dumplings).*

6 cups chicken broth

1 egg, plus 2 egg whites

⅔ cup 2 percent milk or skim milk

⅓ cup freshly grated Parmigiano-Reggiano cheese, plus 2 tablespoons for serving

1 ounce prosciutto, finely chopped

3 tablespoons finely chopped parsley

salt and freshly ground black pepper

6 cups finely diced stale crustless white bread

½ cup dried bread crumbs, plus ¾ cup for rolling the dumplings

1. Bring the stock to a simmer in a deep saucepan.

2. In a mixing bowl, whisk together the egg, egg whites, milk, cheese, prosciutto, parsley, salt, and pepper. Stir in the diced bread and enough bread crumbs to obtain a mixture you can mold into balls with your hands.

3. Wet your hands with cold water and roll the bread mixture into dumplings a little larger than walnuts. Transfer the finished dumplings to a sheet of waxed paper and chill for 30 minutes. Place the remaining bread crumbs in a shallow bowl.

4. Just before cooking, roll each dumpling in the remaining bread crumbs, shaking off the excess. Gently lower the dumplings into the simmering broth. Poach over medium-low heat until firm, 10 to 15 minutes. Be sure the dumplings remain covered by broth.

5. To serve, transfer the dumplings to soup bowls and ladle the broth over them. Sprinkle the remaining cheese on top and serve at once.

Makes 12 1½-inch dumplings, enough to serve 4 to 6

307 CALORIES PER SERVING;* 19 G PROTEIN; 7 G FAT; 2.6 G SATURATED FAT; 41 G CARBOHYDRATE; 1,029 MG SODIUM; 45 MG CHOLESTEROL

Analysis is based on 6 servings.

....

PUMPKIN AGNOLOTTI

Agnolotti are round ravioli. This version features a savory pumpkin filling I first sampled in Parma. The crumbled amaretti (almond cookies) provide a sweet, nutty touch. Amaretti are available at Italian markets and most gourmet shops.

FOR THE FILLING:

1½ pounds trimmed fresh pumpkin or butternut squash (1½ cups puréed cooked flesh)

2 to 3 amaretti, crumbled (about 2 tablespoons)

3 tablespoons freshly grated Parmigiano-Reggiano cheese

1 egg white

salt and freshly ground black pepper

a whisper of nutmeg

3 to 5 tablespoons toasted bread crumbs (or as needed)

TO FINISH THE AGNOLOTTI:

1 recipe any of the homemade pastas on pages 125–128

1 egg white, lightly beaten

1. Prepare the filling: Preheat the oven to 400°F. Loosely wrap the pumpkin in foil and bake until soft, about 40 minutes. Transfer to a plate and let cool. Purée the pumpkin and amaretti in a food processor or mash with a fork in a mixing bowl. Still using the processor, work in the cheese, egg white, salt, pepper, and nutmeg to taste: the filling should be highly seasoned. Add enough bread crumbs to obtain a soft but dry filling: it should be the consistency of soft ice cream.

2. Roll out the pasta dough through the thinnest setting on your machine to make 2 sheets about 40 inches long and 5 inches wide. Lay one of these sheets on a work surface and brush the top with the beaten egg white. Using a piping bag fitted with a ½-inch round tip or using a spoon, place small mounds of the filling (about 1 tablespoon each) in 2 neat rows on top of the dough strip, 1½ inches apart. Bring 4 quarts lightly salted water to a boil in a large pot.

3. Lay the second sheet of pasta on top. Press with your fingertips between the mounds of filling to seal the two pasta sheets together. Using a fluted round pastry cutter (1½ inches in diameter), cut out the agnolotti and transfer them to a wire rack. Pasta scraps can be gathered together and rerolled. (If you wish to freeze the agnolotti for later use, place them on a baking sheet in the freezer. Once frozen, pack in a zip-top plastic bag.)

4. Cook the agnolotti in rapidly boiling water until they are al dente, about 6 minutes. Drain in a colander and serve at once. I like to serve these agnolotti in bowls with chicken broth or vegetable broth to cover and a grating of Parmesan cheese.

Makes 32 to 40 agnolotti, enough to serve 6 to 8 as an appetizer, 4 to 5 as an entrée

283 CALORIES PER SERVING;* 12 G PROTEIN; 5 G FAT; 1 G SATURATED FAT; 45 G CARBOHYDRATE; 161 MG SODIUM; 73 MG CHOLESTEROL

Analysis is based on 6 servings as an appetizer.

RAVIOLI RAPIDISSIMO

*Authenticity versus convenience. Nutrition versus taste.
As an author writing about low-fat cooking in a hurried age,
I constantly wrestle with conflicting values. On the one hand,
I certainly strive to chronicle the proper way to cook a particular
dish. On the other, I want to write recipes that people will
actually cook. While writing my* High-Flavor, Low-Fat
Pasta *book, I discovered that Italian ravioli could be made
with Chinese eggroll wrappers and dumpling skins. The result
isn't really Italian, of course, but it's quite tasty. Wonton
wrappers enable you to enjoy traditional Italian fillings, such
as the mushroom filling on page 150 and the pumpkin filling
on page 132, in a fraction of the time that it would take to
make Italian pasta from scratch. I offer the following recipe to
the time-harried cook who doesn't mind mixing cultures.
A replacement for real ravioli? No. But my wife and I enjoy
ravioli rapidissimo from time to time, and so will you.*

salt

40 3-inch Chinese dumpling wrappers or wonton wrappers
(round or square) or 10 large eggroll wrappers
(if using eggroll wrappers, cut each in quarters)

1 egg white, lightly beaten

one of the following fillings:
pumpkin filling (page 135)
mushroom filling (page 150)

1. Bring 4 quarts salted water to a boil. Lay the wrappers
out on a work surface. Very lightly brush the edges of
each wrapper with egg white. Place a small spoonful of
filling in the center of each. Fold the wrapper in half
and pinch the edges, starting at one side and working
around to the other, to seal in the filling. (If using a
square wrapper, fold it in half on the diagonal.)

2. Cook the ravioli in boiling water until tender, about
2 minutes. Drain in a colander and serve with any of the
sauces on pages 160–164.

**Makes 40 ravioli, enough to serve 8 to 10 as an appetizer,
4 to 5 as an entrée**

171 CALORIES PER SERVING;* 6 G PROTEIN; 3 G FAT; 1 G SATURATED FAT;
28 G CARBOHYDRATE; 93 MG SODIUM; 3 MG CHOLESTEROL

Analysis is based on 8 servings as an appetizer.

SHRIMP RAVIOLI WITH ROASTED RED PEPPER SAUCE

*East meets West in this recipe—ravioli filled with gingery
shrimp mousse and served on a colorful pepper sauce.
For speed and convenience, I make the ravioli with wonton
wrappers, which are widely available in the produce section of
most supermarkets. (Good brands include Leasa and Frieda's.)
The purist can certainly use homemade pasta.*

FOR THE SHRIMP MOUSSE:

1 8-ounce can water chestnuts, drained

8 ounces peeled, deveined shrimp

1 garlic clove, minced

1 scallion, minced

2 teaspoons minced fresh ginger

1 teaspoon soy sauce

½ teaspoon sugar

salt and freshly ground black pepper

Roasted Red Pepper Sauce (see below)

1 package wonton wrappers (36 three-inch squares)

¼ cup coarsely chopped fresh cilantro or scallion greens

1. Finely chop the water chestnuts in a food processor and
transfer to a mixing bowl. Purée the shrimp in the food
processor. Add the garlic, scallion, ginger, soy sauce, sugar,
and salt and pepper and purée again. Stir the shrimp mousse
into the water chestnuts. Correct the seasoning, adding salt to
taste: The mixture should be highly seasoned. (**Note:** To
taste the mixture for seasoning without eating raw shrimp,
cook a tiny bit of mousse on the end of a spoon in boiling
water.) Prepare the Roasted Red Pepper Sauce. Bring 4
quarts of water to a boil in a large pot for cooking the ravioli.

2. Spread a few wonton wrappers on a work surface. Lightly
brush the edges with water. Place a teaspoon of shrimp
mousse in the center of each and fold it in half on the
diagonal. Starting at one end and continuing to the other,
seal the edges by gently patting with your fingers. It's important to make a hermetic seal. Assemble the remaining ravioli
in this fashion. Transfer the finished ravioli to a cake rack.

3. Cook the ravioli in the boiling water until the pasta is
translucent and the filling is firm and white, about 2 to 3
minutes. Drain the ravioli in a colander. Spoon the pepper

sauce on plates or a platter and arrange the ravioli on top. Sprinkle with cilantro or scallion greens and serve at once.

Makes about 36 ravioli, which will serve 9 as an appetizer or 4 to 6 as an entrée

234 CALORIES PER SERVING;* 17 G PROTEIN; 5 G FAT; 1 G SATURATED FAT; 30 G CARBOHYDRATE; 157 MG SODIUM; 139 MG CHOLESTEROL

Analysis is based on 4 servings.

ROASTED RED PEPPER SAUCE

This is the one dish in this book you can burn. Indeed, charring the bell peppers gives them an inimitable sweet-smoky flavor that makes the sauce delicious enough to eat straight off a spoon. A yellow bell pepper sauce can be made the same way.

- 2 large red bell peppers
- 1 garlic clove, chopped
- 1 cup Vegetable Stock or Chicken Stock (see pages 382, 379), or as needed
- 1½ tablespoons balsamic or wine vinegar, or to taste
- 1 tablespoon extra-virgin olive oil
- ¼ teaspoon saffron threads soaked in 1 tablespoon warm water (optional)
- salt and freshly ground black pepper
- pinch of cayenne pepper

1. Roast the peppers over high heat on a barbecue grill, under a broiler, or directly over a gas or electric burner until charred and black on all sides. Turn as necessary with tongs: The whole process should take 8 to 10 minutes. Wrap the charred peppers in wet paper towels and let cool.

2. Scrape the charred skin off the peppers, using the tip of a paring knife. (Don't worry if you leave a few charred bits behind.) Core the peppers and scrape out the seeds, working over a strainer and bowl to catch the juices.

3. Place all the ingredients for the sauce (including the pepper juices) in a blender and purée until smooth. The sauce should be pourable: If too thick, add a little more stock. Correct the seasoning, adding salt, vinegar, or cayenne to taste: The sauce should be highly seasoned.

Makes 1½ cups

43 CALORIES PER SERVING; 1 G PROTEIN; 3 G FAT; 0 G SATURATED FAT; 3 G CARBOHYDRATE; 3 MG SODIUM; 0 MG CHOLESTEROL

QUICK SUMMER PASTA WITH TOMATOES AND ARUGULA

Here's a perfect pasta dish for the dog days of summer. All you need to cook are the noodles. The sauce—a coarse purée of fresh tomatoes and herbs—is "cooked" by the warm pasta. My favorite cheese for serving with this pasta is ricotta salata—a firm, snappy grating or shaving cheese made by pressing and aging ricotta.

- 3 cups ridged tube-shaped pasta, like penne rigati
- salt
- 2 ripe tomatoes, peeled and very finely chopped (about 1½ cups)
- 1 to 2 cloves garlic, minced
- 1 tablespoon capers, drained
- 1½ tablespoons extra-virgin olive oil
- 1 tablespoon balsamic vinegar, or to taste
- freshly ground black pepper
- 1 bunch arugula, washed, stemmed, and thinly slivered (see the box on page 69)
- 1 to 2 ounces ricotta salata or Pecorino Romano cheese

1. Cook the pasta in a large pot in at least 4 quarts rapidly boiling salted water until al dente, about 8 minutes. Meanwhile, combine the tomatoes, garlic, capers, oil, and vinegar in a large heatproof serving bowl. Add salt and pepper to taste.

2. When the pasta is cooked, drain well in a colander and stir it into the tomato mixture. Stir in the arugula. Correct the seasoning, adding salt or vinegar to taste. Serve at once, with shaved or grated ricotta salata on top.

Serves 4

199 CALORIES PER SERVING; 7 G PROTEIN; 8 G FAT; 1 G SATURATED FAT; 25 G CARBOHYDRATE; 119 MG SODIUM; 33 MG CHOLESTEROL

SPAGHETTI WITH RED-HOT TOMATO SAUCE

Does the world really need another recipe for tomato sauce? If it's this thick, spicy red sauce, pepped up with olives, capers, and pepper flakes, the answer is unequivocally yes! This recipe is loosely modeled on my friend Myrna Mirow's putanesca sauce.

FOR THE SAUCE:

2½ pounds fresh ripe tomatoes (4 to 6 regular tomatoes, or 12 to 16 plum tomatoes), or 1½ 28-ounce cans

1 tablespoon olive oil

5 shallots, minced (⅓ cup)

5 cloves garlic, minced (5 teaspoons)

1 tablespoon tomato paste

3 tablespoons finely chopped capers

3 tablespoons finely chopped pimiento-stuffed green olives

1 teaspoon hot red pepper flakes (or to taste)

⅓ cup finely chopped fresh herbs (basil, oregano, tarragon, chervil, parsley, and/or chives); reserve 2 tablespoons for garnish

salt and freshly ground black pepper

salt

1 pound spaghetti or dried bucatini, or 1½ pounds fresh

3–4 tablespoons freshly grated Parmigiano Reggiano (or other Parmesan-style cheese)

To make the sauce, peel, seed, and finely chop the tomatoes, working over a strainer and bowl to collect the juice. Heat the oil in a large saucepan. Cook the shallots and garlic over medium heat for 2 to 3 minutes, or until soft but not brown.

Stir in the tomatoes, 3 to 4 tablespoons reserved tomato juice, tomato paste, capers, olives, and pepper flakes, and cook over medium-low heat for 10 minutes, or until reduced to a thick sauce. If the mixture seems too dry, add a little reserved tomato juice or water. Stir in the herbs. Season with salt and pepper.

Just before serving, bring at least 4 quarts water to a boil in a large pot. Add salt to taste. Boil the pasta for 6 to 8 minutes, or until cooked but still al dente. Drain and transfer it to a large bowl. Spoon the sauce over it and sprinkle with the reserved herbs. Serve the cheese on the side.

Serves 4 to 6

605 CALORIES PER SERVING; 21 G PROTEIN; 9 G FAT; 112 G CARBOHYDRATE; 357 MG SODIUM; 4 MG CHOLESTEROL

Spaghetti with Red-Hot Tomato Sauce

FUSILLI WITH MINTED TOMATO SAUCE

This dish should be made only at the height of tomato season, when the gardens and farm stands are brimming with luscious, vine-ripened tomatoes. The virtue of this sauce lies in its simplicity: it isn't even cooked!

FOR THE SAUCE:

4 fresh ripe tomatoes, seeded and coarsely chopped

1 clove garlic, minced (1 teaspoon)

3 scallions, whites minced, greens finely chopped

1–3 jalapeño chilies (or to taste), seeded and minced or thinly sliced

1 cup finely chopped fresh mint or cilantro

½ teaspoon ground cumin

3 tablespoons fresh lime juice

1½ tablespoons extra-virgin olive oil

salt and freshly ground black pepper

salt

½ pound dried fusilli

2–3 tablespoons thinly sliced black olives, for garnish (optional)

To make the sauce, place the tomatoes, garlic, scallions, chilies, mint, cumin, lime juice, and oil in a food processor and grind to a coarse purée. Correct the seasoning, adding salt, pepper, and lime juice to taste.

Just before serving, bring at least 4 quarts water to a boil in a large pot. Add salt to taste. Boil the fusilli for 6 to 8 minutes, or until cooked but still al dente. Drain the pasta and transfer it to a large bowl. Stir in the sauce. Sprinkle the olive slices (if using) on top and serve at once.

Serves 4

306 CALORIES PER SERVING; 9 G PROTEIN; 7 G FAT; 53 G CARBOHYDRATE; 15 MG SODIUM; 0 MG CHOLESTEROL

CUBAN SPAGHETTI

No book of mine would be complete without at least one recipe from our friend and recipe tester extraordinaire, Elida Proenza. Here's how a fine Cuban cook makes spaghetti.

1 tablespoon olive oil

1 small onion, finely chopped

2 garlic cloves, minced

½ red bell pepper, finely chopped

½ teaspoon cumin

½ teaspoon oregano

1 large ripe tomato, finely chopped

1 tablespoon capers, drained

10 pitted black olives, cut in half

¼ cup chopped cilantro or flat-leaf parsley

1 8-ounce can tomato sauce

salt and freshly ground black pepper

1 pound shrimp, peeled and deveined

8 ounces spaghetti or other long, thin pasta

1. Bring 4 quarts of water to a boil in a large pot for cooking the spaghetti. Heat the olive oil in a large sauté pan. Add the onion, garlic, pepper, cumin, and oregano and cook over medium heat until just beginning to brown, about 4 minutes, stirring often. Add the tomato, capers, olives, and half the cilantro and cook until the tomato liquid begins to evaporate, about 2 minutes.

2. Add the tomato sauce and salt and pepper and simmer the mixture until rich and flavorful, about 5 minutes. Stir in the shrimp and simmer until cooked, about 3 minutes. Correct the seasoning, adding salt, pepper, and a little more cumin if necessary. The sauce should be highly seasoned.

3. Meanwhile, cook the spaghetti in the boiling water until al dente, about 8 minutes. Drain in a colander. Stir the spaghetti into the sauce and simmer for 1 minute. Sprinkle with the remaining cilantro and serve at once.

Serves 4

509 CALORIES PER SERVING; 27 G PROTEIN; 8 G FAT; 1 G SATURATED FAT; 83 G CARBOHYDRATE; 610 MG SODIUM; 122 MG CHOLESTEROL

PENNE PIPERADE

Piperade is a Basque specialty, a stunning sauté of red, green, and yellow bell peppers scrambled with eggs and fortified with paprika. Why not replace the eggs with pasta, I reasoned, as I set out to create a low-fat version. You can certainly omit the ham if you're trying to reduce your meat intake.

1 pound penne

FOR THE SAUCE:

1 tablespoon extra-virgin olive oil

1 green bell pepper, cored, seeded, and cut into penne-size pieces

1 red bell pepper, cored, seeded, and cut into penne-size pieces

1 yellow bell pepper, cored, seeded, and cut into penne-size pieces

1 medium onion, thinly sliced

3 garlic cloves, thinly sliced

2 to 3 thin slices prosciutto, Black Forest ham, or Canadian bacon, cut into thin slivers (1 to 2 ounces—optional)

2 large ripe tomatoes, finely chopped (with juices)

1 to 3 teaspoons hot paprika

salt and freshly ground black pepper

½ cup chopped flat-leaf parsley

1 ounce feta, Manchego, or other sheep's milk cheese (optional)

1. Cook the penne in at least 4 quarts of rapidly boiling water until al dente, about 8 minutes. Drain the pasta in a colander, refresh under cold water, and drain well again.

2. Heat the olive oil in a large sauté pan, preferably nonstick. Add the peppers, onion, garlic, and prosciutto and cook over medium heat until lightly browned, about 5 minutes. Stir in the tomatoes, paprika, salt and pepper, and half the parsley. Cook until the tomatoes yield their juices and the mixture is moist and saucy, about 5 minutes.

3. Stir in the penne and bring to a boil. Correct the seasoning, adding salt or paprika to taste. The mixture should be highly seasoned. Sprinkle the penne with the remaining parsley. Grate the cheese on top, if using, and serve at once.

Serves 4

277 CALORIES PER SERVING; 9 G PROTEIN; 5 G FAT; 1 G SATURATED FAT; 51 G CARBOHYDRATE; 16 MG SODIUM; 0 MG CHOLESTEROL

TEX-MEX ARRABBIATA

The name of this Italian dish literally means "angry." The more hot pepper flakes you add, the "angrier" the sauce will be. That set me thinking about another part of the world where emotions are expressed with chili peppers.
The result is Tex-Mex Arrabbiata.
There are several possibilities for pasta here, including fusilli, penne rigate *(ridged penne),* spaghetti, *or* eliche *(helixes).*

FOR THE SAUCE:

1 28-ounce can imported peeled tomatoes

1 tablespoon extra-virgin olive oil

3 garlic cloves, finely chopped

2 ounces thinly sliced Canadian bacon, cut into ¼-inch slivers

1 to 4 jalapeño or serrano chilies, thinly sliced (for a milder arrabbiata, seed the chilies and finely chop)

2 tablespoons fresh lime juice

1 teaspoon chili powder, preferably chipotle (see Note)

½ cup washed cilantro leaves, plus 4 sprigs for garnish

salt and freshly ground black pepper

8 ounces long fusilli or other dried pasta

3 to 4 tablespoons freshly grated romano cheese

PAPPARDELLE WITH EXOTIC MUSHROOMS

When I was growing up, mushrooms meant button mushrooms. My, how times have changed!
Today's cook has access to a dazzling range of exotic mushrooms, many available at your local supermarket. For the following
recipe you can use shiitakes, creminis, portabellos, oyster mushrooms, chanterelles, porcinis, and/or morels. Better still,
use a combination. Pappardelle are wide (½- to 1-inch) egg noodles. The dish would also be good with fettuccine.

1 pound fresh exotic mushrooms

1½ tablespoons extra-virgin olive oil

3 garlic cloves, minced

2 shallots, minced

¼ cup madeira or cognac

¾ cup Vegetable Stock or Chicken Stock
(see pages 369, 372)

¾ cup no-fat sour cream

½ cup finely chopped flat-leaf parsley

salt and freshly ground black pepper

1 pound fresh pappardelle or 8 ounces dried

¼ cup freshly grated Parmigiano Reggiano
(parmesan) cheese for serving

1. Bring 4 quarts of water to a boil in a large pot for cooking the pasta. Trim off the ends of the mushroom stems and gently wipe any dirt off the caps with a damp cloth. Thinly slice the mushrooms.

2. Heat the olive oil in a large nonstick skillet over medium heat. Add the garlic and shallots and cook over medium heat until soft but not brown, about 2 minutes. Increase the heat to high, add the mushrooms, and cook until the mushrooms are soft, about 3 minutes. Stir in the madeira and boil until reduced by half, about 2 minutes.

3. Stir in the stock, sour cream, and half of the parsley and bring to a boil. Simmer the mixture until thick and well flavored, about 10 minutes. Correct the seasoning, adding salt and pepper to taste.

4. Meanwhile, cook the pappardelle until al dente. Fresh pasta will take 2 to 3 minutes to cook; dried pasta about 8 minutes. Drain the pasta well in a colander and stir it into the mushroom sauce. Cook for 1 to 2 minutes, stirring well, to heat the pasta and thoroughly coat it with sauce. Sprinkle the remaining parsley on top and serve at once, with the cheese on the side for sprinkling.

Serves 4

349 CALORIES PER SERVING; 14 G PROTEIN; 10 G FAT; 2 G SATURATED FAT; 48 G CARBOHYDRATE; 210 MG SODIUM; 54 MG CHOLESTEROL

1. Prepare the sauce: Drain the tomatoes in a colander, reserving the juice. Coarsely chop the tomatoes; you should have about 2 cups. Bring 4 quarts of water to a boil in a large pot for cooking the pasta.

2. Heat the olive oil in a large nonstick skillet. Add the garlic and cook over medium heat until fragrant but not brown, about 1 minute. Stir in the bacon and chilies and cook until lightly browned, about 3 minutes. Stir in the chopped tomatoes with 1 cup juice and bring to a boil. Reduce the heat and simmer the sauce until richly flavored, about 3 minutes. Stir in the lime juice, chili powder, half the cilantro, and salt and pepper and cook for 30 seconds. Correct the seasoning, adding salt or lime juice to taste.

3. Cook the fusilli in the boiling water until al dente, about 8 minutes. Drain in a colander. Stir the fusilli into the sauce and cook until thoroughly heated and coated with sauce, about 2 minutes. Stir in the remaining cilantro and sprinkle the grated cheese on top.

Note: My favorite chili powder for this recipe is chipotle, made with dried smoked jalapeño chilies. Chipotle chili powder can be found at Mexican markets and gourmet shops.

Serves 4

431 CALORIES PER SERVING; 17 G PROTEIN; 9 G FAT; 2 G SATURATED FAT; 71 G CARBOHYDRATE; 567 MG SODIUM; 12 MG CHOLESTEROL

PASTA PIQUANTE

This dish started as a low-fat version of Italy's classic aglio e olio *(pasta with oil and garlic).*
Most of the oil was replaced with chicken stock. To make up for the lost richness, I started adding intense flavorings: anchovies,
capers, olives, garlic, and hot peppers. The result is a far cry from the original, but it sings with flavor!

FOR THE SAUCE:

1½ tablespoons extra-virgin olive oil

6 to 8 garlic cloves, cut widthwise into paper-thin slices

1 small can anchovy fillets, drained, blotted dry, and cut widthwise into ¼-inch pieces

½ teaspoon hot pepper flakes

2 tablespoons red wine vinegar, or to taste

3 tablespoons capers, drained

8 pitted oil-cured or Kalamata olives, thinly sliced

1 large or 2 small ripe tomatoes, peeled, seeded, and cut into ¼-inch dice

1 teaspoon grated lemon zest

1 cup chopped flat-leaf parsley

2 cups Chicken Stock (see page 379)

salt and freshly ground black pepper

10 ounces linguini

¼ to ½ cup freshly grated romano cheese for serving

1. Bring 4 quarts of water to a boil in a large pot for cooking the pasta.

2. Heat the olive oil in a large nonstick skillet. Add the garlic, anchovy pieces, and hot pepper flakes and cook over medium heat until the garlic is golden brown, about 2 minutes. Add the vinegar and bring to a boil. Stir in the capers, olives, tomato, lemon zest, half the parsley, and chicken stock and bring to a boil. Simmer the sauce until richly flavored, about 3 minutes. Correct the seasoning, adding salt or vinegar to taste.

3. Meanwhile, cook the linguini in the rapidly boiling, lightly salted water until just shy of al dente, about 7 minutes. Drain the pasta in a colander.

4. Stir the linguini into the sauce and cook it over high heat until thoroughly heated and some of the stock is absorbed, about 2 minutes. Serve it in bowls (the sauce is quite soupy), with the remaining parsley on top. Serve at once, with grated cheese on the side for sprinkling.

Serves 4

411 CALORIES PER SERVING; 17 G PROTEIN; 11 G FAT; 3 G SATURATED FAT; 62 G CARBOHYDRATE; 825 MG SODIUM; 19 MG CHOLESTEROL

A NEW SPAGHETTI WITH CLAMS

Here's a New England twist on classic Italian spaghetti alle vongole *(spaghetti with clams). The potatoes and Canadian bacon recall Yankee chowder, and they add substance to the dish, enabling you to reduce the oil and omit the traditional butter. For best results, use fresh littlenecks or other small clams.* Note: *Canned clams will work in a pinch.*
(You'll need two 6.5-ounce cans.)

- 36 littleneck clams (the smaller the better)
- 1 tablespoon extra-virgin olive oil
- 3 garlic cloves, minced
- 1 ounce thinly sliced Canadian bacon or smoked ham
- ¼ teaspoon hot pepper flakes
- ½ cup dry white vermouth or dry white wine
- 1 cup bottled clam broth or fish stock
- 1 baking potato (about ½ pound), peeled and cut into ¼-inch dice
- 8 ounces spaghetti, spaghettini, or linguini
- ½ cup chopped flat-leaf parsley

1. Bring 4 quarts of water to a boil in a large pot for cooking the pasta. Scrub the clam shells under cold water with a stiff bristle brush.

2. Heat the olive oil in a large nonstick skillet. Add the garlic and cook over medium heat until fragrant but not brown, about 1 minute. Stir in the bacon and pepper flakes and cook for 1 minute. Add the vermouth and bring to a boil. Add the clam broth and bring to a boil. Stir in the potatoes and clams, tightly cover the pan, and cook until the shells open and the potatoes are tender, about 8 minutes.

3. Cook the spaghetti in the boiling water until al dente, about 8 minutes. Drain the pasta in a colander. Stir it into the sauce and cook until thoroughly heated and coated with sauce, about 2 minutes. Stir in the parsley and serve at once.

Note: For a spicier dish, you can substitute 2 cups slivered arugula leaves for the parsley.

Serves 4

394 CALORIES PER SERVING; 18 G PROTEIN; 6 G FAT; 1 G SATURATED FAT; 61 G CARBOHYDRATE; 263 MG SODIUM; 60 MG CHOLESTEROL

SPAGHETTINI WITH RED CLAM SAUCE

When most Americans hear the words "spaghetti with clam sauce," they think of a white butter- or oil-based sauce. Fresh tomato gives this version an inviting red color and so much flavor that you don't need a lot of fat. Buy the tiniest clams you can find for this recipe. The shellfish of choice in Italy would be a vongole, *a small clam with a brown-striped shell.*

- 36 littleneck or 24 cherrystone clams in the shell (see Note)
- 1½ tablespoons extra-virgin olive oil
- 3 cloves garlic, thinly sliced
- ¼ to ½ teaspoon hot pepper flakes
- 1 cup dry white wine
- 1 ripe tomato, peeled, seeded, and puréed in a food processor
- ½ cup chopped flat-leaf parsley
- salt and freshly ground black pepper
- 10 ounces spaghettini (thin spaghetti)

1. Scrub the clam shells with a stiff brush, discarding any clams with cracked shells or shells that fail to close when tapped. Put 4 quarts salted water on to boil for the pasta.

2. Heat the oil in a large nonstick frying pan. Add the garlic and pepper flakes and cook over medium heat until the garlic begins to turn golden, about 2 minutes. Add the wine, tomato, and half the parsley and bring to a boil. Tightly cover the pan and cook the clams over high heat until the shells open, 6 to 8 minutes. Uncover the pan and season the sauce to taste with salt, pepper, and additional pepper flakes. Discard any clams that do not open.

3. Meanwhile, put the spaghettini on to boil. Cook until al dente, about 7 minutes. Drain the pasta in a colander and stir it into clam sauce. Cook until thoroughly heated, about 2 minutes. Sprinkle the remaining parsley on top and serve at once.

Note: If fresh clams aren't available, substitute 2 6.5-ounce cans of canned.

Serves 4

462 CALORIES PER SERVING; 20 G PROTEIN; 7 G FAT; 1 G SATURATED FAT; 68 G CARBOHYDRATE; 52 MG SODIUM; 26 MG CHOLESTEROL

SPICY MUSSEL CAPELLINI

This colorful dish, a study in red and black, recalls an Italo-American favorite: fra diavolo. You can also prepare it with shrimp or scallops, or any type of seafood: you'll need about 1 pound. Capellini (also known as capelli d'angelo, *"angel hair") is a super-thin spaghetti. I've called for a range of pepper flakes: ¼ teaspoon will give you a mild heat; ½ teaspoon, a mild sweat. My favorite vermouth for this dish is Noilly Prat.*

2 pounds mussels

2 cups dry white vermouth or white wine

1 tablespoon extra-virgin olive oil

¼ to ½ teaspoon hot pepper flakes, or more

1 large onion, finely chopped (about 1½ cups)

4 garlic cloves, thinly sliced

1 green bell pepper, cored, seeded, and finely chopped

1 stalks celery, finely chopped

2 tablespoons tomato paste

4 ripe tomatoes, seeded and finely chopped

1 tablespoon wine or balsamic vinegar, or to taste

1 teaspoon fresh or dried thyme

½ cup finely chopped fresh parsley, preferably flat leaf

salt and freshly ground black pepper

8 ounces capellini or other long, thin dried pasta

1. Scrub the mussels, discarding any with cracked shells or shells that fail to close when tapped. Remove any threads found at the hinges of the mussel shells. (A needlenose pliers works well for this task.) Bring the wine to a boil. Add the mussels, tightly cover the pan, and cook over high heat until the mussel shells open, 4 to 6 minutes, stirring once or twice. Transfer the mussels to a colander with a slotted spoon. Strain the cooking liquid into a measuring cup. You'll need 2 cups. (Extra broth can be frozen for future use in any recipe that calls for fish stock or clam broth.) Bring 4 quarts of water to a boil for cooking the pasta.

2. Heat the olive oil with the hot pepper flakes in a large sauté pan. Add the onion, garlic, green bell pepper, and celery. Cook the mixture, uncovered, over medium high heat, stirring often, until golden brown, about 6 minutes.

Add the tomato paste after 3 minutes and cook with the vegetables.

3. Increase the heat to high and stir in the tomatoes. Cook until the tomato liquid begins to evaporate, about 1 minute. Stir in the 2 cups of mussel liquid, vinegar, thyme, half of the parsley, and salt and pepper. Briskly simmer the sauce until thick and flavorful, about 5 minutes. Stir in the mussels and correct the seasoning, adding salt, vinegar, or hot pepper flakes to taste. The mixture should be highly seasoned. The recipe can be prepared ahead to this stage.

4. Meanwhile, cook the capellini in the boiling water until al dente, 4 to 6 minutes. Drain in a colander and transfer to a platter. Spoon the mussels and sauce on top and sprinkle with the remaining parsley. Serve at once.

Note: For an even richer taste, you can simmer the cooked pasta in the sauce for a minute or two before serving.

Serves 4

417 CALORIES PER SERVING; 18 G PROTEIN; 7 G FAT; 1 G SATURATED FAT; 65 G CARBOHYDRATE; 292 MG SODIUM; 18 MG CHOLESTEROL

Spicy Mussel Capellini

CAVATELLI, CANNELLINI, AND MUSSELS

I first tasted this dish in a remarkable setting, a sixteenth-century wine cellar at a country estate in Apulia. The barrel-vaulted stone room was lit only by candles. A whole lamb spun on a turnspit in the fireplace. Equally stunning was this casserole of cavatelli (small pasta shaped like cowry shells), cannellini (white kidney beans), and mussels. Don't be frightened by the seemingly large number of ingredients. This dish is quite quick and easy to prepare.

3 pounds mussels

1 cup dry white wine

1 small onion, peeled and quartered

2 bay leaves

1 cup cavatelli or small pasta shells

salt

1½ tablespoon extra-virgin olive oil

1 small onion, finely chopped (about ½ cup)

1 stalk celery, finely chopped

1 carrot, finely chopped

2 cloves garlic, minced

2 ripe tomatoes, peeled, seeded, and chopped

¼ cup finely chopped flat-leaf parsley

2 cups cooked cannellini beans (or other white beans)

about 1 cup mussel cooking liquid (reserved from above)

1 tablespoon tomato paste

¼ teaspoon chopped fresh rosemary, or to taste

salt and freshly ground black pepper

Serves 4 to 6

385 CALORIES PER SERVING;* 26 G PROTEIN; 8 G FAT; 0.9 G SATURATED FAT; 63 G CARBOHYDRATE; 349 MG SODIUM; 64 MG CHOLESTEROL

Analysis is based on 4 servings.

1. Scrub the mussels, discarding any that fail to close when tapped. Remove the cluster of strings at the hinge of each mussel shell. (This is most easily done with needlenose pliers.)

2. Bring the wine, quartered onion, and bay leaves to a boil in a large heavy pot. Add the mussels, tightly cover the pot, and cook over high heat—stirring the mussels occasionally, so that all cook evenly—until the shells open, about 8 minutes. (Discard any that do not open.) Transfer the mussels with a slotted spoon to a bowl to cool. Shell most of the mussels, leaving 12 in the shells for garnish. Strain the mussel cooking liquid through a strainer lined with cheesecloth and reserve.

3. Cook the cavatelli in a large pot in 4 quarts rapidly boiling salted water until al dente, about 8 minutes. Drain the cavatelli in a colander and rinse with cold water. Drain well.

4. Meanwhile, heat the oil in a large saucepan. Cook the chopped onion, celery, carrot, and garlic over medium-low heat until lightly browned, stirring often, about 5 minutes. Stir in the tomatoes and half the parsley and continue cooking until the tomato has lost its rawness, about 2 minutes.

5. Stir in the beans, pasta, shelled mussels, mussel cooking liquid, tomato paste, rosemary, and salt and pepper to taste. Cook the mixture for a couple of minutes to blend the flavors. The casserole should be moist but not soupy. If too dry, stir in a little more mussel liquid. Correct the seasoning, adding salt, pepper, or rosemary to taste.

6. Transfer the mixture to an ovenproof dish. Preheat the oven to 400°F. Bake until thoroughly heated, 10 to 15 minutes. Garnish with whole mussels and sprinkle with the remaining parsley. Serve at once.

PENNE WITH SMOKED SALMON AND PEPPER VODKA

This dish sounds more Slavic than Italian, but I've seen it at trendy trattorie in Milano and elsewhere. It took some doing to create a low-fat version of a dish whose primary ingredients are butter, cream, and smoked salmon. My first step was to replace the butter and cream with stock and no-fat sour cream. (The latter certainly meshes with the Russian overtones of the dish.) The next step was to use kippered (baked) salmon instead of cold smoked salmon: both have a smoky flavor, but the kippered, which is hot smoked, contains a fraction of the fat. Please note that this is an extremely forgiving recipe. Sometimes, I finish the dish with pepper vodka, sometimes with dry white vermouth. Sometimes I use spinach for a green garnish, sometimes sugarsnap peas or asparagus. As for broth, at one point or another I've used fish broth, chicken broth, vegetable broth, and bottled clam broth—all with delectable results.

3 cups penne or
other tube-shaped pasta

salt

FOR THE SAUCE:

1½ tablespoons extra-virgin olive oil

3 to 4 large shallots, minced (½ cup)

3 tablespoons dry white vermouth or white wine

1 cup fish broth, chicken broth, vegetable broth, or bottled clam broth

6 tablespoons no-fat sour cream

6 ounces kipper style (hot smoked) salmon, flaked

freshly ground black pepper

2 cups stemmed washed spinach leaves or 1 cup cooked sugarsnap peas or asparagus (cut into 2-inch pieces)

1 to 2 tablespoons pepper vodka or more vermouth

1. Cook the penne in 4 quarts rapidly boiling salted water until al dente, about 8 minutes. Drain in a colander, rinse well, and drain again.

2. Meanwhile, heat the olive oil in a nonstick frying pan. Add the shallots and cook over medium heat until soft but not brown, about 2 minutes. Add the vermouth and bring to a boil. Add the broth, sour cream, smoked salmon, and pepper and briskly simmer until the sauce is reduced, thick, and richly flavored, about 5 minutes. Stir in the spinach (or other vegetables) and cook until wilted. Remove the pan from the heat and stir in the vodka and salt and pepper to taste.

3. Stir the penne into the sauce and cook to warm. Serve at once.

Serves 4

449 CALORIES PER SERVING; 22 G PROTEIN; 8 G FAT; 1 G SATURATED FAT; 66 G CARBOHYDRATE; 454 MG SODIUM; 10 MG CHOLESTEROL

BOW TIES WITH SALMON, SPINACH, AND BLACK MUSHROOMS

Here's a colorful dish loaded with protein, vitamins, and healthful fish oils. I like the smoky flavor you get from Chinese dried black mushrooms, which are available at most supermarkets. But you can also use fresh shiitakes or even button mushrooms if you omit the soaking in step 1.

8 Chinese black mushrooms (see Note), fresh shiitakes, or large button mushrooms

8 ounces pasta bow ties (farfalle)

FOR THE SAUCE:

¼ cup Chicken Stock or Vegetable Stock (see pages 379, 382)

3 tablespoons oyster sauce (see Note)

3 tablespoons rice wine or sake

1 tablespoon soy sauce

½ teaspoon chili oil or hot sauce (optional)

2 teaspoons sugar

2 teaspoons cornstarch

1 tablespoon canola oil

3 garlic cloves, minced

3 scallions, white part minced, green part finely chopped

2 teaspoons minced fresh ginger

12 ounces boneless, skinless salmon fillets, cut into ¼- by 1-inch slivers

5 cups fresh spinach leaves (about 4 ounces), stemmed and washed

FETTUCCINE WITH CAVIAR AND SMOKED SALMON

Here's an extravagant pasta dish that's perfect for New Year's Eve. (But don't wait for New Year's to try it!) A hot smoked salmon (kippered or Pacific Northwest–style) is lower in fat than Scottish smoked salmon or Nova, but the latter may be used in moderation. Salmon caviar (sometimes called salmon roe) is available at Japanese markets, gourmet shops, and most supermarkets.

FOR THE SAUCE:

1 tablespoon extra-virgin olive oil

¼ cup minced shallots (3 or 4 whole shallots)

½ cup dry white vermouth

1 cup bottled clam broth or fish stock

1 cup no-fat sour cream

4 to 8 ounces smoked salmon, flaked or thinly slivered

1 teaspoon grated lemon zest

2 tablespoons chopped dill or flat-leaf parsley

salt and freshly ground black pepper

TO FINISH THE PASTA:

8 ounces dried fettuccine or 1 pound fresh fettuccine

2 ounces salmon caviar

1. Prepare the sauce: Heat the oil in a large nonstick skillet. Add the shallots and cook over medium heat until soft, but not brown, about 3 minutes. Add the vermouth and bring to a boil. Boil the vermouth until reduced by half. Whisk in the clam broth and sour cream and briskly simmer the sauce until thickened to the consistency of heavy cream. Stir in the smoked salmon, lemon zest, and parsley and simmer until the sauce has a rich smoky flavor, 1 to 2 minutes. Stir in salt and pepper to taste.

2. Cook the pasta in 4 quarts of rapidly boiling water until al dente. Dried pasta will take about 8 minutes to cook; fresh pasta, 2 to 3 minutes. Drain the pasta well in a colander and stir it into the smoked salmon sauce. Cook until thoroughly heated, 1 to 2 minutes. Dot the fettuccine with the caviar and serve at once.

Serves 6 as an appetizer, 4 as an entrée

368 CALORIES PER SERVING;* 18 G PROTEIN; 9 G FAT; 2 G SATURATED FAT; 44 G CARBOHYDRATE; 677 MG SODIUM; 139 MG CHOLESTEROL

Analysis is based on 4 servings.

---

1. Soak the black mushrooms in 1 cup warm water until soft, about 20 minutes. Drain the mushrooms, remove and discard the stems, and quarter the caps.

2. Meanwhile, bring 4 quarts of lightly salted water to a boil in a large pot for cooking the pasta. Cook the bow ties until al dente, about 8 minutes. Drain the bow ties in a colander, rinse with cold water to cool, and drain well. Combine the ingredients for the sauce in a small bowl and stir to mix.

3. Just before serving, heat a wok or large nonstick frying pan to smoking. Swirl in the oil. Add the garlic, scallion whites, and ginger. Stir-fry over high heat until fragrant but not brown, about 15 seconds. Add the salmon and mushrooms and stir-fry until the fish is almost cooked, 1 to 2 minutes.

4. Stir the ingredients of the sauce to redissolve the sugar and cornstarch. Add the sauce to the wok with the spinach and bring to a boil. Stir in the bow ties and cook until the spinach is cooked and the noodles are thoroughly heated, about 1 minute. Sprinkle the dish with the scallion greens and serve at once.

Note: Black mushrooms are dried shiitake mushrooms. Oyster sauce is a tangy brown sauce flavored with oysters and used often in Cantonese cooking. (If unavailable, use soy sauce.) Both are available at Asian markets, natural foods stores, and in the ethnic foods sections of most supermarkets.

Serves 4

375 CALORIES PER SERVING; 22 G PROTEIN; 8 G FAT; 1 G SATURATED FAT; 52 G CARBOHYDRATE; 834 MG SODIUM; 16 MG CHOLESTEROL

ORECCHIETTE WITH BROCCOLI RABE AND ANCHOVIES

Orecchiette are one of Italy's most whimsically named pastas: literally, "little ears."
With a little imagination, these tiny concave disks of dough do indeed look like tiny ears. Orecchiette are often paired
with members of the cabbage family, such as cauliflower and broccoli rabe. The latter, also known as rapini
and Italian broccoli, is a leafy cousin of broccoli. Look for it in the supermarket, or use regular broccoli.

1 pound broccoli rabe or 1 bunch broccoli

salt

2 cups dried orecchiette (about 8 ounces) or
   1 recipe fresh orecchiette (see page 128)

1½ tablespoons extra-virgin olive oil

1 to 2 cloves garlic, minced

2 to 4 anchovy fillets, rinsed, blotted dry,
   and finely chopped

2 tablespoons toasted fine dry bread crumbs

freshly ground black pepper

2 to 4 tablespoons grated Pecorino Romano cheese,
   or to taste

1. Holding the broccoli rabe by the stems, wash it in a deep bowl of cold water by plunging it up and down. Change the water, as necessary, until completely free of grit or sand. Trim any large tough stems from the broccoli rabe (save them for soup or stock).

2. Bring 4 quarts lightly salted water to a boil in a large pot. Cook the orecchiette until al dente, about 10 minutes for dried and 4 to 5 minutes for fresh. With a slotted spoon, transfer the orecchiette to a colander, rinse with cold water, and drain. Reserve the pasta cooking water.

3. Add the broccoli rabe to the boiling pasta water and cook until just tender, 2 to 4 minutes. Drain the broccoli rabe in a strainer or colander, refresh under cold water, and drain well. Blot the broccoli rabe dry and finely chop.

4. Just before serving, heat the olive oil in a large nonstick frying pan. Add the garlic and anchovies and cook over high heat until just beginning to brown, about 1 minute. Stir in the broccoli rabe and cook until thoroughly heated, about 2 minutes. Stir in the orecchiette and bread crumbs and cook until thoroughly heated, about 2 minutes. Add salt and pepper to taste. Serve the orecchiette at once, with the cheese on the side for sprinkling.

Serves 4

301 CALORIES PER SERVING; 12 G PROTEIN; 9 G FAT; 2 G SATURATED FAT; 45 G CARBOHYDRATE; 196 MG SODIUM; 53 MG CHOLESTEROL

SPAGHETTI WITH ANCHOVIES

One of the most famous restaurants in Liguria—indeed, on the whole Adriatic coast—is Puny in Portofino. Since 1880, a cosmopolitan clientele has flocked to this harborside eatery to see and be seen, while enjoying gutsy Ligurian specialties such as this spaghetti with anchovies. To reduce the fat in the original recipe, I've replaced some of the olive oil with clam broth. One of the best brands of dried pasta is De Cecco.

1 2-ounce can anchovy fillets

1½ tablespoons olive oil

3 cloves garlic, minced (1 tablespoon)

½ teaspoon cracked black peppercorns

1 cup bottled clam broth

salt

½ pound (8 ounces) imported spaghetti

⅔ cup finely chopped flat-leaf parsley

3–4 tablespoons freshly grated
   Parmigiano Reggiano, or other
   Parmesan-style cheese (optional)

1. Drain the anchovy fillets in a strainer, blot dry with paper towels, and coarsely chop them. Heat the oil in a small saucepan. Add the anchovies, garlic, and cracked pepper, and cook over medium heat for 2 minutes, or until the garlic just begins to color. Add the clam

Pepper Confetti Macaroni and Cheese

PEPPER CONFETTI MACARONI AND CHEESE

Diced red, green, and yellow bell peppers give this macaroni the festive look of confetti. The flavor of the vegetables enables you to reduce the amount of cheese.

8 ounces macaroni
or rigatoni

FOR THE SAUCE:

1 tablespoon olive oil

1 large onion, finely chopped

3 garlic cloves, minced

2 red bell peppers

2 yellow bell peppers

1 green bell pepper
(or 2 ancho chilies for
a little more spice)

¼ cup flour

3 cups skim milk

1 to 1½ cups crumbled
feta cheese (or other
strong-flavored cheese)

2 tablespoons
chopped fresh dill
(or 1 tablespoon dried)

1 tablespoon Dijon-style
mustard

salt and freshly ground
black pepper

dash cayenne pepper and
freshly grated nutmeg

vegetable spray oil

½ cup toasted bread crumbs

1. Bring 4 quarts of lightly salted water to a rolling boil in a large pot. Cook the macaroni until al dente, about 8 minutes. Drain the macaroni in a colander, rinse with cold water to cool, and drain well. Preheat the oven to 400°F.

2. Meanwhile, prepare the sauce. Heat the olive oil in a large sauté pan, preferably nonstick. Add the onion, garlic, and peppers and cook over medium heat until the vegetables are soft and aromatic, but not brown, about 4 minutes. Stir in the flour and cook for 1 minute more. Stir in the skim milk and bring to a boil, stirring steadily. Simmer the sauce until thickened, about 1 minute. Stir in the cheese, dill, mustard, salt and pepper, and cayenne and nutmeg to taste. The sauce should be highly seasoned.

3. Stir the macaroni into the sauce. Spoon the mixture into an attractive 8- by 12-inch baking dish you've lightly sprayed with oil. Sprinkle the top with bread crumbs. Bake the macaroni and cheese until bubbling, crusty, and golden brown, 30 to 40 minutes.

Serves 6

408 CALORIES PER SERVING; 18 G PROTEIN; 13 G FAT; 7 G SATURATED FAT; 55 G CARBOHYDRATE; 665 MG SODIUM; 40 MG CHOLESTEROL

broth and bring to a boil. Simmer the sauce for 2 to 3 minutes, or until reduced to about 1 cup.

2. Just before serving, bring at least 4 quarts water to a boil in a large pot. Add salt to taste. Boil the spaghetti for 6 to 8 minutes, or until cooked but still al dente. Drain the pasta and transfer it to a large bowl. Pour the sauce over it and stir in the parsley. Serve the cheese on the side (if using).

Serves 4

330 CALORIES PER SERVING; 12 G PROTEIN; 7 G FAT; 54 G CARBOHYDRATE; 768 MG SODIUM; 12 MG CHOLESTEROL

MUSHROOM MANICOTTI

The earthy flavor of mushrooms in these rich-tasting manicotti compensates for the reduced quantities of butter and cheese. For a special treat, use fresh porcini or other exotic mushrooms.

8 crêpes

FOR THE FILLING:

8 ounces fresh button mushrooms, porcini, cremini, shiitakes, or a mix of mushrooms

2 teaspoons fresh lemon juice

1 tablespoon extra-virgin olive oil

1 small onion, finely chopped

1 clove garlic, minced

2 tablespoons chopped flat-leaf parsley

salt, freshly ground black pepper, and a hint of freshly grated nutmeg

1¼ cups low-fat or no-fat ricotta cheese

1 egg white

1 cup reduced-fat béchamel (page 275) or one of the tomato sauces on pages 160–163

1. Prepare the crêpes as described on page 109.

2. Wipe the mushrooms clean with a damp cloth and finely chop in a food processor with the lemon juice. (See Note. If using shiitakes, remove and discard the stems.) Heat the olive oil in a nonstick frying pan. Add the onion and garlic and cook over medium heat until soft but not brown, about 4 minutes.

3. Add the mushrooms and parsley to the onion mixture and increase the heat to high. Cook the mixture until all the mushroom liquid has evaporated. Add salt, pepper, and nutmeg to taste; the mixture should be highly seasoned. Transfer the mushroom mixture to a mixing bowl and let cool slightly. Stir in the ricotta and egg white.

4. Place 3 to 4 tablespoons filling on the bottom third of each crêpe (the crêpe should be pale side up). Roll the crêpe into a tube. Arrange the tubes in a baking dish that's been lightly sprayed or brushed with oil. The recipe can be prepared ahead to this stage and stored in the refrigerator for 6 hours.

5. Preheat the oven to 400°F. Spoon the béchamel or tomato sauce in a row down the center of the crêpes, leaving the ends exposed. Bake the manicotti until they are puffed and the filling is set, 15 to 20 minutes. Serve at once.

Note: To chop mushrooms in a food processor, cut any large mushrooms in quarters, medium-size mushrooms in half. You can leave the small ones whole. Don't fill the processor bowl more than one-quarter of the way. Run the machine in brief bursts. Overcrowding the bowl or overprocessing the mushrooms will result in a watery mess.

Makes 8 manicotti, enough to serve 8 as an appetizer, 4 as an entrée

130 CALORIES PER PIECE OF MANICOTTI; 8 G PROTEIN; 4 G FAT; 0.6 G SATURATED FAT; 15 G CARBOHYDRATE; 275 MG SODIUM; 15 MG CHOLESTEROL

BARBARA'S SMOKED CHEESE LASAGNA

My wife and I saw a sign for smoked cheese lasagne on the blackboard menu of a trattoria in the Trastevere district of Rome. Unfortunately, we'd already eaten dinner, but we took the idea home with us. Barbara created her version, using a caramelized-onion tomato sauce and smoked mozzarella. As in other recipes, if your fat budget allows it, use low-fat, not no-fat, ricotta.

FOR THE TOMATO SAUCE:

2 tablespoons extra-virgin olive oil

1 large onion, finely chopped

3 shallots, finely chopped

4 cloves garlic, finely chopped

2 tablespoons balsamic vinegar

4 to 5 ripe tomatoes (2½ to 3 pounds), peeled and finely chopped, with their juices

5 tablespoons tomato paste

1 tablespoon dark brown sugar

½ teaspoon dried oregano

¼ teaspoon red pepper flakes

2 tablespoons finely chopped fresh basil

salt and freshly ground black pepper

12 dried lasagne noodles (3 x 13 inches)

2 cups low-fat or no-fat ricotta

2 egg whites

3 ounces smoked cheese, shredded

1 9 x 13-inch baking dish sprayed with spray oil

1. Heat the olive oil in a large nonstick frying pan. Add the onion and cook over medium heat for 5 minutes, or until a deep golden-brown. Reduce the heat slightly, add the shallots, and cook for 2 minutes, or until golden-brown. Add the garlic and cook for 1 minute.

2. Deglaze the pan with the balsamic vinegar. Add the tomatoes, tomato paste, sugar, oregano, pepper flakes, basil, salt, and pepper. Gently simmer the sauce until thick and richly flavored, about 10 minutes, scraping the sides of the pan often with a rubber spatula. Remove the pan from the heat and let stand for 30 minutes.

3. Cook the lasagne noodles in 4 quarts lightly salted boiling water until al dente, about 8 minutes. Drain in a colander, rinse with cold water, and let cool. When the noodles are cool enough to handle, drape them over the sides of the colander to keep them from sticking together.

4. Combine the ricotta and egg whites in a mixing bowl and stir to mix. Add salt and pepper to taste.

5. Assemble the lasagne. Spoon a little tomato sauce on the bottom of the baking dish. Arrange a layer of noodles on top. Spread a thin layer of the ricotta mixture on each noodle. Sprinkle on a little smoked cheese. Spoon on a little tomato sauce. Add another layer of pasta, followed by more ricotta, smoked cheese, tomato sauce, and a lasagna noodle. The last layer should be tomato sauce topped with a little smoked cheese.

6. Bake the lasagna, uncovered, in a 350°F. oven until thoroughly heated and the top is bubbling, 30 to 40 minutes. Serve at once.

Serves 6 to 8

336 CALORIES PER SERVING;* 19 G PROTEIN; 12 G FAT; 2 G SATURATED FAT; 39 G CARBOHYDRATE; 406 MG SODIUM; 7 MG CHOLESTEROL

Analysis is based on 6 servings.

BUCKWHEAT NOODLES WITH SPICY SESAME SAUCE

This refreshing dish, made with soba *(chewy buckwheat noodles from Japan), is one of my favorite warm-weather lunches. (Look for soba in Japanese markets, natural food stores, and the Oriental food sections of most supermarkets.) It can also be made with spaghetti or linguine.*

8 ounces soba

salt

1 teaspoon sesame oil

1 red bell pepper, cored, seeded, and cut into strips

1 yellow bell pepper, cored, seeded, and cut into strips

1 small cucumber, peeled, halved, seeded, and cut into strips

FOR THE SAUCE:

¼ cup sesame seeds

1 tablespoon minced fresh ginger

2 cloves garlic, minced (2 teaspoons)

3 scallions, whites minced, greens cut into ½-inch pieces for garnish

¼ cup peanut butter

3–4 tablespoons warm water

3 tablespoons soy sauce

2 tablespoons rice or cider vinegar

1 teaspoon Thai or other hot sauce (or to taste)

1 tablespoon sugar

Cook the soba in 4 quarts rapidly boiling salted water for 4 to 6 minutes, or until tender. Drain in a colander, refresh under cold water, and drain well. Transfer to a large bowl and toss with the sesame oil.

To make the sauce, lightly toast the sesame seeds in a dry skillet over medium heat. Transfer to a mixing bowl to cool. Reserve 2 tablespoons for garnish.

Add the remaining sauce ingredients (except the scallion greens) and whisk until smooth. Correct the seasoning, adding sugar, vinegar, soy sauce, and hot sauce to taste. The sauce should be sweet-tart, salty, and spicy. If it's too thick, add a little water. The recipe can be prepared ahead to this stage.

Just before serving, toss the noodles with half the peppers, cucumber, and sauce. Arrange on a platter. Spoon the remaining sauce on top. Decorate the noodles with the remaining peppers and cucumber, the scallion greens, and the reserved sesame seeds.

Serves 4

383 CALORIES PER SERVING; 16 G PROTEIN; 14 G FAT; 56 G CARBOHYDRATE; 1,309 MG SODIUM; 0 MG CHOLESTEROL

SINGAPORE-STYLE NOODLES

This popular noodle dish reflects the cosmopolitan cuisine of Singapore; the Indian passion for curry powder, the Thai fondness for chili paste, and the Indonesian use of a sweet soy sauce called kejap maris. *To simplify the recipe, I've substituted regular soy sauce and molasses.*

RICE STICKS WITH BARBECUED PORK

Rice noodle stews are as popular in Southeast Asia as hamburgers are in the West. My favorite meat for this dish is the sweet barbecued pork tenderloin found at Chinese markets, but any cooked meat or seafood will do. Dried shrimp can be found at Asian and Hispanic markets.

8 ounces rice sticks,
   ideally ¼-inch wide

2 teaspoons canola oil

2 cloves garlic, thinly sliced

5 cups chicken stock

¼ cup fish sauce

1–3 teaspoons Thai chili paste or
   hot sauce

3 tablespoons sugar

1 tablespoon fresh lime juice
   (or to taste)

2 cups bean sprouts

6–8 ounces Chinese barbecued pork
   or cooked chicken, beef, shrimp,
   or scallops, thinly sliced

½ cup finely chopped cilantro

3 tablespoons finely chopped
   dried shrimp (optional)

3 tablespoons finely chopped
   dry-roasted peanuts

1 lime, quartered

Soak the rice sticks in cold water to cover for 30 minutes, or until pliable. Heat the oil in a large saucepan and cook the garlic until golden brown. Add the stock and bring to a boil. Stir in the fish sauce, chili paste, sugar, and lime juice. Correct the seasoning, adding chili paste and lime juice to taste.

Bring 2 quarts water to a boil in a large pot. Just before serving, drain the rice sticks and cook in boiling water for 1 minute, or until tender. Add the bean sprouts and cook for 10 seconds. Drain the noodles and sprouts, and transfer them to 4 large bowls or soup plates. Arrange the barbecued pork slices on top. Fill each bowl with broth and sprinkle with cilantro, dried shrimp (if using), and chopped peanuts. Serve at once, with lime wedges and hot sauce on the side.

Serves 4

478 CALORIES PER SERVING; 28 G PROTEIN;
9 G FAT; 71 G CARBOHYDRATE; 627 MG SODIUM;
43 MG CHOLESTEROL

---

8 ounces rice vermicelli or very thin Chinese wheat noodles

¼ cup soy sauce

½–1 teaspoon sambal ulek (Indonesian chili paste),
   Thai chili paste, or hot sauce

2 tablespoons molasses

2 tablespoons rice wine vinegar or lemon juice

1½ tablespoons canola oil

1 tablespoon curry powder

1 tablespoon minced fresh ginger

2 cloves garlic, minced (2 teaspoons)

4 scallions, whites minced, greens cut into 1-inch pieces

6 ounces lean pork loin (partially frozen), thinly sliced
   across the grain and cut into ¼-inch pieces

6 ounces shrimp, peeled and deveined

1 red bell pepper, cored, seeded,
   and cut into ¼-inch strips

2 cups bean sprouts

salt and freshly ground black pepper

Soak the rice vermicelli in cold water to cover for 20 minutes or until pliable. (If using wheat noodles, cook in 3 quarts boiling water for 2 to 4 minutes, or until tender. Drain in a colander, refresh under cold water, and drain well.)

Combine the soy sauce, sambal ulek, molasses, and vinegar in a small bowl and stir to mix.

Drain the rice vermicelli. Heat a wok over high heat. Swirl in the oil. Stir-fry the curry powder, ginger, garlic, and scallion whites for 20 seconds, or until fragrant but not brown. Add the pork, shrimp, and pepper, and stir-fry for 1 to 2 minutes, or until cooked. Stir in the vermicelli, soy sauce mixture, scallion greens, and bean sprouts. Stir-fry for 1 to 2 minutes, or until the noodles are soft. Add salt and pepper to taste. Serve at once.

Serves 4

412 CALORIES PER SERVING; 23 G PROTEIN; 10 G FAT; 59 G CARBOHYDRATE;
620 MG SODIUM; 84 MG CHOLESTEROL

KOREAN SESAME NOODLES WITH BEEF

This dish, called chap chae, *could be thought of as Korean chop suey. It's traditionally made with a silvery gray sweet potato starch noodle called* dang myun *(available in Asian markets), but you can use 8 ounces of any thin cooked noodle.*

- 8 ounces dang myun
- ½ teaspoon plus 1 tablespoon sesame oil
- 5 Chinese dried black mushrooms
- 3 tablespoons sesame seeds
- 3 cloves garlic, minced (1 tablespoon)
- 1 onion, thinly sliced
- 1 large carrot, peeled and cut into julienne strips
- 6 ounces beef tenderloin or sirloin (partially frozen), thinly sliced across the grain and cut into ½-inch strips
- 5 ounces fresh spinach
- 4–5 tablespoons soy sauce
- 2–3 tablespoons sugar
- salt and freshly ground black pepper

Cook the dang myun in 3 quarts boiling water for 3 to 4 minutes, or until tender. Drain in a colander, refresh under cold water, and drain well. Cut the dang myun 3 or 4 times with scissors and toss with ½ teaspoon oil. Soak the mushrooms in hot water to cover for 20 minutes.

Lightly toast the sesame seeds in a dry skillet over medium heat. Stem the mushrooms and cut into thin slivers.

Heat the 1 tablespoon oil in a wok or skillet over medium heat. Add the garlic, onion, carrot, and mushrooms, and stir-fry for 2 minutes, or until soft but not brown. Increase the heat to high and add the beef. Stir-fry for 1 minute, or until cooked. Transfer the beef mixture to a platter with a slotted spoon and keep warm.

Add the spinach, soy sauce, and sugar to the wok and cook for 2 minutes, or until the spinach is wilted. Stir in the dang myun and the beef mixture. Cook for 1 to 2 minutes, or until the noodles are soft. Correct the seasoning, adding salt, pepper, soy sauce, and sugar to taste. The mixture should be a little sweet and a little salty. Sprinkle with sesame seeds and serve at once.

Serves 4

416 CALORIES PER SERVING; 13 G PROTEIN; 10 G FAT; 69 G CARBOHYDRATE; 590 MG SODIUM; 24 MG CHOLESTEROL

PAD THAI

Pad thai, or stir-fried noodles, is one of the national dishes of Thailand. My version uses less oil than the original, but it's tasty enough to have become a once-a-week special at our house.

- 8 ounces rice sticks, ideally ⅛-inch wide
- 4 tablespoons fresh lime juice
- 3 tablespoons fish sauce
- 1 tablespoon soy sauce
- 1 tablespoon sugar
- 1–2 teaspoons Thai hot sauce (or to taste)
- 1½ tablespoons canola oil
- 3 cloves garlic, minced (1 tablespoon)
- 1 tablespoon minced fresh ginger or galangal
- 4 scallions, whites minced, greens cut into ½-inch pieces for garnish
- 1 or 2 hot chilies, seeded and minced
- 4 ounces skinless, boneless chicken breast, thinly sliced across the grain
- 4 ounces shrimp, peeled, deveined, and cut into 1-inch pieces
- 1 red or yellow bell pepper, cored, seeded, and diced
- 1 medium-sized onion, thinly sliced
- 2 carrots, peeled and thinly sliced
- 2 cups mung bean sprouts
- 3 tablespoons chopped dry-roasted peanuts, for garnish

Soak the rice sticks in cold water to cover for 30 minutes, or until pliable. Combine the lime juice, fish sauce, soy sauce, sugar, and hot sauce in a small bowl and whisk to mix.

Just before serving, drain the rice sticks. Heat a wok over high heat. Swirl in the oil. Add the garlic, ginger, scallion whites, and chilies, and stir-fry for 15 seconds, or until fragrant. Add the chicken, shrimp, pepper, onion, and carrots, and stir-fry for 1 to 2 minutes, or until the chicken is cooked.

Stir in the rice sticks and bean sprouts, and cook for 30 seconds. Stir in the sauce and cook for 30 seconds, or until the rice sticks are tender.

Correct the seasoning, adding fish sauce, lime juice, and sugar to taste. The dish should be a little sweet, a little sour, and a little salty. Transfer the pad thai to a platter or plates. Sprinkle with the scallion greens and peanuts, and serve at once.

Serves 4

434 CALORIES PER SERVING; 22 G PROTEIN; 11 G FAT; 64 G CARBOHYDRATE; 508 MG SODIUM; 58 MG CHOLESTEROL

VIETNAMESE NOODLE STIR-FRY

Here's a quick, home-style dish from central Vietnam. I learned how to make it at a cozy restaurant called Vietfood, run by a soft-spoken couple named Tan and Gam Thi Doan in the Boston suburb of Watertown. Vegetarians can omit the pork and shrimp, substituting 4 ounces thinly sliced tofu.

- 8 ounces pre-steamed Chinese egg noodles (see previous Note) or dried wheat noodles
- 1 tablespoon canola oil
- 2 garlic cloves, minced
- 3 scallions, white part minced, green part thinly sliced
- 1 tablespoon minced fresh lemongrass or 1 teaspoon grated lemon zest (optional)
- 1 onion, thinly sliced
- 2 carrots, cut into matchstick slivers (julienned)
- 4 ounces lean pork or chicken breast, thinly sliced
- 12 small or 8 medium shrimp, peeled and deveined
- 3 tablespoons fish sauce or soy sauce, or to taste
- 2 cups mung bean sprouts
- 12 fresh basil leaves or mint leaves, thinly sliced
- 2 to 3 tablespoons coarsely chopped dry roasted peanuts

1. Cook the noodles in 4 quarts of rapidly boiling water until al dente, 6 to 8 minutes for pre-steamed noodles, 8 minutes for dried noodles. Drain in a colander, rinse with cold water, and drain again.

2. Just before serving, heat a wok (preferably nonstick) over a medium-high flame. Swirl in the oil. Add the garlic, scallion whites, lemongrass, if using, and onion and stir-fry until fragrant but not brown, about 30 seconds. Add the carrots, pork, and shrimp and stir-fry until cooked, 1 to 2 minutes.

3. Stir in the noodles and fish sauce and stir-fry until the noodles are heated, about 2 minutes. If using grated lemon zest, add it now. Stir in the bean sprouts and basil and cook until the sprouts are just tender, about 30 seconds. Correct the seasoning, adding fish sauce to taste. Sprinkle with the scallion greens and peanuts and serve.

Serves 4

367 CALORIES PER SERVING; 22 G PROTEIN; 9 G FAT; 1 G SATURATED FAT; 50 G CARBOHYDRATE; 895 MG SODIUM; 107 MG CHOLESTEROL

Nonya Noodles

NONYA NOODLES

Nonya is the Malay word for "grandmother." The term refers to a unique Singaporean style of cooking that combines Chinese cooking techniques, such as stir-frying, with the Malay love of spices and coconut milk. To reduce the fat, I use a "lite" coconut milk; one good brand is made by A Taste of Thai.

salt

4 ounces long beans (see Note), green beans, or haricots verts

2 large carrots, peeled and thinly sliced on the diagonal

8 ounces pre-steamed Chinese egg noodles (see Note) or dried wheat noodles

4 garlic cloves, finely chopped

3 shallots, finely chopped

4 teaspoons finely chopped fresh ginger

1 to 3 hot chilies, finely chopped (for milder noodles, seed the chilies)

1 tablespoon canola oil

¾ cup "lite" coconut milk

¾ cup Chicken Stock or Vegetable Stock (see pages 379, 382)

3 tablespoons Asian fish sauce or soy sauce

freshly ground black pepper

3 tablespoons finely chopped scallion greens

1. Bring 4 quarts of salted water to a boil in a large pot for cooking the vegetables and noodles.

2. Snap the ends off the beans. If using long beans, cut them into 3-inch pieces. Cook the beans in the boiling water until crispy-tender, about 2 minutes. Transfer the beans to a colander with a slotted spoon, rinse with ice water, and drain again. Cook, drain, and chill the carrots the same way.

3. Add the noodles to the boiling water and cook until tender, 6 to 8 minutes. Drain the noodles in a colander, rinse with cold water, and drain again.

4. Purée the garlic, shallots, ginger, and chilies in a mortar and pestle or food processor. Heat the oil in a nonstick wok or frying pan. Add the garlic paste and stir-fry until fragrant, about 2 minutes. Stir in the coconut milk, stock, fish sauce, and pepper. Boil the mixture until slightly thickened and very flavorful, about 2 minutes.

5. Stir in the noodles and simmer until most of the sauce is absorbed, 2 to 3 minutes. Stir in the long beans and carrots and cook until heated. Correct the seasoning, adding fish sauce or pepper to taste. Sprinkle the noodles with the scallion greens and serve at once.

Note: Long beans are Asian green beans that grow up to two feet in length. Look for them in Asian and West Indian markets or use regular green beans.

Chinese egg noodles are a thin yellow pasta made from flour, eggs, and a little oil. Most supermarkets carry pre-steamed egg noodles, which are partially cooked and conveniently packaged in sealed plastic bags. One widely available brand is Leasa. Other possibilities for noodles include udon, ramen, or even fettuccine.

Serves 4

305 CALORIES PER SERVING; 10 G PROTEIN; 8 G FAT; 2 G SATURATED FAT; 49 G CARBOHYDRATE; 808 MG SODIUM; 49 MG CHOLESTEROL

THAI NOODLE "BOUILLABAISSE"

The Thai love of explosive flavors is apparent in this dish—a cross between stir-fried noodles and bouillabaisse. The delicate interplay of sweet (honey and peanuts), sour (lime juice), salty (fish sauce or soy sauce), and aromatic (chilies and basil) will send you rushing back for seconds. The noodle of choice is a rice stick (see Note), but you can also use cooked linguini or fettuccine. This recipe can be prepared with any type of seafood, from shrimp or fish (you'll need about 1 pound) to the selection listed below. Vegetarians can replace the seafood with tofu and cooked vegetables.

8 ounces rice sticks

2 pounds mussels or clams in the shell

1 cup rice wine or white wine

½ pound shrimp

½ pound squid or scallops

FOR THE SAUCE:

1 cup mussel juice (or chicken or vegetable stock)

5 tablespoons Asian fish sauce or soy sauce

5 tablespoons lime juice

3 tablespoons honey or sugar

TO FINISH THE NOODLES:

1 tablespoon canola oil

1 to 3 Thai or jalapeño chilies, minced (for a milder dish, seed the chilies before mincing)

3 garlic cloves, minced

1 tablespoon minced fresh ginger

3 scallions, white part minced, green part finely chopped

1 carrot, thinly sliced on the diagonal

4 ounces snow peas, strings and stems removed

2 cups fresh mung bean sprouts

1 bunch basil, stemmed

2 to 3 tablespoons coarsely chopped dry roasted peanuts

1. Soak the rice sticks in cool water to cover, for 20 minutes.

2. Scrub the mussels, discarding any with cracked shells or shells that fail to close when tapped. Remove any tufts of threads found at the hinges of the mussel shells. (A needle-nose pliers works well for this task.) Bring the wine to a boil. Add the mussels, tightly cover the pan, and cook over high heat until the mussel shells open, 4 to 6 minutes, stirring once or twice. Transfer the mussels to a colander with a slotted spoon. Shell most of them, reserving 12 in the shell for garnish. Strain the cooking liquid into a measuring cup. You'll need 1 cup. (Extra broth can be frozen for future use in any recipe that calls for fish stock or clam broth.) Peel and devein the shrimp. Thinly slice the squid or scallops.

3. Combine the ingredients for the sauce and stir until mixed.

4. Just before serving, heat a large wok (preferably nonstick) or skillet over high heat and swirl in the oil. Add the chilies, garlic, ginger, and scallion whites and stir-fry until fragrant, about 15 seconds. Add the carrot, snow peas, and shrimp and stir-fry for 2 minutes, or until the shrimp starts to turn pink.

5. Stir in the sauce and bring to a boil. Add the rice sticks and squid and cook until the noodles are almost soft, 2 to 3 minutes. Stir in the bean sprouts and basil leaves and stir-fry until the sprouts lose their rawness and all the seafood is cooked, about 1 minute more. Stir in the mussels. Transfer the Thai noodle "bouillabaisse" to a platter and sprinkle with the chopped peanuts and scallion greens. Serve at once.

Note: Rice sticks are noodles made from rice flour and water. They come in a broad range of widths: from capellini-thin strands to fettuccine-thick ribbons. I like a rice stick that's ⅛- to ¼-inch wide for this recipe. Thin rice sticks will need only a minute of cooking, thick rice sticks, 2 to 4 minutes. If rice noodles are unavailable, you can use spaghetti or linguini. (You'll need about 8 ounces of dried.)

Serves 4

514 CALORIES PER SERVING; 35 G PROTEIN; 9 G FAT; 2 G SATURATED FAT; 74 G CARBOHYDRATE; 1,624 MG SODIUM; 211 MG CHOLESTEROL

MR. KEE'S LAMB CHOW MEIN

When I lived in Boston, one of my favorite restaurants in Chinatown was barely a restaurant at all. King Fung Garden consisted of a single dining room with five tables in a building so rickety, it looked as though it might blow down in the next snowstorm. The kitchen was even smaller and more rickety, but from it emerged some of the most wondrous noodle dishes I've eaten on three continents. The man behind this culinary pleasure was a Mr. Fung Kee, a quiet, elderly man, who was born in northern China, trained in Hong Kong, and spent several decades in Boston. Mr. Kee used a variety of fresh wheat noodles. If you live in an area with a large Chinese population, you may be able to find them. This recipe has been designed for the steamed egg noodles sold in plastic bags in supermarket produce sections.

Note: *Partially freezing the lamb helps facilitate slicing.*

8 ounces pre-steamed Chinese egg noodles (see Note on page 157)

½ pound lean leg of lamb

FOR THE SAUCE:

½ cup Chicken Stock or Vegetable Stock (see pages 379, 382)

3 tablespoons soy sauce

3 tablespoons Chinese rice wine or dry sherry

1 tablespoon honey or sugar

1 to 3 tablespoons chili paste or hot bean paste (optional; see Note)

1 tablespoon cornstarch

salt and freshly ground black pepper

1 tablespoon canola oil

3 garlic cloves, minced

1 tablespoon minced fresh ginger

3 scallions, white part minced, green part cut on the diagonal into ½-inch slivers

1 cup thinly sliced green cabbage or nappa (Chinese cabbage)

1 carrot, cut into matchstick slivers

1 cup snow peas, stems and strings removed

1. Cook the noodles in 4 quarts of boiling water in a large pot until tender, 6 to 8 minutes. Drain the noodles in a colander and rinse with cold water.

2. Cut the lamb across the grain into paper-thin slices. Combine the ingredients for the sauce in a small bowl and stir until the honey and cornstarch are dissolved.

3. Heat a large wok (preferably nonstick) over a high flame and swirl in the oil. Add the garlic, ginger, and scallion whites and stir-fry until fragrant but not brown, about 15 seconds. Add the lamb and stir-fry until pink, 1 to 2 minutes. Add the cabbage, carrot, and snow peas and continue cooking until the vegetables are tender, about 1 minute. Stir in the noodles. Stir the sauce to redissolve the cornstarch and add it to the noodles. Stir-fry the mixture until thoroughly heated, about 2 minutes. The sauce should boil. Sprinkle the noodles with the scallion greens and serve at once.

Note: Chili paste and hot bean paste are fiery Chinese condiments. Both contain chilies, salt, and garlic; the latter contains soy beans as well. I've made them optional; by now you've probably gathered I love fiery food. Both are available at Asian markets and in the ethnic foods sections of most supermarkets.

Serves 4

393 CALORIES PER SERVING; 21 G PROTEIN; 8 G FAT; 1 G SATURATED FAT; 59 G CARBOHYDRATE; 370 MG SODIUM; 91 MG CHOLESTEROL

MEE GORING—MUSLIM-STYLE NOODLES WITH LAMB

Singapore may well be the world's noodle capital. The residents of this tiny nation eat noodles for breakfast, lunch, dinner, midnight snack, and at just about any time in between. Mee goring *is a Muslim specialty of Indonesian origin, a popular dish at Newton Circus and Singapore's other hawker centers. Chicken or tofu can be substituted for the lamb.*

8 ounces pre-steamed Chinese egg noodles (see Note on page 157) or dried wheat noodles

FOR THE SAUCE:

¼ cup ketchup

¼ cup Singaporean or Thai chili sauce (see Note)

2 tablespoons soy sauce

1 tablespoon chili paste (optional—see Note)

2 teaspoons sugar

salt and freshly ground black pepper to taste

1 tablespoon canola oil

3 garlic cloves, minced

1 onion, thinly sliced

8 ounces lean lamb, very finely chopped or minced

2 cups thinly sliced nappa (Chinese cabbage) or Savoy or green cabbage

2 cups snow peas, strings and stems removed

2 cups mung bean sprouts

1 cucumber, peeled, seeded, and cut into fine dice

¼ cup cilantro leaves or chopped scallion greens

1. Cook the noodles in 4 quarts of boiling water until tender, 6 to 8 minutes for fresh or pre-steamed noodles, 8 minutes for dried noodles. Drain the noodles in a colander, rinse with cold water until cool, and drain again.

2. Combine the ingredients for the sauce in a small bowl and whisk until smooth.

3. Heat a large wok (preferably non-stick) over a high flame and swirl in the oil. Add the garlic and onion and stir-fry until just beginning to brown, about 1 minute. Add the lamb, cabbage, and snow peas and stir-fry until the lamb is cooked, about 2 minutes. Add the noodles, bean sprouts, and sauce and stir-fry until the noodles are thoroughly heated, 2 to 3 minutes. Correct the seasoning, adding chili sauce or soy sauce. The mixture should be highly seasoned. Sprinkle the noodles with the diced cucumber and cilantro and serve at once.

Note: Chili sauce is a relatively mild hot sauce that tastes a little like spicy ketchup. Chili paste is a devilishly hot condiment made with puréed red chilies, vinegar, garlic, and salt. A Singaporean would use the Indonesian version: sambal ulek. You can also use Chinese chili garlic sauce or Vietnamese hot sauce.

Serves 4

219 CALORIES PER SERVING; 15 G PROTEIN; 6 G FAT; 1 G SATURATED FAT; 28 G CARBOHYDRATE; 913 MG SODIUM; 29 MG CHOLESTEROL

BASIC RED SAUCE WITH BASIL

Here's a good, basic all-purpose red sauce—the sort consumed by the gallon by pasta lovers from Siena to Seattle. Serve it over spaghetti, linguini, and other smooth noodles or with lasagna or baked stuffed shells. For the best results, use canned plum tomatoes from Italy.

2 tablespoons extra-virgin olive oil

1 onion, minced (about 1 cup)

3 garlic cloves, minced

1 stalk celery, minced

¼ green bell pepper, minced

2 tablespoons tomato paste

1 28-ounce can imported peeled plum tomatoes

1½ teaspoons dried oregano

1 tablespoon balsamic vinegar

1 to 2 teaspoons sugar or honey (optional)

salt and freshly ground black pepper

12 to 16 fresh basil leaves, thinly slivered (optional)

1. Heat the olive oil in a large heavy saucepan. Add the onion, garlic, celery, and bell pepper and cook over medium heat until lightly browned, 6 to 8 minutes. Add the tomato paste after 4 minutes and cook it with the vegetables. Meanwhile, purée the tomatoes with their juices in a food processor or put them through a vegetable mill.

2. Stir the tomatoes with their juices, oregano, balsamic vinegar, sugar, if using, and salt and pepper into the vegetable mixture. Simmer the sauce, uncovered, over medium heat until thick, and flavorful, about 10 to 15 minutes, stirring often. Stir in the basil, if using, and cook for 1 minute. Correct the seasoning, adding salt or sugar to taste.

Note: Refrigerated, the sauce will keep for 4 or 5 days. To put it up for future use, spoon the boiling sauce into canning jars that have been sterilized in boiling water for 10 minutes. Place sterile lids on top and screw on the caps. Invert the jars for 10 minutes (this sterilizes the lids), then reinvert.

Makes about 4 cups. Serving is ½ to 1 cup

74 CALORIES PER SERVING;* 1 G PROTEIN; 5 G FAT; 1 G SATURATED FAT; 6 G CARBOHYDRATE; 153 MG SODIUM; 0 MG CHOLESTEROL

Analysis is based on ½ cup serving.

Big Flavor Tomato Sauce and Enlightened Pesto

FRESH (UNCOOKED) TOMATO SAUCE

Here's a fresh uncooked tomato sauce for dishes and occasions when you simply don't feel like cooking. The sauce can literally be made in a matter of minutes. It's delicious with frittatas, sformati (savory custards), and grilled seafood. For the best results, use tomatoes so ripe and juicy, they would go splat if you dropped them.

2 large, juicy, red ripe tomatoes (about 1¼ pounds), quartered (reserve juices)

1 clove garlic, minced

8 fresh basil leaves, thinly slivered

4 fresh oregano leaves, or ¼ teaspoon dried

1½ tablespoons extra-virgin olive oil

1 tablespoon balsamic vinegar

salt and freshly ground black pepper

Place all the ingredients in a blender or food processor and grind to a coarse or smooth purée. Correct the seasoning, adding salt or vinegar to taste.

Makes 2 cups, enough to serve 4 to 6

83 CALORIES PER SERVING;* 1 G PROTEIN; 6 G FAT; 0.7 G SATURATED FAT; 8 G CARBOHYDRATE; 14 MG SODIUM; 0 MG CHOLESTEROL

Analysis is based on 4 servings.

BIG FLAVOR TOMATO SAUCE

Here's a robust, rib-sticking tomato sauce for pasta that demands more substance. I prefer to use fresh tomatoes, but only when they're squishily ripe and in season. Otherwise, use good imported canned tomatoes. A recipe for homemade dried tomatoes can be found in my book High-Flavor, Low-Fat Vegetarian Cooking.

4 dried tomatoes

1 cup warm Vegetable Stock or Chicken Stock (see pages 382, 379) or tomato juice

1½ tablespoons extra-virgin olive oil

1 medium onion, finely chopped (about 1 cup)

1 carrot, finely chopped

2 stalks celery, finely chopped

5 garlic cloves, minced

2 tablespoons tomato paste

4 large ripe tomatoes (about 2½ pounds), peeled, seeded, and finely chopped, with juices

1 tablespoon balsamic vinegar

2 teaspoons sugar or honey, or to taste

salt, freshly ground black pepper, and a pinch of cayenne pepper

1 tablespoon capers, drained

2 tablespoons chopped pitted black olives

2 anchovy fillets, finely chopped (optional)

¼ cup flat-leaf parsley, washed, stemmed, and finely chopped

1. Soak the dried tomatoes in the stock for 20 minutes, or until soft. Finely chop or sliver the dried tomatoes and return them to the stock. Set aside.

2. Heat the oil in a large saucepan. Cook the onion, carrot, celery, and garlic over medium heat until just beginning to brown, about 8 minutes. Add the tomato paste after 5 minutes and cook it with the vegetables.

3. Stir in the chopped tomatoes, stock with dried tomatoes, vinegar, sugar or honey, salt, pepper, and cayenne. Gently simmer the sauce until thick and very flavorful, 5 to 10 minutes, stirring as needed. Stir in the capers, olives, anchovies, and parsley and simmer for 2 minutes. Correct the seasoning, adding salt, vinegar, or sugar to taste. Refrigerated, the sauce will keep for 4 or 5 days.

Makes about 5 cups. Serving is ½ to 1 cup

85 CALORIES PER SERVING;* 2 G PROTEIN; 4 G FAT; 0.5 G SATURATED FAT; 12 G CARBOHYDRATE; 179 MG SODIUM; 0 MG CHOLESTEROL

Analysis is based on ½ cup serving.

SMOOTH TOMATO SAUCE
(SUGO DI POMODORO)

Sugo di pomodoro (literally, "tomato juice") is the simplest of all Italian tomato sauces, a smooth, light, velvety sauce perfect for spooning over spaghetti, gnocchi, and other simple pastas. What's remarkable about this recipe is that it is virtually fat-free. Traditionally, the onion and garlic would be sautéed in a generous amount of olive oil. Here they're roasted in a hot oven. But if your fat budget allows it, add one or two tablespoons of extra-virgin olive oil at the end for extra flavor.

1 small onion, peeled and quartered

3 cloves garlic, in their skins

½ teaspoon extra-virgin olive oil, plus (optional) 1 to 2 tablespoons for adding at end

salt and freshly ground black pepper

1 28-ounce can imported peeled plum tomatoes, with their juices

6 basil leaves, thinly slivered, or ½ teaspoon dried

½ teaspoon sugar (optional)

1. Preheat the oven to 400°F. Toss or brush the onion and garlic with ½ teaspoon olive oil and season with salt and pepper. Roast the onion in a roasting pan for 10 minutes. Add the garlic and continue roasting until both onion and garlic are soft and golden-brown, an additional 10 to 15 minutes. Turn once or twice to ensure even roasting.

2. Grind the onion, garlic, and tomatoes with their juices through a vegetable mill or purée in a food processor or blender until smooth. Strain the mixture through a strainer or sieve back into the saucepan. (Straining is not necessary if you use a vegetable mill.)

3. Add the basil and sugar (if using), and simmer the sauce, uncovered, over medium heat, stirring occasionally, until it is well flavored and slightly thickened, 4 to 6 minutes. Correct the seasoning, adding salt and pepper to taste. If using additional oil, add it 1 minute before you remove the sauce from the heat.

Makes 3½ cups, enough to serve 8 to 10

26 CALORIES PER SERVING;* 1 G PROTEIN; 0.3 G FAT; 0 G SATURATED FAT; 6 G CARBOHYDRATE; 162 MG SODIUM; 0 MG CHOLESTEROL

Analysis is based on 8 servings.

TURKEY BOLOGNESE SAUCE

Here's a rich, meaty red sauce that contains only a fraction of the fat found in a traditional bolognese. The secret is to use ground turkey and prosciutto instead of sausage and pork. If you buy the turkey preground, make sure it's freshly ground lean turkey breast. I've seen packaged ground turkey that contains as much fat as pork sausage! If you're in doubt, buy turkey breast and grind it yourself. For best results, use imported plum tomatoes. **Note:** *A food processor works well for mincing the prosciutto and chopping the canned tomatoes.*

1 tablespoon olive oil

1 medium onion, finely chopped

3 garlic cloves, finely chopped

2 stalks celery, finely chopped

1 carrot, finely chopped

½ pound lean ground turkey breast

1 ounce prosciutto, minced

3 tablespoons tomato paste

¼ cup madeira

1 28-ounce can peeled tomatoes, finely chopped, with juices

1 tablespoon balsamic vinegar

1 teaspoon dried oregano

salt and freshly ground black pepper

3 tablespoons chopped fresh basil or flat-leaf parsley

BOLOGNESE MEAT SAUCE
(RAGÙ)

This rich, meaty sauce is one of the glories of Bolognese cooking. The traditional version would contain butter, cream, liver, and other fat-laden ingredients.

My low-fat version uses lean cuts of veal, pork, and/or turkey, which I chop at home to make sure they're completely devoid of fat. (For the richest flavor, use 4 ounces of each type of meat.) In place of the traditional cream, I enrich this sauce, too, with a thoroughly non-Italian ingredient, evaporated skim milk. I like the way the slight sweetness of this product cuts the acidity of the tomatoes. The easiest way to chop the tomatoes is in a food processor.

1 tablespoon extra-virgin olive oil

1 medium onion, finely chopped

2 stalks celery, finely chopped

2 small or 1 large carrot, finely chopped

12 ounces lean veal, pork, and/or turkey, minced with a cleaver or in the food processor

1 ounce prosciutto, minced

1 tablespoon tomato paste

1 cup dry white wine

1 cup evaporated skim milk

1 28-ounce can imported peeled plum tomatoes, with their juices, finely chopped

3 tablespoons finely chopped flat-leaf parsley

2 fresh basil leaves, or ½ teaspoon dried

1 bay leaf

salt and freshly ground black pepper

1 cup Chicken Stock (page 379) or veal stock (optional)

a little freshly grated nutmeg

1. Heat the olive oil in a large, heavy saucepan (preferably nonstick). Add the onion, celery, and carrot and cook over medium heat until lightly browned, about 5 minutes.

2. Stir in the meat and prosciutto and cook until crumbly and browned, 5 to 10 minutes, breaking the meat apart with the edge of a metal spatula or with a wooden spoon. Add the tomato paste after 4 minutes. Add the wine and bring to a boil. Reduce the heat and simmer the sauce until the wine is completely absorbed, about 5 minutes. Add ½ cup of the evaporated skim milk and simmer until completely absorbed, about 5 minutes.

3. Stir in the chopped tomatoes with their juices and the parsley, basil leaves, bay leaf, salt, and pepper. Reduce the heat and gently simmer the sauce until it is well reduced and richly flavored, 30 to 40 minutes. If the sauce becomes too thick, add a little chicken stock or water. Stir in the remaining ½ cup of evaporated skim milk and continue simmering the sauce until the milk is absorbed and reduced. Correct the seasoning, adding salt and pepper to taste. Add a hint, just a hint of freshly grated nutmeg. Discard the bay leaf before serving.

Makes 4 cups, enough to serve 6 to 8 people

226 CALORIES PER SERVING;* 20 G PROTEIN; 6 G FAT; 2 G SATURATED FAT; 17 G CARBOHYDRATE; 437 MG SODIUM; 55 MG CHOLESTEROL

Analysis is based on 6 servings.

1. Heat the olive oil in a large heavy saucepan (preferably nonstick). Add the onion, garlic, celery, and carrot and cook over medium heat until lightly browned, about 5 minutes.

2. Stir in the turkey and prosciutto and cook until the turkey is crumbly and nicely browned, 5 to 10 minutes, stirring and breaking up the meat with the edge of a wooden spoon. Add the tomato paste after 4 minutes. Add the madeira when the turkey is browned and bring to a boil.

3. Stir in the chopped tomatoes with juices, vinegar, oregano, and salt and pepper and simmer the sauce until richly flavored, about 10 minutes. Stir in the basil or parsley and cook for 1 minute. Correct the seasoning, adding salt, pepper, or vinegar as needed. Refrigerated, this sauce will keep for 3 to 4 days.

Makes 4 cups. Serving is ½ to 1 cup

119 CALORIES PER SERVING;* 8 G PROTEIN; 6 G FAT; 1 G SATURATED FAT; 8 G CARBOHYDRATE; 246 MG SODIUM; 23 MG CHOLESTEROL

Analysis is based on ½ cup serving.

PARMESAN CHEESE SAUCE

Cheese isn't normally an ingredient one associates with high-flavor, low-fat cooking. But real Parmigiano-Reggiano has so much flavor (thanks to the lengthy aging) that just a little will give you a satisfying cheese flavor. Another plus: Parmigiano-Reggiano is made with part-skim milk.

1 recipe reduced-fat béchamel (page 275)

6 to 8 tablespoons freshly grated Parmigiano-Reggiano cheese

1 to 2 teaspoons mustard (nonsweetened or Dijon-style)

Prepare the béchamel sauce. Whisk all but 1 tablespoon cheese into the sauce. Whisk the mustard in. Just before serving, sprinkle the remaining cheese over the sauce. That way, the first taste that hits your tongue will be cheese, and it will trick your mouth into thinking there's more cheese in the sauce than there really is.

Makes 2 cups, enough to serve 8

70 CALORIES PER SERVING; 5 G PROTEIN;
2 G FAT; 1.7 G SATURATED FAT;
6 G CARBOHYDRATE; 130 MG SODIUM;
9 MG CHOLESTEROL

ENLIGHTENED PESTO

Like most Americans who came of culinary age in the 1970s, I cut my teeth on pesto. I remember it as a thick, garlicky paste, rich with cheese and chunky with pine nuts. My first taste of pesto in its birthplace, Genoa, came as a shock. It was a smooth, thin, emerald-colored elixir. It was much lighter than the North American version—made with very little cheese and no pine nuts. Traditionally, the ingredients for pesto were pounded to a smooth paste in a marble mortar and pestle.
Nothing produces a smoother, more mellow-tasting pesto than this method. (Realizing this, restaurateurs in northern Italy have devised a mechanized version of a mortar and pestle: a rotating drum with a heavy marble tumbler to crush the basil leaves.) But delicious results can be obtained by puréeing the ingredients in a blender. To further lighten the pesto, I've substituted broth for some of the olive oil.

4 cloves garlic, peeled, trimmed, and sliced

½ teaspoon salt, or to taste

1 large or 2 medium bunches fresh basil, washed, stemmed, and blotted dry (about 4 cups leaves)

2 tablespoons freshly grated Parmigiano-Reggiano cheese

2 tablespoons extra-virgin olive oil

3 to 4 tablespoons Basic Vegetable Stock (page 382) or Chicken Stock (page 379)

½ teaspoon freshly ground black pepper, or to taste

With a mortar and pestle, pound the garlic and salt to a smooth paste. Add the basil leaves and pound to a smooth paste. Pound in the cheese. Work in the olive oil, stock, and pepper, stirring the pestle in a circular motion. The pesto can also be made in a blender. Correct the seasoning, adding salt and pepper to taste.

Makes ¾ to 1 cup, enough to serve 4

88 CALORIES PER SERVING; 3 G PROTEIN; 8 G FAT; 2 G SATURATED FAT; 3 G CARBOHYDRATE; 196 MG SODIUM; 2 MG CHOLESTEROL

FISH

MESQUITE-GRILLED TUNA WITH FLAME-CHARRED TOMATO SALSA

*If you like smoke and fire, you'll love this simple grilled tuna dish from the north of Mexico.
The mesquite gives the fish a heady smoke flavor—a flavor reinforced by the northern Mexico–style fire-charred tomato salsa.
Chiles de árbol are long, slender, fiery, dried red chilies.*

6 chiles de árbol, stemmed

1½ pounds fresh tuna, cut into 4 (½-inch-thick) steaks

2 cloves garlic, minced

1 teaspoon salt

½ teaspoon black pepper

2 tablespoons chopped cilantro, plus a few sprigs for garnish

¼ cup fresh lime juice

FOR THE FLAME-CHARRED SALSA:

2 large ripe red tomatoes

½ small white onion, cut in half lengthwise

1 clove garlic, peeled

¼ cup coarsely chopped cilantro

1 to 2 tablespoons fresh lime juice

salt and black pepper

1 teaspoon oil for the grill grate

warm flour tortillas for serving

Mesquite wood chunks for building your fire, or 1½ cups mesquite chips to toss on the coals

1. Place the chiles de árbol in a small bowl with warm water to cover. Let soak until they are soft and pliable, about 30 minutes.

2. Rinse the tuna and blot dry. With a pestle in a mortar or in a small bowl, mash together the garlic, salt, pepper, and chopped cilantro. Coarsely chop two of the soaked chiles de árbol and add them to the garlic mixture with the lime juice. Arrange the tuna steaks in a baking dish just large enough to hold them, and pour the marinade over the fish. Marinate in the refrigerator for 20 minutes, turning once.

3. If you are using mesquite chunks, build a brisk fire. If you're using a charcoal or gas grill, preheat to high. Toss ½ cup of the mesquite chips on the coals.

4. To make the salsa, grill the tomatoes until the skins are dark and blistered, 8 to 10 minutes, turning with tongs. Thread the onion and garlic onto a skewer and grill until lightly browned, 4 minutes per side. Transfer the tomatoes, onion, and garlic to a plate and let cool. Scrape any really burnt bits off the tomatoes. Drain the remaining chiles de árbol and tear them into pieces. (For a milder salsa, discard the seeds.) Combine the chilies, tomatoes, onion, garlic, cilantro, and lime juice in a blender and purée until smooth. Add salt, pepper, and lime juice to taste; the salsa should be highly seasoned.

5. Oil the grill grate. Toss the remaining 1 cup of mesquite chips (if using) on the charcoal or in the smoker box of a gas grill. Grill the tuna until it's cooked to taste: about 3 minutes per side for medium-rare. (That's how I like my tuna.) Warm the tortillas on the grill. (You'll need about 20 seconds per side.) Serve the tuna with the salsa and tortillas.

Note: Grill shops and hardware stores sell chunks of mesquite wood that you can light and use like charcoal. (Light them in a chimney starter, just as you would charcoal.) If you can't find these, use mesquite chips, which are available at gourmet shops and cookware shops. I suppose you could use oak or hickory, but the flavor wouldn't be quite the same.

Serves 4

289 CALORIES PER SERVING; 41 G PROTEIN; 9 G FAT; 2 G SATURATED FAT; 9 G CARBOHYDRATE; 609 MG SODIUM; 64 MG CHOLESTEROL

BASIL-GRILLED TUNA WITH BITTER GREENS

This quick, attractive dish combines the fish and salad course. I've called for the most readily available bitter greens: arugula, radicchio, and Belgian endive. You could certainly augment the blend with other greens.

1½ pounds fresh tuna, cut into ½-inch-thick steaks

2 cloves garlic, peeled

12 fresh basil leaves

salt

4 tablespoons fresh lemon juice, plus 1 lemon cut in slices or wedges for garnish

1½ tablespoons extra-virgin olive oil

freshly ground black pepper

1 bunch arugula, washed and stemmed

1 small bunch radicchio, broken into leaves

2 Belgian endives, broken into leaves

1. Trim any bloody spots or sinews off the tuna. Arrange the fish steaks in a glass baking dish. In a mortar and pestle, combine the garlic, basil, and salt and pound to a smooth paste. Work in 3 tablespoons lemon juice, ½ tablespoon olive oil, and the pepper. (If you don't have a mortar and pestle, purée the ingredients for the marinade in a blender or even finely chop them and stir to mix.) Pour the mixture over the fish and marinate for 20 to 30 minutes, turning the tuna steaks two or three times.

2. Slice all the bitter greens crosswise into ¼-inch strips. Place the greens in a bowl with the remaining 1 tablespoon olive oil, 1 tablespoon lemon juice, and salt and pepper, but do not toss. Preheat the grill to high.

3. Grill the tuna steaks until cooked to taste, about 1 minute per side for medium-rare, basting with marinade. (Alternatively, the fish can be cooked in a ridged skillet or under the broiler.) Just before serving, toss the bitter greens with the dressing, adding salt and pepper to taste. Arrange the tuna on a platter or plates and top with the bitter greens. Garnish with lemon slices or wedges and serve at once.

Serves 4

246 CALORIES PER SERVING; 40 G PROTEIN; 7 G FAT; 1 G SATURATED FAT; 4 G CARBOHYDRATE; 70 MG SODIUM; 74 MG CHOLESTEROL

SESAME SEARED TUNA

With an investment of a few minutes, you get a dish that looks fabulous and tastes even better. This recipe is a specialty of Mark's Place in North Miami, Florida, where chef Mark Militello serves the tuna blood-rare in the center, like sushi. (Don't try this unless you have access to impeccably fresh tuna.) Japanese pickled ginger would make an appropriate garnish.

- 4 5–6-ounce tuna steaks
- 2 teaspoons sesame oil
- salt and freshly ground black pepper
- 3 tablespoons white sesame seeds, lightly toasted
- 3 tablespoons black sesame seeds
- 4 teaspoons wasabi (or to taste)
- 2 teaspoons warm water
- small carafe soy sauce

Preheat the oven to 400°F. Brush the tuna steaks on all sides with the sesame oil and season with salt and pepper. Combine the white and black sesame seeds in a shallow bowl. Dip each steak in sesame seeds, thickly encrusting the top, bottom, and sides. Transfer the tuna to a nonstick frying pan or roasting pan. Bake for 20 minutes, or until cooked to taste. (To test for doneness, press the steaks with your finger. At medium-rare, they'll yield gently.)

Combine the wasabi and warm water in a small bowl and stir to form a thick paste. Let stand for 5 minutes. Wet your fingers and shape the paste into 4 balls.

To serve, transfer the tuna to plates. (For a more elaborate presentation, cut the steaks into ¼-inch slices and fan them out across the plate.) Garnish each with a ball of wasabi. Provide each guest with a small ramekin or saucer, and invite everyone to pour a little soy sauce into the ramekin and stir in wasabi to taste. Dip each bite of tuna into the wasabi soy sauce before eating.

Note: Wasabi is very hot. Use it sparingly the first time you try it.

Serves 4

318 CALORIES PER SERVING; 39 G PROTEIN; 16 G FAT; 2 G CARBOHYDRATE; 377 MG SODIUM; 59 MG CHOLESTEROL

TUNA WITH SICILIAN MINTED TOMATO SAUCE

This is one of the most popular Sicilian ways of preparing tuna. Traditionally, it would be made with a tuna "roast" (a fist-thick steak weighing a couple of pounds). But 1-inch tuna steaks, which are more readily available in the United States, work well, too. Mint is popular in Sicily and Apulia, perhaps a legacy of the Moors. Of course you'll try to use fresh mint for this recipe. But lacking fresh mint, I've raided mint tea bags and still produced fine results.

- 1½ pounds fresh tuna in 1 large, thick (2-inch) chunk, or 2 to 4 steaks, each 1 inch thick

FOR THE STUFFING:

- ⅓ cup washed, stemmed, finely chopped fresh mint leaves, or 4 teaspoons dried mint
- 3 cloves garlic, minced
- salt and freshly ground black pepper

FOR THE SAUCE:

- 1 tablespoon extra-virgin olive oil
- 1 large onion, finely chopped
- ¼ to ½ teaspoon hot pepper flakes (optional)
- 2 tablespoons tomato paste
- ½ cup dry white wine
- 1 28-ounce can imported peeled plum tomatoes, with their juices, puréed in a food processor or put through a vegetable mill
- ½ teaspoon ground coriander, or to taste
- ½ teaspoon sugar (optional)

1. Using the tip of a paring knife, make ½-inch-deep holes in the tuna on both sides, spaced 1 inch apart. Combine half the mint with the garlic, salt, and pepper. Mash these ingredients together in a bowl with the back of a spoon to form a coarse paste. Stuff this paste into the holes you've made in the tuna. Season the outside of the tuna with salt and pepper.

2. Prepare the sauce: Heat the olive oil in a large nonstick frying pan. Add the onion and pepper flakes (if using) and cook over medium heat until the onion is soft and translucent but not brown. Add the tomato paste and sauté for 2 minutes. Add the wine and bring to a boil, stirring to dissolve the tomato paste. Add the puréed tomatoes, the coriander, the sugar (if using), the remaining 2½ tablespoons fresh mint, and a little salt and pepper. Simmer the sauce until thickened and richly flavored, about 10 minutes. Correct the seasoning, adding salt, sugar, or mint to taste.

3. Place the tuna in the pan, spooning the sauce over it. There are two ways to cook the fish. You can gently simmer it on top of the stove over medium-low heat, turning once with a large spatula. In this case, you'll need about 10 to 15 minutes per side. Or you can bake the tuna under the sauce in a preheated 350°F. oven for about 30 minutes. Unlike Asian and many North American preparations of tuna, Sicilian-style tuna is served fully cooked, not rare in the center. Serve at once with the sauce spooned over the fish.

Serves 4

299 CALORIES PER SERVING; 41 G PROTEIN; 4 G FAT; 1 G SATURATED FAT; 16 G CARBOHYDRATE; 147 MG SODIUM; 74 MG CHOLESTEROL

SALMON WITH YOGURT-TAHINI SAUCE

This recipe, loosely inspired by a Lebanese sauce called tara-toor, *calls for the fish to be baked, but it can also be grilled. (If you grill it, spread the sauce on the fish after you've turned it.) Tahini (sesame paste) can be found at Middle Eastern markets, natural food stores, and most supermarkets.*

- **4 6–8-ounce salmon fillets or steaks**
- **salt and freshly ground black pepper**
- **1 small clove garlic, minced (½ teaspoon)**
- **3 tablespoons tahini**
- **3 tablespoons nonfat yogurt**
- **3 tablespoons fresh lemon juice**
- **2 teaspoons soy sauce**
- **2 tablespoons finely chopped fresh chives or scallion greens, for garnish**
- **½ cup pomegranate seeds, for garnish (optional)**

WOK SMOKED SALMON

Smoking salmon is easy. I should know; I do it every weekend for Sunday brunch. This recipe produces a kipper-style salmon to eat with bagels or serve on toast points. To make smoked salmon pâté, purée leftovers with a little low-fat cream cheese.

- **1 1-pound salmon fillet**
- **5 tablespoons brown sugar, honey, molasses, or maple syrup**
- **2½ tablespoons kosher or sea salt**
- **1 teaspoon freshly ground white pepper**
- **2 tablespoons oak, alder, or other hardwood sawdust or small wood chips**
- **¼ teaspoon oil**

Skin the salmon fillet (if necessary) and remove any bones, using needlenose pliers or tweezers. Combine the brown sugar, salt, and white pepper in a shallow bowl

and whisk to mix. Marinate the salmon in this mixture for 3 to 4 hours, turning several times. Drain the salmon on a rack, wiping off any crystallized salt with a moist paper towel, and let dry for 30 minutes.

Line a wok with foil and place the sawdust at the bottom. Place a circular wire rack in the wok 2 inches above the sawdust. Oil the rack and place the salmon, exterior side down, on top.

Place the wok over high heat. When the wood begins to smoke, reduce the heat to medium and tightly cover the wok. Smoke the fish for 20 to 30 minutes, or until cooked. (A skewer inserted in the center will come out hot to the touch.) Do not overcook, or the salmon will be dry.

Transfer the fish to a wire rack to cool. Wrap it in foil and refrigerate overnight.

Serves 4

117 CALORIES PER SERVING; 16 G PROTEIN; 4 G FAT; 3 G CARBOHYDRATE; 960 MG SODIUM; 20 MG CHOLESTEROL

Preheat the oven to 400°F. If using salmon fillets, run your fingers over the fish, feeling for bones. Remove any you find with needlenose pliers. If using salmon steaks, leave the bones intact—they'll help hold the fish together. Season the fish with salt and pepper, and arrange it in a lightly oiled baking dish just large enough to hold it.

Combine the garlic, tahini, and yogurt in a small bowl and whisk until smooth. Whisk in the lemon juice, soy sauce, salt, and pepper. Spoon the sauce over the fish.

Bake the salmon for 20 minutes, or until a skewer inserted in the center comes out very hot to the touch. (Another test for doneness is to press the fish with your finger. When cooked, it will break into flakes.) Sprinkle the fish with chives and pomegranate seeds (if using), and serve at once.

Serves 4

234 CALORIES PER SERVING; 27 G PROTEIN; 12 G FAT; 5 G CARBOHYDRATE; 1,232 MG SODIUM; 31 MG CHOLESTEROL

BAKED SALMON WITH MINTED SALSA VERDE

Salmon isn't particularly traditional or even popular in Mexico, but many Mexican preparations lend themselves to this dark, rich, widely available fish. Consider the following recipe— salmon baked under a blanket of mint-flavored salsa verde. I love the contrast of colors and flavors in this recipe: the bright green of the salsa against the electric pink of the salmon, and the way the piquancy of the salsa cuts the richness of the fish.

FOR THE MINTED SALSA VERDE:

8 to 10 tomatillos (8 ounces), husked

1 small onion, peeled and quartered

3 cloves garlic

1 poblano chili, stems, seeds, and veins removed

1 to 2 serrano chilies, stems and seeds removed (for a hotter salsa, leave in the seeds)

4 scallions, trimmed, white part cut into 1-inch pieces, green part finely chopped

3 tablespoons chopped fresh spearmint or peppermint, plus 4 whole sprigs

3 tablespoons chopped fresh cilantro

3 tablespoons chopped fresh flat-leaf parsley

½ teaspoon ground cumin

¼ teaspoon sugar

1 tablespoon olive oil

salt and freshly ground black pepper

4 (6-ounce) salmon steaks or fillets

spray oil

¼ cup no-fat sour cream

1. To prepare the salsa verde, bring 3 cups of water to a boil in a large saucepan. Add the tomatillos, half the onion, and the garlic, chilies, and scallion whites. Simmer until tender, about 5 minutes. Remove the pan from the heat.

2. With a slotted spoon, transfer the tomatillos, onion, garlic, chilies, and scallion whites to a blender, reserving the cooking liquid. Add the scallion greens, chopped mint, cilantro, parsley, cumin, sugar, and 1 cup of the cooking liquid. Purée until smooth. The salsa should be thick but pourable; add the reserved cooking liquid as needed.

3. Finely chop the remaining onion. Heat the oil in a large saucepan. Add the onion and cook over medium heat until soft but not brown, about 3 minutes. Add the salsa verde and boil until it's richly flavored, 3 to 5 minutes, stirring with a wooden spoon. Add salt and pepper to taste.

4. Preheat the oven to 400°F.

5. Spray with oil an attractive baking dish just large enough to hold the fish. Spoon one third of the salsa verde on the bottom. Arrange the salmon on top. Spoon the remaining salsa verde over the fish. Place a dollop of sour cream in the center of each piece of fish. Bake the salmon until it is cooked and the salsa verde is bubbling, 12 to 15 minutes. (To test for doneness, insert a skewer in the center of a piece of fish: It will come out very hot to the touch when the fish is cooked.) Garnish each portion of fish with a mint sprig and serve at once.

Serves 4

397 CALORIES PER SERVING; 37 G PROTEIN; 22 G FAT; 5 G SATURATED FAT; 12 G CARBOHYDRATE; 96 MG SODIUM; 112 MG CHOLESTEROL

SNAPPER IN THE STYLE OF LIVORNO WITH CAPERS, OLIVES, AND TOMATOES

Livorno (Leghorn in English) is a port city on the Tuscan coast famed for its seafood. While precise definitions of Livornese-style fish vary, the preparation generally includes a colorful assortment of capers, tomatoes, and black olives. There are lots of possibilities for fish. The locals would use branzino (sea bass). Here in Florida, we like snapper. But you could also use striped bass, sea bass, cod, grouper—almost any delicate white fish.

1½ pounds snapper fillets

salt and freshly ground black pepper

3 to 4 tablespoons all-purpose unbleached white flour

1½ tablespoons extra-virgin olive oil

1 small onion, thinly sliced

3 cloves garlic, thinly sliced

1 ripe tomato, peeled, seeded, and diced

12 black olives

2 tablespoons drained capers

3 tablespoons chopped flat-leaf parsley

1 cup dry white wine

1. Wash and dry the fish fillets. Run your fingers over the fillets, feeling for bones. Pull out any bones you find with tweezers or pliers. Season the fish with salt and pepper and dust with flour, shaking off the excess. I do this on a paper towel.

2. Heat half the oil in a nonstick frying pan over high heat. Add the fish fillets and quickly brown on both sides, about 1 minute per side. Transfer the fish to a plate. Add the remaining oil, the onion, and the garlic and cook over medium heat until the vegetables are soft but not brown, about 4 minutes. Add the tomato, olives, and capers and half the parsley and cook until most of the tomato juices boil away, about 3 minutes.

3. Return the fish to the pan, add the wine, and bring to a boil. Briskly simmer the fish until cooked, about 3 minutes per side. Most of the wine should evaporate and the sauce should thicken. If the fish cooks before the sauce thickens, transfer the fish to plates or a platter and boil down the sauce. Stir in the remaining parsley and correct the seasoning, adding salt and pepper to taste. Spoon the sauce over the fish and serve at once.

Note: To test for doneness, press the fish with your finger: it should flake easily. Another test is to insert a slender metal skewer into the thickest part of the fish. When the fish is ready, the skewer will be very hot to the touch.

Serves 4

310 CALORIES PER SERVING; 37 G PROTEIN; 12 G FAT; 2 G SATURATED FAT; 5 G CARBOHYDRATE; 298 MG SODIUM; 62 MG CHOLESTEROL

SNAPPER WITH MEDITERRANEAN VEGETABLE SAUTÉ

This colorful dish was inspired by one I enjoyed at the restaurant Robuchon in Paris, where chef Joël Robuchon dices the vegetables literally as fine as grains of sand. This version requires far less precision. The fish is browned with the skin on, which creates a crisp crust.

1½ tablespoons olive oil

1 clove garlic, minced (1 teaspoon)

1 red bell pepper, cored, seeded, and minced

1 yellow bell pepper, cored, seeded, and minced

1 small zucchini, cut in half lengthwise, seeded, and minced

1 small yellow squash, cut in half lengthwise, seeded, and minced

¼ teaspoon saffron threads, soaked in 3 tablespoons hot water

1 teaspoon chopped fresh thyme (or 1 teaspoon dried)

salt, freshly ground black pepper, and cayenne pepper

1½ pounds snapper fillets (skin left on)

½ cup flour (approximately)

GRILLED SNAPPER WITH AVOCADO SAUCE

You may not find this dish in traditional Mexican cookbooks, but the flavors of the smokily grilled fish served with a silken salsa of avocado, chilies, and fried garlic are as ancient as the country itself. I've called for snapper here, but you can really use any fish. For ease in turning the fish on the grill, cook it in a wire fish basket.

4 (6-ounce) boneless, skinless snapper fillets

salt and freshly ground black pepper

2 cloves garlic, minced

¼ cup fresh orange juice

¼ cup fresh grapefruit juice

FOR THE SALSA:

1 poblano chili

1 jalapeño chili

½ medium white onion, cut in half

5 cloves garlic (2 cloves peeled, 3 cloves thinly sliced)

1 tablespoon olive oil

1 small or ½ large avocado, peeled and seeded

3 tablespoons chopped cilantro, plus 4 sprigs for garnish

¼ teaspoon ground cumin

½ cup no-fat sour cream

½ cup water, fish broth, or bottled clam juice

1 tablespoon fresh lime juice, or to taste

spray oil

1. Season the fish fillets with the salt and pepper and sprinkle with the garlic. Arrange the fillets in a baking dish and pour the orange and grapefruit juice over them. Marinate for 1 hour, turning once or twice.

2. Meanwhile, prepare the salsa. Heat a comal or cast-iron skillet over a medium-high flame. Roast the chilies, onion, and the 2 peeled garlic cloves until nicely browned: 8 to 10 minutes for the poblano and onion; 4 to 6 minutes for the garlic and chilies. Transfer to a plate and let cool. Seed the chilies.

3. Heat the oil in a small skillet over medium heat. Fry the sliced garlic until it is lightly browned, 1 to 2 minutes. Do not let it burn. Drain the fried garlic in a colander.

4. Place the roasted chilies, onion, and garlic in a blender with the avocado, chopped cilantro, cumin, sour cream, water or fish broth, and lime juice. Purée until smooth, adding water as needed to obtain a thick but pourable sauce. Correct the seasoning, adding salt, pepper, and lime juice to taste. Add the fried garlic and pulse the blender just to mix.

5. Preheat the grill to high. Place the fish in an oiled fish basket. (Spray it with oil.) Grill the fish until it's cooked to taste, about 4 minutes per side. Arrange the fish fillets on plates or a platter and pour the salsa over them. Garnish with cilantro sprigs and serve at once.

Serves 4

249 CALORIES PER SERVING; 36 G PROTEIN; 7 G FAT; 1 G SATURATED FAT; 9 G CARBOHYDRATE; 118 MG SODIUM; 62 MG CHOLESTEROL

Heat ½ tablespoon oil in a nonstick frying pan. Add the garlic, peppers, zucchini, and yellow squash, and cook over high heat for 1 minute. Stir in the saffron, thyme, salt, pepper, and cayenne. Lower the heat to medium and cook the vegetables for 3 to 4 minutes, or until tender but not soft. Correct the seasoning, adding salt, pepper, and cayenne to taste. The mixture should be very flavorful.

Preheat the oven to 400°F. Cut the snapper into 4 pieces and season with salt and pepper. Dredge the pieces in flour, shaking off any excess. Heat the remaining 1 tablespoon oil in a nonstick frying pan with a metal handle. Add the fish, skin side down, and cook over medium heat for 3 to 4 minutes, or until the skin is very crisp. Turn the fish and place the pan in the oven. Bake for 10 to 15 minutes, or

until cooked. (When done, it will flake easily when pressed.)

To serve, transfer the fish, skin side up, to plates or a platter. Spoon the vegetable mixture around it and serve at once.

Serves 4

273 CALORIES PER SERVING; 37 G PROTEIN; 8 G FAT; 12 G CARBOHYDRATE; 16 MG SODIUM; 62 MG CHOLESTEROL

SWORDFISH BRAISED AND GLAZED WITH BALSAMIC VINEGAR

When I was growing up, few people had ever heard of balsamic vinegar. Today, we can't seem to cook without it! This sweet-sour condiment from the province of Emilia-Romagna has captured our culinary fancy, turning up in dishes all over the world. Not bad for an ingredient that, until recently, was made by hand in tiny batches in farmhouse attics and virtually unknown outside its birthplace, Modena. The following recipe is also delicious with salmon.

4 6-ounce pieces of swordfish steak
    (each about ¾-inch thick)

salt and freshly ground black pepper

3 tablespoons all-purpose unbleached white flour

1 tablespoon extra-virgin olive oil

3 to 4 tablespoons balsamic vinegar

3 tablespoons dry white wine

1 cup Fish Stock (page 381) or bottled clam broth

2 sprigs fresh rosemary, or 2 teaspoons dried

1 clove garlic, minced

2 tablespoons finely chopped flat-leaf parsley

1. Preheat the oven to 400°F. Season the fish steaks on both sides with salt and pepper. Dust the fish with flour, shaking off the excess. (I like to do this on a paper towel.)

2. Heat the olive oil in a large, nonstick frying pan. Lightly brown the swordfish steaks on both sides over high heat, 1 to 2 minutes per side. Add 3 tablespoons vinegar and the wine and bring to a boil. Add the fish stock, rosemary, and garlic and bring to a gentle simmer.

3. Place the pan in the oven and bake until the swordfish is cooked, 15 to 20 minutes. Alternatively, you can cook the fish on the stove, 4 to 5 minutes per side. (When the fish is cooked, it will flake easily when pressed with your finger. Another test is to insert a slender metal skewer into the thickest part of the fish. When the fish is ready, the skewer will be very hot to the touch.)

4. Transfer the fish to a platter or plates. Boil the pan juices until about ½ cup liquid remains. Correct the seasoning, adding salt and pepper to taste. If a more lively balsamic vinegar flavor is desired, add ½ to 1 tablespoon vinegar, but be sure to bring the sauce to a boil to mellow its sharpness. Strain or spoon the sauce over the fish. Sprinkle with the parsley and serve at once.

Serves 4

283 CALORIES PER SERVING; 35 G PROTEIN; 10 G FAT; 2 G SATURATED FAT; 8 G CARBOHYDRATE; 157 MG SODIUM; 67 MG CHOLESTEROL

SWORDFISH "FIG PICKERS"
(SICILIAN SWORDFISH ROULADES)

This dish, a specialty of Sicily, has a curious name and history. Beccafico (literally "fig picker") refers to a thrush or other tiny game bird. Throughout Italy, small roulades of meat or seafood are called beccafico on account of their resemblance to trussed, roasted game birds. The traditional fish for this recipe is fresh sardine—a quintessential Mediterranean fish that is almost impossible to find fresh in this country. For this reason, I call for another popular Sicilian fish—swordfish—but you could also use boneless fillets of snapper, mahi-mahi, or sole. (If using sole, you don't need to slice it on the diagonal.)

1½ pounds skinless swordfish (cut in a rather thick steak); or large boneless fillets of snapper, mahi-mahi, or sole; or fresh scaled and cleaned sardines (gutted and heads removed)

FOR THE STUFFING:

1½ tablespoons extra-virgin olive oil, plus a little oil or spray oil for the pan

1 medium onion, finely chopped

1 stalk celery, finely chopped (about 3 tablespoons)

2 tablespoons currants or chopped raisins

2 tablespoons toasted pine nuts

1 cup toasted bread crumbs

3 tablespoons minced flat-leaf parsley

½ teaspoon grated fresh lemon zest, plus 1 tablespoon fresh lemon juice, plus lemon wedges for serving

2 tablespoons Parmigiano-Reggiano cheese

salt and freshly ground black pepper

1. Cut the fish sharply on the diagonal into ¼-inch-thick slices. Each slice should be about 2 inches wide and 2½-inches long. You should have 20 to 24 slices in all. Place each piece of fish between 2 sheets of plastic wrap and gently flatten with the side of a cleaver. The new pieces should be about 2½- to 3-inches wide and 3½- to 4-inches long. (Don't worry if the pieces come out a little larger or smaller. The important thing is to obtain pieces of uniform size.)

2. Prepare the stuffing: Heat 1 tablespoon oil in a non-stick frying pan. Add the onion, celery, currants, and pine nuts and cook over medium heat until the onion is soft but not brown, about 4 minutes. Add the bread crumbs, parsley, lemon zest, and Parmesan and cook until toasted

and flavorful, about 5 minutes. Stir in salt and pepper to taste.

3. Preheat the oven to 400°F. Arrange one of the fish slices on the work surface, narrow edge toward you. Spread a spoonful of stuffing on top of the fish. Starting at the edge closest to you, roll it up to form a compact roll. Place the roll, seam side down, in an attractive, lightly oiled, 8 x 12 inch baking dish. Continue rolling and stuffing the fish slices until all are used up.

4. Drizzle the lemon juice and remaining ½ tablespoon oil over the roulades. Sprinkle any remaining stuffing on top. Season with salt and pepper. Bake the roulades until fish is cooked through, 15 to 20 minutes. (One way to test for doneness is to press a roulade with your finger. When cooked, it will break into flakes. Another test is to insert a metal skewer. When the roulades are cooked, the skewer will come out very hot to the touch.) Serve the roulades with lemon wedges for squeezing. If a sauce is desired, consider one of the tomato sauces on pages 160–162.

Note: If you're lucky enough to live in a city where fresh sardines are available, by all means use them. Bone them and spread the filling over the fish. Roll each sardine up widthwise (the long way), so that the tails stick up over the roulades.

Makes 20 to 24 rolls, enough to serve 6 as a first course, 4 as an entrée

279 CALORIES PER SERVING;* 27 G PROTEIN; 11 G FAT; 3 G SATURATED FAT; 17 G CARBOHYDRATE; 303 MG SODIUM; 96 MG CHOLESTEROL

Analysis is based on 6 servings as a first course.

Shark in Lemon Parsley Broth

GRILLED SWORDFISH WITH RED ONION "JAM"

Here's a contemporary Italian dish with a Californian twist. The "jam" is a sort of chutney—made by glazing sliced red onions in balsamic vinegar and honey.

FOR THE ONION JAM:

2 teaspoons extra-virgin olive oil

2 medium red onions, thinly sliced

⅔ cup balsamic vinegar

⅓ cup dry red wine

1 to 2 tablespoons honey

salt and freshly ground black pepper

1½ pounds swordfish, cut into ½-inch-thick steaks

2 teaspoons extra-virgin olive oil

1 tablespoon fresh lemon juice

4 sprigs flat-leaf parsley

1. Prepare the onion jam: Heat the 2 teaspoons oil in a nonstick skillet. Add the onions and cook over high heat for 2 minutes. Add the vinegar, wine, and honey and bring to a boil. Reduce the heat and gently simmer the onions until reduced to a jamlike consistency; the vinegar and wine should be completely absorbed. This will take 30 to 45 minutes. Correct the seasoning, adding honey for sweetness and salt and pepper to taste: the jam should be tart, a little sweet, and highly seasoned. The jam can be prepared several days ahead of time and stored in the refrigerator.

2. Brush the swordfish slices with the 2 teaspoons olive oil and season with salt and pepper. Arrange the fish on a plate and squeeze the lemon juice on top. Marinate the fish for 15 minutes. Preheat the grill to high.

3. Grill the swordfish until cooked, 2 to 3 minutes per side, turning each steak 45 degrees after 30 seconds of grilling to create an attractive crosshatch of grill marks. Transfer the steaks to plates or a platter and place a heaping spoonful of onion jam on top. Garnish each with a parsley sprig and serve at once.

Serves 4

348 CALORIES PER SERVING; 35 G PROTEIN; 11 G FAT; 2 G SATURATED FAT; 21 G CARBOHYDRATE; 175 MG SODIUM; 67 MG CHOLESTEROL

SHARK IN LEMON PARSLEY BROTH

This delicate stew takes its inspiration from Greek avgolemono, egg lemon soup. You can make it with any delicate white fish, from shark to cod to haddock. Serve with crusty Italian bread for dipping in the broth.

1½ pounds shark, cod, or haddock fillets

1½ teaspoons olive oil

3 cloves garlic, minced (1 tablespoon)

4 cups water

1 pound baby red potatoes, cut into 1-inch chunks

salt and freshly ground black pepper

½ cup finely chopped flat-leaf parsley

3–4 tablespoons freshly grated Parmigiano-Reggiano (or other Parmesan-style cheese)

2–3 tablespoons fresh lemon juice (or to taste)

Cut the shark into ¼-inch slices. (If using cod or haddock, cut into 2-inch pieces.)

Heat the oil in a large sauté pan. Cook the garlic over medium heat for 1 minute, or until soft but not brown. Add the water, potatoes, salt, and pepper. Bring to a boil, reduce the heat, and simmer, uncovered, for 6 to 8 minutes, or until almost tender.

Add the shark, parsley, and cheese, and simmer for 2 minutes, or until the fish is just cooked. (It should flake easily when pressed.) Remove the pan from the heat, stir in the lemon juice, and let the stew sit for 2 minutes. Correct the seasoning and ladle the fish and broth into bowls.

Serves 4

268 CALORIES PER SERVING; 32 G PROTEIN; 4 G FAT;
25 G CARBOHYDRATE; 147 MG SODIUM; 67 MG CHOLESTEROL

GRILLED SHARK AND PINEAPPLE IN THE STYLE OF TACOS AL PASTOR

The taco al pastor is one of Mexico's national snacks: thin slices of rotisseried pork served with sweet grilled pineapple on soft corn tortillas, with diced cabbage and onions for crunch. (A pastor is a shepherd and, by extension, someone from the Middle East. The taco al pastor is the Mexican version of Middle Eastern shwarma or Turkish donner kebab: The Arabic roots of this dish are obvious.) Here's a seafood taco al pastor made with shark that's been marinated with spices, chilies, and pineapple juice and grilled smokily over coals. We in the United States are just now discovering what Mexicans have known for centuries: that shark is a delectable, economical, low-fat seafood. You can also make this dish with tuna, snapper, grouper, or halibut.

2¼ pounds shark steaks

1 fresh pineapple

FOR THE SPICE MIX:

2 tablespoons pure chili powder (preferably quajillo chili powder)

1 teaspoon salt (or to taste)

1 teaspoon fresh black pepper

1 teaspoon ground cumin

1 teaspoon dried oregano

3 cloves garlic, minced

1 cup pineapple juice (reserved from cutting the pineapple)

2 cups finely shredded green cabbage

1 large white onion, finely chopped

1 bunch cilantro, washed, dried, and stemmed

1 batch of your favorite salsa (I like the Salsa Chipotle, page 7)

32 small corn tortillas (preferably fresh)

1. Cut the shark into ¼-inch-thick steaks. Peel the pineapple and cut widthwise into ½-inch slices. (Reserve any juice.) Combine the chili powder, salt, pepper, cumin, oregano, and garlic in a mixing bowl and blend well. Rub the shark slices with this mixture and place them in a nonreactive baking dish. Pour the pineapple juice over the shark and let marinate for 1 hour. Place the cabbage, onion, cilantro, and salsa in individual serving bowls.

2. Preheat the grill to high. Grill the shark and pineapple slices over high heat until the shark is cooked through and the pineapple is lightly browned. (This will take 2 to 3 minutes per side for the shark, 4 to 5 minutes per side for the pineapple.) Transfer the shark to a platter and cut it into slivers. Place in a serving bowl and keep warm. Sliver the pineapple and place it in a bowl. Warm the tortillas on the grill (10 to 20 seconds per side) or in the oven until they are soft and pliable, and place them in a cloth-lined basket.

3. To serve, have each guest place a spoonful of shark and pineapple on a tortilla. Sprinkle the shark and pineapple with cabbage, onion, cilantro, and salsa, then roll the tortillas into tubes or fold them in half. And pop in your mouth.

Serves 8

446 CALORIES PER SERVING; 34 G PROTEIN; 9 G FAT; 2 G SATURATED FAT; 62 G CARBOHYDRATE; 856 MG SODIUM; 65 MG CHOLESTEROL

POACHED STRIPED BASS WITH POBLANO CORN SALSA

I didn't catch her name, but she sure looked like she was in showbiz. We were flying to Mexico City and she was reading a book on low-fat cooking, so we got to chatting. It turned out she was a Mexican soap opera star, and she told me that one of the secrets to her trim figure was poaching her food instead of frying or sautéing it. A case in point: the following fish dish, which she poaches in an aromatic mixture of vegetables, chilies, and vinegar. My own contribution to this dish is the salsa, a colorful and spectacularly flavorful blend of fire-roasted corn and poblano chilies. If you live on the Eastern seaboard, you should make this dish with striped bass: Its soft flesh absorbs the flavors of the poaching liquid splendidly. Other possibilities include sea bass, salmon, and bluefish.

1½ pounds skinless striped bass, sea bass, or other fish fillets

FOR THE SALSA:

2 poblano chilies

2 ears of corn, husked

2 plum tomatoes

4 scallions

3 tablespoons chopped cilantro

3 tablespoons fresh lime juice

salt and freshly ground black pepper

FOR THE POACHING LIQUID:

4 cups water

2 tablespoons distilled white vinegar

1 medium white onion, thinly sliced

1 carrot, thinly sliced

1 tomato, thinly sliced

2 stalks celery, thinly sliced

2 cloves garlic, thinly sliced

2 serrano chilies, seeded and thinly sliced

1 (2-inch) piece poblano chili

2 sprigs cilantro

1 bay leaf

2 allspice berries

1. Run your fingers over the fish, feeling for bones. Pull out any you find with pliers or tweezers. Rinse the fish and blot it dry.

2. To prepare the salsa, preheat a grill to high. Cook the chilies, corn, tomatoes, and scallions until nicely browned on all sides, 2 to 3 minutes per side (8 to 12 minutes in all). Transfer to a plate and let cool.

3. Scrape any really burnt bits off the poblanos, then core, seed, and cut them into ¼-inch dice. (A little black is fine.) Transfer to a mixing bowl. Cut the kernels off the corn and add them to the bowl. Dice the tomatoes and scallions and add them to the bowl. Add the cilantro, lime juice, and salt and pepper to taste. Toss to mix. Set aside the salsa.

4. Combine the ingredients for the poaching liquid in a fish poacher or sauté pan and bring to a boil. Reduce the heat and simmer the poaching liquid until richly flavored, about 10

SEA BASS A LA VERACRUZANA
(IN A SPICY SAUCE OF FRESH TOMATOES, OLIVES, CAPERS, AND PICKLED PEPPERS)

This is one of the most famous fish dishes in Mexico, and it's easy to see why. You start with the freshest possible fish. You bake or simmer it in a sauce that jolts your taste buds with electrifying bursts of flavor from salty capers, tangy olives, pickled jalapeño peppers, and even sweet spices, such as cinnamon and cloves. Despite the large number of ingredients, Veracruz-style fish is relatively quick and easy to make. (I wouldn't hesitate to prepare it on a week night.) There are many possibilities for fish here, including sea bass, snapper, and pompano. Any mild whitefish will do.

minutes. Add salt and pepper to taste.

5. Lower the fish into the poaching liquid. Poach over medium heat (the liquid should be barely simmering) until the fish is cooked, about 10 minutes. Drain off the poaching liquid and carefully transfer the fish to a platter or plates, using a spatula. The fish can be served hot or chilled.

6. Mound the salsa in the center of the fish and serve at once.

Serves 4

290 CALORIES PER SERVING;
35 G PROTEIN; 5 G FAT; 1 G SATURATED FAT;
30 G CARBOHYDRATE; 156 MG SODIUM;
136 MG CHOLESTEROL

4 (6-ounce) boneless, skinless sea bass fillets

salt and freshly ground black pepper

1 clove garlic, minced

3 tablespoons fresh lime juice

FOR THE SAUCE:

8 to 10 ripe red plum tomatoes or 4 regular tomatoes (about 2 pounds)

1 tablespoon olive oil

1 medium white onion, finely chopped

2 cloves garlic, finely chopped

1 tablespoon drained capers

1 tablespoon chopped pitted green olives

1 to 2 pickled jalapeño chilies, finely chopped

1 to 2 tablespoons picked jalapeño juice

2 tablespoons chopped fresh flat-leaf parsley, plus 4 sprigs for garnish

½ teaspoon dried oregano

1 bay leaf

1 (2-inch) piece cinnamon stick

⅛ teaspoon ground cloves

1 cup fish stock (page 381) or bottled clam juice

1. Rinse the fish and blot it dry. Season the fillets with salt and pepper and arrange them in a baking dish. Sprinkle with the garlic, pour the lime

juice over the fish, and let marinate for 15 minutes. Preheat the oven to 400°F. Bring 2 quarts of water to a boil in a large saucepan.

2. Place the tomatoes in the boiling water for 30 seconds. Dip them in a bowl of cold water, drain well, then pull off the skins. Cut the tomatoes in half and squeeze out the seeds. Coarsely chop the tomatoes.

3. Heat the oil in a large, nonstick frying pan. Add the onions and cook over medium heat until they are just beginning to brown, 4 to 5 minutes, adding the garlic halfway through. Increase the heat to high and add the tomatoes. Cook until most of the tomato juices are evaporated, 3 minutes. Stir in the capers, olives, jalapeños, jalapeño juice, parsley, oregano, bay leaf, cinnamon stick, cloves, and fish stock. Simmer the sauce until it is thick and richly flavored, 5 to 8 minutes, stirring with a wooden spoon. Correct the seasoning, adding salt and pepper to taste. For extra heat and sharpness, add a little more pickled jalapeño juice.

4. Spoon one third of the sauce over the bottom of a baking dish. Arrange the fish on top and spoon the remaining sauce over it. Bake the fish until it is cooked (when done, it will break into clean flakes when pressed with your finger), 10 to 15 minutes. Remove and discard the bay leaf and cinnamon stick. Serve the fish at once, garnishing each fillet with a sprig of parsley.

Serves 4

285 CALORIES PER SERVING; 38 G PROTEIN; 7 G FAT; 1 G SATURATED FAT; 18 G CARBOHYDRATE; 398 MG SODIUM; 62 MG CHOLESTEROL

MAHIMAHI TIKEN-XIK
(WITH A MAYAN MARINADE OF SOUR ORANGE AND ANNATTO)

The cooking of the Yucatán is unlike that of anywhere else in Mexico. Consider tiken-xik *("tee-ken-SHEEK"). Named for the Mayan words for "marinated" and "turned" (as in flipped with a spatula), this ancient preparation features a fish flavored with a Mercurochrome-orange* recado *(spice paste), flavored with annatto seeds and sour orange juice, then cooked on a griddle or grill. Annatto is a rust-colored Caribbean seed that has the sort of tangy, iodiney flavor one associates with French oysters. Sour orange is a citrus fruit that looks like an orange but tastes like a cross between a lime and a grapefruit. Put them together and you get a dish that screams with exotic Caribbean flavors, yet is immediately accessible to anyone who likes fish.* Note: *I call for mahimahi here, but you could also use snapper, pompano, or another mild white fish.*

FOR THE RECADO:

½ teaspoon annatto seeds

½ teaspoon black peppercorns

2 allspice berries

2 cloves

1 (½-inch) piece cinnamon stick

½ teaspoon dried oregano

1 bay leaf

¼ cup sour orange juice or lime juice

2 tablespoons fresh orange juice

¼ medium white onion

2 cloves garlic

1 teaspoon salt

¼ cup water

1½ pounds boneless, skinless mahimahi fillets, cut sharply on the diagonal into 4 pieces

1 tablespoon olive oil

½ medium white onion, thinly sliced

1 clove garlic, thinly sliced

1 tomato, peeled, seeded, and diced

1 tablespoon chopped epazote or cilantro, plus 4 whole sprigs for garnish

salt and freshly ground black pepper

4 lime wedges for garnish

1. To prepare the recado, place the annatto seeds, peppercorns, allspice, cloves, cinnamon, oregano, and bay leaf in a coffee grinder or spice mill and grind to a fine powder. Transfer the mixture to a blender and add the sour orange juice, fresh orange juice, onion, garlic, salt, and water. Purée to a smooth paste.

2. Arrange the fish in a nonreactive baking dish. Pour the recado over it, turning once or twice to coat both sides. Marinate in the refrigerator for 1 hour.

3. Preheat your barbecue grill to high.

4. Shortly before serving, heat the oil in a nonstick skillet. Add the sliced onion and garlic and cook over medium heat until they're soft but not brown, 3 minutes. Increase the heat to high and add the tomato and chopped epazote. Cook for 1 minute. Add salt and pepper to taste.

5. Grill the fish until done, 4 to 6 minutes per side, turning with a spatula. Place the fish on a platter. Spoon the onion-tomato mixture on top. Garnish each piece of fish with an epazote sprig and serve at once with wedges of lime for squeezing.

Serves 4

218 CALORIES PER SERVING; 33 G PROTEIN; 5 G FAT; 1 G SATURATED FAT; 11 G CARBOHYDRATE; 690 MG SODIUM; 124 MG CHOLESTEROL

BLUEFISH PUTTANESCA

Puttanesca traditionally refers to a Roman pasta dish, a lively sauté of tomatoes, olives, capers, hot peppers, and anchovies *tossed with spaghetti. The preparation is said to have originated in a former Red Light district called the Trastevere. As you probably know, the dish takes its name from* puttana, *prostitute, although whether that's because it's hot and spicy or because it can be made in a matter of minutes remains a matter of debate. One day, when I was presented with some gorgeous bluefish by a fisherman friend, it struck me that the flavorings in spaghetti puttanesca would be perfect for full-flavored seafood. The result is this bluefish puttanesca, which would be delectable with any rich fish, from mackerel to salmon to tuna.*

1½ pounds boneless, skinless bluefish or salmon fillets

salt and freshly ground black pepper

1½ tablespoons extra-virgin olive oil

1 to 2 cloves garlic, minced

8 anchovy fillets, cut into ¼-inch pieces

½ teaspoon hot pepper flakes, or to taste

2 tablespoons drained capers

8 chopped pitted black olives

1 pound ripe tomatoes, peeled, seeded, and coarsely chopped

3 tablespoons chopped flat-leaf parsley

spray olive oil

1. Run your fingers over the fish, feeling for bones, and remove any you find with plies or tweezers. Sprinkle the fillets with salt and pepper. Preheat the oven to 400°F.

2. Heat the olive oil in a large nonstick frying pan. Add the garlic, anchovy fillets, and pepper flakes and cook over medium heat for 20 seconds. Add the capers, olives, and tomatoes, increase the heat to high, and cook until most of the tomato liquid evaporates, 3 to 5 minutes. Stir in half the parsley and salt and pepper to taste.

3. Lightly spray a baking dish with oil. Spoon one-third of the mixture into the baking dish and arrange the fish pieces on top. Spoon the remaining puttanesca mixture over the fish. The recipe can be prepared ahead to this stage and be refrigerated for a few hours. (If you do prepare it ahead, let the sauce cool to room temperature before putting it over the fish.)

4. Bake the fish until the sauce is bubbling and the bluefish is cooked, 15 to 20 minutes. (When done, it will flake easily when pressed with your fingers. Another test is to insert a slender metal skewer into the thickest part of the fish. When the fish is ready, the skewer will be very hot to the touch.) Sprinkle the remaining parsley on top and serve at once.

Serves 4

294 CALORIES PER SERVING; 38 G PROTEIN; 13 G FAT; 2 G SATURATED FAT; 6 G CARBOHYDRATE; 604 MG SODIUM; 107 MG CHOLESTEROL

BRAISED COD WITH TUNISIAN SPICES

This dish spans two continents: cod is a native of the icy North Atlantic; coriander, caraway, and cumin are ingredients in a popular Tunisian spice mixture called tabil. *You can also make this dish with snapper, hake, or bluefish.*

1½ pounds cod fillets

½ teaspoon coriander seeds

½ teaspoon cumin seeds

½ teaspoon hot red pepper flakes

½ teaspoon caraway seeds

½ teaspoon salt (or to taste)

3 cloves garlic, thinly sliced

1 medium onion, thinly sliced

2 ripe tomatoes, thinly sliced

1 cup bottled fish stock, clam broth, or chicken stock

juice of ½ lemon (or to taste)

3 tablespoons chopped flat-leaf parsley, for garnish

Run your fingers over the fish, feeling for bones. Remove any you find with tweezers or needlenose pliers. Cut the fish into 4 pieces.

Combine the coriander seeds, cumin seeds, pepper flakes, caraway seeds, and salt in a small, dry skillet. Roast over medium heat for 2 to 3 minutes, or until the spices are fragrant. Grind the spices in a blender or spice mill. Rub the fish with the spice mixture and let stand for 10 minutes.

Oil a baking dish just large enough to hold the fish and arrange half the garlic, onion, and tomato slices over the bottom. Place the fish pieces in the dish and top with the remaining garlic, onion, and tomato slices. Pour the fish stock and lemon juice over the fish. The recipe can be prepared to this stage up to 2 hours ahead.

Preheat the oven to 400°F. Bake the fish for 20 to 30 minutes, or until cooked to taste. Sprinkle with parsley and serve at once.

Serves 4

162 CALORIES PER SERVING; 30 G PROTEIN; 2 G FAT; 6 G CARBOHYDRATE; 568 MG SODIUM; 67 MG CHOLESTEROL

ANNATTO-GLAZED "GRIDDLED" POMPANO

Mexicans love foods that are cooked on a plancha *(griddle). The proof of this assertion lies no farther than the nearest sidewalk food vendor or market. The problem from the health-conscious eater's point of view is the fat used to oil the griddle: often margarine, sausage drippings, or pork fat. That set me thinking about a low-fat method for giving foods the buttery crisp crust associated with griddling without a lot of fat. I took to doing my "griddling" on a lightly oiled, preheated baking sheet in a superhot oven. The following recipe calls for pompano, but you could really use any thin fish fillet or even thin fish steaks. As for the recado (seasoning), it owes its piquancy to vinegar and orange juice; its fragrance to cumin, cloves, and oregano; and its distinctive flavor and bright orange color to a Caribbean spice called annatto.*

Serves 4

317 CALORIES PER SERVING; 33 G PROTEIN; 17 G FAT; 6 G SATURATED FAT; 8 G CARBOHYDRATE; 384 MG SODIUM; 86 MG CHOLESTEROL

MONKFISH "SPLENDIDO" BAKED WITH PINE NUTS, OLIVES, AND SAGE

I'm of the school that holds that fish tastes best when eaten in sight of water. Few sites are more apt or lovely than the Splendido Hotel in Portofino, which has a terrace restaurant that offers bird's-eye views of the boat-studded harbor and the craggy cliffs around it. Like so many Italian recipes, this one uses a few simple flavors to reinforce the primal taste of the fish. There's one unexpected ingredient—Worcestershire sauce—perhaps a throwback to the days when Portofino was almost exclusively an English resort. There are lots of possibilities for fish here: the Splendido normally uses sea bass. I've crafted the recipe for monkfish; good choices would include mahi-mahi, cod, salmon, and tilefish.

FOR THE RUB AND RECADO (MARINADE):

½ teaspoon annatto seeds

½ teaspoon black peppercorns

½ teaspoon cumin seeds

3 cloves

2 allspice berries

½ teaspoon dried oregano

½ teaspoon salt, plus salt for the salsa

1 large red ripe tomato

½ medium white onion

3 cloves garlic

⅓ cup fresh orange juice

1 tablespoon fresh lime juice

1 tablespoon red wine vinegar

Freshly ground black pepper

4 (6-ounce) pompano fillets

spray oil or 1 tablespoon olive oil

¼ cup chopped fresh cilantro

1. To prepare the rub and the recado, in a comal or dry skillet, roast the annatto seeds, peppercorns, cumin, cloves, and allspice over medium heat until they are toasted and fragrant, 2 to 3 minutes. Transfer to a coffee grinder or spice mill and grind to a fine powder. Add the oregano and ½ teaspoon salt. Rub this mixture into the fish fillets and place them in a roasting pan. Marinate for 15 minutes. Bring 1 quart of water to a boil in a saucepan.

2. Cook the tomato, onion, and garlic in the boiling water until tender, about 5 minutes. Drain well. Combine the tomato, onion, garlic, orange juice, lime juice, and vinegar in a blender and purée to a smooth paste. Add salt and pepper to taste. Pour half this mixture over the pompano and marinate in the refrigerator for 4 to 6 hours, turning the fillets two or three times.

3. Preheat the oven to 400°F. Place a baking sheet (preferably nonstick) in the oven, preheating it as well. Remove the fish from the marinade and let it drain.

4. Just before serving, spray the preheated baking sheet with oil or drizzle with olive oil. Arrange the fish fillets on top. Spray or drizzle the fish with more oil. Bake the fish until it's cooked, 6 to 8 minutes per side, turning once with a spatula. Transfer the fish to plates or a platter and spoon the remaining tomato mixture on top. Sprinkle with cilantro and serve at once.

1½ pounds monkfish, washed, patted dry, and cut into ½-inch-thick medallions

salt and freshly ground black pepper

2 to 3 tablespoons all-purpose unbleached white flour

1 tablespoon extra-virgin olive oil

8 fresh sage leaves or basil leaves

1 bay leaf

1 tablespoon toasted pine nuts

8 black olives

1 cup dry white wine

1 tablespoon Worcestershire sauce

1. Preheat the oven to 400°F. Season the fish with salt and pepper and dust with flour, shaking off the excess. (I do this on a paper towel.)

2. Heat the oil in a nonstick frying pan over a high flame. Add the fish pieces and lightly brown on both sides, about 1 minute per side. Place the sage leaves, bay leaf, pine nuts, and olives on top of the fish. Add the wine, Worcestershire sauce, and additional salt and pepper to the pan and bring to a boil.

3. Transfer the pan to the oven and bake, uncovered, until the fish is tender, 12 to 15 minutes. (When done, it will flake easily when pressed with your finger. Another test is to insert a slender metal skewer into the thickest part of the fish. When the fish is ready, the skewer will be very hot to the touch.)

4. Transfer the fish to plates or a platter. Boil the pan juices down to a syrupy glaze. Spoon this over the fish and serve at once.

Serves 4

212 CALORIES PER SERVING; 25 G PROTEIN; 5 G FAT; 0 G SATURATED FAT; 6 G CARBOHYDRATE; 109 MG SODIUM; 41 MG CHOLESTEROL

WHOLE FISH BAKED IN A SALT CRUST

Rarely does the confluence of so few ingredients result in such a dramatic dining showpiece. This dish contains only two ingredients—fish and salt—but it never fails to dazzle guests at home or in restaurants. The theory is that the salt crust seals in the moisture and freshness of the fish. One common choice for fish in Italy is branzino (sea bass). But the species of fish is really less important than its freshness. Because of the simplicity of the presentation, there is nothing to mask the flavor of fish that is less than impeccably fresh. Here in Florida, I prepare the recipe with snapper. Elsewhere in the country, you could use porgies, scups, black bass, small striped bass, or even trout.

1 large whole fish (2½ to 3 pounds) or 4 small fish (1½ pounds each)

10 to 12 cups coarse sea salt or kosher salt

Salsa Verde (page 8)

1. Preheat the oven to 450°F. Trim the fins off the fish, wash it, and pat it dry. Spread half the salt in an attractive baking dish or baking sheet just large enough to hold the fish. Place the fish on top, pressing it into the salt. Spread the remaining salt over the fish to completely envelop it. Compact the salt by patting it.

2. Bake the fish until cooked, 25 to 40 minutes or as needed. (To test for doneness, insert a slender metal skewer into the thickest part of the fish. When the fish is cooked, it will come out very hot to the touch.)

3. To serve, present the fish to your guests at the table. Using 2 large spoons, remove the top of the salt crust. Brush off any excess salt with a pastry brush. Transfer the fish to a platter and remove the skin. (This eliminates all the excess sodium from the fish.) Fillet the fish and serve it on plates with Salsa Verde on the side.

Serves 4

340 CALORIES PER 4 SERVING; 53 G PROTEIN; 12 G FAT; 2 G SATURATED FAT; 1 G CARBOHYDRATE; 785 MG SODIUM; 118 MG CHOLESTEROL

Fish in a Foil Bag (Branzino in Cartuccio)

FISH IN A FOIL BAG
(BRANZINO IN CARTUCCIO)

Here's a high-tech Italian version of fish en papillote, the specialty of a wonderful open-air seafood restaurant called Rosa, high on a cliff overlooking the town of Camoglie. The chef had prepared a large whole sea bass in cartuccio, *and it was served to a party of eight. It certainly makes a festive party dish—one that can be prepared for unexpected company in 10 to 15 minutes. But you can also make the fish* in cartuccio *in individual portions, which my wife and I often do for a casual midweek supper. I've written the following recipe for individual portions: preparation of one large fish is explained below. Once again, there are lots of possibilities for fish: sea bass, black bass, snapper, or fillets or steaks of mahi-mahi, swordfish, or cod—to name just a few.*

2 medium potatoes (about 12 ounces),
    peeled and very thinly sliced

1½ tablespoons extra-virgin olive oil

salt and freshly ground black pepper

4 4- to 6-ounce portions of boneless fish fillets

1 tomato, cut into ¼-inch dice

4 sprigs fresh thyme, or 1 teaspoon dried

4 sprigs fresh basil, or 1 teaspoon dried

4 bay leaves

½ cup dry white wine

Serves 4

259 CALORIES PER SERVING; 22 G PROTEIN; 8 G FAT; 1 G SATURATED FAT; 19 G CARBOHYDRATE; 87 MG SODIUM; 91 MG CHOLESTEROL

1. Preheat the oven to 400°F. Arrange a large (12 x 20 inches) rectangle of heavy-duty foil on a work surface, shiny side down. In the center, spread out one-quarter of the sliced potatoes. Drizzle with a little oil and season with salt and pepper. Place a piece of fish on top and season with salt and pepper. Arrange one-quarter of the diced tomatoes, a sprig each of thyme and basil, and a bay leaf on top. Drizzle with a little more oil and a final sprinkling of salt and pepper.

2. Bring together the short edges of the foil rectangle high over the fish without sealing. Crimp or pleat the sides to form an airtight seal. Add 2 tablespoons wine in the top, then crimp or seal the top edges to form an airtight seal. Prepare the remaining packages the same way.

3. Place the *cartucci* on a baking sheet. Bake until the foil is puffed and the fish inside is cooked, 20 to 25 minutes. (To test for doneness, you can open one of the packets, but 20 minutes of baking should do the trick.) Serve the *cartucci* on plates or a platter. Have each person open the packet and slide the fish, vegetables, and juices onto his plate.

Note: To make one large *cartuccio*, you'll need a whole fish weighing 3 to 4 pounds. Trim the fins off the fish (or have your fishmonger do it). Wash it thoroughly inside and out and pat dry. Season the fish inside and out with salt and pepper. You'll also need to make a much larger foil rectangle. To do so, attach several sheets together, folding joining edges over several times to make a tight seal. Assemble as described above, but use only 2 bay leaves. You'll need to bake a large fish for 40 to 60 minutes.

SHRIMP WITH CHERRY TOMATOES

La Vela Bianca (The White Sail) in Sorrento is the sort of Italian trattoria that lives in our collective imaginations: down-to-earth, homey, with red-checkered curtains and tablecloths and wide windows overlooking the water. What it lacks in glitz, it makes up for in good, simple, honest food. La Vela Bianca uses fish broth to make the sauce for the following shrimp. A slightly different but equally delectable dish can be made using white wine, which is more readily available in many American homes than fish broth. Use the smallest, ripest cherry tomatoes you can find.

1½ pounds shrimp

1 tablespoon extra-virgin olive oil

3 cloves garlic, peeled and flattened with the side of a cleaver

¼ teaspoon hot pepper flakes, or to taste

8 large or 12 small cherry tomatoes, cut in half

½ cup Fish Stock (page 381) or dry white wine

3 tablespoons chopped flat-leaf parsley

1. Peel and devein the shrimp. Heat the olive oil in a large nonstick frying pan. Add the garlic and sizzle in the oil over high heat until it just begins to brown, about 1 minute. Add the pepper flakes and cook for 10 seconds.

2. Add the shrimp and tomatoes and cook over high heat for 1 minute. Add the fish stock and bring to a boil. Continue cooking at a boil until the shrimp are done, 1 to 2 minutes more. Stir in the parsley and serve at once.

Serves 4

175 CALORIES PER SERVING; 29 G PROTEIN; 5 G FAT; 0.9 G SATURATED FAT; 2 G CARBOHYDRATE; 301 MG SODIUM; 262 MG CHOLESTEROL

Shrimp with Cherry Tomatoes

Shrimp Kebabs with Sun-Dried Tomatoes and Basil

SHRIMP KEBABS WITH SUN-DRIED TOMATOES AND BASIL

These kebabs are as delectable as they are easy to make. Sun-dried tomatoes are a sort of vegetarian prosciutto.
They're made by slicing, salting, and drying tomatoes, sometimes in the sun, more often in a food drier.
Look for them in gourmet shops, natural food stores, and most supermarkets.

1 tablespoon extra-virgin olive oil

½ teaspoon freshly grated lemon zest

2 tablespoons fresh lemon juice

2 teaspoons chopped fresh thyme (or 2 teaspoons dried)

salt and freshly ground black pepper

24 large shrimp (about 1½ pounds), peeled and deveined

1 bunch basil (24 large leaves)

24 1-inch pieces of sun-dried tomato,
   drained and blotted dry

Combine the oil, zest, lemon juice, thyme, salt, and pepper in a bowl. Add the shrimp and marinate for 15 to 20 minutes. Thread the marinated shrimp onto skewers, placing a basil leaf and a piece of sun-dried tomato between each (as pictured on the cover of this book).

Season with salt and pepper. Preheat the grill. Just before serving, grill the kebabs, basting with marinade, for 1 to 2 minutes per side, or until the shrimp are cooked.

Serves 4 to 6

207 CALORIES PER SERVING; 30 G PROTEIN; 5 G FAT; 11 G CARBOHYDRATE; 319 MG SODIUM; 261 MG CHOLESTEROL

SHRIMP WITH BEANS AND ROSEMARY

I often muse on why Italian cuisine is so universally popular. I believe there are three reasons: its simplicity and directness, its emphasis on great raw materials, and the speed with which so many dishes can be prepared. All three factors come into play in this Tuscan dish—a favorite at our house when dinnertime arrives and no one has made any special plans for cooking. Note the optional use of fish, chicken, or clam broth to replace some of the oil in the traditional recipe, reducing the fat but maintaining the flavor.

1½ tablespoons extra-virgin olive oil

1 clove garlic, minced

3 tablespoons chopped flat-leaf parsley

2 teaspoons chopped fresh rosemary or sage

1 pound shrimp, peeled and deveined

2 cups cooked cannellini beans

salt and freshly ground black pepper

½ cup Fish Stock (page 381), Chicken Stock (page 379), or bottled clam broth (juice) (optional)

Serves 4

261 CALORIES PER SERVING; 27 G PROTEIN; 6 G FAT; 1 G SATURATED FAT; 23 G CARBOHYDRATE; 205 MG SODIUM; 175 MG CHOLESTEROL

1. Heat 1 tablespoon of the olive oil in a large nonstick skillet. Add the garlic, 2 tablespoons of the parsley, and the rosemary and cook over medium heat until fragrant but not brown, about 1 minute. Stir in the shrimp, beans, salt, and pepper and cook for 1 minute. Add the fish stock and simmer until the shrimp are firm, pink, and cooked, 2 to 3 minutes more. Correct the seasoning, adding salt and pepper to taste.

2. Drizzle the remaining ½ tablespoon olive oil over the shrimp and beans, sprinkle with the remaining tablespoon parsley, and serve at once.

SHRIMP SAAG

Saag is a mild Indian curry made with spinach. Indians tend to cook spinach much longer than we do, so frozen spinach will work fine for this recipe.

1 tablespoon olive or canola oil

1 onion, finely chopped

2 teaspoons minced fresh ginger

2 cloves garlic, minced (2 teaspoons)

½ teaspoon cumin seeds

½ teaspoon ground coriander

½ teaspoon ground turmeric

¼ teaspoon ground cinnamon

¼ teaspoon ground cardamom

pinch of ground cloves

1 bay leaf

1 cup clam broth or fish stock (approximately)

2 12-ounce bags fresh spinach, finely chopped (or 2 packages frozen)

1½ pounds large shrimp, peeled and deveined

salt and freshly ground black pepper

3 tablespoons finely chopped cilantro or parsley, for garnish

Heat the oil in a sauté pan. Add the onion, ginger, garlic, spices, and bay leaf, and cook over medium heat for 3 minutes, or until soft but not brown. Add the clam broth and bring to a boil. Stir in the spinach and cook for 10 to 15 minutes, or until the spinach is soft and mushy. If the mixture dries out too much, add more clam broth.

Stir in the shrimp and simmer for 1 to 2 minutes, or until cooked. Remove and discard the bay leaf. Season with salt and pepper. Transfer to a serving dish, garnish with the cilantro, and serve at once.

Serves 4

198 CALORIES PER SERVING; 34 G PROTEIN; 3 G FAT; 9 G CARBOHYDRATE; 414 MG SODIUM; 261 MG CHOLESTEROL

SEAFOOD CHILES RELLENOS

In the United States, chiles rellenos *means poblano chilies stuffed with artery-clogging globs of melted cheese and soggily fried in egg batter—hardly the stuff of a healthy diet. You might be surprised to learn that Mexicans have dozens of different types of stuffed chilies—some filled with seafood, others with chicken or vegetables, and not all of them deep-fried. Consider the following seafood chiles rellenos, which make an inviting light entrée. I owe a special thanks to my friend Elida Proenza, for it was she who had the idea of adding rice to thicken the cooking liquid without using cream or cornstarch.*

8 large poblano chilies

FOR THE FILLING:

1 tablespoon canola oil

1 medium onion, finely chopped

2 cloves garlic, minced

1 jalapeño chili, seeded and minced

8 ounces button mushrooms, trimmed, wiped clean
   with a damp cloth, and cut into ½-inch dice

8 ounces shrimp, peeled, deveined,
   and cut into ½-inch dice

8 ounces scallops, cut into ½-inch dice

2 tablespoons chopped fresh cilantro

1½ cups fish stock or bottled clam broth

½ cup evaporated skim milk

½ cup Valencia-style or arborio rice
   (short-grain rice)

salt and freshly ground black pepper

1 batch Cooked Tomato Salsa (page 6)
   or Salsa Ranchera (page 7)

1. Roast the chilies over a high flame or under the broiler, until the skins are charred all over. This will take 8 to 10 minutes. Place the chilies in a bowl and cover with plastic wrap. Let cool for 15 minutes. Scrape the burnt skin off each chili, using a paring knife.

2. Cut the top (the stem end) three fourths of the way off each chili. (Leave it attached at the bottom.) Fold back the top and, using a grapefruit spoon or paring knife, scrape out the seeds and veins.

3. Meanwhile, prepare the filling. Heat the oil in a sauce-pan. Add the onion, garlic, and jalapeño and cook over medium heat until soft but not brown, about 4 minutes. Stir in the mushrooms, shrimp, scallops, and cilantro and cook for 2 minutes. Stir in the fish stock, evaporated milk, and rice.

4. Gently simmer the seafood mixture over medium-low heat, uncovered, until the rice is soft, the shellfish is cooked, and most of the liquid has been absorbed, 18 to 20 minutes. Add salt and pepper to taste.

5. Fill each chili with the seafood mixture, using a spoon, and arrange the chilies in a nonstick baking dish. Spoon any excess filling over the chilies. The recipe can be prepared ahead to this stage.

6. Preheat the oven to 400°F. Bake the chiles rellenos until they are thoroughly heated, 10 to 15 minutes. Spoon the salsa on plates or a platter and arrange the chiles rellenos on top. (Alternatively, spoon the salsa over them.)

Serves 8 as an appetizer, 4 as an entrée

349 CALORIES PER PEPPER; 42 G PROTEIN; 6 G FAT; 1 G SATURATED FAT; 36 G CARBOHYDRATE; 382 MG SODIUM; 194 MG CHOLESTEROL

SHRIMP IN GARLIC TOMATO SAUCE
(CAMARONES AL AJILLO)

Shrimp in garlic sauce is a popular Mexican entrée. Most versions are awash in a sea of butter.
Mexico City–born Los Angeles restaurateur Frank Romero offers a low-fat twist on this fat-laden favorite, flavoring his sauce
with fried garlic and roasted tomatoes and onion. It lets you enjoy a rich garlic flavor with only a fraction of the fat.
Note: *This preparation works equally well with fish.*

1½ pounds ripe red tomatoes
(3 to 4 tomatoes)

1 small onion, peeled and quartered

1 to 2 jalapeño chilies

3 tablespoons chopped cilantro,
plus 2 tablespoons for garnish

½ teaspoon oregano
(preferably Mexican)

1 tablespoon olive oil

6 cloves garlic, peeled and thinly
sliced widthwise

salt and freshly ground black pepper

1¼ pounds large shrimp,
peeled and deveined

1. Heat a comal or cast-iron frying pan over medium-high heat. Roast the tomatoes, onion, and chilies until nicely browned on all sides: 8 to 10 minutes for the tomatoes and onion; 4 to 6 minutes for the jalapeños. Transfer to a plate and let cool.

2. Seed the chilies. (For a more fiery sauce, leave in the seeds.) Purée the tomatoes, onion, chilies, 3 tablespoons of the cilantro, and the oregano in a food processor.

3. Heat the olive oil in a nonstick frying pan. Add the garlic and cook over medium heat until it is lightly browned, stirring steadily, 2 to 3 minutes.

Do not let the garlic burn. Stir in the tomato purée and simmer until it is slightly thickened and richly flavored, about 5 minutes. Add salt and pepper to taste. The recipe can be prepared ahead to this stage.

4. Just before serving, stir in the shrimp. Gently simmer until the shrimp are firm and pink, about 3 minutes. Correct the seasoning, adding salt and pepper to taste. Sprinkle the shrimp with the remaining cilantro and serve at once.

Serves 4

209 CALORIES PER SERVING; 25 G PROTEIN; 7 G FAT; 1 G SATURATED FAT; 14 G CARBOHYDRATE; 185 MG SODIUM; 172 MG CHOLESTEROL

CASCABEL CHILI AND ORANGE-MARINATED SHRIMP FAJITAS

The first fajitas were made with beef (skirt steak, to be exact). Indeed, faja *is the Spanish word for skirt steak (literally, it means "girdle"). These days, anything goes when it comes to fajitas. Consider the following, made with shrimp marinated with fiery cascabel chilies. The cascabel is a cherry-shaped dried chili whose seeds rattle when you shake it. (Cascabel means "sleighbell.") Orange juice and annatto (a small, orange, squarish, seed spice that has an earthy, iodiney flavor. It's often used in the cooking of the Yucatán) round out the flavor of this fiery chili to make a shrimp fajita you won't soon forget.*

FOR THE MARINADE:

1 cup fresh orange juice

2 cascabel chilies or 2 small dried hot red peppers, stemmed

2 cloves garlic

½ teaspoon annatto seeds

2 teaspoons chopped fresh marjoram, or 1 teaspoon dried

½ teaspoon salt, or to taste (optional)

¼ teaspoon freshly ground black pepper

¼ teaspoon ground cumin

TO SERVE THE FAJITAS:

1 cup no-fat sour cream

1 large ripe tomato, seeded and finely chopped

½ avocado, diced and sprinkled with a few drops of lime juice to prevent browning

1½ cups Chipotle Salsa (page 7), or your favorite salsa

2 poblano chilies

1 red bell pepper

1 yellow bell pepper

1 large white onion, peeled and cut lengthwise in eighths (leave the furry root end intact)

2 bunches of scallions, roots trimmed off

1 pound large shrimp, peeled and deveined

8 (8-inch) fat-free flour tortillas

1. To prepare the marinade, in a small saucepan combine the orange juice, chilies, garlic, and annatto seeds. Briskly simmer over medium-high heat until the chilies have softened and only ½ cup of juice remains, 5 to 8 minutes. Transfer the mixture to a blender and add the marjoram, salt, pepper, and cumin. Purée until smooth. Strain the mixture through a fine strainer into a large bowl and let cool completely. Correct the seasoning, adding salt and pepper to taste. The marinade should be very spicy. Stir the shrimp into the marinade and let marinate for 20 minutes.

2. Meanwhile, build a hot fire in your barbecue grill. Place the sour cream, tomato, avocado, and salsa in separate serving bowls.

3. Grill the poblano chilies and bell peppers until they are nicely charred on all sides, 2 to 3 minutes per side, 8 to 12 minutes in all. Transfer to a cutting board. Grill the onion wedges until they are nicely browned, 3 to 4 minutes per side. Transfer to the cutting board. Grill the scallions until they are charred and wilted, 2 minutes per side. Transfer to the cutting board. Scrape any really burnt skin off the peppers and cut the flesh off the cores and seeds. Cut the flesh into long, thin strips. Thinly slice the onions, discarding the furry root end. Leave the scallions whole. Arrange the vegetables on a platter and keep warm.

4. Thread the shrimp onto skewers and grill until cooked, 2 to 3 minutes per side. Transfer the shrimp to the platter and remove them from the skewer.

5. Warm the tortillas on the grill until they're soft and pliable, 10 to 20 seconds per side.

6. To serve the fajitas, invite each guest to place a few shrimp and grilled vegetables on a tortilla. Spoon the tomato, avocado, and salsa on top and roll the tortilla into a tube for eating.

Note: Fajitas are often served on theatrically sizzling skillets. To achieve this at home, preheat a cast-iron skillet in a 400°F. oven for about 30 minutes. Just before serving, transfer the grilled shrimp and vegetables to the skillet: They will sizzle at once. Warn your guests not to touch the skillet.

Makes 8 fajitas, enough to serve 4

439 CALORIES PER SERVING; 37 G PROTEIN; 7 G FAT; 1 G SATURATED FAT; 66 G CARBOHYDRATE; 790 MG SODIUM; 172 MG CHOLESTEROL

MUSSELS STEAMED WITH ROSEMARY AND ROASTED PEPPERS

One of the most appealing aspects of Italian cuisine is its reliance on a few bold, simple flavors. I was recently thumbing through a Sri Lankan cookbook and was struck by the difference in approach the two countries take to mussels. The Sri Lankan version contains over a dozen spices and seasonings, and the resulting dish is magnificent. Then I remembered the steamed-mussel dish I tasted in Santa Margherita on the Ligurian coast. It contained only two primary flavorings and it was magnificent, too, perhaps even more magnificent in its simplicity. If you're in a hurry, you could use bottled or canned pimientos.

4 pounds mussels

2 cups dry white wine

1 onion, finely chopped

1 roasted or grilled red bell pepper, cut into ¼-inch strips

2 branches fresh rosemary, or 1 tablespoon dried

1. Scrub the mussels, discarding any with cracked shells or shells that fail to close when tapped. Use needlenose pliers to remove any black threads attached to the hinge end. Bring the wine, onion, roasted pepper, and rosemary to boil in a large, heavy pot. Add the mussels and cover the pot tightly.

2. Cook the mussels until the shells open wide, about 8 minutes, stirring once or twice to give the mussels on the bottom room to open. Discard any mussels that do not open. Transfer the cooked mussels and vegetables with a slotted spoon to serving bowls. Ladle the broth on top, taking care to leave the grit in the bottom of the pot. Serve the mussels with crusty bread for dipping and bowls for holding the empty shells.

Serves 4

161 CALORIES PER SERVING; 20 G PROTEIN; 3 G FAT; 0 G SATURATED FAT; 11 G CARBOHYDRATE; 379 MG SODIUM; 74 MG CHOLESTEROL

SAFFRON STEAMED MUSSELS

This fragrant dish is a variation on classic French moules marinière. *Serve it with crusty bread for dunking in the broth.*

3 pounds fresh mussels

1 onion, finely chopped

1 leek, trimmed, washed, and finely chopped

1 carrot, finely chopped

2 stalks celery, finely chopped

1 small fennel bulb, finely chopped (optional)

1 red bell pepper, cored, seeded, and finely chopped

3 cloves garlic, minced (1 tablespoon)

½ cup finely chopped flat-leaf parsley

⅛ teaspoon saffron threads soaked in 1 tablespoon warm water

1½ cups dry white wine

1½ cups clam broth, fish stock, or water

2 bay leaves

1 teaspoon chopped fresh thyme (or 1 teaspoon dried)

salt and freshly ground black pepper

Scrub the mussels and discard any with cracked shells or shells that fail to close when tapped. Remove the cluster of threads at the hinge of each mussel. (Pinch it between your thumb and the back of a paring knife and pull.)

Shortly before serving, combine all the ingredients except the mussels in a large pot. Bring to a boil and cook for 5 minutes. Add the mussels, tightly cover the pot, and cook over high heat for 5 minutes, or until the mussels open. Stir the mussels once or twice, so those on the bottom have room to open.

Remove and discard the bay leaves. Serve the mussels with their cooking liquid in bowls, and provide extra bowls to hold the empty shells. When the mussels are finished, use empty half shells to spoon up the broth and vegetables.

Serves 4 as an appetizer, 2 to 3 as an entrée

262 CALORIES PER SERVING; 22 G PROTEIN; 4 G FAT; 19 G CARBOHYDRATE; 355 MG SODIUM; 48 MG CHOLESTEROL

MUSSELS STEAMED WITH CHIPOTLES AND TEQUILA

This recipe is simplicity itself, but it never fails to elicit raves. I use canned chipotles, adding a tablespoon of the adobo (can juices) to the broth. I also like to use small mussels; they're sweeter and more tender than the large ones.

4 pounds mussels

1 cup dry white wine

½ cup water

¼ cup tequila

2 tablespoons fresh lime juice

1 large ripe red tomato, diced

1 medium white onion, finely chopped

2 cloves garlic, thinly sliced

1 to 3 chipotle chilies, minced

1 to 3 teaspoons chipotle juices

½ cup chopped fresh cilantro

1. Scrub the mussels, discarding any with cracked shells or shells that fail to close when tapped. Remove the cluster of threads at the hinge of the mussels. (Pinch the threads between your thumb and the back of a paring knife and pull, or use needlenose pliers.)

2. To prepare the broth, combine the wine, water, tequila, lime juice, tomato, onion, garlic, chipotles, chili juices, and cilantro in a large pot and bring to a boil.

3. Add the mussels and cook, covered, over high heat until the shells open wide, about 8 minutes, stirring the mussels once or twice to give the ones on the bottom room to open.

4. With a slotted spoon, transfer the mussels to a serving bowl. Spoon most of the broth over them, leaving behind any sandy dregs. Serve at once with tortillas or bread for dunking in the broth, and extra bowls for the empty mussel shells.

Serves 4

208 CALORIES PER SERVING; 17 G PROTEIN; 3 G FAT; 0 G SATURATED FAT; 11 G CARBOHYDRATE; 333 MG SODIUM; 64 MG CHOLESTEROL

CLAMS IN GREEN SAUCE

Camogie is one of the best-kept secrets on the Ligurian coast, a thoroughly Italian seaside community on a curved pebble beach ringed with tall, pastel-colored, green-shuttered nine-teenth-century apartment buildings. A spacious promenade runs from one end of the half-mile-long cove to the other, and best of all, there are no cars. This dish turns up at the homey trattorie that line the promenade. For the best results, use the smallest clams you can find, because they're the sweetest and most tender. Mussels or shrimp could be cooked the same way.

48 littleneck clams or 40 cherrystone clams

1½ tablespoons extra-virgin olive oil

2 cloves garlic, flattened with the side of a cleaver and peeled

½ teaspoon hot pepper flakes

1 bunch flat-leaf parsley, stemmed and finely chopped (about 1 cup)

1½ cups dry white wine

freshly ground black pepper

1. Scrub the clams with a brush under cold running water. Discard any clams with cracked shells or shells that fail to close when tapped.

2. Heat the olive oil in a large, heavy saucepan. Add the garlic and cook over medium heat until fragrant, about 1 minute. Add the pepper flakes and most of the parsley and cook for 30 seconds. Add the wine and bring to a boil. Add the clams, tightly cover the pan, and cook over high heat until the clam shells open wide, about 8 minutes. Stir the clams once or twice to give the shells on the bottom space to open. Discard any clams that do not open.

3. Serve the clams in bowls with the broth ladled on top. Sprinkle with the remaining parsley. Serve with crusty bread for dipping and bowls for the empty shells.

Serves 4

193 CALORIES PER SERVING; 14 G PROTEIN; 6 G FAT; 0.8 G SATURATED FAT; 5 G CARBOHYDRATE; 73 MG SODIUM; 36 MG CHOLESTEROL

SEAFOOD COCKTAIL IN THE STYLE OF VERACRUZ

Served in oversize wine goblets, these seafood cocktails are guaranteed show-stoppers.
You can pretty much use any seafood you fancy: shrimp, crabmeat, and squid rings if you like your seafood cooked; oysters,
clams, and raw scallops if your taste runs to sushi and ceviche. Whatever seafood you choose, it will benefit greatly
from the dual sauces: a piquant mixture of lime and orange juice and a smoky tomato salsa fired up with chipotle chilies.
Serve this in the biggest wine- or martini glasses you have and prepare to wow your guests.

**FOR THE SMOKY
TOMATO SALSA:**

2 tomatoes

¼ white onion

1 clove garlic

2 canned chipotle chilies

salt

**FOR THE LIME-ORANGE
MARINADE:**

⅓ cup fresh lime juice

⅓ cup fresh orange juice

½ teaspoon salt

½ pound lump crabmeat, picked
    through to remove any shell

½ pound cooked baby shrimp
    (or diced large shrimp)

½ pound cooked squid rings

12 shucked oysters (optional)

2 ripe tomatoes, seeded and cut
    into ¼-inch dice

1 medium red onion,
    cut into ¼-inch dice

1 to 2 jalapeño chilies, seeded
    and minced (for a hotter cocktail,
    leave in the seeds)

½ cup chopped fresh cilantro

½ avocado, peeled and diced

1. To prepare the smoky tomato salsa, heat a comal or cast-iron skillet over medium-high heat. Roast the tomatoes, onion, and garlic until they are lightly charred on all sides: about 8 minutes for the tomatoes and onions, 4 minutes for the garlic. Transfer to a plate and let cool. Purée the charred vegetables and chilies in a blender, adding salt to taste.

2. To make the lime-orange marinade, combine the lime juice, orange juice, and salt in a mixing bowl and whisk until the salt is dissolved. Add the crab, shrimp, squid, the optional oysters, the tomatoes, red onion, jalapeños, cilantro, and avocado and gently stir to mix.

3. Spoon the seafood mixture into four wine goblets. Spoon a little smoky tomato salsa over each. Serve at once, instructing each guest to lightly mix the cocktail in the glass with a fork before eating.

Serves 4

259 CALORIES PER SERVING; 33 G PROTEIN; 6 G FAT; 1 G SATURATED FAT; 18 G CARBOHYDRATE; 652 MG SODIUM; 276 MG CHOLESTEROL

Seafood Cocktail in the Style of Veracruz

SPICY CRAB SALPICÓN
(SALPICÓN DE JAIBA)

Salpicón *is the Spanish word for "hodgepodge" or "medley." Depending on where you order it in Mexico, you might get an appetizer of spiced shredded beef (in central Mexico) or a fiery onion and habanero chili relish (in the Yucatán). I'm partial to the coastal version, made with fresh sweet crab teased into tiny shreds and spiced up with celery, onions, cilantro, and chilies. This recipe makes a wonderful summertime appetizer or salad.*

    1 pound backfin crabmeat

    2 red ripe tomatoes, thinly sliced

    12 large basil leaves, washed and stemmed

    1 tablespoon olive oil

    ½ small onion, finely chopped

    1 clove garlic, finely chopped

    1 stalk celery with leaves, finely chopped

    1 to 3 serrano chilies, finely chopped
      (for a milder salpicón, seed the chilies)

    1 tomato, peeled, seeded, and finely diced

    ¼ cup coarsely chopped fresh cilantro,
      plus 4 sprigs for garnish

    1 tablespoon lime juice, or to taste

    salt and black pepper

1. Pick through the crabmeat, discarding any pieces of shell. Tease large pieces into fine shreds. Line four salad plates with tomato slices (three or four slices to a plate) and arrange three large basil leaves in the center of each, points facing out.

2. Heat the oil in a nonstick skillet. Add the onion, garlic, celery, and chilies and cook over medium heat until the vegetables are soft but not brown, about 2 minutes.

3. Increase the heat to high and stir in the crab, diced tomato, and cilantro. Cook until the crab is hot, about 3 minutes. Stir in the lime juice and salt and pepper to taste.

4. Mound the crab mixture in the center of the tomato slices on top of the basil. (Let a little basil peek out from the edges.) Garnish each salpicón with a sprig of cilantro and serve at once.

Serves 4

161 CALORIES PER SERVING; 21 G PROTEIN; 5 G FAT; 1 G SATURATED FAT; 8 G CARBOHYDRATE; 353 MG SODIUM; 67 MG CHOLESTEROL

LOBSTER FRA DIAVOLO

I've never seen lobster fra diavolo *on a menu in Italy, but when I was growing up in Baltimore, no dish seemed more quinessentially Italian. Here's an updated version of this childhood favorite. A professional chef would probably cut up the lobsters alive. This can be disconcerting to home cooks, so I've called for the lobster to be parboiled before cutting. I've also given instructions for making shrimp* fra diavolo *(see below), for people who are squeamish about cooking lobster.*

    2 2- to 2½-pound Maine or Florida lobsters
      (or 4 1¼-pound lobsters)

    1½ tablespoons extra-virgin olive oil

    ½ to 1 teaspoon hot pepper flakes, or to taste

    1 large onion, finely chopped

    4 cloves garlic, minced

    1 green bell pepper, cored, seeded, and finely chopped

    2 red ripe tomatoes, peeled, seeded, and finely chopped

    3 tablespoons good-quality brandy or grappa

    ½ cup dry white wine

    about 1 tablespoon balsamic vinegar

    3 tablespoons tomato paste

    2 bay leaves

    ¼ cup finely chopped flat-leaf parsley

    1½ cups reserved lobster cooking liquid
      (or chicken, fish, or vegetable broth)

    salt and freshly ground black pepper

1. Place the lobsters in a large pot with 2 inches of cold water (at least 2 cups). Cover the pot tightly and bring to a boil. Cook the lobsters until they begin to turn red, about 3 minutes. Transfer the lobsters to a colander and let cool, reserving the cooking liquid. When the lobsters have cooled, break off the claws, break into 2 sections, and crack each. Twist the tail and body in separate directions to remove the tail. Using a large knife or cleaver, cut the lobster tails in half lengthwise. Remove the vein running the length of the tail.

2. Heat the olive oil in a large sauté pan. Add the pepper flakes, onion, garlic, and green pepper. Cook the mixture over medium heat until it begins to brown, about 6 minutes, stirring often.

3. Increase the heat to high and stir in the tomatoes. Cook until the tomato liquid begins to evaporate, about 1 minute. Stir in the brandy and bring to a boil. Stir in the wine and vinegar and bring to a boil. Stir in the tomato paste, the bay leaves, half the parsley, 1½ cups of the lobster cooking liquid, salt, and pepper. Simmer this mixture until thick and richly flavored, about 10 minutes.

4. Add the lobster pieces. Gently simmer until the lobster is cooked (the meat will be firm and white), about 5 minutes. Season the sauce to taste, adding salt, vinegar, or pepper flakes. The mixture should be highly seasoned.

Sprinkle the remaining 2 tablespoons parsley on top and serve at once. I like to serve lobster fra diavolo over cooked linguine or spaghetti.

Note: To make shrimp fra diavolo, start at step **2.** Instead of adding lobster cooking liquid in step 3, add 1½ cups chicken, fish, or vegetable broth. Add 1½ pounds shrimp in place of the lobster in step **4.**

Serves 4

540 CALORIES PER SERVING; 89 G PROTEIN; 8 G FAT; 1 G SATURATED FAT; 18 G CARBOHYDRATE; 1,719 MG SODIUM; 305 MG CHOLESTEROL

VENETIAN-STYLE SQUID IN BLACK INK SAUCE

Baby squid simmered in a dark, rich ink sauce is a classic dish of Venice. The ink adds not only color, but a pleasing briny flavor that gives this dish a unique taste. Once you know how to clean squid (see below), the dish is a cinch to make. You could ask your fishmonger to clean the squid for you, saving the silvery ink sacs.

2 pounds small, uncleaned squid (or 1½ pounds cleaned squid, with ink sacs reserved)

1½ tablespoons olive oil

1 to 2 cloves garlic, minced

1 small onion, finely chopped

¼ cup chopped flat-leaf parsley

1 red ripe tomato, peeled, seeded, and finely chopped, with its juices

1 cup dry white wine

salt and freshly ground black pepper

1. Clean the squid, following the directions below. Cut the body crosswise into ½-inch rings. Cut the tentacles into 1-inch sections. Reserve the ink sacs.

2. Heat the olive oil in a nonstick skillet. Add the garlic, onion, and half the parsley and cook over medium heat until golden-brown, about 6 minutes. Add the tomatoes and cook until most of the juices have boiled away, about 3 minutes.

3. Stir in the squid and sauté for 1 minute. Add the wine, salt, and pepper and simmer until the squid are very tender, 20 to 30 minutes. Halfway through, squeeze the squid ink from sacs into the sauce. Correct the seasoning, adding salt and pepper to taste. Sprinkle the remaining parsley over the squid and serve at once.

Serves 4

310 CALORIES PER SERVING; 36 G PROTEIN; 8 G FAT; 1 G SATURATED FAT; 1 G CARBOHYDRATE; 108 MG SODIUM; 528 MG CHOLESTEROL

HOW TO CLEAN SQUID

Here's a simple way to clean squid. First, cut off the tentacles just above the eyes. Squeeze the base of the tentacles to remove the "beak," the squid's mouth, which looks like a celluloid chickpea. Discard it.

Next, hold the body by the tail and scrape it lengthwise toward the head with the back of a knife. Turn the squid over and scrape again. This loosens the entrails, which will come out when you pull out the head. Any entrails that remain can be scraped out with a small spoon.

The ink is found in a small, elongated, silvery sac amid the entrails. Gently cut it away with a paring knife and squeeze it into a sauce or stew. (Soap and water will wash off any ink that gets on your fingers.) Better still, wear rubber gloves when handling squid ink.

Finally, stab the "pen" (the transparent quill) that protrudes from the head end with the knife. Pull the body away, and the quill should slip right out. Discard it. Pull off any reddish skin on the body or tentacles with your fingers. (The skin is edible, but many people find it unaesthetic.) Rinse the body inside and out: it is now ready for stuffing or cutting into rings.

A QUICK CALAMARI SAUTÉ

As a foodie who came of age in Boston in the 1970s, I remember with fondness a postage-stamp-sized eatery called the Daily Catch. Located in the heart of Boston's "Little Italy," the North End, the Daily Catch specialized in calamari (squid) and almost single-handedly popularized this tentacled sea fare to Boston's non-Italian community. It was the sort of no-frills eatery where the chef served his food right in the skillet in which it was cooked. This quick calamari sauté is a great way to get people to try squid—even if they think they don't like it.

1½ pounds cleaned calamari

salt and freshly ground black pepper

1½ tablespoons all-purpose unbleached white flour

1 tablespoon extra-virgin olive oil

1 clove garlic, minced

¼ teaspoon hot pepper flakes

¾ cup dry white wine

2 tablespoons toasted pine nuts

2 tablespoons drained capers

1 teaspoon grated lemon zest

3 tablespoons chopped flat-leaf parsley

1. Wash the calamari and blot dry. Cut the bodies crosswise into ½-inch rings. Leave the heads whole, but cut any long tentacles into 1-inch pieces. Season the calamari with salt and pepper and lightly dust with flour.

2. Heat the olive oil in a large nonstick frying pan. Add the garlic and pepper flakes and cook over high heat until fragrant, about 30 seconds. Add the calamari and sauté for 1 minute. Add the wine, pine nuts, capers, lemon zest, and half the parsley and simmer until the calamari are cooked and the sauce is reduced, thickened, and richly flavored, 2 to 3 minutes. Do not overcook, or the calamari will become tough.

3. Correct the seasoning, adding salt or pepper to taste: the mixture should be highly seasoned. Serve at once. The Daily Catch used to serve this dish over linguine.

Note: Instructions on cleaning calamari can be found in preceding box.

Serves 4

259 CALORIES PER SERVING; 28 G PROTEIN; 8 G FAT; 1 G SATURATED FAT; 0 G CARBOHYDRATE; 236 MG SODIUM; 396 MG CHOLESTEROL

THAI SQUID SALAD

Part stir-fry and part salad, this dish is 100 percent delicious. I first tasted it at the streetside restaurant Panawan in the village of Mai Sariang in northwestern Thailand. Scoring the squid helps tenderize it and creates an attractive pattern.

FOR THE SAUCE:

1 tablespoon fish sauce (or to taste)

1 tablespoon fresh lime juice (or to taste)

2–3 teaspoons Thai chili paste (or to taste)

1 teaspoon sugar

3 stalks fresh lemongrass, or 2 tablespoons dried

4 large lettuce leaves

1 large ripe tomato, cut into wedges

1 tablespoon canola oil

2 cloves garlic, minced (2 teaspoons)

1–3 Thai or serrano chilies (or to taste), thinly sliced

1 onion, cut into thin wedges

1 pound squid, cleaned, cut into 1-inch pieces, and lightly scored in a crosshatch pattern

½ cup fresh mint leaves, for garnish

To make the sauce, combine the fish sauce, lime juice, chili paste, and sugar in a small bowl. Whisk until the sugar is dissolved.

Cut the top ⅓ off each lemongrass stalk, trim off the outside leaves and roots, and thinly slice the cores on the diagonal. If using dried lemongrass, soak it in warm water for 20 minutes. Arrange the lettuce leaves on a platter or salad plates, and place the tomato wedges on top. The dish can be prepared ahead to this stage.

Just before serving, heat a wok over high heat. Swirl in the oil. Add the garlic and chilies, and stir-fry for 10 seconds. Add the onion, squid, and lemongrass, and stir-fry for 1 to 2 minutes, or until the squid is firm and opaque.

Spoon the squid mixture over the tomatoes and lettuce leaves. Sprinkle with mint leaves and spoon the sauce on top. Serve at once.

Serves 4

172 CALORIES PER SERVING; 19 G PROTEIN; 5 G FAT;
12 G CARBOHYDRATE; 129 MG SODIUM; 265 MG CHOLESTEROL

BAKE-FRIED SQUID

If squid has gone from being a geek food to a chic food, it is largely thanks to a single Italian dish: calamari fritti *(fried squid). My low-fat version uses a technique I call "bake-frying": the squid is breaded as it would be for frying, but is then cooked in a hot oven rather than in oil. Instructions for cleaning squid are found in the box on page 197.*

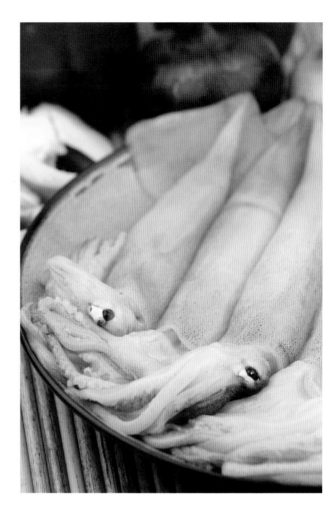

2 pounds cleaned squid

salt and freshly ground black pepper

1¾ cups all-purpose unbleached white flour

1 egg, plus 2 egg whites

¾ cup very fine white cornmeal

2 tablespoons extra-virgin olive oil or spray oil

1. Preheat the oven to 450°F. Cut the squid bodies widthwise into ¼-inch rings. Blot dry. Leave the tentacles whole. Season the squid with salt and pepper.

2. Place 1 cup of the flour in a shallow bowl and season with salt and pepper. Place the egg and whites in another bowl and beat well with a fork. Combine the remaining ¼ cup flour with the cornmeal in a third shallow bowl. Add salt and pepper and whisk to mix.

3. Use about ⅔ tablespoon of the oil to oil a large nonstick baking sheet. Dip each piece of squid first in flour, shaking off the excess, then in the egg mixture, and finally in the cornmeal, again shaking off the excess. Place the squid in a single layer on the baking sheet. Drizzle or spray the remaining oil on top.

4. Bake the squid until crisp and golden-brown, 8 to 10 minutes, turning with a spatula to ensure even browning. Serve at once.

Serves 6 to 8

385 CALORIES PER SERVING;* 31 G PROTEIN; 8 G FAT; 2 G SATURATED FAT; 44 G CARBOHYDRATE; 101 MG SODIUM; 388 MG CHOLESTEROL

Analysis is based on 6 servings.

POULTRY

. . . .

CHICKEN ALLA DIAVOLA

Sightly, succulent, and mercifully simple is this flattened, marinated grilled chicken—a dish with a parentage claimed by both the Florentines and the Romans. The traditional recipe calls for a whole chicken to be spatchcocked (cut down the backbone and opened like a book). If your fat budget allows, use the whole bird. Because chicken skin and dark meat are high in fat, I call for boneless, skinless chicken breasts below. I've also turned up the heat a few notches by adding mustard and hot pepper flakes to the traditional marinade. After all, alla diavola *means "in the style of the devil"!*

4 half chicken breasts (6 ounces each)

FOR THE MARINADE:

¼ cup fresh lemon juice

2 teaspoons dry mustard

1 tablespoon extra-virgin olive oil

2 teaspoons cracked black peppercorns, or to taste

½ teaspoon hot pepper flakes

coarse sea salt

Serves 4

320 CALORIES PER SERVING; 53 G PROTEIN; 9 G FAT; 2 G SATURATED FAT; 2 G CARBOHYDRATE; 159 MG SODIUM; 144 MG CHOLESTEROL

1. Trim any fat or sinews off the chicken breasts. Gently flatten each breast between 2 sheets of plastic wrap to achieve a uniform thickness, using a scalopine pounder or the side of a cleaver. Arrange the chicken breasts in a nonreactive baking dish.

2. Combine the lemon juice and mustard in a mixing bowl and whisk to mix. Whisk in the oil, peppercorns, and pepper flakes. Pour the marinade over the chicken, turning the breasts once or twice. Marinate the chicken, refrigerated, for at least 30 minutes or as long as 2 hours.

3. Preheat the grill to high. Oil the grate. Grill the chicken breasts until cooked, 2 to 3 minutes per side, seasoning with salt and basting with any extra marinade. I like to serve chicken alla diavola with arugula salad.

Chicken Adobo with Spicy Black Bean Salsa

CHICKEN ADOBO WITH SPICY BLACK BEAN SALSA

Here's a summery chicken dish from my hometown, Miami. The chicken is steeped in a tangy Cuban marinade called adobo. *(The basic ingredients for* adobo *are garlic, cumin, and sour orange or lime juice.) The chicken is then grilled, sliced, and served with a colorful salsa of mango and black beans. Scotch bonnets are the world's hottest peppers, but you can certainly use a milder chili if desired.*

1 to 1½ pounds boneless, skinless chicken breasts

FOR THE ADOBO MARINADE:

3 cloves garlic, minced

1 teaspoon ground cumin

½ teaspoon dried oregano

½ cup fresh lime juice

salt and freshly ground black pepper to taste

FOR THE SALSA:

1½ cups cooked black beans, rinsed and drained

1 ripe mango, peeled, seeded, and diced

¼ cup chopped red onion

¼ cup chopped fresh cilantro, mint, or basil

½ scotch bonnet chili, seeded and minced (optional)

salt, to taste

3 tablespoons lime juice, or to taste

1 tablespoon extra-virgin olive oil (optional)

2 to 3 teaspoons brown sugar

1. Wash and dry the chicken breasts and trim off any fat. Combine the ingredients for the marinade in a blender and purée until smooth. Correct the seasoning, adding salt and pepper to taste. The mixture should be highly seasoned. Combine the chicken and marinade in a non-reactive bowl and stir to mix. Cover the bowl with plastic wrap and marinate the chicken for 1 to 2 hours, turning occasionally.

2. Combine the ingredients for the salsa in a mixing bowl and toss to mix. Correct the seasoning, adding salt, lime juice, or sugar to taste. The salsa should be highly seasoned. It tastes best made shortly before serving. You can certainly have all the ingredients ready ahead of time and mix them at the last minute.

3. Preheat the barbecue grill or broiler to high. Drain the chicken breasts and blot dry, reserving a little marinade. Grill the breasts until cooked, about 2 minutes per side, basting with the marinade. Transfer the breasts to a cutting board and thinly slice across the grain.

4. Mound the salsa onto plates or a platter. Arrange the chicken slices on and around the salsa and serve at once.

Note: For convenience in serving, you can also grill the chicken ahead of time and serve at room temperature.

Serves 4

256 CALORIES PER SERVING;
27 G PROTEIN; 3 G FAT; 1 G SATURATED FAT;
32 G CARBOHYDRATE; 52 MG SODIUM;
55 MG CHOLESTEROL

GRILLED CHICKEN WITH TANGERINE GLAZE

Here's a Floridian twist on a Chinese classic. The perfumed sweetness of the tangerines counterpoints the saltiness of the soy sauce. (If tangerines aren't in season, you can use oranges.) The best way to remove the zest (the oil-rich outer rind) from the tangerines is to use a vegetable peeler.

2 boneless, skinless chicken breasts (about 1½ pounds)

FOR THE MARINADE/GLAZE:

½ cup soy sauce

½ cup fresh tangerine juice, plus 5½-inch strips tangerine zest

6 tablespoons honey

4 cloves garlic, minced

3 scallions, white part minced, green part thinly sliced for garnish

1 tablespoon minced fresh ginger

1 cinnamon stick

2 star anises (available at Asian markets—optional)

1 teaspoon sesame oil

2 teaspoons sesame seeds, toasted

1. Wash and dry the chicken breasts and trim off any fat or sinew. Cut the breasts into halves.

2. Combine the ingredients for the marinade/glaze in a mixing bowl and whisk until the honey has dissolved. Arrange the chicken breasts in a glass baking dish. Pour half the marinade on top. Marinate the chicken breasts in this mixture in the refrigerator for 1 to 2 hours, turning several times.

3. Prepare the glaze: Place the remaining marinade in a saucepan and boil until thick and syrupy, about 3 minutes. Strain the glaze into a small bowl.

4. Just before serving, preheat the grill to high.

5. Drain the chicken breasts and blot dry. Brush the breasts with sesame oil. Grill the chicken until cooked, about 2 minutes per side, brushing generously with glaze. Sprinkle the chicken with chopped scallion greens and sesame seeds and serve at once.

Note: To toast sesame seeds, place them in a dry skillet over medium heat. Cook, shaking the pan, until aromatic and the white seeds are lightly browned, 1 to 2 minutes.

Serves 4

297 CALORIES PER SERVING; 29 G PROTEIN; 5 G FAT; 1 G SATURATED FAT; 33 G CARBOHYDRATE; 2,124 MG SODIUM; 73 MG CHOLESTEROL

TANDOORI CHICKEN

Tandoori refers to a style of cooking that originated in northeast India. Meats were marinated in a tangy mixture of yogurt and spices, then grilled on vertical spits in an urn-shaped oven called a tandoor. *In recent years, tandoori has spread far beyond the boundaries of India. Indeed, many Western chefs have adopted this high-flavor, high-heat method of cooking. Most Indian cooks use food coloring to obtain the Day-Glo orange hue associated with traditional tandoori. I prefer the natural if somewhat paler look of tomato paste, but you can certainly use food coloring if you desire.*

1½ pounds boneless, skinless chicken breasts

1 medium onion, peeled

1 green bell pepper, seeded and cored

FOR THE MARINADE:

1-inch piece of fresh ginger, peeled and thinly sliced

1 shallot or ½ small onion, peeled and thinly sliced

4 cloves garlic, peeled

1 to 3 bird peppers or other hot chilies, thinly sliced (optional; see Note)

2 cups plain non-fat yogurt

¼ cup fresh lemon juice

2 tablespoons tomato paste

1 teaspoon ground cumin

1 teaspoon ground coriander

1 teaspoon ground turmeric

1 teaspoon freshly ground black pepper

½ teaspoon ground cardamom

salt to taste

lemon wedges for serving

1. Wash and dry the chicken breasts and trim off any fat. Cut the breasts into 1-inch squares. Cut the onion lengthwise in quarters, then cut each quarter widthwise in half. Cut the pepper into 1-inch squares.

2. Prepare the marinade. Finely chop the ginger, shallot, garlic, and chilies in a food processor or by hand. Work in the yogurt, lemon juice, and tomato paste. Purée to a smooth paste. Add the spices and salt to taste. The mixture should be highly seasoned. Transfer the marinade to a nonreactive bowl and stir in the chicken. Marinate the chicken in this mixture for at least 3 hours or as long as overnight.

3. Thread the chicken pieces onto metal or bamboo skewers, alternating with the onion and bell pepper. Preheat the grill to high. Grill the kebabs until the chicken is cooked, 2 to 3 minutes per side. Transfer the tandoori to a platter and serve with lemon wedges and rice.

Note: Bird peppers are fiery, tiny, ridged chilies sold in Indian and Asian markets. But any hot peppers will do. For a milder tandoor, omit the chilies. For extra flavor, use whole spices. Roast them in a dry skillet until fragrant, then grind them in a spice mill.

Serves 4

278 CALORIES PER SERVING; 39 G PROTEIN; 4 G FAT; 1 G SATURATED FAT; 21 G CARBOHYDRATE; 292 MG SODIUM; 84 MG CHOLESTEROL

JERK CHICKEN

Ten years ago, few people had ever heard of jerk. Today, we can barely live without it. Born in Boston Beach in northeast Jamaica, this fiery barbecue has taken the world by storm. The heart and soul of Jamaican jerk is the "seasoning," a fiery marinade made from dozens of tropical herbs and condiments. The dominant flavors in jerk seasoning are the tongue-blistering Scotch bonnet chili, the fragrant pimiento (as Jamaicans call allspice), and escallions (pungent Caribbean chives—these are hard to find in the U.S., but scallions make a good substitute). But equally important is the cooking method: a slow smoky grilling over fruitwood. Here's a simplified recipe that can be cooked on a barbecue grill. The wood chips help give your jerk the traditional smoky flavor, but the recipe can be prepared without them.

8 chicken legs (drumsticks and thighs attached) or
  4 chicken breasts (bone in)

3 tablespoons lime juice or distilled white vinegar

FOR THE SEASONING:

2 to 4 Scotch bonnet chilies (stemmed—for a milder jerk, seed the chilies before grinding)

2 bunches scallions, trimmed and cut into 1-inch pieces

1 small onion, peeled, trimmed, and cut into 1-inch pieces

1 tablespoon minced fresh garlic

1 tablespoon minced fresh ginger

1 tablespoon fresh thyme (or 2 teaspoons dried)

2 teaspoons ground allspice

1 teaspoon freshly ground black pepper

½ teaspoon freshly grated nutmeg

¼ teaspoon ground cinnamon

¼ cup lime juice or distilled white vinegar

3 tablespoons soy sauce

1 tablespoon olive oil

1 tablespoon brown sugar

kosher salt or coarse sea salt to taste

1 cup hardwood chips, such as hickory or mesquite (optional)

1. Trim off any lumps of fat from the chicken legs. If using chicken breasts, cut them in half, but leave the rib bones in. (To further reduce the fat, remove the skin.) Wash the chicken with lime juice or vinegar. Using the tip of a paring knife, make ¼-inch-deep holes in the meat. Place the chicken in a glass or ceramic baking dish.

2. Prepare the jerk seasoning. Finely chop the chilies, scallions, onion, garlic, and ginger in a food processor fitted with a chopping blade. Mix in the remaining ingredients. Correct the seasoning, adding lime juice, brown sugar, or salt. (Jamaicans use a *lot* of salt. You can certainly be more moderate.) The seasoning should be intensely flavorful and almost unbearably hot.

3. Spread the seasoning over the chicken with a rubber spatula, stuffing it into the holes. Marinate the chicken for 3 to 6 hours, turning several times. (The longer you marinate it, the stronger the jerk flavor will be.) Soak the wood chips in cold water for 1 hour.

4. Preheat the barbecue grill to low. Loosely wrap the wood chips in heavy-duty foil (or place in a foil pie pan) and place on the coals away from where you'll be grilling the chicken. Grill the chicken until cooked, 10 to 15 minutes per side, turning to ensure even cooking. Keep the grill covered to hold in the smoke. Serve the chicken at once, with a cold Jamaican beer such as Dragon Stout or Red Stripe.

Note: To achieve the right flavor, you must use scotch bonnet chilies, or their cousins, Mexican habaneros. If you can't find scotch bonnets, use fresh jalapeño chilies and a few tablespoons of a scotch bonnet–based hot sauce, such as Busha Browne's Pukka Sauce or Matook's from Trinidad. Warning: If you have sensitive skin, wear rubber gloves when handling scotch bonnets. (The scotch bonnet is fifty times hotter than a jalapeño!) Scotch bonnets are available at West Indian and Mexican markets, gourmet shops, and at many supermarkets.

Serves 8

228 CALORIES PER SERVING; 27 G PROTEIN; 10 G FAT; 2 G SATURATED FAT; 7 G CARBOHYDRATE; 476 MG SODIUM; 89 MG CHOLESTEROL

CHICKEN GRILLED IN HOJA SANTA LEAVES AND SERVED WITH OAXACAN MOLE VERDE

This exact dish may never have been served in Mexico, but it features a uniquely Mexican ingredient, an herb so divinely flavored that its Spanish name is hoja santa, *meaning "holy leaf." Imagine a soft, silky, emerald green, heart-shaped leaf with a peppery anise flavor that may remind you a little of sassafras. Then simply take your imagination to a Mexican market and you'll have a gustatory experience that borders on the religious. If you can't find fresh* hoja santa, *you can approximate the flavor by grilling the chicken wrapped in lettuce leaves with sprigs of fresh fennel leaves or thin slices of bulb fennel.* Note: *I like to serve the grilled chicken over Oaxacan Mole Verde (in the following recipe), but if you're pressed for time, the chicken is quite tasty without it.*

FOR THE CHICKEN AND MARINADE:

1½ pounds boneless, skinless chicken breasts

1 tablespoon extra-virgin olive oil

2 cloves garlic, minced

salt and freshly ground black pepper

½ cup fresh orange juice

8 fresh hoja santa leaves or 8 large Boston lettuce leaves, 8 sprigs fennel leaves, or 8 paper-thin slices fennel

1 batch Oaxacan Mole Verde (page 228) (optional)

Serves 4

331 CALORIES PER SERVING;* 54 G PROTEIN; 10 G FAT; 2 G SATURATED FAT; 5 G CARBOHYDRATE; 127 MG SODIUM; 144 MG CHOLESTEROL

Analysis is based on 4 servings.

1. Trim any sinews or fat off the chicken breasts. Cut each half breast section in half lengthwise to obtain pieces about 4 inches long and 1½ inches wide.

2. Toss the chicken breasts with the oil and garlic in a shallow baking dish. Season generously with salt and pepper. Pour the orange juice over the chicken and marinate for 30 minutes, turning once or twice. Meanwhile, light your grill and build a hot fire.

3. If you are using hoja santa leaves, wash them and blot dry, but don't blanch. If you're using lettuce leaves, you'll need to blanch them in rapidly boiling salted water for 30 seconds, then refresh them under cold water, drain, and blot dry. Wrap each piece of chicken in one hoja santa leaf and tie shut with string or secure with a toothpick. If you're using lettuce leaves, place a sprig of fennel or fennel slice on top of a piece of the chicken and wrap in the lettuce leaf. Tie with string or pin shut with a toothpick.

4. Grill the chicken bundles until the meat is cooked, 4 to 6 minutes per side, turning with tongs. If you are serving the chicken with mole verde, spoon it onto four plates and set two chicken bundles on top of each. Be sure to remove the string or toothpicks.

MANGO AND CHICKEN STIR-FRY

Asia meets the Caribbean in this tropical fruity stir-fry. Let mangoes ripen at room temperature until squeezably soft and very fragrant. **Note:** *Some people are allergic to mango sap, so wear gloves if you have sensitive skin.*

1¼ pounds skinless chicken thighs or 1¼ pounds boneless, skinless chicken breasts

1 large or 2 small ripe mangoes

¼ pound young asparagus or slender green beans

3 tablespoons soy sauce

2 tablespoons fresh orange or tangerine juice

1 tablespoon honey

1 teaspoon cornstarch

1 to 1½ tablespoons canola oil

2 cloves garlic, minced

1 tablespoon minced fresh ginger

2 scallions, white part minced, green part finely chopped

½ cup stemmed fresh mint leaves or cilantro

Mango and Chicken Stir-Fry

1. Wash and dry the chicken and trim off any fat. If using chicken thighs, cut the meat off the bones and slice as thinly as possible. If using chicken breasts, cut across the grain on the diagonal into ¼-inch strips. Cut these strips into 2-inch pieces.

2. Peel the mango and cut the flesh off the seed. Cut the mango into ½-inch cubes and set aside. Snap the fibrous ends off the asparagus and cut the stalks on the diagonal into 1-inch pieces. If using green beans, remove the ends and strings and cut on the diagonal into 1-inch pieces.

3. Combine the soy sauce, orange juice, honey, and cornstarch in a small bowl and stir until the cornstarch is dissolved. The recipe can be prepared ahead to this stage.

4. Just before serving, heat a nonstick wok or frying pan over high heat. Swirl in the oil. Add the garlic, ginger, and scallion whites and stir-fry until fragrant but not brown, about 15 seconds. Add the chicken and asparagus or green beans and stir-fry for 2 minutes. Stir the sauce again and add it to the wok. Continue stir-frying until the chicken is cooked and nicely coated with sauce, 1 to 2 minutes. Stir in the mango, scallion greens, and mint leaves and cook for 20 seconds. Serve at once.

Serves 4

240 CALORIES PER SERVING; 18 G PROTEIN; 11 G FAT; 2 G SATURATED FAT; 19 G CARBOHYDRATE; 832 MG SODIUM; 58 MG CHOLESTEROL

GINGERY CHICKEN AND GREEN BEAN STIR-FRY

For the best results use "young" ginger, the kind that's very tender and juicy, with a thin skin and virtually no fibers. Look for young ginger in Asian markets. My favorite bean for this dish is the skinny French haricot vert, but any slender green bean will do. Oyster sauce is a tangy condiment available in the ethnic-foods section of most supermarkets.

1 pound boneless, skinless chicken breasts

8 ounces haricot verts or green beans

FOR THE SAUCE:

¼ cup chicken stock (see page 379)

2 tablespoons rice wine or sherry

1½ tablespoons soy sauce

1½ tablespoons oyster sauce (optional)

2 teaspoons honey

2 teaspoons cornstarch

TO FINISH THE DISH:

1 tablespoon canola oil

1 tablespoon minced fresh ginger

1 tablespoon thinly slivered fresh ginger

3 cloves garlic, minced

3 scallions, white part minced, green part cut into 1-inch pieces for garnish

1. Wash and dry the chicken and trim off any fat. Cut the chicken breasts across the grain on the diagonal into thin ⅛-inch strips. Snap the ends off the green beans.

2. Combine the ingredients for the sauce in a small bowl and stir until the cornstarch is dissolved. The recipe can be prepared ahead to this stage.

3. Just before serving, heat a nonstick wok or frying pan over high heat. Swirl in the oil. Add the gingers, garlic, and scallion whites and stir-fry until fragrant but not brown, about 15 seconds. Add the chicken and green beans and stir-fry until almost cooked, about 2 minutes. Stir the sauce again to redissolve the cornstarch and add it to the wok. Continue stir-frying until the chicken is cooked and nicely coated with sauce, 1 to 2 minutes. Stir in the scallion greens and serve at once.

Serves 4

204 CALORIES PER SERVING; 22 G PROTEIN; 6 G FAT; 1 G SATURATED FAT; 12 G CARBOHYDRATE; 440 MG SODIUM; 55 MG CHOLESTEROL

THAI CHICKEN, BASIL, AND CHILI STIR-FRY

This explosively flavorful dish is one of the glories of Thai cuisine. To be strictly authentic, use Thai basil, which has smaller leaves and a more pronounced licorice flavor than Western basil. Thai basil is available at Asian markets, but regular basil makes a perfectly delectable stir-fry. I've given a range of chilies: My readers have probably gathered by now that I have an asbestos palate. For a milder stir-fry, use just 1 chili and remove the seeds.

1 pound boneless, skinless chicken breasts

1 bunch fresh basil (2 cups leaves)

FOR THE SAUCE:

¼ cup chicken stock (see page 379)

2 tablespoons fish sauce (see page 381) or soy sauce

2 teaspoons sugar or honey

¼ to ½ teaspoon freshly ground black pepper

2 teaspoons cornstarch

1 tablespoon canola oil

3 cloves garlic, minced

3 scallions, white part minced, green part thinly sliced

1 to 4 jalapeño or Thai chilies, thinly sliced

6 ounces Asian eggplant, cut in half lengthwise, then thinly sliced on the diagonal (see Note)

6 ounces snow peas, stems and strings removed

LEMONGRASS CHICKEN

Lemongrass chicken is to Vietnamese cooking what coq au vin is to French cooking. This simple dish was a mainstay of my diet during my student days in Paris. Native to Southeast Asia, lemongrass is a fibrous, scallion-shaped herb with a delicate grassy-lemony flavor that has none of the acidity found in lemon juice. Fresh lemongrass can be found at Asian markets, specialty greengrocers, and at many supermarkets. If unavailable use dried lemongrass (soak in hot water for 20 minutes). Or use 1 teaspoon grated lemon zest.

1¼ pounds boneless, skinless chicken breasts

1½ tablespoons honey

3 tablespoons fish sauce or soy sauce

1 to 2 stalks fresh lemongrass (2 tablespoons minced)

1½ tablespoons canola oil

3 cloves garlic, minced

1 large onion, thinly sliced (about 2 cups)

3 tablespoons chopped fresh cilantro or mint for garnish (optional)

1. Wash and dry the chicken breasts and trim off any fat. Cut the chicken breasts across the grain on the diagonal into ¼-inch strips. Cut these strips into 2-inch pieces. Wash, dry, and stem the basil.

2. Combine the ingredients for the sauce in a small bowl and stir until the sugar is dissolved.

3. Just before serving, heat a nonstick wok or frying pan over high heat. Swirl in the oil. Add the garlic, scallion whites, and chilies and stir-fry until fragrant but not brown, about 15 seconds. Add the chicken, eggplant, and snow peas and stir-fry for 2 minutes. Stir in the basil, scallion greens, and sauce and continue stir-frying until the chicken is cooked, 1 to 2 minutes.

Note: This dish is supposed to be a little soupy. Serve it in bowls over rice.

Note: Asian eggplant is a long, slender, purplish eggplant. Look for it in Asian markets and many supermarkets or use a small Italian-style eggplant.

Serves 4

202 CALORIES PER SERVING; 24 G PROTEIN; 6 G FAT; 1 G SATURATED FAT; 13 G CARBOHYDRATE; 573 MG SODIUM; 55 MG CHOLESTEROL

1. Wash and dry the chicken and trim off any fat. Cut the chicken breasts across the grain on the diagonal into ⅛-inch strips. Cut these strips into 2-inch pieces. Combine the chicken, honey, and 1 tablespoon fish sauce in a bowl and stir to mix. Let marinate for 5 to 10 minutes.

2. Trim the green leaves and root end off the lemongrass stalk and strip off the outside leaves. What remains will be a greenish cream-colored core 4- to 5-inches long and ¼- to ½-inch thick. Mince this core finely; you'll need about 2 tablespoons.

3. Just before serving, heat a wok (preferably nonstick) over high heat and swirl in the oil. Add the garlic and lemongrass and stir-fry until fragrant but not brown, about 15 seconds. Add the chicken and stir-fry until the pieces turn white, about 1 minute.

4. Move the chicken to the sides of the wok and add the onion to the center. Stir-fry until the onion loses its rawness, about 1 minute. Mix the chicken back in the center of the wok, add the remaining fish sauce, continue stir-frying until the chicken is cooked, 2 to 3 minutes. Correct the seasoning, adding honey or fish sauce to taste. The dish should be a little sweet and salty. Sprinkle the chicken with the cilantro, if desired, and serve at once.

Serves 4

274 CALORIES PER SERVING; 32 G PROTEIN; 9 G FAT; 1 G SATURATED FAT; 15 G CARBOHYDRATE; 185 MG SODIUM; 85 MG CHOLESTEROL

CHICKEN AND WILD MUSHROOM STIR-FRY

Lest anyone doubt we live in the age of the global village, consider this lively dish. It unites two thoroughly Western flavorings (madeira and wild mushrooms) with the venerable Asian cooking technique of stir-frying. You can use use almost any type of exotic mushroom: shiitakes, oyster mushrooms, morels, portabellos, creminis, porcini (also known as boletus)—or even regular button mushrooms. Better still, use a blend. The important thing is that the mushrooms be fresh. Mushroom soy sauce is a thick, mushroom-flavored soy sauce. Look for it at Asian markets and gourmet shops.

1¼ pounds boneless, skinless chicken breasts

12 to 16 ounces exotic mushrooms

FOR THE SAUCE:

¼ cup Chicken stock (see page 379)

3 tablespoons madeira or sherry

3 tablespoons mushroom soy sauce or a mixture of regular soy sauce and oyster sauce

2 teaspoons cornstarch

1½ tablespoons olive oil

3 cloves garlic, minced

2 shallots, minced (about 2 tablespoons)

2 teaspoons minced fresh ginger (optional)

½ cup chopped fresh flat-leaf parsley

SINGAPORE BLACK PEPPER CHICKEN

*Black pepper crab is one of the national dishes of Singapore.
This recipe combines the robust flavor of the seafood dish with America's favorite meat for stir-frying, chicken.*

1 pound boneless, skinless chicken breasts

FOR THE SAUCE:

2 tablespoons chicken stock (see page 379) or water

2 tablespoons oyster sauce

2 tablespoons soy sauce

2 tablespoons rice wine

2 teaspoons sugar or honey

2 teaspoons cornstarch

1 to 1½ tablespoons canola oil

3 cloves garlic, minced

1 tablespoon chopped fresh ginger

1 to 3 chili peppers, minced
(for a milder dish, seed the chilies)

2 scallions, white part minced,
green part finely chopped for garnish

2 to 3 teaspoons coarsely ground black peppercorns

1 red or yellow bell pepper, cored, seeded,
and cut into 1-inch dice

4 ounces snow peas, snapped, strings removed

1. Wash and dry the chicken breasts and trim off any fat. Cut the breasts across the grain on the diagonal into ¼-inch strips and cut these strips into 2-inch pieces. Combine the ingredients for the sauce in a small bowl and stir to mix.

2. Just before serving, heat a wok to smoking. Swirl in the oil. Add the garlic, ginger, chilies, scallion whites, and black pepper. Stir-fry over high heat until fragrant but not brown, about 15 seconds. Add the chicken and stir-fry for 1 minute. Add the red bell pepper and snow peas and stir-fry for 1 minute or until the chicken is almost cooked.

3. Stir the ingredients for the sauce to redissolve the sugar and cornstarch. Stir the sauce into the chicken mixture and bring to a boil. Simmer until the chicken is cooked, about 1 minute. Correct the seasoning, adding pepper if necessary. The chicken should be highly seasoned. Sprinkle the chicken with the scallion greens and serve at once.

Serves 4

206 CALORIES PER SERVING; 23 G PROTEIN; 8 G FAT; 1 G SATURATED FAT; 10 G CARBOHYDRATE; 641 MG SODIUM; 57 MG CHOLESTEROL

1. Wash and dry the chicken breasts and trim off any fat. Cut the breasts across the grain on the diagonal into ¼-inch strips and cut these strips into 2-inch pieces. Trim the stem ends off the mushrooms and wipe the caps clean with a damp cloth. Cut any large mushrooms in half or quarters; the idea is to have pieces that are all the same size.

2. Combine the ingredients for the sauce in a small bowl and whisk until the cornstarch is dissolved. The recipe can be prepared ahead to this stage.

3. Just before serving, heat a large nonstick wok over high heat. Swirl in the oil. Add the garlic, shallots, and ginger and stir-fry until fragrant but not brown, about 15 seconds. Add the chicken and stir-fry for 1 minute. Add the mushrooms and stir-fry until crispy-tender, about 2 minutes.

4. Stir the sauce again and add it to the wok. Continue stir-frying until the chicken and mushrooms are cooked and nicely coated with sauce, 1 to 2 minutes. Stir in the parsley and cook for 15 seconds. Serve at once.

Serves 4

240 CALORIES PER SERVING; 29 G PROTEIN; 9 G FAT; 2 G SATURATED FAT; 10 G CARBOHYDRATE; 511 MG SODIUM; 70 MG CHOLESTEROL

CHICKEN VERDICCHIO

When I lived in Boston, this simple sauté was a favorite at the family restaurants in the North End (Boston's "Little Italy"). Verdicchio is a pungent, crisp white wine from central Italy. It goes particularly well with the earthy flavor of artichokes. Naturally, the dish will be best if made with fresh artichokes. But canned or frozen artichokes will produce a perfectly tasty version of this dish, too. (Skip step 1 and add them 5 minutes before the chicken is done.) I've written the recipe for boneless, skinless chicken breasts, but if your fat budget allows it, make it with a cut-up whole chicken for an even richer flavor.

Serves 4

439 CALORIES PER SERVING; 40 G PROTEIN; 10 G FAT; 2 G SATURATED FAT; 27.5 G CARBOHYDRATE; 183.6 MG SODIUM; 96 MG CHOLESTEROL

1 pound boneless, skinless chicken breasts, cut into 2-inch diamond-shaped pieces, or 1 chicken, cut into 8 even pieces

salt and freshly ground black pepper

2 tablespoons all-purpose unbleached white flour

1½ tablespoons extra-virgin olive oil

1 onion, finely chopped

1 clove garlic, minced

3 tablespoons chopped flat-leaf parsley

2 to 3 cups Verdicchio or other dry white Italian wine

½ pound baby red potatoes (8 potatoes), scrubbed and cut in halves or quarters to obtain 1-inch pieces)

3 large or 4 medium artichokes, trimmed, quartered, and cooked, or 1 14-ounce can artichoke hearts, rinsed and drained

8 black olives (optional)

1. In a mixing bowl, toss the chicken with salt and pepper and the flour. Heat half the olive oil in a nonstick frying pan. Brown the chicken pieces over a high flame, 1 to 2 minutes per side. Transfer the chicken to a plate lined with paper towels to drain.

2. Add the remaining oil to the pan and heat. Add the onion, the garlic, and half the parsley and cook over medium heat until soft and translucent but not brown, about 4 minutes.

3. Return the chicken to the pan with 2 cups wine and the potatoes and bring to a boil. Reduce the heat and simmer until the chicken and potatoes are cooked and the sauce reduced and flavorful, 15 to 20 minutes. (If the chicken starts to dry out, add a little more wine: the dish should be quite saucy.) Add the cooked artichokes and olives the last 5 minutes. Correct the seasoning, adding salt or pepper to taste. Garnish with the remaining parsley and serve.

CHICKEN CACCIATORE

When I was growing up, chicken cacciatore was probably the best-known Italian dish. For that matter, it was the only Italian dish many Americans had ever heard of. This was long before the pasta revolution, before our discovery of regional Italian cooking, before the explosive proliferation of Italian restaurants in this country. Today, cacciatore sounds dated if not clichéd, and I bet it's been a good long time since you've sampled this soulful dish— chicken "in the style of a hunter." I've written the following recipe for boneless, skinless chicken breasts, but if your fat budget allows it, make it with a cut-up whole chicken; the bones will produce an even richer flavor.

1½ pounds boneless, skinless chicken breasts

salt and freshly ground black pepper

1½ tablespoons olive oil

½ teaspoon hot pepper flakes, or to taste

1 medium onion, finely chopped

1 stalk celery, finely chopped

1 green bell pepper, cored, seeded, and cut into ¼-inch dice

5 ounces thinly sliced porcini, shiitake, or portobello mushrooms, or regular button mushrooms

½ cup dry white wine

1 28-ounce can imported peeled plum tomatoes with their juices

1 bay leaf

3 tablespoons finely chopped flat-leaf parsley

2 to 3 teaspoons red wine vinegar

1. Rinse and dry the chicken breasts and cut into 2-inch pieces. Season with salt and pepper. Heat half the oil in a large nonstick frying pan over high heat. Add the chicken pieces and brown on both sides, about 1 minute per side. Transfer the chicken to a plate with a slotted spoon.

2. Heat the remaining oil in the pan. Add the pepper flakes, onion, celery, and bell pepper and cook over medium heat until the vegetables are soft and translucent, about 5 minutes. Add the mushrooms and cook until tender and most of the mushroom liquid has evaporated, about 3 minutes. Stir in the chicken and the white wine and bring to a boil.

3. Purée the tomatoes with their juices in a food processor or through a vegetable mill. Add them to the chicken with the bay leaf and half the parsley. Gently simmer the cacciatore over medium heat until the chicken is cooked and the sauce is thick and richly flavored, about 20 minutes. Add vinegar to taste the last 5 minutes. Remove and discard the bay leaf. Correct the seasoning, adding salt and pepper to taste. Sprinkle the remaining parsley on top and serve at once.

Serves 4

347 CALORIES PER SERVING; 47 G PROTEIN; 10 G FAT; 2 G SATURATED FAT; 17 G CARBOHYDRATE; 429 MG SODIUM; 104 MG CHOLESTEROL

CHICKEN WITH BALSAMIC VINEGAR

Balsamic vinegar owes its sweetness to the fact that it's made with grape must (partially fermented juice), not wine. This leaves a considerable amount of residual sugar in the vinegar, which makes it ideal for reducing for sauces. Simple but incredibly flavorful, this is high-flavor, low-fat Italian cooking at its best.

1½ pounds boneless, skinless chicken breasts

salt and freshly ground black pepper

2 to 3 tablespoons all-purpose unbleached white flour for dredging, or as needed

1 tablespoon extra-virgin olive oil

1 cup balsamic vinegar

1 cup Chicken Stock (page 379)

2 tablespoons finely chopped flat-leaf parsley

CHICKEN WITH ASPARAGUS, LEMON, AND PARMESAN

Asparagus sprinkled with Parmesan cheese is a popular vegetable in Florence—especially in springtime, when the first of the crop comes into season. That gave me the idea for a more substantial dish, a chicken, asparagus, and Parmesan sauté. (This is a good place to use up the chicken tenderloins reserved from other recipes.) Time-conscious cooks will appreciate the fact that this dish can be made in its entirety in a single pan.

1 pound asparagus stalks

salt

1 tablespoon extra-virgin olive oil

1½ pounds skinless, boneless chicken breasts,
   cut crosswise into ½-inch strips

freshly ground black pepper

1½ tablespoons all-purpose unbleached white flour

1 medium onion, thinly sliced

1 cup dry white vermouth or white wine

1 cup Chicken Stock (page 379)

1 to 2 tablespoons fresh lemon juice

3 to 4 tablespoons freshly grated Parmigiano-Reggiano
   cheese

1. Snap the asparagus stalks (see box). Discard the stem ends. Cut the stalks sharply on the diagonal into 2-inch pieces. Bring 3 cups lightly salted water to a boil in a 12-inch nonstick frying pan. Cook the asparagus until crisp-tender, about 3 minutes. Drain the asparagus in a colander, refresh under cold water, and drain again. Rinse out the pan.

2. Heat half the olive oil in the pan. Season the chicken pieces with salt and pepper and toss with the flour. Lightly brown the chicken pieces on all sides over medium-high heat, 1 to 2 minutes per side. Transfer the chicken to a plate lined with paper towels to drain.

3. Add the remaining olive oil to the pan. Add the onion and cook over medium heat until soft but not brown, about 4 minutes. Return the chicken to the pan, add the vermouth, and bring to a boil. Add the stock. Reduce the heat and gently simmer the chicken until cooked and tender, until the wine and stock have reduced to a thick, flavorful sauce, about 10 minutes.

4. Stir in the asparagus and the lemon juice and cook for 1 minute. Correct the seasoning, adding salt or lemon juice to taste. Just before serving, sprinkle the chicken and asparagus with the Parmesan cheese. Serve at once.

Serves 4

431 CALORIES PER SERVING; 60 G PROTEIN; 12 G FAT; 3 G SATURATED FAT; 9 G CARBOHYDRATE; 315 MG SODIUM; 148 MG CHOLESTEROL

HOW TO SNAP ASPARAGUS

The easiest way to snap asparagus is to grasp each stalk firmly by the cut end and bend the stalk over; it will snap at the natural point of tenderness.

---

1. Cut each chicken breast (if whole) into halves and trim off any fat or sinews. (For a neater appearance, remove the tenderloins and reserve them for other recipes.) Season each half breast with salt and pepper and lightly dust with flour, shaking off the excess.

2. Heat the oil in a nonstick frying pan. Lightly brown the breasts on both sides over high heat, about 2 minutes per side. Add the vinegar and bring to a boil. Reduce the heat to medium and simmer until the vinegar is reduced by two-thirds.

3. Add the chicken stock and continue simmering, uncovered, until the chicken is tender, about 10 minutes. Transfer it to a platter. Boil the sauce until reduced, thick, and flavorful, about 10 minutes. Add salt and pepper to taste. Spoon the sauce over the chicken and sprinkle with the parsley. Serve at once.

Serves 4

391 CALORIES PER SERVING; 54 G PROTEIN; 10 G FAT; 2 G SATURATED FAT; 17 G CARBOHYDRATE; 220 MG SODIUM; 144 MG CHOLESTEROL

CHICKEN ALMENDRADA

(IN OAXACAN ALMOND SAUCE)

Her nickname was La Abuelita ("Little Grandmother") and her lunch counter in the November 20 Market in Oaxaca was always crowded with locals. When she saw my notebook, she insisted I sit down to try her almendrada, *a soulful stew flavored with toasted almonds, sesame seeds, and roasted vegetables.*

(This dish takes its name from the Spanish word for almond, almendra.*)*

Little Grandmother makes her almendrada *with chicken, but you could also use pork or veal. For that matter, you could serve the sauce over any type of grilled seafood. In terms of the flavor profile, we're playing sweet against sour here: the sweetness of almonds, raisins, and cinnamon in counterpoint to the acid tang of the tomatoes and tomatillos. To reduce the fat in the traditional recipe, I use a fraction of the lard and almonds, boosting the nutty taste of the latter with a few drops of almond extract. To further boost the flavor, I cook the chicken right in the sauce. (A Mexican would cook it separately.) Even with these modifications, you'll find this an irresistible dish with a delectably creamy consistency, bursting with unexpected flavors.* Note: *I know we're a little high on the fat grams here (although the fat still accounts for less than 30 percent of the calories). Make this a splurge dinner.*

FOR THE ALMOND SAUCE:

4 medium tomatoes, stemmed (about 1¼ pounds)

3 tomatillos, peeled and washed (about 3 ounces)

6 cloves garlic, peeled

½ small onion, peeled and cut in half lengthwise

3 tablespoons slivered almonds (about ⅔ ounce)

2 tablespoons sesame seeds

1 slice white bread (with crust), lightly toasted

2 sprigs cilantro

2 sprigs parsley

½ teaspoon cinnamon

½ teaspoon dried oregano

⅛ teaspoon dried cloves

1 teaspoon salt, or to taste

½ teaspoon black pepper, or to taste

½ to 1 teaspoon sugar, or to taste

1 tablespoon lard or olive oil

¼ teaspoon almond extract

½ cup chicken stock, or as needed

TO FINISH THE ALMENDRADA:

1½ pounds boneless, skinless chicken breasts

2 tablespoons raisins

1 tablespoon sliced pickled jalapeño chilies

1 tablespoon sliced pimiento-stuffed olives

1 tablespoon drained capers

4 tortillas, warmed

1. Heat a comal or cast-iron skillet over medium-high heat. Cook the tomatoes and tomatillos until they are darkly browned on all sides, about 10 minutes. Transfer to the bowl of a blender. Roast the garlic and onion until they're darkly browned on all sides, about 6 minutes. Transfer to the blender. Toast the almonds until they are lightly browned, shaking the pan, 2 to 3 minutes. Transfer to the blender. Toast the sesame seeds until they're lightly browned, 1 to 2 minutes. Transfer half the sesame seeds to the blender. Set aside the remaining seeds for garnish.

2. Add the bread, cilantro, parsley, cinnamon, oregano, cloves, salt, pepper, and ½ teaspoon of the sugar to the blender. Purée until smooth.

3. Heat the lard or oil in a deep pot over high heat. Add the sauce and fry it until it's thick and flavorful, about 10 minutes, stirring often. Lower the heat to medium if the sauce spatters too much. Add the almond extract and ½ cup of stock after 5 minutes. The sauce should be thick but pourable: Add additional stock as needed. The recipe can be prepared up to a day ahead to this stage. (If preparing ahead, let the sauce cool to room temperature, then refrigerate.)

4. Trim any fat from the chicken. Wash each breast and blot dry. Cut each breast into 2-inch pieces. Add the chicken, raisins, pickled jalapeños, olives, and capers to the sauce. Gently simmer over medium heat until the chicken is cooked, about 10 minutes. Correct the seasoning, adding salt and pepper to taste. Check the sweetness, adding sugar if needed; the sauce should have just the tiniest bit of sweetness. Transfer the chicken and sauce to a platter or plates and sprinkle with the remaining sesame seeds. Serve at once with the warm tortillas.

Serves 4

435 CALORIES PER SERVING; 58 G PROTEIN; 13 G FAT; 3 G SATURATED FAT; 21 G CARBOHYDRATE; 773 MG SODIUM; 145 MG CHOLESTEROL

CHICKEN WITH TOMATILLOS AND CILANTRO

I first tasted this dish—or one very much like it—at a charming Mexican restaurant in Boston called the Casa Romero. The Casa was one of the nation's first upscale Mexican restaurants, and this dish epitomizes its light approach to Mexican cooking. If you like cilantro, you'll love the explosive flavors of this simple stovetop sauté.

1 pound tomatillos, husked

1¼ pounds boneless, skinless chicken breasts, trimmed of any fat

salt and freshly ground black pepper

1 tablespoon olive oil

½ white onion, finely chopped (about ½ cup)

4 scallions, finely chopped

1 jalapeño chili (seeded and minced)

1 tablespoon fresh lime juice, or to taste

½ teaspoon sugar, or to taste

¼ cup chopped fresh cilantro

1. Heat a comal or cast iron skillet over a medium flame. Roast the tomatillos until lightly browned and soft, about 8 minutes in all, turning with tongs. Transfer the tomatillos to a food processor and grind to a coarse purée.

2. Wash the chicken breasts, blot dry, and cut into 2-inch diamonds. Season with salt and pepper.

3. Heat the olive oil in a nonstick skillet. Add the onion, scallions, and chili and cook over medium heat until soft but not brown, 4 minutes, stirring as needed. Increase the heat to high, add the chicken, and cook until lightly seared, 2 minutes. Stir in the tomatillos, lime juice, and sugar and simmer until the chicken is cooked, 2 minutes.

4. Stir in the cilantro and cook for 1 minute. Correct the seasoning, adding salt or sugar to taste. (Use the sugar to balance the tartness of the tomatillos.) Serve with white or Mexican rice.

Serves 4

314 CALORIES PER SERVING; 46 G PROTEIN; 10 G FAT; 2 G SATURATED FAT; 10 G CARBOHYDRATE; 105 MG SODIUM; 120 MG CHOLESTEROL

JAPANESE STEAK HOUSE–STYLE CHICKEN

Here's a home version of Japanese teppan *(steak house–style) chicken that both kids and adults will enjoy, especially if you cook it at the table in an electric frying pan or large skillet. Serve with steamed white or brown rice.*

1½–2 tablespoons canola oil

1 large onion, thinly sliced

8 ounces shiitake or button mushrooms, stemmed and thinly sliced

4 scallions, whites minced, greens thinly sliced

2 cloves garlic, minced (2 teaspoons)

1 tablespoon minced fresh ginger

1–1½ pounds skinless, boneless chicken breasts, thinly sliced

3 tablespoons sesame seeds

2 tablespoons sake (rice wine) or sherry

2 tablespoons soy sauce (or to taste)

2 tablespoons fresh lemon juice

3 cups mung bean sprouts

salt and freshly ground black pepper

Just before serving, heat a large wok over high heat. Swirl in 1 tablespoon of the oil. Add the onion and mushrooms, and cook for 2 minutes, or until the onion is tender-crisp. Transfer the mixture to a platter with a slotted spoon.

Swirl the remaining oil in the wok. Add the scallion whites, garlic, and ginger, and cook for 20 seconds, or until fragrant but not brown. Add the chicken and sesame seeds, and cook for 1 minute, stirring with a wooden spoon. Add the sake and flambé. (If working over a gas burner, simply tilt the pan toward the flame, and the wine will catch fire. If using an electric burner, light the wine with a match.)

When the flame dies down, stir in the soy sauce and lemon juice, and continue cooking for 2 to 3 minutes, or until the chicken is done. Add the bean sprouts and cook over high heat for 30 seconds, or until the sprouts lose their rawness. Stir in the onion, mushrooms, scallion greens, salt, and pepper. Correct the seasoning, adding soy sauce and lemon juice to taste.

Serves 4

245 CALORIES PER SERVING; 23 G PROTEIN; 11 G FAT; 14 G CARBOHYDRATE; 566 MG SODIUM; 46 MG CHOLESTEROL

PEKING CHICKEN

Andrew Swersky, owner/chef of the Morada Bar & Grill in Boca Raton, Florida, had the idea of using chicken, instead of fatty duck, in this classic Chinese recipe. I've lightened and simplified his version, using flour tortillas instead of Mandarin pancakes. The result is a great party dish, with scallion brushes providing some of the crunch of the duck skin in the traditional recipe.

5 cloves garlic, minced (5 teaspoons)

2 tablespoons minced fresh ginger

1 cup hoisin sauce

¼ cup soy sauce

¼ cup rice wine vinegar

¼ cup honey

2 pounds skinless, boneless chicken breasts, thinly sliced across the grain

12 scallions

1 tablespoon sesame oil

12 flour tortillas

Serves 6 to 8

436 CALORIES PER SERVING; 42 G PROTEIN; 8 G FAT; 47 G CARBOHYDRATE; 1,519 MG SODIUM; 96 MG CHOLESTEROL

Combine the garlic, ginger, hoisin sauce, soy sauce, vinegar, and honey in a small bowl. Whisk to mix. Set aside half of this mixture to use as a sauce. Marinate the chicken in the remaining mixture for 1 to 2 hours, stirring several times.

Meanwhile, make the scallion brushes. Cut the roots and greens off the scallions. (Reserve the latter for another recipe in this book.) There should be 3-inch pieces of scallion white remaining. Make a series of 1-inch length-wise cuts in each end, gradually rotating the scallion, to form the individual "bristles" of the brush. Soak the scallions in a bowl of ice water for a couple of hours to swell the ends of the brushes.

Just before serving, heat the oil in a large nonstick frying pan. Cook the chicken over medium heat for 2 minutes, or until done. Set aside and keep warm. Lightly brush each tortilla with water and toast in a nonstick frying pan over high heat (or warm in a steamer). Divide the reserved marinade among 6 small ramekins or dishes.

Mound the chicken in the center of a platter. Arrange the tortillas (fold them in quarters or halves) and scallion brushes around the chicken. Invite guests to use a scallion to brush a tortilla with hoisin sauce. Have them place a spoonful of chicken and the scallion brush in a tortilla and roll it into a cone.

TURKEY PICCATA

When I set out to write this book, I despaired of being able to include some of my favorite Italian dishes, such as veal piccata. After all, how could you possibly cut enough fat in a dish that consists of scalopine dipped in an egg-and-cheese batter and pan-fried in oceans of butter? My first step was to use lean turkey breasts instead of veal. Then I cut the number of egg yolks in the batter. (For a dish even lower in fat, you could eliminate them completely.) Finally, I cook the scalopine in olive oil instead of butter. I think you'll be pleasantly surprised at how tasty a low-fat version can be.

1½ pounds turkey scalopine (see Note)

1 whole egg plus 4 egg whites, or ¾ cup egg substitute

¼ cup all-purpose unbleached white flour, plus ¾ cup for dredging

⅓ cup freshly grated Parmigiano-Reggiano cheese

salt and freshly ground black pepper

1½ to 2 tablespoons extra-virgin olive oil

¼ cup fresh lemon juice

¼ cup Chicken Stock (page 379)

2 tablespoons drained capers

lemon wedges for serving

1. Rinse the turkey and pat dry. If necessary, place each scalopine between sheets of plastic wrap and pound with a scalopine pounder or the side of a cleaver to a thickness of ⅛ inch.

2. Make the batter: Lightly beat together the egg and whites in a shallow bowl. (Beat just to mix.) Stir in ¼ cup flour, the cheese, and salt and pepper. The batter should be just a little thicker than heavy cream: if necessary, thin with 1 or 2 tablespoons of water. Place the remaining ¾ cup flour in another shallow bowl or on a paper towel.

3. Just before serving, preheat the oven to 400°F. Heat half the olive oil in a nonstick skillet over a medium-high heat. Season the scalopine with salt and pepper. Lightly dust each scalopine with flour, shaking off the excess. Using 2 forks, dip each scalopine in the batter, shaking off the excess. Pan-fry the scalopine until cooked, 1 to 2 minutes per side, adding olive oil as needed. As the scalopine are cooked, transfer them to an ovenproof serving platter and keep warm in the oven.

4. When all the scalopine are cooked, discard any oil and add the lemon juice, stock, and capers to the pan. Boil this sauce until reduced to about 6 tablespoons and slightly thickened, about 2 minutes. Add salt and pepper to taste. Pour the sauce over the scalopine and serve at once, with lemon wedges on the side.

Note: Many butcher shops sell turkey scalopine. If not, it's easy to cut your own from boneless, skinless turkey breast. Cut the breast across the grain into ¼-inch slices. It's important to cut across the grain, so the scalopine will be tender. Place each slice between 2 sheets of plastic wrap and pound with a scalopine pounder or the side of a cleaver.

Serves 4

319 CALORIES PER SERVING; 43 G PROTEIN; 14 G FAT; 4 G SATURATED FAT; 2 G CARBOHYDRATE; 1,022 MG SODIUM; 125 MG CHOLESTEROL

TURKEY WIENERSCHNITZEL

By substituting turkey for the veal, egg whites for the whole eggs, and olive oil for the butter, I came up with a tasty and healthy remake of this Austrian classic.

1½ pounds turkey cutlets

salt and freshly ground black pepper

½ cup flour (approximately)

2 egg whites

½ cup bread crumbs (approximately)

2 tablespoons olive oil

2 tablespoons capers, for garnish

lemon wedges, for garnish

Place each cutlet between two pieces of plastic wrap and pound with a scalopine pounder or the side of a cleaver to ¼-inch thick. Season the cutlets on both sides with salt and pepper.

Place the flour, egg whites, and bread crumbs in three shallow bowls. Dip each turkey cutlet first in flour, shaking off any excess, then in the egg whites, and then in the bread crumbs.

Heat the oil in a nonstick frying pan over high heat. Pan-fry the schnitzel for 30 seconds per side, or until golden brown. Drain on paper towels. Sprinkle the schnitzel with capers and serve with lemon wedges on the side.

Serves 4

342 CALORIES PER SERVING;
37 G PROTEIN; 11 G FAT; 21 G CARBOHYDRATE;
219 MG SODIUM; 74 MG CHOLESTEROL

POACHED CHICKEN/POACHED TURKEY

Many recipes in this book call for cooked chicken, so I always try to keep some on hand. A Mexican would poach a whole chicken, but leaner results can be obtained with boneless, skinless breasts. Because these have a tendency to dry out, poaching is a great way to impart flavor while keeping them moist. I like to cool the chicken breasts in the broth to prevent drying out.

1½ pounds boneless, skinless chicken breasts or turkey breast

FOR THE BROTH:

6 cups water

1 tomato, quartered

1 small onion, quartered

2 cloves garlic, peeled

1 stalk celery, cut into 1-inch pieces

1 carrot, cut into 1-inch pieces

2 sprigs cilantro

1 bay leaf

6 black peppercorns

salt

Makes 4 cups, enough to serve 4 as an entrée. But for many dishes, as in tacos and panuchos, you'll be using only a few shreds of chicken per piece.

309 CALORIES PER SERVING;
54 G PROTEIN; 6 G FAT; 2 G SATURATED FAT;
6 G CARBOHYDRATE; 154 MG SODIUM;
144 MG CHOLESTEROL

1. Wash the chicken breasts and blot them dry. Trim off any visible fat or sinews.

2. In a large shallow pan, combine the water, tomato, onion, garlic, celery, carrot, cilantro, bay leaf, and peppercorns and bring to a boil. Reduce the heat and simmer until the broth is richly flavored, 10 minutes, adding salt to taste.

3. Add the chicken or turkey breasts and poach (gently simmer) over medium heat until the meat is firm, white, and cooked through, 8 to 12 minutes. Remove the pan from the heat and let the chicken or turkey cool in the broth.

4. With a slotted spoon, transfer the chicken or turkey to a cutting board and tear the meat into coarse shreds with your fingers. Wrap in plastic and store for up to 3 days in the refrigerator or up to a month in the freezer. Don't forget to strain the broth and use it for soups and sauces.

CHICKEN CHILI

Here's a bowl o' red for people who love the gutsy flavor of chili, but don't want the fat found in traditional ground beef versions. I offer a range of jalapeño chilies and chili powder to suit individual tastes and heat tolerance. The chicken can be ground in a meat grinder or food processor. This chili is also delicious made with lean ground turkey.

1 tablespoon olive oil

1 large onion, finely chopped

4 cloves garlic, minced

1 green bell pepper, cored, seeded, and finely chopped

1 to 3 jalapeño chilies, seeded and minced (for a hotter chili, leave the seeds in)

2 to 4 tablespoons pure chili powder

1½ teaspoons ground cumin

1 teaspoon dried oregano

1 pound very finely chopped or coarsely ground chicken or turkey breast

1 14.5-ounce can peeled tomatoes, with juice

1 cup beer

2 cups cooked black beans (1 16-ounce can)

½ teaspoon Tabasco sauce or your favorite hot sauce (optional)

salt and freshly ground black pepper to taste

½ cup no-fat sour cream for garnish

4 scallions, finely chopped, for garnish

1. Heat the oil in a large sauté pan, preferably nonstick. Add the onion, garlic, green pepper, and jalapeños and lightly brown over medium-high heat, about 5 minutes.

2. Stir in the chili powder, cumin, and oregano and cook for 1 minute. Add the chicken and cook it until white, about 3 minutes, breaking it up with a wooden spoon.

3. Drain the tomato liquid into the chili. Finely chop the tomatoes and add them with their juices and the beer. Simmer the chili, uncovered, over medium heat until the chicken is cooked, about 15 minutes.

4. Rinse and drain the beans and stir them into the chili with the hot sauce, if desired. Simmer until the chili is thick and well flavored, about 10 minutes. Correct the seasoning, adding hot sauce, salt, and pepper to taste. Serve the chili in bowls, topped with dollops of sour cream and chopped scallions.

Serves 4 to 6

336 CALORIES PER SERVING;* 26 G PROTEIN; 7 G FAT; 1 G SATURATED FAT; 38 G CARBOHYDRATE; 265 MG SODIUM; 42 MG CHOLESTEROL

Analysis is based on 4 servings.

CHICKEN WITH SAFFRON AND MUSSELS

Here's a dish from my nouvelle cuisine days in Paris. The year was 1976 and Young Turks of French cuisine were promoting a sort of designer equivalent of surf and turf. The combination of land and sea flavors became one of the hallmarks of the new style of cooking. The black of the mussel shells against the orange of the saffron sauce makes this dish as gorgeous to look at as it is good to eat.

1 pound boneless, skinless chicken breasts

2 pounds mussels

½ cup dry white vermouth

1½ tablespoons extra-virgin olive oil

salt and freshly ground black pepper

¼ cup flour, for dredging

2 to 3 shallots, finely chopped (about 3 tablespoons)

2 stalks celery, very thinly sliced

½ cup chicken stock (see page 379)

⅛ teaspoon saffron threads, soaked in 1 tablespoon hot water

3 tablespoons no-fat sour cream

2 tablespoons chopped fresh flat-leaf parsley

1. Wash and dry the chicken breasts and trim off any fat. Cut the breasts into 1-inch diamond-shaped pieces.

2. Cook the mussels. Sort through them, discarding any with cracked shells or shells that fail to open when tapped. Scrub the mussels and remove the threads at the hinge of the shells. (This is most easily done with a pliers.) Place the mussels and vermouth in a large pot. Tightly cover the pot and cook the mussels over high heat until the shells open, 5 to 8 minutes, stirring once or twice. Remove the pan from the heat and let the mussels cool. Shell most of the mussels, leaving twelve to sixteen in the shell for garnish. Strain the mussel juices through a double layer of cheesecloth or a coffee filter. You should have about 1 cup mussel juice.

3. Heat half the olive oil in a nonstick sauté pan. Season the chicken pieces with salt and pepper and dredge in flour, shaking off the excess. Lightly brown the chicken pieces in the olive oil over medium heat, about 2 minutes per side. Transfer the chicken to a platter with a slotted spoon. Discard the oil and wipe out the pan.

4. Add the remaining oil to the pan and cook the shallots and celery over medium heat until soft but not brown, about 4 minutes. Stir in the chicken, mussel juice, stock, and saffron and bring to a boil. Reduce the heat and gently simmer the chicken until very tender, about 15 minutes. Transfer the chicken back to the platter with a slotted spoon.

5. Stir the sour cream into the pan. Boil the cooking liquid until thickened and reduced to about 1¼ cups. Stir in the chicken, shelled mussels, and mussels left in the shell for garnish. Simmer the stew for 2 minutes to heat these ingredients. Correct the seasoning, adding salt and pepper to taste. Transfer to a platter or serve it right out of the pan. Sprinkle with parsley and serve at once. Noodles or rice will make a nice accompaniment.

Serves 4

288 CALORIES PER SERVING; 31 G PROTEIN; 9 G FAT; 1 G SATURATED FAT; 11 G CARBOHYDRATE; 275 MG SODIUM; 92 MG CHOLESTEROL

CHICKEN-SHIITAKE STROGANOFF

Beef stroganoff was one of the first "gourmet" dishes I learned to prepare. The advent of no-fat sour cream has enabled me to return this quick, easy, and flavorful dish to my repertoire. I'm not sure what Pavel Stroganoff, the nineteenth-century Russian diplomat for whom this dish is named, would make of the shiitake mushrooms, but I find them infinitely more flavorful than the traditional button mushrooms. Portobello mushrooms would make another good alternative.

1½ pounds boneless, skinless
   chicken breasts

salt and freshly ground black pepper

8 ounces shiitake mushrooms

1 tablespoon extra-virgin olive oil

1 onion, thinly sliced

3 tablespoons cognac or dry sherry

1 cup chicken stock (see page 379)

1 cup no-fat sour cream

1 tablespoon Dijon-style mustard

3 tablespoons chopped flat-leaf parsley

1. Wash and dry the chicken breasts and trim off any fat or sinews. Cut the breasts across the grain on the diagonal into ¼-inch slices. Season the chicken

with salt and pepper. Stem the shiitakes and cut the caps in quarters.

2. Heat the oil in a large nonstick sauté pan or skillet. Add the onion and cook over medium heat until just beginning to brown, about 5 minutes, stirring often.

3. Stir in the chicken and shiitakes and cook over high heat until the chicken turns white, 1 to 2 minutes. Stir in 2 tablespoons cognac and bring to a boil. Stir in the stock and sour cream and bring to a boil.

4. Reduce the heat and gently simmer until the chicken is cooked and the sauce is nicely thickened and well flavored, about 10 minutes. Stir in the mustard

and the remaining 1 tablespoon cognac. Correct the seasoning, adding salt and pepper to taste. Sprinkle the chicken stroganoff with the parsley and serve at once over boiled noodles.

Note: For an interesting variation use dried Chinese black mushrooms instead of shiitakes. You'll need twelve large black mushrooms. Soak in hot water for 30 minutes before stemming and quartering the caps.

Serves 4

303 CALORIES PER SERVING; 35 G PROTEIN; 8 G FAT; 2 G SATURATED FAT; 11 G CARBOHYDRATE; 240 MG SODIUM; 82 MG CHOLESTEROL

COQ AU VIN

Coq au vin (*chicken cooked in red wine*) was one of the first dishes I ever learned to cook. The place was La Varenne Cooking School in Paris. The year was 1976 and no one seemed to care about how much butter or bacon fat you used in order to obtain rich flavors. As my eating became more healthful over the years, I forgot about coq au vin. Perhaps it's time to revive a classic. Here's a low-fat coq au vin that uses lean Canadian bacon in place of the traditional belly bacon. (Be sure to trim off any visible fat.) I've also increased the proportion of vegetables to the meat. I dedicate this recipe with affection to La Varenne's founder, Anne Willan.

- **1 3½- to 4-pound chicken, cut into 8 equal-size pieces**
- **salt and freshly ground black pepper**
- **¼ cup flour**
- **2 tablespoons olive oil**
- **1 ounce sliced Canadian bacon (2 to 3 slices), cut into 1-inch by ¼-inch slivers**
- **4 shallots, minced (about ¼ cup)**
- **3 cloves garlic, minced**
- **3 cups dry red wine, or as needed (you don't need an expensive Burgundy, but use a wine that you would drink)**
- **1 bouquet garni of bay leaf, thyme, and parsley**
- **24 baby onions, peeled**
- **16 baby carrots**
- **½ pound button mushrooms, trimmed**
- **¼ cup finely chopped flat-leaf parsley**

1. Remove the skin from the chicken and trim off any visible pieces of fat. Wash the chicken and blot dry. Season the chicken pieces with salt and pepper and toss with the flour in a mixing bowl.

2. Heat 1 tablespoon olive oil in a large nonstick sauté pan. Brown the chicken in the oil over medium heat, turning the pieces with tongs, working in several batches as needed to avoid crowding the pan. Transfer the chicken to a platter lined with paper towels. Brown the bacon in the same pan and transfer to the platter. Pour off any fat and rinse and dry the pan.

3. Heat the remaining 1 tablespoon oil in the pan and add the shallots and garlic. Cook over medium low heat until soft but not brown, about 3 minutes, stirring often.

4. Return the chicken to the pan. Add the wine and bouquet garni and bring to a boil, scraping the bottom of the pan with a wooden spoon to dissolve any congealed pan juices. Reduce the heat and gently simmer the chicken for 20 minutes, stirring occasionally. Skim off any fat that may rise to the surface with a spoon.

5. Meanwhile, prepare the vegetables. Cook the baby onions in 1 quart rapidly boiling salted water until tender, about 5 minutes. Transfer the onions with a slotted spoon to a colander to drain. Cook the carrots in the same water until tender, about 3 minutes. Transfer the carrots to the colander with a slotted spoon. Cut any large mushroom caps in quarters; medium-size caps in half; leave the small ones whole. Boil the mushrooms until tender, about 1 minute, and transfer to the colander.

6. Add the onions, carrots, mushrooms, and Canadian bacon to the coq au vin. Continue simmering until the chicken is cooked and tender and the sauce is reduced and well flavored, about 10 minutes more. The total cooking time will be 30 to 40 minutes. Correct the seasoning, adding salt and pepper to taste. Discard the bouquet garni. Just before serving, transfer the coq au vin to a platter and sprinkle with the chopped parsley.

Note: When cutting up a whole chicken, I like to leave a 2-inch piece of breast meat attached to each wing. This makes the wing section a more generous portion. By using 1½ pounds boneless, skinless chicken breasts for this recipe, instead of a whole chicken, you can reduce the calories per serving to 504, the fat to 11 grams, and the saturated fat to 2 grams.

Serves 4 heartily. Makes a light lunch for 6 to 8

686 CALORIES PER SERVING;* 60 G PROTEIN; 21 G FAT; 5 G SATURATED FAT; 37 G CARBOHYDRATE; 365 MG SODIUM; 163 MG CHOLESTEROL

Analysis is based on 4 servings.

BASQUE CHICKEN

The Basque region lies in the Pyrenees Mountains, straddling the border of France and Spain. The local cooking is characterized by the assertative flavors of bell peppers, dried chilies, and country ham. This recipe calls for a cut-up whole chicken, but you can certainly use straight legs, thighs, or breast meat.

1 3½- to 4-pound chicken, cut into 8 equal-size pieces

salt and freshly ground black pepper

2 tablespoons flour

4 teaspoons extra-virgin olive oil

1 onion, finely chopped

3 cloves garlic, thinly sliced

1 red bell pepper, cored, seeded, and cut into strips or 1-inch dice

1 green bell pepper, cored, seeded, and cut into strips or 1-inch dice

1 yellow bell pepper, cored, seeded, and cut into strips or 1-inch dice

1 to 2 ounces thinly sliced prosciutto, Smithfield ham, or Canadian bacon, cut into matchstick slivers

1 tablespoon paprika (preferably hot), or to taste

¼ to ½ teaspoon hot pepper flakes (optional—use them if using mild paprika)

1 large ripe tomato, cut into ½-inch dice (about 1 cup)

1 cup chicken stock (see page 379)

¼ cup chopped fresh flat-leaf parsley

1. Remove the skin from the chicken and trim off any visible pieces of fat. Wash the chicken pieces and blot dry. Season the chicken with salt and pepper and lightly sprinkle with flour.

2. Heat 2 teaspoons olive oil in a large nonstick sauté pan. Brown the chicken in the oil over medium-high heat, turning the pieces with tongs, working in several batches as needed to avoid crowding the pan. Transfer the chicken to a platter lined with paper towels to drain. Pour off any remaining fat and rinse out and dry the pan.

3. Heat the remaining 2 teaspoons olive oil in the pan. Add the onion, garlic, bell peppers, and ham and cook over medium-high heat until the vegetables begin to brown, about 5 minutes. Stir in the paprika, hot pepper flakes, and tomato and cook for 2 minutes.

4. Stir in the chicken and stock. Gently simmer the stew loosely covered, until the chicken is cooked, 20 to 30 minutes. Uncover the pan the last 10 minutes to concentrate the sauce. Skim off any fat that may rise to the surface with a spoon. Correct the seasoning, adding salt or paprika to taste. The sauce should be highly seasoned. Stir in half the parsley and remove the pan from the heat. Sprinkle the chicken with the remaining parsley and serve at once. I like to serve Basque Chicken over rice, noodles, or spaetzle.

Note: When cutting up a whole chicken, I like to leave a 2-inch piece of breast meat attached to each wing. This makes the wing section a more generous portion. By using 1½ pounds boneless, skinless chicken breasts for this recipe, you can reduce the calories per serving to 243, the fat to 8 grams, and the saturated fat to 2 grams.

Serves 4

451 CALORIES PER SERVING; 56 G PROTEIN; 18 G FAT; 4 G SATURATED FAT; 14 G CARBOHYDRATE; 215 MG SODIUM; 163 MG CHOLESTEROL

Basque Chicken

CHICKEN COLOMBO

Colombo is the French West Indian word for curry. (The preparation is named for the capital of Sri Lanka.) Colombo arrived in the Caribbean in the 1830s, when Indian and Sri Lankan workers were brought to Guadeloupe to work the sugarcane plantations after the abolition of slavery. Today it's enjoyed throughout the French West Indies, where it's made with a variety of ingredients, from seafood to goat. If you live in an area with a large West Indian community, you may be able to find colombo powder, but any good curry powder will do.

2 pounds chicken thighs or boneless, skinless breasts

salt and freshly ground black pepper

2 tablespoons fresh lime juice, or to taste

2 tablespoons canola oil

1 medium onion, finely chopped

4 cloves garlic, minced

2 bunches of scallions, finely chopped

1 tablespoon minced ginger

1 to 2 tablespoons colombo powder or curry powder

2 teaspoons fresh thyme or 1 teaspoon dried

4 to 5 cups chicken stock (see page 379)

2 tablespoons tomato paste

1½ pounds pomatoes, peeled and cut into 1-inch pieces

2 tablespoons chopped fresh cilantro for garnish

1. If using chicken thighs, remove the skin and trim off any fat. Wash and blot dry. If using chicken breasts, wash, blot dry, and cut into 2-inch pieces. Season the chicken with salt and pepper and marinate in 1 tablespoon lime juice for 5 minutes.

2. Heat 1 tablespoon oil in a large, nonstick skillet or sauté pan. Brown the chicken pieces on all sides over high heat, working in several batches to keep from crowding the pan. Transfer the chicken pieces to a platter with a slotted spoon. Pour off any fat and rinse and dry the pan.

3. Heat the remaining 1 tablespoon oil in the pan. Add the onion, garlic, scallions, and ginger and cook over medium heat until soft but not brown, 3 to 4 minutes. Stir in colombo or curry powder and cook until fragrant, about 2 minutes.

4. Return the chicken to the pan with the thyme, stock, and tomato paste. Bring the mixture to a boil, reduce the heat, and gently simmer the chicken for 10 minutes. Stir in the potatoes and continue cooking until the chicken and spuds are tender, 20 to 25 minutes, stirring often. Add stock as needed to keep the stew moist. The stew can be prepared up to 48 hours ahead to this stage and reheated.

5. Just before serving, stir in the remaining 1 tablespoon lime juice. Correct the seasoning, adding salt, pepper, or curry powder to taste. Garnish the colombo with the cilantro and serve over rice.

Serves 6

303 CALORIES PER SERVING; 20 G PROTEIN; 12 G FAT; 2 G SATURATED FAT; 29 G CARBOHYDRATE; 118 MG SODIUM; 62 MG CHOLESTEROL

CHICKEN PAPRIKÁS

Chicken paprikás is one of the glories of Hungarian cuisine. Thanks to the advent of no-fat sour cream, it can now be a part of a healthful low-fat diet. Chili peppers were native to the New World, of course, and they arrived in Hungary in the sixteenth century, where they were adopted with gusto. For best results, use an imported Hungarian paprika.

1½ pounds boneless, skinless chicken breasts

salt and freshly ground black pepper

1 tablespoon olive oil

1 large onion, finely chopped

3 cloves garlic, minced

1 large red bell pepper, cored, seeded, and thinly sliced

4 to 6 teaspoons paprika (preferably imported), or to taste

1 tomato, peeled, seeded, and finely chopped

1 bay leaf

1 cup chicken stock (see page 379)

1 cup no-fat sour cream

2 tablespoons chopped flat-leaf parsley for garnish (optional)

1. Wash and dry the chicken breasts and trim off any fat. Cut the breasts across the grain on the diagonal into ¼-inch slices. Season the chicken with salt and pepper.

2. Heat the olive oil in a large non-stick sauté pan or skillet. Add the onion, garlic, and pepper and cook over medium heat until the vegetables are very soft and just beginning to brown, about 5 minutes, stirring often.

Add the paprika and tomato after 3 minutes.

3. Stir in the chicken and sauté for 1 minute. Stir in the bay leaf, stock, and most of the sour cream, reserving 2 tablespoons for garnish. Gently simmer until the chicken is cooked and the sauce is nicely thickened, about 10 minutes. Discard the bay leaf and add salt, pepper, and paprika to taste.

4. Transfer the paprikás to plates or a platter. Garnish with dollops of sour

cream sprinkled with paprika or parsley, if desired. Serve the paprikás over noodles or rice.

Note: One good brand of Hungarian paprika is Pride of Sceged. That's the brand my Hungarian aunt, Judy, uses.

Serves 4

266 CALORIES PER SERVING; 34 G PROTEIN; 7 G FAT; 2 G SATURATED FAT; 13 G CARBOHYDRATE; 190 MG SODIUM; 82 MG CHOLESTEROL

CHICKEN TAGINE

Vibrantly spiced with ginger and saffron and chock-full of interesting root vegetables, this dish is modeled on a Moroccan stew called tagine. Enjoy it as is (it's great on a cold winter day), or add extra broth and serve as part of a traditional couscous (page 300).

1 tablespoon olive oil

1 large onion, finely chopped

3 cloves garlic, minced (1 tablespoon)

2 tablespoons minced fresh ginger

1½ teaspoons ground turmeric

1½ teaspoons ground cumin

1½ teaspoons ground coriander

1 cinnamon stick

6–8 cups chicken stock (page 379) or water

2 tablespoons fresh lemon juice

½ pound turnips, peeled and cut into ¾-inch dice

½ pound carrots, peeled and cut into ¾-inch dice

½ pound parsnips, peeled and cut into ¾-inch dice

½ pound celeriac, peeled, cut into ¾-inch dice, and sprinkled with 1 tablespoon lemon juice

1 tablespoon chopped Pickled Lemons, page 308 (optional)

½ cup raisins

salt and freshly ground black pepper

2 pounds skinless, boneless chicken breasts, cut into 2-inch pieces

½ cup cooked chick-peas (optional)

⅓ cup chopped cilantro or flat-leaf parsley, for garnish

CHICKEN POACHED WITH STAR ANISE

If you think the first chicken poached in this fragrant broth is good, wait until you taste the second. The flavor improves each time you use it. Star anise is a hard, star-shaped spice with a smoky, licorice flavor. Look for it in Asian and Hispanic markets. I first learned of this cooking method from Bruce Cost, author of a fascinating and invaluable book called Asian Ingredients: A Guide to the Foodstuffs of China, Japan, Korea, Thailand and Vietnam. *For the lowest possible fat, skin the chicken. For a pretty presentation, truss it.*

6 cups water

1¼ cups soy sauce

1¼ cups Chinese rice wine or dry sherry

1 cup honey

2 teaspoons salt

4 star anise

1 cinnamon stick

2 strips orange zest

1 whole 3½–4-pound chicken

5 scallions, whites left whole, greens finely chopped for garnish

¼ cup finely chopped cilantro, for garnish

2 teaspoons sesame oil (optional)

Heat the oil in a large casserole dish. Add the onion, garlic, ginger, turmeric, cumin, coriander, and cinnamon stick. Cook over medium heat for 3 to 4 minutes, or until the onion is soft but not brown. Add 6 cups of the stock and the lemon juice, root vegetables, pickled lemons (if using), raisins, salt, and pepper. Simmer for 20 minutes, or until the root vegetables are almost tender. Add stock or water as necessary to keep the stew from drying out.

Just before serving, remove the cinnamon stick and stir in the chicken and chick-peas (if using). Simmer for 2 to 3 minutes, or until cooked. Correct the seasoning, adding salt, pepper, and lemon juice to taste. The stew can be prepared ahead to this stage. (It just gets better with age.) Garnish with cilantro and serve at once.

Note: To serve this stew as a couscous, use 10 cups stock. Prepare the couscous (page 300) and mound it on a platter or plates. Ladle the stew on top and serve with *harissa* (North African hot sauce, available at Middle Eastern markets and gourmet shops), Yemenite Hot Sauce (page 316), or even sambal ulek (Indonesian chili paste) or Vietnamese hot sauce.

Serves 6 to 8

359 CALORIES PER SERVING; 43 G PROTEIN; 8 G FAT;
29 G CARBOHYDRATE; 942 MG SODIUM; 96 MG CHOLESTEROL

Chicken Tagine

Combine all the ingredients except the chicken, sesame oil, and garnishes in a deep pot just large enough to hold the chicken. Bring to a boil. Add the chicken and simmer for 40 to 50 minutes, or until cooked, turning the bird from time to time to make sure it poaches evenly. Skim the mixture often with a shallow ladle to remove any fat that rises to the surface. To test the chicken for doneness, insert a skewer into the thick part of the thigh; the juices should run clear.

Drain the chicken, remove the trussing string, and carve it or cut it into pieces. Sprinkle it with scallion greens and cilantro. Serve hot, at room temperature, or chilled.

Tasty as this chicken is, it looks rather drab. To jazz up the presentation, serve it in large, shallow soup bowls with broth ladled over it. Sprinkle with chopped scallions and cilantro. Or brush the chicken pieces with sesame oil and brown them on the grill or under the broiler, then sprinkle with chopped scallions and cilantro.

Note: The broth can and should be reused. Strain it and let it cool to room temperature. Chill overnight in the refrigerator and skim off any fat that collects on the surface. Freeze until you're ready to use again. To reuse, bring the broth to a boil, adding seasonings and water as necessary.

Serves 4

408 CALORIES PER SERVING; 53 G PROTEIN; 13 G FAT;
14 G CARBOHYDRATE; 758 MG SODIUM; 161 MG CHOLESTEROL

CHICKEN A LA MEXICANA

This robust stew contains only six main ingredients, but the finished dish fairly bursts with flavor. The secret is to use bone-in chicken breasts (the bones add extra flavor), cooking them in a sealed pot in the oven. To slash the overall fat, I remove the chicken skin. **Note:** *If you don't like bones with your chicken, feel free to use boneless breasts.*

1¾ pounds bone-in but skinless chicken breasts (or 1½ pounds boneless, skinless breasts)

2 ripe tomatoes, peeled and quartered

1 large baking potato, peeled and cut into 2-inch pieces

1 medium white onion, peeled and cut into 8 wedges

4 cloves garlic, peeled and cut in half

1 poblano chili or green bell pepper, seeded and cut into 1-inch pieces

2 jalapeño chilies, cut in half and seeded

1 bay leaf

½ teaspoon oregano

½ teaspoon cumin

¼ teaspoon ground cinnamon

salt and freshly ground black pepper

1. Preheat the oven to 350°F.

2. Cut each chicken breast into 2-inch pieces, using a cleaver to chop through the bones. Place the chicken, tomatoes, potato, onion, garlic, poblano, jalapeños, bay leaf, oregano, cumin, and cinnamon in a deep casserole or pot and stir to mix. Add 1 cup of water, and the salt and pepper to taste.

3. Tightly cover the pot and place it in the oven. Bake the chicken until done, about 45 minutes, stirring once or twice to ensure even cooking. Correct the seasoning, adding salt and pepper to taste.

Serves 4

352 CALORIES PER SERVING; 55 G PROTEIN; 7 G FAT; 2 G SATURATED FAT; 16 G CARBOHYDRATE; 135 MG SODIUM; 144 MG CHOLESTEROL

CHICKEN IN PUEBLA-STYLE MOLE

Until you have feasted on this dish, you haven't experienced Mexican cuisine. Hyperbole, perhaps, but this dark, rich, sonorous sauce—bitter with cocoa powder, sweet with raisins and honey, nutty with almonds and sesame seeds, earthy and gently piquant with five different types of dried chilies— is one of the glories of Mexican cookery. The chocolate (cocoa powder in this case) acts more like a spice than a sweetener. I've eliminated more than ½ cup of lard from the traditional recipe, but the mole is still so flavorful that you won't for a moment miss the fat.

TO COOK THE CHICKEN:

8 half chicken breasts (6 to 7 ounces each), trimmed of all fat and sinew

1 bay leaf

¼ white onion

1 clove

1 clove garlic

1 sprig cilantro

1 batch of mole poblano (see below)

1 tablespoon toasted sesame seeds

1. To cook the chicken, arrange the breasts in a single layer in a large sauté pan. Pin the bay leaf to the onion quarter with a clove. Add it to the chicken with the garlic, cilantro, and water to cover by 1 inch (4 to 6 cups). Gently simmer the chicken over medium heat until it is cooked through, about 10 minutes. Remove the pan from the heat and let the chicken cool in the broth.

2. Prepare the mole, following the instructions on this page. Preheat the oven to 400°F.

3. Just before serving, spoon one third of the mole into an attractive baking dish. Arrange the chicken breasts on top and spoon the remaining mole over them. Bake the chicken until it's thoroughly heated, 10 to 15 minutes. Sprinkle the chicken with sesame seeds and serve at once.

Serves 8

444 CALORIES PER SERVING; 80 G PROTEIN; 10 G FAT; 3 G SATURATED FAT; 4 G CARBOHYDRATE; 202 MG SODIUM; 216 MG CHOLESTEROL

Chicken a La Mexicana

CHOCOLATE CHILI MOLE FROM PUEBLA
(MOLE POBLANO)

Mole poblano is one of the most notorious and misunderstood dishes in the Mexican repertoire. It usually occasions squeals of incredulity (chocolate and chilies?), followed by sighs of pleasure upon actually tasting it. Yes, it contains chocolate (cocoa powder in this recipe, to keep a lid on the fat grams). But it also contains five different kinds of chilies, six different spices, raisins, nuts, tomatoes, toasted tortillas—in short, more than twenty ingredients whose sole purpose is to create a thick, creamy, dark, fragrant sauce with a symphonic range of flavors. The addition of chocolate to what is basically a savory sauce isn't as strange as it sounds. In pre-Columbian times, chocolate was used as a spice, not as a sweet. Its fruity, bitter flavor goes well with the pungency of the chilies. **Note:** *Several recipes in this book call for mole poblano, so I'll often make a double batch and freeze it in 1-cup containers, to always have some on hand.*

3 ancho chilies

3 pasilla chilies

2 mulato chilies (or more anchos)

2 guajillo chilies

1 dried chipotle chili (optional)

1 teaspoon coriander seeds

½ teaspoon black peppercorns

½ teaspoon anise seeds

¼ teaspoon cumin seeds

4 cloves

1 (1-inch) piece cinnamon stick (or ½ teaspoon ground)

1 bay leaf

3 tablespoons slivered almonds

2 tablespoons sesame seeds

2 corn tortillas, torn into 1-inch pieces

1 medium white onion, quartered

5 cloves garlic, peeled

3 medium ripe red tomatoes

¼ cup chopped fresh cilantro

¼ cup yellow raisins

1½ tablespoons lard or vegetable oil

2 cups chicken or vegetable stock, or as needed

2½ tablespoons unsweetened cocoa powder

1 tablespoon honey, or to taste

2 teaspoons red wine vinegar, or to taste

salt

1. Stem the chilies, tear them in half, and remove the veins and seeds. Place the chilies in a bowl with warm water to cover. (You may need to place a saucer on top of the chilies to keep them submerged.) Soak the chilies until they are soft and pliable, about 30 minutes. Drain off the water.

2. Meanwhile, place the coriander, peppercorns, anise seeds, cumin, cloves, cinnamon, and bay leaf in a comal or dry frying pan. Roast over medium heat until toasted and fragrant, 2 to 3 minutes, shaking the pan to keep the spices from burning. Place the roasted spices in a spice mill or coffee grinder and grind to a fine powder.

Note: If you're in a hurry, use preground spices but roast them in a skillet briefly to boost their flavor.

3. Place the almonds in the comal or frying pan. Roast over medium heat until they are toasted and fragrant,

2 to 3 minutes, shaking the pan to prevent scorching. Transfer to a plate. Roast the sesame seeds and tortilla pieces separately the same way.

4. Roast the onion pieces, garlic, and tomatoes in the comal or frying pan until nicely browned on all sides: 8 to 10 minutes for the onion and tomatoes, 4 to 6 minutes for the garlic. Transfer the vegetables to a plate to cool.

5. Place the tomatoes, onion, garlic, soaked chilies, ground spices, almonds, sesame seeds, tortillas, cilantro and raisins in a blender. Purée to a smooth paste, adding a little stock if needed. (You may need to work in several batches. Scrape down the sides of the blender bowl as you work.)

Note: You must use a blender for puréeing; a food processor does not produce a fine enough purée.

6. Heat the lard in a large saucepan. Add the mole mixture and fry it over high heat, stirring with a wooden spoon, for 5 minutes. Stir in the stock, cocoa powder, honey, vinegar, and salt to taste. Reduce the heat to medium and briskly simmer the mole until it is thick and flavorful, about 10 minutes. If the mole thickens too much, add a little more stock; it should remain pourable. Correct the seasoning, adding salt, vinegar, or honey to taste—the mole should be very flavorful. (The honey serves more to round off any sharp edges than to actually sweeten the mole.)

Makes about 4 cups, enough to serve 8 to 12

128 CALORIES PER SERVING;* 3 G PROTEIN; 5 G FAT; 1 G SATURATED FAT; 18 G CARBOHYDRATE; 26 MG SODIUM; 2 MG CHOLESTEROL

Analysis is based on 8 servings.

CHICKEN IN MOLE VERDE
(GREEN HERB MOLE FROM OAXACA)

This chicken dish features the lightest and most refreshing of the seven great Oaxacan moles, a handsome green sauce built on roasted tomatillos and onions, lightly thickened with masa, and enlivened with fresh Mexican herbs. (The herbs are puréed and added to the mole at the end to preserve their bright green color.) To be completely authentic, you'll need to ferret out a few special ingredients, including epazote and hoja santa ("holy leaf"—a large flat leaf with a pleasant licoricy flavor). Fortunately, these can be ordered by mail. If unavailable, omit the epazote and substitute fresh basil for the hoja santa. Although I call for the mole to be served with poached chicken here, you could certainly serve it with grilled chicken or fish, shrimp, veal, or pork.

2¼ pounds boneless, skinless chicken breasts

5 cups chicken stock (see page 380)

FOR THE MOLE:

6 large tomatillos (about 8 ounces), peeled and halved

6 cloves garlic

4 jalapeño chilies (for a milder mole, seed the chilies)

1 small white onion, quartered

1 teaspoon salt, or to taste

1 teaspoon dried oregano

½ teaspoon dried thyme

½ teaspoon ground cumin

¼ teaspoon ground cloves

½ cup masa harina

1 bunch flat-leaf parsley, washed and stemmed

1 bunch fresh cilantro, washed and stemmed

2 tablespoons chopped epazote, fresh or dried

4 hoja santa leaves or 16 fresh basil leaves

1. Wash the chicken and blot dry: Cut the breasts into 2-inch diamonds. Heat the chicken stock in a large saucepan. Add the chicken and gently simmer until cooked, 3 to 5 minutes. Transfer the chicken to a plate with a slotted spoon. Reserve the broth.

2. In a blender, purée the tomatillos, garlic, chilies, onion, salt, oregano, thyme, cumin, cloves, and 1 cup stock. Transfer the mixture to a saucepan and cook over high heat until thick and aromatic, about 3 minutes, stirring with a wooden spoon.

3. Add 2 cups stock and boil the sauce for 5 minutes.

4. Combine the masa and 1 cup stock in a bowl and whisk until smooth. Whisk this mixture into the mole. Simmer the mole until thick and creamy, 5 to 10 minutes.

5. Combine the parsley, cilantro, epazote, hoja santa leaves, and remaining 1 cup stock in the blender. Purée until smooth. Stir this purée into the mole and simmer for 3 minutes, or until the herbs have lost their rawness, but kept their bright green hue. Correct the seasoning, adding salt and pepper to taste.

6. Return the chicken pieces to the mole and simmer until heated through, 3 to 5 minutes. Serve at once.

Makes about 5 cups, enough to serve 4 to 6

358 CALORIES PER SERVING;* 56 G PROTEIN; 7 G FAT; 2 G SATURATED FAT; 15 G CARBOHYDRATE; 501 MG SODIUM; 144 MG CHOLESTEROL

Analysis is based on 4 servings.

AUNT ANNETTE'S DEMFTED CHICKEN

"Demfing" refers to a venerable Eastern European Jewish cooking technique—braising a chicken or a roast in a sealed heavy pot on the stove. And no one does it better than my great-aunt Annette Farber. The secret to making a rich brown gravy is to let the onions "catch" and caramelize several times before adding more water. Aunt Annette probably wouldn't bother with a gravy separator (see note), but it does help reduce the fat.

1 3½- to 4-pound frying chicken

salt and freshly ground black pepper

2 cloves garlic, thinly sliced

2 medium onions, peeled and cut into ¼-inch slices (about 2 cups)

2 carrots, scrubbed and cut into ¼-inch slices

2 stalks celery, washed and cut into ¼-inch slices

1½ pounds potatoes, peeled and cut into 1-inch pieces

1. Remove any lumps of fat from the cavity of the chicken, wash the bird inside and out, and blot dry. To further reduce the fat you could remove the skin. Season the cavity with salt and pepper and add 3 slices of garlic. Tightly truss the bird.

2. Arrange the sliced onions, carrots, and celery on the bottom of a heavy pot (large enough to hold the bird) with a tightly fitting lid. Place the chicken on top and season all over with salt and pepper. Place a few more garlic slices on top of the chicken and add the rest to the vegetables. Add 2 tablespoons water to the pan and tightly cover.

3. Cook the chicken over medium-high heat until the onions are a dark golden brown, 10 to 15 minutes. You'll need to check the onions often (you don't want them to burn), stirring as needed to ensure even browning. Add ¼ cup water and stir to dissolve the dark onion juices. Baste the chicken with this mixture.

4. Continue cooking the bird until the onions dry out and brown again, 5 to 10 minutes. Add another ¼ cup water. Repeat the procedure again: The idea is to wind up with a rich, dark brown gravy. Add 1½ cups water and stir well. Baste the chicken with this mixture.

5. Stir in the potatoes, tightly cover the pot, and continue cooking until the chicken and potatoes are cooked, about 30 minutes. (When the chicken is cooled, the juices will run clear and the internal temperature of the bird will be 160°F.) Transfer the chicken to a platter and remove the trussing string. Season the vegetable mixture with salt and pepper. Transfer the vegetables to the platter and pour the gravy into a gravy separator. Let stand for 3 minutes. Pour the gravy into a gravy boat (or over the vegetables), leaving the fat behind.

Note: A gravy separator is a gravy boat with the spout attached to the bottom of the server. Fat floats on water, of course, so you can pour off the meat juices from the bottom, leaving the fat behind. Gravy separators are sold at most cookware shops.

Serves 4

578 CALORIES PER SERVING; 63 G PROTEIN; 15 G FAT; 4 G SATURATED FAT; 45 G CARBOHYDRATE; 214 MG SODIUM; 179 MG CHOLESTEROL

CHICKEN SALTIMBOCCA

Saltimbocca is a traditional Roman dish, a tiny veal scalopine rolled with a sage leaf and prosciutto. My low-fat version features thinly sliced chicken breast that is cooked in wine and chicken stock instead of butter. The result is so tasty, it "jumps in your mouth," which is what the word saltimbocca literally means in Italian. For ease in slicing, buy the largest chicken breasts you can find. If fresh sage is unavailable, you can use fresh basil or another herb.

1½ pounds boneless, skinless chicken breasts

4 paper-thin slices prosciutto (1 to 1½ ounces)

1 bunch fresh sage leaves

salt and freshly ground black pepper

about ⅓ cup flour, for dusting

1 tablespoon olive oil

½ cup marsala wine

½ cup chicken stock (see page 379)

1. Cut each half chicken breast very sharply on the diagonal into ¼-inch scaloppine. You should wind up with four slices per breast—sixteen slices in all. Place one slice between two sheets of plastic wrap and gently pound with a scaloppine pounder or the side of a cleaver to form a rectangle 3- to 4-inches long and 2-inches wide. Pound the remaining slices in this way. Cut the prosciutto into 2- by 3-inch rectangles.

2. Place a piece of prosciutto on each chicken slice. Lay two to three sage leaves on top. Starting at one narrow end, roll the chicken into a compact roll and pin it shut with a lightly oiled toothpick. Prepare the other saltimboccas the same way. Season the saltimboccas with salt and pepper and lightly dust with flour, shaking off the excess.

3. Heat the olive oil in a nonstick skillet. Lightly brown the saltimboccas on all sides. Add the marsala and bring to a boil. Add the chicken stock and bring to a boil. Reduce the heat and gently simmer the chicken for 10 minutes, or until tender. Transfer the chicken to a platter and keep warm. Remove the toothpicks.

4. Boil the cooking liquid until reduced by half. (It should be thick and flavorful.) Correct the seasoning of the sauce, adding salt and pepper to taste. Spoon the sauce over the chicken and serve at once.

Serves 4

263 CALORIES PER SERVING; 33 G PROTEIN; 7 G FAT; 2 G SATURATED FAT; 9 G CARBOHYDRATE; 191 MG SODIUM; 86 MG CHOLESTEROL

Chicken and Shiitake Rollatini

CHICKEN AND SHIITAKE ROLLATINI

In this recipe, a chicken breast is pounded into a broad thin sheet, then rolled up with a mushroom stuffing called duxelles. *(The preparation is named for the Marquis d'Uxelles, patron of the great seventeenth-century French chef La Varenne.) The resulting rolls form colorful pinwheels when sliced. You can certainly improvise on the stuffing, using other exotic mushrooms. Similarly, rollatini can be made with spinach and sun-dried tomatoes or prosciutto and fresh basil leaves.* Note: *To further reduce the fat in this recipe, you can omit browning the rollatini in olive oil and bake them directly in the oven.*

2 large boneless, skinless chicken breasts (4 halves—1¼ to 1½ pounds)

salt and freshly ground black pepper

FOR THE FILLING:

½ pound shiitake mushrooms, stemmed

½ pound button mushrooms, stemmed (or more shiitakes)

1 tablespoon extra-virgin olive oil

3 shallots, finely chopped

1 clove garlic, minced

3 tablespoons finely chopped flat-leaf parsley

pinch of cayenne pepper

TO FINISH THE ROLLATINI:

1 cup flour, for dredging (in a shallow bowl)

2 teaspoons olive oil

1. If using whole (double) chicken breasts, cut them in half. Remove the fillets (the finger-shaped muscles running the length of each breast) and reserve for another use (for example, the satays on page 24). Place each breast between two large pieces of plastic wrap. Using a scaloppine pounder or the flat side of a heavy cleaver, pound one breast into a large (at least 4 to 5 inches) rectangle ⅛ to ¼ inch thick. Pound gently but firmly, taking care not to tear the breast. Pound all the other chicken breasts in this fashion. Lightly season the breasts with salt and pepper.

2. Meanwhile, prepare the mushroom filling. Finely chop the shiitakes and button mushrooms in the food processor. (Work in several batches and run the processor in bursts. You want to finely chop the mushrooms, not reduce them to a watery purée.) Heat the olive oil in a large, nonstick frying pan. Add the shallots and garlic and cook over medium heat until soft and fragrant but not brown, about 3 minutes. Add the mushrooms and increase the heat to medium-high. Cook the mushrooms, stirring, until most of the liquid is evaporated and the mixture is concentrated and reduced, about 10 minutes. Stir in the parsley and cook for 1 minute. Season the mixture with salt, pepper, and cayenne. It should be highly seasoned. Let the mixture cool.

3. Preheat the oven to 400°F. Lay out the chicken breasts on a work surface, wide side toward you, and spread the mushroom mixture in a thin layer over the chicken. Leave ½-inch border at the top edge (the wide edge furthest away from you). Starting at the bottom wide edge, roll the chicken breast into a tight cylinder. Pin it closed with lightly oiled toothpicks. Stuff and roll all the breasts in this fashion. Season with more salt and pepper.

4. Dip each rollatini in flour, shaking off the excess. Heat the oil in a large nonstick skillet with an ovenproof handle. Lightly brown the rollatini on all sides over medium-high heat, working in several batches if necessary to avoid crowding the pan. Pour off any excess fat. Place the pan with the rollatini in the oven and bake until cooked, 15 to 20 minutes.

5. Transfer the rollatini to a cutting board and remove the toothpicks. Cut each rollatini widthwise into ½-inch slices. (An electric knife works great for slicing.) Fan the slices out on plates or a platter. Wild rice or couscous will make a nice accompaniment.

Note: A good source for exotic mushrooms is Aux Délices Des Bois in New York City. For mail order, visit www.auxdelices.com

Serves 4

345 CALORIES PER SERVING; 33 G PROTEIN; 10 G FAT; 2 G SATURATED FAT; 32 G CARBOHYDRATE; 68 MG SODIUM; 73 MG CHOLESTEROL

CHICKEN BREASTS STUFFED WITH SPINACH AND CHEESE

This quick, easy dish was inspired by the famous cima *(stuffed veal breast) of Parma. For the best results, use fresh tender young leaf spinach (the sort sold in bunches).*

2 large boneless, skinless chicken breasts (4 halves—about 1½ pounds)

4 slices country-style white bread, crusts removed

½ cup skim milk

3 ounces stemmed, washed fresh spinach or ¼ package frozen

salt

8 fresh basil leaves, thinly slivered (optional)

¼ cup freshly grated Parmigiano-Reggiano cheese

freshly ground black pepper

1 tablespoon extra-virgin olive oil or spray olive oil

¾ cup toasted bread crumbs

1. Preheat the oven to 400°F. Wash and dry the chicken breasts. Remove the "tenderloins" (the long, cylindrical strips of meat on the inside of the breasts) and reserve for another recipe. Cut each breast into halves. Lay one of the half breasts lengthwise on a cutting board at the edge of the board. Cut a deep horizontal pocket in the breast, taking care not to pierce the top, bottom, or far side. It helps to hold the breast flat with your free hand while cutting the pocket. Cut pockets in the remaining breasts the same way.

2. Prepare the stuffing: Place the bread in a shallow bowl and pour the milk over it. Let stand for 10 minutes. Cook the spinach in ½ inch boiling salted water until tender, about 1 minute. Drain well and let cool. Squeeze the spinach between your fingers to wring out all the water. Finely chop the spinach and transfer to a mixing bowl. Squeeze the bread between your fingers to wring out the milk. Add it to the mixing bowl with the basil and cheese and add salt and pepper to taste. Mix well.

CHICKEN ROLLATINI IN RED, WHITE, AND GREEN

Italians love meats that are stuffed and rolled. This one produces colorful pinwheels of red prosciutto, white fontina cheese, and bright-green escarole leaves. (It's important to use imported Italian fontina, which has an intense, robust flavor.) If escarole is unavailable, you could substitute twelve fresh spinach leaves.

2 large chicken breasts (4 halves—about 1½ pounds in all)

salt and freshly ground black pepper

4 escarole leaves, washed

2 very thin slices prosciutto, cut in half crosswise

1½ ounces fontina cheese, thinly sliced

1 cup all-purpose unbleached white flour for dredging (in a shallow bowl)

1 tablespoon extra-virgin olive oil

1. Preheat the oven to 400°F. If using whole (double) chicken breasts, cut them in half. Remove the "tenderloin" (the finger-shaped muscle running the length of each breast) and reserve for another recipe. Place each half breast between two large pieces of plastic wrap. Using a scaloppine pounder or the flat side of a heavy cleaver, pound the breast into a large (at least 4 x 6 inches) rectangle ⅛- to ³⁄₁₆-inch thick. Pound gently but firmly, taking care not to tear the breast. Pound all the chicken breasts in this fashion. Lightly season the breasts with salt and pepper.

2. Cook the escarole leaves in 2 quarts salted water until tender, about 1 minute. Refresh under cold water and drain. Blot dry. Cut the escarole leaves to the size of the chicken breasts.

3. Lay out the chicken breasts on a work surface, wide side toward you. Place an escarole leaf, a slice of prosciutto, and a couple of slices of fontina on top. Starting at the bottom wide edge, roll the chicken breast into a tight cylinder. Pin it closed with toothpicks. Stuff and roll all the breasts in this fashion. Season with more salt and pepper.

3. Place a spoonful of stuffing mixture in the pocket of each chicken breast. Pin the pockets shut with lightly oiled toothpicks. Brush the chicken breasts on both sides with half the olive oil and dredge in bread crumbs, shaking off the excess. Transfer the chicken breasts to a lightly oiled nonstick baking dish. Drizzle the remaining oil over the chicken breasts.

4. Bake the chicken breasts until cooked, 20 to 25 minutes. (To test for doneness, press breasts with your finger—they should be firm, yet a little yielding. Another way to test for doneness is to insert a metal skewer: it should come out very hot to the touch.) There are three ways to serve chicken breasts: whole, cut in half, or sliced with a sharp knife or electric knife and fanned out.

Serves 4

429 CALORIES PER SERVING; 12 G PROTEIN; 12 G FAT; 3 G SATURATED FAT; 30 G CARBOHYDRATE; 559 MG SODIUM; 109 MG CHOLESTEROL

4. Dip each rollatino in flour, shaking off the excess. Heat the oil in a large nonstick frying pan with an oven-proof handle. Lightly brown the rollatini on all sides over medium-high heat, working in several batches if necessary to avoid crowding the pan. Pour off any excess fat. Place the pan with the rollatini in the oven and bake until cooked, 15 to 20 minutes.

5. Transfer the rollatini to a cutting board and remove the toothpicks. Cut each rollatino crosswise into ½-inch slices. (An electric knife works great for slicing.) Fan the slices out on plates or a platter. The Braised New Potatoes with Garlic and Bay Leaves on page 283 would make a good accompaniment.

Note: To further reduce the fat in this recipe, you could omit browning the rollatini in olive oil before baking them in the oven.

Serves 4

318 CALORIES PER SERVING; 43 G PROTEIN; 12 G FAT; 4 G SATURATED FAT; 6 G CARBOHYDRATE; 308 MG SODIUM; 122 MG CHOLESTEROL

QUARTET OF STUFFED CHICKEN BREASTS

A skinless, boneless chicken breast is like a blank painter's canvas: uninteresting by itself but full of promise when the cook adds his or her colors. I love the surprise of cutting into a chicken breast and discovering a tangy layer of sage and prosciutto or a crimson pocket of sun-dried tomato. Here are 4 of my favorite stuffings. Use them as a springboard for your own creations. Each of these recipes can easily be adapted to serve 1, 2, or a multitude.

2 large skinless, boneless chicken breasts (double-sided)

your choice of stuffing (see next page)

salt and freshly ground black pepper

½ cup flour (approximately)

1½ tablespoons olive oil

¼ cup balsamic vinegar

¾ cup chicken stock

Trim the "tenderloins" (the long, thin, cylindrical muscles on the inside of the breast—save them for stir-fries) and any fat off the chicken breasts and cut the breasts in half. Place each half flat on a cutting board and, using the palm of one hand to hold the breast flat, cut a deep horizontal pocket in the side with a slender knife. Make the pocket as large as you can without piercing the top or bottom of the breast.

Choose one of the stuffings given on the next page and stuff the chicken breasts as indicated. Pin the breasts closed with toothpicks and season with salt and pepper. Dredge each breast in flour, shaking off any excess.

Heat the oil in a nonstick frying pan and brown the breasts on both sides. Add the balsamic vinegar and bring to a boil. Add the stock and bring to a boil. Reduce the heat and gently simmer the chicken breasts for 2 to 3 minutes per side, or until cooked. (A skewer inserted in the center will come out hot to the touch.) Transfer to a platter and remove the toothpicks.

Season the sauce with salt and pepper and spoon it over the chicken. Serve at once.

Serves 4

PROSCIUTTO AND SAGE STUFFING

4 very thin slices prosciutto (about 1 ounce)

12 fresh sage leaves

Place a slice of prosciutto and 3 sage leaves in the pocket of each half breast.

253 CALORIES PER SERVING; 30 G PROTEIN; 9 G FAT; 12 G CARBOHYDRATE; 158 MG SODIUM; 77 MG CHOLESTEROL

SAUERKRAUT AND SMOKED CHEESE STUFFING

½ cup sauerkraut, drained

4 thin slices low-fat smoked mozzarella or other smoked cheese

Place a spoonful of sauerkraut and a slice of cheese in the pocket of each half breast.

279 CALORIES PER SERVING; 34 G PROTEIN; 9 G FAT; 13 G CARBOHYDRATE; 306 MG SODIUM; 77 MG CHOLESTEROL

BASIL AND SUN-DRIED TOMATO STUFFING

eight 1-inch pieces sun-dried tomato (drained)

16 large basil leaves

Place 2 pieces of sun-dried tomato and 4 basil leaves in the pocket of each half breast.

262 CALORIES PER SERVING; 29 G PROTEIN; 8 G FAT; 16 G CARBOHYDRATE; 81 MG SODIUM; 73 MG CHOLESTEROL

RICOTTA AND SPINACH STUFFING

5 ounces fresh spinach, washed and stemmed

salt

½ cup low-fat ricotta cheese

½ small clove garlic, minced (¼ teaspoon)

freshly ground black pepper

freshly grated nutmeg

Cook the spinach in ½ cup boiling salted water for 2 minutes, or until limp. Drain, refresh under cold water, and drain again. Squeeze the spinach in your hands to wring out as much water as possible. Finely chop the spinach and mix it with the ricotta, garlic, salt, pepper, and nutmeg in a small bowl. Stuff the ricotta mixture into the pocket of each half breast using a spoon.

291 CALORIES PER SERVING; 32 G PROTEIN; 11 G FAT; 14 G CARBOHYDRATE; 130 MG SODIUM; 83 MG CHOLESTEROL

CHICKEN BREASTS STUFFED WITH PROSCIUTTO AND FIGS

In this recipe a beloved Italian appetizer becomes a stuffing for boneless chicken breasts. The balsamic vinegar sauce picks up the sweetness of the figs. If fresh figs are in season, by all means use them. But dried figs work well, too. (If using dried figs, soften them in warm water or port wine.) **Note:** *To further reduce the fat in this recipe, you can bake or grill the chicken breasts instead of sautéing them.*

2 large boneless, skinless chicken breasts (4 halves—1¼ to 1½ pounds)

4 fresh or dried figs

2 very thin slices prosciutto or Smithfield ham (about 1 ounce)

8 fresh sage or basil leaves

1 tablespoon olive oil

CHICKEN BREASTS STUFFED WITH FETA CHEESE AND FRESH MINT

Sometimes the best dishes are the ones that are the simplest. Consider these stuffed chicken breasts, which contain just two ingredients: feta cheese and fresh mint. As a rule, I generally avoid cheese when cooking low-fat, but feta has so much flavor, a tiny amount will do the trick. This recipe comes from a former cooking student, Dina Hanna, who learned to make it in a Peloponnesian village in Greece.

salt and freshly ground black pepper

½ cup flour, for dredging

FOR THE SAUCE:

¼ cup balsamic vinegar

1 cup chicken stock (see page 379)

1. Wash and dry the chicken breasts and trim off any fat. Remove the tenderloins (the long cylindrical strips of meat on the inside of the breasts) and reserve for another recipe, such as the Sesame Chicken Fingers on page 25. Cut each breast lengthwise into two halves. Lay one of the half breasts at the edge of a cutting board. Cut a deep horizontal pocket in the breast, taking care not to pierce the top, bottom, or far side. It helps to hold the breast flat with your free hand while cutting the pocket. Cut pockets in the remaining breasts the same way.

2. Stem the figs and thinly slice widthwise. Place 1 sliced fig, ½ slice prosciutto, and 2 sage leaves in the pocket of each chicken breast. Pin the pockets shut with lightly oiled toothpicks. Stuff all the chicken breasts the same way.

3. Heat the olive oil in a nonstick skillet. Season the chicken breasts with salt and pepper and lightly dredge in flour, shaking off the excess. Lightly brown the chicken breasts over high heat, about 2 minutes per side. Add the balsamic vinegar and bring to a boil. Add the stock and bring to a boil.

4. Reduce the heat and gently simmer the chicken breasts until cooked, about 10 minutes, turning once. Transfer the chicken breasts to a cutting board and keep warm. Boil the sauce until reduced, thick, and richly flavored, about 3 minutes. Add salt and pepper to taste.

5. Remove the toothpicks and thinly slice the chicken breasts widthwise. (The best tool for slicing is an electric knife.) Fan the sliced chicken breasts out on plates or a platter. Spoon the sauce over or around the chicken and serve at once.

Serves 4

289 CALORIES PER SERVING; 30 G PROTEIN; 7 G FAT; 2 G SATURATED FAT; 24 G CARBOHYDRATE; 165 MG SODIUM; 77 MG CHOLESTEROL

---

2 large boneless, skinless chicken breasts
(4 halves—1¼ to 1½ pounds)

1 ounce feta cheese, thinly sliced

1 cup fresh mint leaves, stemmed and washed

1 tablespoon fresh lemon juice

2 teaspoons extra-virgin olive oil

salt and freshly ground black pepper

1. Wash and dry the chicken breasts and trim off any fat. Remove the fillets (the long cylindrical strips of meat on the inside of the breasts) and reserve for another recipe, such as the satays on page 25. Cut each breast in half. Lay one of the half breasts at the edge of a cutting board. Cut a deep horizontal pocket in the breast, taking care not to pierce the top, bottom, or far side. It helps to hold the breast flat with your free hand while cutting the pocket. Cut pockets in the remaining breasts the same way.

2. Place two or three slices of feta cheese and six or eight mint leaves in the pocket of each chicken breast. Pin the pockets shut with lightly oiled toothpicks. Place the breasts in a glass or ceramic baking dish. Finely chop the remaining mint and sprinkle it over the breasts with the lemon juice, olive oil, and salt and pepper. Marinate the chicken breasts in this mixture for 20 minutes, turning once or twice.

3. Preheat a grill or broiler to high. Reseason the chicken breasts with salt and pepper. Grill or broil until cooked, 2 to 3 minutes per side. Remove the toothpicks with tongs or a pliers and serve at once.

Note: The chicken breasts can also be baked.

Serves 4

186 CALORIES PER SERVING; 28 G PROTEIN; 7 G FAT; 2 G SATURATED FAT; 1 G CARBOHYDRATE; 143 MG SODIUM; 79 MG CHOLESTEROL

CHICKEN TAQUITOS

A taquito *is the cousin of the popular Tex-Mex taco. The difference is that the filling is served in a soft corn tortilla, not in a deep-fried shell. At our house we like to add shiitake mushrooms to the filling.*

FOR THE FILLING:

10 ounces boneless, skinless chicken breasts

1 tablespoon extra-virgin olive oil

1 small onion, finely chopped

1 clove garlic, finely chopped

1 to 2 jalapeño chilies, seeded and finely chopped (optional)

½ teaspoon cumin

4 ounces shiitake or button mushrooms, stemmed and diced

TO FINISH THE TAQUITOS:

8 corn tortillas

2 cups shredded lettuce

1 large ripe tomato, seeded and finely chopped

3 scallions, finely chopped

¼ cup shredded smoked cheese or cheddar (preferably low fat—optional)

1½ cups Salsa Mexicana (see page 6), or use your favorite bottled brand

½ cup no-fat sour cream

1. Prepare the filling. Wash and dry the chicken breasts and trim off any fat. Dice the chicken breasts as finely as possible or cut into thin slivers. Heat the oil in a nonstick skillet. Add the onion, garlic, chili, and cumin and cook over medium heat until the vegetables just begin to brown, 4 to 5 minutes. Stir in the chicken and mushrooms and continue sautéing until the chicken and mushrooms are cooked, about 3 minutes. Transfer the mixture to a serving bowl with a spoon.

2. Warm the tortillas on a baking sheet in a 350°F. oven or toaster oven until soft and pliable, about 5 minutes. Place the lettuce, tomato, scallions, cheese, salsa, and sour cream in separate bowls.

3. To serve the taquitos, let each guest place a spoonful of chicken and the various garnishes on a tortilla. Fold the tortilla in half or roll into a tube for eating.

Note: To make crisp tortilla shells for tacos, fold the tortillas in half around cannelloni molds or other tube-shaped molds and bake on a nonstick baking sheet in a 350°F. oven until crisp, 8 to 10 minutes.

Makes 8 taquitos

304 CALORIES PER SERVING;* 21 G PROTEIN; 8 G FAT; 1 G SATURATED FAT; 40 G CARBOHYDRATE; 202 MG SODIUM; 35 MG CHOLESTEROL

*Analysis is based on 4 servings.

TURKEY TAQUITOS WITH SALSA VERDE

A taquito is a baby taco. This ubiquitous street food is as popular in Mexico as sandwiches are in North America. Unlike our version of tacos, taquitos are always served in soft tortillas, so they're much lower in fat. They feature a piquant green salsa made with tomatillos. A tomatillo is a small, green tomatolike fruit recognizable by its papery skin. There's nothing quite like its tart, perky flavor. If you can't find fresh or canned tomatillos, you can substitute plum tomatoes, but the look and taste will be quite different.

2 teaspoons olive oil

1 onion, finely chopped

2 cloves garlic, minced (2 teaspoons)

1 or 2 serrano or jalapeño chilies (or to taste),
   seeded and minced

1 pound fresh tomatillos, husked and finely chopped

½ cup chicken stock or water

¼ cup chopped cilantro

¼ teaspoon ground cumin

½ teaspoon sugar (or to taste)

1 tablespoon lime juice (or to taste)

salt and freshly ground black pepper

1 pound skinless, boneless turkey, ground, finely
   chopped, or cut into slivers

1 cup tightly packed chopped flat-leaf parsley

⅓ cup nonfat yogurt

12 flour or corn tortillas

Heat the oil in a saucepan. Add the onion, garlic, and chilies, and cook over medium heat for 2 to 3 minutes, or until soft but not brown. Add the tomatillos and chicken stock. Simmer, covered, 6 to 8 minutes, or until the tomatillos are soft. Stir in the cilantro, cumin, sugar, lime juice, salt, and pepper. Purée the salsa in a blender or food processor. If the salsa seems too tart, add sugar. If it's too thick, add a little water.

Stir the turkey into the salsa verde and simmer 2 to 3 minutes, or until the turkey is just cooked. Correct the seasoning. Purée the parsley in a spice mill or blender. (A food processor does not work particularly well for this procedure.) Blend in the yogurt and salt to obtain a bright green sauce. (If you want to get fancy, place the sauce in a plastic squirt bottle for squirting whimsical designs.)

Just before serving, heat a nonstick frying pan over medium-high heat. Very lightly brush each tortilla with water and toast it in the pan. The trick is to brown it slightly without making it brittle. Place spoonfuls of the turkey-tomatillo mixture in each rottilla and fold in quarters (or serve in corn tortillas folded in half, as you would for tacos). Arrange the taquitos on a platter and decorate with squiggles of parsley sauce.

Serves 4

442 CALORIES PER SERVING; 26 G PROTEIN; 10 G FAT;
63 G CARBOHYDRATE; 150 MG SODIUM; 38 MG CHOLESTEROL

Turkey Taquitos with Salsa Verde

ASIAN ROAST CHICKEN

This recipe is simplicity itself, but it never fails to fetch raves. The secret ingredient is the small, rust-colored seed of the Zanthoxylum simulans, better known as the Sichuan peppercorn. Available at Asian markets and most gourmet shops, Sichuan peppercorns are the size and shape of common black peppercorns, but their flavor is piny and aromatic and not in the least bit hot. The salt and peppers are roasted to intensify the flavor. Note: Inserting the garlic paste under the skin gives the chicken extra flavor. If you're in a hurry, you can omit this step, placing the ingredients for the paste in the bird's cavity.

1 roasting chicken (3½ to 4 pounds)

FOR THE SEASONED SALT:

2 teaspoons Sichuan peppercorns

1 teaspoon black peppercorns

1½ teaspoons kosher salt

FOR THE GARLIC PASTE:

3 cloves garlic, minced

2 scallions, trimmed and minced

2 teaspoons minced fresh ginger

1 tablespoon minced cilantro

1 tablespoon soy sauce

1 teaspoon sesame oil

1. Wash the chicken inside and out and blot dry. (Reserve the giblets for stock.) Remove any lumps of fat from the cavity. Preheat the oven to 400°F.

2. Prepare the seasoned salt. Place the peppercorns and salt in a dry skillet or wok and cook over medium heat until the peppercorns begin to crackle and smoke, about 3 minutes, shaking the pan to prevent scorching. Transfer the mixture to a spice mill or blender and grind to a coarse powder.

Note: This will make more seasoned salt than you actually need. Store any leftovers in a jar.

3. Prepare the garlic paste. Combine the garlic, scallions, ginger, and cilantro in a mortar and pestle and pound to a smooth paste or purée in a food processor. Add the soy sauce and 1 teaspoon seasoned salt.

4. Loosen the skin from the chicken by gently working your finger under it, starting at the hole at the neck. Loosen the skin from the breast and thighs, working as gently as possible so as not to tear the skin. Spread most of the garlic mixture under the skin. Place the remainder in the cavity. Sprinkle a little of the seasoned salt in the cavity of the chicken. Truss the bird with string. Brush the outside of the chicken with the sesame oil and sprinkle with seasoned salt.

5. Place the bird on a rack in a roasting pan, breast side up, and place in the oven. Roast the chicken until cooked, about 1 hour. (When cooked the juices in the chicken will run clear. The internal temperature will be 160°F.) Halfway through cooking (after 30 minutes), tip the bird, using tongs or a carving fork (insert them in the cavity), to drain any juices in the cavity into the roasting pan. Cut the chicken into bite-size pieces with a cleaver and serve with tiny dishes of seasoned salt for sprinkling.

Note: By using 2 bone-in chicken breasts instead of a whole chicken (you can still stuff the garlic paste under the skin), you can reduce the calories per serving to 211, the fat to 9 grams, and the saturated fat to 2.3 grams.

Serves 4 to 6

455 CALORIES PER SERVING;* 67 G PROTEIN; 18 G FAT; 5 G SATURATED FAT; 2 G CARBOHYDRATE; 632 MG SODIUM; 205 MG CHOLESTEROL

Analysis is based on 4 servings.

HERB-ROASTED GAME HENS

A platter of game hens makes a dramatic centerpiece for a dinner party, while a single bird is a perfect serving for 1. This recipe features an aromatic paste of garlic and herbs stuffed under the skin of the hens before roasting. It's important to use fresh herbs.

8 large cloves garlic, peeled

½ cup chicken stock

½ cup finely chopped fresh herbs (rosemary, basil, thyme, oregano, chives, and/or parsley)

1 tablespoon fresh lemon juice (or to taste)

1 tablespoon olive oil

salt and freshly ground black pepper

4 Cornish game hens (about 1¼ pounds each)

1 very small onion or shallot, quartered

8 sprigs fresh rosemary of thyme

Combine the garlic and chicken stock in a saucepan and gently simmer, covered, for 20 minutes, or until the garlic is soft. Let cool. Purée the garlic and stock with the herbs in a food mill or blender. Work in the lemon juice, oil, salt, and pepper. The mixture should be highly seasoned.

Remove any lumps of fat from inside the birds. Season the cavities with salt and pepper, and place an onion quarter in each. Starting at the neck of each bird, work your finger under the skin to create a pocket between the skin and the breast meat. Try to loosen the skin over the breasts, thighs, and drumsticks. Work carefully so as not to tear the skin. Preheat the oven to 400°F.

Spread 1 tablespoon herb mixture under the skin of each bird. (This is most easily done with a small spoon.) Tightly truss each bird with string, tucking sprigs of rosemary or thyme between the legs. Season the outside of the birds with salt and pepper, and brush with the remaining herb mixture.

Roast the birds on a rack in a roasting pan for 40 minutes, or until golden brown. To test for doneness, insert a trussing needle into the thickest part of the thigh. The juices will run clear when the bird is cooked. Transfer the birds to a platter and let stand for 3 minutes. For a really

Herb-Roasted Game Hens

low-fat dish, remove the skin before serving. Remove the trussing string and serve at once.

Serves 4

265 CALORIES PER SERVING; 34 G PROTEIN; 12 G FAT; 3 G CARBOHYDRATE; 199 MG SODIUM; 102 MG CHOLESTEROL

TUSCAN ROAST PHEASANT

Pheasant is the perfect bird for health-conscious eaters, offering rich flavor with dramatically less fat than chicken. Once available only to hunters, pheasant can now be found at gourmet shops, specialty butchers, and many supermarkets. And because virtually all of the pheasant sold in the United States is farm-raised, you never have to worry about an unpleasantly strong gamy flavor. This recipe uses a wet-roasting technique: the wine keeps the bird from drying out.
Note: Pancetta is Italian bacon. I use just a little for flavor. You could further reduce the fat in the dish by substituting prosciutto for the pancetta or omitting it entirely.

2 fresh pheasants

2 to 3 teaspoons extra-virgin olive oil

salt and freshly ground black pepper

1 tablespoon chopped fresh rosemary

1 tablespoon chopped fresh thyme

2 cloves garlic, minced

2 thin slices pancetta (Italian bacon), each cut in half crosswise (optional)

1 cup dry white wine, or as needed

2 tablespoons good-quality brandy or grappa

1. Prepare the pheasants for roasting. Normally they are sold ready to cook, but sometimes you will need to pull out the tiny pin feathers around the wings and legs. Do this with tweezers or pliers. Remove any lumps of fat from the cavities. Preheat the oven to 350°F.

2. Brush the outside of the pheasants with olive oil. Season the inside and outside with salt and pepper. Mash together the rosemary, thyme, and garlic in a mortar and pestle or mix in a small bowl. Place half this mixture in the cavities of the birds (a little in the front cavity, more in the rear cavity). Spread the remaining mixture over the outside of the birds. If using the pancetta, place 2 half strips over each pheasant breast. Truss the birds with string.

3. Place the pheasants on their sides on a rack over the pan. Roast in the oven for 30 minutes, turning the birds from one side to the other after 15 minutes.

4. Add the wine to the pan and continue roasting the birds for another 20 minutes, turning once. (If too much wine in the pan evaporates, add a little more.) Turn the pheasants on their backs (breasts up) and increase the oven temperature to 450°F. Roast the birds in this position for 6 to 8 minutes to brown the skin.

5. Remove the pheasants from the oven and cut each one in half with a large sharp knife or poultry shears. Place the halves, cut side down, in the roasting pan with the wine. Pour the brandy over them. Roast for 3 to 4 minutes more, or until there are no traces of pink in the meat.

6. Transfer the pheasant halves to plates or a platter. Strain the pan juices into a sauce boat for serving on the side. Polenta or risotto would make an excellent accompaniment.

Serves 4

805 CALORIES PER SERVING; 91 G PROTEIN; 40 G FAT; 11 G SATURATED FAT; 1 G CARBOHYDRATE; 165 MG SODIUM; 0 MG CHOLESTEROL

CHICKEN BAKED IN PARCHMENT PAPER WITH AVOCADO LEAVES AND CHILIES (MIXIOTES)

Let the French have their papillotes, the Italians their cartuccias. I raise my fork for mixiotes. Mexicans have a longstanding tradition of roasting or grilling foods wrapped in plant leaves. (See the pibil on page 262.) The mixiote—*native to central Mexico—may be the most ingenious such preparation of all. The term (pronounced "mee-she-OH-tay") refers to a paperlike membrane that covers the maguey cactus leaf, which is traditionally used to wrap meats marinated in chili paste for pit roasting or steaming. Cactus membranes are hard to come by in the United States, but you can use parchment paper or even aluminum foil with similar results. You'll need to know about one other offbeat ingredient here—avocado leaves, which have a smoky, licorice flavor. You can find them at Mexican grocery stores, but a thin slice of fresh fennel makes an acceptable substitute. This dish may sound complicated, but the actual cooking time is quite brief and the presentation is off the charts in wow power. Few dishes can compete with these dramatically puffed paper pouches, which release a heady scent of chilies and anise when opened before your guests at the table.* Note: *As parchment paper can be hard to find in some parts of the country, I call for aluminum foil below.*

6 boneless, skinless chicken breast halves (5 to 6 ounces each)

FOR THE ADOBO:

8 guajillo chilies (about 2 ounces) or 2½ tablespoons sweet paprika

1 ancho chili

1 pasilla chili

6 cloves garlic, peeled

¼ onion

½ teaspoon dried oregano (preferably Mexican)

¼ teaspoon dried thyme

¼ teaspoon ground cumin

¼ teaspoon ground cinnamon

¼ teaspoon ground allspice

⅛ teaspoon ground cloves

1 teaspoon salt

½ cup chicken broth

2 tablespoons distilled white vinegar

6 avocado leaves or thin (⅛-inch-thick) slices fresh fennel

6 (13 x 24 inch) rectangles of aluminum foil

1. Wash the chicken breasts and blot them dry. Trim off any excess fat or sinews.

2. To prepare the adobo, stem the chilies, tear them open, and remove the veins and seeds. Soak the chilies in warm water to cover until they are soft and pliable, about 20 minutes. Drain the chilies and place them in a blender with the garlic, onion, oregano, thyme, cumin, cinnamon, allspice, cloves, salt, broth, and vinegar. Purée to a smooth paste. Place the chicken pieces in a roasting pan and pour the adobo over them. Marinate for 2 hours, turning once or twice.

3. Preheat the oven to 400°F.

4. Place a sheet of foil (the shiny side should be down) on your work surface and place an avocado leaf or slice of fennel in the center of one half. Place a piece of chicken on top. Spoon one sixth of the adobo mixture on top. Fold the long side of the foil over the chicken, matching up the edges. Pleat (tightly fold over) the edges to form a hermetic seal. Prepare the other mixiotes the same way.

5. Arrange the mixiotes on baking sheets and bake until dramatically puffed and the chicken is cooked, 15 to 20 minutes. Slide the mixiotes onto six plates and present them this way to your guests. Have handy a pair of scissors and use them (or have your guests use them) to open the mixiotes. (Keep your face and hands averted to avoid the escaping steam.) Slide the chicken and sauce out of the foil before eating. Serve with white rice, Mexican rice, or tortillas.

Note: Sometimes this dish is prepared with parchment paper. You'll need six 20-inch squares. Place the avocado leaf, chicken, and adobo in the center. Bring the sides of the parchment up over the chicken to encase it. Twist the raised ends of the parchment paper to seal in the chicken and tie with string: The idea is to create a hermetically sealed package. What results will look like a giant beggar's purse.

Serves 6

307 CALORIES PER SERVING; 54 G PROTEIN; 6 G FAT; 2 G SATURATED FAT; 5 G CARBOHYDRATE; 485 MG SODIUM; 144 MG CHOLESTEROL

CHICKEN CUTLETS

This recipe is dedicated fondly to our children,
Jake and Betsy, who grew up on these crispy cutlets.
Back then, of course, we fried the cutlets in butter.
Today we use egg whites, not whole eggs, for the
breading and we bake the breasts in the oven.

Serves 4

367 CALORIES PER SERVING; 35 G PROTEIN; 5 G FAT; 2 G SATURATED
FAT; 42 G CARBOHYDRATE; 329 MG SODIUM; 71 MG CHOLESTEROL

2 large whole, boneless, skinless chicken breasts
(1¼ to 1½ pounds)

salt and freshly ground black pepper

2 tablespoons freshly grated parmesan cheese

approximately 1 cup flour, for dredging

2 egg whites, lightly beaten with a fork

approximately 1 cup bread crumbs
(preferably homemade), or cracker crumbs

spray oil

lemon wedges for serving

small bowl of capers for serving

NOT FRIED CHICKEN

By baking the chicken instead of deep-frying it and by using buttermilk and spices to bolster the flavor, we create a tasty,
delectably crisp chicken that won't jeopardize your health. **Note:** *By using boneless, skinless chicken breasts for this recipe,*
you could reduce the calories to 444 per serving, the fat to 7 grams, and the saturated fat to 2 grams.

1 3½- to 4-pound chicken

FOR THE SPICE MIX:

1 tablespoon Cajun spice

1 tablespoon paprika

1 tablespoon garlic powder

1 teaspoon freshly ground black pepper

salt to taste

2 cups low-fat buttermilk

FOR THE BREADING:

1 cup bread crumbs, preferably
homemade

½ cup flour

½ cup cornmeal

spray oil

1. Cut the chicken into eight even pieces or have your butcher do it. (When I cut off the wings, I include a 2-inch piece of the breast meat. This gives you a meatier wing.) Remove all the skin from the chicken and cut away any pieces of fat.

2. Combine the Cajun spice, paprika, garlic powder, pepper, and salt in a shallow bowl and stir to mix. Rub one-third of this spice mix on the chicken pieces and let stand for 10 minutes in a metal mixing bowl. Stir in the buttermilk and place the bowl in the freezer. Marinate the chicken in the buttermilk for 30 minutes, stirring once or twice.

3. Combine the ingredients for the breading and the remaining spice mix in a mixing bowl and stir or whisk to

mix. Spray a nonstick baking sheet with spray oil. Preheat the oven to 400°F.

4. Drain the chicken pieces in a colander. Dredge each piece of chicken in the crumb mixture, shaking off the excess. Arrange the chicken pieces on the baking sheet in a single layer. Lightly spray the tops of the chicken pieces with oil.

5. Bake the chicken until golden brown and cooked, 30 to 40 minutes, turning several times to ensure even browning. Serve at once. Mashed potatoes will make a great accompaniment.

Serves 4

667 CALORIES PER SERVING; 69 G PROTEIN; 18 G
FAT; 5 G SATURATED FAT; 53 G CARBOHYDRATE;
488 MG SODIUM; 184 MG CHOLESTEROL

1. Wash and dry the chicken breasts and trim off any fat and sinew. Cut each breast in half down the middle (you want four halves) and remove the fillets—the long cylindrical muscle running the length of each breast. (Reserve the fillets for the chicken fingers on page 25.) Place each half breast between two sheets of plastic wrap and pound to a thickness of ¼ inch, using a scalopine pounder or the side of a heavy cleaver or frying pan. Season the chicken breasts with salt and pepper and sprinkle with the grated parmesan.

Note: If you don't want to use cheese, sprinkle the breasts with a little paprika and garlic powder instead.

2. Place the flour in one shallow bowl, the egg whites in another, and the bread crumbs in a third. Lightly spray a nonstick baking sheet with spray oil. Preheat the oven to 400°F.

3. Just before baking, dip each breast first in flour, shaking off the excess, then in egg white, and finally in bread crumbs, shaking off the excess. Transfer the chicken breasts to the baking sheet. Lightly spray the tops with spray oil. Bake the cutlets until cooked, about 15 minutes, turning once or twice. Serve the chicken cutlets with lemon wedges and capers.

STOVETOP-SMOKED CHICKEN

Smoking is one of my favorite ways to cook chicken. You don't even need any special equipment; here is a tried-and-true method for smoking a chicken in a stovetop smoker or wok. When doing stovetop smoking, be sure to run the hood exhaust fan on high. **Note:** *By removing the chicken skin you can reduce the calories in this recipe to 382, the fat to 15 grams, and the saturated fat to 4 grams. This dish is a little on the high end in terms of fat, so enjoy it for a splurge or use the smoked chicken in smaller amounts in other recipes in this book.*

1 3½- to 4-pound chicken

salt and freshly ground black pepper

3 to 4 tablespoons hardwood chips or sawdust

1. Remove any lumps of fat from the chicken and thoroughly wash inside and out. Blot the chicken dry with paper towels and season inside and out with salt and pepper. Truss the chicken to give it a neat appearance.

2. Place a 6-inch square of foil in the bottom of a stovetop smoker or a wok. Place the wood on top. Place a wire rack (a round cake rack works well in a wok) over the wood and place the chicken on top. Place the smoker or wok over high heat until the first wisps of smoke appear. Reduce the heat to medium, tightly cover the wok or smoker, and smoke the chicken until cooked, about 1 hour. (The juices will run clear when the chicken is cooked; the internal temperature should be 160°F.) If the smoker lid isn't tall enough, you can tent the bird with heavy-duty aluminum foil. (Crimp the edges to make a hermetic seal.)

Makes 1 chicken, which will serve 4

509 CALORIES PER SERVING; 64 G PROTEIN; 26 G FAT; 7 G SATURATED FAT; 0 G CARBOHYDRATE; 191 MG SODIUM; 202 MG CHOLESTEROL

Stovetop-Smoked Chicken

SMOKED HOLIDAY TURKEY

*Smoking adds a wonderful flavor to turkey, and the wet heat keeps the meat—even the breast—succulent and tender.
It's also very fast. Using a stovetop smoker, you can cook a 10-pound turkey in less than 2 hours. One good stovetop smoker
is a Cameron smoker cooker, available at cookware shops. If you have an outdoor smoker, follow the manufacturer's instructions,
or improvise a stovetop smoker using the procedure outlined below. Don't be intimidated by the length of the recipe.
This will probably be the easiest holiday turkey you've ever made.*

1 10-pound turkey

2 teaspoons garlic salt

2 teaspoons paprika

½ teaspoon freshly ground black pepper

⅓ cup hardwood sawdust (such as alder or maple)

2 cups turkey or chicken stock

½ cup dry vermouth

3 tablespoons soy sauce

1½–2 teaspoons cornstarch

3 tablespoons Madeira

Wash and dry the turkey. Remove the wishbone to facilitate carving. Sprinkle the outside of the turkey with garlic salt, paprika, and pepper. Place the sawdust in the bottom of the smoker. Combine the stock, vermouth, and soy sauce, and pour into the drip pan. Place the turkey on a rack over the liquid. Tightly cover the smoker with a lid or foil tent. Place the smoker over medium heat and smoke the turkey for 1½ hours.

Preheat the oven to 400°F. Uncover the turkey and roast it for 20 minutes, or until the skin is crisp. (This step is optional, but the skin won't be crisp without it.) Whether you roast the turkey or simply smoke it without roasting, cook it until the internal temperature registers 185°F.

To make the gravy, strain the liquid from the drip pan into a heavy saucepan. Skim off any fat. Boil the pan liquid until reduced to about 2 cups. Dissolve the cornstarch in the Madeira. Whisk into the simmering liquid and bring to a boil. Boil for 1 minute. Correct the seasoning, adding salt and pepper to taste.

Let the turkey stand for 5 minutes before carving. Serve the gravy on the side.

Note: To rig up a smoker, you'll need a turkey roaster, Dutch oven, or heavy roasting pan; a smaller pan to catch the drips; two wire racks; lots of heavy-duty foil; and hardwood sawdust or small chips. Place the sawdust on a large piece of foil in the bottom of the roasting pan. Place a wire rack over the wood. Place a smaller pan (or a cake pan) on the rack to hold the steaming liquid and catch any drips. Place a second rack on top of the drip pan to hold the turkey. Place the bird on the rack and cover the roasting pan with a tight-fitting lid or a tent made of heavy-duty foil. Tightly seal the edges of the foil to keep in the smoke and steam.

Serves 10 to 12

226 CALORIES PER SERVING; 33 G PROTEIN; 9 G FAT; 1 G CARBOHYDRATE; 390 MG SODIUM; 84 MG CHOLESTEROL

WATCH POINTS FOR STOVETOP SMOKING

Stovetop smoking generates some stray smoke. Keep the exhaust fan on high. (You may need to disconnect nearby smoke alarms temporarily.)

Line the roasting pan and drip pan with aluminum foil and coat the drip pan and wire racks with vegetable oil spray to facilitate cleaning.

When you're finished smoking, let the ash cool completely before discarding it in the trash. (Smoldering wood can set fire to your garbage.)

Smoked turkey and other meats remain pink at the bone, even when fully cooked. Use an instant-read meat thermometer to make sure that a safe internal temperature—185°F.—has been reached.

MEAT

GRILLED VEAL CHOPS WITH BITTER GREENS

This colorful dish combines the meat and salad course. The veal chops are pounded so thin that they all but bury the plate. Marinated in an aromatic mixture of lemon, garlic, and rosemary, they're topped with a colorful salad of radicchio, arugula, and endives.

4 10- to 12-ounce veal chops, with the bone

2 lemons

3 cloves garlic, thinly sliced

3 sprigs fresh rosemary (about 3 tablespoons leaves), stemmed and lightly crushed

1½ tablespoons olive oil

salt and freshly ground black pepper

1 small radicchio, cored

1 bunch arugula, stemmed

2 Belgian endives, ends trimmed

Make a ¼-inch cut in the rounded edge of each chop opposite the bone. (This prevents the chops from curling during cooking.) Place each chop between 2 sheets of plastic wrap and pound with a scalopine pounder or the side of a cleaver until ¼ to ⅓ inch thick. (Better still, have your butcher do it.)

Remove the zest from 1 lemon in broad strips using a vegetable peeler. Juice the peeled lemon (there should be about 3 to 4 tablespoons juice). Cut the second lemon into slices or wedges for garnish. Combine the zest, garlic, rosemary, 1 tablespoon of the oil, and all but 2 teaspoons of the lemon juice in a small bowl. Stir in plenty of salt and pepper. Rub the flattened veal chops with this mixture and marinate in a shallow pan for 20 minutes.

Slice the greens widthwise into ¼-inch strips. Place in a bowl with the remaining ½ tablespoon oil, 2 teaspoons lemon juice, and salt and pepper. Do not toss. Preheat the grill.

Grill the veal chops over high heat, basting with marinade, for 3 to 4 minutes per side, or until cooked. (Alternatively, cook the chops in a ridged skillet or under the broiler.)

Just before serving, toss the greens with the dressing. Arrange the chops on a platter or plates, and top with the dressed greens. Garnish with lemon slices or wedges, and serve at once.

Serves 4

230 CALORIES PER SERVING; 28 G PROTEIN; 11 G FAT; 4 G CARBOHYDRATE; 84 MG SODIUM; 100 MG CHOLESTEROL

A NEW VEAL MARSALA

Veal marsala was one of the first Italian dishes I learned to make. Thanks to its simplicity and speed (ten minutes' preparation time and not much more for cooking), it remains popular at our house on work nights. What's "new" about this veal marsala is the addition of shiitake mushrooms and the use of low-fat half-and-half. If unavailable, you could add 2 to 3 tablespoons evaporated skim milk.

1 pound veal scaloppine (8 scaloppine)

salt and freshly ground black pepper

about ¼ cup all-purpose unbleached white flour

1½ tablespoons extra-virgin olive oil

½ red onion, finely chopped (about ¾ cup)

6 ounces shiitake mushrooms, stemmed and cut in half

1½ cups marsala wine

3 tablespoons low-fat half-and-half or evaporated skim milk

1 tablespoon chopped flat-leaf parsley or rosemary

1. Season the scalopine on both sides with salt and pepper and lightly dust with flour, shaking off the excess. (I like to do the dusting—actually more rubbing than dusting—on a paper towel.)

2. Heat half the olive oil in a nonstick skillet over high heat. Quickly sear the scalopine on both sides, about 30 seconds per side, working in several batches, if needed, to avoid crowding the pan. Transfer the veal to a platter.

3. Heat the remaining oil in the skillet. Add the onion and mushrooms and cook over medium heat until just beginning to brown, about 4 minutes. Return the veal to the pan. Add the marsala and half-and-half and bring to a boil. Reduce the heat and gently simmer the veal until it is very tender and the sauce is reduced and thick, 8 to 10 minutes. Correct the seasoning, adding salt and pepper to taste. To reinforce the marsala flavor you can add a fresh splash of marsala at the end. Sprinkle the parsley on top and serve at once.

Serves 4

347 CALORIES PER SERVING; 24 G PROTEIN; 12 G FAT; 3 G SATURATED FAT; 17 G CARBOHYDRATE; 144 MG SODIUM; 102 MG CHOLESTEROL

SPICY STEW OF SHREDDED VEAL AND CHIPOTLE CHILIES
(TINGA POBLANA)

Tinga is one of those versatile dishes you always want to have in your kitchen. (It stores well in the refrigerator and freezer.) Left whole or coarsely shredded, tinga makes the sort of rib-sticking stew that's great to serve on a cold winter evening. Finely shred the meat, as is done at street stalls throughout Mexico, and it becomes a succulent, flavorful, chili-fired filling for tacos and tortillas. To decrease the amount of fat, I've cut back on the chorizo and lard used in the traditional recipe. But I think you'll find the rich, meaty taste of the pork and the smoky sting of chipotle chilies and roasted tomatoes to be right on the money.

Note: Here, as in other recipes, I call for a range of chilies and chipotle can juices. Adjust the heat to suit your taste. Also, this is a rather upscale tinga, using veal instead of pork. But pork would certainly be fine, too.

TO COOK THE MEAT:

1¼ pounds lean veal, cut into 1½-inch cubes

1 bay leaf

¼ medium white onion

1 clove

2 sprigs fresh thyme, or ½ teaspoon dried

2 sprigs fresh marjoram, or ½ teaspoon dried

2 sprigs fresh oregano, or ½ teaspoon dried

TO FINISH THE TINGA:

8 to 10 plum tomatoes (about 2 pounds)

¾ medium white onion (remaining from above), quartered

6 cloves garlic

3 tablespoons chopped fresh cilantro or parsley

1 tablespoon lard

1 (1-inch) piece chorizo sausage, finely chopped

1 teaspoon fresh oregano, chopped, or ½ teaspoon dried

1 teaspoon fresh marjoram, chopped, or ½ teaspoon dried

1 teaspoon fresh thyme, chopped, or ½ teaspoon dried

¼ teaspoon ground cinnamon

1 to 3 canned chipotle chilies, minced

1 to 3 teaspoons canned chipotle juices (adobo),
   or to taste

salt and freshly ground black pepper

½ teaspoon sugar (optional)

1. Place the veal in a pot with 8 cups of water to cover. Pin the bay leaf to the onion with the clove and add it to the veal. Add the sprigs of thyme, marjoram, and oregano. Bring the water to a boil. Skim off any foam that rises to the surface. Reduce the heat to medium and gently simmer the veal until very tender, 40 minutes to 1 hour.

2. Remove the pan from the heat and let the veal cool in the cooking liquid. When the veal is cool, transfer it to a platter or cutting board with a slotted spoon. Tear it into shreds with a fork or your fingers. Reserve the cooking liquid.

3. Meanwhile, heat a comal or cast-iron frying pan over a medium-high flame. Roast the tomatoes, onion, and garlic in the comal until they are nicely browned: 8 to 10 minutes for the tomatoes and onion, 4 to 6 minutes for the garlic. Transfer the roasted vegetables to a food processor, add half the cilantro, and coarsely chop.

4. Heat the lard in a large sauté pan. Add the chorizo and cook until it's fragrant and browned, 3 minutes. Add the shredded veal and cook for 3 minutes. Add the chopped tomato mixture, the chopped oregano, marjoram, and thyme, the cinnamon, and the chipotles with their juices. Fry the mixture until it is very fragrant and the tomato juices have been absorbed by the meat, about 5 minutes. Add 1 cup of the reserved veal cooking liquid and simmer to obtain a rich moist stew, 5 to 10 minutes. (Add more cooking liquid as needed; the tinga should be very moist.) Season with salt and pepper to taste. To round out the flavor, add a pinch of the optional sugar. For a hotter tinga, add more chipotle chilies or chili juices. Stir in the remaining cilantro and serve at once.

Makes about 4 cups, enough to stuff 16 tortillas or to top 16 tostadas, or to serve 4 as a light main-course stew

325 CALORIES PER SERVING;* 35 G PROTEIN; 14 G FAT; 5 G SATURATED FAT; 17 G CARBOHYDRATE; 362 MG SODIUM; 89 MG CHOLESTEROL

Analysis is based on 4 servings.

OSSO BUCO
(BRAISED VEAL SHANKS)

The mere mention of osso buco *is enough to set a Milanese's mouth watering. Nothing tastes better on a cold winter night than a steaming plate of veal shanks braised with wine and vegetables. Cooking the dish will warm your kitchen. The aroma will perfume your whole house. The only remotely challenging aspect to this recipe is finding a butcher who sells osso buco.* **Note:** *The initial boiling helps melt away some of the fat in the shanks.*

4 veal shanks (about 3 pounds)

1 tablespoon extra-virgin olive oil,
   plus a little oil for brushing

1 large onion, finely chopped

2 carrots, peeled and finely chopped

2 stalks celery, finely chopped

2 cloves garlic, minced

½ cup chopped flat-leaf parsley

3 large ripe tomatoes, peeled, seeded, and chopped,
   or 1 28-ounce can imported peeled plum tomatoes,
   drained of their can juice and chopped in the food
   processor (about 2 cups)

2 tablespoons tomato paste

1 cup dry white wine

4 to 5 cups water or, for a richer sauce, Chicken Stock
   (page 379)

1 herb bundle comprising a bay leaf,
   a sprig of rosemary, a sprig of flat-leaf parsley,
   and a few sage leaves

salt and freshly ground black pepper

the finely grated fresh zest of 1 lemon for serving

1. Using a paring knife, cut any visible pieces of fat off the veal shanks. Place the shanks in a large pot with cold water. Bring to a boil and cook for 3 minutes. Rinse the shanks under cold water and drain. Preheat the oven to 350°F.

2. Heat the olive oil in a large, ovenproof sauté pan. Add the onion, carrot, celery, garlic, and half the parsley and cook over medium heat until lightly browned, about 6 minutes. Stir in the chopped tomatoes and cook for 1 minute. Stir in the tomato paste and cook for 1 minute.

Osso Buco (Braised Veal Shanks)

3. Add the veal shanks and white wine and bring to a boil, stirring with a wooden spoon. Add 4 cups water, the herb bundle, salt, and pepper and bring the mixture back to a boil. Cover the pan tightly and place it in the oven. Combine the remaining parsley and the lemon zest in a small bowl and stir to mix.

4. Bake the veal shanks until they are falling-off-the-bone tender, stirring from time to time to make sure nothing burns, 2 to 3 hours. Uncover the pan the last 45 minutes to allow any excess liquid to evaporate. You should wind up with about 2 cups sauce. Correct the seasoning, adding salt and pepper to taste.

5. Serve the braised lamb shanks over rice or another absorbent grain. Sprinkle each shank with the parsley-lemon mixture and serve at once.

Serves 4

393 CALORIES PER SERVING; 45 G PROTEIN; 13 G FAT; 3 G SATURATED FAT; 15 G CARBOHYDRATE; 230 MG SODIUM; 155 MG CHOLESTEROL

FONDUE RAPPERSWIL WITH SPICY SOY SAUCE

The citizens of Rapperswil on the Zurichsee in northern Switzerland cook paper-thin slices of beef in simmering broth instead of oil, using a fraction of the fat found in traditional fondue bourguignonne. What makes fondue fun are the sauces. Here's a Spicy Soy Sauce to get you started. Other sauce possibilities include, Lemon Chili Sauce (page 316), and Romesco Sauce (page 315). The more the merrier!

1 pound beef tenderloin or sirloin, partially frozen

sprigs of parsley, for garnish

FOR THE SAUCE:

1 or 2 jalapeño chilies (or to taste), seeded and minced

2 cloves garlic, minced (2 teaspoons)

2 scallions, minced

1 tablespoon minced fresh ginger

¾ cup chicken or veal stock

2 tablespoons soy sauce

2 tablespoons rice vinegar

1 tablespoon honey

6 cups beef, veal, or chicken stock (page 379)

salt and freshly ground black pepper

CARNITAS
(FIRE-SEARED BEEF ON TORTILLAS)

Carnitas were the first dish I ever ate in Mexico. To this day, these robustly spiced, fire-seared bits of beef, served on flame-softened tortillas with salsa and onions, remain one of the quickest routes I know to gastronomic nirvana. And few dishes are better suited to a cookout or to summer entertaining. I like to cook the carnitas on the barbecue grill, but you can also use a broiler or nonstick frying pan.

1 pound skirt steaks or thinly sliced sirloin

FOR THE SPICE MIX AND SEASONING:

1 tablespoon pure chili powder

1 teaspoon salt

½ teaspoon ground cumin

½ teaspoon dried oregano

½ teaspoon cayenne (or to taste)

1 small onion, thinly sliced

2 cloves garlic, thinly sliced

½ cup fresh lime juice

1½ cups of your favorite salsa (I use the Salsa Chipotle on page 7 or fire-charred tomato Chile de Árbol Salsa on page 8)

1 bunch cilantro, washed, dried, stemmed, and coarsely chopped

1 tomato, seeded and cut into ¼-inch dice

1 cup jícama, cut into ¼-inch dice

½ ripe avocado, cut into ½-inch dice

1 teaspoon fresh lime juice

3 medium white onions, peeled and cut crosswise into ½-inch slices

16 corn tortillas (preferably homemade)

Serves 4

135 CALORIES PER SERVING; 9 G PROTEIN; 4 G FAT; 1 G SATURATED FAT; 18 G CARBOHYDRATE; 313 MG SODIUM; 12 MG CHOLESTEROL

Slice the meat across the grain as thinly as possible (If you have a good relationship with your butcher, ask him to slice it on a meat slicer.) Arrange the sliced beef in an attractive pattern on a platter. Garnish with parsley sprigs, cover with plastic wrap, and refrigerate until using.

To make the sauce, combine all the ingredients and stir until the honey is dissolved.

Just before serving, bring the broth to a boil in a fondue pot. (If the fondue flame isn't strong enough, bring the broth to a boil on the stove.) Add salt and pepper to taste. Invite each guest to cook the beef to taste in the simmering broth.

Note: Most fondue burners aren't hot enough to keep the broth boiling. Use an electric hot plate, tabletop gas burner, or camping stove.

Serves 4

193 CALORIES PER SERVING; 23 G PROTEIN; 8 G FAT; 7 G CARBOHYDRATE; 869 MG SODIUM; 64 MG CHOLESTEROL

1. Trim any fat off the steaks. Combine the chili powder, salt, cumin, oregano, and cayenne in a mixing bowl and rub this mixture on the meat. Place the meat in a nonreactive baking dish with the sliced onion and garlic. Add the lime juice and marinate 1 to 2 hours, turning the steaks once to ensure even seasoning.

2. Place the salsa, cilantro, tomato, and jícama in separate serving bowls. Place the avocado in a serving bowl and toss with the teaspoon of lime juice to prevent discoloring.

3. Preheat the grill or broiler to high. Place the onions on the grate and grill until they're nicely browned, about 4 minutes per side, turning carefully with a spatula. Add the steaks and cook to taste, about 4 minutes per side for medium-well. (Mexicans tend to eat their carnitas well done.) Transfer the meat and onions to a cutting board and cut or chop into ¼-inch pieces. Arrange the meat and onions on a platter. Warm the tortillas on the grill (or in the oven), until they are soft and pliable, 1 to 2 minutes per side, and place them in a cloth-lined basket.

4. To serve, have each guest spoon some carnitas and grilled onions onto a tortilla and top with cilantro, tomato, jícama, avocado, and salsa. The tortilla is folded in half or rolled up into a tube, ready to eat.

INVOLTINI OF BEEF

Many countries have a version of stuffed, braised beef rolls. This one comes from the Locanda del Gallo restaurant in the sleepy town of Acaja, near the west coast of Apulia. The easiest way to cut the beef is to have your butcher slice it on a meat slicer. You want slices that are about 6-inches long, 3-inches wide, and ¼-inch thick.

12 thin slices of beef (about 1 pound) (have it cut from the top or bottom of the round)

salt and freshly ground black pepper

2 cloves garlic, coarsely chopped

½ red onion, finely chopped

1 tomato, peeled, seeded, and finely chopped

⅓ cup coarsely grated Sardo, Pecorino, Romano, or other tangy sheep's-milk cheese

1½ tablespoons extra-virgin olive oil

FOR THE SAUCE:

1 onion, finely chopped

3 cloves garlic, very finely chopped

½ cup dry white wine

½ cup beef broth or Chicken Stock (page 379)

2 red ripe tomatoes, peeled, seeded, and finely chopped

1 bay leaf

3 tablespoons chopped flat-leaf parsley

1. Place each piece of beef between sheets of plastic wrap and pound with a scalopine pounder or the side of a cleaver to flatten and tenderize the meat. Arrange the meat slices on a work surface and sprinkle with salt and pepper, the coarsely chopped garlic, the red onion, the 1 chopped tomato, and the Sardo cheese. Roll up the beef slices into compact rolls. Pin the rolls closed with toothpicks.

2. Heat half the oil in a large non-stick frying pan over high heat. Lightly brown the rolls on all sides, seasoning with salt and pepper. (This will take about 5 minutes.) Transfer the rolls to a plate.

3. Make the sauce: Add the remaining oil to the pan. Add the onion and garlic and cook over medium heat until just beginning to brown. Return the beef rolls to the pan. Add the wine and bring to a boil. Stir in the stock, the 2 chopped tomatoes, and the bay leaf.

4. Gently simmer the beef rolls, covered, for 30 to 40 minutes, or until tender. Uncover the pan the last 10 minutes to allow the sauce to cook down. Correct the seasoning, adding salt and pepper to taste. Remember to remove the bay leaf and the toothpicks (needlenose pliers work well for this) before serving. Sprinkle with the parsley and serve at once.

Makes 12 rolls, enough to serve 4 to 6

304 CALORIES PER SERVING;* 27 G PROTEIN; 16 G FAT; 5.2 G SATURATED FAT; 6.8 G CARBOHYDRATE; 224 MG SODIUM; 72 MG CHOLESTEROL

Analysis is based on 4 servings.

WHEAT BERRIES WITH BEEF

Here's the Italian version of what a Latino would call picadillo or a North American would call hash. I sampled it in Ostuni in Apulia, where it was made with a local grain called farro *(emmer). Wheat berries are quite similar and are more widely available in this country. This is an ideal recipe for people who are trying to incorporate more grains into their diet and increase the ratio of plant-based foods to meats. The beef serves more as a flavoring than principal ingredient. I like to chop the beef myself to ensure getting the leanest possible cut.*

1 cup wheat berries

1 tablespoon extra-virgin olive oil

1 small onion, finely chopped

1 stalk celery, finely chopped

1 carrot, peeled and finely chopped

1 clove garlic, finely chopped

½ pound lean beef or veal, finely chopped

1 cup dry white wine

2 cups puréed canned imported peeled plum tomatoes with their juices (see Note)

1 bay leaf

3 tablespoons minced flat-leaf parsley

½ to 1 cup Chicken Stock (page 379) or Basic Vegetable Stock (page 382) or water, or as needed

1. Rinse the wheat berries. Cook them in a pressure cooker until tender, about 20 minutes. If you don't have a pressure cooker, soak the wheat berries in cold water for at least 4 hours or overnight. Cook them, covered, in a large pot in 3 quarts briskly simmering water until tender, 1 to 1½ hours. Rinse the wheat berries in a colander and drain well.

2. Heat the olive oil in a sauté pan. Add the onion, celery, carrot, and garlic and cook over medium heat until just beginning to brown, about 5 minutes. Add the beef and cook until crumbly and cooked, chopping the meat into small pieces with the edge of a metal spatula or wooden spoon. Add the wheat berries and wine and bring to a boil. Cook until the wine has almost evaporated. Add the puréed tomatoes, bay leaf, and half the parsley and bring to a boil.

3. Reduce the heat and gently simmer the mixture until the wheat berries and beef are very tender and the sauce is reduced and richly flavored, 30 to 40 minutes. If the mixture dries out too much, add ½ to 1 cup stock. Correct the seasoning, adding salt and pepper to taste. To serve, discard the bay leaf and sprinkle the remaining parsley on top.

Note: The best way to purée the tomatoes is to place them, juices and all, in the food processor.

Serves 4

318 CALORIES PER SERVING; 18 G PROTEIN; 6 G FAT; 1 G SATURATED FAT; 40 G CARBOHYDRATE; 326 MG SODIUM; 32 MG CHOLESTEROL

CARDAMOM BEEF WITH CARAMELIZED ONIONS

Cardamom is generally used in desserts in this country, but in India and the Near East, the fragrant spice is often paired with meat. This recipe was inspired by one of my cooking students, Dina Hannah. Think of it as Levantine beef Stroganoff.

1–1½ pounds lean beef (such as tenderloin or sirloin)
2 cloves garlic, minced (2 teaspoons)
½ teaspoon ground cardamom
freshly ground black pepper
1 cup nonfat yogurt
1 tablespoon Dijon-style mustard
1 tablespoon cognac
1½ teaspoons flour
1½ tablespoons olive oil
1 large or 2 medium-sized onions, thinly sliced
½ teaspoon sugar
salt
3 tablespoons chopped fresh chives or scallions, for garnish

Trim any fat or sinew off the meat and cut into thin (2-inch by ½-inch by ¼-inch) strips. Place the meat in a mixing bowl with the garlic, cardamom, and pepper, and marinate for 15 minutes. Combine the yogurt, mustard, cognac, and flour in a small bowl and whisk until smooth.

Heat the oil in a large nonstick frying pan. Cook the onions over medium-low heat for 10 minutes, or until they turn a deep golden brown, stirring often. Add the sugar after 5 minutes to help the onions brown.

Just before serving, season the beef with salt and pepper. Increase the heat to high, add the beef to the onions, and sauté for 1 to 2 minutes, or until cooked to taste. Stir in the yogurt mixture and bring to a boil. Correct the seasoning, adding salt and pepper to taste. Sprinkle the beef with the chives and serve at once.

Serves 4

268 CALORIES PER SERVING; 26 G PROTEIN; 13 G FAT; 10 G CARBOHYDRATE; 144 MG SODIUM; 65 MG CHOLESTEROL

BEEF BRAISED IN BAROLO

The wine country around Barolo boasts some of the most stunning vineyards in the world. The vines seem not so much trained to grow down the vertiginously steep hillsides as coiffed with a giant comb. The soil, climate, and steep topography conspire to produce intense, powerful wines that go well with the stewed and braised meats so beloved in the region. You don't need to use a super-costly Barollo for this recipe (to drink with it, maybe), but try to use a wine from the region. Traditionally, the beef would be braised and served by itself, but I've added vegetables to reduce the overall proportion of meat.

1 eye-of-the-round roast
   (about 3 pounds), trimmed
   of fat and sinew

3 cloves garlic, each cut into 6 slivers

2 sprigs fresh rosemary

1½ tablespoons olive oil

salt and freshly ground black pepper

1 onion, finely chopped

1 carrot, peeled and finely chopped

2 stalks celery, finely chopped

¼ cup chopped flat-leaf parsley

1 bottle Barolo or other powerful,
   dark-red wine

FOR THE GARNISH:

18 pearl onions, peeled

18 baby carrots, peeled

12 baby potatoes, or
   6 small red potatoes, scrubbed

1. Preheat the oven to 350°F. Using the tip of a paring knife, make 18 tiny slits all over the roast. Insert a sliver of garlic and a few leaves from one sprig of rosemary in each hole.

2. Heat half the oil in a large, deep, ovenproof casserole. Season the roast with salt and pepper and brown it on all sides over high heat. Transfer the beef to a platter and blot with paper towels. Discard the oil.

3. Add the remaining oil to the pan and heat. Add the chopped onion, carrot, and celery and half the parsley. Cook over medium heat until soft but not brown, about 4 minutes, stirring often. Return the beef to the pan. Add the wine and the remaining rosemary sprig and bring to a boil.

4. Tightly cover the pan and place it in the oven. Cook the beef for 1½ hours. Add the pearl onions, baby carrots, and potatoes. Cover the pan and continue braising until the beef and vegetables are tender, 1 to 1½ hours more. If the vegetables become tender before the beef, transfer them to a platter with a slotted spoon.

5. Transfer the beef to a carving board and let stand for 5 minutes. Cut it crosswise into ¼-inch slices. Arrange the slices on a platter with the vegetables. Boil the braising liquid down until reduced to 1½ cups. Season it to taste with salt and pepper. Strain it on top of the beef and serve at once.

Serves 6

479 CALORIES PER SERVING; 54 G PROTEIN;
12 G FAT; 4 G SATURATED FAT;
8 G CARBOHYDRATE; 238 MG SODIUM;
126 MG CHOLESTEROL

OXTAILS OR SHORT RIBS SMOTHERED IN ONIONS AND BRAISED IN WINE

In the course of writing this book, I've thought a great deal about the difference between cooking in Italy and in North America. It's not only about flavors and ingredients. It's also about a notion of time. Italians are willing to devote much more time on a daily basis to food preparation than most North Americans are. As a result, Italians still enjoy the sort of long, slow, oven-braised dishes so characteristic of country cooking that have almost disappeared in the United States. Here's a recipe for braised oxtails, a cut of meat that is tough and cheap but incredibly flavorful. The same preparation can be used for another wonderful tough, cheap, flavorful cut of beef: short ribs. This is a great dish to make when you're home on a cold, rainy or snowy day: the oven warms your kitchen and the soulful aromas will fill your whole house. The initial boiling of the oxtails helps melt away some of the fat.

3 pounds oxtails

1 tablespoon extra-virgin olive oil

3 medium onions, thinly sliced

1 28-ounce can imported peeled
plum tomatoes, finely chopped,
with their juices (see Note)

1 tablespoon tomato paste

3 cups dry white wine, or
as needed (or for a less
traditional but tremendously
flavorful touch, dry red wine)

1 bay leaf

1 sprig rosemary

⅓ cup finely chopped flat-leaf parsley

salt and freshly ground black pepper

1½ pounds small potatoes, cut in
halves or quarters (to obtain
1-inch pieces)

1. Using a paring knife, cut any visible pieces of fat off the oxtails. Place the meat in a large pot with cold water. Bring to a boil and cook for 3 minutes. Rinse the meat under cold water and drain. Preheat the oven to 350°F.

2. In a large ovenproof pot with a tightly fitting lid, heat the olive oil. Add the onions and cook until nicely browned and richly caramelized, about 20 minutes. You'll want to start on high heat, reducing the heat to medium after a few minutes, then to low, to prevent the onions from burning.

3. Stir the oxtails into the onions. Add the tomatoes, tomato paste, wine, bay leaf, rosemary sprig, half the parsley, and salt and pepper. Bring the mixture to a boil, scraping the bottom of the pan with a wooden spoon to dissolve any congealed

onion juices. Tightly cover the pot and place it in the oven.

4. Braise the oxtails, covered, for 2 hours. Remove the pan from the heat and skim off any fat that has risen to the surface. Stir in the potatoes (and more wine if needed to keep the mixture moist).

5. Cover the pan and continue baking until the oxtails and potatoes are very tender, about 1 hour. Uncover the pot the last 30 minutes to allow the pan juices to cook down to a thick gravy. Remove the bay leaf and the rosemary sprig. Correct the seasoning, adding salt and pepper to taste. I like to serve the braised oxtails right in the pan in which they were cooked, but you can also transfer them to a platter. Sprinkle the remaining parsley on top and serve at once.

Note: The best way to purée the tomatoes is to place them, juices and all, in the food processor.

Serves 6

327 CALORIES PER SERVING; 14 G PROTEIN;
7 G FAT; 0.4 G SATURATED FAT;
35 G CARBOHYDRATE; 253 MG SODIUM;
31 MG CHOLESTEROL

VARIATION:
BRAISED BEEF
SHORT RIBS

Prepare as above, using 3 pounds beef short ribs instead of oxtail. Trim any visible fat off the short ribs. Use red wine instead of white.

BRAISED BRISKET
WITH DRIED FRUITS

Ask a Jewish person about his favorite meat, and he'll probably name brisket. It is customary to eat this dish at Rosh Hashanah, the Jewish New Year. The fruit symbolizes the promise of sweetness for the coming year. Miami publicist Barbara Seldin taught me how to make this brisket and it's one of the best. I should know. She's my wife!

1 3½–4-pound brisket

salt and freshly ground black pepper

1 tablespoon canola oil

1 large onion, finely chopped

3 carrots, finely chopped

3 stalks celery, finely chopped

2 cloves garlic, minced (2 teaspoons)

½ cup port, kosher concord grape
wine, or marsala

3 cups beef stock, chicken stock,
or water (approximately)

bouquet garni of bay leaf, thyme,
and parsley

8 ounces dried apricots (1½ cups)

1½ cups pitted prunes

1 cup sultanas

¼ cup chopped flat-leaf parsley,
for garnish

Trim the fat from the brisket and season with salt and pepper. Preheat the oven to 325°F. Heat the oil in a nonstick frying pan. Cook the onion, carrots, celery, and garlic over medium heat for 4 to 5 minutes, or until golden.

Transfer the vegetables to a large roasting pan. Add the brisket, port, stock, and bouquet garni. Bring the liquid to a boil on the stovetop.

Tightly cover the pan and bake the brisket in the oven for 1½ hours.

Transfer the brisket to a cutting board and thinly slice it on the diagonal. (An electric knife works great for slicing.) Return the brisket to the roasting pan and stir in the dried fruit. (Make sure the fruit is submerged in the cooking liquid. Add stock, as necessary, to cover it completely.) Cover the pan and bake for 1 to 2 hours more, or until the meat is tender. Add stock or water as necessary to keep the meat and fruit moist. If there's too much cooking liquid, uncover the pan for the last half hour to allow some of it to evaporate.

Arrange the meat on a platter. Using a slotted spoon, transfer the fruit to the platter around the meat. Pour the pan juices into the sort of gravy boat that allows you to pour the broth off from the bottom, leaving the fat on top. If you don't have one of these, pour the gravy into a bowl or measuring cup and skim the fat off the top with a ladle. Spoon some of the gravy over the meat and fruit, serving the rest on the side. Garnish with parsley.

Serves 6 to 8

522 CALORIES PER SERVING; 31 G PROTEIN;
12 G FAT; 74 G CARBOHYDRATE;
492 MG SODIUM; 79 MG CHOLESTEROL

ROSEMARY-ROASTED PORK LOIN

Visit a weekly market in Umbria or Tuscany and you're sure to find a crowd lined up in front of the mobile rotisserie. This truck travels from market to market, selling porchetta, *savory slices of a young pig that has been stuffed and rubbed with herb paste and roasted in a wood-fired oven. I've cut the pork down to a manageable size (a pork loin) in the following recipe and trimmed a lot of fat.*

8 cloves garlic

2 tablespoons fresh rosemary leaves, plus 4 sprigs fresh rosemary

4 fresh sage leaves, or 1 teaspoon dried

salt and freshly ground black pepper to taste

1 3-pound boneless pork loin roast

1 tablespoon extra-virgin olive oil

1 cup dry white wine, plus ¼ cup for deglazing the pan

1 cup Chicken Stock (page 379), Basic Vegetable Stock (page 382),
   or water, or as needed

1. Preheat the oven to 400°F. Pound the garlic, rosemary, and sage to a smooth paste in a mortar and pestle or purée in a spice mill. Add salt and pepper to taste.

2. Insert a long, slender object, such as sharpening steel, through the roast, from one end of the loin to the other. The idea is to make a tunnel through the center. Stuff half the herb paste into this tunnel, working from both ends, pushing it in with your fingers. Rub the roast with the olive oil, season with salt and pepper, and rub the remaining herb paste on top of the roast. Tie the rosemary sprigs on the roast lengthwise with butcher's string.

3. Place the roast on a rack in a roasting pan in the oven. Roast at 400°F. for 20 minutes. Reduce the heat to 325°, add the 1 cup wine and the stock to the roasting pan, and continue roasting until the pork is cooked, 1¼ to 1½ hours. Add stock and wine as necessary to keep about ½ inch liquid in the roasting pan. Baste the pork often with the pan juices. (This is most easily done with a bulb baster.) When the pork is cooked, the internal temperature will register about 160°F. Transfer the roast to a carving board, cover with foil, and let stand for 5 minutes.

4. Meanwhile, strain the pan juices into a gravy separator. (Deglaze the roasting pan by placing it over a top burner at high heat, adding the ¼ cup wine, and bringing it to a boil. Simmer for 2 minutes, scraping the bottom of the pan to dissolve any congealed juices.) Add this mixture to the gravy separator. Pour off the pan juices into a sauce boat, leaving the fat behind. Season the juices with salt and pepper.

5. To serve, remove the string and rosemary sprigs. Slice the roast widthwise and serve with the pan juices on the side.

Serves 6 to 8

143 CALORIES PER SERVING;* 12 G PROTEIN; 6.6 G FAT; 2 G SATURATED FAT; 2 G CARBOHYDRATE;
187 MG SODIUM; 36 MG CHOLESTEROL

*Analysis is based on 6 servings.

GRILLED PORK TENDERLOIN IN THE STYLE OF THE YUCATÁN
(POC CHUK)

Thinly sliced, brine-cured pork, smokily grilled, served with grilled pickled onions and a fiendishly hot salsa of grilled tomatoes and habanero chilies: Such is the legendary poc chuk—a specialty of the restaurant Los Almendros in the Yucatán. Mexican pork dishes aren't usually the stuff of heart-healthy diets, but this one fairly bursts with flavor and is naturally low in fat. For the best results, grill the pork and vegetables over charcoal. **Note:** *Don't be put off by the seemingly large amount of salt used for curing the pork; most of it will be discarded.*

3 pork tenderloins (about 1½ pounds)

3 tablespoons salt

1 cup water

FOR THE PICKLED ONIONS:

1 large red onion, peeled and quartered (leave the furry root intact)

½ cup fresh lime juice

2 tablespoons fresh grapefruit juice

½ teaspoon salt

FOR THE SALSA:

2 ripe red tomatoes

1 to 2 habanero or Scotch bonnet chilies

3 tablespoons chopped fresh cilantro

2 tablespoons fresh lime juice

salt

1 teaspoon oil for the grill grate

4 warm corn or flour tortillas for serving

1. Preheat the grill or broiler to high.

2. Cut each pork tenderloin in half widthwise. Cut each half almost in half lengthwise through the side and open it up like a book. Place each opened piece of tenderloin between two sheets of plastic wrap and pound with a scaloppine pounder or the side of a cleaver to a thickness of ¼-inch. The idea is to create broad, thin sheets of pork.

3. Arrange the pork in a baking dish. Combine the salt and water in a jar with a tightly fitting lid and shake until the salt crystals are dissolved. Pour the salt water over the pork and marinate for 15 minutes.

4. Meanwhile, prepare the pickled onions. Grill the onion quarters until they are nicely charred on all sides, 4 to 5 minutes per side. Transfer the onions to a cutting board and let cool. Thinly slice the onions widthwise and place them in a serving bowl. Stir in the lime juice, grapefruit juice, and salt. Marinate for 10 minutes.

5. To prepare the salsa, grill the tomatoes and habaneros until nicely charred on all sides: 8 to 10 minutes for the tomatoes, 4 to 6 minutes for the chilies. Transfer to a plate and let cool. Scrape any burnt bits of skin off the tomatoes and cut the tomatoes in quarters. For a milder salsa, seed the chilies; for an authentically fiery salsa, leave them in. Finely chop the tomatoes and chilies in a food processor. Add the cilantro, lime juice, and salt to taste. Okay: You've done the hard part.

6. Remove the pork from the brine and blot it dry with paper towels. Lightly oil the grill grate. Grill the pork until cooked, about 2 minutes per side. Transfer the pork to plates or a platter and top with the grilled onions. Warm the tortillas on the grill, about 20 seconds per side. Serve the pork with the salsa and tortillas on the side.

Serves 4

342 CALORIES PER SERVING; 40 G PROTEIN; 9 G FAT; 3 G SATURATED FAT; 22 G CARBOHYDRATE; 382 MG SODIUM; 99 MG CHOLESTEROL

Grilled Pork Tenderloin in the Style of the Yucatán (Poc Chuk)

LEAN ROAST PORK WITH MUSTARD AND APRICOTS

This dish has something for everyone: the spice of mustard, the sweetness of dried apricots, and the crispness of a garlic crumb crust. Wild Rice Stuffing (page 292) would make a nice accompaniment.

1 1–1½-pound lean pork tenderloin

10 large dried apricots

¼ cup minced fresh herbs (oregano, tarragon, thyme, chives, and/or flat-leaf parsley)

3 cloves garlic, minced (1 tablespoon)

1 cup lightly toasted bread crumbs (preferably homemade)

salt and freshly ground black pepper

3 tablespoons Dijon-style mustard

Preheat the oven to 375°F. Trim any fat off the pork. Using a sharpening steel, boning knife, or other long, slender object, poke a hole through the center of the roast from end to end. Insert the apricots in this hole, pushing them in with your finger. (This gives you a pretty patch of orange when you slice the roast.)

Combine the herbs, garlic, and bread crumbs in a shallow bowl. Season the roast all over with salt and pepper, and paint it on all sides with mustard. Dredge the roast in the bread crumb mixture, turning with two forks to coat all sides.

Place the roast on a wire rack over a roasting pan. Bake for 1 hour, or until cooked. Transfer the roast to a cutting board and let stand for 5 minutes. Cut into ½-inch slices and serve.

Note: People tend to overcook pork. It's safe to eat when the internal temperature reaches 160°F., a point at which it will still be juicy.

Serves 4

267 CALORIES PER SERVING; 21 G PROTEIN; 9 G FAT; 25 G CARBOHYDRATE; 379 MG SODIUM; 51 MG CHOLESTEROL

OAXACAN-STYLE PORK IN RED MOLE
(PUERCO EN MOLE COLORADO)

This simple pork recipe features one of the seven great moles (sauces) of Oaxaca— mole colorado, a thick, dark red gravy made with ground nuts, dried chilies, and roasted vegetables. Like most moles, this one plays to every taste bud on your tongue: There are raisins and cinnamon for sweetness, ancho chilies for gentle heat, almonds and sesame seeds for a nutty flavor, onions and garlic for pungency, even avocado leaves for a touch of smoke and licorice sweetness. Thanks to all these flavorings, I was able to eliminate most of the lard used in the traditional recipe and still wind up with a dish that's bursting with richness.

FOR COOKING THE PORK:

- 2 pounds boneless pork loin, cut into 1½-inch cubes
- 4 cups chicken broth
- 1 bay leaf
- ¼ white onion
- 1 clove
- salt and freshly ground black pepper
- 2 baking potatoes, peeled and cut into 1½-inch cubes

FOR THE MOLE:

- 5 ancho chilies
- 4 guajillo chilies
- 2 tablespoons raisins
- 2 large or 3 medium ripe red tomatoes (about 1¼ pounds)
- ½ large white onion, cut in half again
- 4 cloves garlic, peeled
- 1 corn tortilla
- 2 to 3 tablespoons sesame seeds
- 2 to 3 tablespoons slivered almonds
- 1 slice white bread, darkly toasted
- ½ teaspoon dried oregano
- ½ teaspoon dried marjoram
- ¼ teaspoon dried thyme
- ¼ teaspoon ground allspice
- ⅛ teaspoon ground cloves
- 1 tablespoon lard or olive oil
- 1 (2-inch) piece cinnamon stick
- 1 avocado leaf (optional)

1. Place the pork in a saucepan with the chicken broth. Pin the bay leaf to the onion quarter with a clove and add it to the broth. Add a little salt and pepper. Simmer the pork over medium heat for 20 minutes. Add the potatoes and continue simmering until the pork and potatoes are tender, 10 to 15 minutes more. With a slotted spoon, transfer the pork and potatoes to a plate and keep warm. Strain the broth and set aside.

2. To prepare the mole, stem the chilies, tear them open, and discard the seeds. Place the chilies and raisins in a bowl with hot water to cover. Let soften for 30 minutes.

3. Meanwhile, heat a comal or cast-iron skillet over a medium-high flame. Roast the tomatoes, onion, and garlic until nicely browned: 8 to 10 minutes for the tomatoes and onion, 4 to 6 minutes for the garlic. Transfer the roasted vegetables to a blender.

4. Roast the tortilla in the pan until it is nicely browned, 2 to 4 minutes, turning with tongs. Tear the tortilla into pieces and transfer to the blender. Roast the sesame seeds and almonds until they are lightly browned, 2 to 3 minutes. Set aside 1 tablespoon of the sesame seeds for garnish. Add the remaining sesame seeds and almonds to the blender. Drain the chilies and raisins and add them to the blender. Add the bread, oregano, marjoram, thyme, allspice, and clove and purée to a smooth paste.

5. Heat the lard in a deep saucepan over medium heat. Add the puréed vegetable mixture, cinnamon stick, and the optional avocado leaf. Fry until thick, dark, and fragrant, 5 to 8 minutes, stirring with a wooden spoon to prevent splattering. Add 2½ cups of the reserved pork cooking liquid and simmer until thick and richly flavored, 5 to 8 minutes. The mole should be thick, but pourable; if it's too thick, add a little more stock or water. Correct the seasoning, adding salt and pepper to taste.

6. Just before serving, warm the pork and potatoes in the mole. Discard the cinnamon stick and avocado leaf. Transfer to plates or a platter. Sprinkle the pork with the remaining sesame seeds and serve at once.

Serves 6

452 CALORIES PER SERVING; 43 G PROTEIN; 18 G FAT; 5 G SATURATED FAT; 30 G CARBOHYDRATE; 155 MG SODIUM; 103 MG CHOLESTEROL

MA PO TOFU
(SICHUAN-STYLE BEAN CURD WITH PORK)

Here's a tofu dish for people who are meat eaters. It's traditionally prepared with custardlike soft tofu, but you can also use the more readily available firm tofu. Tree ears are a dark, thin, round fungus with a crisp, chewy texture and mild taste. Look for them in Chinese markets and gourmet shops. If they're unavailable, simply omit from the recipe.

1 cup chicken stock or water

3 tablespoons soy sauce

3 tablespoons rice wine vinegar

3 tablespoons rice wine or sherry

1 teaspoon Chinese hot bean paste, Thai chili paste, or hot sauce

1 teaspoon sugar

1½ tablespoons canola oil

1 tablespoon minced fresh ginger

3 cloves garlic, minced (1 tablespoon)

1–3 hot chilies, seeded and minced (optional)

4 scallions, whites minced, greens sliced on the diagonal for garnish

6 ounces pork tenderloin (or other lean cut), finely chopped

1 pound tofu, rinsed, drained, and cut into ½-inch dice

½ cup dried tree ears, soaked in warm water for 1 hour (optional)

2 teaspoons cornstarch, dissolved in 1 tablespoon water

1 teaspoon Sichuan peppercorns, lightly toasted and crushed, for garnish

Combine the stock, soy sauce, vinegar, wine, bean paste, and sugar in a bowl. Stir to make a smooth sauce.

Heat a wok over high heat and swirl in the oil. Add the ginger, garlic, chilies (if using), and scallion whites, and stir-fry for 15 seconds, or until fragrant. Add the pork and stir-fry for 1 minute, or until the meat changes color. Add the tofu and stir-fry for 30 seconds.

Stir in the sauce and tree ears (if using), and bring to a boil. Reduce the heat and simmer gently for 5 minutes. Stir the dissolved cornstarch into the tofu and cook for 30 seconds. Correct the seasoning, adding soy sauce, vinegar, and bean paste to taste. The mixture should be hot, tart, and salty. Transfer to a deep platter or bowls and sprinkle with the scallion greens and peppercorns.

Note: It's best to chop the pork by hand with a cleaver or chef's knife. A food processor tends to mash the meat.

Serves 4 as an appetizer, 2 as an entrée
213 CALORIES PER SERVING; 20 G PROTEIN; 12 G FAT; 9 G CARBOHYDRATE; 821 MG SODIUM; 30 MG CHOLESTEROL

PORK IN MEXICAN GREEN PUMPKIN-SEED SAUCE
(PUERCO EN PIPIÁN VERDE)

Here's another of the great moles of Oaxaca—
this one made nutty with pumpkin seeds, tangy and tart
with tomatillos and green chilies, and fragrant with fresh
green herbs. Pumpkin seeds are a traditional flavoring and
thickener in Mexican cuisine, and there's nothing quite
like the rich, earthy, nutty flavor they impart to a sauce.
Men, take note: There's growing scientific evidence that
pumpkin seeds can help relieve prostate woes.

FOR COOKING THE PORK:

2¼ pounds pork loin, cut into 1-inch-thick slices

4 cups chicken stock (page 379)

1 bay leaf

¼ medium white onion

1 clove

1 clove garlic

2 sprigs cilantro

salt and freshly ground pepper

FOR THE PIPIÁN VERDE:

⅓ cup hulled pumpkin seeds

12 fresh or canned tomatillos (about 1 pound), husked

¾ medium white onion, cut into quarters

1 poblano chili

3 to 6 fresh jalapeño chilies, cut in half lengthwise
and seeded

4 scallions, trimmed and cut into 1-inch pieces

3 cloves garlic

3 leaves romaine lettuce, thinly sliced

½ cup finely chopped fresh cilantro, plus 6 sprigs for
garnish

½ cup finely chopped flat-leaf parsley, plus 6 sprigs for
garnish

½ teaspoon ground cumin

2 to 3 tablespoons fresh lime juice

1½ tablespoons lard or olive oil

3 sprigs epazote, finely chopped (optional)

1. To cook the meat, place the pork slices in a large frying pan with the chicken stock. Pin the bay leaf to the onion wedge with a clove. Add it to the pork with the garlic, cilantro, and a little salt and pepper. Gently simmer the pork over medium heat until it is tender, 20 to 30 minutes. Let the pork cool in the broth. Strain the broth.

2. Prepare the pipián (green pumpkin-seed sauce). Roast the pumpkin seeds in a comal or dry frying pan over medium heat until they begin to brown and pop, about 3 minutes, shaking the pan to ensure even cooking. Set aside 1 tablespoon of the pumpkin seeds for garnish and transfer the remainder to a blender.

3. Roast the tomatillos, onion, poblano and jalapeño chilies, scallions, and garlic in the comal or frying pan until nicely browned: 8 to 10 minutes for the tomatillos, onions, and poblanos; 4 to 6 minutes for the jalapeños, scallions, and garlic. (Turn with tongs.) You'll need to work in several batches. Place the roasted vegetables in the blender. Add the lettuce leaves, half the cilantro, half the parsley, the cumin, and 2 tablespoons of the lime juice. Purée until smooth.

4. Heat the lard in a large saucepan or sauté pan over medium-high heat. Add the pumpkin seed–tomatillo mixture and fry until it is thick and fragrant, 5 minutes, stirring often. Strain in 3 cups of the reserved pork broth and simmer until it is somewhat thickened and richly flavored, about 10 minutes. The last 3 minutes, stir in the optional epazote and the remaining chopped cilantro and parsley. The mole should be highly seasoned: Add salt, pepper, and additional lime juice to taste.

5. Just before serving, warm the pork in the pumpkin-seed sauce. Transfer to plates or a platter. Sprinkle the pork with the remaining 1 tablespoon of pumpkin seeds and garnish with the sprigs of cilantro and parsley. Serve at once.

Serves 6

347 CALORIES PER SERVING; 40 G PROTEIN; 15 G FAT; 5 G SATURATED FAT;
13 G CARBOHYDRATE; 122 MG SODIUM; 103 MG CHOLESTEROL

"PIT"-ROASTED PORK TENDERLOIN IN THE STYLE OF THE YUCATÁN
(PIBIL)

Mention pibil to someone from the Yucatán and his mouth will water and his eyes light with pleasure. Pibil describes an ancient Mayan method of cooking: Pork or other meat is slathered with a rich recado (spice paste), wrapped in banana leaves, then roasted in a pib, a flame-heated hole in the ground. Visit the market in Merida and you can still find pit-roasted pibil, although most cooks today bake their pork in the oven. (I've also done the preparation on my barbecue grill.) If you can find banana leaves for wrapping, your pibil will have an even richer flavor, but foil wrapping produces a highly tasty pibil too.

FOR THE RECADO (SPICE PASTE):

½ medium white onion, cut in half

4 cloves garlic

½ teaspoon annatto seeds

½ teaspoon black peppercorns

3 cloves

2 allspice berries

1 (½-inch) piece cinnamon stick

1 bay leaf

½ teaspoon oregano

⅓ cup fresh orange juice

⅓ cup fresh grapefruit juice

1 tablespoon red wine vinegar

1 teaspoon salt

1½ pounds pork tenderloin (3 tenderloins)

3 (8-inch by 16-inch) pieces banana leaf
   or aluminum foil

1. To prepare the recado, heat a comal or frying pan over a medium-high flame. Roast the onion and garlic until they are nicely browned on all sides: 8 to 10 minutes for the onion, 4 to 6 minutes for the garlic. Set aside.

2. Add the annatto, peppercorns, cloves, allspice, cinnamon, and bay leaf to the comal and roast until all are fragrant and toasted, 2 to 3 minutes. Transfer the spices to a coffee grinder or spice mill and grind to a fine powder. Place the roasted spices in a blender with the oregano, roasted onion and garlic, the orange and grapefruit juices, vinegar, and salt. Purée until smooth.

3. Trim any fat off the pork and arrange the tenderloins in a baking dish. Pour the recado over them and marinate for at least 4 hours or even overnight, turning two or three times. Preheat the oven to 350°F.

4. Wrap the tenderloins in banana leaves or foil (securing the ends with toothpicks if using leaves). Place the pork on a baking sheet. Bake until cooked, 30 to 40 minutes. (Use an instant-read thermometer to test for doneness. The internal temperature should be 165°F.) Transfer the pibils to a cutting board and let them sit for 5 minutes.

5. Unwrap the pibils and cut the pork, on the diagonal, into ¼-inch slices. (Take care not to burn yourself on the escaping steam as you open the packages.) Serve the pibils with warm tortillas and the xni pec (fiery dog's nose salsa) on page 9.

Serves 4

287 CALORIES PER SERVING; 38 G PROTEIN; 10 G FAT; 4 G SATURATED FAT; 8 G CARBOHYDRATE; 643 MG SODIUM; 99 MG CHOLESTEROL

SPICY PORK STIR-FRY WITH CABBAGE

I love the Asian approach to meat eating—combining small amounts of meat with large amounts of vegetables. This colorful stir-fry pairs pork with ginger, chilies, and Chinese cabbage.

1 1-pound pork tenderloin

2 tablespoons soy sauce

2 tablespoons rice wine

2 tablespoons rice wine vinegar

1 tablespoon brown sugar

1½ tablespoons canola oil

3 cloves garlic, minced (1 tablespoon)

1 tablespoon minced fresh ginger

3 scallions, whites minced, greens cut into ½-inch pieces for garnish

1 or 2 fresh hot chilies, seeded and minced (or ½ teaspoon hot red pepper flakes)

12 ounces nappa (Chinese cabbage) or savoy cabbage, cut widthwise into ½-inch strips

1 red bell pepper, cored, seeded, and cut into ½-inch strips

2 carrots, peeled, thinly sliced on the diagonal, and cut into ½-inch strips

⅓ cup chicken stock

1 teaspoon cornstarch, dissolved in 1 tablespoon rice wine or water

Trim any fat off the pork and thinly slice across the grain. Cut the slices into ½-inch strips. Combine the soy sauce, wine, vinegar, and brown sugar, and marinate the pork for 30 minutes. Drain, reserving the marinade.

Just before serving, heat a wok over high heat. Swirl in the oil. Add the garlic, ginger, scallion whites, and chilies, and cook for 15 seconds, or until fragrant but not brown. Add the pork and stir-fry for 1 to 2 minutes. Add the nappa, pepper, and carrots, and stir-fry for 1 to 2 minutes more. Stir in the reserved marinade and chicken stock. Bring to a boil and cook for 1 minute, or until the vegetables are tender-crisp. Stir in the dissolved cornstarch and bring to a boil. Sprinkle the stir-fry with scallion greens and serve at once.

Serves 4

269 CALORIES PER SERVING; 28 G PROTEIN; 10 G FAT;
17 G CARBOHYDRATE; 617 MG SODIUM; 81 MG CHOLESTEROL

GUAJILLO CHILI-MARINATED PORK TAQUITOS

These tangy taquitos (baby tacos) turn up everywhere in Mexico: at markets, bus stations, sidewalk stalls—wherever an enterprising cook has room to set up a grill or griddle. The meat ranges from beef to pork to innards. The following recipe features pork marinated in a Oaxacan-style adobo. An adobo is an aromatic but not particularly fiery paste of guajillo chilies, garlic, and vinegar. What's remarkable from a healthy eater's point of view is the modest proportion of meat to grains and vegetables. For taquitos are eaten on corn tortillas mounded with shredded cabbage, onions, cilantro, and salsa. A few shreds of meat per tortilla is all it takes to create a perfect dish.

FOR THE ADOBO:

4 guajillo chilies

3 tablespoons distilled white vinegar

2 tablespoons chopped onion

2 cloves garlic

½ teaspoon salt

½ teaspoon freshly ground black pepper

½ teaspoon dried oregano

¼ teaspoon ground cinnamon

Pinch of ground cloves

2 pounds lean pork loin, thinly sliced across the grain

⅓ head green cabbage, thinly shredded (2 to 3 cups)

1 medium red onion, finely diced

1 bunch cilantro, washed, stemmed, and coarsely chopped

8 radishes, washed and finely diced

2 cups of your favorite salsa (good options include the roasted Tomato Salsa on page 7 and the Salsa Chipotle, page 7)

24 corn tortillas

1. Tear open the chilies and remove the veins and seeds. In a bowl, soak the chilies in warm water to cover until soft, about 30 minutes. Drain the chilies and place them in a blender with the vinegar, onion, garlic, salt, pepper, oregano, cinnamon, and cloves. Purée to a smooth paste.

Arrange the pork in a baking dish and pour the chili mixture over it. Marinate in the refrigerator for 2 hours, turning the pork once or twice.

2. Place the shredded cabbage in a serving bowl. Place the onion, cilantro, and radishes in another serving bowl and toss to mix. Place the salsa in a third serving bowl. Place spoons in each bowl.

3. Preheat the grill to high. (Mexicans grill over wood or charcoal, but you can also use gas.) Grill the pork until it is browned and well done, 2 to 3 minutes per side. Transfer it to a cutting board and chop into thin slivers

with a cleaver. Place the pork in a serving bowl and keep warm. Warm the tortillas on the grill until they are soft and pliable, 1 to 2 minutes per side. Arrange the tortillas in a cloth-lined basket.

4. To eat the taquitos, each guest takes a tortilla, folds it in half, and spoons in pork, cabbage, some of the onion-cilantro-radish mixture, and salsa.

Serves 8

431 CALORIES PER SERVING (THREE TAQUITOS); 33 G PROTEIN; 9 G FAT; 3 G SATURATED FAT; 57 G CARBOHYDRATE; 668 MG SODIUM; 66 MG CHOLESTEROL

MEXICAN-STYLE PICADILLO
(FLAVORED WITH OLIVES, RAISINS, AND ALMONDS)

Picadillo is Mexican hash—finely chopped meat spiced up with onions, tomatoes, spices, and chilies. (Picar is the Spanish word for "to chop" or "mince.") Like picadillos throughout Latin America, this recipe offers an intricate interplay of sweet and salty flavors—sweet in the form of raisins, almonds, cinnamon, and cloves, salty in the capers and olives. What results is one of the most flavorful mincemeats ever to grace a tortilla or be stuffed into a roasted pepper. To lighten the traditional recipe, I combine lean ground pork and turkey, and I've dramatically slashed the cooking fat. But thanks to all the spices and seasonings, this picadillo still fairly explodes with flavor.

12 ounces lean pork loin, ground

12 ounces turkey breast, ground

1 teaspoon salt

½ teaspoon freshly ground black pepper

½ teaspoon dried oregano

½ teaspoon ground cumin

½ teaspoon ground cinnamon

⅛ teaspoon ground cloves

3 tablespoons slivered almonds

4 to 6 ripe red plum tomatoes or 2 large ripe tomatoes (about 1 pound)

1 tablespoon lard or olive oil

1 medium white onion, finely chopped (about 1 cup)

3 cloves garlic, minced

1 to 2 jalapeño or serrano chilies, finely chopped (for a milder picadillo, seed the chilies)

2 tablespoons chopped cilantro, plus 1 tablespoon for garnish

4 pimiento-stuffed green olives, finely chopped

1 to 2 pickled jalapeño chilies, finely chopped (optional)

½ cup raisins

1 tablespoon drained capers

1. Combine the pork, turkey, salt, pepper, oregano, cumin, cinnamon, and cloves in a bowl and mix with a spoon. Let stand for 10 minutes.

2. Meanwhile, heat a comal or cast-iron skillet over medium-high heat. Roast the almonds until they are lightly browned, shaking the pan to ensure even cooking, 3 minutes. Transfer the almonds to a plate and let cool. Roast the tomatoes until they are browned and blistered on all sides, 8 to 10 minutes, turning with tongs. Core the tomatoes, scrape off any really burned bits of skin, and purée in a blender or food processor. Set aside.

3. Heat the lard in a large, nonstick frying pan over medium heat. Add the onion, garlic, and fresh jalapeño pepper. Cook until just beginning to brown, 4 to 5 minutes. Add the meat mixture, breaking it up with a wooden spoon, and cook until it starts to turn white, about 3 minutes. As it cooks, chop the meat mixture into small pieces with the end of the spoon.

4. Stir in 2 tablespoons of the almonds, the puréed tomato mixture, cilantro, olives, pickled jalapeño (if using), and the raisins and capers. Gently simmer the picadillo until the meat is cooked through and the mixture is richly flavored, about 10 minutes. The picadillo should be moist but not soupy; if necessary, add a few tablespoons of water. Correct the seasoning, adding salt or pepper to taste.

Serve the picadillo with warm tortillas.

Note: Some cooks like to add a further element of sweetness in the form of a diced ripe plantain or banana.

Serves 6 to 8 on tostadas or in tortillas

288 CALORIES PER SERVING;* 32 G PROTEIN; 10 G FAT; 3 G SATURATED FAT; 18 G CARBOHYDRATE; 477 MG SODIUM; 83 MG CHOLESTEROL

Analysis is based on 6 servings.

CHIPOTLE CHILI–MARINATED PORK LOIN

Here's yet another adobo-marinated pork dish, this one featuring pork loin marinated in a fiery paste of chipotles (smoked jalapeño chilies). To balance the heat, I like to serve the pork on a sweet corn salsa. If you use dried chipotles, soak them in warm water until they are soft and pliable, about 30 minutes, then drain, stem, and seed.

FOR THE ADOBO:

4 canned chipotle chilies with 1 tablespoon can juices (or 4 dried chipotles)

2 cloves garlic

½ teaspoon grated orange zest

½ cup fresh orange juice

½ cup fresh grapefruit juice (or more orange juice)

2 tablespoons red wine vinegar

2 tablespoons tomato paste

1 teaspoon dried oregano

½ teaspoon ground cumin

salt and freshly ground black pepper

1¼ pounds lean pork loin, cut into ½-inch-thick steaks

Sweet Corn Salsa (page 9)

4 sprigs cilantro, for garnish

1. To prepare the adobo, combine the chilies, garlic, orange zest, orange juice, grapefruit juice, vinegar, tomato paste, oregano, and cumin in a saucepan and boil until reduced by a third, about 3 minutes. Transfer the mixture to a blender and purée to a smooth paste. Add salt and pepper to taste. Let the mixture cool to room temperature.

2. Arrange the pork slices in a roasting pan and generously spread them with adobo on both sides. Cover with plastic wrap and marinate in the refrigerator for at least 4 hours, or as long as overnight. Prepare the corn salsa.

3. The pork can be grilled or broiled. Preheat the grill or broiler to high. Grill or broil the pork loin until it is cooked through, 2 to 3 minutes per side, or until done to taste.

4. To serve, spoon the corn sauce on plates or a platter. Arrange the pork slices on top. Garnish with the cilantro sprigs and serve at once.

Serves 4

375 CALORIES PER SERVING; 39 G PROTEIN; 9 G FAT; 3 G SATURATED FAT; 35 G CARBOHYDRATE; 587 MG SODIUM; 85 MG CHOLESTEROL

RACK OF LAMB WITH INDIAN SPICES

This spicy dish makes a nice change from the usual rack of lamb served at French restaurants. Loosely modeled on Indian tandoori, it's marinated in an aromatic mixture of yogurt and spices, then smokily charred on the grill. Rack of lamb is a relatively expensive and fatty cut of meat. It's more a dish for splurging than for everyday eating. A more economical version could be made with shoulder lamb chops.

1 8-rib rack of lamb

1 small onion

3 cloves garlic, minced (1 tablespoon)

1 tablespoon minced fresh ginger

¼ cup finely chopped cilantro, plus ¼ cup for garnish

1 cup nonfat yogurt

3 tablespoons fresh lemon juice

2 teaspoons ground turmeric

2 teaspoons paprika

2 teaspoons ground cumin

2 teaspoons ground coriander

1 teaspoon salt (or to taste)

freshly ground black pepper and cayenne pepper

1 lemon cut into wedges, for garnish

Trim as much of the exterior fat off the rack as possible and scrape the ribs clean. (Better still, have your butcher do it.) Combine the remaining ingredients (except the cilantro and lemon for garnish) in a large bowl. Whisk to a smooth paste. Add salt and pepper to taste. Marinate the lamb for 8 to 24 hours (the longer the better), turning 3 or 4 times.

Preheat the grill. Grill the lamb over medium-high heat, basting with the marinade, for 8 to 10 minutes per side for medium-rare, or until cooked to taste. The lamb can also be roasted in a 400°F. oven for 20 to 30 minutes. Medium-rare lamb will register 130°F. on an instant-read meat thermometer; medium lamb will register 140°F.

To serve, carve the rack into chops. Sprinkle each with cilantro and serve with lemon wedges.

Serves 2 to 4

324 CALORIES PER SERVING; 30 G PROTEIN; 14 G FAT;
19 G CARBOHYDRATE; 1,224 MG SODIUM; 81 MG CHOLESTEROL

BRAISED LAMB SHANKS

This recipe, made with lamb shanks instead of veal, might be thought of as a Greek osso buco. The shanks are parboiled to melt off the excess fat. Ask your butcher to cut each shank into 3-inch pieces. Serve the braised shanks over rice, orzo or other pasta, or another absorbent grain.

4 lamb shanks

1 tablespoon olive oil

1 large onion, finely chopped

2 carrots, finely chopped

2 stalks celery, finely chopped

2 cloves garlic, finely chopped

3 large ripe tomatoes, peeled, seeded, and chopped, or 1 28-ounce can peeled plum tomatoes, drained and chopped

1 tablespoon flour

1 cup dry white wine

3 cups chicken or veal stock or water

1 tablespoon tomato paste

bouquet garni of bay leaf, thyme, and parsley

salt and freshly ground black pepper

½ cup minced flat-leaf parsley, for garnish

freshly grated zest of 1 lemon, for garnish

Place the shanks in a large pot with cold water. Bring to a boil and cook for 3 minutes. Rinse under cold water and drain. Using a paring knife, cut off any pieces of fat. Preheat the oven to 350°F.

Heat the oil in a large sauté pan. Add the onion, carrots, celery, and garlic, and cook over medium heat for 4 to 5 minutes, or until lightly browned. Stir in the tomatoes and cook for 1 minute. Stir in the flour.

Add the lamb shanks and wine, and bring to a boil, stirring with a wooden spoon. Add the stock, tomato paste, bouquet garni, salt, and pepper, and bring back to a boil. Tightly cover the pan and place it in the oven. Combine the parsley and zest in a small bowl.

Bake the lamb shanks, stirring occasionally, for 1½ to 2 hours, or until the meat is fall-off-the-bone tender. Uncover the pan for the last 45 minutes to allow the excess liquid to evaporate. (There should be about 2 cups sauce.)

Braised Lamb Shanks

Correct the seasoning, adding salt and pepper to taste. Sprinkle each shank with the parsley-zest mixture and serve at once.

Note: A whole lamb shank will weigh about 1 pound and be 6- to 8-inches long. Some butchers sell foreshanks—the bottom half of the shank—which weighs about ½ pound. If you use foreshanks, you'll need 8 for this recipe. There is no need to cut them in half.

Serves 4

292 CALORIES PER SERVING; 26 G PROTEIN; 10 G FAT;
16 G CARBOHYDRATE; 140 MG SODIUM; 74 MG CHOLESTEROL

MONGOLIAN HOT POT

China's glorious fondue gets the guests involved with the cooking. Aficionados might argue that the best part of Mongolian Hot Pot is enjoying the broth as soup at the end of the meal. The traditional hot pot is a bundt pan-shaped pot heated over a charcoal brazier. You can use a fondue pot, but you'll need an electric hot plate or a tabletop butane burner to keep the broth boiling. Feel free to substitute other vegetables for the ones listed.

10 cups chicken stock (page 379)

1-inch piece fresh ginger, thinly sliced

4 scallions

3 star anise

1 1-pound lamb loin, partially frozen

1 1-pound pork loin, partially frozen

1 1-pound beef tenderloin, partially frozen

1 small nappa (Chinese cabbage) or bok choy, broken into leaves and cut widthwise into 1-inch strips

1 bunch watercress, broken into large sprigs

10 ounces fresh spinach

12 ounces shiitakes or button mushrooms, stemmed and cut into quarters or halves

FOR THE DIPPING SAUCE:

½ cup hoisin sauce

2 tablespoons soy sauce

2 tablespoons rice wine vinegar

2 tablespoons honey

FOR THE SOUP (OPTIONAL):

1 tablespoon cornstarch

2 egg whites (or 1 whole egg), beaten

salt and freshly ground black pepper

Combine the broth, ginger, scallions, and star anise in a large pot. Simmer for 15 minutes and strain.

Trim any fat and sinew off the meat. Cut the lamb, pork, and beef across the grain into the thinnest possible slices. Attractively arrange the slices, overlapping slightly, around the perimeter of a large platter. (If the platter swivels, like a lazy Susan, so much the better.)

Arrange the nappa, watercress, spinach, and mushrooms in the center.

Combine the ingredients for the dipping sauce in a small bowl and whisk until smooth.

Fill the hot pot with the strained broth and bring to a boil over a tabletop gas burner. Invite your guests to dip the meat and vegetables in the simmering broth and cook each to taste. Use chopsticks for dipping the meat slices. Use the small wire baskets sold at Asian markets and natural food stores for dipping fragile ingredients. Dip the ingredients in the sauce before eating. Add broth as necessary.

For an extra treat, at the end of the meal turn the broth into soup. Dissolve the cornstarch in 2 tablespoons cold water. Whisk into the broth and bring to a boil. Whisk in the beaten egg whites in a thin stream and bring to a boil. Correct the seasoning, adding salt and pepper to taste. Ladle the broth into soup bowls for serving.

Serves 8

366 CALORIES PER SERVING; 43 G PROTEIN; 11 G FAT;
14 G CARBOHYDRATE; 795 MG SODIUM; 87 MG CHOLESTEROL

VENISON WITH CRANBERRIES

Leaner than beef, pork, or veal, venison is great for a low-fat diet. Here it is served with a New England–style fruit sauce flavored with cranberries and maple syrup. Beef, pork, or veal medallions could be prepared the same way.

1 1–1½-pound venison loin

3 tablespoons fresh orange juice

3 tablespoons gin

1 12-ounce bag cranberries

⅔ cup dry red wine

⅔ cup maple syrup

3 strips lemon zest

3 strips orange zest

1 cinnamon stick

salt, freshly ground black pepper, and cayenne pepper

coarse salt and cracked black peppercorns

1½ tablespoons olive oil

sprigs of fresh tarragon, chervil, or parsley, for garnish

Cut the venison into ½-inch-thick medallions. Marinate in the orange juice and gin in a shallow dish for 20 to 30 minutes.

Pick through the cranberries, removing any stems. Combine the wine, maple syrup, zests, and cinnamon stick in a heavy saucepan and bring to a boil. Add the cranberries, reduce the heat, and gently simmer for 3 to 4 minutes, or until barely cooked. (Remove the pan from the heat the moment the cranberry skins begin to split; they should not be mushy.)

Strain the berries over another heavy saucepan. Discard the zests and cinnamon stick, and boil the sauce until thick and syrupy. (There should be about ¼ cup sauce.) Let it cool slightly and stir in the cranberries. Add salt, pepper, and cayenne pepper to taste. Keep the sauce warm.

Just before serving, drain the venison and thoroughly blot dry. Season each medallion with coarse salt and cracked black pepper. Heat the oil in a nonstick skillet over high heat. Cook the venison for 1 to 2 minutes per side, or until cooked to taste. (I like the meat charred on the outside and still quite rare inside). Spoon the cranberry sauce on a platter or plates, and arrange the venison medallions on top. Garnish with herb sprigs and serve at once.

Note: You can also grill the venison.

Serves 4

414 CALORIES PER SERVING; 25 G PROTEIN; 7 G FAT; 53 G CARBOHYDRATE; 117 MG SODIUM; 0 MG CHOLESTEROL

VEGETABLES

STUFFED ARTICHOKES

The Italian love for artichokes can scarcely be overstated. Italians have as many ways to prepare artichokes as we do potatoes. I've called for small artichokes in this recipe, but you could also use full-size globe artichokes (see Note).

6 small artichokes

½ lemon, plus 1 teaspoon grated fresh lemon zest for the stuffing

salt

FOR THE STUFFING:

1 tablespoon extra-virgin olive oil

1 small onion, finely chopped

1 stalk celery, finely chopped

1 ounce prosciutto, finely chopped

1 cup toasted bread crumbs, preferably homemade (page 385)

3 tablespoons minced flat-leaf parsley

¼ cup freshly grated Parmigiano-Reggiano cheese

salt and freshly ground black pepper

1. Cut the ends off the artichoke stems, leaving about 1-inch of stem. Rub the cut end with lemon. Cut off the top third of each artichoke and rub with lemon. Cut each artichoke lengthwise in half and scrape out the "choke" (the fibrous center) with a melon baller. Rub the artichokes with lemon as you work to keep them from discoloring. Put the trimmed artichokes in a bowl of cold water with a squeeze of lemon juice until you're ready to cook them.

2. Cook the artichokes in 4 quarts boiling salted water until tender, 6 to 8 minutes. Drain in a colander, rinse under cold water, and drain again. Arrange the artichoke halves, cut side up, in an attractive baking dish.

3. Prepare the stuffing: Heat half the olive oil in a nonstick frying pan. Add the onion, celery, and prosciutto and cook over medium heat until soft but not brown, about 4 minutes. Stir in the bread crumbs, the parsley, half the Parmesan, and salt and pepper to taste. Distribute the stuffing evenly among the cavities of the artichoke halves. The recipe can be prepared ahead to this stage and stored in the refrigerator for several hours.

4. Preheat the oven to 400°F. or heat the broiler. Just before serving, drizzle the remaining olive oil over the stuffed artichokes or lightly spray with oil. Sprinkle with the remaining Parmesan cheese. Bake the artichokes until thoroughly heated and the stuffing is lightly browned, 10 to 15 minutes. The artichokes can be served either hot or at room temperature.

Note: To make this dish using full-size globe artichokes, cut them lengthwise in quarters. Trim off the tough parts of the leaves and the fibrous choke. Arrange the artichoke quarters in a baking dish, leaf side down, and mound the stuffing where the choke used to be.

Makes 12 pieces

79 CALORIES PER PIECE; 4 G PROTEIN; 3 G FAT; 0.8 G SATURATED FAT; 11 G CARBOHYDRATE; 193 MG SODIUM; 4 MG CHOLESTEROL

RAPINI WITH GARLIC AND OYSTER SAUCE

Here's a great street dish I encountered on my culinary peregrinations through Thailand. In Asia, it is made with Chinese broccoli (gai lan). In this country, it's easier to find a related vegetable, a leafy cousin of broccoli called rapini (also known as broccoli rabe, brocoletto, and brocoletti de rape).

1 pound rapini

1½ tablespoons canola oil

1 tablespoon minced fresh ginger

8 cloves garlic, peeled

½ pound fresh shiitake, straw, or button mushrooms, stemmed and thinly sliced

4 teaspoons oyster sauce (or to taste)

2 teaspoons fish sauce (or to taste)

freshly ground white pepper

Wash the rapini well and dry. Trim off the ends and cut into 2-inch pieces.

Just before serving, heat a wok over high heat. Swirl in the oil. Add the ginger and garlic, and cook for 20 seconds, or until fragrant. Add the rapini and mushrooms, and stir-fry for 1 minute. Add the oyster sauce, fish sauce, and white pepper, and stir-fry for 1 minute more, or until the greens are tender-crisp. Correct the seasoning, adding oyster sauce and fish sauce to taste, and serve at once. (You're not supposed to eat the garlic cloves, but you certainly can if you want to. I do!)

Serves 4

79 CALORIES PER SERVING; 5 G PROTEIN; 4 G FAT; 9 G CARBOHYDRATE; 475 MG SODIUM; 1 MG CHOLESTEROL

BLUE CABBAGE

Trudy Cutrone, who once owned New Hampshire's Snowvillage Inn, introduced me to blaukraut ("blue cabbage"). The cabbage isn't so much blue as pale lavender—a color that results when you add the vinegar. The Old World version is made with bacon fat, which I've replaced with olive oil.

1 tablespoon olive oil

1 onion, finely chopped

3 tablespoons sugar (or to taste)

¼ cup red wine vinegar

¼ cup plus 1 tablespoon dry red wine

1 head red cabbage (about 2 pounds), cored and thinly sliced

salt and freshly ground black pepper

¼ teaspoon ground cinnamon

⅛ teaspoon ground cloves

1½ cups water (approximately)

2 tart apples, peeled, cored, and coarsely grated

1 teaspoon freshly grated lemon zest

3–4 tablespoons bread crumbs

Heat the oil in a large, nonreactive sauté pan (not aluminum or cast iron). Cook the onion over medium heat for 3 to 4 minutes, or until soft. Stir in the sugar and cook for 2 to 3 minutes, or until lightly caramelized.

Stir in the vinegar and ¼ cup wine, and bring the mixture to a boil. Add the cabbage, salt, pepper, spices, and water (barely to cover). Bring the cabbage to a boil, reduce the heat, and gently simmer, covered, for 20 minutes, or until the cabbage is tender-crisp.

Add the apples and simmer, uncovered, for 5 to 10 minutes or until most of the liquid is absorbed and the cabbage is tender but not mushy. Stir in the zest, remaining 1 tablespoon wine, and enough bread crumbs to absorb any excess liquid. Correct the seasoning, adding salt, vinegar, and sugar to taste. The cabbage should be a little sweet and a little sour.

Serves 6 to 8

135 CALORIES PER SERVING; 2 G PROTEIN; 3 G FAT; 26 G CARBOHYDRATE; 15 MG SODIUM; 0 MG CHOLESTEROL

ROSEMARY-ROASTED CARROTS

Like so much other Italian cooking, this recipe is simplicity itself. But I know of no other cooking method that produces tastier carrots (or other root vegetables). High-heat roasting is a great way to intensify the flavor of vegetables, evaporating the water in them to concentrate the flavor and caramelizing the natural sugars.

1 pound carrots

1 head garlic

1 tablespoon extra-virgin olive oil

2 sprigs fresh rosemary, or 1 tablespoon dried

salt and freshly ground black pepper

Serves 4

95 CALORIES PER SERVING; 2 G PROTEIN; 4 G FAT; 0.5 G SATURATED FAT;
15 G CARBOHYDRATE; 75 MG SODIUM; 0 MG CHOLESTEROL

1. Preheat the oven to 450°F. If using whole carrots, peel them and cut them into 2-inch sections. Break the garlic into individual cloves, leaving the skin intact on each. Place the carrots, garlic, olive oil, rosemary, salt, and pepper in a roasting pan or baking dish just large enough to hold them. Toss to mix.

2. Roast the carrots, stirring from time to time, until browned and tender, 20 to 30 minutes. Serve at once.

CAULIFLOWER WITH POOR MAN'S "PARMESAN"

*Italy, at least the north of Italy, is one of the prosperous regions in Europe.
It's hard to imagine an age when grating cheese would have been considered an unaffordable luxury, but such was the case in southern Italy until the early part of this century. Cheese may have been in short supply, but two staples of the southern Italian diet—anchovies and stale bread—were not. Ingenious cooks combined them to make the following poor man's "Parmesan," which makes a delectable topping for all sorts of vegetables.*

1½ tablespoons extra-virgin olive oil

1 clove garlic, minced

2 to 4 anchovy fillets, rinsed, blotted dry, and minced

¾ cup dry toasted bread crumbs

salt

1 small or ½ large head cauliflower

1. Heat the oil in a large nonstick skillet. Add the garlic and anchovies and cook over medium heat until just beginning to brown, 2 to 3 minutes. Stir in the bread crumbs. Reduce the heat to medium low and cook the mixture until crisp, toasted, and aromatic, about 10 minutes, stirring often.

2. Bring 4 quarts lightly salted water to a boil in a large pot. Stem the cauliflower and break it into small florets. Boil the cauliflower until tender, about 5 minutes, then drain well in a colander.

3. Stir the cauliflower into the crumb mixture and cook over high heat until thoroughly heated, about 2 minutes. Serve at once.

Serves 4

167 CALORIES PER SERVING; 8 G PROTEIN; 7 G FAT; 1 G SATURATED
FAT; 21 G CARBOHYDRATE; 321 MG SODIUM; 2 MG CHOLESTEROL

BRAZILIAN-STYLE COLLARD GREENS

Brazilians have developed one of the best ways to prepare collard greens; they slice them paper-thin and sauté them in garlicky olive oil. The roll-cut method outlined here works well for thinly slicing any leafy green vegetable.

1 bunch collard greens (about 1½ pounds)

1½ tablespoons olive oil

2 cloves garlic, minced (2 teaspoons)

2 shallots, minced

salt and freshly ground black pepper

Wash the collard greens well. Remove the stems and roll up the leaves lengthwise into a tight tube. Cut the greens widthwise into the thinnest possible slices. Fluff the slices in a large bowl and sprinkle with a little water.

Just before serving, heat the oil in a large, heavy skillet over high heat. Add the garlic and shallots, and cook for 20 seconds, or until fragrant but not brown. Add the collard greens, salt, and pepper. Cook the greens for 1 to 2 minutes, or until just tender, stirring well. If the greens look too dry, add a tablespoon or so of water. Do not overcook; the collards should remain bright green. Correct the seasoning and serve at once.

Serves 4

107 CALORIES PER SERVING; 3 G PROTEIN; 5 G FAT;
14 G CARBOHYDRATE; 33 MG SODIUM; 0 MG CHOLESTEROL

GRILLED CORN IN THE STYLE OF OAXACA

I've always loved corn on the cob—especially when it's grilled over an open fire. But I've never had anything quite like the corn served by the street vendors of Oaxaca: the ears charred over charcoal braziers, slathered with mayonnaise, then sprinkled with grated cheese, chili powder, and lime juice. The combination will surely strike you as weird, but I promise that you'll grow to love it. I've pretty much left the recipe intact; however, I mix the mayonnaise with a little no-fat sour cream to reduce the overall fat.

6 ears of corn

2 tablespoons mayonnaise

2 tablespoons no-fat sour cream

3 tablespoons finely grated queso añnejo, Parmesan cheese, or Romano cheese

1 to 2 tablespoons pure chili powder

2 limes, cut into wedges

spray oil

salt and freshly ground black pepper

1. Preheat your grill to high. Shuck the corn by peeling the husks back like banana skins. Leave them attached to the base of the cobs. Tie the husks together; the idea is to create a handle for holding the ear of corn as you eat it.

2. Place the mayonnaise and sour cream in a small serving bowl and stir to mix. Place the cheese, chili powder, and

lime wedges in small serving bowls. Have these ingredients ready on the table, with a pastry brush or butter knife for spreading the mayonnaise mixture.

3. Lightly spray each ear of corn with oil and season with the salt and pepper. Grill the corn until it is nicely browned on all sides, 3 to 5 minutes per side, turning with tongs. (Position the corn so that the tied husks hang over the edge of the grill away from the hot coals.) Transfer the corn to a platter.

4. To serve, have each guest brush or spread the mayonnaise mixture on his corn. Sprinkle the ears with cheese and chili powder and squeeze on lime juice to taste.

Serves 6

178 CALORIES PER SERVING; 6 G PROTEIN; 6 G FAT; 1 G SATURATED FAT;
33 G CARBOHYDRATE; 107 MG SODIUM; 5 MG CHOLESTEROL

SICILIAN STUFFED EGGPLANT
(MELANZANA ALLA SICILIANA)

The Italian word for eggplant is melanzana, *from the Latin words* malum insanum *(literally, "mad apple"). In the Middle Ages, eggplants were believed to cause madness, a fear that may have been based on the plant's close parentage with several highly toxic plants, including deadly nightshade. Times have changed: today, eggplant is almost synonymous with Italian cooking. I like to prepare this dish with baby eggplants (each 3- to 4-inches long), so you can serve individual halves as an antipasto or a vegetable side dish. Baby eggplants are available at Italian markets, specialty greengrocers, and many supermarkets. But larger eggplants could be prepared the same way.*

- 1 to 1¼ pounds eggplant (preferably 4 to 6 baby eggplants), unpeeled
- 1 tablespoon extra-virgin olive oil
- 1 medium onion, finely chopped
- 1 stalk celery, finely chopped
- 1 Italian pepper or cubanelle (a small light-green pepper), or ½ green bell pepper, cored, seeded, and finely chopped
- 2 cloves garlic, finely chopped
- 1 large or 2 medium red ripe tomatoes, finely chopped (about 1 cup), with their juices
- 6 pitted black olives, chopped
- 1 tablespoon drained capers
- 6 basil leaves, thinly slivered, or 3 tablespoons chopped flat-leaf parsley
- a few drops red wine vinegar or fresh lemon juice (optional)
- 2 tablespoons freshly grated Parmigiano-Reggiano cheese
- salt and freshly ground black pepper

1. Preheat the oven to 400°F. Roast the eggplants in a baking dish in the oven until very tender (squeezably soft on the sides), 20 to 40 minutes (depending on the size of the eggplants). Transfer the eggplants to a cutting board to cool. Cut each in half lengthwise and scoop out the flesh with a spoon, taking care not to pierce the shell. Reserve the shells and chop the flesh.

2. Meanwhile, prepare the filling: Heat the olive oil in a large nonstick frying pan. Add the onion, celery, pepper, and garlic and cook over medium heat until just beginning to brown, about 5 minutes. Add the tomato, olives, capers, and chopped eggplant flesh and cook until the eggplant is soft and most of the tomato juices have been absorbed, about 5 minutes. Stir in the basil and vinegar (if using) and cook for 1 minute. Remove the pan from the heat and stir in the cheese and salt and pepper to taste: the filling should be highly seasoned. Stuff the filling into the eggplant shells. The eggplants can be served hot or at room temperature. (As part of an antipasto, they'd probably be served at room temperature.) To warm, bake them in a 400°F. oven until thoroughly heated, about 10 minutes.

Serves 8 as an appetizer, 4 as a vegetable side dish

58 CALORIES PER SERVING;* 2 G PROTEIN; 3 G FAT; 0.6 G SATURATED FAT; 7 G CARBOHYDRATE; 92 MG SODIUM; 1 MG CHOLESTEROL

Analysis is based on 8 servings as an appetizer.

FENNEL GRATIN

Many Americans live their entire lives without having tasted fennel. Gennaro Villella can hardly imagine a meal without it. The Umbrian-born founding chef of the restaurant Fantino at the Ritz-Carlton Hotel in New York slices fennel into salads, simmers it in soups, and even poaches it in sugar syrup to make an offbeat dessert. Here's a more traditional preparation from Umbria: a creamy fennel gratin that makes a great cool-weather side dish or vegetarian entrée. This recipe features a nontraditional element, a butterless béchamel sauce.

- 1 large or 2 medium fennel bulbs (1¼ to 1½ pounds)
- 2 cups skim, 1 percent, or 2 percent milk
- 1 teaspoon salt

FOR THE BÉCHAMEL SAUCE:

- 3 tablespoons all-purpose unbleached white flour
- ⅛ teaspoon freshly grated nutmeg, or to taste
- 1 bay leaf
- ½ onion
- 1 clove
- 2½ cups 2 percent or whole milk or low-fat half-and-half
- 1 clove garlic
- 1 stalk celery, trimmed
- freshly ground white pepper
- ½ cup freshly grated Parmigiano-Reggiano cheese
- spray oil

1. Trim the stems, base, and outside leaves off the fennel. Cut the bulb crosswise into ¼-inch-thick slices.

Place the fennel in a deep, heavy saucepan with the milk, salt to taste, and enough water (3 to 4 cups) to cover the fennel completely. Loosely cover the pan. Simmer the fennel over medium heat until very tender, 10 to 15 minutes.

2. Prepare the béchamel sauce: Have ready a bowl of cold water. Place the flour and nutmeg in a large nonstick saucepan. Cook over medium heat, stirring steadily with a wooden spoon, until the flour has a pleasant, toasted aroma, about 3 minutes. Do not let it brown or burn. Plunge the pot in the bowl of water to stop the cooking. Let the flour cool completely. Pin the bay leaf to the onion with the clove. Whisk the cold milk into the flour, a little at a time, to create a smooth mixture free of lumps. Return the mixture to the saucepan with the onion, garlic, and celery. Gradually bring the mixture to a boil, whisking steadily. Reduce the heat and gently simmer the sauce until thick and well flavored, about 10 minutes. (It should thickly coat the back of a spoon.) Add salt and pepper (and a little more nutmeg if desired) to taste. Remove the pan from the heat and fish out and discard the onion, garlic, and celery. Whisk in half the Parmesan.

3. Spray a 12-inch baking dish with oil and spoon ⅓ of the béchamel sauce into the baking dish. Arrange the fennel slices on top, slightly overlapping. Spoon the remaining sauce on top and sprinkle with the remaining Parmesan. The recipe can be prepared ahead to this stage.

4. Preheat the oven to 400°F. Bake the fennel gratin until thoroughly heated and browned on top, about 20 minutes. Serve at once.

Note: For a crustier gratin, you can sprinkle the top with 2 to 3 tablespoons toasted bread crumbs before baking.

Serves 6

169 CALORIES PER SERVING; 11 G PROTEIN; 5 G FAT; 3 G SATURATED FAT; 21 G CARBOHYDRATE; 659 MG SODIUM; 14 MG CHOLESTEROL

GRILLED PORTOBELLO MUSHROOMS WITH GARLIC AND SAGE

The Italian food revolution of the 1980s introduced many new ingredients to the American larder, including the Portobello mushroom, a jumbo, dark-gilled cousin of Agaricus bisporus, *the common white mushroom. Portobellos are great for grilling, thanks to their large size, and they acquire a smoky, meaty flavor when cooked over fire. The antipasto version of this dish calls for the portobellos to be cut into triangles and served at the end of bamboo skewers. I like to top them with strips of grilled red peppers. You can also serve the portobellos sliced into strips in salads or whole as a first course.*

4 large Portobello mushrooms (4 inches across)

4 cloves garlic, cut into slivers

4 sage leaves, cut widthwise into thin strips

1½ tablespoons extra-virgin olive oil

1 tablespoon balsamic vinegar or fresh lemon juice

salt and freshly ground black pepper

1 red bell pepper (optional)

1. Cut the stems off the mushrooms (reserve for stock). Using the tip of a paring knife, make 10 to 12 narrow slits in the top (rounded part) of each Portobello. Insert a sliver of garlic and a strip of sage leaf into each slit. Combine the olive oil and vinegar in a mixing bowl and whisk in salt and pepper to taste. Add any leftover garlic or sage. Place the portobellos in a baking dish and brush or spoon the marinade over the mushrooms, turning to coat both sides. Let marinate for 1 hour.

2. Preheat the grill to medium-high. Grill the portobellos until nicely charred on the outside and cooked through, 3 to 4 minutes per side. (Start grilling with the rounded part down.) Brush the bell pepper, if using, with any leftover marinade and grill it until nicely charred, about 2 minutes per side. Transfer the vegetables to a plate to cool.

3. Cut the portobellos into bite-sized wedges or triangles. Core and seed the pepper, if using, and cut into wedges, strips, or triangles smaller than the mushrooms. Place a piece of pepper on top of each Portobello and impale with a small bamboo skewer.

Makes 24 to 32 pieces, enough to serve 8 to 12

47 CALORIES PER SERVING;* 2 G PROTEIN; 3 G FAT; 0.3 G SATURATED FAT; 3 G CARBOHYDRATE; 4 MG SODIUM; 0 MG CHOLESTEROL

Analysis is based on 8 servings.

SWEET AND SOUR CIPPOLINI

Cippolini *are small flat onion-like bulbs that have an elegant, shalloty flavor. They were once available only at Italian greengrocers, but you can find them in gourmet shops, natural-foods stores, and many supermarkets. If you can't find* cippolini, *use pearl onions.*

1 pound cippolini or pearl onions

salt

1 tablespoon extra-virgin olive oil

3 tablespoons balsamic vinegar, or to taste

2 tablespoons honey

1 clove

1. Cook the cippolini in their skins in a pot of boiling slated water until just tender, 6 to 8 minutes. Rinse well, refresh under cold water, and drain. Peel the cippolini with a paring knife.

2. Heat the olive oil in a nonstick frying pan. Add the cippolini and cook over high heat until lightly browned, about 3 minutes. Add the vinegar, honey, and clove and continue cooking until the pan juices are reduced to a thick, sweet, syrupy glaze, 3 to 5 minutes. Remove the clove before serving.

Serves 4

116 CALORIES PER SERVING; 1 G PROTEIN; 4 G FAT; 0.5 G SATURATED FAT; 21 G CARBOHYDRATE; 6 MG SODIUM; 0 MG CHOLESTEROL

STUFFED ONIONS IN THE STYLE OF SAN GIMIGNANO

San Gimignano is one of the most scenic hill towns in Tuscany, a medieval walled city with tall towers (once used for hanging and drying dyed fabrics) that create an almost Manhattanesque silhouette against the Tuscan sky. I watched these stuffed onions being made through the back door of a restaurant kitchen and was invited in to try them. They make a wonderful accompaniment to the Rosemary-Roasted Pork Loin on page 256.

3 medium onions (each weighing about 6 ounces), unpeeled

salt

1 carrot, peeled and cut into ¼-inch dice

spray oil (or a little olive oil)

1 tablespoon extra-virgin olive oil

1 medium zucchini or yellow squash, scrubbed and cut into ¼-inch dice

1 red bell pepper, cored, seeded, and cut into ¼-inch dice

4 basil leaves, thinly sliced, or ½ teaspoon dried

3 tablespoons freshly grated Parmigiano-Reggiano cheese (optional)

freshly ground black pepper

2 tablespoons dried bread crumbs (optional)

1. Cook the onions in their skins in boiling salted water to cover until tender, about 15 minutes. Add the carrots the last 2 minutes. Drain the onions and carrots, rinse with cold water, and let cool.

2. Using a sharp knife, cut ¼-inch off the top and bottom of each onion (so it will sit straight without wobbling), then cut the onion in half crosswise. Slip off the skin. Gently remove the inside layers of the onions to create a hollow cup. Cut the inside layers into ¼-inch dice and reserve for the stuffing. Work gently and carefully, as the onion will have a tendency to fall apart. Place the onion halves in an attractive oven-proof baking dish lightly sprayed or brushed with oil.

3. Prepare the stuffing: Heat half the olive oil in a nonstick frying pan. Add the diced onion, carrot, zucchini, and bell pepper. Cook over medium heat until the vegetables are just tender, 3 to 5 minutes. Stir in the basil, Parmesan (if using), and black pepper. Correct the seasoning, adding salt if needed. Stuff this mixture into the onion halves. Sprinkle the bread crumbs on top, if using, and drizzle with the remaining olive oil. The onions can be prepared ahead to this stage.

4. Just before serving, preheat the oven to 400°F. Bake the onions until thoroughly heated, about 10 minutes.

Makes 6 pieces

79 CALORIES PER PIECE; 2 G PROTEIN; 3 G FAT; 0.3 G SATURATED FAT; 12 G CARBOHYDRATE; 7 MG SODIUM; 0 MG CHOLESTEROL

SWEET AND SOUR ROASTED PEPPERS

Roasted peppers are such a part of Italy's culinary landscape, it's hard to image an antipasto spread without them. This recipe features one of my favorite techniques for high-flavor, low-fat cooking: high-heat roasting. The process is easier and cleaner than grilling peppers, but you still get the sweet, smoky flavor that comes from charring the pepper skins and caramelizing the natural sugars in the peppers.

2 red bell peppers

2 yellow bell peppers

2 green bell peppers

1½ tablespoons extra-virgin olive oil

2 springs fresh thyme or ½ teaspoon dried

salt and freshly ground black pepper

⅓ cup balsamic vinegar

1 to 2 tablespoons honey

1. Preheat the oven to 450°F. Cut the pepper flesh off the core and seeds. To do so, make four broad cuts from the top of the pepper to the bottom, one on each side. (The core and scraps can be saved for the Basic Vegetable Stock on page 382.) Cut each side in half lengthwise to obtain strips that are 3 inches long and 1 inch wide.

2. Place the peppers in a nonstick roasting pan and toss with 2 teaspoons of the olive oil, the thyme, salt, and pepper. Roast the peppers in the oven until nicely browned, 10 to 15 minutes, gently stirring from time to time to prevent burning. Remove the pan from the oven and let the peppers cool.

3. Prepare the sauce: Boil the balsamic vinegar until reduced by half. Whisk in the honey, the remaining olive oil, any pepper juices that have accumulated in the roasting pan, and salt and pepper to taste. Cook for 1 minute. Correct the seasoning, adding salt or honey to taste.

4. To serve, arrange the peppers on a platter in rows or circles, with the pieces overlapping to create a colorful design. Spoon the sauce over the peppers and serve. The recipe can be prepared several hours ahead to this stage.

Note: You can make a virtually fat-free version of this dish by tossing the peppers with 1 teaspoon olive oil before roasting and omitting the remaining olive oil from the sauce.

Serves 6 to 8

104 CALORIES PER SERVING;* 2 G PROTEIN; 4 G FAT; .5 G SATURATED FAT; 18 G CARBOHYDRATE; 4 MG SODIUM; 0 MG CHOLESTEROL

Analysis is based on 6 servings.

A QUICK SAUTÉ OF YELLOW PEPPERS AND SUGAR SNAP PEAS

This recipe is simplicity itself, but the colors are breathtaking. Sugar snap peas are sweet enough to eat pods and all. You can also use snow peas, substitute sliced jícama for the peppers, or add thinly sliced shiitake mushrooms.

1 pound sugar snap peas, strung

1½ tablespoons extra-virgin olive oil

1 large clove garlic, minced (1 teaspoon)

½ teaspoon freshly grated lemon zest

2 yellow or red bell peppers, cored, seeded, and cut into pea pod–sized strips

1 tablespoon chopped fresh tarragon, thyme, or basil (or 1 teaspoon dried)

salt and freshly ground black pepper

Blanch the peas in 1 quart boiling salted water for 30 seconds. Drain in a colander and refresh under cold water. Drain and blot dry.

Just before serving, heat the oil in a large sauté pan. Add the garlic and zest, and cook over medium heat for 30 seconds, or until fragrant. Add the peppers and sauté for 30 seconds. Add the peas, tarragon, salt, and pepper. Cook just long enough to heat the peas. Serve at once.

Serves 4

87 CALORIES PER SERVING; 4 G PROTEIN; 4 G FAT; 10 G CARBOHYDRATE; 5 MG SODIUM; 0 MG CHOLESTEROL

MUSHROOM-STUFFED ANAHEIM CHILIES WITH SWEET CORN SALSA

These mushroom-stuffed chilies make a stunning vegetarian appetizer—especially when coupled with the creamy sweet corn sauce on page 9. There are lots of options for chilies: You can use Anaheim chilies, New Mexican green chilies, even small poblanos. Don't be intimidated by the large number of ingredients; the recipe is really just a series of simple steps. The contrast in flavors—gently fiery chilies, earthy mushrooms, sweet corn—is breathtaking.

8 long, slender, fresh green chilies,
   such as Anaheim or New Mexican

FOR THE MUSHROOM STUFFING:

12 ounces button mushrooms, trimmed

2 teaspoons fresh lime juice

1 tablespoon vegetable oil

¼ cup chopped white onion

1 clove garlic

3 tablespoons minced fresh cilantro,
   plus 4 sprigs for garnish

salt and freshly ground black pepper

1 batch sweet corn sauce (Salsa de Maíz); see page 9

1. Roast and peel the peppers. Make a T-shaped cut in the side of each chili. (The long side of the T should run the length of the chili.) Pinch together the ends of the chili to open the slit. Using a grapefruit spoon or the tip of a small paring knife, remove the seeds and veins.

2. To prepare the filling, wipe the mushrooms clean with a damp paper towel. Cut any large mushrooms in quarters, medium-size ones in half. Finely chop the mushrooms by hand or in a food processor. (If using the processor, work in several batches, so as to not fill the bowl more than a third of the way. Run the machine in short bursts. Over-filling the processor bowl, or overprocessing, will turn the mushrooms to mush.) Sprinkle with lime juice.

Assorted Chili Peppers

3. Heat the oil in a nonstick skillet. Add the onion and garlic and cook over medium heat until they are soft but not brown, 3 minutes. Increase the heat to high and add the mushrooms and cilantro. Cook until all the mushroom liquid has evaporated and the mixture is thick, 5 to 8 minutes, stirring often. Correct the seasoning, adding salt and pepper to taste. Let the mixture cool to room temperature. Using a small spoon, stuff the mushroom mixture into the chilies.

4. To serve, warm the chilies in a preheated 400°F. oven. Spoon the corn sauce over the bottom of four plates. Arrange two chilies side by side on top of the sauce, the first going one way, the second going the other way. Garnish with the sprigs of cilantro and serve at once.

Serves 4 (2 chilies per person)

257 CALORIES PER SERVING; 12 G PROTEIN; 5 G FAT; 1 G SATURATED FAT; 46 G CARBOHYDRATE; 370 MG SODIUM; 3 MG CHOLESTEROL

ROASTED POBLANO CHILIES STUFFED WITH FRUITED PICADILLO
(SERVED WITH POMEGRANATES AND WALNUT SAUCE) (CHILES EN NOGADA)

This complex dish—created more than a century ago by the Augustine nuns of Puebla—is one of the high holies of Mexican cuisine: fire-charred poblano chilies stuffed with a spiced, fruited picadillo and cloaked in a thick, creamy sauce flavored with walnuts. It's also a patriotic dish, as the white sauce, green chilies, and ruby red pomegranate seeds echo the colors of the Mexican flag. Alas, chilies en nogada is a nutritional nightmare, as the traditional version contains fatty pork, batter-fried chilies, and a sauce whose main ingredients are heavy cream and cheese. Fortunately, it's a dish that lends itself to a high-flavor, low-fat makeover. To decrease the amount of fat in the filling, I use lean pork loin. The chilies are served in all their fire-charred glory, but without the batter and deep-frying. (As far as I'm concerned, the batter just camouflages the smoke flavor.) As for the sauce, my low-fat version is built from evaporated skim milk, no-fat sour cream, and low-fat cream cheese. Here, then, is a dish that would make a proud centerpiece for any dinner, with much less fat than found in the original. Note: *Ringing in at 14 grams of fat per serving, this recipe is on the higher end of the high-flavor, low-fat spectrum. When you stop to consider that traditional chiles en nogada contain 524 calories and a whopping 36 grams of fat per serving, the makeover represents an enormous improvement.*

8 large poblano chilies

1 batch Fruit and Nut Picadillo (following)

FOR THE WALNUT SAUCE:

⅓ cup walnuts (2 ounces)

¾ cup evaporated skim milk

¾ cup no-fat sour cream

2 ounces low- or no-fat cream cheese

1 ounce queso fresco or feta cheese

1 clove garlic

1 tablespoon chopped onion

1 tablespoon chopped cilantro

1 tablespoon cream sherry

⅛ teaspoon ground cinnamon

salt and freshly ground black pepper

1 fresh pomegranate, broken into seeds

4 sprigs parsley

1. Roast, peel, and seed the chilies for stuffing, as described in the previous recipe. Make the picadillo (following) and let cool.

2. To prepare the sauce, toast the walnuts in a 400°F. oven until they're fragrant and just beginning to brown, 3 to 5 minutes. (Toasting the nuts enhances their flavor.) Combine the nuts, evaporated milk, sour cream, cream cheese, queso fresco, garlic, onion, cilantro, sherry, and cinnamon in a blender and purée until smooth. Add salt and pepper to taste. The recipe can be prepared ahead to this stage and then refrigerated. The sauce is traditionally served at room temperature, so 1 hour before serving, let it warm to room temperature.

3. Just before serving, preheat the oven to 400°F. Using a spoon, stuff the filling through the slits on the sides of the chilies. Place the chilies in an ovenproof serving dish and bake until they're thoroughly heated, 10 to 15 minutes. Spoon the sauce over the chilies and sprinkle with the pomegranate seeds and sprigs of parsley.

Serves 4

387 CALORIES PER SERVING; 31 G PROTEIN; 14 G FAT; 2 G SATURATED FAT; 38 G CARBOHYDRATE; 266 MG SODIUM; 38 MG CHOLESTEROL

FRUIT AND NUT PICADILLO

This fragrant picadillo (meat hash) is the traditional filling for chiles en nogada (page 280). I so like the contrast of flavors—the acidic sweetness of pears and peaches, the nutty crunch of toasted almonds, the meatiness of the pork—that I often use it as a stuffing for tortilla dishes (see the flautas on page 118) and even as a dish by itself.

8 ounces lean pork or veal loin, trimmed of all fat

1 large red ripe tomato

1 (2-inch) piece cinnamon stick

3 cloves

2 allspice berries

¼ white onion, finely chopped

2 cloves garlic, minced

2 tablespoons lightly toasted slivered almonds

2 tablespoons raisins

2 tablespoons chopped citron (optional)

2 tablespoons chopped flat-leaf parsley,
   plus 12 whole leaves for garnish

½ teaspoon dried oregano

½ pear or apple, coarsely grated or finely chopped

½ peach, coarsely grated or finely chopped
   (or more apple or pear)

½ cup water

salt and freshly ground black pepper

1. Finely chop the pork by hand or in a food processor. Place it in a large saucepan. Cut the tomato in half widthwise and squeeze out the water and seeds. Grate the tomato, skin side out, on the coarse side of a grater. (This grates the tomato flesh, leaving the skin behind.) Add the tomato to the pork.

2. Tie the cinnamon stick, cloves, and allspice berries in a piece of cheesecloth (or wrap them in foil and perforate it with a fork) and add them to the pork. Add the onion, garlic, almonds, raisins, citron if using, and the chopped parsley, oregano, pear, peach, and water.

3. Bring the mixture to a boil, reduce the heat, and simmer until the pork is cooked and the excess liquid has evaporated (the filling should be moist but not soupy), about 20 minutes. Remove and discard the spice bundle. Correct the seasoning, adding salt and pepper to taste; the filling should be highly seasoned.

Serves 2 as an appetizer or 4 as a filling

161 CALORIES PER SERVING; 15 G PROTEIN; 6 G FAT; 1 G SATURATED FAT; 14 G CARBOHYDRATE; 47 MG SODIUM; 30 MG CHOLESTEROL

BAKER'S STYLE POTATOES

In trying to come up with a low-fat gratin, I remembered a recipe I had learned at the La Varenne cooking school in Paris. The potatoes were simmered in veal stock, which made them rich and meltingly tender. The dish was called pommes boulangère, "baker's-style potatoes," after a practice popular in the rural France of yesteryear: housewives would drop their casseroles at the local bakery to be cooked while they attended church. Sautéed onions provide as much flavor as the cheese used in traditional gratins. You can make this dish with a variety of root vegetables, including yams and sweet potatoes. It's a great party dish.

1½ tablespoons extra-virgin olive oil

2 onions, thinly sliced (about 2 cups)

4 large potatoes (about 2 pounds)

salt and freshly ground black pepper

2–3 cups chicken or veal stock (approximately)

¼ cup bread crumbs

Preheat the broiler. Heat the olive oil in a 10-inch nonstick frying pan with a metal (not plastic) handle. Add the onions and cook, stirring often, over medium heat for 4 to 6 minutes, or until golden brown.

Meanwhile, peel the potatoes and cut into ¼-inch slices. Stir the potatoes into the onions and season with salt and pepper. Add enough stock to cover the potatoes and bring to a boil. Reduce the heat and simmer for 15 minutes, or until soft. Flatten the potatoes with a fork and sprinkle with bread crumbs. Place the pan under the broiler. Broil for 1 minute, or until the top is crusty and golden brown.

Serves 4

303 CALORIES PER SERVING; 7 G PROTEIN; 6 G FAT; 57 G CARBOHYDRATE; 87 MG SODIUM; 0 MG CHOLESTEROL

Baker's Style Potatoes

POTATO TOMATO GRATIN

Potatoes and tomatoes make a delicious combination, the acidity of the latter cutting the starchiness of the former. In this recipe, they're layered with a little olive oil and cheese in a casserole. The potatoes poach in the liquid from the tomatoes. I like the touch of richness imparted by the little heavy cream. (Who doesn't!) But don't worry if your fat budget precludes cream— the casserole will still be delicious without it.

spray olive oil

1 pound starchy potatoes, like Idahos, peeled and thinly sliced

salt and freshly ground black pepper

2 to 4 tablespoons freshly grated Parmigiano-Reggiano cheese

1 tablespoon extra-virgin olive oil

1 to 2 tablespoons heavy cream (optional)

1 pound red ripe tomatoes, thinly sliced

3 tablespoons toasted bread crumbs

1. Preheat the oven to 400°F. Lightly spray a 6 x 10-inch baking dish with oil. Arrange a layer of potato slices in the bottom, using about one-third of the potatoes. Sprinkle with salt, pepper, and a little cheese. Drizzle a little olive oil and heavy cream (if using) on top. Add a layer of tomatoes, using about one-third of the tomatoes. Sprinkle with a little more salt, pepper, cheese, oil, and cream. Repeat the process twice with the remaining potatoes and tomatoes. (The top layer should be tomatoes.) Sprinkle the bread crumbs on top.

2. Bake the casserole until the potatoes are very soft, 1 to 1¼ hours. Serve hot or at room temperature.

Serves 4 to 6 as a side dish

197 CALORIES PER SERVING;* 5 G PROTEIN; 5 G FAT; 1 G SATURATED FAT; 34 G CARBOHYDRATE; 118 MG SODIUM; 2 MG CHOLESTEROL

Analysis is based on 4 servings.

BRAISED NEW POTATOES WITH GARLIC AND BAY LEAVES

This dish offers a perfect example how Italians use one or two seasonings to create a dish with symphonic flavors. The potatoes are studded with slivers of bay leaf, which gives them a futuristic appearance. To make a low-fat version of this dish (the original was roasted in butter), I had the idea to braise the potatoes in chicken broth. For extra richness, you could brush the potatoes with a little melted butter or olive oil and still wind up with a low-fat dish.
Note: The bay leaves are for flavor and show only. Be sure to have everyone remove them before eating.

8 small red potatoes (about 1 pound), scrubbed

2 fresh bay leaves

8 cloves garlic, peeled

1 cup Chicken Stock (page 379),
   or Basic Vegetable Stock (page 282), or as needed

salt and freshly ground black pepper

1 tablespoon melted butter or extra-virgin olive oil

1. Preheat the oven to 400°F. Make 2 lengthwise cuts in the top of each potato, each about ¼ inch deep. Cut the bay leaves crosswise into ¼-inch slivers. Place a sliver of bay leaf in each slit. Place the potatoes in a roasting pan just large enough to hold them. (A loaf pan works well.) Add the garlic cloves, the chicken stock, and a little salt and pepper.

2. Braise the potatoes, uncovered, until soft, 45 to 60 minutes. During this time, most of the stock will evaporate or be absorbed into the potatoes, but a little should remain to form a sauce. If using the butter, brush it on top of the potatoes. Serve at once, with the sauce and garlic spooned on top. The garlic is edible; *the bay leaves are not.* HAVE EVERYONE REMOVE THEM BEFORE EATING THE POTATOES.

Serves 4

153 CALORIES PER SERVING; 3 G PROTEIN; 4 G FAT; 2 G SATURATED FAT; 28 G CARBOHYDRATE; 284 MG SODIUM; 12 MG CHOLESTEROL

LACY POTATO PANCAKE

This crisp potato pancake was one of my first ventures into low-fat cooking, so it's on the higher end of the fat register. Instead of deep-frying, I bake it in a nonstick frying pan to reduce the fat. Shred the potato on a mandoline, or use the julienne disk of a food processor. (You can use a hand grater, but the pancake won't be as delicate.)

1 large baking potato

2 scallions, chopped

2 tablespoons olive or canola oil

salt and freshly ground black pepper

Preheat the oven to 400°F. Peel the potato and shred it into a fine julienne. Gently squeeze the shredded potato in your hands to wring out as much liquid as possible. Stir the scallions into the potato.

Pour half the oil into a 9-inch nonstick frying pan and spread it around with a pastry brush. Heat the pan over medium heat. Spread the potato over the bottom of the pan. Season with salt and pepper. Cook the pancake for 2 to 3 minutes, or until the bottom is lightly browned. Shake the pan often to prevent the pancake from sticking.

Flip the pancake with a flick of the wrist; if this gesture seems too daunting, place a plate on top of the pan and invert the pancake onto it. Slide the pancake back into the pan and add the remaining 1 tablespoon oil at the edges of the pancake. Season with salt and pepper, and cook for 2 to 3 minutes more to brown the bottom of the pancake.

Place the pan in the oven and bake for 10 to 12 minutes, or until crisp. Transfer to a platter and cut into wedges for serving.

Serves 2 to 4

177 CALORIES PER SERVING; 2 G PROTEIN; 9 G FAT; 23 G CARBOHYDRATE; 5 MG SODIUM; 0 MG CHOLESTEROL

POTATOES WITH ROASTED PEPPERS
(PAPAS CON RAJAS)

Every country has its version of potatoes au gratin. Mexico's offers the electrifying addition of roasted poblano chilies. To decrease the amount of fat, I've cut back on the cheese, adding nonfat sour cream and chicken stock (or vegetable stock) for richness. I also try to use Yukon Gold potatoes, which have a naturally buttery flavor, so you don't need a lot of extra fat.

6 poblano chilies

4 to 5 Yukon Gold potatoes (about 2 pounds), peeled and cut into 1½-inch chunks

salt

1½ tablespoons lard or canola oil

1 large white onion, thinly sliced

3 cloves garlic, thinly sliced

1 cup chicken or vegetable stock

½ cup nonfat sour cream

Freshly ground black pepper

¼ cup grated queso fresco or sharp white cheddar cheese (optional)

1. Roast the chilies over a high flame or under the broiler, until the skins are charred all over, 8 to 10 minutes. Place the chilies in a bowl and cover with plastic wrap. Let cool for 15 minutes. Scrape the burnt skin off each chili, using a paring knife. Seed and devein the chilies, cutting each into ¼-inch-wide strips.

2. Meanwhile, place the potatoes in a pot with lightly salted cold water to cover. Gradually bring to a boil, reduce the heat slightly, and briskly simmer the potatoes until they are just tender, about 10 minutes. Drain the potatoes, rinse with cold water until they're cool, and drain well again.

3. Heat the oil in a large nonstick frying pan. Start the onions over a medium flame, lowering the heat as needed to prevent them from burning. Cook until the onions are a deep golden brown, about 8 minutes, adding the garlic halfway through.

4. Add the chicken stock and sour cream and bring to a boil. Stir in the potatoes and chili strips. Boil the mixture until the sauce is thick and richly flavored, 6 to 8 minutes. Season with salt and pepper to taste. Transfer the mixture to a platter or serving bowl and sprinkle the optional cheese on top. Serve at once.

Serves 6

208 CALORIES PER SERVING; 5 G PROTEIN; 4 G FAT; 1 G SATURATED FAT; 41 G CARBOHYDRATE; 32 MG SODIUM; 3 MG CHOLESTEROL

MASHED POTATOES WITH SUN-DRIED TOMATOES

Italians often pair potatoes and tomatoes—perhaps because the two foods aren't native to Italy, both having been imported from the New World. The following recipe uses broth for moistening the potatoes, with just a little olive oil added at the end for flavor.

8 dried tomato halves (page 383) or 12 to 15 store-bought dried tomato halves

1 cup warm Chicken Stock (page 379), Basic Vegetable Stock (page 382), or low-fat buttermilk

2 pounds starchy dry potatoes, like Idahos

1 to 2 tablespoons extra-virgin olive oil

salt and freshly ground black pepper

1. Soak the dried tomatoes in the stock in a bowl until soft, about 30 minutes. Remove the tomatoes with a slotted spoon and squeeze out the stock with your fingers over the bowl. Reserve the stock. Transfer the tomato halves to a cutting board and thinly slice.

2. Peel the potatoes and cut into 1-inch pieces. Place the potatoes in cold, lightly salted water and bring to a boil. Briskly simmer the potatoes until very tender, 10 to 15 minutes. Drain in a colander. Return the potatoes to the pot and cook over low heat for a few minutes to dry them out. Mash the potatoes with a potato masher.

3. Stir in the tomatoes, half the oil, and enough broth to obtain light, fluffy mashed potatoes. Add salt and pepper to taste. Just before serving, drizzle the remaining oil over the potatoes.

Serves 4 to 6

235 CALORIES PER SERVING;* 5 G PROTEIN; 4 G FAT; 0.6 G SATURATED FAT; 67 G CARBOHYDRATE; 267 MG SODIUM; 5 MG CHOLESTEROL

Analysis is based on 4 servings.

VENETIAN SWEET AND SOUR SQUASH

You've probably never tasted the likes of zucca *in* agro-dolce, *Venetian-style sweet and sour squash. Chocolate may seem like a strange ingredient, but used in tiny amounts, it brings out the natural sweetness of pumpkins and squashes. This recipe was inspired by Washington, D.C., chef Roberto Donna.*

- 3 tablespoons raisins
- 1 tablespoon olive oil
- 2 cloves garlic, peeled and cut in half
- 1 pound winter squash (such as butternut or Hubbard), peeled and cut into ½-inch dice (about 3 cups)
- 2 tablespoons honey
- 1 teaspoon finely chopped semisweet chocolate
- 2 tablespoons balsamic vinegar (or to taste)
- 2 tablespoons pine nuts, lightly toasted
- 4 fresh basil leaves
- 4 fresh mint leaves (or more basil)
- salt

Place the raisins in hot water to cover for 5 minutes, then drain. Heat the oil in a nonstick frying pan. Add the garlic and cook over medium heat for 2 to 3 minutes, or until tender and lightly browned. Discard the garlic. Add the squash and sauté for 4 to 6 minutes, or until lightly browned and tender.

Stir in the honey and bring to a boil. Add the chocolate and vinegar, and stir until the chocolate melts. Add the raisins and pine nuts, and cook for 1 minute more, or until the sauce forms a syrupy glaze. Just before serving, finely chop the basil and mint, and stir them into the squash with salt to taste. Serve warm or at room temperature.

Serves 4 to 6

171 CALORIES PER SERVING; 3 G PROTEIN; 7 G FAT;
27 G CARBOHYDRATE; 7 MG SODIUM; 0 MG CHOLESTEROL

TOMATOES STUFFED WITH PIPERATA AND GOAT CHEESE

Piperata *refers to a savory sauté of peppers and onions. It's found in one form or other throughout the northern Mediterranean, from Spanish sofrito to French pipérade.* Piperata *can be served as a* contorno *(vegetable side dish) in its own right, but I like to use it as a stuffing for tomatoes. Stuffed tomatoes can also be served as part of an antipasto.*

- 8 roma (plum) tomatoes
- salt and freshly ground black pepper

FOR THE PIPERATA:

- 1 tablespoon extra-virgin olive oil, plus ½ tablespoon for drizzling
- 1 onion, finely chopped
- 1 clove garlic, minced
- ½ red or yellow bell pepper, finely diced
- ½ green bell pepper, finely diced
- 2 tablespoons chopped flat-leaf parsley
- salt and freshly ground black pepper
- 1 ounce soft creamy goat cheese or thinly sliced Pecorino Romano

1. Preheat the oven to 400°F. Cut a ½-inch slice off the top (end opposite the stem) of each tomato. Trim the bottoms as necessary so that the tomatoes stand upright. Using a melon baller or small spoon, hollow out each tomato. Coarsely chop the tomato tops and flesh. Season the inside of the tomatoes with salt and pepper.

2. Prepare the *piperata:* Heat 1 tablespoon olive oil in a nonstick frying pan. Add the onion, garlic, bell peppers, and parsley. Cook over the medium heat until soft but not brown, about 4 minutes. Add the chopped tomato flesh and cook until the tomato juices evaporate, about 2 minutes. Add salt and pepper to taste. Stuff this mixture into the tomatoes and place a piece of cheese on top. The recipe can be prepared ahead to this stage and stored in the refrigerator.

3. Bake the stuffed tomatoes until the sides are soft and the topping is browned, 10 to 15 minutes. Serve hot or at room temperature.

Makes 8 pieces, enough to serve 4 to 8

72 CALORIES PER TOMATO; 2 G PROTEIN; 4 G FAT; 0.9 G SATURATED FAT;
9 G CARBOHYDRATE; 25 MG SODIUM; 2 MG CHOLESTEROL

CIDER-GLAZED TURNIPS

This is a good dish for people who don't think they like turnips. The cider sweetens the root and neutralizes its radishy aftertaste. For the best results, use tiny new turnips or choose the smallest ones you can buy. Rutabagas, those giant yellow cousins, can be prepared the same way.

1½ pounds turnips

1½ cups fresh apple cider (approximately)

salt and freshly ground black pepper

1 tablespoon extra-virgin olive oil (optional)

2 tablespoons chopped fresh tarragon and/or chives

Peel the turnips. Quarter the larger ones and cut the smaller ones in half to obtain uniform-sized pieces. Place the turnips in a heavy saucepan with cider to cover. Add the salt, pepper, and olive oil (if using).

Cook the turnips, uncovered, over high heat for 10 minutes, or until tender, stirring from time to time. The cider should be reduced to a syrupy glaze. If the liquid evaporates before the turnips are completely cooked, add more cider. If the turnips are soft before the cider forms a glaze, remove them with a slotted spoon. Boil the cider down to a glaze, then return the turnips to the pan. Sprinkle the turnips with the chopped herbs and serve at once.

Serves 4 to 6

101 CALORIES PER SERVING; 1 G PROTEIN; 4 G FAT; 18 G CARBOHYDRATE; 87 MG SODIUM; 0 MG CHOLESTEROL

ZUCCHINI WITH MINT

We don't often think of mint as a traditional Italian seasoning, but fresh mint is popular throughout southern Italy, including Sicily, where it's used for seasoning everything from tuna to vegetables. Here's a zucchini recipe, elegant in its simplicity, that can be made in 5 minutes. Try to choose smallish zucchini (6 to 8 ounces each): they're more delicate and succulent than the larger ones.

1 pound zucchini

1 tablespoon extra-virgin olive oil

1 clove garlic, smashed with the side of a knife or cleaver and peeled

12 fresh mint leaves, thinly slivered, or 2 teaspoons dried mint

salt and freshly ground black pepper

1 teaspoon fresh lemon juice (optional)

1. Scrub the zucchini and cut into matchstick slivers or ¼-inch slices. Heat the olive oil in a nonstick frying pan. Add the garlic and cook over medium heat until fragrant, about 1 minute.

2. Add the zucchini, mint, salt, and pepper and continue cooking until the zucchini is tender, 2 to 4 minutes. The zucchini should give off their own juices to make a little sauce. If they seem too dry, add 1 to 2 tablespoons water. Correct the seasoning, adding salt and pepper to taste and the lemon juice if desired.

Note: If you don't have fresh or dried mint in the house, open a mint tea bag. This dish could also be prepared using other herbs, such as basil, oregano, and rosemary.

Serves 4

49 CALORIES PER SERVING; 1 G PROTEIN; 3 G FAT; 0.5 G SATURATED FAT; 4 G CARBOHYDRATE; 4 MG SODIUM; 0 MG CHOLESTEROL

MEXICAN PICKLED VEGETABLES
(ESCABECHE)

These tangy pickled vegetables turn up in Mexico wherever drinks are served, whenever Mexicans sit down to the table. Given, the snappy crispness and piquant tartness of these colorful vegetables, it's easy to understand why. Here's the basic formula; the vegetables and seasonings vary from cook to cook and region to region. The amarillo chili is a small, waxy yellow, cone-shaped chili that's especially popular for pickling. Serranos and jalapeños work well, too.

2 large carrots, cut into ¼-inch slices

2 stalks celery, cut into ¼-inch slices

1 small zucchini, cut into ¼-inch slices

1 medium white onion, cut in half lengthwise, then widthwise into ¼-inch slices

1 cup cauliflower florets, cut into 1-inch pieces

½ to 1 cup amarillo chilies or serranos, stemmed but left whole

2 cups distilled white vinegar

2 tablespoons kosher salt

2 bay leaves

½ teaspoon oregano

1. Combine the carrots, celery, zucchini, onion, cauliflower, and chilies in a large bowl and toss to mix. Transfer the vegetables to clean jars. Press sheets of plastic wrap on top to keep vegetables submerged.

2. Combine the vinegar, salt, bay leaves, and oregano in the bowl and whisk until the salt is dissolved. Pour the vinegar mixture over the vegetables and cover the jars. Let the vegetables pickle at room temperature for 48 hours, stirring once or twice. If you plan to keep the vegetables for longer, store them in the refrigerator (pickled vegetables will keep for several weeks).

3. Serve the pickled vegetables in earthenware bowls with drinks or at any Mexican meal.

Serves 10 to 12

23 CALORIES PER SERVING;* 1 G PROTEIN; 0 G FAT; 0 G SATURATED FAT; 1 G CARBOHYDRATE; 1,289 MG SODIUM; 0 MG CHOLESTEROL

Analysis is based on 10 servings.

WINTER VEGETABLE PURÉE

This purée calls for parsnips and celeriacs (celery root), but you can substitute any starchy root vegetable, even winter squash. Serve with Herb-Roasted Game Hens (page 239) or Braised Brisket with Dried Fruits (page 255).

1 or 2 celeriacs (1 pound)

1 tablespoon lemon juice

1 pound parsnips or turnips, peeled and cut into ½-inch dice

salt

1 tablespoon extra-virgin olive oil (optional)

¼–½ cup skim milk, warmed

salt and freshly ground white pepper

pinch of cayenne pepper

freshly grated nutmeg

2 tablespoons chopped fresh chives or scallion greens, for garnish

Peel the celeriacs with a paring knife and cut into ½-inch dice. Toss the celeriacs with the lemon juice to prevent browning. Place the celeriacs and parsnips in a saucepan with cold salted water or stock to cover. (For extra flavor, but a bit more fat, use part or all chicken stock instead of water.)

Boil the vegetables for 6 to 8 minutes, or until very tender. Drain well (save the liquid for soup), then purée in a food processor or food mill (or mash with a potato masher right in the pot). Work in the oil (if using) and enough warm milk to obtain a cream purée. Correct the seasoning, adding salt, white pepper, cayenne, and nutmeg to taste. Sprinkle the purée with chives and serve at once.

Serves 4 to 6

145 CALORIES PER SERVING; 4 G PROTEIN; 4 G FAT; 26 G CARBOHYDRATE; 129 MG SODIUM; 0 MG CHOLESTEROL

RICE, GRAIN, AND BEAN DISHES

WHITE RICE

(ARROZ BLANCO)

*White rice is, of course, a staple throughout Latin America. Even in its most basic incarnation,
Mexicans give it distinction in the form of sautéed onion and garlic. Sautéing the rice imparts a nutty flavor.
Now get ready for some of the tastiest basic white rice in the western hemisphere.*

1 tablespoon olive oil or vegetable oil

1 small onion, finely chopped

1 clove garlic, minced

1½ cups long-grain white rice (like Uncle Ben's)

2½ cups chicken or vegetable stock

½ teaspoon salt

1. Heat the oil in a large heavy saucepan. Add the onion and cook over medium heat for 2 minutes, stirring with a wooden spoon. Add the garlic and continue cooking until the onion is soft and translucent but not brown, 2 minutes more, stirring as needed. Add the rice and cook until the grains are shiny and aromatic, 2 minutes.

2. Add the stock and salt and bring to a boil. Reduce the heat to the lowest setting. Cover the pan and cook until the rice is tender, 18 minutes. Do not stir. Check the rice after 15 minutes; if it appears too wet, partially uncover the pot to let some of the liquid evaporate.

3. Remove the rice from the heat and uncover. Drape a dishcloth over the pot and cover the rice again. Let stand for 2 minutes. Fluff the rice with a fork and serve at once.

Serves 4

309 CALORIES PER SERVING; 6 G PROTEIN; 4 G FAT; 1 G SATURATED FAT; 62 G CARBOHYDRATE; 282 MG SODIUM; 0 MG CHOLESTEROL

Mexican-Style Rice (Arroz a la Mexicana)

MEXICAN-STYLE RICE
(ARROZ A LA MEXICANA)

It's hard to imagine a Mexican meal without a mound of this red-hued rice. And if you're accustomed to restaurant versions—made with bottled salsa—this one, bursting with the brash flavors of fresh tomato, garlic, onion, cilantro, and chilies, will come as a revelation. Remember that the rice will only be as good as the raw materials, so try to use luscious ripe tomatoes. If you like your rice with a little heat, don't bother to seed the chili.
Note: *The cinnamon stick isn't traditional, but I like its spicy sweetness. I've made it optional.*

1 ripe red tomato, stemmed and quartered

¼ white onion (about 2 ounces)

1 clove garlic

1 fresh jalapeño chili, seeded

3 sprigs cilantro

1 teaspoon salt

1 tablespoon canola oil

1½ cups long-grain white rice

1 (1-inch) piece cinnamon stick (optional)

1½ cups chicken stock or water

1. Place the tomato, onion, garlic, jalapeño, cilantro, and salt in a blender and purée to a smooth paste.

2. Heat the oil in a large pot. Add the rice and cinnamon stick and cook over medium heat until the rice grains are shiny, 2 to 3 minutes, stirring with a wooden spoon.

3. Increase the heat to high. Stir in the tomato mixture and bring to a boil. Reduce the heat to medium and cook the rice without stirring until most of the tomato liquid has evaporated and holes appear in the surface of the rice. Add the stock or water and bring to a boil.

4. Tightly cover the pot and reduce the heat to low. Cook the rice, without stirring, until it is tender, about 18 minutes. Check the rice after 15 minutes; if it looks too wet, leave the lid ajar to allow some of the excess liquid to evaporate. If it looks too dry, add a tablespoon or so of stock or water.

5. Remove the pan from the heat and uncover. Drape a dishcloth over the pot and cover the rice again. Let the rice stand for 2 minutes. Fluff the rice with a fork and serve at once.

Serves 4

303 CALORIES PER SERVING; 6 G PROTEIN; 4 G FAT; 1 G SATURATED FAT; 60 G CARBOHYDRATE; 547 MG SODIUM; 0 MG CHOLESTEROL

BLACK RICE
(ARROZ NEGRO)

This gray-black rice—popular in Caribbean coastal Mexico and the Yucatán—won't win any beauty contests. But when it comes to flavor, few grain dishes can compete. The rice owes its richness to the cooking liquid: the broth left over from preparing black beans.

1 tablespoon olive oil or vegetable oil

1 small onion, finely chopped

3 cloves garlic, minced

1 cup long-grain white rice (like Uncle Ben's)

1⅔ cups black bean cooking liquid

½ cup cooked black beans (optional)

½ teaspoon salt

1. Heat the oil in a large heavy saucepan. Add the onion and cook over medium heat for 2 minutes, stirring with a wooden spoon. Add the garlic and continue cooking until the onion is soft and translucent but not brown, 2 minutes more, stirring as needed. Add the rice and cook until the grains are shiny and aromatic, 2 minutes.

2. Stir in the bean broth, black beans (if using), and salt and bring to a boil. Reduce the heat to the lowest setting. Cover the pan and cook until the rice is tender, 18 minutes. Do not stir. Check the rice after 15 minutes; if it appears

RICE WITH SHRIMP
(ARROZ CON CAMARONES)

Part pilaf and part stew, this simple rice dish turns up throughout coastal Mexico. When it comes to making a quick, colorful, satisfying supper, few dishes can top it. The rice gets a double blast of flavor, first from the fish stock, which is simmered with the shrimp shells for extra richness, then from the roasted tomato salsa. For extra color, you could add 16 to 20 mussels.

1 pound large shrimp, peeled and deveined (save the shells)

2 cups fish stock (see page 381) or bottled clam broth

2 ripe red tomatoes

½ medium white onion, cut in half

2 to 4 jalapeño chilies

3 cloves garlic

½ cup chopped fresh cilantro

1 teaspoon salt, or to taste

freshly ground black pepper

1 tablespoon extra-virgin olive oil

1½ cups long-grain white rice

½ teaspoon ground cumin

too wet, partially uncover the pot to let some of the liquid evaporate.

3. Remove the rice from the heat and uncover. Drape a dishcloth over the pot and re-cover the rice. Let stand for 2 minutes. Fluff the rice with a fork and serve at once.

Serves 4

232 CALORIES PER SERVING; 4 G PROTEIN; 4 G FAT; 1 G SATURATED FAT; 45 G CARBOHYDRATE; 306 MG SODIUM; 0 MG CHOLESTEROL

1. Wash the shrimp and blot dry. Place the fish stock and shrimp shells in a saucepan and gently simmer, covered, for 10 minutes.

2. Roast the tomatoes, onion, chilies, and garlic in a comal or frying pan over medium heat until nicely browned on all sides: 8 to 10 minutes for the tomatoes and onions, 4 to 6 minutes for the chilies and garlic; or roast under the broiler or on a barbecue grill. Transfer to a plate to cool. Seed the chilies. (For a spicier rice dish, leave the seeds in the chilies.) Place the roasted vegetables in a blender with two thirds of the cilantro and the salt and pepper and purée to a smooth paste.

3. Heat the oil in a large, nonstick frying pan or deep sauté pan. Add the rice and cumin and fry over medium-high heat until the rice grains are shiny, about 2 minutes. Add the tomato mixture and bring to a rolling boil. Strain in the fish stock and bring to a boil. Stir in the shrimp and bring to a boil.

4. Reduce the heat to its lowest setting and cover the pan. Cook until the rice is tender and the shrimp is done, 18 to 20 minutes. Remove the pan from the heat and uncover. Drape a dishcloth over the pot and cover the rice again. Let stand for 2 minutes. Add the remaining cilantro and salt and pepper to taste, stirring them into the rice and fluffing it with a fork. Serve at once.

Serves 4

440 CALORIES PER SERVING; 29 G PROTEIN; 6 G FAT; 1 G SATURATED FAT; 65 G CARBOHYDRATE; 719 MG SODIUM; 172 MG CHOLESTEROL

GREEN RICE
(ARROZ VERDE)

Rice is a relatively recent import to Mexico (it arrived with the Spanish), but few cuisines make such extensive or colorful use of this nourishing grain. Here's a green rice traditionally served at festivals and celebrations. The rice owes its offbeat hue and distinctive flavor to the addition of spinach, parsley, cilantro, and scallions.

salt

10 spinach leaves, washed and stemmed (or ¼ cup cooked frozen spinach)

¼ cup fresh parsley leaves

¼ cup fresh cilantro leaves

1 poblano chili, roasted, peeled, and seeded

2¼ cups chicken stock

freshly ground black pepper

1½ tablespoons olive oil

4 scallions, finely chopped

1 stalk celery, finely chopped

1 clove garlic, minced

1 cup long-grain white rice

1. Bring 2 cups of salted water to a rolling boil. Add the spinach, parsley, and cilantro and cook for 1 minute. Drain in a colander, rinse well with cold water, and drain again. Squeeze the spinach and herbs between your fingers to wring out any excess liquid.

2. Place the herbs in a blender with the chili and ¼ cup of the chicken stock. Purée until smooth. Add the remaining chicken stock and salt and pepper to taste.

3. Heat the oil in a nonstick sauté pan. Add the scallions, celery, and garlic and cook over medium heat until soft but not brown, about 3 minutes. Add the rice and cook until the grains are shiny, about 1 minute. Stir in the stock-herb mixture and bring to a boil.

4. Reduce the heat to the lowest setting and cover the pan. Cook the rice until it's tender, about 18 minutes. Check after 15 minutes: If the rice looks too soupy, set the lid ajar to allow the excess cooking liquid to evaporate. If the rice seems too dry, add a little water. Remove the rice from the heat and uncover. Drape a dishcloth over the pot and cover the rice again. Let stand for 2 minutes. Fluff the rice with a fork, adding salt and pepper to taste, and serve at once.

Serves 4

238 CALORIES PER SERVING; 5 G PROTEIN; 6 G FAT; 1 G SATURATED FAT; 42 G CARBOHYDRATE; 35 MG SODIUM; 0 MG CHOLESTEROL

WILD RICE STUFFING

Wild rice is something of a culinary misnomer, being neither wild (it's cultivated in paddies) nor rice (botanically speaking, it's an aquatic grass seed). Nevertheless, it's a uniquely American food—it was first harvested by the Indians of Minnesota. I like to presoak the rice to shorten the cooking time. You can omit this step and lengthen the cooking time, but you'll have to add more water.

- 2 cups wild rice
- 1 firm apple (such as a Granny Smith), peeled and finely diced
- 1 teaspoon lemon juice
- 2 ears fresh corn (1 cup kernels)
- 1½ tablespoons olive oil
- 1 large onion, finely chopped (1 cup)
- 3 stalks celery, finely chopped
- 3 cloves garlic, minced (1 tablespoon)
- 4–5 cups water or chicken stock (approximately)
- 1 small green bell pepper, cored, seeded, and cut into ½-inch dice
- 1 small red bell pepper, cored, seeded, and cut into ½-inch dice
- 1 small yellow bell pepper, cored, seeded, and cut into ½-inch dice (optional)
- 2 tablespoons finely chopped fresh herbs (sage, thyme, basil, oregano, parsley, and/or chives)
- 2 tablespoons freshly grated Parmigiano-Reggiano, or other Parmesan-style cheese (optional)
- salt and freshly ground black pepper

Rinse the wild rice in a strainer with cold water and drain. Soak the rice in cold water to cover for at least 4 hours. Drain again. Toss the apple pieces with the lemon juice to prevent browning.

If using fresh corn, cut the kernels off the cobs.

Heat the oil in a large, heavy saucepan. Add the onion, celery, and garlic, and cook over medium heat for 3 to 4 minutes, or until soft but not brown. Stir in the rice and 4 cups water, and bring to a boil. Reduce the heat and simmer for 20 minutes.

Stir in the peppers, apple, and corn, and continue simmering, uncovered, for 10 minutes, or until the rice is tender but not too soft. If the rice begins to dry out, add more water. If the rice is too wet, increase the heat to high to evaporate the excess water.

Just before serving, stir in the herbs, cheese (if using), salt, and pepper. The stuffing should be highly seasoned.

Note: This stuffing can be simmered until done and then baked inside a turkey, chicken, or game hens, but I usually prepare it ahead of time and warm it in a baking dish on the side.

Serves 6 to 8

216 CALORIES PER SERVING; 7 G PROTEIN; 3 G FAT; 42 G CARBOHYDRATE; 25 MG SODIUM; 0 MG CHOLESTEROL

HERB RISOTTO

Risotto is the rice dish that thinks it's pasta. My low-fat risotto calls for less butter and cheese than the traditional recipe. To boost the flavor, I add chopped fresh herbs or saffron. Arborio rice is a starchy, short-grain rice that has the unique ability to absorb 5 times its volume in liquid without becoming mushy. It is widely available at gourmet shops and Italian markets. You can also use short-grain Valencia, which is found at Hispanic markets.

1 tablespoon olive oil

1 onion or 2 leeks, finely chopped (about 1 cup)

1 clove garlic, minced (1 teaspoon)

1½ cups arborio rice

½ cup dry white wine

5–6 cups chicken stock (page 379), heated to simmering

¼ cup chopped fresh herbs (or ¼ teaspoon saffron threads soaked in 1 tablespoon warm water)

¼–½ cup freshly grated Parmigiano-Reggiano (or other Parmesan-style cheese)

salt and freshly ground black pepper

Heat the oil in a large saucepan over medium heat. Cook the onion and garlic for 3 to 4 minutes, or until soft but not brown, stirring well. Stir in the rice and cook for 1 minute, or until all the grains are shiny. (Do not wash arborio rice. You need the starch to thicken the sauce.)

Add the wine and bring to a boil, stirring steadily. When most of the wine is absorbed, add ½ cup stock. Cook the rice at a gentle simmer, stirring steadily. When most of the liquid is absorbed, add another ½ cup stock. Continue adding the stock, ½ cup at a time, until 5 cups are used up. If the rice is still hard, add ½ to 1 cup more stock. Add the herbs or saffron during the last 3 minutes of cooking. The whole process should take 18 to 20 minutes. Properly prepared risotto will be soft and creamy, but you should still be able to taste the individual grains of rice.

Remove the pan from the heat and stir in the cheese, salt, and pepper. Serve immediately. Guests may wait for risotto, but risotto does not wait for the guests!

Serves 4

400 CALORIES PER SERVING; 14 G PROTEIN; 7 G FAT; 62 G CARBOHYDRATE; 1,094 MG SODIUM; 5 MG CHOLESTEROL

Herb Risotto

RISOTTO WITH SAFFRON AND SQUASH BLOSSOMS

Risotto originated in the Po Valley in northern Italy, where its invention, so legend goes, is associated with a stained-glass window maker named Valarius. The master craftsman achieved exceptionally brilliant colors by adding saffron to his paints. One day, at the wedding of Valarius's daughter, one of his apprentices persuaded the cook to add saffron to the rice. Soon the guests were eating a first for the region, a mountain of saffron-colored rice. Valarius pronounced the dish "risus optimus," Latin for "excellent rice." The words were eventually shortened to risotto.
To this day, saffron-flavored risotto remains a Milanese specialty.
In addition to saffron, traditional risotto alla milanese *contains poached marrow, an admittedly tasty ingredient that is off the charts in terms of fat and cholesterol. I've replaced the marrow with another popular northern Italian risotto ingredient: zucchini blossoms. These are available in Italian markets and greengrocers in early summer. But don't worry if you can't find zucchini blossoms: saffron risotto is plenty delicious by itself.*

½ teaspoon saffron threads

1½ tablespoons extra-virgin olive oil

1 medium onion, finely chopped (1 cup)

1 clove garlic, minced

1½ cups arborio rice

½ cup dry white wine

5 to 6 cups Chicken Stock (page 379) or Basic Vegetable Stock (page 382), heated to simmering in another pot

8 to 10 zucchini or squash blossoms, washed, patted dry, and cut crosswise into ½-inch slices

¼ to ½ cup freshly grated Parmigiano-Reggiano cheese

salt and freshly ground black pepper

1. Place the saffron threads in a small bowl and pulverize them with the end of a wooden spoon. Add 1 tablespoon hot water and let stand for 10 minutes.

2. Meanwhile, heat the olive oil in a large, heavy saucepan (preferably nonstick) over medium heat. Cook the onion and garlic until soft and translucent but not brown, about 4 minutes. Stir in the rice, and cook for 1 minute, or until all the grains are shiny.

3. Add the wine and bring to a boil, stirring constantly. Add the saffron. When most of the wine is absorbed, add the first ½ cup stock. Cook the rice at a brisk simmer, stirring steadily. When most of the liquid is absorbed, add another ½ cup stock. Gradually add salt and pepper as you add the stock. Continue adding the stock, ½ cup at a time, until 5 cups are used up. Stir in the zucchini blossoms after 12 minutes of cooking. If the rice is still hard, add ½ to 1 more cup stock. When ready, the risotto will have a creamy sauce, but the individual grains of rice will still be discernible. Remove the pan from the heat. You'll need about 18 minutes of cooking in all.

4. Stir in the cheese, and salt and pepper to taste. Serve at once.

Serves 6 as a first course or side dish, 4 as an entrée

281 CALORIES PER SERVING;* 7 G PROTEIN; 7 G FAT; 2 G SATURATED FAT; 43 G CARBOHYDRATE; 909 MG SODIUM; 18 MG CHOLESTEROL

Analysis is based on 6 servings as a first course.

SEAFOOD RISOTTO

Black mussels, white squid, and pink shrimp make this one of the prettiest risottos in Italy. For a more extravagant risotto, you could add clams, scallops, and/or lobster tails.

1½ pounds mussels

1 pound cleaned squid (calamari) (see box on page 197)

1 pound large shrimp

2 medium onions, finely chopped

4 cloves garlic, minced

½ cup finely chopped flat-leaf parsley

1½ cups dry white wine

5 to 6 cups Fish Stock (page 381), Chicken Stock (page 379), or bottled clam broth (juice)

½ teaspoon saffron threads

1½ tablespoons extra-virgin olive oil

1½ cups arborio rice

salt and freshly ground black pepper

1. Scrub the mussels, discarding any with cracked shells or shells that fail to close when tapped. Remove any threads that may cluster at the hinge of the mussel shells (pull them out with needlenose pliers). Cut the squid bodies crosswise into ¼-inch rings. Leave the heads (tentacle sections) whole. Peel and devein the shrimp, reserving the shells.

2. Place 1 chopped onion, 2 garlic cloves, and 3 tablespoons parsley in a large saucepan with the shrimp shells and wine. Bring to a boil. Add the mussels and tightly cover the pan. Cook the mussels over high heat until the shells are open and the mussels are cooked: about 8 minutes. Stir the mussels once or twice to allow the shells on the bottom to open. Transfer the mussels with a slotted spoon to a colander over a bowl to drain and cool.

3. When the mussels are cool, take ½ of them out of the shells, discard the shells, and place with the squid and shrimp. Leave the remaining mussels in the shell for garnish. Strain the mussel cooking liquid through a strainer lined with cheesecloth or a paper towel into a large measuring cup. Add enough fish stock to obtain 6 cups liquid. Place this liquid in a pot and bring to a simmer. Place the saffron threads in a small bowl and pulverize them with the end of a wooden spoon. Add 1 tablespoon hot broth and let stand for 10 minutes.

4. Heat the olive oil in a large heavy saucepan (preferably nonstick) over medium heat. Cook the remaining onion, 2 cloves garlic, and 3 tablespoons parsley until soft and translucent but not brown, about 4 minutes. Stir in the rice and cook for 1 minute, or until all the grains are shiny.

5. Add ½ cup mussel broth mixture and the saffron and bring to a boil, stirring steadily. When most of the liquid is absorbed, add another ½ cup broth. Gradually add salt and pepper as you add the broth. Cook the rice at a brisk simmer. Continue adding the broth, ½ cup at a time, until 5 cups are used up. If the rice is still hard, add ½ to 1 more cup broth. When ready, the risotto will have a creamy sauce, but the individual grains of rice should still be discernible. You'll need about 18 minutes of cooking in all.

6. The last 5 minutes, stir in the shrimp. The last 3 minutes, stir in the squid. When both are cooked, stir in the shelled mussels and salt and pepper to taste. Warm the mussels in the shells in any remaining broth. Transfer the risotto to plates or a platter and garnish with the mussels in the shells. Sprinkle with the remaining 2 tablespoons parsley and serve at once.

Serves 6 as a first course or side dish, 4 as an entrée

440 CALORIES PER SERVING;* 34 G PROTEIN; 6 G FAT; 1 G SATURATED FAT; 69 G CARBOHYDRATE; 268 MG SODIUM; 311 MG CHOLESTEROL

Analysis is based on 6 servings as a first course.

MILANESE RISOTTO PIE

We had just landed in Milan, and tired as I was after a night of flying, I couldn't dream of going straight to our hotel room. So I found a bar where huge wedges of risotto pie were being sold as a snack. Risotto pie is easy to make (not to mention a great way to use up leftovers) and makes a fine dish for a brunch or buffet.

1 recipe basic risotto (page 293)

1 to 2 ounces prosciutto, trimmed of all fat
 and thinly slivered

½ cup cooked peas

1 roasted red bell pepper, cored, seeded, and diced,
 or ½ cup diced pimiento

1 egg, plus 2 egg whites, lightly beaten
 (or ½-cup egg substitute)

¼ cup finely chopped flat-leaf parsley

salt and freshly ground black pepper

spray olive oil

2 to 3 tablespoons toasted bread crumbs (page 385)

1. Preheat the oven to 400°F. Prepare the risotto. Into it stir the prosciutto, peas, bell pepper, eggs, whites, and parsley. Add salt and pepper to taste.

2. Spray a 12-inch nonstick frying pan with spray oil and line it with bread crumbs, shaking out the excess. Add the risotto, smoothing the top with the back of a spoon. Spray the top of the risotto with oil.

3. Bake the risotto pie until set, 20 to 30 minutes. The sides should be crusty and brown. Remove the pan from the heat and let cool for 5 minutes. Invert the pie onto a platter, taking care not to burn your arm on the handle. Risotto pie can be served hot or at room temperature. Cut into wedges for serving.

Serves 6

333 CALORIES PER SERVING;* 12 G PROTEIN; 8.6 G FAT;
2.6 G SATURATED FAT; 50 G CARBOHYDRATE; 1,045 MG SODIUM;
57 MG CHOLESTEROL

Analysis is based on 6 servings.

ARANCINE
(SICILIAN STUFFED RICE "FRITTERS")

Arancine means "little oranges." With a little imagination, these round, golden brown rice fritters from Sicily do, indeed, resemble tiny citrus fruits. My low-fat version features a filling of sautéed vegetables instead of the traditional ground beef. (For a virtually no-fat version of the dish, you could roast or grill the vegetables instead of sautéing them.) There are two ways to cook the arancine: sautéed in a little olive oil or "bake-fried" in a hot oven. If your fat budget allows it, go for the former, which produces crisper, more succulent fritters. But bake-frying makes tasty arancine, as well. This dish is a great way to use up leftover risotto.

1 batch basic risotto (page 293)

FOR THE FILLING:

2 to 3 teaspoons extra-virgin olive oil

½ small onion, minced

1 clove garlic, minced

½ red bell pepper, cut into the finest imaginable dice

½ yellow bell pepper, cut into the finest imaginable dice

2 teaspoons drained chopped capers

1 tablespoon tomato paste

salt and freshly ground black pepper

TO FINISH THE ARANCINE:

1 egg plus 4 egg whites (or ¾ cup egg substitute),
 lightly beaten with a fork

approximately 1 cup toasted bread crumbs

1 to 2 tablespoons extra-virgin olive oil
 (if sautéing the fritters) or

spray olive oil (if baking)

1. Prepare the risotto and let cool completely. Prepare the filling. Heat the olive oil in a nonstick frying pan. Add the onion, garlic, and bell peppers. Cook over medium heat until peppers are tender and most of the juices have evaporated, about 5 minutes. Add the capers and tomato paste and cook for 2 minutes. Add salt and pepper to taste. Let the mixture cool to room temperature.

2. Pinch off a walnut-size piece of risotto mixture and roll it into a ball between the palms of your hands. (Wet your hands with a little water to prevent sticking.) Make a deep depression in one side of the ball with your thumb. Place a tiny spoonful of filling in the depression. Pinch the hole shut and roll the rice back into a round ball. Repeat until all the risotto and filling are used up. The recipe can be prepared ahead to this stage. Place the beaten egg mixture in one shallow bowl, the bread crumbs in another.

3a. If pan-frying the arancine, flatten each ball between the palms of your hands into a thick pancake. (OK, this is no longer an orange shape, but it facilitates pan-frying.) Dip each fritter first in egg mixture, then in crumbs, shaking off the excess. Heat 1 tablespoon olive oil in a nonstick frying pan. Cook the arancine over medium-high heat until crusty and golden brown on both sides, 2 to 4 minutes per side, turning with a spatula. Work in several batches to avoid crowding the pan, adding oil as needed. Drain the arancine on paper towels, sprinkle with a little more salt and pepper, and serve at once.

3b. If bake-frying the arancine, preheat the oven to 425°F. Dip the arancine in egg, then in crumbs, as described above, shaking off the excess. Bake-fried arancine can be left as balls. Arrange them on a nonstick baking sheet sprayed with oil. Generously spray or brush the sides and tops of the arancine with oil. Bake the arancine until sizzling hot and lightly browned, 10 to 15 minutes. Transfer to a platter and serve at once.

Makes 28 to 30 arancine, which will serve 8 to 10

249 CALORIES PER SERVING; 10 G PROTEIN; 6 G FAT; 1 G SATURATED FAT; 36 G CARBOHYDRATE; 395 MG SODIUM; 23 MG CHOLESTEROL

BASIC POLENTA

Polenta has very ancient roots in Italy, although its primary ingredient—cornmeal—didn't arrive until the sixteenth century (after a Genoese sea captain named Columbus set sail for a shorter route to Asia and happened upon the Americas!). Polenta seems to have originated with the Etruscans as a sort of porridge called puls *or* pulmentum. *Corn, like tomatoes, may have been a New World food, but it was adopted by northern Italians with gusto. Following are two polenta recipes: one for a firm polenta you can cut into fanciful shapes for grilling, the other for a soft polenta you can eat like mashed potatoes. Over the years, I've found that the best way to prevent lumps is to make a slurry by dissolving the cornmeal in a few cups cold water, rather than adding it directly to boiling liquid. For extra flavor, you could cook the polenta in chicken or vegetable broth instead of water.*

FIRM POLENTA

This polenta is prepared ahead of time, poured onto an oiled baking sheet to harden, and cut into fanciful shapes for baking, broiling, or grilling. There are lots of possibilities for sauces here, including Sugo di Pomodoro (page 162).

2 cups coarse yellow cornmeal, preferably stone-ground

7 cups water, Chicken Stock (page 379), or Basic Vegetable Stock (page 382)

salt and freshly ground black pepper

½ to 1 tablespoon extra-virgin olive oil or butter for cooking (optional)

1. In a mixing bowl, combine the cornmeal with 2 cups cold water and whisk to a smooth paste. Bring the remaining 5 cups water to a boil in a large heavy saucepan (preferably nonstick). Add the cornmeal mixture to the boiling water in a thin stream, whisking steadily. Boil the polenta over high heat, whisking steadily, until thick, 2 to 3 minutes. Add a little salt and pepper.

2. Reduce the heat to medium or medium-low and gently simmer the polenta until the mixture thickens enough to pull away from the sides of the pan. It should be the consistency of soft ice cream. It isn't necessary to whisk the polenta continuously, but you should give it a stir every 5 minutes or so. As the polenta thickens, switch from a whisk to a wooden spoon for stirring. The whole cooking process will take 30 to 40 minutes. Correct the seasoning, adding salt and pepper to taste; the polenta should be highly seasoned.

3. You can certainly eat the polenta at this stage and it will be delicious. But tradition calls for pouring it onto a baking sheet that's been lightly brushed or sprayed with oil, then covering it with plastic wrap and chilling it until firm, 2 to 3 hours. The polenta is then cut into strips, squares, rectangles, stars, or other shapes with a knife or cookie cutter.

4. To reheat the polenta for serving, bake it in a baking dish with a sauce on top, sauté it in a little olive oil or butter in a nonstick frying pan, or brush it with oil and grill it. I particularly like grilling, as the polenta picks up a smoky flavor.

Serves 6 to 8 as an appetizer, 4 as an entrée

147 CALORIES PER SERVING;* 3 G PROTEIN; 1.5 G FAT; 0 G SATURATED FAT; 31 G CARBOHYDRATE; 14 MG SODIUM; 0 MG CHOLESTEROL

Analysis is based on 6 servings as an appetizer.

POLENTA WITH CALABRIAN SAUSAGE SAUCE

This recipe takes me back to my restaurant-critic days in Boston— in particular, back to a homey, no-frills trattoria (long since gone) in Boston's "Little Italy," the North End. It was here that I first tasted polenta, and it was smothered with a red sauce sweet with fennel seed and aromatic with bell peppers. My low-fat version calls for turkey sausage, which is considerably leaner than pork. A vegetarian could substitute mushrooms or zucchini for the meat.

1 recipe Firm Polenta (preceding), prepared through step 3

spray oil or a few drops of extra-virgin olive oil

1 turkey sausage (6 to 8 ounces)

1 tablespoon extra-virgin olive oil

1 medium onion, finely chopped

3 cloves garlic

¼ to ½ teaspoon hot pepper flakes

1 green bell pepper, cored, seeded, and cut into 2-inch by ½-inch strips

1 red bell pepper, cored, seeded, and cut into 2-inch by ½-inch strips

1 28-ounce can imported peeled plum tomatoes, with their juices, finely chopped or coarsely puréed in the food processor or through a vegetable mill

½ teaspoon dried oregano

¼ teaspoon fennel seeds

3 tablespoons chopped flat-leaf parsley

salt and freshly ground black pepper

1. Prepare the polenta following the recipe on page 297. Transfer it to a nonstick baking sheet to cool, then refrigerate until firm. Cut it into rectangles or squares and place the polenta shapes in a lightly oiled baking dish.

2. Prick the sausage on all sides with a toothpick and cook it. You can do so either by baking it on a rack in a baking dish; in a 400°F. oven for 20 minutes, or until no longer pink; or by poaching it in simmering water to cover for 10 minutes. Even better, you could grill the sausage. Blot off any excess fat with a paper towel, then cut the sausage on the diagonal into ¼-inch-thick slices.

3. Heat the 1 tablespoon olive oil in a large nonstick frying pan. Add the onions and cook over medium heat for 2 minutes. Add the garlic and pepper flakes and continue cooking until the onions are just beginning to brown.

CREAM OF WHEAT POLENTA

This dish was inspired by the semolina dumplings of Rome. Cream of Wheat may not be a traditional Italian ingredient (although it resembles semolina), but it produces a lovely, light polenta. It has the added advantage over cornmeal-based polenta of requiring only 5 minutes preparation time. Below are two variations on a theme of polenta. You can use quick-cooking Cream of Wheat for this recipe, but do not use instant.

4. Increase the heat to high. Add the peppers and cook until tender, about 5 minutes. Add the sausage, puréed tomatoes, oregano, fennel, and half the parsley. Reduce the heat to medium and gently simmer the sauce until thick and richly flavored, about 10 minutes. Correct the seasoning, adding salt and pepper to taste. Spoon the sauce over the polenta. The recipe can be made ahead to this stage. Let cool to room temperature, then cover with plastic wrap and refrigerate.

5. Preheat the oven to 400°F. Bake the dish until the polenta is thoroughly heated and the sauce is bubbling. Sprinkle with the remaining parsley and serve at once.

Serves 6 to 8 as a first course, 4 as an entrée

267 CALORIES PER SERVING;* 11 G PROTEIN; 6 G FAT; 1 G SATURATED FAT; 45 G CARBOHYDRATE; 471 MG SODIUM; 18 MG CHOLESTEROL

Analysis is based on 6 servings as a first course.

2 cups skim, 1 percent, or 2 percent milk, or low-fat half-and-half

½ cup quick-cooking Cream of Wheat

¼ cup freshly grated Parmigiano-Reggiano cheese

salt and freshly ground black pepper

spray oil

1 tablespoon extra-virgin olive oil or butter (optional)

1. Bring the milk to a simmer in a heavy saucepan. Add the Cream of Wheat in a thin stream, whisking steadily. Simmer the mixture over medium heat until cooked and thick, about 5 minutes, whisking steadily to obtain a smooth consistency. Whisk in the cheese and salt and pepper to taste.

2. Transfer the mixture to a pie pan lightly sprayed with oil. Let cool to room temperature, then cover with plastic wrap and chill for at least 3 hours.

3. To serve, cut the polenta into wedges. Heat the olive oil or butter in a nonstick frying pan. Pan-fry the polenta wedges until lightly browned on each side, 2 to 3 minutes per side. Alternatively, lightly brush the top of the polenta with the 1 tablespoon oil and broil until lightly browned. Alternatively, brush the polenta wedges on both sides with oil and lightly brown on a preheated grill.

Serves 4

148 CALORIES PER SERVING; 9 G PROTEIN; 2 G FAT; 1 G SATURATED FAT; 22 G CARBOHYDRATE; 235 MG SODIUM; 7 MG CHOLESTEROL

QUICK-COOK COUSCOUS

Couscous is often described as a grain, but it's actually a type of pasta made by mixing flour and water and forcing the dough through a sieve. The tiny pellets that result make a delectable, light, healthy starch. This is the quickest, easiest way to cook couscous, and although the individual grains aren't quite as light as when they are steamed (see the next recipe), the overall convenience of this method makes up for it. Most recipes call for lots of butter, but here celery, currants, and pine nuts bolster the flavor without the fat.

1 tablespoon olive oil

1 small onion, finely chopped (½ cup)

1 stalk celery, finely chopped

3 tablespoons currants

2 tablespoons pine nuts

1 cup couscous

1½ cups chicken stock or water

salt and freshly ground black pepper

Heat the oil in a heavy saucepan. Add the onion, celery, currants, and pine nuts, and cook over medium heat for 3 to 4 minutes, or until the onion is soft but not brown. Stir in the couscous and cook for 1 minute, or until lightly toasted.

Add the stock, salt, and pepper. Bring the mixture to a boil, stirring gently. Cover the pan, remove it from the heat, and let the couscous stand for 5 minutes. Just before serving, fluff the couscous with a fork and correct the seasoning. Serve at once.

Serves 4

353 CALORIES PER SERVING; 12 G PROTEIN; 8 G FAT; 58 G CARBOHYDRATE; 407 MG SODIUM; 0 MG CHOLESTEROL

COUSCOUS—TRADITIONAL METHOD

If you want to experience couscous in all its glory, try this method, which uses a series of steamings and soakings to swell the grains to four times their original size. This recipe is loosely modeled on Paula Wolfert's method for preparing Moroccan-style couscous. It tastes similar to Quick-Cook Couscous (see previous recipe) but is much lighter.
A couscousiere is a large pot bowed out in the middle like a barrel, with a steamer that fits in the top. Calphalon makes one; other models are available at cookware shops. Alternatively, you can rig up a steamer using 2 large saucepans and 2 large strainers or colanders. Serve with Chicken Tagine (page 224).

3 cups couscous (1½ pounds)

salt and freshly ground black pepper

2 cups skim milk

2 cups cold water

Start 4 to 5 hours or even a day before you plan to serve the dish. Place the couscous in a strainer and rinse thoroughly under cold water. Spread it out in a large roasting pan and let it dry for 10 minutes. Gently rake the couscous with your fingers, lifting and sifting, to break up any lumps.

In the bottom of a couscousiere or in 2 large saucepans, bring 3 inches salted water to a boil over high heat. Set the steamer or colanders on top; the fit should be snug. (To guarantee a tight fit, wrap the base of the steamer with wet, rolled paper towels.) Add the couscous and steam for 15 minutes, or until hot and moist. Remove the couscousiere from the heat (leave the water in it) and dump the couscous back into the roasting pan.

Spread out the couscous using a long-pronged fork. Sprinkle it with salt, pepper, and 1 cup milk. Gently rake the couscous with the fork, stirring and sifting to break up any lumps. Sprinkle on the remaining milk and rake again. Let the couscous stand for 1 hour, or until no longer wet to the touch, raking occasionally to break up lumps.

Replenish the water in the couscousiere or saucepans.

Return the couscous to the couscousiere or colanders, and steam for another 15 minutes. Dump it back into the roasting pan and gradually rake in 1 cup cold water. Sprinkle on the remaining water and rake again.

Let the couscous dry for 1 hour, or until no longer wet to the touch. Rake it occasionally to break up any lumps. The couscous can be prepared to this point up to 24 hours in advance. Cover it with a dish towel and set it aside at room temperature. (For longer than 6 hours, cover and refrigerate.)

About 20 minutes before serving, wet your hands and rake the couscous again to break up any lumps. Return it to the couscousiere and steam for 20 minutes. Some people like to do the third steaming over a stew.

Note: This couscous may be softer than what you're accustomed to. Unlike other pasta, it isn't supposed to be eaten al dente. It's also extremely mild; the flavor comes from the stew served on top of it.

Serves 8 to 10

281 CALORIES PER SERVING; 11 G PROTEIN; .6 G FAT; 56 G CARBOHYDRATE; 305 MG SODIUM; 1 MG CHOLESTEROL

Quinoa Pilaf

QUINOA PILAF

Quinoa *(pronounced KEEN-wa) is a grain native to the Andes Mountains, where it has been cultivated for 5,000 years. It contains more protein than wheat, oats, millet, rye, and barley. Unlike most grains, it is rich in lysine, an essential amino acid seldom found in the vegetable kingdom.*

1 cup quinoa

1 tablespoon olive oil

1 small onion, finely chopped

1 stalk celery, finely chopped

2 tablespoons pine nuts (optional)

2 cups chicken stock or water

salt and freshly ground black pepper

Place the quinoa in a strainer, rinse with cold water, and drain. Heat the oil in a saucepan or sauté pan. Add the onion, celery, and pine nuts, and cook over medium heat for 2 to 3 minutes, or until the onion is soft but not brown. Add the quinoa and toast for 30 seconds.

Add the stock, salt, and pepper, and bring to a boil. Reduce the heat to a low simmer and cover the pan. Cook the quinoa for 15 to 20 minutes, or until all the liquid is absorbed and the grain is tender. Fluff with a fork and correct the seasoning. Serve at once.

Serves 4 to 6

277 CALORIES PER SERVING; 11 G PROTEIN;
7 G FAT; 42 G CARBOHYDRATE; 542 MG SODIUM;
0 MG CHOLESTEROL

POSOLE A LA MEXICANA

Few people in the United States have tasted hominy (posole) if they don't live in the South or Southwest. Even in these regions, this hulled parched corn is generally served for breakfast (grits are nothing more than ground-up hominy). Here's a Mexican-style hominy—electrified with garlic and cilantro—that you can serve as a starch or a side dish. For the sake of convenience, I call for canned hominy (which is available at select supermarkets).

1¾ cups cooked hominy (one 14½-ounce can)

1 tablespoon canola oil

½ white onion, thinly sliced

2 cloves garlic, minced

3 scallions, white part minced, green part thinly sliced

½ teaspoon ground cumin

½ teaspoon dried oregano

¼ teaspoon ground cinnamon

1 tomato, peeled, seeded, and chopped

¼ cup chopped fresh cilantro

½ cup chicken stock

salt and freshly ground black pepper

1 lime, cut into wedges

1. If you are using canned hominy, drain it well in a strainer, rinse with cold water, drain well again, and set aside.

2. Heat the oil in a nonstick frying pan. Add the onion, garlic, scallion whites, cumin, oregano, and cinnamon and cook over medium heat until the onions are lightly browned, 4 to 6 minutes, stirring with a wooden spoon. Increase the heat to high and add the tomato. Cook for 1 minute.

3. Stir in the cilantro, scallion greens, stock, and hominy. Cook over high heat until most of the stock is absorbed and the hominy is richly flavored, about 4 minutes. Add salt and pepper to taste. Serve at once, with lime wedges for garnish.

Serves 4

116 CALORIES PER SERVING; 3 G PROTEIN; 5 G FAT; 1 G SATURATED FAT; 19 G CARBOHYDRATE; 216 MG SODIUM; 0 MG CHOLESTEROL

RED PORK AND CHICKEN POSOLE
(HOMINY STEW)

Posole (hominy) is one of the most satisfying corn preparations ever to grace a fork. Popular in Mexico and the American South and Southwest, it's virtually ignored in the rest of the United States. This is a shame, for few grains offer a more inviting texture (softly chewy) or flavor (starchy and cornlike, with a pleasing grainy sweetness). Here's a traditional northern Mexican way of serving posole: stewed with chicken and pork and spiced up with cinnamon, cumin, and chili powder. For speed and convenience, this recipe calls for canned hominy, which is available at select supermarkets.

1 tablespoon lard or vegetable oil

1 medium white onion, finely chopped

3 cloves garlic, finely chopped

1 tablespoon pure New Mexican or guajillo chili powder

1 teaspoon dried oregano (preferably Mexican)

½ teaspoon ground cumin (or to taste)

¼ teaspoon ground cinnamon

⅛ teaspoon ground cloves

1 bay leaf

1 tomato, cut in half, seeded, and grated

6 ounces boneless, skinless chicken breast, cut into 1-inch cubes

6 ounces pork loin or tenderloin, cut into 1-inch cubes

5 cups chicken broth or water, or as needed

3½ cups cooked hominy or 2 (14½-ounce) cans hominy, drained and rinsed

salt and freshly ground black pepper

FOR THE GARNISH:

½ ripe avocado, cut into ½-inch dice

1 teaspoon fresh lime juice

1 ripe tomato, seeded and cut into ¼-inch dice

½ white onion, cut into ¼-inch dice

¼ cup chopped scallions (green part only)

¼ cup chopped cilantro

¼ cup sliced radishes

1 lime, cut into wedges

1. Heat the lard or oil in a large, nonstick sauté pan. Add the onion and garlic and cook over medium heat until the onions begin to brown, 3 to 4 minutes. Add the chili powder, oregano, cumin, cinnamon, cloves, and bay leaf and cook for 1 minute. Increase the heat to high and add the tomato. Cook until the tomato juices evaporate, 1 minute. Stir in the chicken and pork and cook until lightly browned, 3 to 4 minutes more.

2. Add the chicken broth and bring to a boil. Reduce the heat and gently simmer the mixture until the chicken and pork are tender, 20 to 30 minutes. Stir in the hominy for the last 10 minutes. Remove and discard the bay leaf. Correct the seasoning, adding salt and pepper to taste; the posole should be highly seasoned.

3. Meanwhile, toss the avocado with the lime juice and place in a small bowl. Arrange the tomato, onion, scallions, cilantro, and radishes in small individual bowls. Alternatively, arrange the vegetables in small mounds on a platter.

4. Serve the posole in shallow bowls, garnishing each serving with a wedge of lime. Serve the avocado, tomato, onion, scallions, cilantro, and radishes on the side with spoons for sprinkling the garnishes over the posole.

Serves 4

345 CALORIES PER SERVING; 27 G PROTEIN; 10 G FAT; 3 G SATURATED FAT; 36 G CARBOHYDRATE; 377 MG SODIUM; 63 MG CHOLESTEROL

HOW TO COOK BEANS

Italians love beans and have ready access to fresh favas, cannellini, and other beans. In this country, most of us have to settle for dried beans or canned beans. The latter certainly are convenient and can be used in any recipe calling for beans in this book. Their drawback is that most brands are very salty. If using canned beans, drain them in a colander and rinse well with cold water. If you have the time, you may wish to start with dried beans. If you like your beans on the firmer side, cook them uncovered, but watch that the cooking water doesn't evaporate to a level below the beans. If you like them on the softer side, cook loosely covered. Always add the salt or any acidic flavorings— such as wine, vinegar, or tomatoes—at the end: these ingredients cause the skins of the beans to toughen if added at the beginning. Cooking times vary according to the freshness of the beans.

1 cup dried beans
1 bay leaf
1 small onion, peeled
1 clove
salt to taste

1. Spread the beans on a baking sheet and pick through them, removing any twigs, stones, or misshapen beans. Rinse the beans in a colander. Soak the beans for at least 4 hours, preferably overnight, in 8 cups water in a large bowl. (This rids the beans of some of their flatulence-causing complex starches.)

2. Drain the beans. Pin the bay leaf to the onion with the clove. Place the beans and onion in a large, heavy pot with 12 cups water. Bring the beans to a boil, reduce the heat, loosely cover the pot, and simmer until the beans are tender, even soft, but not mushy. Add water as necessary to keep the beans submerged. Add salt to taste the last 5 minutes. **Note:** The cooking time can be shortened substantially in a pressure cooker.

Note: To test for doneness, squeeze a bean between your thumb and forefinger: it should crush easily. There's nothing worse than eating undercooked beans.

Makes about 2½ cups cooked beans

159 CALORIES PER SERVING;* 10 G PROTEIN; 1 G FAT; 0 G SATURATED FAT; 29 G CARBOHYDRATE; 2 MG SODIUM; 0 MG CHOLESTEROL

Analysis is based on 4 servings. Slight variation among the different types of beans.

HEALTHY BAKED BEANS

This traditional New England dish is usually made with artery-clogging doses of bacon or salt pork. I've reworked the recipe using smoked turkey for flavor and apple cider instead of pork fat for moistness. My favorite bean for baking is the anasazi, *a handsome red-and-white speckled bean that is high in minerals and protein.*

- 1 pound anasazi or other dried beans
- 1 pound skinless smoked turkey or chicken
- 1 tablespoon olive oil
- 1 large onion, finely chopped
- 2 cloves garlic, minced (2 teaspoons)
- 1 tablespoon minced fresh ginger
- 1 or 2 jalapeño chilies, seeded and minced
- 2 cups apple cider
- 1 cup cider vinegar
- 1 cup water
- ¼ cup molasses (or to taste)
- ¼ cup brown sugar
- 1 tablespoon dry mustard
- 1 tablespoon Dijon-style mustard
- 2 bay leaves
- 1 teaspoon dried thyme
- ¼ teaspoon ground allspice
- ⅛ teaspoon ground cloves
- salt and freshly ground black pepper

Pick through the beans, removing any twigs or stones. Wash the beans well and soak them overnight in a large bowl with cold water to cover.

The next day, cut the turkey into ½-inch dice. Heat the oil in a frying pan and cook the onion, garlic, ginger, and chilies over medium heat for 4 to 5 minutes, or until golden brown. Preheat the oven to 300°F.

Transfer the onion mixture to a bean pot or casserole dish. Drain the beans and add them to the pot. Stir in the remaining ingredients. Tightly cover the pot and bake for 3 hours, or until the beans are very tender. Stir the beans from time to time, adding liquid as necessary to keep

them covered. Leave the pot uncovered for the last 30 minutes to allow the beans to brown and excess liquid to evaporate. Baked beans should be moist but not soupy.

Just before serving, correct the seasoning. The beans should be a little sweet, a tiny bit sour, and faintly spicy. Add brown sugar, vinegar, mustard, salt, and pepper to taste.

Serves 8 to 10

396 CALORIES PER SERVING; 22 G PROTEIN; 9 G FAT; 62 G CARBOHYDRATE; 35 MG SODIUM; 0 MG CHOLESTEROL

Stewed Pinto Beans with Epazote (Frijoles De Olla)

STEWED PINTO BEANS WITH EPAZOTE
(FRIJOLES DE OLLA)

An olla *is an earthenware pot—the kind traditionally used to cook beans in Mexico, where it would be nestled in the coals of a wood fire. Even if you use a more modern metal pot and a gas or electric burner, the combination of flavors—earthy beans, smoky lard, aromatic onion, and pungent epazote—will raise these simple stewed beans to something on the level of art. Epazote is one of the most distinctive seasonings in the Mexican pantry—a ragged-edged, green-leafed herb with a piny, pleasantly bitter, antiseptic taste. Besides the virtue of its unique flavor, it's said to reduce the tendency of beans to cause flatulence. Will your* frijoles de olla *be terrible without epazote? Of course not. But to achieve the authentic flavor, do make an effort to find this distinctive herb.*

2 cups dried pinto beans (about 12 ounces)

1 bay leaf

½ small onion

1 clove

1 tablespoon lard (see Note below) or 1 slice (1 ounce) Canadian bacon, minced

1 clove garlic, peeled

7 to 8 cups water

2 sprigs fresh epazote

1 to 2 whole serrano chilies (optional)

salt and freshly ground black pepper

fresh tortillas

1. Spread the beans on a baking sheet and pick through them, removing any twigs or pebbles. Transfer the beans to a colander and rinse well with cold water.

2. Place the beans in a bowl with enough cold water to cover by 2 inches. Soak the beans in the refrigerator at least 4 hours or as long as overnight. Discard any beans that float on the surface. Drain the beans in the colander and rinse well.

3. Pin the bay leaf to the onion with the clove. Place the soaked beans in a large heavy pot with the lard, onion, garlic, and 7 cups of water. Gradually bring the beans to a boil, reduce the heat, loosely cover the pot, and simmer the beans for 1 hour. Add fresh water as needed, to keep the beans covered by 1 inch of liquid.

4. Add the epazote and the optional serrano chilies and continue simmering until the beans are very tender. (You should be able to squish one easily between your thumb and forefinger.) Uncover the pot for the last 15 minutes, to let some of the cooking liquid evaporate. (The beans should be covered by at least ½ inch of broth.) Using a slotted spoon, remove and discard the onion, garlic, and epazote. Season the beans with salt and pepper to taste.

5. Serve the beans with their broth in earthenware bowls, with fresh tortillas for dipping in the broth.

Note: For the best results, use soupy, freshly rendered lard—the kind you'd get at a neighborhood *carniceria*. Alternatively, a slice of Canadian bacon will give you a similar smoky pork flavor with less fat.

Makes 5 to 6 cups, enough to serve 6

245 CALORIES PER SERVING; 14 G PROTEIN; 3 G FAT; 1 G SATURATED FAT; 42 G CARBOHYDRATE; 16 MG SODIUM; 2 MG CHOLESTEROL

COWBOY-STYLE PINTO BEANS
(CHARROS)

Charros—cowboy-style pinto beans—are Mexico's answer to baked beans, a popular accompaniment to the grilled beef so popular in northern Mexico. The traditional recipe owes its smoky campfire flavor to a generous dose of bacon and bacon fat. My low-fat version uses Canadian bacon, which has all of the smoke flavor of conventional bacon and virtually a fraction of the fat. For speed and convenience I call for canned pinto beans, but you can certainly cook the beans from scratch, following the frijoles de olla *recipe on page 305.*

4 cups cooked pinto beans (two 15-ounce cans)

1 tablespoon lard or olive oil

1 medium onion, minced

2 cloves garlic, minced

2 ounces (2 slices) Canadian bacon, finely chopped

1 large ripe tomato, seeded and finely chopped (for extra richness, roast the tomato in a comal before chopping)

1 cup beer

1 cup chicken stock or bean cooking liquid

1 to 2 tablespoons chopped pickled jalapeño chilies, or to taste

½ cup chopped fresh cilantro

salt and freshly ground black pepper

1. Drain the beans, rinse well, and drain again. Heat the lard in a large heavy saucepan. Add the onion, garlic, and bacon and cook over medium heat until the onion is nicely browned, about 5 minutes. Increase the heat to high and add the tomato. Cook until the tomato juices are evaporated.

2. Stir in the beans, beer, stock, jalapeño, and half the cilantro. Briskly simmer the beans until they are richly flavored and most of the cooking liquid has been absorbed, 10 to 15 minutes. Stir in the remaining cilantro and correct the seasoning, adding salt and pepper to taste.

Serves 4 to 6

345 CALORIES PER SERVING;* 19 G PROTEIN; 6 G FAT; 2 G SATURATED FAT; 53 G CARBOHYDRATE; 266 MG SODIUM; 11 MG CHOLESTEROL

Analysis is based on 4 servings.

REFRIED BEANS
(FRIJOLES REFRITOS)

What can compare to Mexican refried beans? Properly prepared, they're soft and satisfying, rib-sticking, fluffy, and creamy. To make the beans soft and creamy, I beat in chicken stock, which reinforces the meat flavor.

2 corn tortillas

1 tablespoon lard or olive oil

1 small onion, minced

2 to 3 cloves garlic, minced

1 ounce (1 slice) Canadian bacon, minced

2 (15-ounce) cans pinto beans, drained, rinsed under cold water, and drained again

½ to 1 cup chicken or vegetable stock

salt and freshly ground black pepper

2 tablespoons finely grated queso añejo, queso fresco, feta cheese, or Parmesan cheese

1. Preheat the oven to 350°F. Cut the tortillas into strips 1 inch wide. Arrange the strips on a baking sheet and bake until lightly browned, about 10 minutes. Transfer the strips to a cake rack to cool; they'll crisp as they cool.

2. Heat the lard in a nonstick frying pan. Add the onion, garlic, and Canadian bacon and cook over medium heat until just lightly browned, about 5 minutes.

3. Stir half the beans into the onion mixture. With a bean masher or potato masher, mash the beans to a smooth paste. Add the remaining beans and mash to a smooth paste. Stir in ½ cup of the stock and fry the beans until they are thick but creamy, 8 to 10 minutes, stirring with a wooden spoon. If the beans are too thick, add more stock. (The consistency should be that of soft ice cream.) Correct the seasoning, adding salt and pepper to taste.

4. Mound the refried beans on a platter. Sprinkle the top with grated cheese. Stand the tortilla chips upright in the beans. Serve at once.

Makes about 3 cups, enough to serve 6

231 CALORIES PER SERVING; 12 G PROTEIN; 5 G FAT; 1 G SATURATED FAT; 36 G CARBOHYDRATE; 107 MG SODIUM; 9 MG CHOLESTEROL

FAVA BEAN MASH WITH BITTER GREENS

This dish kept turning up on a trip through southern Italy. One restaurant made it with chicory, another with dandelion greens. Yet a third restaurant used arugula. I've even found an Umbrian version made with broccoli rabe and fava beans. I've tried to incorporate the different versions into a single recipe that can be prepared ahead and makes an attractive vegetable dish. The main recipe includes instructions for cooking the beans from scratch. Perfectly tasty results can be obtained with canned beans in a lot less time (see Note).

1¼ cups dried fava beans or small lima beans

1 medium onion, peeled and quartered

1 carrot, peeled and cut into 1-inch pieces

1 celery stalk, cut into 1-inch pieces

1 slice dense white bread, crusts removed, diced

½ clove garlic, minced

1 tablespoon extra-virgin olive oil

¼ to ½ cup Basic Vegetable Stock (page 382) or Chicken Stock (page 379)

salt and freshly ground black pepper

FOR THE GREENS:

salt

1 pound broccoli rabe, dandelion greens, or chicory, or 2 bunches arugula

1 tablespoon extra-virgin olive oil

2 cloves garlic, smashed with the side of a knife or cleaver and peeled

1. Spread the beans on a baking sheet and pick through them, removing any twigs, stones, or misshapen beans. Soak the beans for at least 4 hours, preferably overnight, in cold water to cover.

2. The next day, drain and rinse the beans. Place them in a large, heavy, deep pot with the onion, carrot, celery, and 2 quarts water. Bring the beans to a boil. Reduce the heat to medium, and gently simmer the beans, loosely covered, until soft, about 1½ hours. Drain the beans in a colander.

Note: The cooking time can be shortened considerably by using a pressure cooker.

3. Purée the beans (with the cooking vegetables), the bread, and garlic in a food processor. Add the olive oil and enough vegetable stock to obtain a light, fluffy purée. Add salt and pepper to taste. Spoon this purée into an attractive ovenproof baking dish just large enough to hold a ½-inch-deep layer of purée. (I use a 8-inch oval dish. For ease in cleaning, lightly spray the dish with oil first.)

4. Prepare the greens: Bring 2 quarts salted water to a boil in a large saucepan. Wash the greens in a deep bowl of cold water, holding them by the stems, plunging them up and down. Change the water, as necessary, until completely free of grit or sand. Trim any tough stems off the greens. If using broccoli rabe, dandelion greens, or chicory, cook them in the boiling salted water until just tender, 2 to 3 minutes. Drain in a colander, refresh under cold water, and drain well. Blot them dry and cut crosswise into ½-inch strips. If using arugula, skip the parboiling.

5. Heat the olive oil in a nonstick frying pan. Add the garlic and cook over high heat until just beginning to brown, about 1 minute. Add the greens and cook until thoroughly heated, about 2 minutes. Correct the seasoning, adding salt and pepper to taste. Spoon the greens over the bean purée. If all the ingredients are hot, you can serve them right away. Alternatively, bake the dish in a 400°F. oven until the ingredients are thoroughly heated, about 10 minutes.

Note: To make this dish with canned beans, use 2 15-ounce cans cannellini (white kidney) beans. Drain the beans in a strainer and rinse well. Start the recipe at step 3.

Serves 6 to 8

225 CALORIES PER SERVING;* 12 G PROTEIN; 6 G FAT; 0.8 G SATURATED FAT; 35 G CARBOHYDRATE; 53 MG SODIUM; 0 MG CHOLESTEROL

Analysis is based on 6 servings.

SAUCES AND CONDIMENTS

. . . .

INDIAN YOGURT MARINADE

A tandoor *is a giant urn-shaped clay oven in which kebabs that have been marinated in a tangy mixture of yogurt and spices are roasted on vertical skewers. Most Indian restaurants add food coloring to give the marinated meat its traditional Mercurochrome color. I prefer a natural, if paler, look. This marinade is particularly well suited to lamb, chicken, and shrimp.*

2 cups nonfat yogurt

1½ tablespoons minced fresh ginger

4 cloves garlic, minced (4 teaspoons)

2 jalapeño chilies or other hot chilies, seeded and minced

¼ cup fresh lemon juice

2 bay leaves

2 teaspoons paprika

1½ teaspoons ground cumin

1½ teaspoons ground coriander

1 teaspoon ground turmeric

½ teaspoon ground cinnamon

½ teaspoon freshly ground black pepper

⅛ teaspoon ground cardamom

1–2 teaspoons salt (or to taste)

Drain the yogurt in a yogurt funnel or a cheesecloth-lined colander for 2 hours. Place the ginger, garlic, and chilies in a bowl and whisk in the yogurt, lemon juice, bay leaves, and spices. Add the salt.

Marinate seafood for 2 to 3 hours, poultry for 6 hours, and meat overnight, turning once or twice. Remove and discard the bay leaves before serving.

Note: This marinade also makes a great dressing for grain or pasta salads.

Makes 2 cups, enough marinade for 1½ to 2 pounds seafood, poultry, or meat

13 CALORIES PER TABLESPOON; 1 G PROTEIN; .4 G FAT; 2 G CARBOHYDRATE; 78 MG SODIUM; 1 MG CHOLESTEROL

Berber Marinade

BERBER MARINADE

This thick, spicy paste comes from the nomadic Berbers of North Africa. A little goes a long way! I have used it with great success on tuna, pork tenderloin, and sirloin steak.

- 1 medium-sized onion, diced (1 cup)
- 3 cloves garlic, minced (1 tablespoon)
- 2 tablespoons minced fresh ginger
- ½ cup imported paprika
- 1 tablespoon coriander seeds
- 2 teaspoons cracked black peppercorns
- 2 teaspoons cardamom pods
- 1 teaspoon hot red pepper flakes (or to taste)
- 1 teaspoon fenugreek seeds (optional)
- 1 teaspoon ground cinnamon
- ½ teaspoon allspice berries
- ¼ teaspoon ground cloves
- 1 tablespoon salt (or to taste)
- ¼ cup fresh lemon juice
- ¼ cup olive oil
- 2 tablespoons chicken stock or water (if needed)

Place the onion, garlic, ginger, spices, and salt in a dry skillet. Cook over medium heat for 2 to 3 minutes, or until the spices are lightly roasted and fragrant.

Combine the spice mixture, lemon juice, and oil in a spice mill or blender, and purée to a smooth paste. (If the mixture is too dry to purée, add a little stock or water.)

Spread the paste on the seafood, poultry, or meat, and marinate overnight.

Makes 1 cup, enough marinade for 1½ to 2 pounds seafood, poultry, or meat

42 CALORIES PER TABLESPOON; 0 G PROTEIN; 4 G FAT;
3 G CARBOHYDRATE; 402 MG SODIUM; 0 MG CHOLESTEROL

VIETNAMESE LEMONGRASS MARINADE

Lemongrass is a scallion-shaped herb with a lovely aromatic lemon flavor. If unavailable, you can use thin strips of lemon zest.

- ¼ cup chopped fresh lemongrass (4–6 stalks), ¼ cup dried lemongrass, or 6 strips lemon zest
- 3 cloves garlic, minced (1 tablespoon)
- 2 or 3 shallots, minced (3 tablespoons)
- 2 serrano, jalapeño, or Thai chilies, minced
- 2 teaspoons brown sugar (or to taste)
- 3 tablespoons fish sauce
- 3 tablespoons fresh lime juice
- 1 teaspoon Vietnamese or Thai hot sauce, chili oil, or Tabasco

Cut off the top ⅔ of each lemongrass stalk, trim off the outside leaves and roots, and slice the core thinly. (If the roots are long enough, they can be resprouted in your garden.)

Place the lemongrass, garlic, shallots, chilies, and brown sugar in a spice mill or mortar and pestle, and purée to a coarse paste. Work in the fish sauce, lime juice, and hot sauce. Marinate fish or thinly sliced beef for 1 to 2 hours, turning once or twice.

Makes ¾ cup, enough marinade for 1½ to 2 pounds seafood, poultry, or meat

13 CALORIES PER TABLESPOON; 1 G PROTEIN; 0 G FAT;
3 G CARBOHYDRATE; 52 MG SODIUM; 1 MG CHOLESTEROL

KOREAN SESAME MARINADE

Bool-kogi is to Korea what barbecue is to the American South. To make it, paper-thin slices of beef are marinated in a sweet-salty mixture of soy sauce, sugar, and sesame oil. The meat is traditionally cooked at the table on what looks like an inverted wok, but it can also be grilled on a hibachi or stir-fried in a wok.

¼ cup toasted sesame seeds

3 cloves garlic, minced (1 tablespoon)

1 tablespoon minced fresh ginger

3 scallions, minced

⅓ cup soy sauce

3 tablespoons sugar or honey

1½ tablespoons sesame oil

1 teaspoon hot red pepper flakes

½ teaspoon freshly ground black pepper

Lightly toast the sesame seeds in a dry skillet over medium heat. Combine the sesame seeds and the remaining ingredients in a shallow bowl. Marinate fish for 30 minutes, chicken breasts for 1 hour, and thinly sliced beef for 1 to 2 hours, turning once or twice.

Makes ¾ cup, enough marinade for 1½ to 2 pounds seafood, poultry, or meat

46 CALORIES PER TABLESPOON; 1 G PROTEIN; 2 G FAT; 6 G CARBOHYDRATE; 342 MG SODIUM; 0 MG CHOLESTEROL

RED WINE MARINADE

French chefs use this marinade to give tame meats, such as pork and beef, the sourish tang of wild game. It can also be used with poultry, but it's a little strong for fish. Juniper berries are small, blue-black berries that are the predominant flavoring in gin.

1 onion, finely chopped

2 carrots, finely chopped

2 stalks celery, finely chopped

3 shallots, finely chopped

3 cloves garlic, finely chopped

3 cups dry red wine

½ cup red wine vinegar

20 peppercorns

5 whole cloves

10 juniper berries (or ¼ cup gin)

3 sprigs parsley

5 bay leaves

1½ teaspoons dried thyme

2 tablespoons olive oil

Place all the ingredients in a saucepan and bring to a boil. Let cool completely. Place the meat in a glass or non-metallic dish. Add the marinade and let sit for at least 6 hours, preferably overnight, turning once or twice.

Makes 4½ cups, enough marinade for 2 pounds meat

16 CALORIES PER TABLESPOON; 0 G PROTEIN; .4 G FAT; 1 G CARBOHYDRATE; 3 MG SODIUM; 0 MG CHOLESTEROL

FRESH HERB MARINADE FOR SEAFOOD AND POULTRY

This simple marinade is good for fish, shrimp, scallops, and chicken breasts. The particular variety of herbs you use is less important than that the herbs be fresh.

¼ cup fresh lemon juice

¼ cup dry vermouth

salt and freshly ground black pepper

2 tablespoons extra-virgin olive oil

3 shallots or 1 small onion, thinly sliced

2 cloves garlic, thinly sliced

1 green bell pepper, 1 poblano chili, or 3 jalapeño chilies, thinly sliced

½ cup finely chopped fresh basil, dill, rosemary, parsley, tarragon, and/or other herbs

Combine the lemon juice, vermouth, salt, and pepper in a small bowl and whisk until all the salt is dissolved. Whisk in the olive oil.

Place half the sliced vegetables, herbs, and lemon juice mixture in a shallow glass dish and cover with the food to be marinated. Add the remaining vegetables, herbs, and lemon juice mixture. Marinate seafood for 2 hours and chicken breasts for 4 hours, turning once or twice.

Makes 1 cup, enough marinade for 1½ to 2 pounds seafood or poultry

67 CALORIES PER TABLESPOON; 1 G PROTEIN; 5 G FAT; 5 G CARBOHYDRATE; 8 MG SODIUM; 0 MG CHOLESTEROL

GEORGIAN CINNAMON-ORANGE MARINADE

Tabaka is a cinnamon-orange marinade from the Republic of Georgia (formerly part of the Soviet Union) in the Caucasus Mountains. It is often used for poultry, but it goes well with swordfish, too.

4 or 5 oranges (2 cups juice)

2–4 lemons (½ cup juice)

½ cup dry white wine

3 cloves garlic, minced (1 tablespoon)

1 tablespoon minced fresh ginger

1 medium-sized onion, minced (1 cup)

2 cinnamon sticks

3 tablespoons paprika

1 teaspoon cracked black peppercorns

¼ teaspoon freshly grated nutmeg

1–2 teaspoons sugar (or to taste)

½ teaspoon salt (or to taste)

3 tablespoons olive oil

Grate the zest of 1 orange and 1 lemon. Juice the oranges and lemons. Combine the orange juice, lemon juice, and wine in a saucepan and boil until only ½ cup liquid remains. Let cool.

Combine the garlic, ginger, and onion in a bowl. Stir in the juice mixture, grated zest, spices, sugar, salt, and oil. Marinate swordfish steaks and boneless chicken breasts for 1 to 2 hours, whole chickens or game hens overnight, turning once or twice.

Makes 1½ cups, enough marinade for 1½ to 2 pounds seafood, poultry, or meat

29 CALORIES PER TABLESPOON; 0 G PROTEIN; 2 G FAT; 3 G CARBOHYDRATE; 45 MG SODIUM; 0 MG CHOLESTEROL

MEXICAN SMOKED CHILI MARINADE

Chipotles (smoked jalapeño chilies) add character to this fiery seasoning, which is often used with pork. Chipotles are usually sold canned in tomato paste, but you also see them dried. (If you use dried chilies for this recipe, soften them in hot water and add 2 tablespoons tomato paste.)

1 cup fresh orange juice

¼ cup fresh lime juice

5 canned chipotle chilies, minced, plus 1 tablespoon juice

4 cloves garlic, minced (4 teaspoons)

1 teaspoon freshly grated orange zest

2 teaspoons dried oregano

1 teaspoon cumin seeds

2 tablespoons wine vinegar

½ teaspoon each salt and freshly ground black pepper (or to taste)

Combine the orange juice and lime juice in a saucepan and boil until only ½ cup liquid remains. Place this and the remaining ingredients in a blender and purée to a smooth paste.

Spread this paste on the food to be marinated. Marinate seafood for 2 hours, poultry for 4 to 6 hours, and meat overnight, turning once or twice.

Makes 1 cup, enough marinade for 1½ to 2 pounds seafood, poultry, or meat

6 CALORIES PER TABLESPOON; 0 G PROTEIN; 0 G FAT; 2 G CARBOHYDRATE; 117 MG SODIUM; 0 MG CHOLESTEROL

TERIYAKI MARINADE

Teriyaki could be called the national marinade of Japan. It is equally at home on seafood, poultry, and meat. The traditional sweetener for teriyaki is mirin (sweet rice wine), but if it is unavailable, use sake, sherry, or white wine, and increase the sugar slightly.

1 tablespoon minced fresh ginger

3 cloves garlic, minced (1 tablespoon)

1 or 2 jalapeño chilies, seeded and minced (optional)

3 scallions, finely chopped

¼ cup soy sauce

¼ cup mirin or white wine

1½ tablespoons sesame oil

2 tablespoons maple syrup or brown sugar (or to taste)

Place the ginger, garlic, chilies (if using), and scallions in a bowl and whisk in the soy sauce, mirin, sesame oil, and maple syrup.

Marinate seafood for 2 hours, poultry for 4 hours, and meat overnight, turning once or twice.

Makes 1 cup, enough marinade for 1½ to 2 pounds seafood, poultry, or meat

36 CALORIES PER TABLESPOON; 0 G PROTEIN; 3 G FAT; 3 G CARBOHYDRATE; 260 MG SODIUM; 0 MG CHOLESTEROL

LOW-FAT VINAIGRETTE

Use this recipe on salads, grilled fish or meat, steamed vegetables, or any dish that needs a quick, flavorful sauce.

1 or 2 shallots, minced

1 small clove garlic, minced (½ teaspoon)

2 teaspoons Dijon-style mustard

salt and freshly ground black pepper

1 tablespoon red wine vinegar

1 tablespoon fresh lemon juice

2–6 tablespoons olive oil

2–6 tablespoons chicken stock

Combine the shallots, garlic, mustard, salt, and pepper in a large bowl. Add the vinegar and lemon juice in a thin stream, whisking until all the salt is dissolved. Gradually whisk in the oil and stock in a thin stream. (Or the ingredients can be combined and shaken in a jar with a tight-fitting lid.) There should be ½ cup liquid in all. Correct the seasoning, adding salt and lemon juice to taste.

Makes ¾ cup

24 CALORIES PER TABLESPOON; 0 G PROTEIN; 2 G FAT; 1 G CARBOHYDRATE; 20 MG SODIUM; 0 MG CHOLESTEROL

CUBAN LIME MARINADE

Cubans use this simple marinade on just about everything. It can be made with limes or sour oranges, and it goes especially well with grilled fish.

Makes ½ cup, enough marinade for 1 to 1½ pounds seafood, poultry, or meat

16 CALORIES PER TABLESPOON; 1 G PROTEIN; .2 G FAT; 4 G CARBOHYDRATE; 402 MG SODIUM; 0 MG CHOLESTEROL

6 cloves garlic, minced (2 tablespoons)

1½ teaspoons salt (or to taste)

2 teaspoons ground cumin

1 tablespoon chopped fresh oregano (or 1 teaspoon dried)

½ teaspoon freshly ground black pepper

½ cup fresh lime juice or sour orange juice

Place the garlic in a mortar and pestle with the salt, and mash to a smooth paste. (Or mash these ingredients in a shallow bowl with a fork.) Work in the cumin, oregano, pepper, and lime juice.

Cut small pockets in the food to be marinated and stuff half the marinade inside. Spread the remaining marinade on top. Let marinate for at least 6 hours (meat overnight), turning once or twice. Use any leftover marinade for basting.

ASIAN VINAIGRETTE

Ginger, garlic, and scallions give this vinaigrette an Asian accent. Serve it with salmon, tofu, or cucumber salads.

- 2 cloves garlic, minced (2 teaspoons)
- 1 tablespoon minced fresh ginger
- 2 scallions, minced
- ¼ cup chicken stock
- 2 tablespoons rice wine vinegar
- 1 tablespoon soy sauce
- 1 tablespoon sesame oil (optional)

Combine all the ingredients in a jar with a tight-fitting lid. Shake until well blended. Correct the seasoning, adding soy sauce to taste.

Makes ½ cup

4 CALORIES PER TABLESPOON; 0 G PROTEIN; 0 G FAT; 1 G CARBOHYDRATE; 131 MG SODIUM; 0 MG CHOLESTEROL

VIETNAMESE DIPPING SAUCE

Nuoc cham is a sweet-sour-salty dipping sauce made with fish sauce, lime juice, and sugar. It's as indispensable on the Vietnamese table as ketchup and mustard are on our own.

- 1 carrot
- 2 cloves garlic, minced (2 teaspoons)
- 1 shallot, minced
- 1 fresh hot chili, minced
- 2 tablespoons sugar
- ¼ cup fish sauce
- ¼ cup fresh lime juice
- ¼ cup water
- 3 tablespoons rice wine vinegar

Cut the carrot into the thinnest imaginable shreds. (I mean really thin. The easiest way for a Westerner to do this is to shave the carrot into thin strips with a vegetable peeler. Stack the strips up 3 or 4 high and cut lengthwise into hair-thin slivers.)

Combine the garlic, shallot, chili, and sugar in a mortar and pestle, and pound to a smooth paste. Work in the fish sauce, lime juice, water, and vinegar. (Or the ingredients can be combined and shaken in a jar with a tight-fitting lid.) Transfer the sauce to a pretty bowl (or several bowls) and stir in the carrot.

Makes 1 cup

17 CALORIES PER TABLESPOON; 1 G PROTEIN; 0 G FAT; 4 G CARBOHYDRATE; 52 MG SODIUM; 1 MG CHOLESTEROL

SPICY MIGNONETTE SAUCE

This piquant sauce takes its name from the French word for coarsely cracked peppercorns: mignonette. *Spoon it over raw oysters and clams on the half shell, or serve as a dipping sauce for cooked seafood.*

- 2 teaspoons black peppercorns
- 3 tablespoons minced shallots
- 1 or 2 pickled or fresh jalapeño chilies (or to taste), minced
- ½ cup red wine vinegar
- ½ cup dry white wine
- salt (optional)

Coarsely crush the peppercorns in a mortar and pestle or under a rolling pin or heavy pot. (The idea here is to obtain large pieces of pepper.) Combine the cracked pepper in a bowl with the remaining ingredients. Correct the seasoning, adding salt to taste, if desired.

Makes 1¼ cups

6 CALORIES PER TABLESPOON; 0 G PROTEIN; 0 G FAT; 1 G CARBOHYDRATE; 7 MG SODIUM; 0 MG CHOLESTEROL

ROMESCO SAUCE

A specialty of Tarragona, Spain, romesco is a sauce made of chilies, nuts, and tomatoes. I've reduced the amount of fat by cutting back on the nuts, substituting chicken stock for part of the oil, and toasting rather than frying the bread. Romesco isn't a pretty sauce (it's brown), but it has a wonderful flavor. Serve it with grilled chicken, baked fish, pork or veal, or even on pasta. I like to eat it straight with a spoon!

2 dried red chilies (preferably anchos or pasillas)

1 fresh jalapeño chili, seeded

4 ripe tomatoes, halved and seeded

4 cloves garlic, peeled

2 tablespoons slivered or chopped almonds

2 tablespoons chopped hazelnuts

1 slice country-style white bread (about ¼ cup crumbled)

1 tablespoon olive oil

¼ cup chopped flat-leaf parsley

2 tablespoons red wine vinegar (or to taste)

½ teaspoon sugar

¼ cup chicken stock (approximately)

salt and freshly ground black pepper

Soak the dried chilies in warm water for 1 hour.

Preheat the oven to 350°F. Place the jalapeño, tomatoes, and garlic on a piece of lightly oiled foil in a roasting pan. Roast for 30 minutes, or until the garlic is soft. Toast the nuts on a baking sheet in the oven for 6 to 8 minutes, or until lightly browned. Toast the bread to a dark golden brown in a toaster and crumble it into small pieces.

Drain and chop the soaked dried chilies. (If a milder sauce is desired, remove the seeds.) Sauté the chilies in the oil in a small frying pan for 1 to 2 minutes, or until crisp and fragrant. Let cool.

Grind the nuts and toast to a fine powder in a food processor. Add the fried chilies, jalapeño, tomatoes, garlic, and parsley, and purée to a thick paste. Add the vinegar, sugar, and enough stock to obtain a pourable sauce. Correct the seasoning, adding salt, pepper, and vinegar to taste.

Makes 2 cups

16 CALORIES PER TABLESPOON; 0 G PROTEIN; 1 G FAT; 2 G CARBOHYDRATE; 32 MG SODIUM; 0 MG CHOLESTEROL

MOLASSES BARBECUE SAUCE

Molasses is hardly what one would call a fashionable ingredient these days, but unlike the sugar, fructose, and dextrose used in most commercial barbecue sauces, it has flavor behind its sweetness. This sauce goes particularly well with pork and duck.

1 tablespoon olive oil

1 small onion, minced (½ cup)

1 clove garlic, minced (1 teaspoon)

1 jalapeño chili, seeded and minced

⅔ cup molasses

⅔ cup distilled white vinegar

⅓ cup Dijon-style mustard

1 tablespoon soy sauce

Heat the oil in a large saucepan over medium heat. Add the onion, garlic, and chili, and cook, stirring well, for 2 to 3 minutes, or until soft but not brown.

Stir in the remaining ingredients and simmer for 5 minutes. Let the sauce cool before serving.

Makes 2 cups

25 CALORIES PER TABLESPOON; 0 G PROTEIN; . 5 G FAT; 5 G CARBOHYDRATE; 73 MG SODIUM; 0 MG CHOLESTEROL

LEMON CHILI SAUCE

I first tasted this sauce at the Royal Orchid Sheraton Hotel in Bangkok. It was meant to be served with grilled seafood, but I soon found myself eating it straight with a spoon. For a truly authentic version, use cilantro root, which tastes like a cross between cilantro leaves and parsnips. (Asian and Hispanic markets often sell the whole plant.) Cilantro leaves produce a tasty sauce, too.

- 1 head fresh garlic, minced (¼ cup)
- 4 or 5 fresh hot red chilies, minced (¼ cup)
- 3 tablespoons minced cilantro root or leaves
- ½ cup fresh lemon juice
- ½ cup fish sauce
- 2 tablespoons sugar (or to taste)

Combine all the ingredients in a glass bowl and stir until the sugar is completely dissolved. Add more sugar as necessary. The sauce should be tart, salty, and sweet.

Makes 1¼ cups

17 CALORIES PER TABLESPOON; 1 G PROTEIN; 0 G FAT; 2 G CARBOHYDRATE; 147 MG SODIUM; 3 MG CHOLESTEROL

YEMENITE HOT SAUCE

Zehug is a hot sauce from Yemen, served much the way bottled salsa is in North America. You can use almost any hot chili to make this sauce, including jalapeños, serranos, and Thai peppers. To make a red sauce, use red chilies; to make a green one, use green.

- 6 fresh red or green chilies, seeded
- 6 cloves garlic, peeled
- 2 tablespoons fresh lemon juice (approximately)
- ½ cup finely chopped cilantro or flat-leaf parsley
- 1 teaspoon ground cumin
- salt and freshly ground black pepper

Purée the chilies and garlic in a spice mill or blender, adding enough lemon juice to obtain a smooth paste. (The ingredients can also be pounded to a smooth paste in a mortar and pestle.)

Transfer the chili paste to a bowl and stir in the cilantro, cumin, salt, and pepper.

Makes 1½ cups

4 CALORIES PER TABLESPOON; 0 G PROTEIN; 0 G FAT; 1 G CARBOHYDRATE; 1 MG SODIUM; 0 MG CHOLESTEROL

BRAZILIAN HOT SAUCE

This molho de companha (country hot sauce) could be described as a mildly spicy relish. To be strictly authentic, you'll need an aromatic African chili called pimenta malagueta, whose fiery bite is inversely proportional to its tiny size. But the sauce is perfectly good made with readily available jalapeño or serrano chilies. Serve with grilled meat.

- 1 large red onion, finely chopped
- 1 large ripe tomato, seeded and finely chopped
- 1 green bell pepper, cored, seeded, and finely chopped
- 2 cloves garlic, minced (2 teaspoons)
- 2 *malagueta* or other chilies, minced (or to taste)
- ¼ cup finely chopped flat-leaf parsley
- 1 tablespoon extra-virgin olive oil
- 3 tablespoons fresh lime juice (or to taste)
- 2 tablespoons wine vinegar
- salt and freshly ground black pepper

Combine all the ingredients in a bowl and stir to mix. Correct the seasoning with lime juice and salt to taste. If the sauce seems too thick, stir in a few tablespoons ice water.

Makes 2 cups

8 CALORIES PER TABLESPOON; 0 G PROTEIN; .5 G FAT; 1 G CARBOHYDRATE; 1 MG SODIUM; 0 MG CHOLESTEROL

PICKLED OKRA

Who says okra has to be soft and slimy? These pickles are crisper and crunchier than many cucumber pickles. This recipe is a great way to introduce people who don't think they like okra to this pretty, finger-shaped vegetable. For the best results, choose small, firm, unblemished okra.

- 1 pound small okra
- 2 dried red chilies
- 2 cups white vinegar
- 1 cup water
- 1 tablespoon salt
- 2 teaspoons sugar
- 2 bay leaves
- 1 teaspoon each black peppercorns, coriander seeds, and dill seeds
- ½ teaspoon celery seeds

Wash the okra and trim off the ends of the stems. Place in a large, clean jar with the chilies. Combine the remaining ingredients in a nonreactive saucepan and bring to a boil. Let this mixture cool slightly, then pour it over the okra. Place a small dish or sealed, water-filled plastic bag on top to keep the okra submerged.

Let the okra stand at room temperature for 2 to 7 days. The pickles are ready to eat after 2 days, but the flavor will improve with age. (I've never been able to wait more than a week to see whether they continue to improve!)

Note: Nutritional values for pickled foods are imprecise and, therefore, no analysis is given.

Makes 1 pint

PICKLED LEMONS

Salt-cured lemons are a popular flavoring in Morocco, where they are added to everything from salads to stews. Their explosive flavor is great for enlivening seafood, pasta, and grain dishes, or even for nibbling straight. Pickled lemons will keep almost indefinitely, and a little goes a long way. A tiny spoonful of the juice makes a wonderful addition to salad dressing.

- 3 whole lemons
- ½ cup kosher salt
- ½–1 cup fresh lemon juice
- extra-virgin olive oil (optional)

Scrub the lemons and dry well. Cut each lemon into 8 wedges and each wedge in half. Remove any seeds. Place the lemons in a bowl with the salt and mix well. Transfer the lemon mixture to a clean glass jar with a glass or plastic-coated lid. Add lemon juice to cover.

Seal the jar and let the lemons pickle at room temperature for at least 5 days, shaking the jar from time to time to mix the juices. For extra flavor, stir in a tablespoon or two of olive oil. Store the pickled lemons in the refrigerator.

Note: Nutritional values for pickled foods are imprecise and, therefore, no analysis is given.

Makes 1 pint

PICKLED ONIONS

Homemade pickles are a great way to spice up normally bland low-fat foods such as chicken breasts and fish fillets. I like to use cipollinas— small, flat Italian onions— for pickling, but pearl onions and small silverskins work well, too.

- 2 cups distilled white vinegar
- ⅔ cup water
- 2 teaspoons salt
- 1 tablespoon sugar
- 1½ pounds cipollinas or other small onions, peeled
- 1 or 2 fresh jalapeño chilies, thinly sliced

Combine the vinegar, water, salt, and sugar in a large bowl and whisk until smooth. Place the onions and chilies in a large, clean jar. Add enough of the vinegar mixture to cover the onions completely. If necessary, place a small dish or sealed, water-filled plastic bag on top to keep the onions completely submerged. Let the onions pickle at room temperature for 2 to 3 days.

Note: Nutritional values for pickled foods are imprecise and, therefore, no analysis is given.

Makes 1 pint

Pickled Okra, Pickled Lemons, and Pickled Onions

BANANA-TAMARIND CHUTNEY

Tamarind is a tall tropical tree with a large curved seedpod. The pod contains a sour pulp used in Indian, Asian, and Caribbean cooking. The pulp combines the tartness of lime juice with the sweetness of stewed prunes. To make tamarind water, combine 4 ounces pulp and 2 cups warm water in a blender. Blend for 1 minute and strain well. If you can't find tamarind, substitute balsamic vinegar.

4 ripe bananas

juice of 1 lime

¼ cup tamarind water or tamarind purée (or ¼ cup balsamic vinegar)

2 tablespoons minced fresh ginger

1 or 2 jalapeño chilies, seeded and minced

1 red bell pepper, cored, seeded, and cut into ½-inch dice

1 green bell pepper, cored, seeded, and cut into ½-inch dice

½ cup light brown sugar (or to taste)

¾ cup raisins or currants

2 tablespoons coarsely chopped pecans

1 teaspoon ground cumin

1 teaspoon ground coriander

salt, freshly ground black pepper, and cayenne pepper

Peel and dice 3 of the bananas and sprinkle with lime juice. Prepare the tamarind water.

Combine all the ingredients (except the 4th banana) in a heavy saucepan and gently simmer for 5 minutes. Correct the seasoning with sugar, lime juice, and cayenne to taste. The chutney should be a little sweet, a little sour, and a little spicy.

Let the chutney cool to room temperature. Peel and dice the 4th banana and stir it in. Refrigerate until ready to serve. This chutney tastes best the first week.

Makes 4 cups

24 CALORIES PER TABLESPOON; 0 G PROTEIN; 0 G FAT;
6 G CARBOHYDRATE; 10 MG SODIUM; 0 MG CHOLESTEROL

CORN CHUTNEY

To most people, chutney implies fruit, but fine chutneys are made from onions and other vegetables and herbs. Here's a corn chutney that goes especially well with seafood and roast pork. Dried cherries can be found at gourmet shops or purchased by mail.

4 ears fresh corn (2 cups kernels)

3 shallots, minced

1 or 2 jalapeño chilies, seeded and finely chopped

1 tablespoon minced fresh ginger

1 small green bell pepper, cored, seeded, and chopped

2 stalks celery, finely chopped

¼ cup dried cherries or raisins

3 tablespoons honey (or to taste)

¼ cup cider vinegar

1–2 teaspoons hot sauce

salt and freshly ground black pepper

3 tablespoons chopped fresh chives or scallions

Cut the corn kernels off the cob with a sharp knife. (The easiest way to do this is to lay the ears on their side on a cutting board and make lengthwise cuts with a chef's knife.)

Combine the corn with the remaining ingredients (except the chives) in a saucepan and simmer for 8 to 10 minutes, or until the vegetables are tender. Correct the seasoning, adding salt, honey, vinegar, and hot sauce to taste. The chutney should be a little sweet, a little sour, and decidedly spicy. Remove the pan from the heat and stir in the chives. Transfer the chutney to a clean jar and store in the refrigerator.

Makes 3 cups

15 CALORIES PER TABLESPOON; 0 G PROTEIN; 0 G FAT;
4 G CARBOHYDRATE; 3 MG SODIUM; 0 MG CHOLESTEROL

GINGER PEACH CHUTNEY

Chutney (from the Hindu word chatni) *is a fruit-,
vegetable-, or herb-based condiment traditionally served
with Indian food. North American chefs use it to spice up
everything from roast chicken to baked ham to grilled fish.
Try making this chutney with ripe summer peaches.
It's good enough to eat plain with a spoon! (You can also
make it with nectarines, pears, or other fruits.)*

2 pounds ripe peaches (5 cups diced)

4 slices candied ginger, minced

1 cinnamon stick

4 allspice berries

4 whole cloves

10 black peppercorns

½ red onion, diced (½ cup)

½ red bell pepper, cored, seeded, and diced

½ green bell pepper, cored, seeded, and diced

½ cup raisins

¼ cup rice wine vinegar

3 tablespoons brown sugar (or to taste)

Plunge the peaches in a pot of boiling water for 20 seconds.
Rinse under cold water and slip off the skins. Pit and cut
into ½-inch dice. Tie the ginger, cinnamon stick, allspice,
cloves, and peppercorns in a piece of cheesecloth.

Place the peaches, spice bundle, and remaining ingredients
in a heavy saucepan. Simmer, stirring frequently, for
10 minutes, or until the peaches are soft. Correct the
seasoning, adding vinegar and sugar to taste. The
chutney should be a little sweet and a little sour.

Let the chutney cool to room temperature, then transfer it
to a clean jar. Store in the refrigerator.

Note: The amount of sugar used depends on the sweetness
of the peaches.

Makes 5 cups

10 CALORIES PER TABLESPOON; 0 G PROTEIN; 0 G FAT;
3 G CARBOHYDRATE; 0 MG SODIUM; 0 MG CHOLESTEROL

CRANBERRY CHUTNEY

*Here's an Indian twist on a Thanksgiving favorite.
It's a great accompaniment to Smoked Holiday Turkey
(page 245).*

1 12-ounce bag cranberries

1 tablespoon olive oil

3 shallots, minced

1 tablespoon minced fresh ginger

1 or 2 jalapeño chilies, seeded and minced

1 green bell pepper, cored, seeded,
and cut into ½-inch dice

1 yellow bell pepper, cored, seeded,
and cut into ½-inch dice

½ cup cider vinegar

½ cup brown sugar (or to taste)

½ cup raisins

salt and freshly ground black pepper

Wash and pick through the cranberries, removing
any stems. Heat the oil in a large saucepan. Cook the
shallots and ginger over medium heat for 30 seconds,
or until soft but not brown. Add the remaining
ingredients and gently simmer for 5 minutes, or until
the cranberries are just tender. (They shouldn't be too
soft.) Correct the seasoning, adding sugar and vinegar
to taste. The chutney should be a little sweet and
a little sour.

Store the chutney in clean jars. Refrigerated, it will
keep for several months.

Makes 3 cups

21 CALORIES PER TABLESPOON; 0 G PROTEIN; .5 G FAT;
5 G CARBOHYDRATE; 1 MG SODIUM; 0 MG CHOLESTEROL

Banana-Tamarind Chutney

DESSERTS

MEGA-CHOCOLATE ROULADE

This cake won the approval of the sternest critics, my wife and daughter, both of whom like their chocolate cakes loaded with butter, cream, and egg yolks.

spray oil

½ cup cake flour, plus more for dusting

3 tablespoons unsweetened
  Dutch-processed cocoa powder

Pinch salt

½ cup plus 3 tablespoons granulated sugar

6 large egg whites

½ teaspoon cream of tartar

2 teaspoons vanilla extract

Low-Fat Chocolate Pudding (see page 347)

Confectioners' sugar, for dusting

1. Make sure the rack is in the lower third of the oven and preheat the oven to 375°F. Line a 16 x 11-inch jelly-roll pan with baking parchment or foil, lightly spray it with oil, and dust with flour, shaking off the excess.

2. Sift the ½ cup flour, the cocoa, the salt, and the ½ cup sugar into a mixing bowl. Put the egg whites and cream of tartar in an electric mixer and beat to soft peaks, starting at slow speed, then increasing to medium, then to medium-high. When soft peaks form, add the remaining 3 tablespoons sugar and increase the speed to high. Continue beating until the whites are firm and glossy but not dry, about 30 seconds. (Beating will take about 6 to 8 minutes in all.) Stir in the vanilla. Sift the cocoa mixture into the egg whites in three batches, gently folding after each addition with a rubber spatula. Do not overmix. Spread the batter evenly in the prepared pan and gently tap the pan on the counter to knock out any air bubbles.

3. Bake the roulade until it feels firm and springy to the touch, about 10 minutes. Remove the pan from the oven. Lift the roulade by the corners of the paper or foil and slide it onto a cake rack. Let cool to room temperature. Meanwhile, prepare the Intense Chocolate Pudding.

4. Assemble the roulade: Spread the cake with the chocolate pudding. Beginning at the wide end closer to you, gently roll up the cake, pulling the paper or foil to help you roll it. When it is almost rolled up, transfer it, seam side down, to a long, narrow platter or foil-covered cardboard rectangle a little larger than the cake. The roulade can be prepared up to 3 hours ahead. Just before serving, dust the top with confectioners' sugar. To serve, cut it into ½- or 1-inch slices.

Makes 1 16-inch roulade, which will serve 8 to 10

204 CALORIES PER SERVING; 6 G PROTEIN; 3 G FAT; 10 G SATURATED FAT; 41 G CARBOHYDRATE; 109 MG SODIUM; 27 MG CHOLESTEROL

BASIC SPONGE CAKE

When recrafting traditional recipes for high-flavor, low-fat cooking, I aim for results that equal the original. Sometimes I get lucky and the low-fat version actually tastes better. Such is the case with the following sponge cake, my remake of a French génoise, in which I replaced half the egg yolks in the traditional recipe with whites. The result is an airy cake that's incredibly soft and velvety. (It also lacks the "eggy" taste of a génoise, which I find heavy.) The butter is browned to give it extra flavor, so you only need half as much as for a traditional génoise. I like to bake this cake in a "flan" pan— a cake pan with fluted sides and a depressed center—but you can use a standard round cake pan, too.

spray oil

dry bread crumbs or flour for dusting

1 cup cake flour

2 to 3 tablespoons unsalted butter

2 large eggs plus 4 large egg whites

⅔ cup sugar

2 teaspoons vanilla extract or orange-flower water

2 teaspoons grated lemon or orange zest

1. Preheat the oven to 350°F. Lightly spray an 11-inch flan pan or 9-inch round cake pan (preferably nonstick) with spray oil and place it in the freezer for 5 minutes. Line the bottom of the pan with baking parchment. (If using a flan pan, line only the flat central portion.) Spray the pan with oil again and place it in the freezer for 5 minutes. Sprinkle the pan with bread crumbs and tap it upside down to remove the excess.

2. Sift the flour into a small bowl. Melt the butter in a heavy saucepan set over medium-high heat and continue cooking it until it turns hazelnut brown. Immediately remove from the heat.

3. Put the eggs and sugar in an electric mixer and beat at low speed, gradually increasing to medium, then high. Beat 8 to 10 minutes in all, until the mixture is pale yellow and has tripled in volume, and falls from a raised whisk in a thick, silky ribbon. Stir in the vanilla and zest.

4. Sift the sifted flour onto the egg mixture in three batches, gently folding with a rubber spatula after each addition. Whisk about ½ cup of the batter into the melted butter. Return this mixture to the mixing bowl and fold just to combine. It's important to fold gently and just enough to combine: excess folding will deflate the eggs.

5. Spoon the batter into the prepared pan and bake until the top of the cake feels firm and the sides start to pull away from the pan, and an inserted cake tester comes out clean, about 20 minutes. Remove the pan from the oven and let cool slightly. Invert the cake onto a wire rack and gently tap the pan to unmold it. Let the cake cool to room temperature.

Makes 1 11-inch cake with a depressed center or 1 regular 9-inch cake, which will serve 8 to 10

178 CALORIES PER SERVING; 5 G PROTEIN; 5 G FAT; 2.3 G SATURATED FAT; 29 G CARBOHYDRATE; 61 MG SODIUM; 62 MG CHOLESTEROL

BERRY SPONGE CAKE WITH ORANGE CURD

Easy to make and impressive to serve, this summery cake has something for everyone. The recipe may seem involved, but actually it can be completed in less than an hour. For a great presentation, bake the cake in a "flan" pan—a cake pan with fluted sloping sides and a depression in the center.

Basic Sponge Cake (recipe precedes)

Orange Curd (page 386)

FOR THE GLAZE:

3 tablespoons apricot jam

2 to 3 tablespoons water (enough to thin the jam to brushable consistency)

TO ASSEMBLE THE CAKE:

1 pint fresh raspberries

1 pint fresh blackberries

1 quart strawberries, hulled

1. Prepare the sponge cake and let cool. Prepare the orange curd and let cool.

2. Make the glaze: Put the jam and water in a small heavy saucepan and cook over medium heat, whisking steadily, until the jam is melted and syrupy, about 3 minutes.

3. Assemble the cake: Spoon the orange curd into the depression in the top of the cake. Arrange the berries on the top of the cake in concentric circles, alternating colors. Brush the berries with the apricot glaze. The cake can be prepared several hours ahead.

Makes 1 11-inch cake, which will serve 8 to 10

327 CALORIES PER SERVING; 7 G PROTEIN; 6 G FAT; 2.6 G SATURATED FAT; 65 G CARBOHYDRATE; 71 MG SODIUM; 88 MG CHOLESTEROL

Berry Sponge Cake with Orange Curd

LEMON POPPY CHIFFON CAKE

Chiffon cake might be thought of as angel food that's graduated from finishing school. The addition of oil gives chiffon cake extra refinement and moistness. Chiffon cakes are easy to make, but to be successful you must avoid the three don'ts. Don't overbeat the egg whites (they should be firm and glossy, but not dry). Don't overfold the batter (or you'll deflate it). And don't overbake the cake or it will collapse).

½ cup canola oil

1 cup sugar, plus 3 tablespoons for the egg whites

½ cup fresh lemon juice (3 to 4 lemons)

1 tablespoon grated lemon zest

Pinch salt

¼ cup poppy seeds

1½ cups cake flour

1 tablespoon baking powder

8 egg whites (1 cup)

1 teaspoon cream of tartar

Lemon Glaze (optional) (recipe follows)

1. Preheat the oven to 325°F. Combine the oil, 1 cup sugar, lemon juice, lemon zest, salt, and poppy seeds in a mixing bowl and whisk to mix. Sift in the flour and baking powder and whisk just to mix.

2. Beat the egg whites in an electric mixer at slow speed for 1 minute. Add the cream of tartar and beat for 1 minute. Gradually increase the speed to medium, then medium-high, beating the egg whites to soft peaks. Increase the speed to high, beat in the remaining 3 tablespoons sugar, and beat until the whites are firm and glossy but not dry, about 30 seconds. The whole process should take 6 to 8 minutes. Do not overbeat. If you're not sure when the whites are done, err on the side of underbeating.

3. Gently stir ¼ of the whites into the flour mixture to lighten it. Fold this mixture as gently as possible into the remaining whites, using a rubber spatula. Fold as gently and as little as possible, just to mix. Pour the mixture into a 9-inch tube or bundt pan (preferably nonstick) that has been sprayed with oil and lightly floured and smooth the top with a spatula. Lightly tap the pan on the work surface to knock out any bubbles.

4. Bake the chiffon cake until the top feels firm and an inserted cake tester comes out clean, 30 to 40 minutes. Do not overbake. Remove the pan from the oven, invert it onto a raised wire rack or wine bottle, and let it cool completely, upside down. Gently loosen the cake from the sides of the pan with the tip of a paring knife. Invert it onto a platter and give it a little shake: the cake should slide right out. If you like, drizzle the top with Lemon Glaze (recipe follows).

Makes 1 9-inch cake, which will serve 10 to 12

258 CALORIES PER SERVING; 4 G PROTEIN; 12.7 G FAT; 1 G SATURATED FAT; 35 G CARBOHYDRATE; 188 MG SODIUM; 0 MG CHOLESTEROL

LEMON GLAZE

1 cup confectioners' sugar

About 1½ tablespoons fresh lemon juice

Put the confectioners' sugar in a small bowl and whisk in enough lemon juice to obtain a thick glaze. Spoon the glaze over the cake and let harden before slicing the cake.

PECAN DACQUOISE WITH CHOCOLATE MOUSSE

A dacquoise is a cake made with nut-flavored meringues. This one features Reduced-Fat Chocolate Mousse in place of the traditional buttercream icing. The recipe may seem complicated, but actually it's a series of simple steps. The meringues can be made a day ahead and stored in an airtight cookie tin. Be sure they are completely cool before storing. The pecans raise the fat content but even the most conscientious fat watchers are entitled to an occasional splurge.

2 teaspoons butter, melted (or vegetable oil spray)

1 tablespoon flour

1 cup pecans or other nuts

1 cup sugar

2 tablespoons cornstarch

6 egg whites

¼ teaspoon cream of tartar

Reduced-Fat Chocolate Mousse (page 350)

½ cup unsweetened cocoa

Line 2 or 3 large baking sheets with parchment paper and brush them with the melted butter (or spray with vegetable oil). Sprinkle the paper with flour, shaking off any excess. Cut an 8-inch circle out of cardboard and cover it with foil. Using a pot lid, trace three 8-inch circles on the paper-lined baking sheets, leaving 3 inches between each. (The meringues will spread.) Preheat the oven to 300°F.

Lightly brown the pecans on a baking sheet in the oven. (This will take 4 to 6 minutes.) Grind them with ¼ cup of the sugar to a fine powder in a food processor. (Run the machine in brief spurts. Don't overgrind, or the nuts will become oily.) Mix in the cornstarch.

Beat the egg whites at low speed for 20 seconds. Add the cream of tartar and gradually increase the mixer speed to high. Beat the whites to stiff peaks, adding the remaining ¼ cup sugar as the whites stiffen. Gently fold in the nut mixture. Using a piping bag with a ½-inch round tip, pipe the meringue in circles on the parchment.

Bake the meringues for 50 to 60 minutes, or until firm. Let cool 3 minutes. Using a long spatula, gently loosen the meringues from the parchment paper. Place a plate or pot lid on top of the meringues and trim the edges with a sharp knife to form perfect circles. Transfer to a wire rack to cool.

Prepare the Reduced-Fat Chocolate Mousse.

To assemble the dacquoise, affix one of the meringue rounds to the cardboard with a dab of chocolate mousse. Spread half the mousse on top. Place the second round on top and spread most of the remaining mousse on it. Place the third round, smooth side up, on top. Mask the sides of the dacquoise with the leftover mousse. Sift the cocoa in a thick layer on top.

Let the dacquoise stand for at least 30 minutes before serving to soften the meringue. Cut into wedges and serve with espresso or a tall glass of milk.

Serves 8 to 10

454 CALORIES PER SERVING; 9 G PROTEIN; 21 G FAT; 69 G CARBOHYDRATE; 116 MG SODIUM; 3 MG CHOLESTEROL

Cinnamon Rose Angel Food Cake

CINNAMON ROSE ANGEL FOOD CAKE

This ethereal, uniquely American cake isn't difficult to make, but there are a few tricks to keep in mind. First, let the egg whites warm to room temperature before beating. Second, beat the whites to soft peaks only. You will need a 9-inch tube pan with removable sides for this recipe. Make sure it is completely free of grease. If in doubt, rewash and dry it. Rose water is available at Indian and Middle Eastern grocery stores and at many pharmacies.

1 cup plus 2 tablespoons cake flour (approximately)	¼ teaspoon salt
	12 egg whites (about 1½ cups)
1½ cups sugar	1 teaspoon cream of tartar
1 teaspoon ground cinnamon	2 teaspoons rose water

Preheat the oven to 350°F. Sift the cake flour onto a sheet of wax or parchment paper. Measure out 1 level cup (without packing the cup). Sift the sugar the same way and measure out 1½ cups. Combine the flour with ½ cup sugar and the cinnamon and salt. Sift three times.

Beat the egg whites at low speed for 1 minute. Add the cream of tartar and rose water, and beat until the mixture is frothy. Increase the mixer speed to high and beat the egg whites to soft peaks, adding the remaining 1 cup sugar in a thin stream. Do not overbeat. Sift ¼ cup of the flour mixture into the whites and fold in as gently as possible. Continue sifting and folding in the flour mixture, ¼ cup at a time, until all is used up.

Pour the batter into an ungreased 9-inch tube pan. Bake for 45 minutes without opening the oven door. To check the cake for doneness, press the top with your finger. The top should feel firm to the touch and spring back when you lift your finger. If necessary, cook the cake for 5 to 10 minutes more.

Remove the cake from the oven, invert, and let cool. (Many tube pans have leglike supports on the top to allow the air to circulate underneath when the cake is inverted. If your pan doesn't, invert it onto an upright bottle, with the neck of the bottle in the tube.) Let cool completely.

Gently run a sharp knife around the inside of the pan and around the tube to loosen the cake. Turn the cake out onto a platter. (You may need to give it a gentle shake.) Slice for serving.

Serves 10

169 CALORIES PER SERVING; 5 G PROTEIN; 0 G FAT; 38 G CARBOHYDRATE; 120 MG SODIUM; 0 MG CHOLESTEROL

MEXICAN CARAMEL CHEESECAKE

Here's a contemporary twist on a classic Mexican dessert: a cheesecake flavored with cajeta *(milk caramel). It requires only 10 minutes of preparation time (plus the time it takes the cajeta to cook), but jaws will drop with admiration when your guests taste it. Traditional cajeta is made with goat's milk, which gives it a pleasant sourish aftertaste. To achieve that flavor here, I add a little goat cheese. Not everyone likes goat cheese, however, so I've made it optional.*

1 pound low-fat cottage cheese (1 percent)

1 pound low-fat cream cheese, at room temperature

4 ounces soft goat cheese, like Montrachet (optional)

RICOTTA CHEESECAKE

For me this Italian dessert will always be associated with Boston's Italian neighborhood, the North End. I remember buying lovely ricotta cheesecakes at a tiny bakery (long since defunct) on Salem Street. They were sweet and creamy, fragrant with pine nuts and candied citrus peel, and free of the stick-to-the-roof-of-your-mouth cloy one sometimes encounters with New York–style cheesecakes. (I couldn't resist putting a little cream cheese in the following recipe—a non-Italian touch, perhaps, but it helps give the low-fat ricotta a little more richness.) If your fat budget allows it, use low-fat ricotta and cream cheese, not no-fat. They have substantially more flavor. No-fat cheese will, however, work in a pinch.

¼ cup marsala or other sweet wine

½ cup sultanas (yellow raisins)

2 pounds low-fat or no-fat ricotta cheese

½ pound low-fat cream cheese, at room temperature

1 cup sugar

3 tablespoons all-purpose unbleached white flour

¼ teaspoon salt

2 eggs, plus 5 egg whites, or 1 cup plus 2 tablespoons egg substitute

2 teaspoons finely grated fresh lemon zest

2 teaspoons finely grated fresh orange zest

1 tablespoon vanilla extract

¼ cup diced candied orange peel, lemon peel, or a mixture of both

¼ cup toasted pine nuts

1 8-inch springform pan, lightly sprayed with oil

14 ounces (1 batch) quick cajeta (made with no-fat sweetened condensed milk) (page 387)

1 cup egg substitute, or 2 eggs plus 4 egg whites

¼ cup brown sugar or piloncillo (see Note below) (or even white sugar)

2 tablespoons fresh lime juice

1 tablespoon vanilla extract

1 teaspoon grated lemon zest

1 teaspoon grated orange zest

½ teaspoon ground cinnamon

Pinch of salt

1. Preheat the oven to 350°F. (Set the rack in the lower third of the oven.) Bring 1 quart of water to a boil. Wrap a piece of foil around the bottom and sides of a lightly oiled 8-inch springform pan to prevent water from seeping in when the pan is placed in the water bath.

2. Purée the cottage cheese in the food processor, scraping down the sides.

This may take several minutes. Add the cream cheese, optional goat cheese, and the cajeta and purée until smooth. Add the eggs, egg whites, brown sugar, lime juice, vanilla, lemon and orange zest, cinnamon, and salt and purée. Strain the mixture into the prepared pan. Tap the pan a few times on the work counter to knock out any bubbles.

3. Set the springform pan in a roasting pan in the oven. Add 1 inch of boiling water to the roasting pan and bake the cheesecake until it is set, 40 to 60 minutes. To test for doneness, gently poke the side of the pan—when the top no longer jiggles, the cheesecake is cooked. Another test: An inserted skewer will come out clean when the cheesecake is cooked. Do not overcook, or the cheesecake will become watery.

4. Transfer the cheesecake to a cake rack to cool to room temperature, then

refrigerate until it's cold. To serve, run the tip of a small knife around the inside of the pan and unfasten the sides. Cut the cheesecake into wedges.

Note: *Piloncillo* is Mexican raw sugar; it comes in a cone and has a rich, earthy, malty flavor that's utterly unique. Look for it in Mexican grocery stores. (Dark brown sugar will work in a pinch.)

Variation: For a stunning presentation, pour ½ cup of sweetened condensed milk into a squirt bottle. Place ½ cup of your favorite chocolate sauce in another bottle. Squirt lines of the sauces across the top of the cheesecake to form a zigzag or crosshatch pattern.

Serves 10 to 12

277 CALORIES PER SERVING;* 16 G PROTEIN; 10 G FAT; 6 G SATURATED FAT; 32 G CARBOHYDRATE; 537 MG SODIUM; 24 MG CHOLESTEROL

Analysis is based on 10 servings.

1. Pour the marsala over the raisins in a small bowl and let soak until soft, about 10 minutes. Drain well.

2. Preheat the oven to 350°F. (The rack should be set in the upper third of the oven.) Bring 1 quart water to a boil. Wrap a piece of foil around the bottom and sides of the springform pan. (This prevents water from leaking in.)

3. Purée the ricotta in a food processor, scraping down the sides several times. Add the cream cheese and purée until smooth. Add the sugar, 2 tablespoons of the flour, and the salt and purée. Add the eggs, egg whites, lemon and orange zests, and vanilla and purée. Toss the raisins and candied orange peel with the remaining 1 tablespoon flour in a small bowl. Add the raisins, peel, and pine nuts to the batter and run the machine in short bursts to mix. (Do not purée; you want these ingredients to remain intact.) Pour the mixture into the prepared pan. Tap the pan a few times on the work counter to knock out any bubbles.

4. Set the pan in a roasting pan in the oven. Add 1-inch boiling water to the pan and bake the cheesecake until set, 40 to 60 minutes. To test for doneness, gently poke the side of the pan—when the top no longer jiggles, the cheesecake is done. Another test: A skewer inserted in the center will come out clean when the cheesecake is done. Do not overcook or the cheesecake will become watery.

5. Transfer the cheesecake to a wire rack to cool to room temperature, then refrigerate until cold, at least 4 hours. To serve, run the tip of a small knife around the inside of the pan. Unfasten the sides. Cut into wedges for serving.

Serves 12 to 16

261 CALORIES PER SERVING;* 16 G PROTEIN; 7 G FAT; 1 G SATURATED FAT; 34 G CARBOHYDRATE; 257 MG SODIUM; 47 MG CHOLESTEROL

Analysis is based on 12 servings.

REDUCED-FAT PIE SHELL

There's no way to make a crisp, flaky pie shell completely without fat. In the following recipe, I've replaced some of the butter with canola oil, which is a more healthful type of fat. The cornmeal and cake flour make the crust a little more crumbly than straight all-purpose flour would.

- ¾ cup unbleached all-purpose white flour (plus more as needed)
- 3 tablespoons cake flour
- 3 tablespoons fine cornmeal
- ½ teaspoon salt
- 2½ tablespoons cold unsalted butter (if using salted butter, reduce the salt above to ¼ teaspoon)
- 1 egg white
- 1½ tablespoons canola oil
- 3 tablespoons ice water, or as needed

1. Place the all-purpose flour, cake flour, cornmeal, salt, and butter in a food processor fitted with a chopping blade. Run the machine to cut in the butter: the mixture should feel crumbly, like sand.

2. Add the egg white, oil, and ice water. Pulse until the dough comes together into a smooth ball. (If the mixture looks too dry, add a little more ice water.) Flatten the ball of dough into a disk, wrap in plastic and refrigerate until firm, about 1 hour.

3. Preheat the oven to 400°F. Roll out the dough into an 11-inch circle on a lightly floured work surface, flouring the rolling pin as well. You can also roll it between 2 sheets of plastic wrap. Use the dough circle to line a 9-inch pie pan. Crimp or pleat the edges with your fingers or a fork. Prick the bottom of the crust with a fork and line with a sheet of foil. Freeze the crust for 5 minutes.

4. Fill the foil-lined crust with beans or rice and bake for 15 minutes. (The beans/rice hold the crust in shape during cooking.) Remove the beans or rice and foil and continue baking the crust until golden brown on the sides and bottom, 5 to 10 minutes more. Remove the crust from the oven and let it cool to room temperature before filling.

Makes 1 9-inch pie shell, enough to serve 8 to 10

122 CALORIES PER SERVING; 2 G PROTEIN; 7 G FAT; 2.6 G SATURATED FAT; 14 G CARBOHYDRATE; 141 MG SODIUM; 10 MG CHOLESTEROL

KEY LIME PIE

Key lime pie is one of the world's most refreshing desserts. I'm especially partial to it; it's the official dessert of my home state! The key lime is a small yellow fruit with a flavor that is both sour and bitter. To achieve a similar taste with widely available Persian limes, I add grated lime zest to both the filling and topping.

FOR THE CRUST:

- 1½ cups cinnamon-graham-cracker crumbs (about 15 square crackers)
- 2 tablespoons sugar
- 1 tablespoon butter, melted
- 2 tablespoons canola oil
- 1 large egg white, lightly beaten with a fork

FOR THE FILLING:

- 10 tablespoons fresh lime juice (4 to 6 limes)
- 1 tablespoon grated lime zest

- 2 tablespoons cornstarch
- 1 (14-ounce) can nonfat sweetened condensed skim milk
- 2 eggs

FOR THE MERINGUE:

- 4 egg whites
- ½ teaspoon cream of tartar
- ¾ cup sugar
- 3 tablespoons water
- 1 teaspoon grated lime zest
- spray oil

1. Preheat the oven to 350°F. Lightly spray a 9-inch tart pan with removable sides (preferably nonstick) with spray oil.

2. Make the crust: Put the graham-cracker crumbs, sugar, butter, oil, and egg white in a mixing bowl and combine with your fingers or a fork until moist and crumbly. (Alternatively, you can use a food processor.) Press the crumb mixture into the bottom and sides of the pie pan, using the back of a large spoon to smooth it. Bake until the crust is firm and lightly browned, about 10 minutes. Let cool to room temperature. Leave oven on.

3. While the crust is baking, prepare the filling. Put the lime juice, zest, cornstarch, condensed milk, and eggs in a heavy saucepan and whisk until smooth, about 2 minutes. Bring the filling to a boil, whisking steadily; it will thicken. Remove the pan from the heat and let the filling cool to room temperature. Spoon it into the crust.

4. Prepare the meringue: Place the egg whites in an electric mixer and start beating at low speed, about 1 minute. Add the cream of tartar. Gradually increase the speed to medium and continue beating until frothy, about

30 seconds. Keep the mixer at medium while you cook the sugar.

5. Place ½ cup of the sugar and the water in a saucepan with a lid. Cover and bring to a boil. Uncover and cook over medium-high heat to the softball stage (239°F. on a candy thermometer).

6. When the cooked sugar is ready, increase the mixer speed to high and beat the whites to soft peaks. Add the remaining ¼ cup sugar and beat until the whites are glossy and firm but not dry. The whole process will take about 8 minutes. With the mixer running, pour the hot sugar mixture and 1 teaspoon lime zest into the egg whites and continue beating until cool.

7. Adjust the broiler rack so that it is 6 inches below the heating element and preheat the broiler. (If your rack cannot be lowered sufficiently, bake at 500°F. for 5 to 8 minutes.) Spread or pipe the meringue in decorative swirls or rosettes on top of the filling. Run the pie under the broiler to brown the meringue, 1 to 2 minutes. Watch carefully, because the meringue burns easily. Refrigerate until serving.

Makes 1 9-inch pie, which will serve 8

373 CALORIES PER SERVING; 9 G PROTEIN; 8 G FAT; 1.8 G SATURATED FAT; 68 G CARBOHYDRATE; 205 MG SODIUM; 62 MG CHOLESTEROL

CHOCOLATE SILK PIE

Silk pie is an American classic, but most versions contain an unconscionable amount of butter. The meringue crust gives this one plenty of crunch without the fat. For a splurge, you could serve it with Meringue Whipped Cream (recipe follows).

spray oil

12 chocolate wafer cookies (about ¼ cup cookie crumbs)

⅔ cup sugar

3 tablespoons unsweetened Dutch-processed cocoa powder

3 large egg whites

¼ teaspoon cream of tartar

1 teaspoon vanilla extract

Low-Fat Chocolate Pudding (see page 347)

Meringue Whipped Cream (optional) (recipe follows)

Makes 1 9-inch pie, which will serve 8

337 CALORIES PER SERVING; 6 G PROTEIN; 11 G FAT; 2.7 G SATURATED FAT; 59 G CARBOHYDRATE; 205 MG SODIUM; 39 MG CHOLESTEROL

1. Preheat the oven to 300°F. Lightly spray a 9-inch pie pan with oil. Grind the cookies to a powder in a food processor. Sprinkle with half the cookie crumbs and set aside. Stir together ⅓ cup of the sugar and the cocoa, and set aside.

2. Beat the egg whites in an electric mixer at low speed 1 minute. Add the cream of tartar. Gradually increase the speed and beat the whites to soft peaks. Add the remaining ⅓ cup sugar in a thin stream and continue beating until the whites are firm and glossy but not dry. Stir in the vanilla. Using a rubber spatula, fold in the cocoa mixture as gently as possible. Spoon the meringue into the crumb-lined pie pan, spreading it across the bottom and up the sides.

3. Bake the meringue until crisp, 1½ to 2 hours. Transfer the pan to a wire rack to cool. Meanwhile, prepare the chocolate pudding.

4. Spoon the cooled pudding into the meringue shell and sprinkle with the remaining cookie crumbs. Cut into 8 wedges and serve with Meringue Whipped Cream, if desired.

Banana Cream Pie

MERINGUE WHIPPED CREAM

Lightened with meringue, this whipped topping contains a fraction of the fat found in regular whipped cream. For the best results in whipping the cream, chill the bowl, beaters, and cream in the freezer 20 minutes.

3 large egg whites

¼ teaspoon cream of tartar

½ cup plus 1 tablespoon sugar

3 tablespoons water

1 teaspoon vanilla extract

½ to ¾ cup heavy cream

1. Put the egg whites and cream of tartar in an electric mixer and start beating at low speed. Gradually increase the speed to medium and continue beating while you prepare the sugar syrup.

2. Put the ½ cup sugar and the water in a heavy saucepan with a lid. Cover and bring to a boil. Uncover and cook the sugar until medium-hot, to the softball stage (239°F. on a candy thermometer).

3. Increase the mixer speed to high and beat the whites to soft peaks. Add the remaining 1 tablespoon sugar and beat until the whites are glossy and firm but not dry. The process should take 8 minutes altogether. With the mixer running, pour the hot sugar

syrup into the egg whites. Add the vanilla and continue beating until completely cool.

4. Using a clean bowl and beaters, beat the cream almost until stiff peaks form. Gently fold the meringue into the whipped cream with a rubber spatula.

Makes about 2 cups, which will serve 10 to 12

110 CALORIES PER SERVING; 2 G PROTEIN; 5.5 G FAT; 3.4 G SATURATED FAT; 14 G CARBOHYDRATE; 34 MG SODIUM; 20 MG CHOLESTEROL

BANANA CREAM PIE

*Like most traditional American desserts, banana cream pie is loaded with fat and calories. To reduce the fat in the crust,
I use zwieback crumbs, oil, and cider. A teaspoon of gelatin allows for a substantial reduction of eggs in the filling,
while banana liqueur provides the yellow color lost by reducing the egg yolks.*

FOR THE CRUST:

¾ cup zwieback crumbs (3 ounces cookies)

¾ cup graham cracker crumbs (6 whole crackers)

1 tablespoon brown sugar

½ teaspoon ground ginger

¼ teaspoon ground cinnamon

¼ teaspoon freshly grated nutmeg

1 tablespoon canola oil

1 tablespoon butter, softened

3 tablespoons apple cider or water

FOR THE FILLING:

3 small ripe bananas

1 teaspoon fresh lime juice

1 teaspoon gelatin

2 tablespoons water

1 cup skim milk

3 tablespoons light brown sugar

2 tablespoons flour

2 eggs, separated, plus 1 egg white

1 tablespoon grated fresh ginger
(or 1 tablespoon chopped candied ginger)

2 tablespoons banana liqueur

1 teaspoon vanilla extract

⅛ teaspoon cream of tartar

¼ cup granulated sugar

To make the crust, preheat the oven to 375°F. Combine the zwieback and graham cracker crumbs, brown sugar, and spices in a food processor and process for 1 minute. Add the oil, butter, and cider, and process until the ingredients come together into a crumbly dough. Add a little more cider if necessary. Press the dough into the bottom and sides of a lightly oiled 9-inch pie pan or 10-inch tart pan with a removable bottom. Bake for 10 minutes, or until lightly browned. Remove the pan from the oven and let cool.

To make the filling, peel and thinly slice the bananas. Toss with lime juice to prevent discoloring. Arrange the bananas over the bottom of the crust. Sprinkle the gelatin over the water in a metal measuring cup or small saucepan. Let stand for 5 minutes, or until soft and spongy. Warm over medium heat, stirring, until the gelatin dissolves. Preheat the oven to 500°F.

Scald the milk in a heavy saucepan, whisking constantly. (Skim milk burns easily, so be sure to whisk it as it cooks.) Combine the light brown sugar, flour, egg yolks, and ginger in a bowl and whisk until smooth. Whisk the scalded milk into the sugar mixture in a thin stream. Return the mixture to the pan and boil for 2 minutes, whisking constantly. The mixture will bubble and thicken. Remove the pan from the heat and whisk in the dissolved gelatin, banana liqueur, and vanilla.

Beat the egg whites and cream of tartar at medium speed until the whites begin to stiffen. Increase the speed to high, gradually add the granulated sugar, and beat the whites until firm and glossy. Gently fold ¼ of the whites into the milk mixture. Spoon this mixture into the pie shell over the bananas. Smooth the top with a wet spatula.

Using a piping bag fitted with a large star tip, pipe the remaining meringue on top of the pie in stars or rosettes. Bake 2 to 3 minutes, or until the meringue is well browned. (Watch it closely; meringue burns quickly!) Let cool to room temperature, then refrigerate for at least 3 hours. Cut into wedges and serve.

Serves 6 to 8

353 CALORIES PER SERVING; 8 G PROTEIN; 9 G FAT; 59 G CARBOHYDRATE;
177 MG SODIUM; 80 MG CHOLESTEROL

SWEET-POTATO PIE

This spicy sweet-potato pie is a healthy remake of a Southern classic. High-heat roasting caramelizes the sugars in the sweet potatoes, producing a firm, dense consistency and exceptionally rich flavor.

1½ pounds sweet potatoes
   (3 to 4 potatoes, 2 cups pulp)

¾ cup packed dark-brown sugar

1 large egg plus 4 large egg whites
   or ¾ cup egg substitute

1 cup evaporated skim milk

1 teaspoon ground cinnamon

½ teaspoon ground ginger

⅛ teaspoon ground cloves

⅛ teaspoon grated nutmeg
   (3 passes on a grater)

2 tablespoons dark rum

1 teaspoon vanilla extract

9-inch prebaked Reduced-Fat Pie
   Shell (see page 330)

1. Preheat the oven to 400°F. Scrub the sweet potatoes and put them in a baking dish. Roast until very soft, about 40 minutes. Remove the pan from the oven and reduce the heat to 350°F. (You can roast the sweet potatoes up to 2 days ahead.) When the sweet potatoes are cool enough to handle, peel them and purée the flesh in a food processor. (Alternatively, you can mash them with a potato masher and stir in the remaining ingredients by hand.) You should have 2 cups.

2. Add the sugar and the eggs or egg substitute and process until smooth. Add the milk, cinnamon, ginger, cloves, nutmeg, rum, and vanilla, and process to mix. Spoon the filling into the pie shell.

3. Bake until the filling is set, 20 to 30 minutes. Transfer to a wire rack to cool. Cut into 8 or 10 wedges to serve.

Makes 1 9-inch pie, which will serve 8 to 10

371 CALORIES PER SERVING; 9 G PROTEIN; 9 G FAT; 3.2 SATURATED FAT; 62 G CARBOHYDRATE; 273 MG SODIUM; 39 MG CHOLESTEROL

LEMON RASPBERRY TARTLETS

In my family I'm known as the sourpuss because of my fondness for lemons. I can't resist a good lemon pie. This tart features a topping of fresh raspberries in place of the coying sweetness of the usual meringue. Again, I use Chinese wonton wrappers to make a quick, crisp, virtually fat-free crust.

FOR THE CRUST:

spray oil or 1 tablespoon butter, melted

6 eggroll wrappers (available in the produce section of most supermarkets)

FOR THE FILLING:

1½ cups sugar

2 tablespoons plus 1 teaspoon cornstarch
   (7 teaspoons in all)

2 eggs, plus 2 egg whites (or another egg)

1½ cups fresh lemon juice (5 to 6 lemons)

1½ tablespoons finely grated fresh lemon zest

2 pints fresh raspberries

confectioners' sugar for sprinkling

6 3½-inch tartlet pans

FRESH FIG TARTLETS

These attractive tartlets are completely Italian in spirit, but they call for one thoroughly un-Italian ingredient:
eggroll wrappers. Readers of my High-Flavor, Low-Fat Desserts *book will be familiar with the use of*
eggroll wrappers to make crisp, almost fat-free tartlet shells. These tartlets taste best assembled just prior to serving.
Fortunately, if you have all the components ready, this takes only five minutes.

FOR THE CRUST:

1 tablespoon butter, melted, or spray oil

6 eggroll wrappers (available in the produce section of most supermarkets)

1 recipe Pastry Cream (pg 386) (can be prepared while the crusts are cooling)

1 tablespoon marsala wine or grappa

18 ripe figs
(I like the look of purple figs, but you can also use green)

FOR THE GLAZE:

3 tablespoons commercial strawberry glaze or 3 tablespoons red currant jelly

1 tablespoon chopped toasted pistachio nuts (optional)

6 3½-inch tartlet pans

1. Preheat the oven to 400°F. Brush the tartlet pans with melted butter or spray with oil. Use the eggroll wrappers to line the pans, pushing the dough into the ridges in the sides, trimming off the excess with scissors. Brush the insides of the shells with melted butter or spray with oil. Bake until crisp and golden-brown, 6 to 8 minutes, or as needed. Transfer the shells to a wire rack to cool.

2. Meanwhile, prepare the pastry cream and let cool. Whisk in the marsala.

3. Stem the figs and cut each one lengthwise into quarters. If using red currant jelly for the glaze, melt it in a small saucepan with 1 or 2 tablespoons water, whisking with a wire whisk.

4. To assemble the tartlets, spoon or pipe the pastry cream into the tartlet shells. Stand the fig quarters upright in the cream. Brush the tops of the figs with glaze and sprinkle with pistachio nuts, if using.

Note: Fresh figs are a summer fruit. At other times of the year, a similar tart could be made with fresh strawberries or blackberries.

Serves 6

236 CALORIES PER SERVING; 5 G PROTEIN; 4 G FAT; 2 G SATURATED FAT; 47 G CARBOHYDRATE; 118 MG SODIUM; 42 MG CHOLESTEROL

---

1. Preheat the oven to 400°F. Prepare the tartlet shells: Lightly spray the tartlet pans with spray oil (or brush with melted butter). Use the eggroll wrappers to line the pans, pushing the dough into the ridges in the sides. Trim off the excess with scissors. Lightly spray the insides of the tartlet shells with oil or brush with butter. Bake until crisp and golden brown, 6 to 8 minutes, or as needed. Transfer the shells to a wire rack to cool.

2. Meanwhile, prepare the lemon filling. Combine the sugar and cornstarch in a mixing bowl and whisk to mix. Whisk in the eggs and egg whites. Bring the lemon juice and lemon zest to a boil in a heavy saucepan. Whisk this mixture in a thin stream into the egg mixture. Return the mixture to the pan and bring to a boil, whisking

steadily. Reduce the heat and simmer for 1 minute or until thickened. Transfer the lemon mixture to a bowl and let cool to room temperature. The tartlets can be made ahead to this stage, but they must be assembled at the last minute. Store the shells in an airtight container, and the filling in the refrigerator.

3. Not more than 5 minutes before serving, spoon the lemon filling into the crusts. Arrange the fresh raspberries on top and sprinkle the tartlets with confectioners' sugar. Serve at once.

Serves 6

315 CALORIES PER SERVING; 5 G PROTEIN; 2 G FAT; 95 G SATURATED FAT; 73 G CARBOHYDRATE; 60 MG SODIUM; 71 MG CHOLESTEROL

TIRAMISU

In the late 1980s, tiramisu burst from relative obscurity to international superstardom. The reason? Tiramisu (which literally means "pick me up") has everything a dessert lover could ask for: espresso and brandy-soaked ladyfingers, a silken cream filling, a flavor scale that runs from the bass notes of coffee and cocoa to the clarion tones of cinnamon and vanilla. My reduced-fat version replaces some of the mascarpone (Italian clotted cream) with low-fat pastry cream. For an even lower-fat version of the dish, you could substitute reduced-fat cream cheese for the mascarpone. The traditional brand of ladyfingers for this dish is Vincenzo, which are available at Italian markets and gourmet shops. If unavailable, use slices of sponge cake.

FOR THE CREAM FILLING:

1 cup skim milk

1 3-inch cinnamon stick

1 2-inch piece vanilla bean, cut in half

¼ cup sugar, plus 3 tablespoons for beating the egg whites

1½ tablespoons cornstarch

1 egg, plus 2 egg whites

1½ teaspoons finely grated fresh lemon zest

¼ cup mascarpone (2 ounces) or low-fat or no-fat cream cheese, at room temperature

¼ teaspoon cream of tartar

TO FINISH THE TIRAMISU:

2 dozen ladyfingers or one (basic sponge cake) (page 324), cut into ¼-inch slices

¼ cup cold espresso coffee

2 tablespoons good-quality brandy or rum

1 tablespoon water

2 tablespoons sugar, or to taste

3 to 4 tablespoons unsweetened cocoa powder

Serves 6

311 CALORIES PER SERVING; 10 G PROTEIN; 7 G FAT; 3 G SATURATED FAT; 52 G CARBOHYDRATE; 170 MG SODIUM; 200 MG CHOLESTEROL

1. Prepare the cream filling: Combine the milk, cinnamon, vanilla, and 1 tablespoon of the sugar in a saucepan and gradually bring to a boil, stirring often. (Stirring prevents the milk from scorching.) Meanwhile, in a mixing bowl, whisk together 3 tablespoons sugar and the cornstarch. Add the whole egg and the lemon zest and whisk to mix.

2. Whisk the scalded milk into the egg mixture in a thin stream. Return the mixture to the pan and bring to a boil, whisking steadily. Reduce the heat and cook until thickened, about 2 minutes. The mixture should bubble. Remove the pan from the heat and remove and discard the vanilla bean and cinnamon stick. Whisk in the mascarpone.

3. Beat the 2 egg whites and cream of tartar until firm and glossy but not dry, adding the remaining 3 tablespoons sugar as the whites stiffen. Fold the whites into the warm custard mixture. Let cool to room temperature.

4. Arrange a layer of 12 of the ladyfingers in the bottom of an attractive serving dish or platter (about 12-inches across). Combine the espresso, brandy, water, and 2 tablespoons sugar in a small bowl. Whisk until the sugar is dissolved. (Add sugar to taste.) Brush half this mixture on the ladyfingers, using a pastry brush. Spread half the mascarpone mixture on top and sprinkle with half the cocoa. (Place the cocoa in a sifter or sift it through a strainer.)

5. Place a second layer of ladyfingers on top. Brush with the remaining espresso mixture, and spread with the remaining mascarpone mixture. Refrigerate the tiramisu for 3 to 4 hours to allow the flavors to blend. Just before serving, sift the remaining cocoa on top.

AMAZING LOW-FAT CANNOLI

This popular Sicilian dessert might seem like an unlikely candidate for a low-fat makeover—after all, what could be worse for you than a tube of fried dough stuffed with whipped ricotta cheese? But my low-fat version will shatter into a thousand buttery flakes, just like traditional cannoli. The secret? The pastry tubes are made with Chinese wonton wrappers, which are baked instead of fried. The recipe is extremely easy to make, but you must start the night before to drain the cheese.

FOR THE FILLING:

2 pints no-fat or low-fat ricotta cheese

6 tablespoons sugar, or to taste

1 teaspoon rosewater

½ teaspoon vanilla extract

TO FINISH THE CANNOLI:

spray oil

12 4-inch wonton wrappers

1 teaspoon cornstarch dissolved in 1 teaspoon water

1 tablespoon melted butter or canola oil or more spray oil

1 tablespoon chopped, toasted pistachio nuts

Amazing Low-Fat Cannoli

1. The night before, place the ricotta in a yogurt strainer or cheesecloth- or paper-towel-lined strainer over a bowl. Drain overnight in the refrigerator. Discard the whey.

2. Preheat the oven to 400°F. Lightly spray 12 cannoli tubes with spray oil. Starting with the corner of one wonton wrapper in the center, roll the wrapper around the tube. Glue the opposite corner to the tube with a dab of cornstarch paste. Brush the outside of the cannoli with melted butter or oil, or spray with more oil. Roll up all the wrappers the same way. Bake the cannoli until golden brown and crisp, about 4 to 6 minutes. Let cool slightly, then slide the pastry shells off the tubes. Let the shells cool to room temperature on a wire rack.

3. Finish the filling: In a large bowl, combine the drained ricotta, sugar, rosewater, and vanilla and whisk to mix. Correct the sweetness, adding sugar or rosewater to taste. Transfer the filling to a piping bag fitted with a ½-inch star tip. The recipe can be prepared several hours ahead to this stage. Store the shells in an airtight container. Store the filling in the refrigerator, up to 24 hours.

4. Just before serving, pipe the ricotta mixture into the pastry shells, a little into each end. As you withdraw the piping tube, make a rosette at each end. Sprinkle the ends with chopped pistachios and serve at once.

Note: The perfumed flavoring called rosewater is available in Middle Eastern grocery stores and gourmet shops. If it's unavailable, substitute vanilla or maraschino liqueur.

Makes 12 cannolis, enough to serve 6 to 12

284 CALORIES PER SERVING;* 18 G PROTEIN; 8 G FAT; 1 G SATURATED FAT; 33 G CARBOHYDRATE; 814 MG SODIUM; 7 MG CHOLESTEROL

Analysis is based on 6 servings.

BANANA STRUDEL

Here's a tropical remake of a classic Austrian dessert. My favorite banana for this recipe is the apple banana, but any banana will do.

FOR THE FILLING:

5 large ripe bananas

½ cup raisins

Juice and grated zest of 1 lemon

1 cinnamon stick

2-inch piece vanilla bean, split

1 tablespoon dark rum

¼ cup packed light-brown sugar, or to taste

1 tablespoon cornstarch

1 tablespoon banana liqueur (or more rum)

TO FINISH THE STRUDEL:

1 tablespoon butter, melted

1 tablespoon light olive oil or canola oil

¼ cup cinnamon-graham-cracker crumbs or dry bread crumbs (plus extra for sprinkling)

¼ cup granulated sugar

8 14 x 18-inch sheets filo dough

1. For the filling: Thinly slice the bananas and put them in a heavy nonreactive saucepan. Add the raisins, lemon juice and zest, cinnamon, vanilla, rum, and brown sugar, and stir to combine. Cook over medium heat until the bananas are just tender, 2 to 4 minutes. Correct the sweetness with more brown sugar if necessary.

2. Stir the cornstarch into the banana liqueur and add it to the bananas. Simmer 30 seconds, or until the mixture thickens. Let the filling cool to room temperature and remove the cinnamon stick and vanilla bean. Refrigerate the filling until cold.

3. Preheat the oven to 375°F. Finish the strudel: Combine the melted butter and oil in one small bowl, the graham-cracker crumbs and sugar in another. Place the filo sheets on a work surface that has been covered with plastic wrap. Place a piece of plastic wrap on top of the filo and cover it with a damp dish towel. Keep the sheets of filo covered

until the last possible moment to prevent them from drying out as you work.

4. Lay one sheet of filo dough on a clean dish towel with a long edge toward you. Lightly brush it with some of the butter mixture and sprinkle with a level tablespoon of the crumb mixture. Lay another sheet of filo on top, brush with more of the butter mixture, and sprinkle with the crumb mixture. Repeat with a third and fourth sheet of filo.

5. Mound half the banana filling in a row along the long edge closer to you. Roll up halfway, lifting the dish towel to help. Fold in the short ends and continue rolling the strudel. Carefully transfer it, seam side down, to a baking sheet. Assemble the second strudel the same way. Brush the tops of the strudels with the rest of the butter mixture and sprinkle with the rest of the crumb mixture.

6. Using a sharp knife, lightly score the tops of the strudels (don't cut all the way through to the filling). Bake the strudels until they are crisp and golden brown, 30 to 40 minutes. Let cool slightly, then cut into slices on the diagonal with a serrated knife.

Note: You could also spoon the banana filling into the Filo Nests on page 341.

Makes 2 strudels, which will serve 8 to 10

218 CALORIES PER SERVING; 2 G PROTEIN; 4 G FAT; 1.3 G SATURATED FAT; 46 G CARBOHYDRATE; 61 MG SODIUM; 4 MG CHOLESTEROL

Apple Turnovers

APPLE TURNOVERS

I'll never forget my first "exam" at the LaVarenne cooking school in Paris. I was asked to prepare chaussons aux pommes—*apple turnovers. This required the laborious confection of puff pastry, a process that used more butter for a single dessert than I would now go through in a fortnight. My low-fat version features filo dough lightly brushed with a mixture of butter and oil and layered with bread crumbs and sugar for extra crunch. Leftover turnovers make a great treat for breakfast.*

FOR THE FILLING:

2 pounds firm tart apples, peeled, cored, and cut into ¼-inch dice (about 5 cups)

3 tablespoons fresh lemon juice, plus more as needed

Grated zest of 1 lemon

2 cups apple cider

1 cinnamon stick

2-inch piece vanilla bean, split

⅛ teaspoon ground cloves

¼ cup packed light-brown sugar, or to taste

¾ cup raisins

1 tablespoon cornstarch

1 tablespoon dark rum

1 to 2 tablespoons lightly toasted bread crumbs

TO FINISH THE TURNOVERS:

spray oil

1½ tablespoons butter, melted

1½ tablespoons light olive oil or canola oil

¼ cup lightly toasted bread crumbs or graham-cracker crumbs

¼ cup granulated sugar

12 14 x 18-inch sheets filo dough

Confectioners' sugar for dusting

1. For the filling: In a nonreactive bowl, toss the diced apple with the 3 tablespoons lemon juice to prevent discoloration. Put the zest, cider, cinnamon, vanilla, cloves, and brown sugar in a large nonreactive saucepan and bring to a boil. Reduce the heat to medium, add the apples and raisins, and gently simmer until the apples are tender but not too soft, 3 to 5 minutes.

2. Remove the apples and raisins with a slotted spoon and reserve. Boil the liquid until it is reduced to a thick, syrupy glaze. Remove and discard the cinnamon stick and vanilla bean. Dissolve the cornstarch in the rum and stir the apple mixture into the glaze. Return the apples and raisins to the pot and bring to a boil; the mixture will thicken. Taste and correct the seasoning with brown sugar or lemon juice. Transfer the mixture to a bowl set over ice and stir until cold. The cooled mixture should be fairly dry; if it is too wet, add 1 to 2 tablespoons bread crumbs.

3. Preheat the oven to 400°F. Lightly spray a nonstick baking pan with spray oil. Finish the turnovers: Combine the melted butter and oil in one small bowl, the bread crumbs or graham-cracker crumbs and granulated sugar in another. Place the filo sheets on a work surface that has been covered with plastic wrap. Place a piece of plastic wrap on top of the filo and cover it with a damp dish towel. Keep the sheets of filo covered until the last possible moment to prevent them from drying out as you work.

4. Lay one sheet of filo dough on a cutting board with a short edge toward you. Lightly brush it with the butter mixture and sprinkle with 2 level teaspoonfuls of the bread-crumb mixture. Lay another sheet of filo on top of it, brush with the butter mixture, and sprinkle with a

heaping teaspoonful of the bread-crumb mixture. Cut the sheet lengthwise into 3 strips.

5. Place 2 to 3 tablespoons of the apple mixture 2 inches below the top edge of each strip in the center. Fold a top corner of the strip over the filling, lining up the edges to form a triangle. Continue folding the strip (as you would a flag) to obtain a triangle-shaped turnover. Repeat the process with the other 2 strips, and then with the rest of the filo dough and filling, to make 18 turnovers. Lightly brush the tops of the turnovers with the butter mixture and transfer them to the prepared baking pan. (The turnovers can be frozen at this stage and thawed overnight in the refrigerator.)

6. Bake the turnovers until they are crisp and nicely browned, 15 to 20 minutes. Transfer them to a wire rack to cool slightly. Dust with confectioners' sugar and serve at once.

Makes 18 turnovers (2 to 3 per person)

251 CALORIES PER SERVING; 2 G PROTEIN; 5 G FAT; 1.6 G SATURATED FAT; 54 G CARBOHYDRATE; 84 MG SODIUM; 5 MG CHOLESTEROL

CREAM-FILLED CRÊPES

When I learned to make crêpes at cooking school in Paris, my teachers would compete to see who could put the most butter and eggs in the batter. They'd probably be astonished by the following crêpes, which are virtually fat-free. The trick is to replace most of the eggs with egg whites and use low-fat buttermilk in place of butter. **Note:** *Be very careful when you flambé. Keep your face away from the pan and take care not to spill any of the flaming liquid on the tablecloth, the napkins, or your clothes.*

FOR THE CRÊPES:

1 large egg plus 2 large egg whites

½ cup low-fat buttermilk

¾ cup water, plus more as necessary

½ teaspoon sugar

½ teaspoon salt, or to taste

1 teaspoon canola oil

1 cup unbleached white flour

spray oil

FILO NESTS

Filo nests are the easiest of all filo dough confections to make, yet these freeform pastry shells with their delicately crinkled sides make for a dramatic presentation. Possible fillings include lemon curd or orange curd, Low-Fat Chocolate Pudding (see page 347), Duet of Poached Pears (see page 357), and Banana Strudel filling (see page 338).

4 14 x 18-inch sheets filo dough

spray oil

1 tablespoon light olive oil or canola oil, or a mixture of the two

1. Preheat the oven to 400°F. Lightly spray 8 3½-inch tartlet molds or a muffin tin with spray oil. Place the filo sheets on a work surface that has been covered with plastic wrap. Place a piece of plastic wrap on top of the filo and cover it with a damp dish towel. Keep the sheets of filo covered until the last possible moment to prevent them from drying out as you work.

2. Lay one sheet of filo dough on a cutting board with a long edge toward you. Lightly brush it with the oil. Cut the sheet in half crosswise and then into 6 strips lengthwise, each about 2¼ inches wide. Use these 12 rectangles to line 2 of the tartlet molds. Tuck one end of the strip into a corner of a mold. Bring the remainder of the strip across the bottom, up the side, and into the air, crinkling it slightly. Add a second strip at a 60-degree angle to the first and continue forming the sides of the nest. Continue lining the mold until 6 strips are used up. Line the other mold the same way, and repeat the process with the other sheets of filo dough and other molds.

3. Bake the filo nests until they are crisp and golden brown, about 10 minutes. Transfer to a wire rack to cool. Keep them in a cool, dry place. If they become soggy, recrisp them in a 350°F. oven.

Makes 8 filo nests

25 CALORIES PER NEST; 0.5 G PROTEIN; 1 G FAT; 0.9 SATURATED FAT; 3 G CARBOHYDRATE; 30 MG SODIUM; 4 MG CHOLESTEROL

FOR THE FILLING:
Lemon curd, orange curd, or Low-Fat Chocolate Pudding (see page 347)

FOR THE FLAMBÉING (OPTIONAL):

½ cup rum (preferably 150— see Note)

1. Put the egg and the egg whites in a mixing bowl and whisk to combine. Whisk in the buttermilk, water, sugar, salt, and oil. Sift in the flour and whisk gently just to mix. (Do not overmix, or the crêpes will be rubbery.) If the batter looks lumpy, strain it. It should be the consistency of heavy cream. If it is too thick, thin it with a little more water.

2. Lightly spray a 7-inch frying pan or crêpe pan with oil and heat over a medium flame until a drop of water evaporates in 2 to 3 seconds. Off the heat, add a scant ¼ cup of crêpe batter to the pan all at once. Gently tilt and rotate the pan to coat the bottom with a thin layer of batter. Pour back any excess; the crêpe should be as thin as possible. Cook until the crêpe is lightly browned on both sides, 1 to 2 minutes per side, turning it with a spatula. As the crêpes are done, stack them on a plate. For the best results, spray the pan with oil after each one. The crêpes can be prepared up to 24 hours ahead to this stage. Store in the refrigerator on a plate covered with plastic wrap.

3. Arrange a crêpe, pale side up, on a plate. Place a heaping tablespoonful of filling in the center. Roll up the crêpe or fold it in half, then in half again. Arrange the crêpes on individual plates or a large platter.

4. To flambé the crêpes, gently warm the rum in a small saucepan, being careful not to let it boil or even become too hot to touch. Bring a lighted match to the surface of the rum and stand back: it will ignite. Pour the flaming rum over the crêpes and serve at once.

Note: 150 rum is an ovenproof rum that's great for flambéing because it seems to burn forever, but regular rum or brandy will work, too.

Makes 14 to 16 crêpes

112 CALORIES PER SERVING; 3 G PROTEIN; 1 G FAT; 0.3 G SATURATED FAT; 24 G CARBOHYDRATE; 103 MG SODIUM; 31 MG CHOLESTEROL

INDIVIDUAL ZUPPA INGLESES

*You don't need a degree in Italian gastronomy to know
that* zuppa inglese *means "English soup." And that it's not really soup at all,
but a sort of trifle made by layering liqueur-soaked sponge cake with fresh
fruit and custard. I like to serve zuppa inglese in individual wineglasses, but you
could certainly use a large glass bowl. This is another dessert that actually tastes
best made a few hours ahead of time to allow the flavors to blend.*

FOR THE CUSTARD SAUCE:

- 2 cups skim milk
- 1 2-inch piece vanilla bean, cut in half
- 1 2-inch piece cinnamon stick
- 5 tablespoons sugar
- 2 tablespoons cornstarch
- 2 eggs, plus 1 egg white
- 1 teaspoon finely grated fresh lemon zest

- 1 sponge cake (page 324) or angelfood cake, cut into 1-inch cubes (you'll need 6 to 8 cups diced cake)
- 3 to 4 tablespoons maraschino liqueur or kirsch
- 1½ cups diced fresh ripe fruit, including peaches, plums, pears, or apricots
- 1½ cups fresh berries, including sliced strawberries and/or whole blueberries, raspberries, and blackberries
- 8 sprigs fresh mint

1. Prepare the custard sauce: Combine the milk, vanilla bean, and cinnamon stick and 2 tablespoons of the sugar in a saucepan and gradually bring to a boil, stirring often. (Stirring prevents the milk from scorching.) Meanwhile, in a mixing bowl whisk together the remaining 3 tablespoons sugar and the cornstarch. Add the eggs, egg white, and lemon zest, and whisk to mix. Whisk the scalded milk into the egg mixture in a thin stream. Return the mixture to the pan and bring to a boil, whisking steadily. Reduce the heat and cook until slightly thick, about 2 minutes. The mixture should bubble.

Individual Zuppa Ingleses

2. Remove the vanilla bean and cinnamon stick with tongs. Press a piece of plastic wrap on top of the cream to prevent a skin from forming. Make a slit in it to allow the steam to escape. Let the cream cool to room temperature, then chill.

3. Place a layer of cake cubes in the bottom of 8 large wine goblets or compote glasses. Sprinkle with maraschino liqueur. Spoon in a layer of custard sauce and top with fresh fruit and berries. Sprinkle with more maraschino. Continue layering the cake, custard, and fruit until all are used up, sprinkling with maraschino as you go. The zuppa ingleses can be prepared several hours ahead of time. Store in the refrigerator covered with plastic wrap. Just before serving, garnish each serving with a sprig of fresh mint.

Note: A great recipe for a low-fat sponge cake is found on page 324. To save time, you could use store-bought cake. (I'd use store-bought angel food, as few sponge cakes are as low in fat as mine.) Maraschino is a liqueur made not from cloying maraschino cherries, but from *marascas*, wild sour cherries from northeast Italy. The *marasca* has a nutty flavor reminiscent of almonds. It's well worth the trouble of finding real maraschino—look for it in Italian spirit shops and specialty liquor stores.

Serves 8

298 CALORIES PER SERVING; 9 G PROTEIN; 6 G FAT; 2.7 G SATURATED FAT; 50 G CARBOHYDRATE; 115 MG SODIUM; 115 MG CHOLESTEROL

PANNE COTTA

Panne cotta *(literally, "cooked cream") is a dessert of astonishing simplicity, a sort of Jell-O made with milk and heavy cream. When properly prepared, it will be set—but quivering, not so hard that you can bounce a spoon off of it. My low-fat version uses skim milk—plus a nontraditional ingredient: sweetened condensed skim milk for richness. The real flavor comes from the spices and seasonings: vanilla, cinnamon, almond extract, and lemon zest. For a pretty presentation, serve* panne cotta *on pools of fruit sauce.*

1½ envelopes gelatin, softened over 3 tablespoons cold water

2 cups skim milk

1 cup sweetened condensed skim milk (for an even lower-fat dessert, use no-fat sweetened condensed milk)

1 piece vanilla bean, 2 inches long, split, or 1 teaspoon vanilla extract

1 teaspoon finely grated fresh lemon zest

1 3-inch cinnamon stick, or ½ teaspoon ground cinnamon

½ teaspoon almond extract

spray oil

6 ½-cup ramekins

1. Sprinkle the gelatin over the water in a small bowl. Let stand until spongy, about 5 minutes.

2. Combine the skim milk, condensed milk, vanilla bean, lemon zest, and cinnamon stick in a heavy saucepan. Heat the mixture to simmering but do not let it boil. Simmer the seasonings in the milk over low heat for 10 minutes. Remove the pan from the heat and whisk in the gelatin and almond extract.

3. Spray the ramekins with oil. Strain the panne cotta mixture into the ramekins. Let cool to room temperature, then cover with plastic wrap and refrigerate until firm (at least 4 hours, as long as overnight).

4. To serve the panne cotta, run the tip of a paring knife around the inside of the ramekins. Put a dessert plate over a ramekin, invert, and give a little shake: the panne cotta should slide out easily. Serve with the raspberry or peach sauce on pages 349.

Serves 6

202 CALORIES PER SERVING; 8 G PROTEIN; 5 G FAT; 3 G SATURATED FAT; 32 G CARBOHYDRATE; 109 MG SODIUM; 19 MG CHOLESTEROL

FRUIT SAUCES

Use these colorful fruit sauces the way an artist would paint; to create shimmering pools or whimsical squiggles of color. I always try to keep a few fruit sauces on hand in squirt bottles. Refrigerated, they'll keep for one or two weeks.

STRAWBERRY SAUCE

1 quart ripe strawberries, hulled

2 tablespoons strawberry preserves

2 to 4 tablespoons confectioners' sugar

1 tablespoon fresh lemon juice, or to taste

Purée the berries and strawberry preserves in a food processor or blender, adding sugar or lemon juice to taste. Strain the sauce into a bowl.

Makes about 2 cups (¼ cup per serving)

18 CALORIES PER SERVING;
0 G PROTEIN; 0 G FAT;
0 G SATURATED FAT;
5 G CARBOHYDRATE;
1 MG SODIUM;
0 MG CHOLESTEROL

RASPBERRY SAUCE

3 cups fresh raspberries or 1 10-ounce package frozen, thawed

2 to 4 tablespoons confectioners' sugar, or as needed

1 tablespoon fresh lemon juice, or to taste

Purée the berries in a food processor, adding sugar and lemon juice to taste. Run the machine in brief bursts. Don't overpurée, or you'll crush the raspberry seeds, which would make the sauce bitter. Strain the sauce into a bowl.

Makes about ¾ cup (3 tablespoons per serving)

61 CALORIES PER SERVING;
1 G PROTEIN; 0.5 G FAT;
0 G SATURATED FAT;
15 G CARBOHYDRATE;
0 MG SODIUM;
0 MG CHOLESTEROL

BLACKBERRY SAUCE

3 cups fresh blackberries or 1 10-ounce package frozen, thawed

2 to 4 tablespoons confectioners' sugar, or as needed

1 tablespoon fresh lemon juice, or to taste

1 tablespoon black currant liqueur (optional)

Purée the berries in a food processor, adding sugar, lemon juice, and black currant liqueur to taste. Run the machine in brief bursts. Don't overpurée, or you'll crush the blackberry seeds, which would make the sauce bitter. Strain the sauce into a bowl.

Makes about ¾ cup (3 tablespoons per serving)

72 CALORIES PER SERVING;
1 G PROTEIN; 0.4 G FAT;
0 G SATURATED FAT;
18 G CARBOHYDRATE;
0 MG SODIUM;
0 MG CHOLESTEROL

PEACH SAUCE

2 ripe peaches (about 1 pound—enough to make 2 cups diced peaches)

2 tablespoons confectioners' sugar, or to taste

1 tablespoon fresh lemon juice, or to taste

2 to 4 tablespoons fresh orange juice or water (enough to thin the sauce to a pourable consistency)

Peel the peaches and cut the flesh off the stones. Purée in a food processor, adding sugar and lemon juice to taste and enough orange juice or water to obtain a pourable consistency. Strain the peach sauce into a bowl.

Makes about 2 cups (¼ cup per serving)

20 CALORIES PER SERVING;
0 G PROTEIN; 0 G FAT;
0 G SATURATED FAT;
5 G CARBOHYDRATE;
0 MG SODIUM;
0 MG CHOLESTEROL

TWO FLANS

Like many desserts, flan was brought to Mexico by the Spanish, but Mexican cooks have given it a distinctive personality, adding local spices and seasonings. My low-fat rendition takes advantage of the richness of sweetened condensed milk to compensate for the loss of most of the egg yolks. Below are two versions: an orange anise flan bursting with Arabic flavors and a Oaxacan chocolate flan guaranteed to satisfy the most diehard chocoholic.

ORANGE ANISE FLAN

This recipe has Spanish roots, but the flavorings are Middle Eastern. This isn't as odd as it sounds, given the fact that Spain was occupied by the Moors for several centuries and that Mexico welcomed thousands of Lebanese immigrants in the early 1900s. Orange flower water has a haunting perfumed flavor and can be found at Middle Eastern and Indian markets and in some gourmet shops. You can substitute an orange liqueur, but the flavor won't be quite the same.

1 teaspoon anise seed

1½ cups sugar

1 (14-ounce) can fat-free sweetened condensed milk

1 cup skim milk

2 eggs plus 6 whites or 1¼ cups egg substitute

1 tablespoon orange flower water

2 teaspoons grated fresh orange zest

Pinch of salt

6 (6-ounce) ramekins or custard cups

1. Preheat the oven to 350°F. Grind the anise seed to a fine powder in a spice mill or coffee mill.

2. Place the sugar in a heavy saucepan with ¼ cup of water. Cover the pan and cook over high heat for 2 minutes. Uncover the pan, reduce the heat slightly, and cook the sugar, without stirring, until it is caramelized (it will turn a dark golden brown), about 5 minutes. Pour the caramel into the ramekins, rotating each to coat the bottom and sides. Be careful: Caramel gives a terrible burn. (You may want to wear oven mitts to protect your hands and arms.) Let the caramel cool completely. Bring 1 quart of water to a boil.

3. Combine the condensed milk and the skim milk, the eggs, whites, orange flower water, orange zest, salt, and ground anise in a mixing bowl and whisk to blend. Ladle this mixture into the ramekins. Set the ramekins in a roasting pan and pour ½-inch of boiling water around them. Place the roasting pan in the oven. Bake until the flans are set, 40 to 50 minutes. (To test for doneness, gently poke the side of one of the ramekins; the filling should jiggle.) Transfer the flans to a rack to cool, then refrigerate for at least 6 hours, preferably overnight.

4. To unmold, run the tip of a paring knife around the inside edge of each ramekin. Place a plate over the ramekin, invert, and shake until the flan slips loose. Spoon any caramel left in the ramekin around the flan and serve at once.

Serves 6

440 CALORIES PER SERVING; 13 G PROTEIN; 2 G FAT; 0 G SATURATED FAT; 93 G CARBOHYDRATE; 182 MG SODIUM; 8 MG CHOLESTEROL

OAXACAN CHOCOLATE FLAN

Cocoa beans. Almonds. Sugar. Cinnamon. Cloves. This is what Oaxacans use to prepare hot chocolate, and I've never tasted better anywhere. The combination of sweetened condensed milk and evaporated skim milk creates uncommon richness and depth of flavor.

1½ cups sugar

1 cup evaporated skim milk

2 ounces Mexican chocolate or bittersweet chocolate, finely chopped

1 (14-ounce) can fat-free sweetened condensed milk

⅓ cup unsweetened cocoa powder

2 eggs plus 6 whites or 1¼ cups egg substitute

2 teaspoons vanilla extract

¼ teaspoon almond extract

½ teaspoon ground cinnamon

¼ teaspoon ground cloves

Pinch of salt

6 toasted almonds

6 (6-ounce) ramekins or custard cups

1. Preheat the oven to 350°F.

2. Place the sugar in a heavy saucepan with ¼ cup of water. Cover the pan and cook over high heat for 2 minutes. Uncover the pan, reduce the heat slightly, and cook the sugar, without stirring, until it is caramelized (it will turn a dark golden brown), about

5 minutes. Pour the caramel into the ramekins, rotating each to coat the bottom and sides. Be careful: Caramel gives a terrible burn. (You may want to wear oven mitts to protect your hands and arms.) Let the caramel cool completely.

3. Place the evaporated milk in a saucepan and heat to a simmer. Whisk in the chocolate and cook until melted. Remove the pan from the heat and whisk in the condensed milk and the cocoa powder. Let cool for 5 minutes. Add the eggs, whites, vanilla and almond extracts, cinnamon, cloves, and salt and whisk well to mix.

4. Strain the flan mixture into the ramekins. Set the ramekins in a roasting pan and pour ½ inch of boiling water around them. Place the roasting pan in the oven. Bake until the flans are set, 40 to 50 minutes. (To test for doneness, gently poke the side of one of the ramekins: The filling should jiggle.) Transfer the flans to a rack to cool, then refrigerate for at least 6 hours, preferably overnight.

5. To unmold, run the tip of a paring knife around the inside edge of each ramekin. Place a plate over the ramekin, invert, and shake until the flan slips loose. Spoon any caramel left in the ramekin around the flan.

Serves 6

496 CALORIES PER SERVING; 14 G PROTEIN; 4 G FAT; 2 G SATURATED FAT; 103 G CARBOHYDRATE; 205 MG SODIUM; 8 MG CHOLESTEROL

PUMPKIN FLAN

Here's a low-fat alternative to Thanksgiving pumpkin pie. The purist may wish to make the purée from scratch. To do so, bake a halved, seeded pumpkin, cut side down, on a lightly oiled baking sheet in a moderate oven for 1 hour, or until soft. Peel off the skin and purée the flesh in a food processor.

⅔ **cup granulated sugar**

2 **cups pumpkin purée**

¼ **cup brown sugar (or to taste)**

¼ **cup molasses**

2 **teaspoons vanilla extract**

2 **teaspoons grated fresh ginger**

1 **teaspoon ground cinnamon**

¼ **teaspoon freshly grated nutmeg**

⅛ **teaspoon ground allspice**

⅛ **teaspoon ground cloves**

6 **egg whites (or 3 whites and 2 whole eggs), lightly beaten**

1 **cup skim milk or evaporated skim milk**

2 **tablespoons dark rum**

To make the caramel, combine the granulated sugar with 3 tablespoons water in a heavy saucepan. Cook the mixture, covered, over high heat for 2 minutes. Uncover the pan and continue cooking until the sugar caramelizes (turns a deep golden brown). Pour the caramel into a 9-inch cake pan, gently swirling the pan to coat the bottom and sides with caramel. Work quickly, or the caramel will harden. (Take care not to let the molten caramel touch your skin.)

To make the filling, place the pumpkin in a large bowl and beat in the brown sugar, molasses, vanilla, and spices. Whisk in the egg whites, little by little, followed by the milk and rum. Pour this mixture into the caramel-lined pan.

Bring 1 quart water to a boil. Preheat the oven to 350°F.

Set the cake pan in a roasting pan with ½ inch boiling water. (This is called a water bath, and it helps the flan cook at a moist, even heat.) Place the roasting pan in the oven and bake for 1 hour, or until set. (A skewer inserted in the center should come out clean.) Remove the flan from the roasting pan and let cool to room temperature. Refrigerate for at least 6 hours, preferably overnight.

To unmold the flan, run the tip of a paring knife around the inside of the pan. Place a large round platter over the pan, invert, and give the pan a firm shake. The flan should slide right out. Spoon the caramel sauce around the flan and serve at once.

Serves 8 to 10

170 CALORIES PER SERVING; 4 G PROTEIN; 0 G FAT; 37 G CARBOHYDRATE; 64 MG SODIUM; 1 MG CHOLESTEROL

GASCON CRÈME CARAMELS

*Here's a low-fat version of another classic French dessert. To replace the richness of the egg yolks,
I've added prunes soaked in Armagnac. You can substitute cognac or any other grape brandy.*

⅓ cup Armagnac

6 pitted prunes

1 cup plus 3 tablespoons sugar

3 cups skim milk

1 vanilla bean, split

1 cinnamon stick

3 strips lemon zest (removed with a vegetable peeler)

6 egg whites (or 2 whole eggs and 3 whites), lightly beaten

Warm the Armagnac in a small saucepan. (Do not boil.) Add the prunes, cover the pan, and let soak for 30 minutes.

To make the caramel, combine ⅔ cup sugar with 3 tablespoons water in a heavy saucepan. Cook the mixture, covered, over high heat for 2 minutes. Uncover the pan and continue cooking until the sugar caramelizes (turns a deep golden brown). Pour the caramel into 6½-cup ramekins (or an 8-inch cake pan) and tilt to coat the bottoms and sides. (You may wish to wear heavy gloves during this procedure; molten caramel gives a terrible burn.)

Combine the milk, vanilla bean, cinnamon stick, and zest in the top of a double boiler and cook over low heat for 15 minutes. In a heatproof bowl, whisk together the egg whites and the remaining sugar. Strain the hot milk into the egg mixture, little by little, whisking constantly.

Bring 1 quart water to a boil. Preheat the oven to 350°F.

Drain the prunes. (Save the Armagnac for another purpose.) Place 1 prune in the center of each ramekin (or arrange the prunes evenly around the cake pan). Strain the custard mixture on top, filling each ramekin to within ¼ inch of the top. Set the ramekins in a roasting pan with ½ inch boiling water. This is called a water bath, and it helps the flan cook at a moist, even heat.

Bake for 30 to 40 minutes, or until just set. (A skewer inserted in the center should come out clean. The cake pan will take slightly longer.) Remove the ramekins from the roasting pan and let cool to room temperature. Refrigerate for at least 6 hours, preferably overnight. (The recipe can be prepared up to 2 days ahead to this stage.)

Just before serving, run the tip of a paring knife around the inside of each ramekin. Place a dessert plate over the ramekin, invert, and give the ramekin a firm shake. Lift the ramekin, and the flans will slide right out. If using a cake pan, unmold it onto a platter and cut into wedges for serving.

Serves 6

236 CALORIES PER SERVING; 8 G PROTEIN;
0 G FAT; 48 G CARBOHYDRATE; 119 MG SODIUM;
2 MG CHOLESTEROL

LOW-FAT CHOCOLATE PUDDING

This creamy pudding is actually part of the next recipe (Low-Fat Chocolate Soufflé), but it's so tasty (not to mention easy to make) that I decided to run it as a recipe in its own right. Mexicans use cinnamon and vanilla in their hot chocolate as a counterpoint to the flavor of the cocoa. If you use a fresh vanilla bean, you can rinse it off and use it again.

⅓ cup unsweetened cocoa

⅓ cup sugar

1 tablespoon cornstarch

½ teaspoon ground cinnamon

⅛ teaspoon ground cloves

1 cup skim milk

½ vanilla bean, split (or 1 teaspoon vanilla extract)

Combine the cocoa, sugar, cornstarch, cinnamon, and cloves in a bowl and whisk until smooth. Scald the milk with the vanilla bean in the top of a double boiler.

Whisk the scalded milk into the cocoa mixture in a thin stream. Return this mixture to a heavy saucepan and boil for 1 minute, whisking constantly. (Continuous whisking is important, or the milk will scorch.) Remove the pan from the heat and remove the vanilla bean. (If you're not using a vanilla bean, whisk in the vanilla extract at this point.)

Transfer the pudding to a bowl and press a piece of plastic wrap on top to prevent a skin from forming. Let cool to room temperature, then chill. Spoon into bowls for serving. For a decorative touch, top each pudding with a spoonful of sweetened yogurt cheese.

Note: If you wish to serve 4, simply double the ingredients.

Serves 2

214 CALORIES PER SERVING; 7 G PROTEIN; 2 G FAT; 51 G CARBOHYDRATE; 73 MG SODIUM; 2 MG CHOLESTEROL

Low-Fat Chocolate Soufflé

LOW-FAT CHOCOLATE SOUFFLÉ

In my house, Valentine's Day isn't complete without a chocolate soufflé. It wasn't hard to create a low-fat version by eliminating the egg yolks and replacing the chocolate with unsweetened cocoa. Serve with Pear Sauce (page 348) on the side.

½ tablespoon butter, melted (or vegetable oil spray)

¼ cup sugar

Low-Fat Chocolate Pudding (page 347)

5 egg whites

½ teaspoon cream of tartar

confectioners' sugar

Brush the inside of a 5-cup soufflé dish with the melted butter (or spray with vegetable oil), taking special care to brush the inside rim. Freeze the dish for 5 minutes and brush it again. (This is called double buttering and helps prevent the soufflé from sticking as it rises.) Sprinkle the inside of the mold with ½ tablespoon of the sugar. Preheat the oven to 400°F.

Prepare the Low-Fat Chocolate Pudding and keep it hot. Beat the egg whites at low speed for 20 seconds. Add the cream of tartar and gradually increase the mixer speed to high. Beat the whites to stiff peaks, adding the remaining sugar as the whites stiffen.

Stir ¼ of the whites into the hot pudding mixture to lighten it. Fold the pudding mixture into the remaining whites as gently as possible. Spoon the soufflé mixture into the dish. Smooth the top with a wet spatula. Run the tip of a paring knife around the inside edge of the dish to keep the rising soufflé from sticking.

Bake for 15 minutes, or until puffed and cooked to taste. (I like my soufflés a little runny in the center.) Dust the top with confectioners' sugar and serve at once.

Serves 4

186 CALORIES PER SERVING; 8 G PROTEIN; 2 G FAT; 38 G CARBOHYDRATE; 120 MG SODIUM; 5 MG CHOLESTEROL

FLAMING GRAND MARNIER AND CHOCOLATE CHUNK SOUFFLÉ

Soufflés are the ultimate indulgence. We make them often at our house—not only on account of their elegance, but for the fact that they require only 10 minutes of preparation time and can be made with ingredients you almost always have on hand. The one or two optional egg yolks in the following recipe would give the soufflé added richness, but you can certainly leave them out to make a virtually fat-free dessert. (A "normal" soufflé could contain 4 to 5 egg yolks.) The same is true for the chocolate, which makes a nice surprise to bite into. For heightened drama, I've included instructions for flambéing the soufflé, but you could omit this step, in which case you'd need only 3 tablespoons Grand Marnier. Be very careful when you flambé. Keep your face away from the pan and take care not to spill any of the flaming liquid on the tablecloth, the napkins, or your clothes.

spray oil

½ cup sugar, plus 2 to 3 tablespoons for the ramekins

2 tablespoons cornstarch

2 teaspoons grated orange zest

1 cup skim milk

1 to 2 egg yolks (optional)

1 tablespoon orange marmalade

6½ tablespoons Grand Marnier (or other orange liqueur)

5 egg whites

½ teaspoon cream of tartar

1 to 2 ounces semisweet or bittersweet chocolate, cut into ¼-inch chunks (optional)

1. Lightly spray the insides (bottoms and sides) of eight 3-inch ramekins with spray oil. (Be sure to spray the inside rim.) Sprinkle the insides with sugar, rotating the ramekins to coat the bottom and sides with sugar. (Pour the sugar from one ramekin to another.) Preheat the oven to 400°F.

2. Combine 5 tablespoons of the sugar, 1 tablespoon of the cornstarch, and the orange zest in a small, heavy saucepan and whisk to mix. Gradually whisk in the milk in a thin stream. When all the ingredients are dissolved, place the pan over high heat and bring to a boil, whisking steadily: the mixture will thicken. Simmer for 2 minutes, whisking well.

3. Remove the pan from the heat and whisk in the egg yolk (if using) and the orange marmalade. Combine 2 tablespoons of the Grand Marnier and the remaining 1 tablespoon cornstarch in a small bowl and mix to a smooth paste. Return the pan to the heat and bring the milk mixture just to a boil. Whisk in the Grand Marnier–cornstarch mixture and boil until thick. Remove the pan from the heat.

4. Beat the egg whites in a clean bowl at low speed for 1 minute. Add the cream of tartar. Gradually increase the speed to medium, then to medium-high, and beat the whites to soft peaks. Increase the speed to high, add the remaining 3 tablespoons sugar in a thin stream, and beat the whites until firm and glossy but not dry. Whisk ¼ of the whites into the hot Grand Marnier mixture. Fold this mixture into the remaining whites with a rubber spatula, working as gently as possible. (You don't want to deflate the whites.)

5. Spoon the soufflé mixture into the ramekins to fill halfway. Add the chocolate chunks and sprinkle in 1½ tablespoons of the Grand Marnier. Add the remaining soufflé mixture and smooth the tops with a wet spatula.

6. Bake the soufflés until puffed and nicely browned on the top and cooked in the center, 10 to 15 minutes. (To test for doneness, give one of the ramekins a gentle poke. The soufflé should wobble just a little.) Meanwhile, warm the remaining 3 tablespoons Grand Marnier in a small saucepan, but do not let boil. Serve the soufflé immediately. Touch a lighted match to the warm Grand Marnier and pour the flaming liquid on top.

Serves 8

170 CALORIES PER SERVING; 4 G PROTEIN; 0 G FAT; 0 G SATURATED FAT; 32 G CARBOHYDRATE; 87 MG SODIUM; 0 MG CHOLESTEROL

REDUCED-FAT CHOCOLATE MOUSSE

This chocolate mousse is as rich and creamy as any I've tasted, but it contains not one gram of cholesterol and a reduced amount of fat. The secret is using Italian meringue to thicken and bind the mousse. The meringue has another advantage. Being cooked, it eliminates the risk of salmonella.

6 ounces semisweet chocolate, coarsely chopped

2 ounces unsweetened chocolate, coarsely chopped

FOR THE MERINGUE:

1 cup sugar

6 egg whites

½ teaspoon cream of tartar

Place the semisweet and unsweetened chocolate in a large bowl over a pan of hot water and stir until melted. Let cool slightly.

To make the meringue, combine ¼ cup of the sugar and 3 tablespoons water in a heavy saucepan. Cook over high heat, covered, for 2 minutes. Cover and cook the sugar to the soft ball stage (239°F. on a candy thermometer).

Meanwhile, beat the egg whites at low speed for 1 minute. Add the cream of tartar and beat until the mixture is frothy. Increase the speed to high and beat the egg whites until they form soft peaks. Add the remaining sugar and beat for 30 seconds, or until the whites are firm and glossy.

Pour the hot sugar mixture into the whites in a thin stream and continue beating until almost cool. Gently fold the melted chocolate into the meringue and let cool. Using a piping bag with a large star tip, pipe the chocolate mousse into ramekins or wine glasses.

Note: For a more fanciful presentation, transfer 4 to 6 tablespoons meringue to a second piping bag fitted with a large star tip before incorporating the chocolate. Pipe rosettes of meringue on top of each serving. It will look exactly like whipped cream.

Serves 8

239 CALORIES PER SERVING; 5 G PROTEIN; 10 G FAT; 39 G CARBOHYDRATE; 42 MG SODIUM; 0 MG CHOLESTEROL

GINGER FLOATING ISLAND WITH SHOCKING RED RASPBERRY SAUCE

Here's a modern twist on classic French île flottante, *"floating island." The island is made by baking meringue in a soufflé dish. To lighten the recipe, I've replaced the traditional custard sauce with a colorful raspberry coulis. (A cranberry coulis is nice when cranberries are in season in the fall.)*

FOR THE MOLD:

1–2 teaspoons butter, melted (or vegetable oil spray)

2 tablespoons sugar

FOR THE MERINGUE:

4 extra-large egg whites, at room temperature

1 tablespoon minced candied ginger

1 teaspoon grated fresh ginger

1 teaspoon vanilla extract

½ teaspoon cream of tartar

1 cup sugar

1 teaspoon freshly grated lemon zest

FOR THE SAUCE:

3 cups fresh raspberries (or 1 12-ounce package frozen)

3–4 tablespoons confectioners' sugar (or to taste)

2 tablespoons fresh lemon juice (or to taste)

FOR THE GARNISH:

1 cup fresh raspberries, or 2 ounces toasted, slivered almonds

To prepare the mold, brush the bottom and sides of a 5-cup soufflé dish or charlotte mold with melted butter and freeze for 5 minutes. Brush again with melted butter. (This technique is called double buttering, and it helps keep the meringue from sticking.) Alternatively, thoroughly coat the inside of the mold with vegetable oil spray. Sprinkle the inside of the mold with the 2 tablespoons sugar. Preheat the oven to 350°F. Bring 1 quart water to a boil.

To make the meringue, combine the egg whites, candied ginger, fresh ginger, vanilla, and cream of tartar in the bowl of a mixer. Beat to soft peaks, starting at low speed and increasing to medium. Increase the speed to high, add ¼ cup sugar in a thin stream, and continue beating until the whites are firm and glossy.

Fold in the remaining sugar and the zest, using a rubber spatula. Work as gently as possible so as not to deflate the whites. Spoon the meringue mixture into the soufflé dish. Place the dish in a roasting pan with ½-inch boiling water. Bake for 25 minutes, or until puffed and firm but not brown.

To make the sauce, purée the raspberries in a food processor, running the machine as little as possible so as not to crush the seeds. (Crushing the seeds will make the purée bitter.) Strain the puréed raspberries into a bowl and whisk in the confectioners' sugar and lemon juice.

Remove the floating island from the oven and let cool for 10 minutes. Invert it onto a round platter or shallow bowl, and let cool to room temperature. Just before serving, spoon the raspberry sauce around the floating island and garnish the top with raspberries or toasted almonds. Cut into wedges for serving.

Serves 4 to 5

313 CALORIES PER SERVING; 5 G PROTEIN; 2 G FAT; 74 G CARBOHYDRATE; 96 MG SODIUM; 3 MG CHOLESTEROL

PUDIM DE CLARAS
(APRICOT-CARAMEL MERINGUE)

This dessert is a sort of Brazilian floating island. Any dried fruit could be substituted for the apricots.

1¾ cups sugar

¾ cup dried apricots

2 tablespoons finely chopped candied ginger

2 teaspoons grated lemon zest

6 large egg whites

½ teaspoon cream of tartar

1. Preheat the oven to 350°F. Sprinkle ¾ cup of the sugar in a deep, one-piece, 8-inch, 8-cup-capacity ring mold. Heat the mold directly on the burner over medium-low heat until the sugar melts into a golden-brown caramel, about 10 minutes, rotating the mold to ensure even melting and coating. Use a spoon to coat the tube section. Take care to avoid being burned by the hot caramel. Let cool.

2. Put the apricots in a small saucepan and add water to cover. Gently simmer the apricots until very tender, 6 to 8 minutes. Drain, reserving 3 tablespoons of the water. Purée the apricots with the reserved water in a food processor and stir in the candied ginger and lemon zest.

3. Beat the egg whites in an electric mixer at low speed 1 minute. Add the cream of tartar. Gradually increase the speed to medium, then medium-high, and beat the whites to soft peaks. Gradually add the remaining 1 cup sugar in a thin stream and continue beating until the whites are firm and glossy but not dry. Using a rubber spatula, gently fold the apricot purée into the egg whites. Spoon this mixture into the caramel-lined mold. Set the mold in a roasting pan, place it in the oven, and add boiling water to 1 inch.

4. Bake until the meringue is firm and puffed, about 40 minutes. Avoid opening the oven door. (It's normal for the meringue to rise like a soufflé; it will fall to the proper height as it cools.) Turn off the oven and let the meringue cool 1 hour without opening the oven door.

5. Run the tip of a knife around the inside of the mold. Place a platter over the mold and invert: the meringue should slide out easily. If not, give the mold a gentle shake. Spoon any caramel that remains in the mold on top of the meringue. Cut into wedges and serve.

Makes 6 to 8 servings

277 CALORIES PER SERVING; 4 G PROTEIN; 0 G FAT; 0 G SATURATED FAT; 69 G CARBOHYDRATE; 76 MG SODIUM; 0 MG CHOLESTEROL

FRUIT GAZPACHO

Gazpacho for dessert? Why not! This dessert was inspired by a strawberry "soup" served by Breton chef Louis Leroy, with whom I trained in 1979. Serve with Cinnamon Rose Angel Food Cake (page 327).

2 pints fresh strawberries, hulled and diced

1 ripe banana or peach, peeled

1 tablespoon orange liqueur

juice and grated rind of 1 lemon (or to taste)

2–3 tablespoons sugar (or to taste)

1 cup dessert wine (such as Moscato or Sauternes)

1 cup diced angel food cake

1 cup fresh blueberries, for garnish

¼ cup fresh mint leaves, stemmed and cut into slivers, for garnish

Place the strawberries, banana, orange liqueur, lemon juice and rind, sugar, wine, and angel food cake in a blender and purée until smooth. Correct the seasoning, adding sugar or lemon juice to taste. If the gazpacho seems too thick, add a little more wine or water.

Ladle the gazpacho into 4 large brandy snifters or wine glasses, and garnish with blueberries. Sprinkle slivered mint on top. Serve with long-handled spoons.

Serves 4

275 CALORIES PER SERVING; 3 G PROTEIN; 1 G FAT; 50 G CARBOHYDRATE; 64 MG SODIUM; 0 MG CHOLESTEROL

PEPPERED STRAWBERRIES

For most North Americans, pepper belongs to the realm of savory seasonings. Italians are more broad-minded in their thinking, adding pepper to desserts and confections as diverse as biscotti, spice cakes, and fruit dishes. The pepper bite in this strawberry dessert is as tasty as it is unexpected.

1 quart fresh strawberries (about 3 cups sliced)

¼ cup sugar, or to taste

2 to 3 tablespoons Strego or other Italian liqueur (see Note)

2 to 3 tablespoons orange-flavored liqueur

½ teaspoon coarsely ground black pepper, or to taste

3 cups vanilla frozen yogurt (optional)

1. Wash, drain, and hull the strawberries and cut them lengthwise into ¼-inch slices. Place in a large glass bowl.

2. Shortly before serving, mix in the sugar, liqueurs, and pepper. Let the mixture stand until the juices start to come out of the strawberries, about 10 minutes. If using the frozen yogurt, scoop it into martini glasses or bowls and spoon the strawberry mixture over it. If not, just spoon the strawberries into the glasses or bowls. Grind a little more fresh pepper on top and serve at once.

Note: Strega is an angelica-and-spice-based liqueur made in Benevento in southern Italy and sold in long, slender bottles. If it's unavailable, use another Italian liqueur.

Serves 4 to 6

137 CALORIES PER SERVING;* 1 G PROTEIN; 0.6 G FAT; 0 G SATURATED FAT; 28 G CARBOHYDRATE; 2 MG SODIUM; 0 MG CHOLESTEROL

Analysis is based on 4 servings.

FRESH BERRIES WITH LOW-FAT ZABAGLIONE

The frothy egg dessert known as zabaglione has a curious history. It is named for Baglioni, a fifteenth-century general who defended Florence against a warring neighboring city. Reduced to cooking with eggs and sweet wine (the enemy having captured his provision wagon), the general's chef invented a sweet dessert, which he called zuppa baglioni—"Baglioni's soup." In time the term was shortened to zabaglione (pronounced "tsa-bah-LYO-nay"). Traditionally, zabaglione is a heart-stoppingly rich dessert sauce made with wine and beaten egg yolks. Here's a low-fat version that uses 2 eggs and 2 egg whites instead of the traditional 6 to 8 yolks.

6 cups mixed berries, including strawberries, raspberries, blackberries, and/or blueberries

FOR THE ZABAGLIONE:

2 eggs, plus 2 egg whites

¾ cup Moscato or marsala wine

¼ cup sugar

1. Wash, stem, hull, if necessary, and dry the berries, cutting any large berries, like strawberries, into slices. Toss the berries in a mixing bowl and spoon them into 6 wineglasses or martini glasses. The recipe can be prepared ahead to this stage.

2. Prepare the zabaglione: Bring 4 cups water to a boil in a large, wide saucepan and reduce the heat to a gentle simmer. Combine the egg, egg whites, wine, and sugar in a large metal mixing bowl. Place the bowl with the zabaglione mixture over the pan of simmering water. Beating steadily with a whisk, cook the mixture until thick, moussy, and doubled in volume, 3 to 5 minutes. When the zabaglione is ready, the whisk will leave a clean trace on the bottom of the bowl. Do not overcook, or the mixture will curdle. Remove the bowl from the heat and spoon the zabaglione over the fruit. Serve at once.

Serves 6

144 CALORIES PER SERVING; 4 G PROTEIN; 2 G FAT; 0.6 G SATURATED FAT; 24 G CARBOHYDRATE; 59 MG SODIUM; 71 MG CHOLESTEROL

PEACHES IN ASTI SPUMANTE OR IN MOSCATO

The mere mention of Asti Spumanti is enough to make many North American wine lovers curl their lips with disdain. But the sweet sparkling wine from Piedmont has a wide following in Italy, where its perfumed bouquet and fruity flavor are prized at the conclusion of a meal. This simple dessert takes literally seconds to make, but the contrast of flavors is stunning. Because of its simplicity, you must use fragrant ripe peaches that are at the height of their ripeness. Moscato is a nonsparkling sweet wine. Use it if you prefer a dessert without fizz.

2 to 3 ripe peaches

1 cup fresh raspberries, washed, stemmed, and patted dry with paper towels

3 cups Asti Spumante wine or Moscato wine

4 sprigs fresh mint

1. Peel and pit the peaches. (To pit a peach, cut it in half to the stone around the lengthwise circumference. Twist the halves in opposite directions to separate the peach into halves. Pry out the stone with a spoon.) Dice the peaches and place them in wineglasses.

2. Add the raspberries and Asti Spumante wine to cover. Garnish each glass with a sprig of mint.

Serves 4

154 CALORIES PER SERVING; 1 G PROTEIN; 0.2 G FAT; 0 G SATURATED FAT; 1.3 G CARBOHYDRATE; 0 MG SODIUM; 0 MG CHOLESTEROL

PEARS POACHED IN PEPPERED PORT

Pears poached in red wine are a venerable French bistro dessert. This variation calls for the pears to be cooked in port. Pepper might seem like an odd ingredient in a fruit dessert, but it adds an offbeat spiciness that cuts the sweetness of the port. My favorite pear for this recipe is Comice, but Anjou or Bosc will work well, too.

4 ripe pears

1 lemon

3 cups port wine

¼ cup sugar (or to taste)

20 peppercorns

1 cinnamon stick

5 whole cloves

1 teaspoon cornstarch

8 sprigs fresh mint, for garnish

Peel the pears, cut in half lengthwise, and core with a melon baller. Remove 3 strips zest from the lemon with a vegetable peeler. Cut the lemon in half and rub the pears with one half to prevent browning. Juice the other half.

Combine the lemon zest and juice, port, sugar, and spices in a deep, wide saucepan and bring to a boil. Reduce the heat, add the pears (cut side up), and cover the pan. Poach the pears for 3 to 12 minutes (depending on their ripeness), or until very tender. (They should be easy to pierce with a toothpick.) Use a slotted spoon to transfer the pears, cut side down, to a wire rack to cool.

Boil the poaching liquid until only 1½ cups remain. Dissolve the cornstarch in 1 tablespoon cold water. Whisk into the sauce and boil for 30 seconds. Strain the sauce and chill.

Arrange the pears, cut side down, on a cutting board. Using a sharp knife, starting at the wide end of each pear, make a series of lengthwise parallel cuts almost to the stem end. Do not cut all the way through; the slices should be attached at the end. Gently flatten each pear with the palm of your hand to fan out the slices. Spoon the sauce on a platter or on individual dessert plates. Using a spatula, arrange the fanned-out pears on top. Garnish with mint sprigs and serve at once.

Serves 4 to 8

265 CALORIES PER SERVING; 1 G PROTEIN; 1 G FAT; 49 G CARBOHYDRATE; 4 MG SODIUM; 0 MG CHOLESTEROL

GELATINA DI FRUTA

Da Guido is one of the finest restaurants in Piedmont. And one of the best-hidden! To get there, we embarked on a labyrinthine journey, down winding country roads, through deserted villages (at nighttime, no less). Once there, we embarked on what can only be described as a ten-course food odyssey, complete with a truffle tasting. (It turns out there's a subtle difference in taste between the truffles that grow under different types of trees.) Among the many dishes that stand out in my mind is a dessert of startling simplicity—the description "fruit aspic" or "fruit gelatin" fails to convey how light, refreshing, and welcome at the end of a copious meal such a simple confection can be. Feel free to vary the fruits depending on what's in season.

1½ envelopes unflavored gelatin

2 cups fresh orange juice
 (the juice must be freshly squeezed)

½ cup fresh raspberries, picked over and washed

½ cup fresh blueberries, picked over and washed

½ cup fresh blackberries, picked over and washed
 (or other berry)

3 to 5 tablespoons sugar, or to taste

spray oil

fresh Blackberry Sauce or Peach Sauce
 (page 344) or both for serving

6 ½-cup ramekins

1. Sprinkle the gelatin over ½ cup of the orange juice in a small metal bowl. Let stand until spongy, about 10

BAKED APPLES

Is there any dish more evocative of autumn than baked apples? Unfortunately, most recipes are loaded with butter. My low-fat version uses banana to provide some of the moistness traditionally supplied by the butter. The rose water lends a Near Eastern accent.

2 cups apple cider

4 dried apricots, finely chopped

3 tablespoons raisins

6 firm, tart apples
  (such as Granny Smiths)

¼ cup toasted bread crumbs,
  Grape-Nuts, or other crunch cereal

3 tablespoons brown sugar
  (or to taste)

¼ teaspoon ground cinnamon

freshly grated nutmeg

1 banana

1 teaspoon rose water or vanilla
  extract

2 tablespoons maple syrup

1 teaspoon cornstarch

1 tablespoon rum

Warm the cider in a saucepan. Remove the pan from the heat and add the apricots and raisins. Let soften for 20 minutes.

Meanwhile, core the apples, using an apple corer or melon baller, but don't cut all the way through the bottom. The idea is to create a cavity for stuffing. Preheat the oven to 350°F.

Drain the apricots and raisins, reserving the cider. Combine the apricots, raisins, bread crumbs, brown sugar, cinnamon, and nutmeg in a bowl and crumble with your fingers. Finely chop the banana. Stir the banana and rose water into the crumb mixture. Stuff the filling into the apples. Make a few small holes in each filling with a skewer and pour in the maple syrup.

Place the apples in a baking dish. Pour in enough drained cider to cover the bottom inch of the apples. Reserve any excess cider. Bake the apples for 1 hour, or until soft. If the filling starts to get too brown, cover the apples with a piece of foil.

Transfer the apples to shallow bowls. Strain the pan juices and reserved cider into a small saucepan and bring to a boil. Dissolve the cornstarch in the rum. Whisk this mixture into the pan juices and bring to a boil. Pour the sauce over the apples and serve at once.

Serves 6

216 CALORIES PER SERVING; 1 G PROTEIN; .7 G FAT; 53 G CARBOHYDRATE; 49 MG SODIUM; 0 MG CHOLESTEROL

- -

minutes. Place the bowl in a pan of simmering water to melt the gelatin.

2. Meanwhile, combine the raspberries, blueberries, and blackberries in a mixing bowl and gently toss with the sugar. Let stand for 15 minutes, or until the berries start to become juicy.

3. Warm the remaining 1½ cups orange juice in a saucepan over medium heat. Do not let it boil. Stir the gelatin mixture into the orange juice, followed by the berries. Gently stir until all the sugar is dissolved. Let the mixture cool to room temperature.

4. Meanwhile, lightly spray the insides of the ramekins with spray oil. Line the bottom of each with a small circle of baking parchment and lightly spray with oil

again. Ladle the fruit mixture into the ramekins and place in a baking pan in the refrigerator. Cover and chill until firm, at least 8 hours, preferably overnight.

5. To serve, run the tip of a paring knife around the inside of the ramekins. Put a dessert plate over a ramekin, invert, and give a little shake; the fruit aspic should slide out easily. Pool the fruit sauce around the aspics. (If using two sauces, you can marble them with the point of a knife.)

Serves 6

149 CALORIES PER SERVING; 3 G PROTEIN; 0.7 G FAT; 0 G SATURATED FAT; 35 G CARBOHYDRATE; 4 MG SODIUM; 0 MG CHOLESTEROL

FRUIT "SALSA"

At first glance, this fruit salad really does look like salsa, the tomato red provided by strawberries, the onion white by peach, the cilantro green by fresh mint leaves. I even include a little chili: You'll be amazed how the heat of the jalapeños brings out the sweetness of the fruit. Note: *For extra color and flavor, I like to add blueberries, but then you lose the salsalike appearance.*

1 pint fresh strawberries, washed and hulled

1 large ripe white peach or pear, cut into ½-inch dice

½ cup fresh mint leaves, thinly slivered, plus 6 whole sprigs for garnish

1 jalapeño chili, seeded and minced (for a spicier salsa, leave the seeds in)

3 tablespoons fresh lime juice

2 to 3 tablespoons light brown sugar

1. Cut the strawberries into ½-inch dice and place them in a bowl. Add the peach, mint leaves, chili, lime juice, and brown sugar and gently toss to mix. Correct the seasoning, adding lime juice or sugar to taste; the "salsa" should be a little sweet and a little sour.

Note: You can prepare the ingredients ahead of time, but the salsa tastes best served within 10 minutes of mixing.

Serves 4 to 6

65 CALORIES PER SERVING;* 1 G PROTEIN; 0 G FAT; 0 G SATURATED FAT; 16 G CARBOHYDRATE; 5 MG SODIUM; 0 MG CHOLESTEROL

Analysis is based on 4 servings.

YUCA IN SPICE-SCENTED SYRUP

Here's an offbeat twist to the fruits poached in spice-scented syrup so beloved by Mexicans for dessert. The "fruit" in question is actually a starchy root vegetable—yuca—and its mild buttery flavor and soft creamy texture work surprisingly well for dessert. Actually, the idea of serving yuca as dessert isn't as wacky as it seems; this is the plant from which tapioca is made.
Fresh yuca can be found at Hispanic markets and at many supermarkets. Many stores sell it frozen. When buying fresh yuca, look for firm, heavy tubers free of blemishes, soft spots, and strong odors. If the flesh looks dried out or riddled with black veins, don't buy it.

1½ pounds fresh yuca

pinch of salt

FOR THE SYRUP:

1½ cups water

½ cup sugar

½ cup piloncillo or dark brown sugar

1 cinnamon stick

4 cloves

2 allspice berries

½ teaspoon anise seed

2 strips lemon zest

2 strips orange zest

1. Cut the yuca crosswise into 2-inch pieces and peel with a chef's knife. (Stand the pieces on end and cut off the peel with downward strokes of the knife.) Cut any large pieces in half or quarters, so that all pieces are the same size.

2. Bring 2 quarts of water and a pinch of salt to a boil in a large pot. Add the yuca and cook for 10 minutes. Add 1 cup of cold water. Return the yuca to a boil and cook for 5 minutes. Add another cup of cold water, return to a boil, and cook for 5 minutes, or until the yuca is very soft. (The successive additions of cold water help tenderize the yuca.)

3. Meanwhile, make the syrup. Combine the water, sugar, piloncillo or brown sugar, cinnamon stick, cloves, allspice, anise seed, and lemon and orange zest in a saucepan and bring to a boil. Reduce the heat and simmer for 5 minutes. Remove the pan from the heat and strain the syrup into a heatproof bowl.

Duet of Poached Pears

4. Drain the yuca in a colander and rinse briefly with cold water. Older yuca may have woody fibers running the length of the center: With a fork, scrape out any you find. Add the yuca to the warm syrup and let it cool to room temperature. Refrigerate until serving. To serve, spoon the yuca into individual bowls and generously douse with syrup.

Serves 4 to 6

409 CALORIES PER SERVING;*
5 G PROTEIN; 1 G FAT; 0 G SATURATED FAT;
99 G CARBOHYDRATE; 29 MG SODIUM;
0 MG CHOLESTEROL

Analysis is based on 4 servings.

DUET OF POACHED PEARS

There are two options for poaching liquid in this easy but elegant poached-pear recipe: a more traditional red-wine-and-port mixture, which will produce lovely rose-colored pears, and a lemon-and-Earl-Grey-tea-based mixture, which produces golden pears. Make one or the other, or some of both. As for the pears, I prefer Anjou or Comice, and they should be ripe but still firm. For heightened drama, you could serve the pears in filo nests (see page 341).

4 large pears

½ lemon

FOR ROSE-COLORED PEARS:

1 cup dry red wine

1 cup port

½ cup sugar

1 cinnamon stick

2 whole cloves

2 strips lemon zest

1½ teaspoons cornstarch

1 tablespoon water

FOR GOLDEN PEARS:

2 cups water

1 cup sugar

½ cup fresh lemon juice

2 tea bags Earl Grey tea
   (1½ tablespoons loose tea)

2-inch piece vanilla bean, split

1½ teaspoons cornstarch

1 tablespoon water

FOR THE GARNISH (OPTIONAL):

Fresh mint sprigs

1. Peel the pears, leaving the stems intact. Rub the peeled pears with the lemon to prevent them from discoloring and set aside.

2. To make rose-colored pears, put the wine, port, sugar, cinnamon stick, cloves, and zest in a narrow, deep nonreactive saucepan and bring to a boil. Add the pears, reduce the heat, and gently simmer until tender, 10 to 15 minutes, turning with a slotted spoon to ensure even cooking. (To test for doneness, insert a metal skewer through the bottom of the pear to the center; it should pierce the pear easily.) Transfer the pears to a plate to cool, standing them upright. Continue simmering the poaching liquid until reduced to 1 cup. Dissolve the cornstarch in the water and stir it into the simmering liquid: it will thicken. Strain and let cool.

3. To make golden pears, follow the instructions for rose-colored pears, using the water, sugar, and lemon juice for the liquid and the tea bags and vanilla bean for the seasonings.

4. Arrange the poached pears on individual plates or a large platter. (If you are using Filo Nests, place one pear in each nest.) Spoon the sauce on top and garnish each pear with a sprig of mint, if desired.

Makes 4 servings

465 CALORIES PER SERVING; 1 G PROTEIN;
0.8 G FAT; 0 G SATURATED FAT;
110 G CARBOHYDRATE; 22 MG SODIUM;
0 MG CHOLESTEROL

PEAR SAUCE

Fruit sauces are known as coulis *in French. They became fashionable during the reign of nouvelle cuisine and remain so to this day. I like to make this sauce with fresh pears, but in a pinch you can use canned.*

2 ripe pears

1 tablespoon fresh lemon juice

2 strips lemon zest

1 cup water

2–3 tablespoons sugar (or to taste)

1 teaspoon cornstarch

1 tablespoon pear brandy or water

Peel, core, and dice the pears. Toss them with lemon juice to prevent browning. Combine the pears, zest, water, and sugar in a heavy saucepan. Simmer for 3 to 4 minutes, or until the pears are very soft.

Dissolve the cornstarch in the brandy and whisk it into the pears. Bring the mixture to a boil and remove the pan from the heat. Remove the zest and purée the pear mixture in a blender. Let cool to room temperature, then refrigerate until cold.

Makes 1½ cups

14 CALORIES PER TABLESPOON; 0 G PROTEIN;
0 G FAT; 3 G CARBOHYDRATE; 0 MG SODIUM;
0 MG CHOLESTEROL

LOW-FAT CHOCOLATE FONDUE

I always serve chocolate fondue at my Cook and Ski cooking classes at the Snowvillage Inn in New Hampshire. Despite its decadent reputation, it's really just a fresh fruit salad whose parts are dipped in chocolate sauce. To make the low-fat version, I substitute low-fat vanilla yogurt for the traditional heavy cream. You'd never know the difference!

2 bananas

2 apples or ripe pears

2 kiwis

juice of ½ lemon

2 oranges or tangerines

½ pound seedless red grapes

1 pint strawberries

½ cup nonfat vanilla yogurt

6 ounces semisweet chocolate

2 tablespoons rum or cognac

Peel the bananas, apples, and kiwis, and cut into bite-sized pieces. Sprinkle the banana and apple pieces with lemon juice to keep them from browning. Peel the oranges, break into segments, and carefully remove the seeds. Stem the grapes and hull the strawberries. Attractively arrange the fruit on a platter.

Combine the yogurt and chocolate in the top of a double boiler. Cook over low heat, whisking, until the chocolate is melted and the mixture is hot. Stir in the rum. Keep the chocolate warm over the double boiler until serving.

Serve the fondue warm but not hot. (Do not place it directly over the flame.) Invite guests to dip the fruit in the chocolate.

Serves 4

448 CALORIES PER SERVING; 6 G PROTEIN; 13 G FAT; 85 G CARBOHYDRATE; 23 MG SODIUM; 1 MG CHOLESTEROL

BALINESE BANANA SPLIT

This dish is inspired by a dessert I tasted in Bali called kolek pisang—*bananas in coconut-milk caramel. I've dramatically reduced the fat by using light coconut milk and skim milk instead of the full-fat coconut milk used in Bali. The cinnamon stick and lemongrass aren't strictly traditional, either, but they add a great flavor. I like to make this recipe with finger bananas or apple bananas (available at ethnic markets and some supermarkets), but regular bananas will work, too.*

½ cup packed dark-brown sugar

½ cup light coconut milk (see Note)

1 cup skim milk

1 cinnamon stick

1 stalk lemongrass, trimmed (see Note),
   or 2 strips lemon zest

12 finger bananas, 4 apple bananas, or 2 regular bananas

2 teaspoons cornstarch

1 tablespoon water

1 pint vanilla nonfat frozen yogurt

2 tablespoons unsweetened shredded coconut, toasted
   (see Note)

1. Put the sugar in a large heavy saucepan (preferably nonstick) set over medium heat and, stirring with a wooden spoon, cook until it begins to smoke and turn dark brown. Remove the pan from the heat and add the coconut milk (be careful, as it may spatter). Return the pan to the heat and bring to a boil, stirring to dissolve the sugar. Stir in the skim milk and add the cinnamon stick and lemongrass. Reduce the heat and simmer, stirring from time to time to prevent scorching, until the mixture is richly flavored and you can taste the cinnamon and lemongrass, about 10 minutes.

2. Peel the bananas. If you are using apple bananas, cut them in half on the diagonal. If you are using regular bananas, cut them in thirds or quarters on the diagonal. Keep finger bananas whole. Add the bananas to the milk mixture and simmer until tender, 2 to 3 minutes. Mix the cornstarch with the water and add it to the saucepan. Simmer 1 minute: the sauce will thicken.

3. Divide the frozen yogurt among 4 bowls. Arrange the bananas on top and spoon the sauce around them. Sprinkle the banana splits with the shredded coconut and serve at once.

Note: To toast coconut, spread it on a piece of foil on a baking sheet and bake in a 350°F. oven 3 to 5 minutes, or until golden brown. Light coconut milk is a reduced-fat coconut milk available canned at gourmet shops. One good brand is A Taste of Thai. To trim lemongrass, cut off the dark-green leaves (about the top two-thirds). Strip off the outside layer of leaves.

Makes 4 servings

357 CALORIES PER SERVING; 7 G PROTEIN; 5 G FAT; 1.3 G SATURATED FAT; 71 G CARBOHYDRATE; 136 MG SODIUM; 1 MG CHOLESTEROL

BAKED HAWAII

Here's my low-fat version of a dessert that was popular at hotel restaurants when I was a kid—baked Alaska. And what an extraordinary dessert it seemed at the time! Festooned with rococo swirls of meringue and served flambéed, it combined the best of both hot and cold desserts. My heart-healthy remake uses frozen yogurt instead of ice cream and fresh fruit instead of sponge cake, but it sure doesn't lack for drama. Use your favorite flavor of frozen yogurt—I like cherry.

1 ripe pineapple with leaves attached

1 pint nonfat frozen yogurt or sorbet, softened

5 tablespoons rum or coconut rum (see Note)

FOR THE MERINGUE:

4 large egg whites, at room temperature

½ teaspoon cream of tartar

¾ cup sugar

3 tablespoons water

1 teaspoon vanilla extract

1. Using a large sharp knife, cut the pineapple in half lengthwise, starting at the end opposite the leaves and cutting through the leaves as well. Cut the core out of each pineapple half and discard. Remove the flesh with a grapefruit knife, being careful not to pierce the shell.

2. Cut the pineapple flesh into large dice. Put it in a non-reactive mixing bowl and stir in the frozen yogurt and 2 tablespoons of the rum. Pack this mixture back into the pineapple shells and place them in the freezer.

3. Prepare the meringue: Put the egg whites in an electric mixer and start beating at low speed. Add the cream of tartar. Gradually increase the speed to medium and continue beating while you prepare the sugar syrup.

4. Place ½ cup of the sugar and the water in a small heavy saucepan with a lid. Cover and bring to a boil. Uncover and cook to the softball stage.

5. Increase the mixer speed to high and beat the egg whites to soft peaks. Add the remaining ¼ cup sugar and beat until the whites are glossy and firm but not dry. This will take about 8 minutes in all. With the mixer running, pour the hot sugar syrup and vanilla into the egg whites and continue beating until completely cool.

6. Preheat the oven to 450°F. Transfer the meringue to a pastry bag fitted with a large star tip. Pipe decorative swirls of meringue over the top of the pineapple halves to completely encase the frozen yogurt.

7. Place the pineapple halves on a baking sheet in the oven and bake until the meringue is nicely browned, 3 to 5 minutes. Transfer to a platter and serve at once. To flambé the Baked Hawaii, heat the remaining 3 tablespoons rum in a small saucepan set over medium heat until warm to the touch (do not allow to boil). Touch a lighted match to the surface of the rum and pour the flaming liquid over the pineapple halves. Be very careful when you flambé. Keep your face away from the pan and take care not to spill any of the flaming liquid on the tablecloth, the napkins, or your clothes.

Note: Coconut rum is actually a coconut-flavored rum and is available at most liquor stores. One popular brand is Malibu.

Makes 8 servings

169 CALORIES PER SERVING; 3 G PROTEIN; 0.3 G FAT; 0 G SATURATED FAT; 37 G CARBOHYDRATE; 80 MG SODIUM; 0 MG CHOLESTEROL

Baked Hawaii

CHOCOLATE SORBET

This rich, fudgy chocolate sorbet is the next best thing to chocolate ice cream. Think of it as a low-fat Carvel.

1¼ cups sugar
½ cup unsweetened Dutch-processed cocoa powder
2 cups water
2-inch piece vanilla bean, split
1 ounce unsweetened chocolate, chopped

1. Sift the sugar and cocoa into a large heavy saucepan. Gradually whisk in the water and add the vanilla bean. Bring the mixture to a rolling boil. Add the chocolate and whisk until melted. Let cool to room temperature, then refrigerate until cold.

2. Freeze the mixture in an ice-cream machine, following the manufacturer's instructions. Serve the sorbet in wineglasses or martini glasses.

Makes 3 cups, which will serve 4 to 6

285 CALORIES PER SERVING; 3 G PROTEIN; 5 G FAT; 1.7 G SATURATED FAT; 69 G CARBOHYDRATE; 11 MG SODIUM; 0 MG CHOLESTEROL

GIANDUIA
(CHOCOLATE HAZELNUT)
GELATO

Gianduia *(pronounced jan-DOO-ya) is a classic combination of chocolate and toasted hazelnuts associated with the Piedmont city of Turin. If you think chocolate and hazelnuts are good by themselves, wait until you try them together.*

½ cup hazelnuts

1 cup sugar, or to taste

3 cups water

½ cup unsweetened cocoa powder

½ cup no-fat sweetened condensed milk

2 tablespoons hazelnut liqueur (such as Frangelico), plus 2 tablespoons for serving

1. Preheat the oven to 400°F. Toast the hazelnuts in a roasting pan until fragrant and the skins begin to split (about 5 minutes). Transfer the nuts to a clean dish towel and rub them between your hands to remove the skins. (Don't worry if you can't get all the skins off—the idea is to remove the majority.) Let the nuts cool completely. Place nuts in a food processor with ¼ cup of the sugar and grind to a fine powder, running the machine in short bursts.

2. Combine the water, the remaining ¾ cup sugar, the cocoa powder, and the condensed milk in a heavy saucepan and bring to a rolling boil, whisking as needed. When the sugar is completely dissolved and the mixture is syrupy, remove the pan from the heat and let cool to room temperature. Stir in the hazelnut mixture and the 2 tablespoons hazelnut liqueur.

3. Freeze the mixture in an ice cream machine, following the manufacturer's instructions. Serve the gelato in martini glasses, splashing additional hazelnut liqueur on top.

Makes about 1 quart, enough to serve 6 to 8

319 CALORIES PER SERVING;* 5 G PROTEIN; 8 G FAT; 1 G SATURATED FAT; 59 G CARBOHYDRATE; 32 MG SODIUM; 3 MG CHOLESTEROL

Analysis is based on 6 servings.

LEMON-LIME GRANITA

Granita is, perhaps, the most refreshing dessert on the face of the planet. It consists of nothing more than frozen fruit juice, sugar, and water, scraped into icy crystals as it freezes. These tiny crystals (granita literally means "tiny seed") melt on the tongue like snowflakes, releasing tiny bursts of flavor. This recipe offers the tropical touch of lime (after all, the author lives in Miami), but you could certainly make a traditional lemon granita by using all lemon juice and zest.

2 cups water

⅔ cup sugar, or to taste

6 tablespoons fresh lemon juice

6 tablespoons fresh lime juice

2 teaspoons finely grated fresh lemon zest

2 teaspoons finely grated fresh lime zest

1. Combine the water and sugar in a shallow nonreactive bowl and whisk until the sugar crystals are dissolved. Stir in the citrus juice and zest. Taste the mixture for sweetness, adding sugar or citrus juice as desired. Transfer the granita to the freezer.

2. Freeze the granita, scraping the mixture with a fork three or four times as it freezes to break it into ice crystals. Scrape again just before serving to loosen the crystals.

Serves 6

97 CALORIES PER SERVING; 0 G PROTEIN; 0 G FAT; 27 G CARBOHYDRATE; 3 MG SODIUM; 0 MG CHOLESTEROL

CHAMOMILE GRANITA

Granitas are the world's simplest frozen dessert, consisting of frozen flavored water or wine. The name comes from the Italian granita, *meaning "small seed," a description of the tiny ice crystals that give this dessert its crunch. Cool, light, and refreshing, granitas are perfect for warm weather. This recipe is from my assistant Didi Emmons.*

2¼ cups water

¼ cup loose chamomile tea (or 4 tea bags)

¼ cup fresh lemon juice (or to taste)

¼ cup honey (or to taste)

Bring the water to a boil and remove the pan from the heat. Add the tea and let steep for 5 minutes. Strain into a bowl and stir in the lemon juice and honey to taste.

Place the bowl in the freezer for 6 to 8 hours. Scrape the mixture 2 or 3 times with a fork as it freezes. Just before serving, scrape the mixture again with a fork to obtain loose ice crystals. Serve in chilled wine glasses.

Serves 4 to 6

86 CALORIES PER SERVING; 0 G PROTEIN; 0 G FAT; 23 G CARBOHYDRATE; 3 MG SODIUM; 0 MG CHOLESTEROL

BEAUJOLAIS GRANITA

Granitas are the world's simplest frozen dessert, consisting of frozen sweetened wine or fruit juice flaked into icy crystals with a fork. (Granita means "small seed" in Italian—a fitting description of the tiny bits of ice that make up this grainy sorbet.) Few experiences can match the sensation of these delicate crystals melting on the tongue. This is a great way to use up those bottles of Beaujolais Nouveau you never got around to drinking in November.

1 bottle Beaujolais or other light, fruity red wine

1½ cups cold water

3 tablespoons fresh lemon juice

¾ cup sugar, or to taste

1. Put the wine, water, lemon juice, and sugar in a nonreactive mixing bowl and whisk until the sugar is completely dissolved. Transfer the mixture to a metal bowl and place in the freezer. As the liquid freezes, scrape it two or three times with a fork to break it up.

2. To serve, scrape again and spoon the granita into glasses that have been chilled in the freezer. Serve immediately, as the granita melts quickly.

Makes about 1 quart, which will serve 6 to 8

181 CALORIES PER SERVING; 0.5 G PROTEIN; 0 G FAT; 0 G SATURATED FAT; 27 G CARBOHYDRATE; 82 MG SODIUM; 0 MG CHOLESTEROL

ALMOND BISCOTTI

These hard, dry Italian cookies have taken the country by storm. This recipe comes from a friend and fellow food writer, Lucy Cooper, who lives in Fort Lauderdale, Florida.

2½ cups flour
½ cup yellow cornmeal
1 cup sugar
2 teaspoons baking powder
¼ teaspoon salt
3 egg whites, lightly beaten
¼ cup canola oil
1 teaspoon almond extract
finely grated zest of 1 lemon
finely grated zest of 1 orange
¼–½ cup dry white wine

Preheat the oven to 350°F. Combine the flour, cornmeal, sugar, baking powder, and salt in a large bowl and whisk to mix. In another large bowl, combine the egg whites, oil, almond extract, zests, and ¼ cup of the wine. Whisk to mix.

Gradually stir the flour mixture into the wine mixture, adding wine as necessary to obtain a soft, pliable

CHOCOLATE HAZELNUT BISCOTTI

Chocolate and hazelnuts are classic dessert flavorings in Piedmont, particularly in Turin, where they're combined to make both a pudding and a gelato called gianduia *(pronounced "jan-DOO-ee-ya"). If you've never tasted the combination, you'll be amazed how complex the resulting flavor is. The easiest way to skin hazelnuts is to roast them in a hot oven for a few minutes, then rub them in a clean dish towel.*

½ cup shelled hazelnuts

2 eggs, plus 2 egg whites

1 cup sugar

3 tablespoons canola oil

1 tablespoon hazelnut liqueur (such as Frangelico), or amaretto liqueur

1¼ cups all-purpose unbleached white flour

½ cup unsweetened cocoa powder

¼ cup cornstarch

¼ cup stone-ground cornmeal

¼ teaspoon salt (optional)

1½ teaspoons baking powder

1. Preheat the oven to 400°F. Place the hazelnuts in a roasting pan and roast until fragrant and the skins start to blister, 5 to 8 minutes. Wrap the nuts, a few at a time, in a clean dish towel and rub them between the palms of your hands to loosen the skin. Toss the nuts between your fingers to shake away the skins. Return any hard-to-peel nuts to the oven for additional roasting. (Don't worry if you don't get every last piece of skin off. The purpose of the roasting is as much to intensify the flavor of the nuts as to remove the skins.)

2. Reduce the oven temperature to 350°F. Combine the eggs, egg whites, sugar, oil, and liqueur in a mixing bowl and whisk until smooth. Sift in the dry ingredients. Add the hazelnuts and stir just to mix. You should wind up with a soft, pliable dough.

3. Transfer the dough to the back of a baking sheet and roll it into a log about 16 inches long. Gently pat it into a rectangle 5 to 6 inches wide and ½-inch high, tapering at the edges. Score the top of the rectangle with a knife, making shallow cuts on the diagonal every ½-inch.

4. Bake the biscotti for 25 minutes, or until the tops are firm to the touch. Remove the pan from the oven and let cool for 3 minutes.

5. Using a serrated knife, cut each rectangle into ½-inch slices, following the lines you scored on top. Place the slices, cut side down, on the baking sheet and bake for 10 minutes. Turn the biscotti and bake for 10 minutes more, or until crusty.

6. Transfer the biscotti to a wire rack to cool to room temperature, then store in an airtight container. The traditional way to eat biscotti is to dip them in coffee or wine, but I also like to munch them straight.

Makes 32 to 36 biscotti

74 CALORIES PER PIECE; 2 G PROTEIN; 3 G FAT; 0.3 G SATURATED FAT; 12 G CARBOHYDRATE; 22 MG SODIUM; 12 MG CHOLESTEROL

dough. Divide the dough in two and roll each half between your hands into a 12-inch log. Place the logs on a baking sheet lined with parchment paper, leaving 5 inches between them. Gently flatten the logs with your fingertips to form a ½-inch-thick rectangle.

Bake for 35 to 40 minutes, or until the tops are firm to the touch.

Remove from the oven and let cool for 3 minutes.

Using a serrated knife, cut each log on the diagonal into ½-inch slices. Place the slices, cut side down, on the baking sheet and bake for 10 to 15 minutes, or until golden brown. Turn the biscotti and bake for 10 to 15 minutes more.

Completely cool the biscotti on a wire rack and store in an airtight container. The traditional way to eat biscotti is to dip them in coffee or wine, but I like to munch them straight.

Makes 40 biscotti

72 CALORIES PER BISCOTTI; 1 G PROTEIN; 1 G FAT; 13 G CARBOHYDRATE; 34 MG SODIUM; 0 MG CHOLESTEROL

DRIED-CHERRY BISCOTTI

Biscotti—the crisp, double-baked Italian cookies—have taken America by storm. For an offbeat touch, I flavor them with dried cherries, which are available at gourmet shops and natural foods stores or by mail order from American Spoon Foods, (800) 222-5886. For a New England accent, you could substitute dried cranberries.

2 large eggs plus 2 whites

½ cup granulated sugar

½ cup packed light-brown sugar

3 tablespoons canola oil

1 tablespoon kirsch or 1 teaspoon almond extract

2 teaspoons vanilla extract

1 cup dried cherries

2 teaspoons grated lemon zest

2¾ cups unbleached all-purpose flour, or as needed

¼ cup cornmeal (or more flour)

¼ cup cornstarch

¼ teaspoon salt (optional)

1½ teaspoons baking powder

1 teaspoon ground cardamom or cinnamon

spray oil

1. Preheat the oven to 350°F. Combine the eggs, egg whites, sugars, oil, kirsch, and vanilla in a mixing bowl and stir with a wooden spoon to mix. Stir in the dried cherries and lemon zest. Sift in the flour, cornmeal, cornstarch, salt, baking powder, and cardamom and stir or beat just to mix. You should wind up with a soft, pliable dough. Add more flour if dough is too sticky to handle.

2. Lightly spray a large baking sheet (preferably nonstick) with spray oil. Transfer the dough to the prepared baking sheet and roll it into a log about 16 inches long. Gently pat into a rectangle 5 to 6 inches wide and ½-inch high, tapering at the edges. (You may need to wet your hands to prevent the dough from sticking to them.) Score the top of each rectangle with a knife, making shallow cuts on the diagonal every ½-inch.

3. Bake the biscotti for 25 minutes, or until the top is firm to the touch. Remove the pan from the oven and let cool for 3 minutes.

4. Using a serrated knife, cut the loaf into ½-inch slices, following the lines you scored on top. Place the slices, cut side down, on the baking sheet and bake for 10 minutes. Turn the biscotti and bake for 10 minutes more, or until crusty.

5. Transfer the biscotti to a wire rack to cool to room temperature. Store in an airtight container.

Makes about 3 dozen biscotti

92 CALORIES PER PIECE; 2 G PROTEIN; 1.6 G FAT; 0.2 G SATURATED FAT; 18 G CARBOHYDRATE; 20 MG SODIUM; 12 MG CHOLESTEROL

Dried-Cherry Biscotti

AUNT LINDA'S CINNAMON-CURRANT MANDELBROT

Mandelbrot (literally, "almond bread") could be described as Jewish biscotti. This one features a crumbly cinnamon-sugar filling and is just the thing for dipping in coffee. Readers of my other books will be familiar with the culinary prowess of my Grammie Ethel. This recipe was inspired by her daughter, my aunt Linda Millison, from Philadelphia.

1½ cups sugar

1 teaspoon ground cinnamon

2 large eggs plus 2 large egg whites

¼ cup canola oil

2 teaspoons vanilla extract

1 teaspoon almond extract

¾ cup currants or raisins

3½ cups flour

2 teaspoons baking powder

spray oil

1. Preheat the oven to 350°F. Mix ½ cup of the sugar with the cinnamon in a small bowl and set aside. Put the remaining 1 cup sugar, the eggs, and the egg whites in an electric mixer and beat at medium speed until light and foamy, about 5 minutes. Beat in the oil, vanilla, and almond extract. Stir in the currants. Sift the flour and baking powder into the mixture and stir just to combine. You should wind up with a soft, pliable dough. Add more flour if dough is too sticky to handle.

2. Lightly spray a baking sheet (preferably nonstick) with spray oil. Cut the dough in half. Roll each half into a log 14-inches long and 2-inches wide, and place it on the prepared baking sheet. (You may need to wet your hands to prevent the dough from sticking to them.) Using the side of your hand, make a 1-inch depression in the top running the length of the log. Sprinkle half the cinnamon-sugar into each depression and pinch the depression closed. Pat each log into a loaf shape about 12-inches long, 4-inches wide, and ¼-inch high.

3. Bake until the mandelbrot is firm to the touch and an inserted cake tester comes out clean, about 40 minutes. Transfer the loaves to a cutting board. Using a serrated knife, cut them into ½-inch slices. Transfer the slices to a wire rack to cool. Store the mandelbrot in an airtight container.

Makes about 4 dozen cookies

93 CALORIES PER PIECE; 1.7 G PROTEIN; 1.8 G FAT; 0.2 G SATURATED FAT; 18 G CARBOHYDRATE; 21 MG SODIUM; 11 MG CHOLESTEROL

CHOCOLATE MADELEINES

Madeleines are cake-like, shell-shaped cookies, of course, and they're so beloved by the French that a single bite was enough to inspire French novelist Marcel Proust to write Remembrance of Things Past. *We made lots of madeleines at the La Varenne cooking school in Paris, where the order of the day was "butter, butter, and more butter."*

spray oil

1 cup unbleached all-purpose white flour, plus flour for dusting the mold

¼ cup unsweetened Dutch-processed cocoa powder

1½ teaspoons baking powder

½ teaspoon baking soda

½ cup low-fat buttermilk

2 tablespoons canola oil

1 tablespoon butter, melted

1 teaspoon vanilla extract

1 large egg, plus 1 large egg white

¾ cup sugar

¼ cup confectioners' sugar for sprinkling

madeleine molds

1. Preheat the oven to 400°F. Spray the molds with oil and dust with flour, shaking out the excess. Combine the flour, cocoa, baking powder, and baking soda in a mixing bowl, whisk to mix, and set aside. Combine the buttermilk, oil, melted butter, and vanilla in another bowl and set aside.

2. Combine the egg, egg white, and sugar in an electric mixer. Beat until thick and foamy, starting on medium speed, then high, about 8 minutes in all. When the eggs are ready, the mixture will be pale-yellow and tripled in volume and will fall from a raised whisk in a thick, silky ribbon.

3. Sift the flour mixture into the egg mixture in three batches, alternately adding the buttermilk mixture and folding gently with a rubber spatula between each addition. Spoon the batter into the prepared molds, filling each ¼ of the way. Bake the madeleines until cooked, 12 to 15 minutes; when they are done, the tops will spring back when pressed lightly. Let the madeleines cool in the pans for 1 minute, then unmold onto a cake rack. Let cool completely. Dust the madeleines (the ribbed side) with confectioners' sugar and serve.

Note: Madeleine molds are available at cookware shops. Or you can use small fluted tartlet molds.

Makes about 2 dozen

68 CALORIES PER PIECE; 1.3 G PROTEIN; 2 G FAT; 0.5 G SATURATED FAT; 12 G CARBOHYDRATE; 51 MG SODIUM; 10 MG CHOLESTEROL

TORTILLA CRISPS

Buñuelos, fried dough sprinkled with cinnamon-sugar, are a popular Mexican dessert. Here's a low-fat version made with flour tortillas and baked instead of deep-fried. The recipe is almost embarrassingly simple, requiring just 4 ingredients and 5 minutes' preparation time, but it never fails to delight.

4 flour tortillas

1 tablespoon butter, melted, or canola oil

⅓ cup sugar

1 tablespoon ground cinnamon

1. Preheat the oven to 400°F. Lightly brush the top of each tortilla with butter. Mix the sugar with the cinnamon in a small bowl.

2. Sprinkle 1 tablespoon of the cinnamon-sugar mixture over each tortilla and spread it evenly with a spoon. Cut each tortilla into 8 wedges. Transfer the wedges to a baking sheet lined with foil. Bake until the tortillas are crisp and lightly browned, about 5 minutes. Transfer the tortilla crisps to a wire rack to cool.

Makes 32 crisps

9 CALORIES PER PIECE; 0 G PROTEIN; 0.3 G FAT; 0.2 G SATURATED FAT; 2 G CARBOHYDRATE; 5 MG SODIUM; 1 MG CHOLESTEROL

CINNAMON CHIPS WITH FRUIT "SALSA"

Salsa and chips for dessert? The idea might seem oddball, but this colorful dessert is grounded in Mexican tradition. First, the chips—my version of a crisp, flat fritter called buñuelo. My low-fat recipe calls for flour tortillas to be brushed with a little butter, sprinkled with spiced sugar, and baked crisp in the oven. The "salsa" is actually a fruit salad.

6 (8-inch) flour tortillas

1½ tablespoons melted butter (preferably unsalted) or canola oil

⅓ cup granulated sugar

1½ tablespoons ground cinnamon

½ teaspoon anise seeds

¼ teaspoon ground cloves

Fruit "Salsa" (page 356)

6 sprigs mint, for garnish

COCOA KISSES

I've always loved hard meringues—the kind that make a deafening crunch when you bite into them.
They gave me the idea for a low-fat "kiss": a teardrop of meringue that could be dipped in chocolate for extra richness.
(The kisses are plenty delicious without it.) For truly crisp meringues, I like to bake them at a very low temperature
and allow them to dry out in the oven's residual heat overnight.

spray oil

flour for dusting

⅔ cup sugar

3 tablespoons unsweetened Dutch-processed cocoa powder

½ teaspoon ground cinnamon (optional)

1 tablespoon cornstarch

3 large egg whites

¼ teaspoon cream of tartar

1 teaspoon vanilla extract

1 to 2 ounces semisweet or bittersweet chocolate (preferably Valrhona) (optional)

1. Preheat the oven to 200°F. Line a baking sheet with baking parchment. Lightly spray it with oil and dust with flour, shaking off the excess.

2. Sift ⅓ cup of the sugar and the cocoa, cinnamon, and cornstarch into a small bowl, and set aside. Beat the egg whites in an electric mixer at low speed 1 minute. Add the cream of tartar. Gradually increase the speed and beat the whites to soft peaks, about 6 to 8 minutes. Add the remaining ⅓ cup sugar in a thin stream and continue beating until the whites are firm and glossy but not dry. Stir in the vanilla. Using a rubber spatula, gently fold the cocoa mixture into the beaten whites.

3. Transfer the meringue to a pastry bag fitted with a ½-inch round or star tip. (A star tip will give you a ridged kiss.) Holding the tip ¼-inch above the baking sheet, pipe a 1-inch-wide ball, reducing the pressure and lifting the tip to taper it to a point. (You should wind up with a shape like a Hershey's kiss.) Repeat the process with the rest of the meringue.

4. Bake the meringues until they are firm and crisp, 3 to 4 hours. Turn off the heat and leave the meringues to dry out in the oven overnight. Gently pry the meringues off the baking sheet with a spatula.

5. If dipping the kisses, melt the chocolate in a bowl set over a pan of barely simmering water. (Do not let even a drop of water come in contact with the chocolate, or it may "seize.") Holding a meringue by its base, dip it in the melted chocolate and let the excess drip off. Invert it onto a sheet of wax paper or parchment and let cool. Repeat the process with the other kisses. When they are completely cool, store them in an airtight container away from heat and light.

Makes 5 to 6 dozen kisses

10 CALORIES PER SERVING (1 KISS); 0.2 G PROTEIN; 0 G FAT; 0 G SATURATED FAT; 2.5 G CARBOHYDRATE; 4 MG SODIUM; 0 MG CHOLESTEROL

---

1. Preheat the oven to 400°F. Lightly brush the tortillas on both sides with melted butter and arrange them in a single layer on baking sheets. Combine the sugar, cinnamon, anise, and cloves in a bowl and whisk to mix. Sprinkle 1 tablespoon of the spiced sugar over each tortilla. Cut each tortilla into 6 wedges.

2. Bake the tortillas until they're lightly browned, about 5 minutes. Remove the tortillas from the oven and let cool; the "chips" will crisp as they cool.

3. Spoon the salsa into six ramekins, garnish each with a mint sprig, and place in the center of dessert plates. Arrange the chips around the salsa and serve at once.

Serves 6

202 CALORIES PER SERVING; 4 G PROTEIN; 6 G FAT; 2 G SATURATED FAT; 34 G CARBOHYDRATE; 288 MG SODIUM; 8 MG CHOLESTEROL

BEVERAGES

THE REAL MARGARITA

Who really invented the margarita? There are lots of candidates, including bartenders in Tijuana, Acapulco, and even San Antonio, Texas. One thing's for sure, though: No Mexican meal would be complete without this tangy, sweet-salty tequila and fresh lime thirst quencher. Like most cocktails that are too successful for their own good, the margarita has inspired a great deal of nonsense in recent years: frozen margaritas, banana margaritas, margaritas prepared with bottled mixes. Here's an authentic margarita that will get you back to the basics of good drinking and eating. One tequila I particularly like for margaritas is Herradura Gold.

2 tablespoons sugar

2 strips lime zest

2 strips orange zest

6 ounces (¾ cup) good tequila

⅓ cup Cointreau or other bitter orange liqueur

½ cup fresh lime juice

2 tablespoons water

5 fresh lime wedges

Kosher salt or coarse sea salt (optional)

4 cups ice

1. Place the sugar, lime zest, and orange zest in a mortar and pound with a pestle. The idea is to bruise the zests, extracting the fragrant oils. (If you don't have a mortar, pound the zests with the end of a wooden spoon in a bowl.)

2. Transfer the sugar and zests to a pitcher and stir in the tequila, Cointreau, lime juice, and water. If you have the time, let the mixture sit for a couple of hours in the refrigerator to allow the flavors to meld.

3. Rub the rims of four martini glasses with one of the lime wedges. Spread the salt, if using, in a shallow bowl.

Dip each glass, rim side down, in the salt to coat the rim. Shake off the excess salt and right the glasses.

Note: If you're watching your sodium intake, omit the salt.

4. Just before serving, add the ice to the margarita and stir or shake well, 2 minutes. Strain the margarita into the prepared glasses. Festoon each with a wedge of lime and serve at once.

Serves 4

200 CALORIES PER SERVING; 1 G PROTEIN; 0 G FAT; 0 G SATURATED FAT; 20 G CARBOHYDRATE; 2 MG SODIUM; 0 MG CHOLESTEROL

MIXED-FRUIT MARGARITA

Necessity, goes the saying, is the mother of invention. A margarita made without tequila may seem like a contradiction in terms, but if you have a Mexican restaurant without a liquor license, this is precisely what you may find yourself serving. Mexico City–born Los Angeles restaurateur Frank Romero has risen to the challenge, concocting a margarita from a soothing blend of vermouth and tropical fruit juices. You've probably never had the likes of this margarita, but I wager that you'll find yourself wanting seconds.

1 or 2 wedges fresh lime

Kosher salt or coarse sea salt (optional)

1 cup fresh or canned diced pineapple

1 cup diced honeydew melon

1 cup guava nectar

⅓ cup fresh lime juice, or to taste

⅔ cup dry white vermouth

1½ tablespoons sugar, or to taste

2 cups ice cubes

1. Rub the rims of six martini glasses with the cut lime. Spread the salt, if using, in a shallow bowl. Dip each glass, rim side down, in the salt to coat the rim. Shake off the excess salt and right the glasses.

2. Combine the pineapple, melon, guava nectar, lime juice, vermouth, sugar, and ice in a blender and purée until smooth. Correct the tartness and sweetness, adding lime juice or sugar to taste. Pour the margarita mixture into the glasses without disturbing the salt and serve at once.

Serves 6

90.7 CALORIES PER SERVING; .3 G PROTEIN; .2 G FAT; 0 G SATURATED FAT; 16.6 G CARBOHYDRATE; 10.4 MG SODIUM; 0 MG CHOLESTEROL

SOURPUSS LEMONADE

Nothing goes to waste in this lemonade, which uses both the sour juice and the fragrant zest of the lemon. When choosing lemons, avoid fruits with knobby ends (they tend to be dry) and those with a greenish tinge (they tend to be sour, even for lemons).

4–6 lemons (1 cup juice), plus 1 lemon for garnish

⅓ cup sugar (or to taste)

4 cups water

ice

Wash the lemons and remove the zest of all but the lemon for garnish with a vegetable peeler. (Be sure to take only the yellow outer rind, not the bitter white pith beneath it.) Combine the zest, sugar, and 1 cup of the water in a saucepan. Simmer the mixture for 10 minutes. Strain it into a heat-proof pitcher and let cool.

Cut the zested lemons in half and extract the juice. Stir it and the remaining water into the lemon syrup. Correct the flavoring, adding sugar and lemon juice to taste.

Serve the lemonade in tall glasses with ice. Cut the remaining lemon into wedges or slices for garnish. For a fancier presentation, rub the rim of each glass with cut lemon and dip it in sugar.

Serves 4

75 CALORIES PER SERVING; 0 G PROTEIN; 0 G FAT; 21 G CARBOHYDRATE; 8 MG SODIUM; 0 MG CHOLESTEROL

WALNUT RICE PUNCH WITH MELON
(HORCHATA)

Milky white, nutty and sweet, horchata is one of the most offbeat beverages sold at a Mexican juice bar or lunch counter. Its origins lie a continent and a millennium away: The Moors brought rice to Spain when they invaded in the 8th century A.D. Rice and walnuts may seem like odd flavorings for a beverage, but the combination is amazingly refreshing. Horchata-type drinks can be found throughout the former Spanish empire; the melon is a strictly Mexican touch.

2 cinnamon sticks

4 cloves

4 allspice berries

½ teaspoon anise seed

2 strips orange zest

5 cups water

½ cup uncooked white rice

¼ cup chopped walnuts

⅓ cup sugar, or to taste

½ teaspoon almond extract

2 cups diced honeydew melon

Serves 4

221 CALORIES PER SERVING; 3 G PROTEIN; 3 G FAT; 0 G SATURATED FAT; 46 G CARBOHYDRATE; 20 MG SODIUM; 0 MG CHOLESTEROL

1. Tie the cinnamon, cloves, allspice, anise seed, and orange zest in a piece of cheesecloth. Combine the water, rice, walnuts, sugar, almond extract, and spice bundle in a pitcher and let steep for 6 to 8 hours, preferably overnight.

2. Remove and discard the spice bundle. Place the rice mixture and half the melon in a blender and blend until smooth. Taste for sweetness, adding sugar as needed.

3. Strain the horchata through a fine-mesh strainer into a pitcher. Stir in the remaining melon. Serve chilled.

MINT FIZZ

This drink is a booze-free twist on a classic cocktail made with gin. The mint and lemon flavors are so intense that you won't miss the alcohol.

3 or 4 lemons

¼ cup fresh mint leaves, plus 4 sprigs for garnish

⅓ cup sugar

1 egg white

3½ cups sparkling water

2 cups crushed ice

Juice the lemons. (There should be ¾ cup juice.) Wash and stem the mint leaves. Combine the lemon juice, mint leaves, sugar, and egg white in a blender. Blend at high speed for 1 minute. Add the sparkling water and ice. Blend until the mix-ture is smooth. Pour into glasses and garnish with mint sprigs.

Serves 4

76 CALORIES PER SERVING; 1 G PROTEIN; 0 G FAT; 20 G CARBOHYDRATE; 59 MG SODIUM; 0 MG CHOLESTEROL

MINTED LIMEADE

This drink combines the cooling properties of fresh mint with the thirst-quenching tartness of lime. It's more refreshing than all the beer at Budweiser. Pounding the lime zest and mint with the sugar helps release the fragrant oils.

6–8 limes (1 cup juice)

15 fresh mint leaves, plus 4 sprigs for garnish

⅓–½ cup sugar (or to taste)

4 cups water

ice

Using a vegetable peeler, remove the zest from 3 of the limes. Cut all the limes in half and extract the juice. Combine the zest, mint leaves, and sugar in a mortar or sturdy bowl, and crush with a pestle or the end of a rolling pin to release the aromatic oils.

Place the sugar mixture in a pitcher and whisk in the lime juice and water. Whisk until all the sugar crystals are dissolved. Correct the flavoring, adding sugar to taste. The limeade can be served right away, but the flavor will improve if it stands for 15 minutes. To serve, strain the limeade into ice-filled glasses, garnishing each with mint sprigs.

Serves 4

76 CALORIES PER SERVING; 0 G PROTEIN; 0 G FAT; 21 G CARBOHYDRATE; 8 MG SODIUM; 0 MG CHOLESTEROL

MANGO NECTAR
(AGUA DE MANGO)

This golden drink is one of the delights of a Mexican juice bar, a perfumed nectar made with nature's perfect fruit. But to get the full effect, you must use ripe mangoes— the kind you can smell from the kitchen the moment you walk into the house. Smell alone will tell you a mango's ripeness, as some varieties remain green even when they're ready to eat. To ripen mangoes, place them in a loosely sealed paper bag at room temperature. **Note:** *If you have sensitive skin, wear gloves when working with mangoes. Some people have a violent allergic reaction to mango sap.*

1 large or 2 small ripe mangoes (about 1½ pounds)

2 to 4 tablespoons sugar, or to taste

2 tablespoons fresh lime juice, or to taste

4 cups water

1. Peel the mango and cut the flesh off the seed. Place the flesh in a blender with the sugar, lime juice, and water. Purée until smooth. Taste for sweetness and tartness, adding sugar or lime juice as needed.

2. Strain the mango nectar into a pitcher and refrigerate until you're ready to serve. If it's too thick, add a little more water. Serve over ice in a tall glass. Stir well just before serving.

Serves 4

137 CALORIES PER SERVING; 1 G PROTEIN; 1 G FAT; 0 G SATURATED FAT; 36 G CARBOHYDRATE; 11 MG SODIUM; 0 MG CHOLESTEROL

TAMARIND NECTAR
(AGUA DE TAMARINDO)

Mexicans love fruit drinks. Visit almost any casual restaurant or market stall and you'll see a rainbow-colored assortment of beverages lined up on the bar in handsome glass jars. This brown drink may not look as pretty as the others, but when it comes to quenching a thirst, nothing can beat the smoky, sweet-sour tang of tamarind. This tan, curved, tropical seedpod harbors an orangish brown pulp that tastes uncannily like prunes soaked in lime juice. If you live in a city with a large Hispanic community, you may be able to find whole tamarind pods. (Choose ripe pods—the ones with cracked tan skins.) More commonly, the tamarind pulp is sold peeled but with the seeds in plastic bags. This is what I call for below (see Note).

4 ounces peeled tamarind pulp, or 6 to 8 peeled pods

1 cup hot water

4 cups cold water

4 to 6 tablespoons sugar (or to taste)

1. Place the tamarind pulp in the bowl of a blender or food processor with the hot water and let stand for 5 minutes. Blend the mixture in short bursts at low speed until the seeds are free of pulp, 30 to 60 seconds.

2. Pour the tamarind mixture through a strainer into a pitcher, pressing hard with a wooden spoon to extract the juices and scraping the bottom of the strainer with a rubber spatula.

3. Return the seeds and pulp that remain in the strainer to the blender and mix with the 4 cups of cold water and the sugar. Strain this mixture into the pitcher and stir. Chill well.

4. Just before serving, check the tamarind nectar for sweetness, adding sugar as needed. Stir well and serve at once in tumblers filled with ice.

Note: Hispanic grocery stores often sell packages of frozen tamarind purée (pulpa de tamarindo). If you can find this, place 12 ounces in the pitcher. Stir in the cold water and sugar to taste, omitting the blending in steps 1 and 3.

Serves 4

56 CALORIES PER SERVING; 0 G PROTEIN; 0 G FAT; 0 G SATURATED FAT; 14 G CARBOHYDRATE; 9 MG SODIUM; 0 MG CHOLESTEROL

CAJUN MARY

This drink may lack alcohol, but it's not without a kick.
V-8 Juice has a richer flavor than tomato juice,
but you can certainly use the latter, or even the juice
from canned plum tomatoes.

1 quart V-8 juice

2 tablespoons prepared horseradish

1 tablespoon Worcestershire sauce

1 tablespoon juice from pickled jalapeño chilies
(optional)

1–2 teaspoons Tabasco

1 teaspoon celery seeds

juice of 1 lemon (or to taste)

salt and freshly ground black pepper

ice

Cajun Spice, for garnish

4 pickled jalapeño chilies, for garnish (optional)

Place the V-8 Juice in a pitcher. Stir in the horseradish,
Worcestershire sauce, jalapeño juice, Tabasco, celery seeds,
lemon juice, salt, and pepper. Correct the seasoning,
adding flavorings to suit your taste. The mixture should
be very spicy. Pour into ice-filled glasses. Sprinkle a
pinch of Cajun Spice over each glass and garnish with
a jalapeño chili, if desired.

Serves 4

58 CALORIES PER SERVING; .3 G PROTEIN; .1 G FAT; 12 G CARBOHYDRATE;
950 MG SODIUM; 0 MG CHOLESTEROL

SANGRITA
(SPICED TOMATO JUICE "CHASER")

Sit down to any serious meal in Mexico and you'll be
offered twin glasses of sipping tequila and sangrita.
Sangrita is a spicy "chaser" based on tomato and orange or
lime juice, often with a little chili powder or pickled pepper
juice for punch. The presentation might be rounded out
with a few radishes, scallions, or jícama slices to munch on.

1 cup tomato juice

¾ cup fresh orange juice

¼ cup fresh lime juice, plus 1 or 2 lime wedges

2 tablespoons juice from pickled jalapeño peppers,
or to taste

2 tablespoons finely grated onion with juices (optional)

¼ cup pure chili powder

1. In a pitcher, mix together the tomato, orange, and
lime juices, the jalapeño pepper juice, and onion (if using).
Add lime juice or pepper juice to taste; the sangrita
should be highly seasoned.

2. Moisten the rims of eight straight-sided shot glasses
or cordial glasses with the lime wedges. Spread the chili
powder in a shallow bowl. Invert the glasses and dip them
to the chili powder to coat the rims. Pour the sangrita into
the glasses and serve at once.

Serves 8

31 CALORIES PER SERVING; 1 G PROTEIN; 1 G FAT; 0 G SATURATED FAT;
7 G CARBOHYDRATE; 177 MG SODIUM; 0 MG CHOLESTEROL

LASSI

Lassi is India's answer to the North American milkshake. It's an ideal drink to serve with hot and spicy food. (Contrary to popular belief, dairy products are much more effective than beer at extinguishing chili hellfire.) If rose water is unavailable, use a perfumed liqueur such as Cointreau or triple sec.

1 cup nonfat yogurt

2 tablespoons sugar (or to taste)

1 teaspoon rose water

5 ice cubes

⅛ teaspoon ground cardamom, for garnish

Serves 1

195 CALORIES PER SERVING; 13 G PROTEIN; .4 G FAT; 36 G CARBOHYDRATE; 174 MG SODIUM; 4 MG CHOLESTEROL

Combine the yogurt, sugar, rose water, and ice in a blender. Blend until smooth. Correct the flavoring, adding sugar and rose water to taste. Pour into a tall glass. Lightly sprinkle the top with cardamom and serve at once.

Thai Fruit Shake

THAI FRUIT SHAKE

This refreshing drink can be found at street stalls and open-air markets throughout Southeast Asia. Because of the hot climate and general lack of refrigeration, sweetened condensed milk is the dairy product of choice. Similar shakes can be made with virtually any other fruit.

1 cup diced watermelon

1 ripe banana, peeled and diced

1 cup diced fresh pineapple

1 tablespoon fresh lime juice (or to taste)

2 tablespoons sugar (or to taste)

2 tablespoons sweetened condensed milk

2 cups crushed ice

Combine all the ingredients in a blender and blend until smooth. Correct the flavoring, adding lime juice and sugar to taste.

Serves 2

225 CALORIES PER SERVING; 3 G PROTEIN; 3 G FAT; 52 G CARBOHYDRATE; 27 MG SODIUM; 7 MG CHOLESTEROL

SPICED COFFEE
(CAFÉ DE OLLA)

This dark, sweet, spicy coffee takes its name from the earthenware pot (olla) in which it's traditionally brewed. Cinnamon, cloves, and anise seed impart a beguiling spice flavor, while the piloncillo (Mexican brown sugar) both thickens and sweetens the brew. I can't think of a better beverage to bring a Mexican meal to a close.

5 cups water

1 cinnamon stick, plus 4 sticks for garnish

6 cloves

½ teaspoon anise seeds

2 strips orange zest

3 to 4 ounces piloncillo, chopped, or ⅓ cup brown sugar

½ cup freshly ground dark-roast coffee beans (like a French or Italian roast)

1. Combine the water, 1 stick of the cinnamon, cloves, anise seeds, orange zest, and sugar in a large pot and bring to a boil. Reduce the heat and gently simmer until the sugar is dissolved and the liquid is richly flavored, about 5 minutes.

2. Remove the pan from the heat and stir in the coffee. Let it steep for 5 minutes, then strain it into coffee mugs through a coffee filter, fine-mesh strainer, or a strainer lined with cheesecloth. Garnish each mug with a cinnamon stick and serve at once.

Serves 4

79 CALORIES PER SERVING; 0 G PROTEIN; 0 G FAT; 0 G SATURATED FAT; 21 G CARBOHYDRATE; 17 MG SODIUM; 0 MG CHOLESTEROL

HOT MULLED CIDER WITH GINGER

Here's a great hot mulled cider for serving on Halloween or Thanksgiving, at an après-ski party, or on any cold winter evening. The term mull *is etymologically related to* mill, *as in to mill or grind whole spices. For the best results, use whole spices and fresh, unpasteurized apple cider.*

½ gallon apple cider

⅓ cup brown sugar (or to taste)

1 lemon

2 oranges

4 ¼-inch slices fresh ginger

6 whole cloves

6 allspice berries

2 cinnamon sticks

4 cardamom pods

4 blades mace (or freshly grated nutmeg)

8 long cinnamon sticks, for garnish (optional)

Combine the cider and brown sugar in a large nonreactive pot. Remove the zest from the lemon and 1 of the oranges with a vegetable peeler. Juice the peeled fruits and add the juice to the cider. Cut the remaining orange into slices for garnish.

Tie the spices (except the cinnamon sticks) and zest in cheesecloth and add them to the cider. Bring the cider to a boil, reduce the heat, and simmer for about 20 minutes. Skim off any foam that rises to the surface. Remove the spice bundle before serving. Ladle the mulled cider into mugs and garnish with orange slices and cinnamon sticks (if using).

Serves 8

15 CALORIES PER SERVING; 0 G PROTEIN; 0 G FAT; 38 G CARBOHYDRATE; 20 MG SODIUM; 0 MG CHOLESTEROL

Mexican Hot Chocolate

MEXICAN HOT CHOCOLATE

Mexicans flavor their hot chocolate with cinnamon, cloves, and vanilla, a practice already popular when Cortès visited the court of Montezuma in the 16th century. Thanks to these spices, you won't miss the richness of whole milk. For a prettier presentation, sprinkle cinnamon or grate a little chocolate on top.

4 cups skim or 1 percent milk

⅓ cup unsweetened cocoa

⅓ cup sugar (or to taste)

1 teaspoon ground cinnamon

⅛ teaspoon ground cloves

1 vanilla bean, split (or 2 teaspoons vanilla extract)

Combine all the ingredients (except the vanilla extract, if using) in a heavy saucepan. Slowly bring the mixture to a boil, whisking constantly.

Remove the vanilla bean (you can rinse it off and reuse it) and pour the hot chocolate into mugs. (If using vanilla extract, add it to the hot chocolate after removing the pan from the heat.)

Serves 4

188 CALORIES PER SERVING; 10 G PROTEIN; 4 G FAT; 28 G CARBOHYDRATE; 125 MG SODIUM; 10 MG CHOLESTEROL

BASIC RECIPES

CHICKEN STOCK

Stock or brodo *(broth) is the foundation of much of great low-fat Italian cooking (or even great high-fat Italian cooking). Below is the recipe for the chicken broth used in this book. The cooked chicken meat can be used for stuffings and salads.*

1 3½- to 4-pound chicken

1 bay leaf

1 large onion, quartered (unpeeled)

1 clove

2 carrots, peeled and cut into 1-inch pieces

2 stalks celery, cut into 1-inch pieces

2 cloves garlic, peeled and cut in half

2 sprigs flat-leaf parsley

1 sprig rosemary

4 quarts cold water, or as needed

1. Remove the skin and lumps of fat from the chicken and wash the bird inside and out. Pin the bay leaf to one of the onion quarters with a clove. Place all the ingredients for the stock in a stockpot with enough cold water to cover the chicken.

2. Bring the stock to a boil and skim off any foam that rises to the surface. Lower the heat and gently simmer for 1 hour, adding cold water as necessary to keep the chicken covered and skimming the broth often with a flat ladle to remove any fat or impurities that rise to the surface, especially after you've added water. (The cold water brings the fat to the top.)

3. Ladle the stock through a strainer lined with paper towels into a large container and let cool to room temperature. Transfer the broth to 1- and 2-cup containers and refrigerate or freeze. (Broth will keep for 4 to 5 days in the refrigerator; for several months in the freezer.) The chicken can be pulled off the bone and used for stuffings and salads.

Note: Chicken stock can be made with 1½ pounds chicken parts or bones (such as backs or thighs).

Makes 10 to 12 cups

BASIC CHICKEN STOCK
(CALDO DE POLLO)

Chicken stock is the very soul of Mexican cuisine. Preparing it from scratch not only will make your food taste better and more authentic, but it also will be healthier, because you can eliminate the sodium and fat found in most canned chicken stock. Plus, it will leave you with delicious cooked chicken, which is always handy to have for stuffing into tortillas or piling on tostadas.

1 (3½ pound) chicken or 2 pounds chicken parts (backs, necks, wings)

1 bay leaf

1 medium onion, quartered

1 clove

1 large carrot, cut into 1-inch pieces

1 stalk celery, cut into 1-inch pieces

2 cloves garlic, cut in half

1 tomato, quartered

4 sprigs fresh cilantro

5 black peppercorns

10 to 12 cups cold water, or as needed

1. Remove the skin and any visible fat from the chicken and wash the bird inside and out. Pin the bay leaf to one of the onion quarters with a clove. Place the chicken, onion, carrot, celery, garlic, tomato, cilantro, and peppercorns in a large pot and add water to cover by 2 inches.

2. Bring the mixture to a boil over high heat. Skim off any fat or foam that rises to the surface. Lower the heat and gently simmer the broth until the bird is cooked, about 1 hour, adding cold water as needed to keep the chicken covered. Skim the stock often with a ladle to remove any fat or impurities that rise to the surface. (The best time to skim is after an addition of cold water—the water brings the fat to the surface.)

3. Line a strainer with paper towels and place it over a large bowl. Transfer the chicken to a plate to cool. Pour or ladle the broth through the strainer. Let the strained broth cool to room temperature, then refrigerate until cold. Skim off any congealed fat that rises to the surface. I like to freeze chicken stock in 1- or 2-cup containers, so I always have a premeasured amount on hand.

4. Meanwhile, pull the chicken meat off the bones and tear it into coarse or fine shreds. Use the bird in any recipe calling for cooked chicken.

Makes about 8 cups

16 CALORIES PER SERVING;* 1 G PROTEIN; 0 G FAT; 0 G SATURATED FAT; 4 G CARBOHYDRATE; 17 MG SODIUM; 0 MG CHOLESTEROL

Analysis is based on 8 servings.

FISH STOCK

If you've ever wondered why Italian fish stews have such an incredible depth of flavor, look no further than this recipe. In Italy, fish stock would be made with small, bony rockfish, like gallinella *(sea hen) and* scorfano *(rascasse or wraisse). In this country, use the frames (bones) and heads of any nonoily or dark-fleshed fish. Good candidates include snapper, grouper, halibut, sole, turbot, cusk, hake, sea bass, and striped bass. The more different types of fish you use, the richer your stock will be. In a pinch, you can use bottled clam juice in place of fish stock, or chicken or vegetable stock.*

- **2 pounds frames, scraps, or heads from fine-flavored white fish**
- **1 tablespoon extra-virgin olive oil**
- **1 medium onion, finely chopped**
- **1 small leek, trimmed, washed, and finely chopped**
- **2 stalks celery, finely chopped**
- **1 clove garlic, minced**
- **1 tablespoon tomato paste**
- **1 tomato, finely chopped**
- **1 herb bundle comprising a bay leaf, a sprig of rosemary, a sprig of flat-leaf parsley, and a sprig of fresh thyme**
- **5 cups cold water, or enough to cover the fish and vegetables**

1. Remove any gills from the fish frames and wash thoroughly to eliminate all traces of blood. Using a cleaver, cut the frames into 3-inch pieces.

2. Heat the olive oil in a large saucepan or small stockpot. Add the onion, leek, celery, and garlic and cook over medium heat until soft and translucent but not brown, about 4 minutes. Add the tomato paste and cook for 1 minute. Add the tomato and cook for 1 minute. Add the fish frames, increase the heat to high, and cook until the fish starts to turn opaque, about 2 minutes. Add the herb bundle and cold water to cover.

3. Bring the stock to a boil and skim off any white foam that rises to the surface. Reduce heat and gently simmer the stock until richly flavored, 20 to 30 minutes, skimming often.

4. Ladle the stock through a strainer lined with paper towels into a large container and let cool to room temperature. (If the flavor of the stock is not concentrated enough, continue boiling the stock without the bones, until it is reduced to the taste and consistency you desire.) Transfer the stock to 1- and 2-cup containers and refrigerate or freeze. (Stock will keep for 4 to 5 days in the refrigerator; for several months in the freezer.)

Makes 4 to 5 cups

FISH STOCK

If you've done much eating on Mexico's coasts, you've probably wondered how cooks seem to pack so much flavor into their fish soups and stews. The answer is the fish stock. The time-challenged U.S. cook often resorts to bottled clam stock (indeed, many of the recipes in this book call for it), and fine results certainly can be obtained using this time-saver. But for maximum depth of flavor, there's no substitute for a good homemade fish broth. **Note:** *The best fish for making stock is lean and light fleshed, like snapper, pompano, halibut, hake, and mahimahi. Steer clear of oily, strong-flavored fish, like salmon and mackerel.*

- **2 pounds fish heads and/or bones**
- **10 black peppercorns**
- **2 bay leaves**
- **1 clove**
- **1 allspice berry**
- **1 tablespoon canola oil**
- **1 medium onion, thinly sliced**
- **1 carrot, thinly sliced**
- **1 stalk celery, thinly sliced**
- **2 cloves garlic, thinly sliced**
- **1 tomato, finely chopped**
- **3 sprigs flat-leaf parsley**
- **3 sprigs fresh cilantro**
- **2 quarts cold water**

1. If you are using fish heads, remove the gills or have your fishmonger do it. If the heads are large, cut them in half with a cleaver. (Or again, have your fishmonger do it.) If you're using fish bones, cut them into 3-inch pieces. Rinse the fish pieces under cold water to remove all traces of blood. Tie the peppercorns, bay leaves, clove, and allspice berry in a piece of cheese-cloth (or wrap in aluminum foil and pierce with a fork).

2. Heat the oil in a large pot. Add the onion, carrot, celery, and garlic and cook over medium heat until soft but not brown, about 4 minutes. Add the tomato and cook for 1 minute. Increase the heat to high and add the fish pieces. Cook until the fish pieces are opaque, 3 to 5 minutes.

3. Add the parsley, cilantro, spice bundle, and water and bring to a boil. Skim off any froth or foam that rises to the surface. Reduce the heat and gently simmer the stock, uncovered, until it is richly flavored, about 30 minutes.

4. Line a strainer with paper towels and place it over a large bowl. Strain the broth and let it cool to room temperature. I like to freeze fish broth in 1- or 2-cup containers, so I always have a premeasured amount on hand.

Makes about 6 cups

118 CALORIES PER SERVING (1 CUP);
5 G PROTEIN; 1 G FAT; 0 G SATURATED FAT;
26 G CARBOHYDRATE; 90 MG SODIUM;
0 MG CHOLESTEROL

BASIC VEGETABLE STOCK

Here's a broth for vegetarians. It's even easier to make than chicken or fish broth, because it requires almost no skimming. Almost any vegetable or vegetable trimming is a candidate for stock: tomatoes, fennel tops, corncobs, zucchini, summer and winter squash, red and yellow bell peppers, green beans, mushrooms, collard greens, and kale stalks. Use strong-tasting vegetables— such as green peppers, eggplants, turnips, and cabbage—in moderation, as their flavor can become overpowering. Avoid beets, which will turn a stock red, and asparagus and artichokes, which will make it bitter.

1 large onion, quartered (unpeeled)

1 leek, trimmed, washed, and cut into 1-inch pieces

2 carrots, peeled and cut into 1-inch pieces

2 stalks celery, cut into 1-inch pieces

2 tomatoes, cut into 1-inch pieces

6 cloves garlic, unpeeled, cut in half

2 quarts chopped vegetables or vegetable trimmings (see above for some suggested vegetables)

2 tablespoons tomato paste

1 herb bundle comprising a bay leaf, a sprig of rosemary, a sprig of flat-leaf parsley, and a sprig of thyme

3 quarts water

sea salt and freshly ground black pepper

1. Combine all the ingredients except the salt and pepper in a stockpot and bring to a boil. Reduce the heat and simmer the broth, uncovered, until richly flavored, about 1 hour. Add water as necessary to keep the vegetables covered. (A certain amount of evaporation will take place—this helps concentrate the flavor.) Skim the stock once or twice and season with salt and pepper at the end.

2. Pour the stock through a strainer, pressing with the back of a spoon to extract as much liquid as possible from the vegetables. Let the broth cool to room temperature, then refrigerate or freeze. For a thicker, richer broth, force the liquid and vegetables through a vegetable mill or purée in a blender, then strain.

Note: I like to freeze 1-cup portions of vegetable broth, so I always have the right amount on hand.

Makes 2 to 3 quarts (yield will vary, depending on the vegetables used, the size of the pot, and the length of the cooking time)

DRIED TOMATOES

The hot, dry climate of Sicily makes it possible to dry tomatoes outdoors in the sun. Few of us have backyards with the right climatic conditions for drying tomatoes, but it's easy to make your own in the oven. Homemade dried tomatoes taste much better than the commercial. Plum tomatoes are the traditional fruit for drying, but you can also dry regular tomatoes.

12 ripe roma (plum) tomatoes or 6 large round tomatoes

sea salt and freshly ground black pepper

3 cloves garlic, minced

1 tablespoon chopped fresh rosemary or basil

1 tablespoon extra-virgin olive oil

1. Preheat the oven to 200°F. Wash and dry the tomatoes. If using plum tomatoes, cut them in half lengthwise. If using regular tomatoes, cut in half widthwise and cut out the stem. Arrange the tomatoes on a nonstick baking sheet. Generously sprinkle each tomato with salt, pepper, garlic, and rosemary and drizzle with a little olive oil.

2. Bake the tomatoes at 200°F. until shrunken, wrinkled, and almost dry, 8 to 14 hours. (If you trust your oven, you can bake the tomatoes overnight. But try it first during the daytime hours, so you can make sure the tomatoes don't burn.) Don't let the tomatoes brown, and don't let them dry out completely or they'll be tough.

3. Let the tomatoes cool to room temperature, then transfer to a jar. Some people like to add olive oil to cover. (You can use the resulting tomato oil in salads or over steamed vegetables.) Keep dried tomatoes in the refrigerator.

Makes 24 small or 12 large pieces

21 CALORIES PER PLUM TOMATO PIECE; 1 G PROTEIN; 1 G FAT; 0 G SATURATED FAT; 3 G CARBOHYDRATE; 124 MG SODIUM; 0 MG CHOLESTEROL

HOW TO SOAK, WASH, AND TRIM DRIED PORCINI

Porcini are large, rotund mushrooms from the Italian woodlands. Their earthy aroma and rich, meaty flavor are hallmarks of Italian cuisine. Fresh porcini are available irregularly at Italian markets and gourmet shops, and through mail-order outlets, such as Comptoir Exotique.

But porcini are often used in their dried state; indeed, drying seems to intensify the flavor, adding a dimension that's almost smoky. Many Italian recipes call for both fresh and dried porcini. Dried porcini are widely available at gourmet shops, natural-foods stores, and Italian markets.

Dried porcini are easy to use, but they're often quite gritty. I've developed a two-stage process for cleaning them while retaining the maximum flavor. The first step is to soak the porcini without agitating in warm water or stock for 30 minutes or until soft. The soaking liquid picks up the porcini flavor. It is strained and reserved.

The second step is to transfer the porcini to a bowl of water and agitate them quite vigorously with your fingers. This jars loose any grit. The porcini are then gently lifted out, leaving the grit behind, and the water is discarded.

1 ounce dried porcini mushrooms

1 cup warm stock or water

2 cups cold water

1. Soak the porcini in the warm stock or water until soft, about 30 minutes. Remove the porcini with your fingers, gently wringing the stock back into the bowl. Strain the stock through cheesecloth or a coffee filter into another bowl and reserve.

2. Transfer the porcini to a bowl of cold water. Agitate the mushrooms with your fingers to wash out any grit. If the porcini are really gritty, change the water one or two more times. Lift the porcini out of the water, gently wringing with your fingers, leaving the silt behind. Gently wring out the porcini and transfer to a cutting board. Trim off any gritty parts. The porcini are now ready for adding to sauces or stews, as is the reserved porcini stock.

Makes ¾ cup reconstituted porcini

HOW TO ROAST TOMATOES AND TOMATILLOS

One of the most distinctive techniques in Mexican cuisine is the way cooks roast tomatoes, tomatillos, onions, garlic, and other vegetables before adding them to a salsa or mole to intensify and enrich their flavor. Roasting imparts a distinctive smoke flavor (especially when it's done over a live fire) and helps caramelize the natural plant sugars.

The result is a smoky sweetness that is the true secret to great Mexican cooking. Below are the four methods used by Mexicans to roast tomatoes, tomatillos, and other vegetables.

    ripe tomatoes and tomatillos
        (before roasting tomatillos, peel off and discard
        the papery husk and rinse under cold water)

TRADITIONAL METHOD (PAN·ROASTING)

Heat a comal or dry frying pan over a medium-high flame. When very hot, add the tomatoes and cook until the skins are blackened and blistered, 2 to 3 minutes per side, 8 to 12 minutes in all, turning with tongs. Transfer to a plate to cool.

BROILER METHOD

Preheat the broiler. Cut the tomatoes in half and place them, cut side down, on a nonstick baking sheet or roasting pan lined with foil. Place the tomatoes under the broiler and cook until the skins are blackened and blistered, 6 to 8 minutes. When roasting tomatillos, you can leave them whole, but turn them with tongs. Transfer to a plate to cool. Be sure to reserve the juices.

How to Roast Tomatoes and Tomatillos

GRILL METHOD

Preheat a charcoal or gas grill to high. Place the tomatoes on the grill and roast until the skin blackens and blisters, turning with tongs. This will take 8 to 12 minutes in all. Transfer to a plate to cool.

BURNER METHOD

Place a wire rack over the burner and turn the burner on high. Arrange the tomatoes on the rack over the flame. Roast the tomatoes until the skins are blackened and blistered, 2 minutes per side, turning with tongs. Transfer to a plate to cool.

TO PEEL A TOMATO

Simply pull off the burnt skin with your fingers. Don't try to remove every last bit: A little charred skin adds extra smoke flavor.

HOMEMADE BREAD CRUMBS AND TOASTED BREAD CRUMBS

Cooks are by nature a frugal lot, and Italians are no exception. Many of the recipes in this book call for bread crumbs. The final dish will taste much better if you use homemade instead of store-bought. (The latter are full of preservatives and unnecessary flavorings.) The bread will be easiest to grind if it's stale (a day or two old) but not hard. Crumbs are generally made from white bread.

stale bread, broken into 1-inch pieces

1. Grind the bread in a food processor fitted with a metal blade. Run the machine in bursts and don't overcrowd the chopping bowl. For coarse bread crumbs, grind coarsely; for fine bread crumbs, grind finely, then shake the crumbs through a strainer.

2. To make toasted bread crumbs, preheat the oven to 400°F. Spread the crumbs in a thin layer on a baking sheet and bake until golden-brown, about 5 minutes, raking with a spatula to ensure even browning. Transfer the crumbs to a bowl to cool. I like to store homemade bread crumbs in a plastic container in the freezer.

HOW TO PEEL AND SEED A TOMATO

Many people like to peel and seed tomatoes before adding them to pasta dishes. Why? Cooked tomato skins can form red filaments that get caught in your teeth when you eat them. And some people feel that the watery pulp that holds the seeds dilutes the flavor of the sauce. One general word of advice: Never *refrigerate tomatoes. If they're not completely ripe when you buy them, they will continue to ripen at room temperature. Refrigeration stops the ripening process. If the tomatoes are ripe, refrigerating will make them mealy.*

And now, to peel a tomato. Using the tip of a paring knife, cut the stem end out of the tomato and score a shallow 2 in the rounded end. Plunge the tomato in rapidly boiling water for 15 to 60 seconds. (The riper the tomato, the shorter the time required to loosen the skin.)

Let the tomato cool on a plate until you can comfortably handle it, then pull off the skin with your fingers. It should slip off in broad strips.

To seed a tomato, cut it in half crosswise and squeeze each half in the palm of your hand, cut side down, to wring out the seeds and liquid. Work over a bowl and strainer. Push the pulp through the strainer with the back of a spoon. Reserve the tomato liquid that collects in the bowl for sauces, soups, or even drinking.

1 good-size ripe tomato (8 to 10 ounces)
yields ¾ to 1 cup peeled, seeded, chopped flesh

PASTRY CREAM

The pastry cream I learned to prepare in Paris was dizzyingly rich with egg yolks. The following recipe is a perfect example of the high-flavor, low-fat method: it contains only 1 egg, but the cinnamon stick, vanilla bean, and lemon and orange zest provide all the flavor you could wish for.

1 cup skim milk

1 cinnamon stick

½ inch piece vanilla bean, cut in half

3 strips orange zest (remove it with a vegetable peeler)

3 strips lemon zest (remove it with a vegetable peeler)

4 tablespoons sugar

1½ tablespoons cornstarch

1 egg

1. Combine the milk, cinnamon, vanilla, orange, lemon zest, and 1 tablespoon sugar in a saucepan and gradually bring to a boil, stirring often. (Stirring prevents the milk from scorching.) Meanwhile, in a mixing bowl whisk together the remaining 3 tablespoons sugar and cornstarch. Add the egg and whisk to mix.

2. Whisk the scalded milk into the egg mixture in a thin stream. Return the mixture to the pan and bring to a boil, whisking steadily. Reduce the heat and cook until thickened, about 2 minutes. The mixture should bubble. Force the pastry cream through a strainer into a bowl, pressing with a rubber spatula. (Or remove the vanilla bean, cinnamon stick, and orange and lemon zest strips with tongs.) Press a piece of plastic wrap on top of the cream to prevent a skin from forming, making a slit in the top to allow the steam to escape. Let cool to room temperature.

Note: for added convenience, you could strain the scalded milk into the egg mixture, but I like the extra flavor that results from cooking the spices with the pastry cream.

Makes 1 cup.

ORANGE CURD

Remember orange curd? The rich, tangy filling so laden with butter and egg yolks, it could almost cause cardiac arrest? Here's a tangy orange curd that contains only 1 egg (or 2 if you're feeling splurgy). It's so flavorful, you won't miss the fat.

1/2 cup sugar

1-1/2 tablespoons cornstarch

1 to 2 eggs

¾ cup fresh orange juice

¼ cup lime juice

1 teaspoon grated orange zest

1. Combine the sugar and cornstarch in a mixing bowl and whisk to mix. Add the egg(s) and whisk to mix.

2. Meanwhile, bring the orange juice, lime juice, and orange zest to a boil in a heavy saucepan. Whisk this mixture in a thin steam into the egg mixture. Return the mixture to the pan and bring to a boil, whisking steadily. Reduce the heat and simmer for 1 minute or until thickened. Transfer the orange curd to a bowl. Press a piece of plastic wrap on top of the curd to prevent a skin from forming, making a slit in the top to allow the steam to escape.

Let cool to room temperature.

Makes 1 cup.

QUICK MILK CARAMEL
(CAJETA)

Ok, I know I'm going to take some heat for this one. Cajeta is one of the glories of Mexican confectionery, a tangy, rib-stickingly rich caramel made by boiling down milk (traditionally goats milk) to a thick, sweet, fudgy paste. This presents two problems for the low fat cook: first, you must use whole milk. (Skim milk will burn when you try to reduce it.) Second, the preparation of cajeta requires a major commitment of time and elbow grease. (It takes about 40 minutes of simmering and stirring to cook the milk to the proper consistency.) These difficulties set me thinking about a similar preparation I've enjoyed elsewhere in Latin America: dulce de leche (literally "milk sweet"). This, too, requires lengthy boiling in its traditional version, but cooks from San Juan to Santiago have come up with a tasty shortcut: they boil a can of sweetened condensed milk (fat free condensed milk in this case) until the contents are caramel colored and as thick as fudge. Here, then, is a quick cajeta that's delicious in crepes, ladled over frozen yogurt or fruit, or simply eaten right off a spoon. Note: *to approximate the sourish flavor achieved by making cajeta with goats milk, you can whisk a little soft goat cheese, like a montrachet, into the finished caramel.*

1 14-ounce can fat free sweetened condensed skim milk

1 teaspoon vanilla extract

½ teaspoon ground cinnamon

2 ounces soft goat cheese, like montrachet, at room temperature

1. Place the entire can of condensed milk in a large saucepan with water to cover by 6 inches. Bring to a boil. Reduce the heat to medium and briskly simmer the condensed milk, covered, for 2 hours, adding water as needed to keep the can immersed. It's essential to keep the can covered with 6 inches of water at all times. Alternatively, cook the condensed milk in a pressure cooker for 20 minutes.

2. Transfer the can to the sink with tongs and let cool to room temperature. Open it with a can opener and scrape the dark, thick, sweet caramel inside into a mixing bowl.

3. Stir in the vanilla extract, cinnamon, and goat cheese (if using). Store the cajeta covered in the refrigerator. It will keep for several days (for several weeks if you omit the goat cheese). Let it warm to room temperature before serving.

INDEX

METRIC GUIDELINES

These guidelines were developed to simplify the conversion from Imperial measures to metric. The numbers have been rounded for convenience. When cooking from a recipe, work in the same system throughout the recipe; do not use a combination of the two.*

Metric Symbols

Celsius: C
Liter: L
Milliliter: mL
Kilogram: kg
Gram: g
Centimeter: cm
Millimeter: mm

Oven Temperature Conversions

IMPERIAL	METRIC
250 degrees F	120 degrees C
275 degrees F	140 degrees C
300 degrees F	150 degrees C
325 degrees F	160 degrees C
350 degrees F	180 degrees C
375 degrees F	190 degrees C
400 degrees F	200 degrees C
425 degrees F	220 degrees C
450 degrees F	230 degrees C
475 degrees F	240 degrees C
500 degrees F	260 degrees C

*Developed by the Canadian Home Economics Association and the American Home Economics Committee.

Length

IMPERIAL	METRIC
¼ inch	5 mm
⅓ inch	8 mm
½ inch	1 cm
¾ inch	2 cm
1 inch	2.5 cm
2 inches	5 cm
4 inches	10 cm

Volume

IMPERIAL	METRIC
¼ teaspoon	1 mL
½ teaspoon	2 mL
¾ teaspoon	4 mL
1 teaspoon	5 mL
2 teaspoons	10 mL
1 tablespoon	15 mL
2 tablespoons	25 mL
¼ cup	50 mL
⅓ cup	75 mL
½ cup	125 mL
⅔ cup	150 mL
¾ cup	175 mL
1 cup	250 mL
4 cups	1 L
5 cups	1.25 L

Mass (Weight)

IMPERIAL	METRIC
1 ounce	25 g
2 ounces	50 g
¼ pound	125 g
½ pound (8 ounces)	250 g
1 pound	500 g
2 pounds	1 kg
3 pounds	1.5 kg
5 pounds	2.2 kg
8 pounds	3.5 kig
10 pounds	4.5 kg
11 pounds	5 kg

Some Common Can/ Package Sizes

VOLUME

4 ounces	114 mL
10 ounces	284 mL
14 ounces	398 mL
10 ounces	540 mL
28 ounces	796 mL

MASS

4 ounces	113 g
5 ounces	142 g
6 ounces	170 g
7 ounces	220 g
15 ounces	425 g